SAM HUGHES

The Public Career
of a Controversial Canadian,
1885-1916

SAM HUGHES

The
Public Career
of a
Controversial
Canadian,
1885-1916

*Ronald G.
Haycock*

Canadian War Museum
Historical Publication No. 21

Wilfrid Laurier University Press
in collaboration with
**Canadian War Museum
Canadian Museum of Civilization
National Museums of Canada**

Copyright © 1986 National Museums of Canada

All rights reserved. The use of any part of this publication reproduced, transmitted in any form or by any means, electronic, mechanical, photocopying, recording, or otherwise, or stored in a retrieval system without the proper consent of the publisher is an infringement of the copyright law.

Canadian Cataloguing in Publication Data

Haycock, Ronald Graham, 1942-
  Sam Hughes

(Canadian War Museum historical publication ; no. 21)
Bibliography: p.
Includes index.
ISBN 978-0-88920-177-4 (hbk).—ISBN 978-1-55458-481-9 (pbk).

1. Hughes, Samuel, Sir, 1853-1921. 2. Canada –
Politics and government – 1911-1921.* 3. Canada –
Politics and government – 1896-1911.* 4. Canada –
Militia – Biography. I. Series: Historical
publications (Canadian War Museum) ; no. 21.

FC556.H85H39 1986   971.061′092′4   C86-094401-8
F 1033.H85H39 1986

Cover design: Polygon Design Limited

Wilfrid Laurier University Press

in collaboration with

**Canadian War Museum
Canadian Museum of Civilization
National Museums of Canada**

Printed in Canada

This printing 2014

In the writing of this book the inferences drawn and the opinions expressed are those of the author himself, and the National Museums of Canada are in no way responsible for his presentation of the facts as stated.

*This book is dedicated to my wife, Rita,
to my children, Laura, Bourke, and Judson,
and to the memory of my parents,
Roy and Elva Haycock*

Contents

Abbreviations	ix
Acknowledgments	xi
Introduction	1
1. The Background, 1853-1885	8
2. Journalism, the Militia, and Local Politics, 1885-1890	15
3. Getting Elected, 1890-1892	34
4. In Parliament, 1892-1899	47
5. Hughes, Hutton, and the Contingents for South Africa, 1899	67
6. The Proving Ground: South Africa, 1900	83
7. A Loyal Veteran, 1900-1911	97
8. A Loyal Maverick	114
9. The Peacetime Minister, 1911-1914	135
10. The Critics	154
11. War and Mobilization: One Man's Show, 1914	177
12. Recruiting, 1914-1916	198
13. "Done in Our Own Country": War Supplies, 1914-1916	225
14. Hughes' Hydra Overseas, 1914-1915	258
15. A Nightmare Removed: Reform and Resignation, 1916	288
16. Eclipse	313
Bibliography	325
Index	340

Abbreviations

AG	Adjutant-General
BEF	British Expeditionary Force
BEL	British Empire League
CAMC	Canadian Army Medical Corps
CEF	Canadian Expeditionary Force
CGS	Chief of the General Staff
C-in-C	Commander-in-Chief
CID	Committee of Imperial Defence
CIGS	Chief of the Imperial General Staff
CNR	Canadian Northern Railway
CO	Commanding Officer
DAAG	Deputy Assistant Adjutant General
DM	Deputy Minister
DMD	Department of Militia and Defence
DND	Department of National Defence
DRA	Dominion Rifle Association
FO	Foreign Office
GOC	General-Officer-Commanding
HLRO	House of Lords Records Office
IFL	Imperial Federation League
IY	Imperial Yeomanry
JAG	Judge-Advocate-General
MD	Military District
NDHQ	National Defence Headquarters
NPAM	Non-Permanent Active Militia
OC	Officer Commanding

PAC	Public Archives of Canada
PAO	Public Archives of Ontario
PAM	Permanent Active Militia
PANS	Public Archives of Nova Scotia
PF	Permanent Force
PRO	Public Records Office
QMG	Quarter-Master-General
RCR	Royal Canadian Regiment
SSAC	Standing Small Arms Committee
WPC	War Purchasing Committee

Acknowledgments

This book about Sam Hughes is the culmination of almost two decades of study. However frustrating the digging may have been from time to time, never once during those years has the fascination for the man or his times paled. Yet the manuscript is also a reflection of the debt owed many people. For making publication possible, my gratitude goes to Lee Murray, then the Chief Curator of the Canadian War Museum, and his staff. Without their aid, given through the Canadian Museum of Civilization to fund this book, little of my work would have been accomplished when it was. Two men in particular are responsible for kindling and keeping my interest in Canadian Military History and specifically Sam Hughes. Professor A. M. J. Hyatt is one not only because he is a friend, but also because he provided years of calm council and many insights into Sir Arthur Currie's Canadian Corps; Professor Desmond Morton is another because he is the indisputable dean of the history of the post-Confederation Canadian Militia. While neither man has ever found Sam Hughes an attractive historical figure, both were unswerving in their encouragement. And their penetrating judgments often kept mine in check. As well, Alan R. Capon, the former editor of the Lindsay *Post*, passed on his enthusiasm for Hughes, and willingly let me use his extensive collection of photographs and other archival material. Mrs. Lois Hope arranged interviews for me with her aunt, the late Mrs. Ena MacAdam Macdonald.

There are scores of people in various institutions who contributed their resources, knowledge, and skills. The Canada Council and recently the Social Sciences and Humanities Research Council provided grants for sabbatical and summer research leaves, as did the Department of National Defence through its Military History Post-Doctoral Fellowships awards. At the Public Archives of Canada and at the National Defence Headquarters Directorate of History, individuals such as Barbara Wilson, David Smith, Dr. W. A. B. Douglas, and Brereton Greenhous were indispensable. So were the many archivists at the

Public Record Office and the House of Lords Record Office in the United Kingdom, to name just a few.

To my colleagues at the Royal Military College of Canada there is a particular debt. They always encouraged me to push ahead and found funds from the Arts Division to support my travel and typing needs. One could not ask for better associates and friends than those in the History Department. We talked about Sam Hughes a great deal. Donald Schurman was infectious with his enthusiasm and constant with his support; and Keith Neilson helped in many ways. Karen Brown, in typing many very rough chapters, never once baulked at my handwriting peccadilloes. Special thanks must go to Barry Hunt and to Frederic Thompson. Over the years, they read with good humour every word of the several drafts. The three of us often discussed words and ideas. Their incisive commentary gave this work whatever merit it has. It should also be said that our sometimes planned, sometimes impromptu, gatherings were also just plain fun, even though a little hard on one's liquor cabinet.

Outside of the college, Sandra Woolfrey, the Director of WLU Press, was endlessly patient, and Linda Biesenthal's capable editing kept my prose intelligible. Jennifer Hamilton twice volunteered to type the entire manuscript; in the end, she did it three times and ran a busy household too, all with consummate skill and calmness. In my own family, after a while "working on Sam" became a household phrase: they not only suffered it well, but inspired enthusiasm. They are the project's greatest strength.

Ronald Haycock
"The Pickerel Mash"
Parham, Ontario
12 July 1986

Introduction

Frank Underhill once remembered a teacher who lamented that Canadian history was as "dull as ditch water and Canadian politics full of it." Certainly that comparison could never be applied to Sam Hughes. He is one of the most colourful, even bizarre, figures in Canadian history. Though he died in 1921, his name can still conjure up controversy and not a little misunderstanding. His long career—in so many respects the quintessential story of a poor backwoods Ontario farm boy who made good by his own efforts—continues to exert a fascination that few other Canadian political figures could duplicate. From his beginnings as a schoolteacher and then local newspaper editor, Hughes entered national politics during the final years of Sir John A. Macdonald's last administration. And he stayed at the centre of things until he too died in harness. It was a long public career that revolved around his two abiding preoccupations: federal Conservative politics and the Canadian militia. Through these he rose up the ranks to become a lieutenant-general and the Minister of Militia and Defence in Robert Borden's government. During the First World War, he held his ministry amid increasing controversy until he was unceremoniously fired in 1916.[1]

Sam Hughes was very much a Victorian. He believed in the values of hard work, competition, and strength. He had a precise image of what every man should be: "a highly masculine outdoorsman," as W. L. Morton has said, who is of "independent mind and trained in the habit of authority." Like many Canadians of this period, Hughes had a tenacious and often one-sided view of a few simple ideas. One was the natural superiority of the volunteer citizen-soldiers to better meet the country's defence needs than the regular soldiers with all of their professional and elitist characteristics. Paradoxically, Hughes was a major contributor both to the militia myth that plagued the country for

---

Reference notes for the Introduction are found on p. 7.

years and to military reform. But his military philosophy had a larger dimension: because of its intrinsic moral value, martial training created better citizens and loyal subjects. Military activities could also be exploited to extend Canada's position in the British Empire. Here Hughes was caught in a dilemma. He had a great pride in being part of the imperial world, yet he tried to force it into an odd partnership with his aggressive Canadian nationalism.[2]

Sam Hughes also believed in certain aspects of what John English has described as "old party politics." At a time when government organization was simple and intruded little into the affairs of society, men were often attracted to politics not only by a sense of duty but, in return for their election, by being able to dispense services through the party structure. The epitome of such practices was at the local level, which made constituency politics vital to national party success. In short, patronage was closely linked to victory at the polls and the needs of the people.

In the 1890s when Hughes was first elected and for years after, Parliament placed few demands on MPs. Cabinet ministers were not overly busy, and backbenchers—especially if in opposition—had little to do. Parliamentary sessions lasted about four months, which allowed MPs to carry on a relatively normal private life. Often they had to hold down other jobs because their salaries alone were not sufficient to keep them and their families. Such factors took a toll on the quality of the members. Half of them were new with each election. They were parochial in outlook and sometimes had little talent, so Parliament could be a mixed bag of individuals, with consensus, quality, and discipline hard to achieve.

Sam Hughes shared common roots with the old-party politician. He brought these roots to office at a time when the strains of the Great War were beginning to undermine their acceptability. How well Sam Hughes sensed that great transition is a moot point. But it is clear that his personal political horizons extended well beyond those of most of his contemporaries—as his encouragement of female cadet corps instructors, the regulation of big business, and his progressive views on education indicate. Were it otherwise, his value to Borden's party and government would have been much more circumscribed. As it was, he was important to the Tory party and he was no simple hack.[3]

When Hughes combined his military, imperial, and political ideas, he found himself embroiled in continuous controversy. Much of it was largely a direct function of his own remarkable personality. Contemporaries either admired or hated him, and he could reciprocate hate with equal passion. Frequently he made outlandish and thoughtless public statements, outbursts that reflected his immense and often frustrated personal ambition. During the 1880s and 1890s, he virtually clawed his way to success in the riding of Victoria North after serving several stormy years in local political associations, which often left them fractured and seething with internal intrigues. Ten years later his intemperate tongue ruined his chances of commanding Canadians in the South African war. The desperate Hughes manoeuvred every way he could, even making vague promises to be more friendly with Liberals if given a second chance. Eventually he did serve in that war, but not with Canadians and not for long. Again his public criticism of British superior officers and generalship provoked Lord Roberts to order Hughes home on the first available boat. It was a humiliation he would never forget nor forgive. Thereafter he would always mistrust professional soldiers and some imperial authorities, convinced at times that they were conspiring against him. Once home he continued to press hard in federal politics. In business Hughes had as much energy and drive but evidently not enough talent to get himself into its upper reaches. No doubt this lack of success heightened his political activities. By 1911 his frantic desire to be made a cabinet minister pushed him to even greater heights of self-advertisement. And for the rest of his life, the twin forces of personal ambition and a desire for political power never abated.

In spite of all this, Hughes had several strengths. Not the least was his single-minded energy. In the militia he was known as a progressive, talented officer. With his incredible memory, personal warmth, and natural talent to make friends more often than enemies, he was a hard political and parliamentary worker.

Those who worked close to Sam Hughes, especially in his defence ministry private offices, were devoted to him. Such was the young Ena MacAdam, his personal secretary after 1912. She recalled long visits and checker games between Hughes and her father when Sam visited their house. In the Minister's office, she helped organize his days and bring order and routine to a hectic schedule. Needing little sleep, Hughes was a tireless worker at what interested him. When Colonel C. F. Winter, a regular soldier but a Tory with long militia service, became his military secretary, it was much the same. Both people remembered Hughes as a gregarious, cheery, and mostly calm man who did not always fly off the handle but who could when subjects he felt strongly about were involved. Winter and MacAdam also identified accessibility, compassion, and absolute conviction as other characteristics. Nearly everyone in Ottawa had a favourite story about Hughes which was half-fiction, half-truth, but which captured the essence of the Minister's personality. One came from Tory Colonel W. A. Griesbach in 1912:

Some weeks ago I met an old man in my part of the country who told me that he had learned to shoot while serving in Sam Hughes' battalion of infantry.... He said one day when the men were shooting badly Sam Hughes, who was then a Sergeant, picked up one of the rifles and lay down on the mound. He fired and missed the target. Turning to one of the men he said "That's the way you shoot." Firing again, he again missed the target and turned to another man and said "That's the way you shoot." Firing for the third time, he scored a bull's eye. Speaking to the men, he said: "That's the way I shoot" and walked on.[4]

It was Sam Hughes' great constituency talent that first brought him to Macdonald's notice. Over the years, his continued success at, and instincts for, this sort of politics meant that he could be counted on to deliver his seat election after election. One of the few survivors of the Conservative rout in 1896, by 1911 he was an important political asset for Robert Borden's Ontario organization, the most important one in federal politics.

Sam Hughes had a reputation for bold-faced directness. He was fiercely independent and he prided himself in cutting the "red tape and getting things done." Undoubtedly his common touch attracted many and he went out of his way to portray himself as the champion of democracy and the ordinary Canadian. He often defended what he thought was right, and just as often he was for the underdog. As a young reporter, P. D. Ross, later the editor of the Ottawa *Journal*, remembered an incident in 1881 at the Toronto Exhibition when he and his girlfriend were being pushed around by two tough characters. Just when the unequal contest looked bleakest for Ross, he heard a strong voice behind him: "All right, Ross, I'm with you." It was the muscular Sam Hughes who had a temper similar to "the Irishman who came across a shindy and inquired whether it was a private fight or could anybody get in." Ross' assailants promptly beat a hasty retreat.[5]

Still, whether Hughes would admit it or not, the powerful and famous impressed him most. And he was never shy about pushing himself into the councils of the not-so-common. Though the Governor-General, the Duke of Connaught, thought him a "lunatic," many others including Lionel Curtis, co-founder of the Round Table movement, considered Hughes "a man among men," while General Sir Ian Hamilton thought he recognized some sort of passionate genius in the controversial Canadian.

There were many other ways in which Sam Hughes gained notice. An excellent rifle shot, he served in several of the country's shooting fraternities, including president of the Dominion Rifle Association. He promoted the Cadet Corps movement and his own form of the imperial cause. He believed in Anglo-Saxon values, temperance, and a Protestant and sometimes Orange God. Everyone knew that he loved the militia as much as politics. And Hughes himself realized that such varied participation had the dual advantage of satisfying his own sense of duty and self-aggrandisement as well as the Conservative Party's.

There can be little doubt that Sam Hughes' instinctive sense of theatrical presence and timing combined with his good humour, wit, and ability to laugh at himself inevitably made him a popular figure in rumour-hungry Ottawa. These colourful facets of his character and escapades, however, should never be allowed to overshadow the larger importance of his public career. He was, after all, in charge of one of the most important cabinet posts in government during the greatest war fought by Canada to that time. While many historians have acknowledged his presence, none has examined Sam Hughes on his own terms and within the wider context of his times when Canada itself was being transformed by new forces, including those set loose by the First World War. That Hughes at first imparted great strength then later great weakness to Conservative political fortunes cannot be denied; nor can the fact that as Canadian political and social values matured, Sam Hughes never did—at least not enough. Nevertheless his senior party and cabinet positions provide an unusual vantage point for viewing the complexities of federal political functions and structures in Macdonald's, Laurier's, and Borden's Canada. One such critical issue was French-English relations. Many French-Canadians branded Hughes the "champion of race hatred." Others, however, applauded his moderation on the Manitoba schools question. Still over the long haul he did more to divide the two cultures than to accommodate them. In company with many Ontario Tories, Hughes had a singularly monolithic and English view of Canada that would be, for him and all Canadians, a source of constant frustration.

Hughes was also deeply involved in the fortunes of the British Empire during both the exertions of the new imperialism in the 1890s and the strains of the Great War two decades later. In 1914, of Robert Borden's lieutenants, it was Sam Hughes who had to deal most directly with a new type of war—total war—which no one expected or had any clear understanding of. He could never entirely come to grips with it. It is both tragic and fascinating to watch him try, fail, and then grudgingly be overtaken by others better able to make the transition. During this especially painful part of his life, he was far from alone in his misunderstandings and mistakes.

Even though there has never been a major scholarly study of Sam Hughes, historians and other writers have developed definite opinions about him, and they are held nearly as vigorously as those of his contemporaries. These vary from insisting that Hughes was mentally unbalanced to proclaiming him a genius. Hughes' defenders have rarely been professional historians. For the most part, men like Lord Beaverbrook, Brigadier C. F. Winter (Hughes' wartime military secretary) or the former Conservative Premier of Ontario, Leslie Frost, have written accolades and apologies. To them he was a champion of constitutional freedom and Canadian autonomy who got big things done. He also exposed glaring British incompetence, built a strong militia force, and forged the miracle of Valcartier and shell production during the Great War. But these writings have also been largely unanalytical and based on limited research or on the findings of their predecessors.[6]

On the other side, there are more practised historians. And their view is much more penetrating and hardly so flattering. Roger Graham (Arthur Meighen's biographer) claims that Hughes was a megalomaniac. A popular historian, Ralph Allan, concludes simply that Sam Hughes was "a man who would have had the utmost difficulty in passing a standard medical test for sanity."[7] From here on the opinions mostly vary on the negative side and mostly deal with only specific aspects of Hughes' wartime career. Unlike Sir Sam's apologists, these commentators are usually on their way towards other issues or in search of the careers of other men.

When taken together, both sides have not produced an extensive or definitive literature on Hughes in proportion to other figures of a similar public stature, although recently several works have appeared which add more depth. John English's *Decline of Politics* (1977), Michael Bliss in his sensitive biography of J. W. Flavelle (1978), R. Craig Brown's two volumes on Robert Borden (1975 and 1979), and Desmond Morton's *Canada and War* (1981) and his incisive *A Peculiar Kind of Politics* (1982) have given more realistic glimpses of Hughes' later career.[8]

Whatever side the studies have taken, the assessments are still incomplete because they have not examined the entirety of Sam Hughes' public life. To a large extent these limitations have allowed the folk image of him to persist. But Hughes had fibre and substance beyond this. Since historical figures must be explained in terms of their environment, this study tries to redress the previous imbalances by examining Hughes' public career. It is the only way his historical significance can be explained and reasonable judgments made.

In part the reason for the lack of scholarly studies of Sam Hughes lies in the written sources. The task of any historian is made easier when there is a full range of archival material. This is not the case with Sam Hughes. Personal and public papers, diaries and memoirs are not known to exist, with the exception of a very small collection in the possession of his grandson, Mr. Justice S. H. S. Hughes. And after repeated attempts to see these documents, I was given no access to them. A great many of Hughes' contemporaries left important information about and by him in their correspondence. Much of it is preserved in the Public Archives of Canada. Among the holdings, Robert Borden's papers are the most fruitful; the records of the old Department of Militia and Defence and National Defence are important. The papers of Hughes' cabinet colleagues—Perley, Kemp, White, and Foster, among others—are valuable, and *Hansard* is full of firsthand dialogue. Hughes was an inveterate letter writer, so the files of most of the politicians of the day net something, and nearly all these men had an opinion about him. Overseas the Baron Beaverbrook collection, now in the House of Lords Record Office, Westminister, rates with Borden's papers as an important source, as does the Colonial Office and the War Office files at the Public Record Office, Kew Gardens. One argument for attempting this work is that it tries to bring together as many of the Hughes' sources as possible so that others can make their own judgments and contributions.

No doubt one could go on forever turning up material on Hughes, but there is a point—before old age or indecision or both take over—at which one has to put it in writing. In doing so the limitations of the sources leave only one regret: without personal papers a true biography is not yet possible. According to his long-time secretary, Hughes was devoted to his wife and children, but lack of other such resources allows no close insights into his private life, nor about his activities before he took over the *Victoria Warder* in 1885, nor into his family concerns. Yet Sam Hughes' public career is rich ground and he remains one of the most fascinating and controversial of Canadians.

Reference Notes to Introduction

1 Frank Underhill, "Some Reflections on the Liberal Tradition in Canada," the presidential address in the *Report of the Annual Meeting of the Canadian Historical Association* (Toronto: University of Toronto Press, 1946), *p. 8.*
2 W. L. Morton, ed. *The Shield of Achilles, Aspects of Victorian Canada* (Toronto: McClelland and Stewart, 1968), p. 321.
3 John English, *The Decline of Politics: The Conservatives and the Party System, 1901-1920* (Toronto: University of Toronto Press, 1977), pp.3-30.
4 Personal interviews between author and Ena MacAdam Macdonald, Ottawa, Dec. 11, 1984. MacAdam was born in 1887 in Packenham where her father ran an iron works. She grew up in nearby Ottawa and lived there with her parents during her time in Hughes' office. For years she was silent about Sam Hughes but her loyalty remained unshaken, and she resented his being often portrayed in history as a mere wild man. Also see C. F. Winter, *Lieutenant-General the Hon. Sir Sam Hughes, K.C.B., M.P., Canada's War Minister, 1911-1916* (Toronto: Macmillan, 1931), pp. 11-12; J. H. Bridge, *Millionaires and Grub Street* (New York: Bretanos, 1931), pp. 257-58; Arthur R. Ford, *As the World Wags On* (Toronto: Ryerson, 1950), p. 84; J. Castell Hopkins, ed., *The Canadian Annual Review of Public Affairs for 1912* (Toronto: CAR Publishers, 1912), pp. 177-78 (hereafter cited *CAR*); and W. A. Griesbach, *I Remember* (Toronto: Ryerson, 1946), p. 346.
5 P. D. Ross, *Retrospects of a Newspaper Person* (Toronto: University of Toronto Press, 1931), pp. 186-87.
6 See Winter; Sir Max Aitken, *Canada in Flanders*, vol. I (Toronto: Hodder and Stoughton, 1916); and L. M. Frost, *The Record on Sam Hughes Set Straight* (Fenelon Falls: Fenelon Falls *Gazette*, n.d.).
7 Roger Graham, *Arthur Meighen*, vol. I (Toronto: Clark Irwin: 1960), p. 106; and Ralph Allan, *Ordeal by Fire, Canada, 1910- 1945* (Toronto: Doubleday, 1961), p. 111.
8 These references appear in subsequent chapters.

CHAPTER 1

The Background, 1853-1885

The military funeral was a sombre affair: the troops at slow march, pipers' and buglers' laments, the flag-draped coffin carried on a horse-drawn gun carriage, the riderless horse following with boots reversed in the stirrups, a fifteen-gun salute booming out at the graveside, and the pressing mix of high-ranking military men and civilians with almost 20,000 onlookers. The magnificent ceremony that hot summer day in late August 1921 was one not often witnessed by most townspeople of Lindsay, Ontario. The man who frequently brought unexpected events to the community—Lieutenant-General Sir Sam Hughes—was dead; and it was typical that he would have planned well beforehand most of his own funeral parade.

The death of Sam Hughes ended a remarkable and controversial career of half a century in Canadian national politics and the militia, a career that peaked with his appointment to the portfolio of Militia and Defence in Sir Robert Borden's Conservative government during the Great War. Though he was fired from the post and created many enemies in his long public life, when Hughes died most Canadians sensed that an amazing and colourful personality had passed forever from the scene, and they came to his funeral by the thousands to pay their respect to an old campaigner.[1]

Sam Hughes had been born sixty-nine years earlier on January 8, 1853, in Canada West's Durham County, near Bowmanville. His father, John Hughes, was an Irish Protestant immigrant who had come from county Tyrone in the large wave of Irish immigration in the 1840s. Life in the New World brought the elder Hughes little more success than it had in the old, but he managed to make a living teaching school and

---

Reference notes for Chapter 1 are found on p. 14.

farming in the county. John Hughes had married a Canadian, Caroline Laughlin, of mixed French Huguenot and Irish stock and the daughter of a British artillery officer serving in Canada. The marriage was solid even if the livelihood was meagre, and in time there were four sons and seven daughters in the Hughes family. Sam was the third of the boys.[2]

Life was anything but easy in pre-Confederation Durham County. The area was not far advanced beyond the frontier lumbering and farming stage. Like Victoria County to the north, Durham had its full share of English, Scots, and Irish inhabitants, as well as some French-Canadians and a smattering of other ethnic groups. Most were Protestant, some fiercely so, especially the Ulster Irish who often gave vent to their convictions by joining the Orange Lodges which were proliferating throughout the province. But there were Roman Catholics, and relations between the two groups, especially in the 1870s and 1880s, were often troubled. Such things, however, were of little immediate concern to the young Sam Hughes, although he no doubt was aware his family had come from that "better" part of Ireland which was loyal to the British Crown. Though his youth was full of the satisfactions and hard work of rural life, Hughes' parents encouraged him to reach further. He had an inquisitive mind and learned quickly under his father's guidance; he read widely, especially books on travel and military campaigns. He was fascinated especially by the military adventures of his forebearers. Both his grandfathers had fought at Waterloo, and his maternal great-grandfather—a French general of cuirassiers—and three of his sons had died there defending Bonaparte's return.[3] To an impressionable boy in an age when the truly "great wars" were yet the contests of the Iron Duke and Napoleon, such family history must have been magic, displaying—at least to Victorian minds—daring deeds, honour, and love of country.

The Hughes family also bequeathed its children another Victorian notion: the combination of a sound mind and a sound body. Young Sam Hughes loved outdoor activity and sports of all kinds. He also had the ambition and perseverance to carry his education well beyond that of the average farm boy. By his middle teens, he had most of a high-school education, much of it gained in the self-discipline of home study. Even at this young age, his ambition and energy were apparent. Shortly after his sixteenth birthday, he started to teach primary school, first in Belleville in Hastings County, then in Lifford back in Durham County. While teaching he was also attending the Toronto Normal School where he earned a first-class teacher's certificate. In 1872 at twenty, he married one of his students from Lifford, Caroline Preston, daughter of a prominent local family. A year later she died while Hughes was working for an American railway company in Milwaukee.[4]

This tragedy brought the young widower back to Canada in 1873 where he resumed teaching, this time at Bowmanville. In his two years as schoolmaster in that community, he got to know it well, particularly through the area's sports organizations, which he joined as much to relieve his grief as his need for physical activity. Eventually he fell in love with Mary Burk, whose father Harvey was a well-to-do farmer and former reeve of Durham's Darlington Township. At the time Burk was the Reform member in the federal Parliament for West Durham, having won his seat in the voter outrage in 1874 over the Pacific Scandal that temporarily interrupted the long tenure of Sir John Macdonald's Liberal-Conservative government. The following year Hughes and Mary Burk were married and moved to Toronto, where he again decided to change his vocation. He articled as an apprentice at law, only briefly, likely because it was too dull. And then once more he returned to the classroom.[5]

Sam Hughes had no trouble finding a job in Toronto. The city's rapidly expanding population put a premium on schoolteachers. And his oldest brother James probably helped clear the way. James Hughes had taught at the Normal School for the previous ten years, and by the time Sam arrived he was well on his way to the top educational circles as inspector of Toronto's public schools. The job Sam Hughes landed was as English and history master at what shortly became Toronto Collegiate Institute. In the decade he taught there his classes were as unorthodox as they were exciting; controversy was the tool Hughes used to nurture the inquisitiveness of his students. To some the technique was grating—but it was never dull. Outside of the classroom Hughes eagerly kept improving his own qualifications by adding, on a part-time basis, honours credits in history and modern language from the University of Toronto. At the same time he managed to earn his provincial public school inspector's papers and publish two school works for classroom use.[6]

But Sam Hughes needed more than academic life to keep him content. Like many Victorians, he had a passion for strenuous physical activity. While he liked hunting and fishing, he was best at organized sports. He was a champion runner and earned a formidable reputation as an aggressive lacrosse player. In 1881, as a young reporter, P. D. Ross played lacrosse with Sam Hughes on the famous Toronto Shamrocks team. The first time out for practice, Ross remembered the coach cautioning him about the "black lad" (a name given Hughes by his team-mates because of his swarthy complexion and his habit of wearing a black jersey): "Well, look out for him," the coach advised. "He's some little body-checker. Don't get between him and the fence or the fence is liable to lose a board."[7]

While Sam Hughes lived in Toronto it would be hard to imagine him not following municipal and provincial politics closely, if not actively. Unfortunately there is little known about his involvement in such areas before 1885. The greatest political force of Hughes' time was Sir John A. Macdonald, the Liberal-Conservative Prime Minister of Canada. Certainly at fourteen years of age Hughes would have experienced the excitement of the Confederation celebrations in 1867, and perhaps admired the men of Ontario who appeared to be the prime movers in the union. By 1878, three years after Sam Hughes came to Toronto, Macdonald was concentrating more than ever on consolidating his Confederation dream through the economic and transportation programs of the National Policy. The exploitation of the west, transcontinental railway building, and agricultural and industrial development were all aspects of the political times. The spirit was infectious to anyone like Hughes who had caught a sense of national uniqueness and purpose.

More is known about the other passion of Hughes' life—service in the Active Militia, which he joined when he was only twelve. The Canadian Militia was created in 1868; it was small, based on volunteer local battalions, and was poorly equipped and trained. While it had a long and proud past, the real defenders of colonial Canada had always been regulars from overseas. Despite the false sense of their importance, the Canadian volunteers were meant only to buy time or to flesh out the regular cadres. Since 1783 the enemy had been the Americans. Indeed, invasion fears had been a compelling reason for Confederation. But the Washington Treaty in 1871 diffused Anglo-American tensions, and when the British inland garrisons were withdrawn from Canada, the fledgling Dominion Militia became the prime defender, almost by default. Along with a needless anti-Americanism, this was a role many militiamen cherished because it gave them a rationale for existence. But they were hardly up to the task, for the governments of the day spent little on them and many other Canadians were too absorbed in developing the nation to notice.

One of the forces which kept the Active Militia alive during these years was the creation of a very small permanent corps of instructors in the 1870s and 1880s. But another and more important one for Sam Hughes' career was the influence of prominent citizens—some who were MPs—who joined the Volunteers, then kept up their military reform agitation in government. In the comfort of their own communities, these men often made their militia units as much social clubs as military organizations. The typical emphasis on ceremony and camaraderie was not harmful to military efficiency; it had the merit of attracting others who would not otherwise accept the Queen's shilling. Some also joined because the money which part-time duty gave them could tide them over the vagaries of the Canadian economy; others, caught in the flush of the Confederation spirit, saw military service as an outward manifestation of patriotic duty and good citizenship. There were others still who saw a threat and wanted to be prepared. Certainly personal ambitions to lead or to achieve high offices or public acclaim were also motives; and yet still others loved the vigorous life and martial arts and somehow felt that those who did not participate were less worthy morally and physically. In the half century or more that Sam Hughes served in the Active Militia, he showed signs of all these reasons for joining, and some more than others. But in 1866 few of them were of immediate concern to the twelve-year-old Hughes when he came out to do his duty.[8]

In 1866 during the most serious of the Fenian raids, along with his older brother John, Hughes joined one of the rifle companies of the 45th West Durham Battalion of Infantry. It was a hundred miles away to the west where the Fenians bloodied militiamen at the Battle of Ridgeway on the Niagara peninsula. In 1869 Hughes transferred to the 49th Battalion in Hastings County which was called out in 1870 when the Irish brotherhood made one last incursion into eastern Canada.

Hughes liked the Active Militia and believed that its part-time soldiers were the bulwark of Canadian defence. When peace returned he rejoined his original county unit with his brother and served as its sergeant-major, where he enjoyed field soldiering but not the bureaucratic "red-tape," as he later called it. Since joining he had worked hard at being a Volunteer, and he rose rapidly through the ranks. By 1868 he had completed the short Military School Course, which gave militiamen rudimentary knowledge of military organizations; and in 1870 he successfully sat his Volunteer Board qualifying examinations for a commission. Three years later he was promoted to lieutenant and in 1878 to captain with the position of battalion adjutant. He was always one rank behind his older brother.[9]

The positions Sam Hughes held did not demand a great deal of skill from most militia officers, even less in a rural corps like his. Hughes could comfortably live in Toronto and still do his military job in Durham County. Most of his work as adjutant was the normal routine of military administration, such as bookkeeping, filling the ranks for the annual camp, promulgating orders from Kingston District Headquarters among the six companies stationed throughout the county. Rail connections with Toronto, Bowmanville, and Lindsay were good and Hughes commuted between battalion headquarters at Bowmanville or his company in Lindsay and the city. Occasionally he might have to explain the complexities of the Militia Act or the Queen's Regulations and Orders to members of the regiment, but he could delegate such things to his fellow officers and handle much of the business by mail.

If the job was taken as seriously as Sam Hughes took it, however, it could be frustrating. The vain appeals to Ottawa for more and better equipment, the rules that had the city battalions drilling every year but the rural units at best only every two years, the high annual turnover, and the constant recruiting exertions to keep the ranks as full as possible were all maddening aspects of Sam Hughes' militia world. For Hughes another frustration was the winter which nearly stopped rural regimental activity. Company drill and especially individual study and the occasional rifle shoot were activities that Hughes encouraged among his men in the off-season.

Rifle shooting was Hughes' particular passion. Just after Confederation the Militia Department had begun encouraging civilian rifle training through arms and ammunition subsidies to clubs across the country. Like the government, Hughes believed the activity was an inexpensive way of teaching a basic martial skill without draining the limited regimental resources, and it gave a ready base from which men could be enlisted into the local battalion in an emergency. When civilians and soldiers mixed on the ranges, the experience provided—as it usually did in the long waits between militia camps—the only military field training members of the unit received. And over the years Hughes set up these civilian shooting fraternities in his various communities.[10]

Hughes was a driving force behind his battalion for a great many years; he worked hard at it with an undaunted spirit in spite of all the impediments. While he was teaching in Toronto, he personally organized the first drill squad among students at the Toronto Collegiate and exercised it himself during the school year. Later he claimed that it was he who convinced James Hughes to have drill for all boys made mandatory in the city's school system. Throughout their lives the Hughes brothers continued to be strong advocates of drill for schoolchildren, and they gained a lot of supporters for the activity, which ultimately blossomed into the Cadet Corps movement at the turn of the century.[11]

While Hughes' militia and sports activities continued, he decided to quit teaching in 1885. Classrooms did not satisfy his energy or his gregariousness. Nor did teaching provide enough money for his young family, which eventually included a boy, Garnet, and two girls, Roby and Aileen. Hughes may also have felt that the top posts in education would be denied him without more years of study. But above all he was an ambitious political animal who needed a forum to express his views. Journalism seemed the answer, and he began looking around for a suitable newspaper to buy in the area in which he had grown up. In the spring of 1885, just as Louis Riel was taking his irrevocable steps into rebellion, Hughes bought the *Victoria Warder*, a small newspaper in Lindsay which served both the residents of Victoria County and the Liberal-Conservative cause. By the time the school year was over,

Hughes was ready to move his family to Lindsay and to start careers in journalism and politics.[12]

Reference Notes to Chapter 1

1 *The Evening Post* (Lindsay, Ontario), August 24, 1921, p. 1; and ibid., August 27, 1921, p. 1.
2 Charles G. D. Roberts and A. L. Tunnell, eds., *A Standard Dictionary of Canadian Biography* (Toronto: Trans-Canada Press, 1934), vol. I, p. 272; and A. R. Capon, *His Faults Lie Gently: The Incredible Sam Hughes* (Lindsay: Hall, 1969), pp. 19-20.
3 The *Victoria Warder*, August 28, 1885, p. 1.
4 For a description of Victoria County, see Watson Kirkconnell, *Victoria County Centennial History* (Lindsay: Watchman-Warder Press, 1921), especially p. 234; and *Warder*, Sept. 11, 1885, p. 4.
5 Harvey William Burk (1822-1907) was elected as a Liberal in 1874 and 1878; in 1879 he resigned his seat to let Edward Blake, the national leader, stand in the constituency. See J. K. Johnson, ed., *The Canadian Directory of Parliament, 1867-1967* (Ottawa: Queens Printer, 1968), p. 82. Also see Capon, p. 21.
6 Henry James Morgan, ed., *Men and Women of the Time: A Handbook of Canadian Biography* (Toronto: Briggs, 1898), p. 485.
7 Ibid.; Capon, pp. 20-22; and Ross, pp. 186-87.
8 For a general discussion of the Canadian Militia, see G. F. G. Stanley, *Canada's Soldiers* (Toronto: Macmillan, 1974); Desmond Morton, *Ministers and Generals* (Toronto: University of Toronto Press, 1970) and *Canada and War* (Toronto: Butterworths, 1981), pp. 1-28.
9 Public Archives of Canada (PAC), RG 9, II, BI, vol. 141, F23388, Hughes to AG, July 30, 1888; and ibid., vol. 95, F10397, Memo, DAG, MD 3 and 4, June 24, 1885.
10 Ibid., II, A, vol. 351, F11721; and PAC, Sir John A. Macdonald, *papers*, MG 26, A, vol. 94, Hughes to Macdonald, June 19, 1889.
11 On various aspects of Hughes' regimental career, see RG 9, II A, "Deputy Minister, personal, 1885-1900"; and ibid., BI, "Adjutant General Office." In particular, see ibid., II, BI, vol. 95, F10397, Hughes to Cubitt, June 17, 1885.
12 *Watchman* (Lindsay), February 12, 1891, p. 4.

CHAPTER 2

Journalism, the Militia, and Local Politics, 1885-1890

Sam Hughes was thirty-three when he bought the *Victoria Warder* in 1885. For the next seven years, it was the focus of all his activities and clearly the means by which he intended to get into public office. He used it effectively and was blatantly partisan. Besides reporting community activities, Hughes expressed editorial opinions about anyone and anything, and often sensationally. It all had the calculated effect of quick public notoriety.

While Hughes' brash and pushy personality alienated some, he had obvious charms. One was good looks. Of average height, he was a noticeably muscular man with a swarthy complexion, short steel-grey hair, blue eyes, an angular face, and neatly chiselled features. For most of the next two decades, he wore a thick trimmed mustache. He could be an engaging conversationalist, and humour was his strong point. He had a prodigious memory, and his speech was simple and always littered with homespun phrases and oaths. Usually he spoke with absolute confidence, sometimes without much forethought. When he posed for photographs, which he loved to do, he looked like the stereotype of a North American Calvinist and he was, by way of Methodism. And he neither smoked nor drank.[1]

Whatever impression Sam Hughes left on people, there was no doubt about his preferences after reading his newspaper. His chief interests were politics and the militia. Often men of Sam Hughes' generation used their military and community leadership to qualify themselves for provincial or federal politics, and certainly this was true of Hughes. The quest for news took him to most of the community and

---

Reference notes for Chapter 2 are found on pp. 32-33.

political functions and kept him well informed about local issues. As adjutant of the 45th, he ran the battalion from Lindsay where two of its six companies were headquartered, and he helped found the Victoria County Rifle Association. By 1886 he was an active member of the town's Board of Trade and interested in local educational matters. He also carried on his fraternal associations as a Freemason, an Oddfellow, and an Orangeman. These contacts, especially the latter, helped settle him into the community and made him prominent as he moved into executive positions in these groups.[2]

But party politics was where Hughes moved most deliberately. When he bought the *Warder*, he purchased the goodwill and plant of a Liberal-Conservative newspaper whose previous editor had had the endorsement of Macdonald's government and which had represented Tory interests from the local to the federal level. Though in his youth he had briefly flirted with the Reform Party, there were many reasons why Hughes chose to be a Conservative. His father had been a Tory and so was his elder brother James; his family was also strongly Orange and intensely dedicated to the British connection. As well, Hughes grew up in an area that was overwhelmingly Conservative, and he was part of the generation that responded to Macdonald's national dream in 1867 and in later years to its political application, the National Policy. But there were also practical reasons why he should be a Conservative. It was the party that was in power, and as the government, the Conservatives dispensed patronage to the loyal and hard-working of the party, whether they were seeking office or not. Hughes derived part of his income from government advertising in the *Warder*; in turn, he supported most of their policies. Patronage gave the party discipline, contributed to the distribution of government services, and attracted men to seek elected offices, despite the low salaries of Members of Parliament. Hughes knew how the system operated, and he exploited it well.[3]

Although the *Warder* served both the constituent areas of North and South Victoria (as well as some areas of Haliburton), the town of Lindsay was in the southern part of the county, the area the new editor was most familiar with. When Hughes arrived in the county, both ridings had had long traditions of sending Conservatives to Ottawa, so Hughes joined Victoria South's association and his rise in its ranks was rapid. Within five years he had secured the executive positions of both vice-president and secretary. He was a willing worker in the political structure, donating time and money on behalf of provincial as well as federal candidates. He had a wide association with members of the larger Ontario federal organization, the Liberal-Conservative Union. Frequently he travelled outside his riding to attend meetings or to speak on behalf of other hopefuls. He was part of the patronage system and of the flow of information from the ridings to Ottawa, which helped the national leaders gauge the grass-roots mood, assess potential recruits, and judge the impact of their policies. Hughes was a prodigious correspondent with the Prime Minister; often he sent letters to Sir John to make sure that no local Grit was allowed to stay in public office in Victoria when there was a deserving loyalist who could fill the position. Macdonald sometimes thought Hughes' letters "voluminous"; at other times he thought their bluntness bordered on impertinence. Nevertheless Macdonald knew that Hughes was loyal and that the editor had a wide view of national issues, a perspective sometimes lacking in the constituencies. Macdonald often did what he could to handle Hughes' patronage requests, and in 1888 he confided to his postal minister that "Sam Hughes is one of our best friends." Certainly this was an opinion shared by Robert Birmingham, the federal party organizer in Ontario, and by Charles Hibbert Tupper, the national Minister of Marine and Fisheries.[4]

When the first issues of the *Warder* came off the press in July 1885, Hughes' readers knew instantly that he was a Tory. Every Friday morning the paper was distributed from the *Warder*'s office on Kent Street in Lindsay to about 2,500 subscribers in the town and surrounding area. The local Liberals had their own paper in Lindsay, *The Post*, which functioned much the same as the *Warder*. But Hughes put more aggressive spirit in the local journalism than his competition and his predecessors. Over the next three years, he increased his circulation by giving prizes for new subscriptions and by enlarging both the paper's format and his printing facilities. The improvements also included a new building and a modern and more efficient press. Like most rural and small-town newspapers of its day, the *Warder* was the major and sometimes only regular method of distributing information, as political parties well knew. Hughes also used it as a community teaching device; the lessons, of course, always according to the editor. He had correspondents in all the tiny settlements surrounding Lindsay, such as Fenelon Falls, Omemee, Bobcaygeon, and Kirkfield, and there was always something in the paper for every interest, from serialized children's stories and temperance columns to observations on the latest international events.[5]

One of the most frequent topics of Hughes' editorials was his other passion, the militia. Hughes became a leader in a long debate over the nature of the Canadian militia. On one side were men like professional soldier William Dillon Otter. Hughes had known Otter from his early sports days, and they shared a love of the rigorous life and the militia. But there the similarities stopped. Because of his experience with the Fenians at Ridgeway in 1866, Otter argued that Canada needed a regular, professional military service on the model of the British Army, with all its routine, discipline, order, and subordination—qualities he thought should apply to Canada's part-time soldiers as well as to the few regulars.[6] On the other side was Sam Hughes, enthusiastically defending part-time soldiers as the first line of Canadian defence. Desmond Morton has called Hughes the propagator of the militia myth of the War of 1812.[7] If this is meant to suggest that Hughes believed that irregular troops were better than professionals, indeed he did. But his military ideas contained moral and national connotations and a blending of civil and military roles, which made him something more than a "wild colonial boy" who instinctively disliked regular soldiers for their professional British Army snobbishness. Hughes was concerned with national preparedness, military training, proper equipment, and efficient organization.

The first military news event Hughes reported in the *Warder* was the second Riel rebellion, even though it was nearly over when he put out his first edition in the summer of 1885. Early that spring he had offered his services to the Militia Department, but for unknown reasons they were not accepted. Nevertheless he gave the campaign top coverage. His brother John had been chosen to lead one company of local lads in a composite battalion drawn from various militia units in eastern Ontario. This Midlanders Regiment, as it was called, was commanded by another militia friend and Tory MP for Durham East, Lieutenant-Colonel Arthur Williams. Along with others, the unit had done well at Batoche, justifying Hughes' faith in the superior quality of militiamen. "Regular troops," he proudly proclaimed shortly after the victory, "were all right for police purposes in times of peace and for training schools, but beyond that they are an injury to the nation." While having mostly kind words for the government's response to the crisis and that of GOC Sir Fred Middleton, Hughes at first was mildly critical of the General's slow and set-piece tactics in moving against the rebel headquarters. It is also true that Hughes had not considered that logistics problems and the inexperience of most of the militia troops may have been greater enemies for the GOC than the Métis.[8]

Nevertheless Hughes was delighted that the Volunteers had acquitted themselves so successfully in their first real military test since Confederation. The feat, Hughes advised his readers, could be further cemented if the government gave the troops generous land grants to settle the west. The presence of the veterans would deter "Yankee" interlopers and any further rebellion. Certainly Hughes was overjoyed that the force was almost entirely Canadian and needed little help from the British troops or "standing armies." Again he ignored the fact that even though Canada had had to employ some regulars in the west there were few available, making it impossible to avoid using mostly militiamen. Indeed had it not been for civilian contractors along the

Canadian Pacific Railway, those 5,000 "splendid" militiamen may not have got there at all.[9]

When the campaign was over, Hughes' enthusiasm to improve the Volunteers did not slacken in the *Warder* or elsewhere. Even though he did not agree with them all, he was aware of the latest military trends and he often reprinted war material from international papers. Like many others of his day, he felt that war machinery was becoming so lethal and costly that future conflict would be less frequent and shorter. He used the militia's victory at Batoche to emphasize the need for more rifle practice. Obviously he did not realize that militia numbers and the lack of Métis ammunition counted for the Canadian success; but he was correct about the militia's need for more practical training. When the *Canadian Militia Gazette*, which served the irregular force, first appeared in 1885, he highly recommended it to all militiamen as an important way both of keeping abreast of the latest innovations and also of keeping in contact with each other. The new Canadian paper, he announced, would "someday prove itself the equal of the best British journals."[10]

One thing that bothered Hughes perhaps more than anything else was his fear that the rural militia's primary defence role was being usurped by increases in the Permanent Force and in the city militia battalions. Both in the *Warder* and in private letters to Macdonald and Middleton, he insisted that the rural units train more and receive a larger share of the militia budget. His assessment was correct. But the cause of his worry was not a conspiracy by regular soldiers and a Catholic minister at headquarters—as he complained to Sir John in 1889—but a political reflection of public apathy and limited budgets. It was also due to the fact that Macdonald did not want militia reform. If Hughes recognized this fact, out of loyalty to Sir John he never admitted it. After the Washington Treaty in 1871, the Prime Minister perceived few real threats to Canada, and the militia became a political tool for him, in part because he knew its bulk was made up of militia officers like Sam Hughes who were political individuals. To increase military budgets and the number of units would not result in a corresponding increase in efficiency; it would only augment the partisan demands on his government, all of which would have to be satisfied. There was no better public display of the political nature of the militia than during the Northwest Campaign when prominent Tories demanded and got most of the positions. Hughes was well aware that the two composite units raised from rural Ontario were both commanded by Conservative MPs. It is true that as the apostle of the citizen-soldier he did not expect the militia to be neutral: the citizen had to be political in the national interest. Unfortunately the weakness of Hughes' equation was that not all citizen-soldiers held the same view of politics or the national interest. For Macdonald, therefore, military decisions demanded first political ones, and these were not always compatible with a particular view of progress in the militia. One way to alleviate the prejudice, as Lieutenant-Colonel William Otter then knew, was to build a professional corps to act as a neutral quality control in the militia. But Hughes would not accept that proposal because regulars would then challenge the "real fighters"—the militia.[11]

Still Hughes kept up his agitations; and as was often the case with many of his suggestions, they were spawned as much by his aversion to the permanent soldiers as by the boost given his national pride after the Volunteers' victory in the Northwest Campaign. The recently established Schools of Instruction run by the Permanent Corps, he lamented, were entirely inadequate. They should be expanded and tailored to fit the needs of militiamen instead of catering to "a nucleus of a standing army." So too the Royal Military College at Kingston should represent a national Canadian university, providing education and habits conducive to national development, volunteer service, and good citizenship rather than creating a professional military elite.[12]

Frequently Hughes' editorials in the *Warder* struck out at social problems like the loss of individuality, responsibility, and national toughness because of new labour-saving technologies and urbanization. To reaffirm these older values, he proposed that all farmboys join the Volunteers at eighteen. He chose this group specifically because they could shoot straighter and had more endurance; they were far cheaper to raise as Volunteers, and they had done all of the real military work since the War of 1812.

Hughes was also convinced that military organization needed revamping. Brigade camps should be held more frequently, at least every year. As well, Hughes felt that there should be frequent rotation of the brigade command so that each battalion lieutenant-colonel could practise running larger formations. In 1887 when Middleton suggested that regulars should take precedence over militiamen of the same rank, Hughes was horrified and reminded the General that "the Annals of the North-West do not indicate that the raw militia were a whit behind the regular. Our advice is to get rid of the red-tape and train the boys to spot a bulls-eye at 500 yards." That same year when the question of a replacement for the retiring GOC came up, Hughes supported Lieutenant-Colonel George T. Denison for the post. Denison was a Toronto lawyer of United Empire Loyalist stock, who commanded the Governor-General's Body Guard. Besides being a reformer and an internationally known cavalry expert, he was the most prominent militia enthusiast in the country. Although publicly not a party man, Denison also supported the National Policy and shared many of Hughes' hopes and fears about the country. Hughes also wanted Denison in the GOC post because he was a Canadian.[13]

It was not only Denison's militia ideas and pedigree that shaped Hughes' thinking; more immediately it was the editor's long simmering quarrel with Middleton. During the Riel campaign, the General had not hidden very well his preference for British rather than Canadian soldiers; and he had been unflattering about the quality of his militia officers. Much of his criticism was voiced by Bowen van Straubenzie, a British officer serving on the headquarters staff as deputy assistant adjutant-general. After the war the pretentious van Straubenzie had made some insensitive remarks in the Toronto *Mail* which suggested that he had had to push the Midlanders, including Hughes' brother, into battle at Batoche. When the regiment's commander, Lieutenant-Colonel Arthur Williams, died of natural causes shortly after that fight, not only did the smoldering discord between Canadian militia and British regular soldiers burst to the surface, but back in Lindsay Sam Hughes acridly reminded his readers that Colonel Williams was a maligned Canadian hero—a victim of British arrogance, incompetence, and glory-grabbing.[14]

Yet in 1885 Hughes made no direct public attack on Middleton and even defended the GOC against charges of looting in the west (accusations which ultimately forced the General to resign and leave Canada in 1890). But by the early summer of 1889, the GOC and Hughes had come to a bitter parting of the ways. The cause of the break, however, was more because of the government's refusal to accept Hughes' reform ideas and to call out the 45th for annual training for the third year in a row. As an adjutant and by now a brevet-major, Hughes took the business of running the regiment seriously. To force Middleton to muster the 45th that summer, he used his political influence with Macdonald. The GOC resented this flanking motion by one of his subordinates and promptly censored Hughes. Immediately Hughes complained in writing to Macdonald that if the GOC did not like what he was doing as a citizen in consulting with his own government, the General could court-martial him. Unfortunately Hughes blamed Middleton, but his tirade also implicated the government. The letter contained a combination of implied political threats to his own party, veiled by sharp words for British regular soldiers. In many ways, its message prophesied the storm and controversy which was to typify much of Hughes' later career. He told the Prime Minister:

> General Middleton makes no explanation of why we are dropped out for three years. He does not explain why the "every other year" policy is abandoned for a line of action akin to the Grit regime of 1874-1878....
> I regard it as none of General Middleton's business in any respect whatever, what I as a citizen of Canada and as an elector of Victoria may complain of to you or to the Department of Militia. He gets his salary, has got unmerited honours and has certain duties to perform to this country.... He is our "hired hand"... and we will tolerate no dictation from him. So long as he does his duty

fairly well, we will back him loyally; we will even overlook his trifling faults and impertinent oddities; but too much arrogance we will not suffer. He and his co-workers will find the people want less "flunkyism" and a system more in accord with a free democratic nation. Of late years, since Middleton came out, the Militia Department has been assuming a bureaucratic tone and form that will not do. For several years, as you know, members of the party have been quietly and firmly urging reforms in Sir (Adolphe) Caron's department, but without avail. I tell you in all sincerity, Sir John, and as one who has a very good regard for you, that the actions of those members, your own fellows, will one day surprise you unless a change occurs. . . . There is very much more that you have neither seen nor heard, and that too from men who love and respect *you*, and have sacrificed *time, money, public esteem* and more to *stand by you*. There is a limit however, and their dislike to some may overcome their *love* of *yourself*.[15]

The 45th did not train that year.

To some degree Hughes' reaction in his letter to Sir John was also produced by his own problems within the 45th. Like many other enthusiastic and capable militia officers of his day, he was being crippled in his promotions by a commanding officer who had held the regiment far too long. Lieutenant-Colonel Fred Cubitt had been there since the corps had been formed in 1866. In 1888 Cubitt, who was nearly seventy, had no intention of giving it up, and he did not for nearly another decade. But he thought highly of Hughes as a talented soldier. Several times before 1888 he recommended his adjutant for promotion, reporting that he was a "painstaking, zealous and efficient officer who has really worked hard to perfect his military education" and "who deserves every possible recognition of his services." Once Hughes got his brevet-majority that year, he immediately began agitating to have Cubitt retired. Although he got nowhere, only making Cubitt more determined to stay on, he kept up the pressure in Ottawa. If the deserving subordinate officers were not allowed to get beyond brevet- or junior-major, he reasoned, how could the militia ever rise out of its current malaise. Hughes was correct, but his ego was also involved. "Not to toot my own horn," he calmly told the Prime Minister in 1889, "my brother and I have kept the battalion up for years." He went on to offer a simple solution: instead of his unit being spread all over Victoria and Durham counties, each area should have its own regiment for efficiency's sake. If Colonel Cubitt was retired and Hughes' brother moved over to the 46th, as was recommended in his scheme, then both Sam and John Hughes would become lieutenant-colonels commanding. In the end the Prime Minister typically did nothing, and the next year, when Middleton resigned under a cloud, Sam Hughes was glad to see him go. But he still had to put up with Cubitt.[16]

Closely associated with Sam Hughes' military ideas were his national ones. In his 1888 Dominion Day editorial, he projected a vision of Canada as "the peer of any nation in present benefits and future prospects"; and he was ready to attack all who questioned the country's national greatness—especially if they were Grits. Edward Blake, the federal Reform leader, was labelled a negative force whose leadership was nothing more than "quarrelous [sic] and unpatriotic opposition to national building." The same went for Blake's successor and his trade ideas. After the defeat in the 1887 election, Wilfrid Laurier became mesmerized by the perennial flower of free trade. Never strong on economic theory, the Liberal leader adopted free trade in the form of commercial union with the United States. He was hoping to cash in on the discontent of Ontario farmers over an apparently barren and somewhat shop-worn National Policy. Sam Hughes, however, held no such illusions about the merits of the scheme.[17]

As the free-trade idea gained ground among Victoria County's hard-pressed farmers, Hughes denounced it in the *Warder*. "The question," he said, "of Commercial Union is simply annexation under a softer name." There was no possible economic advantage for Canadians, Hughes warned his readers, for the United States produces many of the same agricultural goods. The fear Hughes had of the economic attraction of commercial union flowed from his passionate desire to prevent Canada from being absorbed if left unprotected and outside the British Empire. He wanted Canadian growth and prosperity, but not at the cost of national self-destruction. By 1888 he was even offering his own solution for any Victoria County farmers who might be seduced by the spurious arguments of Grit economics: stay inside the trading circles of the Empire, build a strong volunteer militia to ward off "Yankees," and seek a commercial union of the Empire, Canada, and the United States, all "under the hereditary kings of Great Britain."[18]

Hughes' concern for Canada's future, entangled with his view of national traditions, ultimately led him to examine the country's relationship within the British Empire itself. In one of his first issues of the *Warder* in 1885, he unfurled a scheme which did not change much over the next thirty-five years. Hughes wanted an imperial federation of Great Britain and all the colonies. Each component was to be autonomous domestically, and each would send delegates to a great imperial parliament sitting in England, which would govern all external interests of the parts. The benefits, he said, would be lower taxes, more local autonomy, better defence with fewer "standing armies," and an increase in trade and commerce.[19]

Hughes' plan typified more than just his enthusiasm for great schemes; it was a revelation about his position in the debate about Canada's future. The mid-1880s saw a resurgence of imperial fervour throughout the Empire. Combining territorial expansion with missionary zeal and a sense of rebirth, imperialists wanted to spread the

Anglo-Saxon benefits of British liberty and justice, state and industrial organization, education, and Christianity to the rest of the world. They also envisioned an integral system of defence and trade. When such promotional organizations as the Imperial Federation League (IFL) were formed in London in 1884, it was only a matter of time before sympathetic Canadians would be preaching a similar message. As Carl Berger cautions, however, Canadian imperialism was different than its British counterpart. In Canada it was a movement "for a closer union of the British Empire through economic and military co-operation and through political changes which would give the dominions influence over imperial policy."[20] In short, nationalism was a prime component of Canadian imperialist thought.

Nowhere is that clearer than in Hughes' 1885 Empire scheme or in his reaction to the commercial union proposals. Like other English-speaking Canadians whose roots lay deep in British traditions, Sam Hughes had an immense sense of pride in belonging to the British Empire. But even this optimistic rhetoric was superficial, for underneath it was a fear that all was not well, especially in Canada. By the time the country was two decades old, the gristle of the national dream had not yet hardened to the bone as Macdonald had hoped; economic hard times had prevented it, so had the developing cultural schism between English- and French-Canadians. Riel on two occasions had pitted east against west and brother against confrère. Having lived through this, Sam Hughes feared for the Dominion's existence. His solution was an imperial consolidation in which Canadians would have sufficient influence to fulfill their national aspirations, a solution that did not take into account the political and cultural problems. In the final analysis, Hughes' imperial dream was closely associated, again in Carl Berger's words, with his conception of his own and Canada's "history, character and destiny."[21]

Sam Hughes was one of the earliest advocates of imperial federation. His position was declared in the *Warder*'s columns only three months after the first Canadian branch of the IFL was established in Montreal. In February 1888 the Toronto IFL was co-founded by James Hughes and D'Alton McCarthy, the Conservative MP for North Simcoe (who would shortly split with the party over the use of French outside Quebec). Another prominent member was G. T. Denison. But in spite of the attraction of these important Torontonians, Sam Hughes needed the impact of the Grit commercial union campaign to join the Toronto branch in November 1888. Shortly after in one of his long letters of advice, Hughes told the Prime Minister:

I like the general outline of the movement, it having for sixteen years been advocated by me. Its growth, to be lasting, must be cautious and yet vigorous—a steady strength so to speak. But give us an English trade influence over our farmers. I claim that there is a market for us, and have got Mr. Hudspeth [Conservative MP for Victoria South], D'Alton McCarthy, the *Empire*, the *World*, and through them the Minister of Agriculture on the war path for that market. Hudspeth is now much interested in that question, Colonel G. T. Denison has forever renounced the Grits. I spent Thursday night at his place in Toronto, and he is very strong for you. He is coming here to give us an imperial federation speech before Xmas.[22]

Not only did Hughes become a member, but he was elected to the federation's organizing committee, which promoted the creation of branches throughout the country. He shared this position with other notables—like Denison, who was the chairman, J. Castell Hopkins, the Tory imperialist observer of Canadian public life; A. R. Creelman, a partner in the Toronto law firm of McCarthy, Osler, Hoskin and Company, and a Liberal; and William Hamilton Merritt, a Toronto mining engineer and another scion of one of Canada's loyalist families. Back home Hughes turned his newspaper's pages to the support of the IFL, which significantly included a resolution that Canada be given more say in determining imperial policy. At the same time Hughes began heading his editorial columns with the Red Ensign and a short jingoistic verse which was the synthesis of his imperial and national ideas. It remained his editorial masthead for as long as he owned the *Warder*:

> A union of hearts and a union of hands
> A union none can sever
> A union of home and a union of lands
> And the flag, the British Union Forever!

In December 1888 and again in January 1889, Hughes brought Denison to Lindsay to spread the IFL gospel. After a few successful rallies, in which attacks against commercial union and arguments for the economic advantages of Empire played a large part, Hughes helped form the Lindsay and County of Victoria Branch of the IFL. Over the next several months, Hughes promoted the IFL so successfully that Castell Hopkins, the secretary of the provincial organizing committee, could satisfactorily report that Victoria County had over sixteen sub-branches—more than any other area in the country.[23]

Though Hughes was to remain a member of the IFL and its successor, the British Empire League, his participation slowly dwindled in the group's official functions over the years. The reasons were in part those that affected McCarthy in 1891 when he was forced to resign as president. As G. M. Grant, the principal of Queen's University and one of the leading intellectuals of the movement, explained at the time to McCarthy: "You see, we wish to keep the league non-partisan till we can persuade Canadians generally that it is in the common interest." D'Alton McCarthy was never neutral in the debate over Canadian cultural politics, and by then neither was Sam Hughes. When he had to match wits with men like G. R. Parkin, principal of Upper Canada College and chief publicist for the IFL, or with Grant, or even with Denison, Hughes was not often successful. Moreover, the movement itself ultimately deviated from what Hughes thought was important in the long run—imperial defence. Most of the other IFL members had put their hopes in an Empire trade scheme because, unlike defence, they knew it had the widest popular appeal. In later years Hughes would reject this as a first step. In this sense, while Hughes remained a vigorous imperialist, like so many in the movement he had his own special brand and went on his own special mission.[24]

Sam Hughes' military and imperial fervour was nothing in comparison to the verbal bashing that went on between the editors of the Liberal *Post* and the Conservative *Warder*, especially over religion and politics. But such "orgies of Billingsgate," as Watson Kirkconnell called them, were accepted as normal political sparring; what caused most of the bitterness was Hughes' strident public comments about Roman Catholics. Victoria County had more Orangemen than many other areas. Already on the local executive and moving in national circles of the Orange Lodge, Hughes could not ignore the potential benefits of a vigorous appeal to the area brethren. He would not be the first or the last political aspirant to tap constituent values for their political returns. When Hughes attacked Catholics, he usually did so claiming that they were all dupes in a priestly conspiracy determined to dominate all levels of society; and mostly it was in a nefarious alliance with Liberals and Fenians to destroy the country.[25]

Invariably Hughes' religious tirades were mixed with and confused by his cultural ideas; and they contributed substantially to the already widening schism between English- and French-Canadians, each side increasingly concerned about the other's threat to its vision of Canada and the world. On his side Hughes strained logic to show that French-Canadians were really "teutonic people," and that priests and Reformers—presumably like Wilfrid Laurier—had hoodwinked them into projecting their "Frenchness." While they need not discard it completely, as far as Hughes was concerned, it was idiocy to perpetuate French "in a country where the vast majority speak English." As soon as Quebec got rid of its "obsolete sixteenth century despotic" ways, the sooner it could adopt the "social improvements that constitute the great blessing of Ontario."[26]

What Hughes meant by the great social "blessing of Ontario" he made clear in a report on an outbreak of smallpox in Montreal in the fall of 1885. The cause of the epidemic, he was convinced, was the Catholic church: "Investigation reveals daily that... the unfortunate French-Canadians are very little better than brutes. The poor creatures have for ages been kept in darkness, ignorance and superstition till now; they are so dulled and blinded as to be insensible to the ordinary feelings of humanity." If all the Quebecois would throw off their oppressive "romanism," the editor suggested, the incidence of disease and famine would decline substantially, and the Canadiens would even become human like people in Ontario.[27]

Direct evidence allows only rare glimpses into Hughes' soul, so how much Sam Hughes actually believed what he broadcast is not clear. Certainly he did not personally endorse Catholicism. His virulence, however, has to be seen as much as a function of constituent political necessity as personal bigotry.

In November 1885 not many of Victoria County's few Catholics were prepared to explore the subtleties of the new editor's motives. Obviously on the verge of violence, a delegation confronted the editor in his office and cursed him roundly as a bigot. Many of them cancelled their subscriptions and called for a similar boycott by the rest of the community. Some answered the call: during several nights Hughes had to put up with torch-lit, placard-carrying protesters denouncing him in several parts of the town. He lost nearly fifty subscriptions. The whole episode only made him dig in his heels. Most "RCs," he lamely snarled, did not read the *Warder* anyhow, so the cancellations were no great loss. In any event the "dogans," as he often called them, should be able to take constructive criticism, which was all his previous editorials had intended. Besides, he claimed, the placards were only a Grit trick meant to discredit him as a Conservative in the eyes of thinking Catholics.[28]

The editorials did not stop then or in the next several years. Indeed in the spring of 1887 Hughes was sued by a local Catholic named Connolly; he eventually lost and was fined $1,000 for libel and costs. A month after the federal election campaign that year—a bitter local contest in which Hughes had carried the Conservative press colours and slammed Grit and Catholic alike—someone tried to burn out the *Warder*. There was little damage done, and in the next edition Hughes gloated that the culprits—"Fenians" no doubt—were so incompetent that they could not even start a good fire. He also reciprocated, presumably aiming his threat at the Liberal *Post* which he suspected of complicity in the deal: "If we undertake to kindle a fire," he wrote, "it will not be a flash in the pan." On another occasion he was shot at in the dark, and on still another, in January 1894, after he had been elected to Parliament, Hughes got into a fist fight on Lindsay's main street with a local political rival named Kylie. For once the editor picked the wrong man: a burly blacksmith, Kylie promptly knocked his attacker off his feet and soundly pummelled him before delighted onlookers. Then he had Hughes arrested for assault, convicted, and fined. All of the area newspapers got into the fray, and nearly all of them were against Hughes. The *Post* ran the caption: "Sammy, Sammy, has our right hand lost its cunning? How this generation has deteriorated!" For weeks after, long epic poems by local Grit and Catholic bards lampooned the great warrior's demise. In turn the sullen Hughes growled back in the *Warder*'s editorial pages that he had lost the fight only because he had just recently recovered from "la grippe" and had a heavy overcoat on. Besides, he said, "sworn evidence will show ... [I] ... received only one mark, while [Kylie] had four besides two heavy blows on the most prominent part of his face." But none of this deterred him, and he kept up his strong anti-Catholic and Liberal tirades.[29]

He even assailed the national Conservative Party when he felt that it was giving in to French-Canadian and Catholic dictates. Such was the case over the Jesuits Estates Bill in the spring of 1889. This issue was an old one for Canadians, dating back to 1774 when the Jesuit order was expelled and its property confiscated by the state. The case was an especially prickly one, for it struck at the very core of differences of religion, education, and language. What to do with the revenues derived from the properties was the question. The newly elected Liberal-Nationalist Premier of Quebec, Honoré Mercier, called for a decision by the Vatican. Anglo-Saxon and Orange Ontarians were incensed, not only because it was a Catholic solution, but also because the legislation involved a foreign interference in a purely domestic affair. They were upset as well because much of the money from the sale of the property was to go in support of Quebec's Catholic school system; for some time the Grand Orange Lodge of British America had passed an annual resolution vowing to fight this kind of use of public funds.

Sam Hughes was no different than other Orangemen when he denounced the Quebec bill, which by then was being hotly debated in the federal House. When John Thompson, the Methodist-turned-Catholic Minister of Justice refused to disallow the bill, arguing that it was a provincial affair, and was supported by most of the cabinet, Hughes was beside himself. In Parliament D'Alton McCarthy and twelve others, including seven Conservative MPs, broke party ranks by offering a motion for disallowance, and Hughes publicly sided with the "noble 13," as they were called. In June he held a public rally in Lindsay in their support, where he threatened the beleaguered Prime Minister personally and in the *Warder* that he would withdraw from the party unless Macdonald backed down on the issue. "Thompson," he heatedly accused Sir John, "controls you all and is really Premier of Canada." It was difficult for Hughes to do otherwise because of both his Protestant Orange instincts and local necessity. J. A. Barron, a Lindsay lawyer and one of the "noble 13," had been the Liberal MP for North Victoria. If

Hughes did not support the proposition, the local Conservative Party would be the loser.[30]

Yet if he remained on his present path, the only step left for Hughes would be a complete break with Macdonald. In spite of the moves of the "noble 13," the government had a large enough majority to override the maverick McCarthy's motion. Moreover, the Prime Minister was backed by Mackenzie Bowell, his Minister of Customs, who was also the former Grand Master of the Grand Orange Lodge; and Bowell was working hard to bring the more moderate lodge members into line. When Hughes took his public hard line on the bill that summer, both Macdonald and Bowell censored him for his political threats and religious extremism. Hughes' reaction in September was to back off and vigorously reaffirm his political loyalty. He did not have any choice. Rebellion would end his political hopes; it would also ruin his four years of hard work as a machine loyalist. No doubt the spectre of losing government printing contracts also helped him make up his mind.[31]

In the early fall Hughes toned down his support of McCarthy. In light of what McCarthy was then trying to do politically, it was a critical move for Sam Hughes. Earlier that year the dissident MP had resigned as head of the powerful Ontario Liberal-Conservative Union and formed his own lobby, the Equal Rights Association, a group dedicated to preventing any groups or religious bodies from acquiring special rights. However, the association quickly filled up with extremists who were both anti-Catholic and anti-French-Canadian. No doubt the new group appealed to Hughes at first, in part because of his strong views but also because his brother James was the co-founder of the Equal Rights Association and its first vice-president. After Macdonald's stern warnings, Sam Hughes steered clear of the body and advised local Tories to do the same. Although he still supported the association's intent, he publicly rationalized, the group was too narrow in limiting its attacks to the Jesuit legislation. By taking such a detached position, Hughes was trying to keep himself in both camps. He needed the support of the more reactionary Tories locally, but he also could not survive easily in business or in politics without government endorsement. Thus Hughes compromised. First he sensibly suggested to Macdonald that the entire question be submitted to a higher court, thereby satisfying both sides and protecting the government. Failing with that, Hughes then publicly admitted that the Jesuits Estates issue belonged under provincial jurisdiction. As a further sign of contrition, Hughes let the Prime Minister know that he was engaged in a heavy but successful struggle to ward off the local Equal Rights Association which was threatening to split Victoria County Tories by forming a third party. Though Hughes was repentant, he made it clear to Macdonald that he was not happy about the Jesuit issue and that the government should "make sure that no grit dogans get Tory offices" in Victoria County or elsewhere. Evidently Macdonald was satisfied because the patronage to the local faithful began to flow through Sam Hughes again—and the Jesuit Estates Bill was overtaken by more pressing national problems.[32]

In the end Hughes survived his first Tory loyalty crisis without any apparent side-effects: he had not become a political victim of his own biases as had McCarthy, and his local reputation was still intact. But it was also evident that Sam Hughes bore the symptoms of racial intolerance, symptoms that were partly the result of a perception of Canada as a secular, Anglo-Saxon, English-speaking country.

While Hughes emerged from the Jesuit Estates crisis largely unstained by his own intolerance, he did encounter local opposition. His direct and personal attacks had upset the local Catholics and some moderate Protestant Tories. At a time when ridings were usually won or lost by a few votes and passions ran deep, there was a small group within the Victoria South constituency association who felt that the fiery editor's thoughtless outbursts had hurt the party, and frequently the few local Catholic Conservatives had expressed their discontent at the riding meetings. But the protests had little effect. Hughes' rapid rise in the executive indicated that he was popular with most of the members who appreciated his vigour and hard work and likely shared many of his biases. Nor was there much visible opposition from non-Catholic Tories until just before the federal election contest in 1887.

When the riding association met to nominate a candidate, Hughes backed a newcomer, Lindsay lawyer Adam Hudspeth, against the incumbent, J. R. Dundas, a wealthy local merchant who had represented the south riding in Parliament since 1882. After a fierce convention fight, Hudspeth got the nomination and subsequently won the election. In turn Hughes got himself into deeper water with Dundas. The antagonism between the two men had begun with Hughes' purchase of the *Warder* in 1885. He had bought it from John Dobson, a prosperous merchant who had been mayor of Lindsay and president of the south riding association for a number of years. Dobson was ambitious for a senate seat (which in fact he got the same day Hughes took his seat in Parliament in 1892). As an Orangeman and a Conservative, perhaps he was dissatisfied with J. R. Dundas' representations in Parliament. Whatever the motive, Dobson was a Sam Hughes' supporter after 1885. In the convention fight in 1887, he had also been a Hudspeth backer. With the local association's executive members, such as Dobson, ranged on Sam Hughes' side, Dundas had little hope of winning with his particular version of Conservatism.[33]

Dundas and two of his nephews and business partners started another Tory newspaper in January 1888. The new independent Conservative sheet, the Lindsay *Watchman*, advertised itself—with more conviction than truth—as the paper of moderation. Dundas installed as the editor Joseph Cooper, who had been the manager of the Victoria *Warder* until Hughes purchased it. A third newspaper in a town as small as Lindsay hurt Hughes financially. Until that time he had made a good yearly profit of about $2,500. The *Watchman* competed for the local advertising trade by charging less than the *Warder*, and it got a share of the government printing largesse. In an election year the printing of voters lists had given Hughes an account worth more than $1,400.[34]

Over the next several years, Dundas frequently lobbied among his ex-fellow MPs in Ottawa to discredit Hughes in the party, always complaining that the aggressive editor's scurrilous press campaigns had "estranged from us the entire Catholic vote." The Catholic Vicar-General in the Lindsay area and an old Tory, P. D. Laurent, added his endorsement to Dundas' frequent protests. Laurent could not understand why the local riding association did not muzzle the "vicious dog." Between the two of them, they had some success with a few of Macdonald's Catholic ministers: Thompson in Justice, Langevin in Public Works, and Adolphe Caron in Militia and Defence. By the height of the Jesuit Estates controversy, Hughes felt the three ministers were conspiring directly against him—a machination supported by the patronage appointment of one or two Catholics to local offices in the county. Macdonald and several of his other cabinet ministers, however, preferred Hughes' party work and his newspaper; and in the riding the bulk of the local association members supported Hughes. They continued to elect him to the executive. Indeed in a letter to the Prime Minsiter, one of them described the minority opposition to Hughes as "partisan nonsense."[35]

The failure to muzzle Hughes did not mean that the infighting between the two lop-sided factions ended. The *Watchman*'s editor sued Hughes in April 1890 for slanderous comments Hughes had made in the *Warder* the previous fall. The affair had begun with Cooper's reference to Hughes as "a drunkard, an unmitigated ass, a braggard, a ruffian and a political montebank." Instead of suing, Hughes could not resist trying to top the insults with some of his own. In a three-column spread across the *Warder*'s front page, Hughes told Cooper in an open letter that "to have noticed you would have gratified your weak intellect, ... your miserable carcass is so puny as to be free of the punishment such craven wretches as you deserve." He also claimed that Cooper had stolen a printing press from nearby Omemee. Hughes hired MP Adam Hudspeth to defend him, but was so impatient with the slow-moving lawyer that he ended up conducting his own case. Several times the presiding judge had to stop the unrepentant Hughes from badgering witnesses and introducing extraneous evidence. The prosecuting lawyer was the famous B. B. Osler, specially imported from Toronto for the case, and in the end the jury was only out a short while before finding Hughes guilty, a verdict that cost him $900. When it was over Hughes whined to Sir John Macdonald that he had lost because the judge was a Grit, that D'Alton McCarthy had influenced the judgment against him, and that Adam Hudspeth was poorly prepared because he had secretly accepted a fee from Dundas "to lose me the case."[36]

In spite of the court defeat and the financial strain, Hughes did not seem to lose much other than money. In the summer of 1890 he was vice-president of the south riding's association. Thereafter he continued to receive Macdonald's support through Robert Birmingham, the Ontario organizer who had already begun to mobilize the provincial machine for the election due in early 1892. Hughes and Cooper continued to spar in their editorial columns, and there were signs that Sam Hughes was winning both the political and the economic struggle against the *Watchman*. That fall Cooper notified his readers that he would have to cut back his political activities in South Victoria because the *Warder* was getting all of the government printing work as well as the official party endorsement.[37] As for Hughes, he was thinking about running for Parliament himself.

Reference Notes to Chapter 2

1. Capon, pp. 19-20.
2. Morton, *Ministers and Generals*, p. 146; and Morgan, 1898, p. 485.
3. Chambers, p. 82; *Watchman*, Feb. 3, 1891, p. 4, editorial; PAC, Sir John Macdonald *papers*, MG 26, A, pp. 221065-66, Hughes to Macdonald, July 7, 1887; and ibid., p. 221298, Hughes to Macdonald, July 10, 1887.
4. PAC, Macdonald *papers*, p. 231829, Macdonald to Haggert, November 1888; ibid., p. 131271, Tupper to Macdonald, June 17, 1889; and ibid., p. 244463, Birmingham to Macdonald, Oct. 6, 1890.
5. For example, see the *Warder*, July 31, 1885, p. 1, Nov. 13, 1885, p. 1, Jan. 15, 1886, p. 4, July 2, 1886, p. 4, Aug. 3, 1886, p. 4, Sept. 30, 1887, p. 1, and Dec. 2, 1887, p. 4.
6. Desmond Morton, *The Canadian General: Sir William Otter* (Toronto: Hakkert, 1974), pp. 79-81.
7. Ibid., pp. 80-81.
8. PAC, Sir A. P. Caron *papers*, MG 27, 1D3, F 7843, 1885, papers missing; PAC, RG 9, II, B 1, vol. 95, F 10397, Cubitt to DAG, MD 3 Kingston, June 22, 1885; and *Warder*, Sept. 11, 1885, p. 4, editorial.
9. PAC, Caron *papers*, vol. 118, Hughes to Caron, Feb. 13, 1888; *Warder*, Aug. 28, 1885, p. 4; and ibid., Sept. 11, 1885, p. 4. Also see C. P. Stacey, ed., *Military History for Canadian Students*, 6th ed. (Ottawa: Queen's Printer, 1973), pp. 75-85.
10. *Warder*, Aug. 28, 1885, p. 4, and July 31, 1885, p. 2; and PAC, Caron *papers*, vol. 108, F 11367, Hughes to Caron, Sept. 5, 1887.
11. PAC, Macdonald *papers*, pp. 36591-96, Hughes to Macdonald, June 19, 1889; and Morton, *Ministers and Generals*, pp. 96-97. One of those Tories was Arthur Williams, the other was Lieutenant-Colonel William O'Brien (Muskoka), a prominent Orangeman. See J. K. Johnson, pp. 447, 602.
12. *Warder*, May 13, 1887, p. 4, and July 6, 1888, p. 4.
13. Ibid., Sept. 11, 1885, p. 4, Jan. 22, 1886, p. 4, Aug. 14, 1885, p. 4, June 24, 1887, p. 4, Aug. 3, 1886, p. 4, Sept. 16, 1887, p. 4, May 16, 1888, p. 4; Morton, *Ministers and*

Generals, p. 107. On Denison, see Berger, *The Sense of Power* (Toronto: University of Toronto Press, 1970), chapters 1-5, 10-11.
14 *Warder*, July 31, 1885, p. 4, Aug. 14, 1885, p. 4, and Aug. 21, 1885, p. 4.
15 PAC, Macdonald *papers*, pp. 36591-92, Hughes to Macdonald, June 19, 1889; and PAC, Caron *papers*, f 11822, Hughes to Hudspeth, May 22, 1889; ibid., Middleton to Caron, June 4, 1889; and ibid., van Straubenzie to AG, June 2, 1889.
16 PAC, RG 9, II, B 1, vol. 25, F 10397, Cubitt to DAG, MD 3 Kingston, June 22, 1885; ibid., vol. 137 F 22807, Hughes to Cubitt, Apr. 20, 1888, Cubitt's marginalia; ibid., vol. 141, F 24388, Sam Hughes to AG Ottawa, July 30, 1888, and Aug. 14, 1888; and ibid., AG to Cubitt, July 24, 1888, and Aug. 26, 1888; PAC, Caron *papers*, F 11822, Hughes to Caron, Feb. 17, 1888; and PAC, Macdonald *papers*, vol. 94, pp. 36591-95, Hughes to Macdonald, June 19, 1889.
17 *Warder*, July 6, 1888, p. 4, and Sept. 4, 1885, p. 2.
18 Ibid., May 27, 1887, p. 4, July 8, 1887, p. 4, and March 28, 1888, p. 4.
19 Ibid., Aug. 14, 1885, p. 4, and Aug. 5, 1887, p. 4.
20 A. D. Johnson, "The Imperial Federation League in Canada, 1885-1899" (Honours BA thesis, Royal Military College of Canada, 1972), chapter 1; and James Morris, *Farewell the Trumpets, An Imperial Retreat* (London: Penguin, 1979), pp. 21-32.
21 Berger, *Sense of Power*, p. 3.
22 *Warder*, Mar. 30, 1888, p. 4; and PAC, Macdonald *papers*, pp. 231823-24, Hughes to Macdonald, Nov. 12, 1888.
23 J. Castell Hopkins, ed. *Canada: An Encyclopedia of the Country* (Toronto: Linscott, 1900), vol. 6, pp. 51-62; PAC, Macdonald *papers*, pp. 232439-41, Hughes to Macdonald, Dec. 18, 1888; and *Warder*, Dec. 7, 1888, p. 4, Dec. 21, 1888, p. 4, Mar. 30, 1888, p. 4, Jan. 11, 1889, p. 4, and Mar. 20, 1891, p. 4.
24 Berger, p. 136; and Johnson, pp. 14-54.
25 Kirkconnell, p. 133; and *Warder*, Nov. 6, 1885, p. 4, and July 2, 1886, p. 4.
26 *Warder*, Aug. 21, 1885, p. 4, and Sept. 4, 1885, p. 4.
27 Ibid., Nov. 6, 1885, p. 4.
28 Ibid., Nov. 13, 1885, p. 4.
29 Ibid., Mar. 25, 1887, p. 4, May 6, 1887, p. 4, and Jan. 19, 1894, pp. 1, 4; PAC, Macdonald *papers*, pp. 221065-66, Hughes to Macdonald, July 7, 1887; "Sam Hughes and the Problem of Imperialism," Canadian Historical Association, *Annual Report*, 1949-1950, p. 32; and Capon, pp. 24-26.
30 Hereward Senior, *Orangeism: The Canadian Phase* (Toronto: McGraw-Hill-Ryerson, 1972), p. 80; PAC, Macdonald *papers*, p. 36595, Hughes to Macdonald, June 19, 1889. See the *Warder*, Feb. 8, 1889, p. 4, Mar. 22, 1889, p. 4, and July 19 and 26, 1889, p. 4—the latter's editorial title is "Country before Party."
31 Senior, p. 79; and PAC, Macdonald *papers*, pp. 79292-93, Bowell to Macdonald, Aug. 1, 1889; ibid., pp. 237509-14, Hughes to Macdonald, Sept. 22, 1889.
32 *Warder*, Nov. 22, 1889, p. 4; PAC, Macdonald *papers*, pp. 234745-46, Hughes to Macdonald, Apr. 7, 1889; ibid., pp. 237509-14, Sept. 22, 1889, and pp. 239205-06, Dec. 27, 1889.
33 Ibid., PAC, Macdonald *papers*, pp. 244514-15, Hughes to Macdonald, Oct. 9, 1890; *Warder*, Dec. 19, 1894, p. 4; Jan. 15, 1896, p. 1; and Johnson, *Directory of Parliament*, pp. 170, 182. Hughes lobbied to get Dobson the Senate seat. See Public Archives of Ontario (PAO), Wallace Family *papers*, MU 3089, Dobson to Wallace, June 3, 1891; PAC, Macdonald, *papers*, pp. 1961-62, Hughes to Macdonald, Oct. 28, 1889.
34 The *Watchman*, Jan. 19, 1888, p. 2; and PAC, Macdonald *papers*, pp. 221065-66, Hughes to Macdonald, July 7, 1887.
35 PAC, Macdonald *papers*, p. 24544, Dundas to Macdonald, Nov. 17, 1890; ibid., pp. 233488-89, Laurent to Macdonald, Feb. 9, 1889; ibid., pp. 218565-66, Laurent to Langevin, Apr. 11, 1887; and ibid., pp. 244979-80, Thompson to Macdonald, Oct. 31, 1890; ibid., pp. 23350-52, Hudspeth to Macdonald, Feb. 11, 1889, and *Supra*, note 4.
36 *Warder*, Oct. 25, 1889, p. 4, and Nov. 8, 1889, p. 1; *Watchman*, Apr. 10, 1890, p. 4; and PAC, Macdonald *papers*, pp. 244514-15, Hughes to Macdonald, Oct. 9, 1890.
37 *Watchman*, Nov. 13, 1890, p. 4.

CHAPTER 3

Getting Elected, 1890-1892

In the summer of 1890, when Sam Hughes confided to Sir John Macdonald that he hoped to seek a federal seat in the election expected in 1892, he had no clear idea of how he would do it.[1] Money was a big problem. Court cases had cost him plenty, so had Dundas' *Watchman*. In the last five years he had spent significant sums on the causes of other Tory candidates in the region. But Hughes felt that his own time was ripe: his standing was good in the local southern association where most of the executive were friends of his; and he had other clear strengths—the Orange Lodge, his willingness to work on behalf of the party throughout the province, his wit and charm, his pugnacious yet forthright manner, and his remarkable memory. But sheer accident pushed him on his way. Earlier that spring the incumbent member for South Victoria, Adam Hudspeth, suddenly died.[2] By September there was a confused scramble for the riding candidacy. Hughes wanted it badly, and a convention was set for the early fall.

The contest was complicated, especially by the discord between Hughes and his old rival in journalism and politics, J. R. Dundas, who supported another candidate for his old seat. There were several other contenders to confuse things further. Since the federal party did not want to lose the seat as they had lost Victoria North three years before, the provincial organizer, Robert Birmingham, had an uncommon interest in the convention. He had to listen to the complaints of Dundas who was afraid of Hughes' popularity among the rank and file. Dundas tried to discredit Hughes with the federal leaders by denouncing his anti-Catholicism as fatal for Tory hopes.[3] But after the Prime Minister's and Bowell's warnings the previous fall, Hughes had softened his public comments on religious issues. For over a year his letters to

---

Reference notes for Chapter 3 are found on pp. 45-46.

Macdonald had contained moderate reminders that he would neither advocate nor support anyone who included the Jesuit Estates issue or Equal Rights planks in their platform. But Hughes was also independent enough to point out to Sir John that both issues were popular enough locally to win on.[4] While there is no evidence that the federal leaders did not want Hughes to throw his hat in the ring, neither is there any that they promoted him. When Birmingham visited the riding several times that fall, he thought Sam Hughes was the most loyal and willing worker there, but he did not list him as one of the candidates. Hughes bided his time as the decision-making process ground slowly through the list of other candidates. While he had some doubts about his financial ability to carry out an open bid, he thought he had one opportunity to raise sufficient funds.[5]

For years Hughes had had a strong interest in railways; coupled with a mechanical skill, it led him to design a relatively simple and effective ventilator system for rail cars. When attached to the roof, his device funnelled air into the front end of the moving rail car, passed it through water filters and ice to cool, extract smoke residue, and reduce its velocity. Air ducts then circulated it evenly throughout the coach; in winter ice was replaced by steam pipes which heated the air before distribution. It was a simple labour- and money-saving apparatus. In 1889 Hughes had it patented in Canada and the United States; in 1890 the French Academie Parisienne des Inventeurs awarded it a bronze medal. Financially it had great potential, at least in Hughes' mind, and he set about trying to sell it to railways in both countries. Though the Americans were interested, but not enough to pay him what he thought it was worth, Hughes wanted it adopted on Canadian roads first.[6] By 1890 libel suits, journalistic competition, and political ambitions had put too much strain on his income, forcing Hughes to lobby for the ventilator's adoption on the Inter-Colonial Railway (ICR) directly with Macdonald and several others who could influence the government line's decisions.

Hughes' invention and his intention to run for Parliament partly explain his substantially moderated political views as well as, in Birmingham's words, his readiness to "do almost anything" for the party.[7] But Hughes had been willing and able long before, and he had enough experience to know that without money he would be handicapped politically in or out of Parliament. As for Macdonald, over the next several months he encouraged Hughes' hopes for the invention by having the ICR test the device on several of its cars, for which the ambitious editor went further into debt. Hughes promised confidentially that if the Prime Minister bent a few rules to see that the ventilator was sold to any Canadian railroad, he would "be only too pleased to give a donation toward the election funds of the Liberal-Conservative party of 5,000 dollars if the ICR gives me 15,000 dollars for the invention, and 10,000 dollars if the CPR gives me 25,000 dollars for theirs."[8]

With all of this going on in September 1890, the question was whether or not Hughes would run in South Victoria's Conservative leadership race. The answer was no. By this time Hughes knew he would not realize any money from the patent soon enough. He also knew that however popular among the rank and file he was, his past activities had caused rivalries potentially harmful to the local Tory cause. Perhaps Birmingham suggested that Hughes should wait out this by-election and seek a seat in 1892 when they expected the next general election. It appears that Hughes decided not to run but to keep his decision private. His letters of early October to Macdonald suggest that he thought Mossom Boyd, a wealthy businessman from Bobcaygeon who had no enemies in the association, was the best choice. The day before Hughes wrote this advice to the Prime Minister, Birmingham had made the same point with Sir John, as if the provincial organizer had been able to convince Hughes privately to stand out of the way.

The problem was that Boyd knew little of this and was not even in the country. If the best candidate was to get the post, someone had to keep things from coming prematurely to a head in the hands of one of the other hopefuls, none of whom impressed either Hughes or Birmingham. The scheduled meeting was thus delayed, and Hughes kept up the illusion that he would seek the post himself by neither denying nor confirming his candidacy, while remaining busily active in the organization. Behind the scenes he and several other like-minded leading Tories, including Birmingham, vigorously worked up Boyd's following. Dundas had earlier challenged Hughes for the association vice-presidency, but Hughes beat him by an overwhelming twelve to one margin. When the nomination convention finally met on October 20, Dundas shoved his own candidate forward. The new vice-president stood up and announced that he would not run, but would support Boyd. Since Hughes' winning of the vice-presidency had excluded Dundas from the council, he was severely handicapped in doing anything about Hughes' tactic; and Hughes' candidate had the quick endorsement of John Dobson, the president, and Robert Birmingham from the provincial organization.[9] The absent Boyd was unanimously elected.

To those few federal Tories like John Thompson who were fearful of Hughes' past anti-Catholicism, his withdrawal was a relief, as was his backing of Boyd who was not part of the Hughes-Dundas schism that had divided the riding. Hughes' apparent magnanimous withdrawal, accompanied by his continued local hard work and public statements that he would support anyone the convention nominated, strengthened his position both in Ottawa and in local circles. There was only one problem: no one had asked Mossom Boyd whether he wanted the job. When cabled in Chicago that he had been elected as the standard-bearer for Victoria South, he refused categorically to accept even the Prime Minister's personal plea.[10] At a hastily called second convention in early November, Hughes—again conveniently silent beforehand, thus raising expectations that he would run himself—campaigned hard for another candidate untainted by local rivalries. Twice before Charlie Fairbairn, Reeve of Verulam Township, had failed to get elected to the provincial legislature in the south riding. At the federal level he was the best compromise in November, and he won both the nomination and a month later the by-election in Victoria South.[11] Much of the credit, he knew, belonged to Sam Hughes.

If Sam Hughes had parliamentary ambitions why did he apparently throw them away? Quite simply, he saw a better opportunity elsewhere. The opportunity was in North Victoria, where Hughes could escape the previous encumberances of the southern riding's politics, and in an assured general election, not in the by-election Fairbairn had fought. The contest would not come for fourteen months, just enough time for Hughes to whip the Victoria North constituency association into shape.

In 1887 the northern riding had been won by the Liberals, and Lindsay lawyer and Grit incumbent, Jack Barron, had had some success in seducing the area's farmers and lumbermen with promises of the financial benefits of unrestricted reciprocity with the United States. Through the columns of the *Warder* (which reached many homes in the riding) and in the local branches of the Imperial Federation League, Sam Hughes had been Barron's chief critic. Hughes had a substantial following among the Orange element in the upper reaches of Victoria and the provisional county of Haliburton, then part of the federal constituency of Victoria North. The north had far fewer Catholics to alienate than the south, and far more Orangemen to impress. They would support him because he never softened his ideas on the contentious religious issues to the point where the north country Protestant enthusiasts thought he had gone soft on Catholics. Since North Victoria had gone Liberal three years before, from closeby Lindsay Hughes had acted as the watchdog for many of the dispossessed local Tories' patronage needs. In the fall of 1890 there seemed no candidate in the northern association capable of presenting a real challenge to Barron.

While Hughes was still considering the nomination for South Victoria, a group from North Victoria approached him to run.[12] There was competition for the northern nomination, and perhaps far more than Hughes bargained for. A local doctor from Kirkfield named Wood, for whom Hughes had once done a patronage favour, also wanted the standard. More importantly so did another man from the same village, William Mackenzie, a burly Scots-Canadian who was embarking on a career which eventually saw him rise to the pinnacle of Canadian business before the First World War. Soon he would become one-half of the dynamic duo of Sir Donald Mann and Sir William Mackenzie, which put together the labyrinthine structure of the transcontinental Canadian Northern Railway. When Sam Hughes knew him in 1890, Mackenzie had already struck it moderately rich in government railway subcontracts in the Northwest and was moving into streetcar transportation in Toronto. Mackenzie also wanted into federal politics at a time when the largest building schemes in the country were railways. In late November when Dr. Wood, as president of the Liberal-Conservative Association of North Victoria, called a nominating convention in Fenelon Falls to choose someone to win back the riding, the ambitions of three very different men were destined to clash.[13]

That cold fall morning in late November when Hughes hitched up his buggy to drive the fifteen miles to Fenelon Falls, he had not yet made up his mind about running in Victoria North. But by the time he got in the hall all doubts had vanished; he knew he could win. Wood, Mackenzie, one other candidate, and Hughes were put on the ballot. To win a candidate had to get two-thirds of the votes cast. On the first poll Hughes took slightly less than half. Mackenzie got only five votes and was retired. In the second round both Wood and Hughes increased their number but neither met the requirement. On the third ballot Hughes fell one vote short and on the fourth—after a vain attempt by the desperate Wood to adjourn the meeting—Hughes beat the association president sixty-three to three in a stormy standing count. A few days later the Prime Minister congratulated Hughes and offered him advice on how to unseat the Grit Barron. The convention had shown that the vast majority wanted Hughes, even though he was not a resident nor had he been a member of the riding association, two points which the disappointed Wood continued to harp on long after his defeat.[14]

When Sam Hughes won that November, little did he know that Macdonald was going to call a general election for early next March. The unsuspecting Hughes plunged into getting Charlie Fairbairn elected in South Victoria and helping others in similar contests elsewhere. Constantly he faced money problems. He continued to push the Prime Minister to pull strings for his invention on the government line and the signs were good. The Inter-Colonial Railway was putting it to trial on several cars in the Maritimes. Twice Hughes travelled there to supervise its installation, yet he had received no return, only increasing debts—debts that were destined to become larger sooner than he thought.

In early February Macdonald surprised most Canadians when he asked the Governor-General to dissolve Parliament. The electors, it seems, were to decide whether their future was best protected by his National Policy or by the Liberal's popular promises of unrestricted reciprocity with the Americans.[15]

From the time of his nomination until Macdonald's unexpected dissolution of Parliament in February, Hughes felt that his way was free in North Victoria. His candidacy had been reaffirmed by a unanimous vote at a second convention held at Coboconk the day after Christmas; and he had already plotted out a campaign strategy. The core of it was to poke holes in Barron's free-trade arguments and to show the local benefits of National Policy and trade with Great Britain. He also wanted to point out the discrepancies in the Grit message. Why would the Americans want to reciprocate anything? They had just passed the McKinley Tariff, the most punitive schedule in their history. Hughes swore to Macdonald that he would work that piece of legislation "for all it was worth."[16] His old party adversary in South Victoria, J. R. Dundas, had been writing both privately and in the *Watchman* disparaging comments about Hughes' "adventurism" and his dim hopes of unseating Barron.[17] As for Dundas' influence in Ottawa, both the executive members of the provincial Liberal-Conservative Union and the Prime Minister made it clear to Dundas that they were not willing to disavow Sam Hughes in any way.[18]

The real trouble came in late January from William Mackenzie, whose ambitions were rekindled when he heard rumours about the unexpected federal election. He wanted Sam Hughes out of the way, and he had enough money to raise a challenge. Both he and Wood tried to get up a petition to call Hughes before another convention, but they got little support. Mackenzie also combined forces with the frustrated Dundas whose paper heaped renewed scorn on Hughes' candidacy, describing it as a "public calamity." The *Watchman*'s columns also charged Hughes with rigging the previous November convention, a claim for which there was no real evidence, except perhaps for Mackenzie's inability to pack it with his own supporters.[19] In early February, the day the Governor-General dissolved Parliament, Mackenzie and five or six other "kickers," as Hughes called them, appeared in his office demanding his withdrawal as a candidate. He refused. Mackenzie then took a small delegation to see the Prime Minister in Ottawa, presumably to point out Hughes' unsuitability and Mackenzie's merits, especially his assets and business connections.[20]

Sam Hughes telegraphed a warning to Macdonald about the delegation, and in a follow-up letter made it clear to the Prime Minister that he was in the field to stay and that he could carry Victoria North against both Barron and Mackenzie. He also pointed out that Mackenzie had offered him "10,000 dollars cash and had 15,000 dollars hinted at to make way and assist him." The more Hughes wrote to Sir John, the more he got fired up. In the end he threatened to run as an independent just to split the Tory vote and let the Grits back in.[21] However emotional his letters were, his charges that Mackenzie had no support in the riding were largely borne out by other evidence in Sir John's correspondence,[22] and by one other significant event.

Faced with the Mackenzie challenge, Hughes appealed directly to the people. Six days after the protest group went to Ottawa, Hughes rallied North Victoria's Tories at Lindsay's town hall where they were to decide once and for all who was going to carry the colours. The tactic worked. The meeting was overwhelmingly for Sam Hughes. As he reported to Macdonald:

The kickers are done. They made a grand final rally on Tuesday night last. William Mackenzie . . . [was] alone. . . . Yet only five in all North Victoria could be got to put their names on paper for a new convention. . . . Finding they could neither buy nor bribe my men, big or little, they apologized on Wednesday night and have fallen into line. . . . He [Mackenzie] now has *a very high opinion of me and* etc. etc.!!![23]

With Mackenzie out of the way, Hughes got down to serious stumping in the area. His platform labelled unrestricted reciprocity as pure annexationist treason. Like most other candidates frightened by the popularity among rural Canadians of free trade with the U.S., he came flat out for "the old flag, the old leader, the old policy and Sam Hughes," as one *Warder* headline put it. On the hustings Hughes was entertaining, well organized, and constantly on the move. He promised local transportation improvements, no taxes on farmland, and more preferential trade in grain and livestock with the United Kingdom. He was aggressive as he travelled through the townships, but he had the good sense not to play up the Jesuit Estates controversy or other religious issues—at least in writing—which might lose moderate or Catholic votes. On several occasions he challenged Barron to public debates and even taunted the unresponsive lawyer by offering to print the Grit handbills free.[24] Unfortunately when polling day came, it was not enough. Though the national Tory party won a substantial victory, in Victoria North Jack Barron beat Sam Hughes by 202 votes.[25]

Hughes' reaction was swift and simple: Barron was corrupt and so had been his campaign. As Hughes had predicted, the strife with Mackenzie had helped give Barron his slim margin. But Hughes took some satisfaction in knowing that he had almost toppled the Grits, and that he would do so yet.[26]

Hughes was left to face his mounting debts, and the fact that Macdonald had not yet managed to get his ventilator adopted on any rail line. The whole situation was made even more desperate for both Hughes and the government when the venerable old chieftain died in June 1891, just after his loyalty campaign against unrestricted reciprocity had snatched another national victory for his tired party. It was a severe blow to Sam Hughes. He considered Macdonald not only a patron but a friend. He also lost his invention's most influential promoter, and had to start the lobby all over again while his major creditor and a Grit newsprint industrialist, John Reid of Buntin, Reid and Company, pressured Hughes for repayment. Hughes was worried that he would not make it through "six months," as he put it to his friend, N. Clarke Wallace, Tory MP for York West and Orange Lodge Grand Master. Hughes' sense of urgency was more acute after the passing of Macdonald because he feared that the death might force another general election soon. Reports at home indicated that Barron was again putting his election organization back into gear.[27]

At the end of September when Parliament was prorogued instead of dissolved, it was a sign that the Tories had managed to weather the loss of their old chieftain by consolidating their ranks behind a compromise leader, the old, sick, and harmless Senator John Abbott. More than ever determined to get into Parliament, during that fall Hughes carefully compiled evidence of Barron's electoral corruption. On December 3, 1891, Hughes put his findings before the two justices of the Queen's Bench who had come to Lindsay to hear the case against Barron. The evidence was overwhelming in favour of the plaintiff. In less than three hours the judges found that Barron had engaged in "a corrupt practice" to win the election; one of the Grit party workers had paid five dollars to some voters—with Barron's knowledge. The decision called for a by-election in Victoria North.[28]

Though Hughes got the verdict he wanted, he still had to fight for the nomination in North Victoria; Barron was out of the way, but there was still William Mackenzie. Having failed to oust Hughes as the Conservative candidate the previous winter, Mackenzie had temporarily made his peace with the editor and even contributed some funds to Hughes' first campaign. But as Hughes gathered the evidence of Barron's election corruption, the possibility of a by-election rekindled Mackenzie's political ambitions. By September 1891 the entrepreneur had made sufficient moves among his Conservative friends in the capital that Hughes began to feel the pressure in Victoria County. As the editor complained to Wallace, there is a "certain ring of Ottawa" which was trying to convince the government "that I am not the kind of man to ... encourage." However, Hughes was too determined, too clever, and too resilient to be discouraged, even though his business worries were so acute that month that he thought that he would have to sell the *Warder* to keep the "ring" in his hat.[29]

Hughes had friends himself in Ottawa and within the Ontario organization. Of the four prominent ones he named in correspondence, all held executive positions in the Liberal-Conservative Union; two were then federal MPs and one a cabinet minister. Robert Birmingham, Clarke Wallace, John Haggert, the Minister of Railways, and J. C. Patterson, the former MP for Essex North, all firmly supported the Lindsay editor. Mackenzie could not easily dispose of the fiery Hughes. All through the fall both men kept lobbying with their separate connections. But Hughes kept working hard on behalf of the party in the riding while Mackenzie did little. When the electoral court decision came out in early December, Mackenzie appeared in the constituency to await the nominating meeting.

As the Boxing Day convention approached, Hughes' worries about Mackenzie increased.[30] The sanguine Mackenzie, who at the time was trying to buy the Toronto Street Railway Company,[31] had promised Robert Birmingham that if he and other Tories pulled a few strings to help Mackenzie in his bid for the railway, he in turn "would not in any way interfere in North Victoria, *except to help me*," Hughes noted.[32] After the contested election decision, Mackenzie went back on his word; and Hughes asked Wallace to convince the Prime Minister "to have Mackenzie side-tracked. I can carry the nomination and riding in spite of him but I want his open support from the start. It is worry that breaks men down and I want none of it more."[33]

What Mackenzie gave was open opposition and no check came down from Abbott in Ottawa. In the meantime Hughes kept on campaigning in the riding's back areas, meeting as many people as he could and keeping the highest possible profile with the busiest possible campaign teams. Even one of Mackenzie's men, as Hughes later boasted to Wallace, expressed "himself as utterly amazed what work I have done." Still Hughes did not know what clout Mackenzie's financial influence would have in the riding, especially when he had so little money himself. Again one of Mackenzie's friends told Hughes that "five thousand" would be made available if he would withdraw from the field. But the offer only fired the editor's determination: "I will never do it," he told a friend, "intrigue is at work and be damned to the whole crew." "But mark me," he went on to another friend a week before the convention, "I can take three-quarters of the votes in the first ballot."[34]

When the convention met at Coboconk, Hughes was correct on several accounts. Mackenzie was there seeking the nomination, so was another old enemy, Dr. Wood of Kirkfield. The three men had their supporters get their names on the slate. But Hughes was much better at the gamesmanship of constituent politics. He trusted no one who was not on his team, and insisted that each delegate's credentials be checked by having the crowd leave the hall and file back in one at a time while their delegate cards were examined. Such organization was not uncommon to Hughes; and because of his effort over the previous months in reforming the whole constituent structure, every sub-polling station in the riding was represented for the first time among the 210 delegates there. After all of these precautions and a few quick speeches by the candidates, in which Wood and Mackenzie played on the deficits of Hughes' non-residency and the benefits of Mackenzie's wealth and national influence, the meeting voted. As he had predicted Hughes won on the first ballot. He took 162 votes, Mackenzie 28, and Wood 20. With such an overwhelming show of strength, neither of Hughes' opponents had any choice but to congratulate the victor and to promise him their public support. It was a happy moment for Sam Hughes. As he recorded in the next issue of the *Warder*, "Cheers for the Queen, Mr. Mackenzie, Dr. Wood, Sam Hughes and Premier Abbott concluded the largest and most harmonious convention ever held in North Victoria or in any similar riding."[35] Privately Hughes was not so happy with Abbott's apparent inability to call off Mackenzie. He flexed his newly won local muscle by telling Wallace that unless Abbott's government quickly endorsed him he would run as an independent Conservative.[36] With such a large local mandate in Hughes' hands, Abbott could hardly do anything else but support him; and Sir John Thompson had been co-operating with him for several months. Likely Hughes' threat was aimed at any renewed ambitions of Mackenzie.

The Coboconk victory did not quiet all opposition to Hughes from within local Conservative circles. Again Dundas and his nephews and business partners, the Flavelle brothers, were vehemently opposed. During the early new year, the *Watchman*'s editor thundered out his denunciations. The "administrator," as he labelled Hughes, had rigged the convention. He was still "an irrepressible political adventurer" whose religious tirades only meant a repetition of the previous year's defeat, and his nomination was incomprehensible when there were talented businessmen of impeccable character like William Mackenzie available. What the *Watchman*'s backers were really confessing was that Hughes was the choice of the rank and file Tory. Their grumbling also pointed out the superiority of Sam Hughes' political organization, his doggedness, and his hard work in the riding.[37]

But Hughes ignored the *Watchman*'s complaints. He had a by-election to win and there was still plenty of work to do before polling day on February 11, 1892. Again J. A. Barron was in the field for the Liberals. The defeat of the previous year had made one point clear to Hughes: the voter's lists were in bad shape. They had not been revised for several years under Dr. Wood's presidency of the north riding. The party simply did not know how many Conservative voters there were. Immediately after his defeat in 1891, Hughes had begun revising the lists. He made sure that as many of the assessors as possible were Tories; he chose reliable teams of workers for each polling subdivision; he personally worked out a new streamlined enrollment procedure which reduced the time it took to record potential voters; then he printed these new forms himself and carefully briefed his crews on how best to use them; finally, he visited every sub-polling area at least three times before the new year, making sure that each citizen who might conceivably vote Conservative was legally on the lists and knew him. At the same time he kept a sharp eye out for Barron's additions to the preliminary rolls. By the first week in January, Hughes was ready to take to the revisions court held in Lindsay his revised lists with their nearly 400 new Conservative names.[38]

Appearing before the judge, Hughes scrutinized every Grit name and defended his own additions. Over the several days that the court convened, the proceedings were never dull as Hughes and Barron haggled over the legitimacy of each other's list. Sometimes their heated exchanges were as ridiculous as they were entertaining, such as Barron's attack and Hughes' long defence of one "Chris Hall," who to the embarrassment of both turned out to be a court clerk's abbreviation for the Christian Hall—a local building. But in all of this, Hughes was the clear winner. Nearly all of his 400 additions were allowed, and his factual and organized presentations, in spite of their occasional flare-ups, simply overwhelmed Barron.[39]

It was the same on the hustings for the next month. Hughes stumped across the townships in his fourth swing in less than a year. Often travelling alone and with cutter and horse, he got into the small and remote settlements like Uphill, Kinmount, and Bury's Green. Frequently his campaign workers had the faithful gathered at pre-determined points when he came through. His memory was so good and he had been so close to the revisions process that he could call nearly everyone he met by name, which gave him a common touch that made him hard to beat in the field. Sometimes, however, his memory backfired. During one visit to Fenelon Falls, he asked a little girl how her father was. She replied, "Father died last week." A few days later on his way back through the village, he met the same little girl and again asked her how her father was. She replied, "He is still dead."[40]

While on the campaign trail, Hughes carried the same message he had in the last contest. He promised the farmers and lumbermen increased prices and protection of their industries. He preached larger injections of National Policy, local improvements, and loyalty. He was not publicly abusive on any of the current religious issues, as the *Watchman* had predicted, but being unable to ignore the deep Orange sentiments in the riding, he likely tailored his remarks to suit his audiences. On the stump Hughes was endorsed by several prominent national and provincial Tories, including Clarke Wallace and Robert Birmingham who visited the riding to speak for him. On the platform Hughes also emphasized Barron's dishonest election practices. In the end he got voters out by organization, team work, persistence, and a common touch, none of which Barron could match. All of it paid off on polling day. As the results came into the campaign headquarters at Fenelon Falls, it was obvious that Hughes was beating Barron in the townships. By late that night there was no doubt. Sam Hughes had won by 242 votes. When he returned to Lindsay the next morning, he and his team-mates were met at the train station by a tumultuous crowd of supporters. The ceremonies continued all afternoon with Hughes' followers combining with those of Charlie Fairbairn who had been re-elected in the southern riding. The crowds, aboard dozens of flag-decorated sleighs and led by the two victors, paraded up and down Lindsay's main street to the delight of the Tories and the chagrin of the local Grits. Sam Hughes had done it: he had reclaimed Victoria North, in spite of them.[41]

Reference Notes to Chapter 3

1 PAC, Macdonald *papers*, pp. 243325-26, Hughes to Macdonald, July 14, 1890.
2 Johnson, p. 281. Hughes claimed Hudspeth was a charlatan who committed suicide rather than face his many creditors. PAC, Macdonald *papers*, pp. 50127-32, Hughes to Macdonald, Oct. 20, 1890; and *Warder*, May 16, 1890, p. 1—both these sources reported that he died of "apoplexy."
3 PAC, Macdonald papers, pp. 245427-28, Dundas to Macdonald, Nov. 17, 1890.
4 Ibid., pp. 244977-78, Hughes to Macdonald, Oct. 29, 1890.
5 Ibid., pp. 244463-64, Birmingham to Macdonald, Oct. 6, 1890; ibid., pp. 244267-68, Hughes to Macdonald, Sept. 22, 1890; and ibid., Hughes to Macdonald, Sept. 23, 1890.
6 Ibid., pp. 244481-84, Hughes to Macdonald, Oct. 7, 1890; ibid., pp. 50133-37, N. C. Wallace to Macdonald, Sept. 25, 1890; and Canada Department of Corporate and Consumer Affairs, Patent Office, patent no. 51024, Sept. 26, 1889.
7 PAC, Macdonald *papers*, pp. 244463-64, Birmingham to Macdonald, Oct. 6, 1890.
8 Ibid., p. 243914, Hughes to Macdonald, Sept. 7, 1890.
9 Ibid., pp. 50137-40, Hughes to Macdonald, Nov. 22, 1890; and ibid., pp. 244481-84, Hughes to Macdonald, Oct. 7, 1890.
10 PAC, Mossom Boyd *papers*, MG 28, III, 1, vol. 191, M. M. Boyd to W. Boyd, Oct. 21, 1890; ibid., Hughes to M. M. Boyd, Oct. 22, 1890; and ibid., Boyd to Macdonald, Oct. 22, 1890.
11 PAC, Macdonald *papers*, pp. 246255-58, S. Hughes to Macdonald, Dec. 28, 1890; and Johnson, p. 195.
12 Ibid., pp. 243911-13, Hughes to Macdonald, Sept. 7, 1890; ibid., pp. 24481-84, Hughes to Macdonald, Oct. 7, 1890—this letter indicates Hughes had made up his mind to run in North Victoria.
13 T. D. Regehr, *The Canadian Northern Railway: Pioneer Road of the Northern Prairies, 1895-1918* (Toronto: Macmillan, 1976), pp. 28-53.
14 PAC, Macdonald *papers*, pp. 250617-18, Hughes to Macdonald, Jan. 20, 1891; and ibid., pp. 247312-23, Hughes to Macdonald, Feb. 1, 1891.
15 Ibid., pp. 50137-40, Hughes to Macdonald, Nov. 22, 1890; ibid., pp. 246255-70, Hughes to Macdonald, Dec. 28, 1890; and J. M. Beck, *Pendulum of Power, Canada's Federal Elections* (Toronto: Prentice-Hall, 1968), pp. 57-71.
16 PAC, Macdonald *papers*, p. 245214, Hughes to Macdonald, Nov. 8, 1890.
17 *Watchman*, Feb. 3, 1891, p. 4.
18 PAC, Macdonald *papers*, pp. 245833-36, Dundas to Macdonald, Nov. 29, 1890; ibid., vol. 530, Macdonald to Dundas, Nov. 24, 1890; ibid., pp. 88613-15, Creighton to Macdonald, Nov. 8, 1890.

19 Ibid., pp. 247312-23. Hughes to Macdonald, Feb. 1, 1891; and *Watchman*, Feb. 3, 1891, p. 4.
20 PAC, Macdonald *papers*, pp. 247419-21, Dobson to Macdonald, Feb. 3, 1891.
21 Ibid., pp. 248605-09, Hughes to Macdonald, Feb. 15, 1891; ibid., pp. 247549-53, Hughes to Macdonald, Feb. 4, 1891.
22 Ibid., pp. 247419-21, Dobson to Mackenzie, Feb. 3, 1891; ibid., pp. 247721-24, Delemere to Macdonald, Feb. 6, 1891; and ibid., pp. 249026-30, McEachern to Macdonald, Feb. 20, 1891.
23 Ibid., pp. 248605-09, Hughes to Macdonald, Feb. 15, 1891; and *Warder*, Feb. 9, 1891, p. 4.
24 *Warder*, Feb. 9, 1891, p. 4; Feb. 13, 1891, p. 4; and Feb. 27, 1891, p. 4.
25 Ibid., Mar. 6, 1891, pp. 1, 4.
26 Ibid.
27 PAO, M. S. S. Wallace Family *papers*, 3089, Hughes to N. C. Wallace, June 9, 1891, June 22, 1891, and July 9, 1891; and PAC, Macdonald *papers*, pp. 252011, Hughes to Macdonald, Apr. 22, 1891; ibid., pp. 251532-34, Hughes to Macdonald, Apr. 10, 1891.
28 PAC, Sir John Thompson *papers*, MG 26, D. vol. 125, p. 15041, Hughes to Thompson, Mar. 30, 1891. *Warder*, Dec. 4, 1891, p. 4, and Canada, Parliament, *Journals of the House of Commons*, Feb. 25, 1892, p. 11.
29 PAO, Wallace *papers*, 3089, f 13, Hughes to Wallace, Sept. 21, 1891.
30 Ibid., Hughes to Wallace, Dec. 6, 1891.
31 Ibid.
32 Ibid., and Regehr, pp. 37-40.
33 PAO, Wallace *papers*, 3089, f 13, Hughes to Wallace, Dec. 6, 1891.
34 Ibid., Hughes to Wallace, Dec. 20, 1891.
35 *Watchman*, Dec. 31, 1891, pp. 1, 4; *Warder*, Jan. 1, 1892, p. 1.
36 PAO, Wallace *papers*, 3089, f. 13, Hughes to Wallace, Dec. 28, 1891.
37 *Watchman*, Dec. 31, 1891, pp. 1, 4.
38 PAO, Wallace, *papers*, 3089, f. 13, Hughes to Wallace, Dec. 20, 1891; and *Warder*, Jan. 15, 1892, p. 1.
39 *Warder*, Jan. 15, 1892, p. 1.
40 Capon, pp. 31-32.
41 *Watchman*, Feb. 18, 1892, p. 1; *Warder*, Feb. 12, 1892, pp. 1, 4; ibid., Oct. 9, 1891, p. 4; ibid., Jan. 29, 1892, p. 4; and ibid., Feb. 5, 1892, p. 4.

CHAPTER 4

In Parliament, 1892-1899

After the by-election there was hardly any time for Sam Hughes to relax at home before the second session of the seventh Parliament opened at the end of February 1892. Rather than dislocate his young family by moving to the capital, he rented a room there. Besides, he had the newspaper to run. But with the good rail connections, and few demands on backbenchers, he could frequently return home. He was anxious to plunge into the often exciting and rumour-filled world of Ottawa politics.

When the session began, Hughes was introduced to the House by two veteran MPs and close friends in the Liberal-Conservative Union, Clarke Wallace, the Orange Lodge Grand Master, and John Haggert, the newly appointed Minister of Railways.[1] As a freshman government backbencher for the next four years, Hughes' House duties were made up mostly of attending sessions and committees where he reacted to the issues of the day or promoted his favourite schemes for national development, the militia and the Empire. Outside the House, constituency patronage and party organization kept him busy.

Though Sam Hughes' maiden speech to the Commons repeated his fear of reciprocity with the U.S. and its threat to Canada and the links between Canada and England, he was not long in getting around to the militia. From the start he made it clear that the non-permanent force was the only workable military system for Canada; if regular soldiers were needed at all, it was only to help train the Volunteers. In pursuing these ideas in the House, Hughes prodded and poked at the smallest details of military affairs. With a wealth of military information at his finger tips, he was always driving at improvement, and always with the Volunteers; and simply because he was on the government

---

Reference notes for Chapter 4 are found on pp. 65-66.

benches, it did not mean his own side escaped criticism when it was due.²

By 1894 his dissatisfaction with the recent disproportionate growth of the regular force led him to level his guns at the British officer commanding the Canadian militia, Major-General Ivor Herbert, who had come to Canada in November 1890 to replace Middleton. It was not by chance that his Dominion posting coincided with British attempts to convince Canadians to do something about their own defence. Thus the not-too-subtle Herbert set out to improve the Canadian militia by trying to make the Permanent Force, instead of the Non-Permanent Active Militia of Canada (NPAM), the nucleus of a regular army. At first Sam Hughes was enthusiastic about a man who was trying to do something positive, unfortunately his support waned as Herbert's plans took shape, especially when he tried to establish his authority over the Militia Department.³ Herbert was a Roman Catholic and spoke French fluently, two factors that likely increased Hughes' misgivings about the new GOC.

But far more important was the personal antagonism between the two men. Like most militia politicians, Hughes had for years used the patronage and "old boy" channels of the militia. He did the same thing with Herbert. Frequently Hughes wrote long letters of advice to the GOC recommending that a militia officer, usually a Tory, be favoured. Herbert took it for a while and then, in the spring of 1893, clamped down hard on the MP's "wire-pulling." "I regret that Major Hughes MP," he caustically reminded the Deputy Minister,

should use the argument that military rank should be granted because "it costs nothing." If military rank is worth anything at all its value cannot be expressed in dollars and cents. This practice of acquiring military rank as a means of obtaining a cheap title is one of the causes which has reduced the Canadian militia to its present unfortunate condition.⁴

About the same time as this slap on the wrist came, Hughes was becoming dissatisfied with the GOC's slowness in reorganizing his own 45th Battalion, especially—to Hughes' mind—in removing that impediment to talent and progress, Fred Cubitt, the commanding officer. In spite of reforming other units, Herbert let Cubitt hang on. Then in early 1893 the GOC promised the frustrated Hughes that if he and his brother would turn out a good battalion in the annual camp that June he would retire old Colonel Cubitt. The Hughes brothers kept their side of the bargain, but Herbert reneged. For the next year he did nothing except ignore the MP's stream of complaints of inaction and unfulfilled promises. Suddenly the GOC gave the older brother command of the 45th instead of shifting him to the head of the neighbouring 46th, letting the younger Hughes have the home battalion, as Sam had long recommended, and it made him boil.⁵

In the spring the disgruntled MP denounced in the Commons the General's recent public comments praising French-Canadian service in the Pontifical Zouaves, which had been made to a largely French-speaking Montreal audience. The MP's attack, if initiated by his religious prejudice, was also an indication of his increasing dissatisfaction with Herbert's general policy. Nor was his own party to escape easily. In waving his finger at J. C. Patterson, the Militia Minister, Hughes reminded him that, as the General's superior, he ought to have the fortitude to censure such statements. "Papist" Zouaves, Hughes implied, had nothing to do with Canada's Volunteer traditions. Hughes was right for all the wrong reasons about the vagaries of the relationship between minister and general.[6] Nevertheless, the more the MP talked, the further his charges reached. He even called Herbert a dictator and again condemned the Militia Minister for allowing the GOC to move towards the establishment of a standing army in place of the militia.[7]

By that summer criticism reached the breaking point when the GOC suspended the popular Adjutant-General, Lieutenant-Colonel Walker Powell, for sending militia orders for the annual training camps to the printers without the General's approval. The overworked Powell was considered by many, especially by Sam Hughes, to be the epitome of the non-permanent soldier and the father of the Canadian militia.[8] It was more than Hughes could tolerate. With substantial sympathy from other disgruntled militia officers, Hughes began another Commons attack on July 6, 1894, again accusing Patterson of not protecting Canadian constitutional freedoms from infringements by the GOC. Suspensions such as Powell's, the MP proclaimed, could only legally be made by the Minister.[9]

Two weeks later, after he found out that Herbert intended to disband or amalgamate some of the more inefficient non-permanent rural regiments, Hughes rammed home the main charge. Efficiency, he pointed out to the House, was not gained by reduction of the militia, but by reorganizing and increasing its numbers, equipment, and training, points Hughes was sure the GOC was slow to comprehend. On the top of this, Hughes told the Commons, Herbert was a callous bully and tyrant who had driven one fellow officer into a sanitorium. He went on to call the GOC "a total failure who suffered from a lack of knowledge and judgement." Worse still, he charged, his own government had stood idly by and let Herbert abuse the rural regiments by increasing the Permanent Corps beyond the numbers needed as instructors. "We do not want to saddle ourselves," he thundered, "with large standing armies such as the countries of Europe have to support." Herbert's new direction, he went on to say, was nothing more than an intolerable step towards a police state. The charges were outlandish. The GOC wanted to make the entire corps more efficient. To do it he saw the necessity of adding professionals to the militia to give continuity, skill, and organization. In retrospect, the General was justified. But at the time Hughes' genuine concern was for the primary role of the militia in national defence and the right of Canadians to determine it.[10] Besides, if there was any way to build stock among militiamen or to carve out an area of expertise in the parliamentary party, however mildly dissident, he had found it.

Hughes was not the immediate cause of the GOC's removal in 1895. Other militia officers had also felt Herbert's sting; they too resented his preference for the regular force. Soon he had few parliamentary supporters. But the determining factor behind his dismissal was Herbert's influence over Patterson. He had convinced the gullible Militia Minister to announce, without cabinet approval, that Canada would send a force to aid the British Army in Hong Kong. Ironically this was a move with which Hughes agreed, for he had long been the advocate of raising battalions for overseas duty. Nevertheless, already sensitive to Hughes' criticism of the GOC, an angry cabinet cut Herbert's term short. In the end the embarrassed and chastened Militia Minister could only complain that in Canada it was often hard to "dissociate the Militia Force from the active politics of the hour." So Herbert resigned and Patterson gave up his portfolio to Arthur Dickey. The forced changes were harmful for the militia, and Hughes contributed to those regressive steps, even though he had hoped the opposite would be true. Faced with the embarrassing Herbert controversy, his party's disorganization and an impending election, the new Militia Minister made serious cutbacks in spending. Immediately Hughes condemned his party for the action, but just as quickly he blamed Herbert for causing it.[11]

In 1892 Sam Hughes may have been a freshman MP, but he was no novice politician. His past record with the party was solid. As he took his place in the parliamentary caucus—the most powerful body in the party structure—he continued to advance within the Ontario Liberal-Conservative Union, itself the largest and most influential provincial organization of the federal structure. In 1896 he was voted chairman of the association of the eight ridings around Victoria North, called the "Midland Counties District 8." He also had a seat on the Union's executive council. These posts represented recognition by Liberal-Conservatives throughout the province of his past services;[12] and in his rise, he participated in some interesting internal contortions of the party and the nation itself, in particular the leadership struggles that plagued the party after Macdonald's death and the Manitoba schools question, which found that leadership wanting.

A product of Canada's longstanding cultural schism, the withdrawal of support for Manitoba's Catholic schools and French-language instruction by the provincial Liberal government in 1890, sparked a destructive six-year political battle in the country. The federal government would be condemned no matter what it did. Ultimately it was a more sympathetic English high court that ordered the government to impose remedial legislation to redress the Catholic grievances in Manitoba.[13]

Long before the English judges' decision, Sam Hughes was deeply involved in the issue. The Orange Lodge was already on record opposing the use of public funds for separate schools and Hughes supported this. But he also saw the need to restore a strong and unified Tory leadership, which had been substantially eaten away by Macdonald's death in 1891 and the bitter passions of the schools debate. Indeed, given his own political ambition, and like many other Protestant Ontario party members, the Manitoba schools issue posed a dilemma for him. To avoid its destructive effects, he would have to tread very carefully.

Even as Macdonald lay dying, Hughes sent John Thompson, the Catholic House Leader and the most talented of Macdonald's ministers, a note declaring his confidence in the Minister's ability to keep the cabinet united until the caucus could find Macdonald's successor.[14] In the past Thompson had been critical of Hughes' anti-Catholic outbursts in Victoria County. Thompson may well have been surprised, therefore, to receive a letter of support from Hughes, and also surprised to receive advice from a very junior Tory and one who had just been defeated. Nevertheless, the note was an early indication that Hughes would try to give the party some resolution and unity. This does not suggest, however, that at that time Hughes wanted Thompson to succeed Macdonald, for he did not. But he soon would.

At the same time he was writing Thompson, Hughes was warning Orange Grand Master Clarke Wallace that Thompson was not acceptable as the next Tory leader because of his support of the Jesuit's Estates bill. The best man for the party, Hughes thought, was Sir Charles Tupper, then the High Commissioner in London; and the best course, Hughes went on, was to send Thompson to the High Commission and bring Sir Charles home as prime minister: "You would fare far better with him than any other man. Quietly hold the boys [in the Orange Lodge] together on those lines. Everyone looks to him." A few days before Macdonald's funeral in Kingston, Hughes again advised Wallace: "I hope I am mistaken but five years from today will prove who was right. The man beyond will be required yet." Hughes' advice for strong leadership was not heeded. Most of the "boys" did not want Tupper. More importantly, neither did most of the cabinet, because "small men did not want a big leader." The compromise was semi-retired Senator John Abbott. For the next eighteen months, he was Prime Minister of Canada because, as he freely admitted, he was not particularly "obnoxious to anybody."[15]

As Abbott half-heartedly governed from the Senate, Hughes watched Thompson do all the work in the Commons. Here was a talented man, Hughes thought, one who gave the party strength even though he was a Catholic. Although Hughes' admiration was genuine, it was also clear that he needed Thompson as House Leader to get his second chance at a federal seat. One of Hughes' earliest letters to the future Prime Minister, written just two months after Macdonald was buried, sets the tone of the relationship between the two men.

[I write] to congratulate you on the manner in which you have conducted the House during the session. Your best friends even are more than pleased, while your worst bitter partisan opponents are dumb. "The country is safe" is the word heard everywhere; while at first, during the transition period from the dear old chieftain to the new, many of our best men would say, "Sir John Thompson is the right man, but it is a d—— pity he is a pervert." That has entirely vanished, and in these parts I feel that the stand I took on the sermon of the clergyman did no harm [Hughes had publicly condemned a Lindsay minister's anti-Catholic attacks on Thompson earlier that spring]. Indeed, I know you seem to be all that is needed to remove prejudice created by that infernal Jesuit Act. I knew at the time Mercier could knock you all out on that and like everyone else, I misconstrued your ideas and motives.[16]

Not that Hughes agreed with all that Thompson did, but he felt that the Minister could strengthen the party far better than the indecisive Abbott. Among his fellow Tories, Hughes was in fact one of the earliest converts to Thompson as party leader.

Between August 1891 and November 1892, when Abbott resigned, Hughes committed himself to getting Thompson into the prime minister's office. He started to publish articles in the *Warder* explaining Thompson's position on the Jesuit's Estates affair. He attacked— "touched up" as he called it—any militant Protestant critics of Thompson, especially D'Alton McCarthy and the Equal Righters, and he ran biographical articles on Thompson, some of which were picked up by other newspapers. These pieces, he privately explained to Thompson, "of necessity refer [to] your change of church and indirectly showing religion, being a matter between man and his maker, is not concerned in churches."

While supporting Thompson, Hughes also lobbied him. He needed Thompson's endorsement in unseating Barron, and Thompson willingly briefed Hughes on the legal points of controverted elections and later advised him on revising the voters lists. Both before and after he took his seat in Parliament, Hughes pushed Thompson to get several of his friends included in the cabinet, namely, N. Clarke Wallace, an MP with Orange connections, and William Mackenzie, because he "owns enormous interests in ... the North West, as well as in Toronto and Montreal.... [He] could carry Winnipeg flying." In Mackenzie's case, the new MP's motive was repayment for his support in Victoria North; it also had the obvious advantage of keeping Mackenzie out of Hughes' bailiwick. Hughes was not entirely successful, although Wallace did become Controller of Customs, a non-cabinet post.[17]

As well, Hughes pressed Thompson to oppose remedial legislation in the Manitoba schools question. Beginning in the summer of 1892, this theme became a constant feature of the MP's voluminous correspondence with Thompson. Hughes' secular stance on the issue had roots in historical Protestant reformism with its separation of church and state; Hughes believed that the state, with its power based on rule by majority, was better equipped to safeguard the commonweal, especially against individual groups seeking special privileges. As he editorialized to Thompson in September 1892, "all churches ... are a simple damned nuisance in a country. Religion is one thing, a church is another.... The Roman Catholic organization ... I fear ... will push on one side and the Protestants and lovers of responsible government on the other will resist, and the devil will be to pay generally." Given this philosophy, Hughes was afraid of what the Manitoba schools question would do to the party and the country. "Believe me" he warned Thompson, "from the bottom of my heart, it [remedial legislation] will never do. Even if the Grand Lodge of Canada with all its masters and chief officers were to hold the premiership and cabinet positions, the public would not for one hour tolerate it.... Even Roman Catholic citizens—not churchmen—do not want it."[18]

Hughes was no less afraid of militant Protestant reaction, especially within the Orange Order, and he told Thompson that he would do all he could to keep control there "in friendly hands," especially at the lodge level where the grass-roots support for the Conservatives was strongest. Already, he pointed out to Thompson, he had suggested to Wallace that a special convention of the Grand Lodge meet in Ottawa to show the members that the issue was separate schools and not French-language instruction, as D'Alton McCarthy and his troublemakers were trying to make it, "for Orangeism owns all languages." He went on to promise Thompson that if he stayed firm against remedial action, "we might possibly be able to elect you honorary member or honorary Grand Master in all our Orange Lodges."[19] Clearly Hughes had not thought about the effect of such a preposterous gesture on Thompson's Catholic supporters. But then again neither had he thought through the inconsistencies and the consequences of his belief in the "public" principle, as he later called it, in a country in which 40 per cent of the population were not likely to accept his secular view.

Thompson was wise enough not to commit himself before he had to; and while the schools grievance was still in the courts, he neither said anything definite nor took any political action on the thorny schools question. Until he did, he got the full support of Hughes, who was co-operating with executive members of the Liberal-Conservative Union, such as Birmingham, W. F. Maclean of the Toronto *World*, and Wallace, in converting public and party opposition to Thompson's leadership.[20]

Sam Hughes represented to Thompson the power of Orange Protestant Ontario, enough of which he had to win over or at least keep neutral to survive politically. At the time Hughes was neither a veteran MP nor even a major power in the Ontario party, but he was climbing and had supporters in both areas as well as in the Orange Lodge. Whether or not Thompson's private opinion of Sam Hughes ever changed after his complaints to Macdonald in 1890, after the old chief's death, there was more than a one-sided dialogue between Thompson and Hughes. On several occasions Thompson wrote candid notes to the Lindsay editor about his political woes, and at times Hughes' letters to Thompson were full of good-natured banter and homespun philosophy, suggesting that the two men had finally reached a better understanding of each other, however far apart they might remain on ideas like religion or the Manitoba bill. In a letter written to Thompson while he was considering the makeup of his first cabinet in 1892, Hughes flatly recommended Wallace, Bowell, Haggert, and William Mackenzie for cabinet posts, while just as bluntly condemning a whole list of other hopefuls and warning Thompson about the dangers of forming a cabinet of "big city" and "Rideau Club" interests which would forever doom talented rural inhabitants to the levels of "hewers of wood and drawers of water." The rest of the letter was more cordial and more typical of the mood of the relationship between the two men.

> You will excuse the sermon, Sir John. There are two travelling soul-savers here [in Lindsay], and I do not care to turn out, so I stay at home and inflict a sermon on you. I can easily do it, you know, you are not here. This soul-saving business, you know costs the country an infernal lot of money.... Clericalism is a curse, always was and always will be.... Each new church too as it becomes orthodox follows in the tyrannical footsteps of its predecessors.... The Christian religion cannot last: Christ's Acts will ever form the basis of sound morality and good citizenship, but the infernal superstitions and glamour that preachers and priests sling around Christ in order to wheedle or scare cowardly sinners into line must vanish. A man's religion concerns only himself and his God. Your mind in Halifax and mine here may exchange ethereal messages.... Thought—not alone words—travels just as light does, and it needs not the intervention of a priest or preachers for my thoughts to pass into space and reach every mind in sympathy. So with every thought; some take root, some do not.
>
> I just thought a left-handed sermon would pass away the time as I am alone with my children.... I made a point of telling old Sir John just what I thought honest right public opinion was. I never curried favours; he took the bitter with the sweet. So you will please to know such are my ways.... My religious views

are my own and I know heterodox.... I have regarded and still regard orthodox churches the greatest enemy of civilization. Those churches represent insane ideas worked out of Christ's life. They do not represent Christ or his Acts. He was simply a reformer of social life and a good one...[21]

After Thompson became Prime Minister at the end of November 1892, the Victoria North MP kept up his support, denouncing where he could Protestant extremists.[22] And while Canadian courts were still considering the schools case, Hughes continued to advise Thompson to avoid remedial legislation. He could not help remembering that Thompson had argued in 1889 that Quebec's Jesuit's Estates bill was legal because it was constitutionally within the jurisdiction of the provincial government. The abolition of separate schools, Hughes reasoned, ought to be within the ambit of the Manitoba government. He had said so in the summer of 1892 in an article on separate schools in *Le Canadien*. By January 1893, he thought that the new Prime Minister should quietly support the secularization process in order to "disarm the villain" before the remedial case got to the British courts. Once there, Hughes warned that the Judicial Committee would likely decide for the minority, which would force the Canadian government into coercing the province. Thompson would then have to battle both remedial legislation and D'Alton McCarthy on the hustings. Hughes was right in as much as the Canadian judges did not decide the issue; by 1894 it was in English hands. As for Hughes, although he never publicly flinched in his support of Thompson and save one plaintive and private note claiming that he had risked his "whole political future ... to back you," his lively and frequent correspondence fell off substantially with the Prime Minister during that year. The relationship between the two men on the Manitoba question had no conclusion; on December 12, 1894, just as the lawyers were beginning to plead before the English justices, Thompson died of a heart attack in Windsor Castle.[23]

If Sam Hughes had had his way Sir Charles Tupper would have succeeded Thompson. Instead Rideau Hall and the cabinet gave the nod to seventy-two-year-old Senator Sir Mackenzie Bowell, who believed he had the talent to lead. Two months after he became Prime Minister, the British courts decided for the Manitoba Catholics. As the government the Conservatives could not afford—as Laurier's smug opposition could—the luxury of inactivity. So in March 1895, with extremists on all sides yelling for action, Bowell tried to be decisive— but not right away. Hinting he would call an election that summer as a sop to dissident caucus members, he got them to agree to the issuance of a remedial order to the Manitoba government. When this was ignored, Bowell threatened federal remedial legislation, but fearing open party revolt, he ended the session in July before introducing it.[24]

Sam Hughes' actions suggest that he supported the issue for the sake of unity and with the hope that a quiet compromise might yet be effected before retreats into principle produced hard-nosed and disastrous decisions. Such moderation was not to be. Few meaningful negotiations between the province and the federal authorities took place; the Liberal government in Manitoba was no longer willing to compromise on anything. To complicate matters, the constitutional clock was running out on the incompetent Bowell government. In December 1895 it started to fall apart. The vital Orange Lodge link went when Clark Wallace quit in December 1895. By early January seven ministers had revolted, including the usually steady George Foster in the Finance Department. And, as Hughes had predicted, the Tory leadership debacle lured Charles Tupper back to Ottawa. His appearance induced the "nest of traitors," as the desperate Bowell called them, to come back into the government on the condition that Tupper act as House leader and that Bowell, the nominal Prime Minister, stay out of the way in the Senate. Tupper's plan was to pass the remedial bill before the clock stopped, then go to the country as Prime Minister.[25]

How did all this affect Sam Hughes? He did not want separate schools. But he did not want the disintegration of the Tory party either. Since the previous spring, he had given reluctant support to Bowell, hoping that a federal election would be called and a quiet negotiated compromise effected before the remedial bill was passed into law. He maintained his complicated position right through Wallace's resignation and the subsequent cabinet revolt. The actions of both, Hughes thought, were a threat to the party; and he told Wallace bluntly that he had been duped by extremists and should have stayed in the government. He also made that point clear to his Orange colleagues elsewhere. A month later he gave the same advice to Foster and crew in the *Warder*'s pages, which for the next six months advised caution and moderation and came down heavily on hard-liners on both sides. In a March letter to the Tory Ottawa *Journal*, he pointed out the destructive effects on both the country and the party. If all sides want "a peaceful settlement," he pleaded with his colleagues, why should "we plunge Canada into a religious war." He avoided lining up with either Bowell's or Wallace's supporters, although, as he privately told the Grand Master, "there must be a change of leadership if the party is to hang together—or there must be some vigour of action."[26]

The "vigour of action" for Hughes was the appearance of Tupper, and he supported Tupper's attempts to reach a compromise by negotiation, especially the two March trips which Sir Donald Smith made to Winnipeg in the hope of reaching a settlement before a final vote was necessary.[27] When these attempts failed, Hughes had to face in one direction or the other. On March 30, 1896, when the remedial bill came up for second reading, Hughes voted against the government. Strong secular convictions and the hard reality of Ontario politics left him little choice. The vote was on the unamended form of Bowell's bill, and Hughes had disagreed with its content for some time because it reaffirmed the vagaries of the pre-1890 educational system; had it been up to him, he would have changed the constitution. But since that was not now possible, he would not endorse separate schools.

The debate over the terms of the bill went on for three weeks. The opposition filibustered as hard as possible; for days members went without sleep or slept at their desks; some were drunk and some sober. Hughes kept to his post most of the time, and when he spoke out, he argued vigorously for conciliation. He even drafted an amendment to allow religious instruction in the schools after hours. His "friendly means," as he called his proposals, were remarkably similar to Laurier's later "sunny ways," which eventually solved the problem. Years later Hughes explained his position in the debate to Sir John Willison, who in 1896 was still with the Liberal *Globe*:

> My stand has always been that no creed organization should have control over secular education. The law only intended that Roman Catholics or Protestants desiring separate schools should have the privilege of teaching religious notions, but the secular education should remain in the hands of the state. For example ... the church concerned teaches all schools subjects and also the creed notions. I maintain they are entitled only to teach their religion. The state should forbid the employment of any teacher to teach religion. Let the churches attend to that and be paid for it if necessary, but they have no right to make the teacher the instrument. The sooner the whole thing is wiped out the better.[28]

Sam Hughes' arguments on the issue make it clear that he was not as sympathetic to minority rights in the first instance as were some of his colleagues. To George Foster, whose "honest broadsword," in the words of Peter Waite, "cut through much of this [constitutional] jungle," the issue was not "hands off Manitoba" but "hands off Manitoba's minority." For him, whether rightly or wrongly, the constitution had given the Catholics in that province those rights and the federal government must first restore them before deciding how legal they were.[29] Hughes, however, saw the crisis as an opportunity, not to redress a wronged minority, but to extend the secular principle. Moreover he felt that his "friendly means" could give the minority the opportunity, within the system, to teach their own creed. Nor did he hold much brief for the language issue. Since deciding to run for Parliament, he had purposefully tried to avoid the matter and to separate it from the Manitoba situation. Frequently in the past he had criticized D'Alton McCarthy for singling out French-language instruction in Manitoba as the problem. It was naive for Hughes to imagine that there could be any such distinction in what was really a minority cultural problem. Nevertheless, his position was consistent with his notion of secularism and his view of Canada outside of Quebec as an English-speaking country. If Manitoba's schools were all public, any language in the service of a minority, like any religion, could be taught after the official daily curriculum.

It did not matter, in the end, what argument Hughes or Foster presented for or against the legislation. After the debate had raged for an exhausting month, Tupper suddenly abandoned the bill in mid-April, and called an election for June 23, 1896.[30] For Sam Hughes this contest was to be an especially hard battle. Indeed it was several battles: one for the party, one within the Orange Lodge, one in Victoria North, and one for himself.

During the intervening two months, Hughes remained an ardent party loyalist, nearly to the point of ruination. After the dissolution, when the Governor-General hesitated to appoint the pompous Tupper as prime minister, Hughes had offered to support Sir Donald Smith for the post, hoping perhaps that if Tupper was not acceptable to the Aberdeens, Smith could both lead and compromise. However, once Tupper got a very reluctant vice-regal nod, Hughes pushed hard to heal the party wounds.

By this time Clark Wallace had broken completely with Tupper and Hughes over the bill. The split between the two Ontarians demonstrated the deep internal divisions that the Manitoba problems had spawned. Hughes and Wallace had been close friends for years. As fellow Orangemen and executive members of the Liberal-Conservative Union, they had worked together for the lodge and the party. Wallace had lent Hughes money for campaigns, had encouraged him over rough spots, and had introduced him to the Commons when Hughes was first elected. In turn Hughes had supported Wallace. But the remedial issue destroyed all of that. Wallace was a militant Protestant; Hughes much less so for the sake of the party. When Wallace bolted in 1895, much of the Orange Order went with him. In the spring of 1896, he and McCarthy joined forces and called meetings across the province, telling Orangemen to vote against the remedialists and to demand that any candidate running on a Tory ticket be an anti-remedialist. For several months, Hughes' brother James, who was Grand Master of the Canada West branch of the Orange Order, had managed to keep the lid on his brethren, but there was only so much he could do.[31]

The crisis came in May at the annual meeting of the Grand Lodge at Collingwood, Ontario. The convention was a stormy one with Wallace's militants gaining the upper hand. It took a lot of courage for Hughes to go before such a hostile crowd with a message they did not want to hear. He tried to explain the government's position on the bill;

he also pleaded for the Order to close ranks behind Tupper before the county went to the polls. It was a much wider view than most constituent Ontario politicians were noted for. But Hughes was shouted down and nearly expelled from the meeting. In the weeks that followed, the animosity towards him spread through many of the more extreme lodges across the province. Even some members of his own county executive publicly branded him as a turn-coat. On top of this, while the political campaign raged back and forth across the province, Wallace pursued Hughes relentlessly from his office as Grand Master. His circular directive to all lodge members in June summed up the bitterness:

Dear Sir and Brother,
   ... It is incumbent on every member of our Order to effectively punish those who were traitors to our cause during the last session of Parliament.
   Eminent among those who aided the Tupper Government in their attempt to defeat the little band who stood up so nobly for the rights in Manitoba were Hughes of North Victoria, Bennett of East Simcoe and McGillvarey.
   I have sent letters to the Masters of a number of the Lodges and find that in some cases they have been suppressed and therefore request you to make this known to the brethren in your lodge.[32]

But Sam Hughes was a fighter and a good tactician. His immediate problem was to win in his own constituency. Since he had already secured the nomination in the riding the previous spring for a contest that never came in 1895, there was no problem with his candidacy. Nor did he feel that there was going to be any difficulty in beating the local Grit opposition. The trouble came in the form of a third candidate. In mid-June Wallace convinced John H. Delemere, the editor of the Minden *Echo* and an anti-remedialist, to run against Hughes on the issue of the MP's support for Tupper. Delemere had reluctantly supported Hughes in 1892, but since that time had been anxious to get Hughes' job. The remedial issue and Hughes' censure by the Order provided the opportunity. To counter the Delemere threat, Hughes avoided the contentious issues during the election campaign; and when he had to, he could point out to one side that he had voted against the bill and to the other that he had loyally supported the Tupper election platform—all of which was true. Local and National Policy matters, Hughes explained carefully to his constituents, were the real issues and not the side "intrigues" of the Manitoba schools question about which he remained purposefully vague. This course was the tactically correct one; he defeated both the other candidates, and Delemere so severely that he lost his deposit, even though Wallace and D'Alton McCarthy had campaigned in the constituency on his behalf. Hughes' majority was slightly larger than it had been in 1892. Quite clearly the local Conservative voters wanted him because they were sick of the Manitoba issue and preferred his moderate if somewhat obscure message.[33] Sam Hughes had done his duty and had held up his end. The federal party, however, had not fared so well.

When the eighth Parliament was summoned in August 1896, Conservative ranks were in shambles. Now sitting on opposition side of the House, Hughes must have sensed the irony as he witnessed Wilfrid Laurier's new government negotiate over the next several months a compromise that was similar to his "friendly means." The past five years of leadership confusion, of in-fighting, and of nearly insoluble cultural questions had left lasting scars in the Conservative organization. Yet there was a brighter side: Hughes had survived politically as a hard-working Tory loyalist and a moderate and, on occasion, as a man who could raise himself above the constituency din and still deliver its strength to the federal party. Even though he was in opposition for the next fifteen years, his party position and parliamentary importance rose slowly but steadily. Soon after the election he was appointed as the chief "organizer"—a word he hated—for the Midland District. In the House he kept a watchful eye on the imperial connection and, enthusiastically, on the militia; he also did his duty in several of the House committees. Outside of Parliament, Hughes remained an active Orangeman, but his brush with the militants in the Lodge in 1896 had tempered his association with it (an association which did not begin to return to normal until Clarke Wallace died in 1901). Hughes continued to try to induce the rebels of 1896, including Wallace, back into the party. He also worked vigorously within the Liberal-Conservative Union on behalf of provincial Tories who had been long out of power, and supported their new leader, Colonel J. P. Whitney, in his campaigns. Hughes often stressed in his district circulars that hard work, preparation, organization, and loyalty were the only things that could restore the party to power provincially and federally.[34]

While politics and the militia were the prime centres of Hughes' life during the decade, his business activities also intensified. By continuous lobbying with his political and business friends, he had managed to have his ventilator applied for trials on several lines by 1893. The results were good, but several problems confounded Hughes. One was how to reduce the cost of production and installation; another was how to find enough capital to float the enterprise without losing control. But previous debts and the journalistic competition which ate into the *Warder*'s profits prevented Hughes from undertaking the project himself. Finally in the fall of 1894, unable to sell it or fund it alone, Hughes convinced William Mackenzie, James Ross, another wealthy railway capitalist from Montreal, and several executives of the Pullman Railcar Company in the U.S. to form a limited stock company. The Hughes' Ventilator Car Company had head offices in Toronto and

$500,000 worth of stock. Sam Hughes was its president, but he was a minority shareholder. Over the next few years he sold most of his shares to other members to pay the debts of the *Warder*. Though Hughes worked hard and travelled widely to make the business succeed, his chronic financial burdens forced him out of the company in 1898.[35]

There were other business enterprises, most of them dealing with railways. In 1898 he sat on the board of directors of the Lindsay, Pontypool, and Bobcaygeon Railway Company, a local line which ran north through Durham and Victoria counties. He had been the chief advocate of the road, and even before getting into Parliament, he had lobbied for government subsidies in its development. Such was the case with another local line, the Lindsay, Haliburton, and Mattawa road. William Mackenzie was a major shareholder in it, and Hughes was the company's president. Hughes' involvement with Mackenzie opened new business vistas for him, especially as Mackenzie's fortunes grew from such enterprises as the Toronto Street Railway and later the Canadian Northern Railway colossus. Hughes was also involved in the Dominion Trust Company along with his railway friends, and he was vice-president of the Canada Mutual Company.[36]

Like many other politicians, Hughes sometimes lobbied in government for friends and interests. He tried to get Prime Minister Thompson to reduce the duty on steel rails for the Toronto Street Railway Company. In 1896 he told C. L. Porteus, Mackenzie's business manager and a former banker from Lindsay, that he had helped swing the Toronto City Council in favour of Mackenzie's bid to take over the street-car system there. He had done so, he confessed, to keep the Kirkfield entrepreneur out of politics in North Victoria. Hughes' effectiveness in winning the contract is doubtful, but his worry about Mackenzie's political aspriations was not. On other occasions, Hughes claimed that he used his influence with the Minister of Railways and the various House committees to make sure favourable legislation was passed. Still, it is doubtful that Hughes was a major force in getting any patronage considerations for these powerful men. He was never in a position to do other than recommend certain actions; there were far more important people to whom William Mackenzie, James Ross, and Donald B. Mann could appeal.[37]

In spite of these activities, his debts were large and pressing. So much so that he frequently begged work from his friends to keep solvent. Typical of this was his December 1896 note to Porteus:

If I could hang on for another six months something might turn up. Perhaps Mr. Ross or William might have some undertaking I could perform. . . . If they have, I am willing to try. I have rarely failed in any undertaking. . . . I fully think I could handle a job like . . . winning a city council in France, Scotland or Ireland or anywhere as well as anyone.[38]

The money trouble persisted, however. It appears that Hughes was a victim of too much ambition and inventiveness and not enough business talent to survive in the same competitive circles as William Mackenzie. In turn Mackenzie may have taken advantage of Hughes' susceptibility. But he did help the MP out in later years. During the election struggles in 1896, Mackenzie saw that some funds went Hughes' way. The next year he evidently considered Hughes for the position of editor-manager of the Toronto *Evening Star*, which was at the time the unabashed supporter of Toronto's business entrepreneurs. It was owned by F. J. Nicholls, president of Canadian General Electric Company, an old-line Tory and a close business partner of Mackenzie. But Hughes did not want the job and nothing came of it.[39]

By 1898 Sam Hughes was in desperate financial shape. Like the dour business manager he was, Porteus smugly moralized to the frantic Hughes that it was his "duty to drop politics entirely and ... give a sure and comfortable home to yourself, your wife and your children.... Politics is a miserable uncertain trade at the best, and unfits a man for steady work, which is necessary for success." By this time Hughes knew that he was not very good at big business and that he was better off in politics and the militia. So in 1899 he sold the financially troubled *Warder* to pay off his debts.[40] After that he dabbled in business only when his casual employment with William Mackenzie's concerns presented an opportunity.

Hughes' financial troubles did not hamper his interest in the militia. With his brother in command of the 45th, he remained the other moving force in the unit as its senior major. For some years he had been vainly trying to have the battalion reorganized so that it was based solely in Victoria County and headquartered at Lindsay. The request made sense. The unit was spread over two counties and there was enough population in both for each to have its own battalion. The opportunity to carry out Hughes' scheme came in March 1897 when the officer commanding the neighbouring 46th retired. Seeing some merit in Hughes' scheme, district headquarters recommended that if John Hughes took over the 46th, the reshuffle could take place. It also meant that Sam Hughes would command the regrouped 45th. It happened so fast that he was caught unprepared for the promotion, and in June he had to take a twelve-day commanding officers course to qualify. The new Liberal Militia Minister, Dr. Fred Borden, approved the changes and, indeed, had no reason not to do so. The regiment needed reorganization and Hughes had earned the promotion.[41]

As a new commander, Hughes took the unit into camp that fall for twelve days of training. During the winter he shifted around the officers, retiring those he thought were dead wood or too old and promoting others. He wanted the battalion to have its full complement, which he succeeded in getting directly from the Minister when the GOC, General Gascoigne, refused. Such moves did not endear Hughes to the headquarters staff. It was not so much his wire pulling, for that was not uncommon among militia colonels. What aggravated the GOC was Hughes' bloated sense of his own command in the smallest things. Soon after taking over the formation, he wanted the name changed to "45th Victoria Regiment of Infantry," while all of the other infantry units were still called battalions. Gascoigne refused. He also refused Hughes' request for a thirty-piece band for the "regiment." In spite of these pretensions, Sam Hughes' battalion was considered to be a very good one.[42]

As the shuffles within the 45th suggest, Hughes had a somewhat special relationship with the Liberal Militia Minister. Like Hughes, Fred Borden had been a long time in the Volunteer corps; he too wanted to make the military force more effective. Also like Hughes, he was part of a political system in which patronage in militia affairs was normal. But each man recognized in the other a kindred spirit that was more concerned about improving the militia than making use of its patronage potentials. Soon after Borden assumed the portfolio, Hughes offered his support for progressive reform of the militia, as long as the Minister's actions coincided with Hughes' notions. Much of the time they were in agreement, and Hughes often supported a Liberal proposal in the Commons which his party opposed. As a knowledgeable critic in the House, Borden considered Hughes too important to ignore and he appreciated Hughes' militia enthusiasm. It was also good politics to cater to Sam Hughes from time to time, since such moves dulled the Conservative Party's attacks on his administration. Consequently Borden often tolerated and sometimes exploited Hughes' vanity and lapses of judgment.[43]

In return for his support, the Minister helped Hughes secure inexpensive militia appointments. The first one appeared with the reorganization of the 45th; the second one came hard on the heels of Hughes' promotion. For Queen Victoria's Diamond Jubilee in 1897, as the senior colony Canada was asked to send an official military contingent of twenty-six militiamen of appropriate ranks to march through London. Upset that he was not chosen, Hughes pressured Borden to send him over as commander of a private contingent. It was too blatant a request and he got nowhere. In April Donald Smith, who liked Hughes for his longstanding imperial ideas and for his brief political support the year before, offered to pay Hughes' way. Hughes eagerly accepted, but quickly added that it would look more appropriate if he went with a militia rank. Smith secured Borden's co-operation, and the newly promoted Lieutenant-Colonel found himself one of the twelve supernumerary officers attached to an official contingent of over 200 "sham warriors."[44]

On Jubilee Day the six-mile-long royal procession passed through a city bedecked in the gaudy trappings of the age as one-quarter of the earth's land surface honoured the "Queen of Earthly Queens." The Empire's heroes were all there: Roberts of Kandahar, Sir Redvers Buller and Wolseley of Ashanti and Tel-el-Kebir. To a Canadian militia colonel from Lindsay, Ontario, such a display reinforced what he knew already: the British Empire was the finest secular agency known for the common good of mankind. Hughes met many of the chief advocates of the new imperialism, like Joseph Chamberlain of the Colonial Office and Lord Milner, and conversations always got around to the merits of imperial defence, trade, and organization.

When he returned to Canada that fall, Donald Smith, now Lord Strathcona, sent Hughes on a tour of British Australasian territories as a travelling Empire evangelist preaching the gospel of colonial military contributions for imperial defence to willing antipodean audiences. When Hughes returned in 1898, his enthusiasm did not lessen. "Real civilization," he confidently proclaimed to an American audience— many of whom had already contracted the imperial disease—"was gained by the British bible and the British bayonet."[45]

Why imperial statesmen—like Joseph Chamberlain—picked Hughes for this job was obvious, but in hoping that he could marshal sentiment for Empire defence, perhaps they were giving him credit for more political influence in Canada than he had. Nevertheless their attention flattered his vanity, added to his reputation, and reaffirmed his resolve to awaken Canadians to militia reform and the need for imperial defence.[46]

Advances in these directions seemed imminent when in 1898 two outstanding British military imperialists were appointed to high posts in Canada: General E. T. H. Hutton as GOC and Lord Minto as the Governor-General. They added considerable influence to Borden's efforts to reform the military establishment. But both men were secretly trying to direct the Canadian government towards active support of Britain in Empire defence. Soon after Hutton's arrival, Hughes offered the GOC sixteen pages of presumptuous, detailed advice on militia reform. Typically his memorandum also repeated an earlier offer to Laurier to raise and lead a Canadian regiment for service in the Sudan.[47]

When the Fashoda crisis faded without a French and English conflict, the tense situation between Briton and Boer in South Africa renewed Hughes' hopes for implementation of his Empire defence scheme; and he spent a lot of time telling the public to be prepared to send troops. Yet when his predictions of war in South Africa came true in 1899, the events affected many careers, including his own.

Reference Notes to Chapter 4

1. *Hansard*, 1892, p. 3.
2. Ibid., pp. 113, 241-92, 443-54, 667-81; ibid., 1894, p. 6169; ibid., 1893, pp. 560, 1524; ibid., 1895, pp. 1163-64, 3187-89, 3809; *Warder*, May 8, 1891, p. 4; and PAC, Sir John Thompson *papers*, MG 26, D, vol. 172, Sam Hughes, memo re: militia, 1893.
3. Morton, *Ministers and Generals*, pp. 95-99, 105-106. Norman L. Penlington, "General Hutton and the Problem of Military Imperialism in Canada, 1898-1900," in the *Canadian Historical Review* XXIV (June 1943), pp. 150-60.
4. PAC, RG 9, II, A 1, vol. 364, f. 45357, Hughes to Patterson, Mar. 27, 1893; and ibid., Herbert to DM:MD, Apr. 11, 1893. For another example, see ibid., 12654, Hughes to Patterson, Mar. 28, 1893.
5. PAC, Ivor John Caradoc Herbert *papers*, MG 29, E 61, vol. 3, Hughes to Herbert, Oct. 7, 1893; ibid., vol. 5, Herbert to Cubitt, Aug. 13, 1894.
6. Morton, *Ministers and Generals*, pp. 95, 104, 106.
7. *Hansard*, 1894, p. 2734.
8. Morton, *Ministers and Generals*, p. 108.
9. *Hansard*, 1894, pp. 5496-97.
10. Ibid., pp. 6161-76; and Morton, *Ministers and Generals*, p. 106.
11. G. F. G. Stanley, *Canada's Soldiers*, p. 269; Morton, *Ministers and Generals*, p. 110; and *Hansard*, 1895, pp. 211, 2207-14.
12. PAO, Wallace *papers*, Mu 3098, f 6, circular notice, District 8, Liberal-Conservative Union, June 20, 1898.
13. For an overview of these events, see P. B. Waite, *Canada, 1874-1898; Arduous Destiny* (Toronto: McClelland and Stewart, 1971), chapter 13.
14. PAC, Thompson *papers*, vol. 130, p. 15733, Hughes to Thompson, June 6, 1891.
15. PAO, Wallace *papers*, Mu 3089, Hughes to Wallace, May 30, 1891, June 6, 1891, and June 9, 1891; Lovell Clark, "The Conservative Party in the 1890's," in the Canadian Historical Association, *Annual Report*, 1961, p. 61; and Beck, *Pendulum of Power*, pp. 73-74.
16. PAC, Thompson *papers*, vol. 135, 16464, Hughes to Thompson, Aug. 15, 1891; *Warder*, June 19, 1891, p. 4; ibid., May 1891, p. 4; and Clark, pp. 58-74.
17. PAC, Thompson *papers*, vol. 159, 19929, Hughes to Thompson, July 30, 1892; ibid., vol. 160, 20018, Hughes to Thompson, Aug. 11, 1892; ibid., vol. 143, 17607, Hughes to Thompson, Dec. 12, 1891; ibid., vol. 171, 21402, Hughes to Thompson, Dec. 27, 1892; and PAC, C. E. L. Porteus *papers*, MG 29, A 32, vol. 4, Hughes to Porteus, Dec. 8, 1896.
18. Ibid., vol. 162, 20238, Hughes to Thompson, Sept. 16, 1892; and ibid., vol. 170, 21363, Hughes to Thompson, Dec. 22, 1892.
19. Ibid., vol. 163, 20314, Hughes to Thompson, Sept. 25, 1892.
20. PAC, Thompson *papers*, vol. 160, 20064, Hughes to Thompson, Aug. 20, 1892.
21. For instance, see ibid., vol. 160, 20064, Hughes to Thompson, Aug. 20, 1892; and ibid., vol. 166, 20753, Hughes to Thompson, Nov. 7, 1892.
22. Ibid., vol. 171, 21402, Hughes to Thompson, Dec. 21, 1892.
23. Ibid., vol. 160, 20018, Hughes to Thompson, Aug. 11, 1892; ibid., vol. 172, 21459, Hughes to Thompson, Jan. 1893; and ibid., vol. 187, 23439, Hughes to Thompson, Oct. 12, 1893.
24. Waite, pp. 255-56.
25. Joseph Schull, *Laurier, The First Canadian* (Toronto: Macmillan, 1965), pp. 303-11.
26. PAO, Wallace *papers*, Mu 3094, f 64, Hughes to Wallace, Dec. 18 and Dec. 30, 1895; *Warder*, Jan. 10, 1896, p. 4, Jan. 17, 1896, p. 4, Feb. 21, 1896, p. 4, and Mar. 13, 1896, p. 4; and the Ottawa *Evening Journal*, in the *Warder*, Mar. 6, 1896, p. 4.
27. *Warder*, Mar. 13, 1896, p. 4.
28. PAC, Sir John Willison *papers*, MG 30, D 14, F 158, Hughes to Willison, July 10, 1905; and *Hansard*, 1896, pp. 4241-52.
29. Waite, p. 267.
30. Ibid., pp. 254-70, traces the events surrounding the bill in the Commons.

31 Beckles Willson, *The Life of Lord Strathcona and Mount Royal* (London: Cassell, 1915), p. 428. Smith was raised to the peerage in 1897. PAO, Wallace *papers*, Mu 3094, editor of the Toronto *World* to Wallace, Apr. 12, 1896; and Senior, pp. 87-89.
32 *Globe*, May 27, 1896, p. 4, May 28, 1896, pp. 1-2, June 5, 1896, p. 5; these cover the Collingwood Convention in detail; and PAO, Wallace *papers*, Mu 3095, f 77, Orange Lodge circular by N. C. Wallace, June 19, 1896.
33 PAO, Wallace *papers*, Mu 3029, Birmingham to Wallace, Mar. 12, 1895; and ibid., Mu 3095, f 76, Delemere to Wallace, June 10, 1896; *Warder*, May 8, 1896, p. 4, June 5, 1896, p. 6, June 12, 1896, p. 1, and June 26, 1896, pp. 1, 4, McCarthy had tried to challenge Hughes' candidacy in 1894 but failed. See PAC, D'Alton McCarthy *papers*, MG 27, 1E7, Fee to McCarthy, May 22, 1894.
34 Schull, *Laurier*, pp. 331-33; and PAO, Wallace *papers*, Mu 3098, f 6, Liberal-Conservative Union, District 8, circular letter, Sam Hughes, June 20, 1893; and *Warder*, July 15, 1898.
35 PAC, Thompson *papers*, vol. 188, 23516, Hughes to Thompson, Oct. 17, 1893; and RG 68, Liber 132, f 432, 433, 434; "Letters Patent Incorporating the Hughes Ventilator Car Company," Oct. 3, 1894.
36 PAC, Porteus *papers*, Hughes to Porteus, Feb. 28, 1897; and Morgan, 1898, p. 485. The Porteus papers and Morgan contain most of what is known about Hughes' business life. Also see *Warder*, Feb. 7, 1896, p. 4, and Feb. 14, p. 4.
37 PAC, Thompson *papers*, vol. 205, 25775, Hughes to Thompson, Apr. 6, 1894; PAC, Porteus *papers*, Hughes to Porteus, Dec. 8, 1896; and personal interview with T. D. Regehr, Ottawa, Dec. 13, 1980.
38 PAC, Porteus *papers*, Hughes to Porteus, Dec. 8, 1896; and ibid., Apr. 19, 1897.
39 Ibid., vol. 25, pp. 143-44, Porteus to Mackenzie, June 25, 1896; ibid., Hughes to Porteus, Mar. 23, 1897; ibid., Hughes to Porteus, Apr. 19, 1897; and Ross Harkness, *J. E. Atkinson of the Star* (Toronto: University of Toronto Press, 1963), pp. 19-39.
40 PAC, Porteus *papers*, Hughes to Porteus, Nov. 16, 1898; and Kirkconnell, pp. 112-13.
41 *Militia Orders*, 1897 (July) G065; PAC, RG 9, II B 1, 250, 65436, DA:AG(HQ) to DOC 3, June 1, 1897; ibid., Cotton to DA:AG(HQ), June 7, 1897; and Public Archives of Nova Scotia, (PANS), Frederick W. Borden *papers*, vol. 140, f 4, p. 2020, AG, June 3, 1897.
42 *Militia Orders*, 1897 (September), GO 83; ibid., GO 87; ibid., GO 88; and ibid. (November), GO 106; PAC, RG 9, II, B 1, vol. 250, 65436, Hughes to F. W. Borden, Apr. 19, 1898; ibid., GOC to Minister, Apr. 26, 1898; ibid., vol. 260, 69806, Hughes to DOC:MD 3 and 4, Nov. 5, 1897; ibid., vol. 256, Hughes to DOC:MD 3 and 4, Nov. 10, 1897; ibid., GOC to AG, Dec. 4, 1897; ibid., vol. 250, GOC to Minister, Apr. 26, 1898, Minute; and ibid., 65436, DOC 3/4 to AG, Apr. 1898.
43 Penlington, *CHR*, XXIV, p. 157; Morton, *Ministers and Generals*, pp. 118-20; and *Hansard*, 1898, pp. 4944-45, 6568-69, contain explanations and examples.
44 *Hansard*, 1897, pp. 841-42, 973, 1083, 1901; PAC, Porteus *papers*, Hughes to Porteus, Apr. 19, 1897; and Morton, *Ministers and Generals*, pp. 123-24.
45 See James Morris, *Farewell the Trumpets: An Imperial Retreat* (London: Penguin, 1978), pp. 21-33, for a vivid portrayal of the emotions and sites of the Diamond Jubilee. Also see PANS, F. W. Borden *papers*, 145, f 2, p. 4172, Hughes to F. W. Borden, Oct. 8, 1897; Willison, p. 428; Penlington, *Canada and Imperialism*, p. 192; and Capon, p. 34.
46 *Hansard*, 1898, pp. 3670, 4944-45, 5324, 6397, 6567-78.
47 PAC, E. T. H. Hutton *papers*, MG 21, G 3, vol. 7, pp. 1101-18, Hughes to Hutton, Nov. 29, 1898. Also see PAC, Sir Wilfrid Laurier *papers*, MG 26, C, C-757, pp. 24358-66, Hughes to Laurier, June 18, 1898.

CHAPTER 5

Hughes, Hutton, and the Contingents for South Africa, 1899

By the spring of 1899, Sam Hughes was sure that the deteriorating situation in Natal would end in fighting. If he thought about it at all, Hughes gave no serious consideration to such ignoble British motives as greed for gold and diamonds or a plain territorial grab from the two Boer republics. But then neither did many other Canadians. To Hughes the sole issues were Canada's military role there and his own participation. In pursuit of these he got into a spectacular quarrel with the new GOC, General Hutton. The affair looked simple, but it involved complex issues of nationalism and imperialism, conflicting constitutional and military ideas, and even British intrigue.

When Hutton received his Canadian post in 1898, Hughes probably believed that he had found another kindred spirit in the reform-minded British GOC, whose goals included making the Canadian "National Army," as he labelled the militia, efficient enough to defend home territory and to fight "whenever British or imperial interests were threatened" in the world.[1] Such ideas, however contrived—of equating nationalism, military reform, and imperial service were very close to Hughes' own. In part they explain why six months before hostilities erupted in Africa Hughes proposed to the Commons that the Laurier government send a brigade for imperial duty if war developed.[2] Hutton and, to a much less enthusiastic extent, the Governor-General were already secretly and separately planning with Joseph Chamberlain, the British Colonial Secretary, a way of ma-

---

Reference notes for Chapter 5 are found on pp. 80-82.

noeuvring the Canadian government into giving official sanction to Britain's policy in South Africa, which made them both react favourably to Hughes' motion. They failed to see, however, the nationalist content of Hughes' suggestion. Hughes wanted Canada to participate largely to demonstrate the country's military prowess rather than its imperial patriotism.[3]

Fortunately for Laurier, the South African situation had remained vague until June 1899 when diplomatic talks between the Boer and British representatives failed and the possibility of war substantially increased. Once war looked imminent to the Canadian public, the offers of volunteers to go off to fight proliferated, profoundly changing the situation for the Liberal administration. As Minto reported to Chamberlain, who had asked if the Canadian government would provide military assistance, such offers embarrassed the cabinet[4] and presented a real dilemma. The Prime Minister had been trying to steer a middle path between the Charybdis of French-Canadian nationalism and the Scylla of imperialism. Laurier's best course was no official course at all, and he tried to do exactly that.

Unfortunately for the government, in July both Hutton and Hughes perceived a rising sentiment to give military aid to Great Britain and both quickly tried to exploit it. On July 17 General Hutton, with Minto's knowledge—at least according to the enthusiastic GOC—circulated among militia officers a scheme to send 1,200 men to the Transvaal, which he would command along with other colonial contingents. Although F. W. Borden was on the side of the imperialists in the cabinet, Hutton had not bothered to inform the Minister of Militia and Defence. But he had confided to his friend Sir Garnet Wolseley, the British Commander-in-Chief, that "I have sub-rosa made arrangements for a squadron of mounted rifles . . . and a regiment of rifles. His excellency [the Earl of Minto] is urging a policy offering help in a practical sense." Hutton's plan designated Hughes as commander of one of the columns. Clearly it was a sop to imperial sentiment and militia fervour. He was soon to regret this decision.[5]

When the government had taken no satisfactory steps by early summer, Hughes was preparing some sensational ones of his own. On July 13, following news that an Australian colonial government had offered the British 250 men for South African service, Hughes impatiently pointed out in the Commons that national shame could only be avoided if the senior Dominion bettered the offer by at least 5,000 men, with himself in command. Eleven days later he sent three letters, all offering to raise and lead a force of Volunteers to the Transvaal: one went directly to Chamberlain, the Colonial Secretary, another went to Hughes' immediate military superior, Hutton, and the last went directly to the Minister of Militia and Defence.[6]

In the letter to F. W. Borden, Hughes volunteered to "enrol and lead in active service a regiment or a brigade of Canadians.... I am further prepared to serve either as leader of a Canadian regiment under pay of Canada or, which I deem better policy, under pay of the Empire." The implication of the last sentence was ominous for Hutton's plans. If Great Britain paid for the contingent, official Canadian government recognition of British policy might not be forthcoming. A clash between Hutton and Hughes seemed inevitable. In the meantime Laurier's government did nothing, except pass a Commons resolution of sympathy for the Uitlanders, mostly British citizens living in the two Boer republics, whose plight some British politicians were manipulating to hide their expansionist intentions in South Africa.[7]

A second factor in the inevitable clash between Hughes and Hutton was the MP's bald presumption of the contingent's command. If anyone was to have it, Hutton was determined it would be himself. Certainly the militia politician's proposal challenged the jealous Hutton's right to make this decision as the GOC. Moreover, in the General's eyes—as his pre-emptive July letters clearly indicated—Hughes was a political meddler and a potential spoiler of imperial plans. The GOC was determined to end both.[8]

Hutton had one clear line of attack. Hughes signed his letters "Sam Hughes, Lieutenant-Colonel commanding 45th Victoria Battalion."[9] This signature on the Chamberlain and Borden letters made them official military business which had failed to go through proper channels. Most of the time Hughes could see no difference between his various careers, and though he may have had no intention of trampling on the GOC's domain, his vanity always made sure that his offices were well noted in public. No doubt he also wanted to give his proposals credibility by emphasizing his qualifications.

As well, there was Hughes' annoying habit of sending the GOC a torrent of unsolicited advice about how best to improve the militia. When Hutton reminded Hughes that he needed no such gospel, the MP accused the GOC of trying to prevent him from introducing his legitimate reforms in Parliament. The two had also tangled over Hughes' aggressiveness and insubordination at the annual Kingston camp in 1899, especially his open criticism of Hutton's timing in calling it for September, the middle of harvest season. The GOC had had experience with contumacious politicians before in New South Wales and he had discovered that he could control them with a strong hand. That success gave the General a haughty disdain for Canadian politicians and militiamen; it also bloated his estimate of his own political prowess.[10]

Both Minto and Hutton had been bending a few rules themselves in pursuit of their plan. When Borden passed Hughes' offer on to Laurier at a cabinet meeting, the Prime Minister quickly requested that

Minto send it to the Colonial Office. The Governor-General was dismayed, and refused the Prime Minister's request. To any one who knew the sometimes pompous Minto, it seemed Hughes had offended his sense of military etiquette by ignoring the proper channels. As well, in returning the Privy Council minute containing the Lieutenant-Colonel's offer, Minto carefully explained to the cabinet that Hughes was incapable of serving with British officers. Minto ordered Hutton to reprimand Hughes for the breach of procedure. Hutton did not need much prodding; he now shared all Minto's ideas about Hughes' qualities. As he told Borden, "I would add that there are many officers with greater experience and equal zeal than that shown by this officer." But Hutton was also concerned about another aspect of the situation. The biggest threat to Chamberlain's hopes was that Laurier would avoid any official commitment by sidetracking Canadian imperial enthusiasm into private offers like Sam Hughes'. Ironically the only praise Hughes' proposal got came from Joseph Chamberlain.[11]

Hughes was not long in feeling the wrath of the GOC. Once he had received the General's official reprimand, he quickly replied with an abusive tirade. His conception of imperialism, Hughes hotly informed the GOC, was "not imperialism in the red-tape narrow sense but in that of broad, tolerant, responsible government, that which develops the principles of intelligent personal liberty to the greatest extent." Clearly Hutton wanted imperialism in the red-tape, narrow sense: official Canadian recognition. Nevertheless, the more lines Sam Hughes penned, the more vehement the letter became. He told Hutton that British regular soldiers were so incompetent that they would be defeated by the Boers; and personal insults followed: "I am desirous of learning where any British officer of note has been promoted to high command on his own merits alone, Lord Roberts alone accepted."[12]

Hughes' vicious rebuttal was also likely the result of Hutton's equally vicious personal comments. On several occasions between writing letters to each other, the two men had met. At one of the encounters, in trying to dissuade the MP from continuing his public agitation for a contingent, the priggish Hutton made some disparaging remarks about the state of Hughes' sanity and the poor fighting qualities of Canadian militiamen. Evidently Hutton also accused Hughes of disingenuously offering a contingent only for his own self-employment. Of course it was not true. Hughes had made many such offers in the past when he had little to gain. Just last year, Hughes burst out in defence of his own maligned military ability, he had refused a high American command in the Spanish American war. If British officers persisted in their out-moded military ways, he wrote, "the old plugs of Boer farmers" would surely defeat them. He then swore up and down that the natural ability of Canada's militia soldiers was far superior to any regular he had ever met. Finally, at the end of all his pejorative comments and warnings, he awkwardly tried to compliment his military chief: "Aside from your being hastily imbued with incorrect notions and a tendency to try to revolutionize everything suddenly, you are, I frankly admit it, by all odds the best officer Canada ever had."[13]

In spite of this personal invective, Hutton managed to keep his temper during August, always basing his case on violations of military procedure and jurisdiction. At the end of the month he informed the stubborn MP, through his superior officer at the Kingston military headquarters, that he had seriously breached militia regulations by his offers of service to Chamberlain and to Frederick Borden. This time Hughes' rebuttal focused on the role of the citizen-soldier: "I have made my official application through you and have yet to read the regulations which deprives a citizen-soldier of Canada from addressing the Minister of Militia on this or any other subject."[14] Of course Hutton did not view the activity of colonial militiamen this way. Nor could he allow it to continue; it was antithetical to military discipline to let his subordinates trot out whatever role they found convenient, especially when they advertised under the aegis of their own military position as Hughes had done.

Hutton had a very low opinion of the battle-worthiness of the militia. On the other hand, Hughes was so blinded by his faith in the natural prowess of these troops that he could not see the GOC's comments, if indeed contemptuous, had considerable merit. Hutton told Laurier that "if the militia went to South Africa they would be a menace" to the British. When Hutton pointed out to Hughes that "Canadian militiamen were unfit to serve in the field short of three year's training as regulars and then only if led by imperial officers,"[15] Hughes was more convinced than ever to show the British professional soldiers just how good colonial militiamen could be. However, it is doubtful that Hughes ever imagined the Canadian militia as a collective whole. He always equated the merit of the entire force with the prowess of some of its individuals. As it turned out, Canadian Volunteers proved to be good soldiers in the Transvaal, but their success was due to the efforts of their leaders, such as William Otter, and to the training and experience they accumulated there. Their achievements had little to do with the fact that they were Canadians.

As the situation between Kruger and the British became more critical in the last days of summer 1899, Hughes stepped up his campaign to lead a Canadian force overseas. While quarrelling with Hutton, he was having no more success convincing the Prime Minister to send a contingent to South Africa. In both August and September, he had visited Laurier to plead his case, but was vigorously rebuffed. According to Hughes' later account, Sir Wilfrid had told him to mind his own business, and that Canadians must not embroil themselves in

British foreign policy which held no interest for them. Evidently the Prime Minister also announced to Hughes that most Canadians did not care about the African issue and that those few who would volunteer for the sake of "adventure and other ignoble causes" should be forcibly restrained. Of course none of this was what the undaunted MP wanted to hear. To him the case was obvious: Empire unity was at stake and the soldiers of the senior Dominion could help the British and show their true mettle. With both the Prime Minister and the GOC against him, Hughes decided to take his case directly to the public. On September 20, with the financial backing of another imperialist, Hugh Graham of the Montreal *Star*, he advertised in many of the major Canadian newspapers for volunteers who would serve with him in South Africa. Once more he signed the public notice with his military rank. The effects were immediate and irrevocable. One of them was to focus public attention on Hughes as chief spokesman for the growing number of Canadians caught up in the spiraling imperial sentiment; another, yet to be seen, was increased public pressure on the waffling Laurier cabinet. Still a third came from Hutton.[16]

If the enthusiasm generated by Hughes's proposition was what the imperialists hoped would push Laurier into action, it did not gain the formal recognition Hutton wanted. He was still in the awkward position of trying to carry out Chamberlain's wishes in the face of Hughes' public offers. Clearly something had to be done to kill Hughes' scheme and overcome the reluctance of the Liberal cabinet if the GOC was to succeed. In late September Hutton tried to stifle Hughes by threatening to prosecute the Colonel under section 98 of the British Army Act. As one of the GOC's aides pointed out in preparing the case, since Colonel Hughes had "offered his military services in his military capacity . . . , it cannot be considered that his application was made as a citizen but as an officer of the Canadian militia." Hutton followed up the aide's observations by informing Hughes that unless he retracted his offers he could be charged, relieved of his duties and rank, fined, and sent to jail.[17]

This did not deter Hughes in the slightest. Again his response was a counter-attack. He wired Laurier and Sir Charles Tupper, the Tory leader, accusing Hutton of persecuting him, and denied the GOC's contention that the British Army Act gave him any rights to act against a Canadian citizen. On October 10 Hughes warned the GOC that he must publicly withdraw his threatening comments, again charging that Hutton had assailed "my freedom as a citizen, my rights as a soldier and my self-respect as a man." He also freely admitted that his campaign tactics had been chosen to prevent his offer from "being pigeon-holed" by men like Hutton. The MP also injected more accusations into the fray by charging that the GOC was against all militiamen exercising their rights as citizens. Not to be outdone, General Hutton stepped up his intimidations, this time telling Hughes that he would fire him from command of the 45th regiment unless he retracted his insubordinate letters. But the GOC did not carry out any of his threats, likely because Hughes was right about the jurisdiction of the Army Act. Moreover any public attempt to prosecute would be a messy affair which could only heighten Hughes' reputation and give more press coverage to his threatening volunteer contingent scheme. What Hutton did was much more subtle and hurtful for Hughes: the GOC struck the Colonel's name off the list of officers he had originally proposed for command in his secret contingent. To rub salt into the wound, he then gave Hughes' spot to a Permanent Force soldier, Lieutenant-Colonel Lawrence Buchan, a man Hughes particularly disliked.[18]

Another reason why Hutton did not tackle Hughes on the law was lack of time. The previous June diplomatic talks between Briton and Boer, held at Bloemfontein in the Orange Free State with the hope of reaching a settlement short of war, had failed. Clearly the Cape Colony's High Commissioner, Alfred Milner, wanted to annex the two gold-rich Boer republics to the British Empire. If it took a war, so be it. His political chief in London, Joseph Chamberlain, while not as bellicose as Milner, sought a similar end. On the opposite side was the ancient "Oom," Paul Kruger, President of the Transvaal. At Bloemfontein he had left the intransigent Milner, protesting, "It is our country you want." He was right, but after those aborted negotiations the stubborn old man saw no use in further serious negotiations. Relations deteriorated sharply during the summer as both sides armed themselves. By the end of September, the Transvaal mobilized; two days later so did the Orange Free State. While no one in Canada understood the machinations of Milner's mind, the mobilization and the plight of the Uitlanders, which the partisan press and Hughes had focused on, put increasing imperialist pressure for action on Laurier's government.

And it did the same thing to the GOC. Hutton was fearful that Laurier might accept Hughes' September offer to raise and lead a force. Speedy action was necessary. On October 3, the day after the Orange Free State's mobilization, and with Hutton conspicuously absent from Ottawa, the GOC arranged the "leak" of a telegram in Ottawa. The wire was from Joseph Chamberlain and was addressed to the Canadian government; conveniently it appeared nearly simultaneously in many Canadian papers. It thanked Canadians for offering a contingent; it also suggested how the contingent should be organized. The announcement was a surprise to nearly everyone in Ottawa. Laurier had made no such offer; and his attempt at neutrality was put in further jeopardy when, upon receipt of Chamberlain's note, the

Canadian Military Gazette, in an apparent "scoop," immediately published a detailed description of the Hutton's secret contingent. Publicly Laurier denied there was any plan and naively he left Ottawa for Chicago convinced it would all blow over. Clearly the editor of the militia journal had been primed by the GOC, for not only did the editorial pages condemn the private offers of "certain individuals," presumably Hughes, as those of "unimportant, self-seeking notoriety hunters," but they continued to argue vigorously for the adoption of Hutton's scheme. Interestingly, in November 1899 when the contingent finally sailed, Hutton appointed the *Gazette*'s editor as the official "Eye-Witness" with the force, and the *Gazette* continued to attack Sam Hughes throughout most of his South African service.[19]

All of this threw the cabinet into a heated debate, which intensified on October 9 with Kruger's forty-eight-hour ultimatum to the British government. Unless mediation and simultaneous British troop withdrawals took place, the old president defiantly proclaimed, the Transvaalers would be in a state of war with Great Britain. The inflexible document was just what Milner desired, but it was not what some men in Laurier's cabinet wanted. They were split three ways: Secretary of State Richard Scott and the French-Canadians were opposed to Canadian involvement; F. W. Borden and Postmaster William Mulock were for an official force, and the moderate advocates of participation led by W. S. Fielding in the Department of Finance found proposals for unofficial, low-cost forces like Hughes' very attractive. A worried Minto thought Scott's group would prevail. Yet two days after the ultimatum expired, the cabinet decided to send a small force of about 1,000 volunteers divided into eight companies at imperial expense: Laurier had given into his fear of electoral defeat in English Canada.[20]

The whole question of official government recognition had become entwined with Hughes' private offer and Hutton's attempts to stifle him. Hughes had friends in the cabinet who also suspected they were being shoved around by a GOC with whom they had already differed for nearly a year over policy, jurisdiction, and political interference. Hutton had once boasted that to put the militia on the right path he would perhaps have to turn out the Canadian government as he had once done with a government in New South Wales. In fact Richard Scott, the Acting Prime Minister, was so incensed at Hutton's apparent vindictive persecution of Hughes that he had summoned the GOC before the cabinet. But Hutton denied everything. While the crisis was averted by the Militia Minister's defence of the General, many of the members still strongly suspected that Hutton was the major force behind the coincidences of early October. If this was true, the arrogant Briton had far exceeded his constitutional authority, and had sacrificed the patriotic Sam Hughes in the process.[21]

As for the Governor-General's role in the Hughes affair, while men like Scott firmly believed that Minto was one of the "imperial conspirators" pushing Canadians into a war that was none of their concern, it was not so. As Carman Miller, the biographer of Minto's Canadian career clearly demonstrates, the Governor-General was at best only a reluctant participant. Since the failure of the Bloemfontein talks, he did not want Canada to get embroiled officially in a remote war where vital imperial interests were not at stake. His view was much more reasoned than that of Sam Hughes, who gave no indication that he ever thought much at all about British motives in South Africa. During the summer and fall, Minto stayed away from the thorny "official" problem. He only joined the serious debate when Hutton was attacked by Scott. Minto's mistakes began with his defence of the GOC against the cabinet's charges of constitutional manipulation; and he became further and unfairly associated with the conspiracy when he abruptly advised Laurier in October that if a contingent was to sail, it should be an official one, representing Canada and commanded by Canadians. Minto was a soldier who was concerned about the military competence of volunteers. After Hughes' outbursts against Hutton, the Governor-General came to believe more and more that Sam Hughes should not, for the sake of Canadians in the field, be involved in the contingent and that the force should be as well and as harmoniously led as possible. This combination of advocating an official force and opposing Hughes catapulted Minto into the conspirator category.[22]

Hughes was shattered when he learned he was not to be part of the contingent. On October 17 the temperamental MP apologized and withdrew his charges against Hutton. But Hutton would not relent. He ignored Borden's direct exhortations to have Hughes reinstated in some lesser capacity in the force.[23] The Governor-General found Hutton's position embarrassing on two accounts: he was ignoring his minister's direction and he was perceived to be attacking a well-known imperialist. However much Minto did not like Sam Hughes and his unofficial schemes, he only wanted Hughes removed from a command position. That had been achieved. Further limitation would only seem to the public to be unnecessary punishment and would jeopardize Minto's already fragile relations with the cabinet. Consequently he tried to get his GOC to see the wisdom of the Borden compromise. At first Minto had little luck. He tried to reason with Hutton: "It would be very advisable to sanction this . . . . Otter agrees; the Minister and the Premier wish it." Still Hutton refused. Finally Minto appealed to the GOC's Empire sentiment, suggesting that, if Hughes the imperialist was "left out, feeling would run high among the Canadian public." With the double pressure of the Militia Minister and the Governor-

General and some added by others like Sir Charles Tupper, Hutton finally gave in to a new proposition that satisfied all three men: Hughes was to go with the contingent but not in a military capacity.[24]

Most of the cabinet were likely relieved when Hutton backed down. They needed no more controversy, especially over the GOC's stand on Hughes, an issue hardly as momentous as the participation of the contingent itself or the threat from the arrogant Hutton. Apparently anxious to get him out of the country as soon as possible, Borden told Hughes that the government would pay his passage to South Africa and that he could sail with the troops, although only in mufti. Borden then added a further strong inducement by hinting to Hughes that he and Minto had arranged some special duty with the British Army once the MP landed at Cape Town. By sending Hughes overseas the Militia Minister removed not only a major source of imperial fervour in Canada, but also a potential critic of an already embarrassed government. If left in the country and unemployed, Hughes would give no peace in public and parliamentary scrutiny of the war effort. As far as Hutton was concerned, his suspicions were confirmed; Borden's act was nothing more than a typical colonial politician's way of getting rid of a parliamentary opponent.[25]

Perhaps it was unfortunate for Hutton, if he had hopes for a rest from the noisy MP, that Hughes had to wait about a week before sailing. During these days the more Hughes thought about Borden's offer, the more he saw his hopes of Canadian involvement in imperial defence being realized without him. Privately he resumed his lobbying for an official role with the contingent. On October 26 the tormented Hughes wrote another letter to his GOC. The communication started with a list of the reasons why the MP thought he should have been allowed to go to South Africa with the force, but soon moved into a diatribe against Hughes' substitute, Lieutenant-Colonel Lawrence Buchan, against regular imperial soldiers, and finally against Hutton himself. "Britishers, remittance men, chance off-spring and others sent to the colonies," Hughes wrote, are "too often placed in positions of trust which they are not capable of filling." Inaccurately he argued that whenever "British regulars have fought with Canadian Volunteers ... victory was ever theirs. Whenever disaster occurred in the War of 1812, there were no Canadians." Hughes focused his last bitter comment on Hutton's organization of the South African corps: the whole force had been ruined by Permanent Force soldiers and by the "fool Englishmen one finds both here and at home."[26]

By the next morning, when Hughes had regained his composure, he apologized to the GOC, saying that he had mistakenly interpreted Hutton's remarks as anti-Canadian. Hughes was not sincere, however, for behind the General's back he renewed his charges of constitutional violations directly with the General's opponents in the cabinet.[27] But the MP's recantation was too late; Hutton was already well into his own spiteful retaliation. Although he could not stop Hughes from sailing to South Africa, he could try to stop him from having any military employment. Privately Hutton wrote the Commander-in-Chief in South Africa that "this officer [Hughes] proceeds as a passenger without military status. I am not prepared to recommend his appointment in any military capacity in South Africa."[28]

Hughes was allowed to travel as a civilian aboard the *SS Sardinian* when it sailed from Quebec on October 30, 1899. Even on board ship, he manoeuvred hard to have his status upgraded and his grievances with Hutton redressed. A stream of letters flowed to Canadian and British politicians. While it is doubtful he was serious, Hughes even hinted to Laurier that he might be more sympathetic in the future to Liberal causes if reinstated to a high position in the force. Such a play was hardly admirable but it was a feature of Hughes' ambitious character which raised its ugly head from time to time. From aboard the *SS Sardinian* Hughes again wasted no opportunity to damn Hutton in the strongest possible language. He told Laurier that the GOC was "only fit to bull niggers."[29]

Hughes' quarrel with Hutton made him a martyr to many Canadians. Fellow imperialists, like those in the Denison clan who had applauded Hughes' contingent promotions, fully supported him. Looking back on the events during the fall, Septimus Denison, then serving in South Africa on Lord Robert's staff, told his brother George in Toronto that he and others "don't care too much for Lord Minto and therefore don't care how much roasting he gets from the press over the Hughes matter." Elsewhere Ontario Orangemen were also sympathetic to Sam Hughes. In the Lindsay area he was lauded as a credit to the militia, the Queen, and the country. The townspeople felt that "as citizens we should all feel proud that an officer [Colonel Hughes], second in command, has been selected from our community." Nothing could have been further from the truth: Hughes had no official or military role with the contingent. Typically his vanity would not let him correct the impression. He accepted praise, gifts, and money from the town in a public farewell to "one of the chief officers of the Canadian Contingent for service in the Transvaal."[30]

With General Hutton working against Sam Hughes, it is surprising that he found any military employment in South Africa. For the first two months Hughes was there, Hutton's interdictions effectively barred him from obtaining any post. But these impediments only made Hughes work harder. As soon as he landed in Cape Town in December 1899, he started writing letters begging employment from influential British soldiers and politicians in South Africa, many of whom, like

Lord Methuen, he had met while at the Diamond Jubilee celebrations in 1897.[31]

Hughes succeeded in laying his case before Sir Alfred Milner, High Commissioner of Cape Colony and later the architect of the Union of South Africa. Hughes not only met one of his future commanding officers, Sir Charles Warren, but later managed to break into the powerful clique which frequented Groote Schuur, the estate of Cecil Rhodes near Cape Town. Even though Rhodes at this time was s comfortable prisoner of the Boers in besieged Kimberley, Hughes was often invited to dine and ride at the Cape Town residence with many politicians, soldiers, and journalists, such as Dr. L. S. Jameson, General Herbert Settle, Lionel Curtis, Leopold Amery of the London *Times*, and General Sir Frederick Forestier-Walker, the commander of the British forces at the Cape. These connections, however, did not immediately produce any employment. In frustration Hughes visited one of the combat zones in early January 1900 only to be stymied once again. Hughes "came up here without leave," wrote one of Minto's friends from the field, "and asked for employment and was sent back with a flea in his ear."[32]

Fortunately for Sam Hughes, the new year produced larger forces which started to work in his favour. The initial one seems to have been Minto himself back in Canada, who interceded on Hughes' behalf. In helping Hughes, Minto may have been trying to demonstrate that he wanted to co-operate with the cabinet and that he did not agree with all of his arrogant GOC's decisions. By this time the Governor-General had accomplished most of what he wanted: official contingents and Hughes' exclusion as a commander of Canadian troops in South Africa. Moreover the vice-regal offer was a favour for Borden, who preferred not having Hughes opposing the government for a while longer. Whatever the reason, the Governor-General fulfilled Borden's hint to Hughes of the previous October by writing directly to the new Commander-in-Chief, Field Marshal Roberts, asking him to find a suitable position for the colonial Colonel in some imperial service, but as far away from the Canadian contingent as possible.[33]

The Colonel's partisans at home, disgruntled with the arrogant Hutton, continued to criticize him for his rough treatment of Hughes, especially over the General's statement in the Ottawa *Citizen* which claimed that Hughes was not in his right mind. Some newspapers charged that Hughes had been robbed by Hutton's unnecessary persecutions of his right to serve Queen and country. At the same time the government inadvertently contributed to the public sympathy for Hughes by granting him the Fenian Raid Medal of 1870. To supporters who could not tell the difference between campaign medals and awards for bravery, not only was Hughes a martyr but now he was a heroic martyr.[34]

Minto was not the only one who was helping Sam Hughes in January 1900. Perhaps because of Hughes' support in the Conservative leadership race in 1896 or because he might be of further use in promoting imperial schemes, Lord Strathcona privately persuaded Hutton through Minto to offer Hughes a captaincy in a new force which he was sponsoring for duty in South Africa, namely, Lord Strathcona's Horse. Even though he was at the time still unemployed, when Hughes received the offer, with typical arrogance he replied, "I would accept with pleasure the command but not a command."[35] Indeed he never even bothered to formally answer Hutton's telegram, probably because he felt that he had the GOC on the run and was not going to back down until he obtained the position he desired. Hughes' egotism made it nearly impossible for him to settle for this position when there was still the possibility of receiving a higher one. There is no indication, however, that the Canadian Militia Minister ever offered Hughes the command of any officially sanctioned force.[36]

Laurier and Borden were having enough trouble with Hutton, and his chief defender Minto, without asking for more from Sam Hughes. The temporary truce between Hutton and the Laurier cabinet came to an end with the organization of additional forces for South Africa. There was obvious evidence of the General's insubordination and disdain for cabinet opinion. The Minister of Militia and Hutton were also at loggerheads over matters of patronage and jurisdiction. Finally in February 1900, when the government could no longer tolerate its authority being challenged by Hutton, Laurier dismissed the General.[37]

As for Sam Hughes, he was guilty of nearly as many transgressions as Hutton. But he was absent and defenceless, and he had national and political legitimacy. Some of those who watched him struggle against arrogant, powerful men like the GOC and Minto failed to recognize that he too was straining another aspect of the normal civil-military equation. To these people, especially the MP himself, Hughes was fighting a "Canadian" fight against the pro-consuls.[38]

Ironically, in mid-February 1900, neither Hughes nor Hutton had a job. They both seemed to be victims of forces they had mutually aggravated in trying to promote support for the war in South Africa. Indeed with Lord Roberts' vigorous assault then taking place directly on the Boer republics, Hutton and Hughes especially may have thought that events were passing them by.

Reference Notes to Chapter 5

1 Canada, *Sessional Paper*, no. 19, *Annual Report of the Militia Department for 1898* (Ottawa: Queen's Printer, 1899), p. 40. Hereafter cited *Militia Report*.
2 *Canadian Military Gazette*, Oct. 18, 1898, p. 9; *Militia Report*, 1898, p. 42; and *Hansard*, 1899, pp. 2335-58.
3 PAC, Hutton *papers*, pp. 964-97. Hutton to Chamberlain, Feb. 20, 1899; and ibid., Chamberlain to Hutton, Mar. 14, 1899. For an explanation of the complexity of Minto's role see Carman Miller, *The Canadian Career of the Fourth Earl of Minto: The Education of a Viceroy* (Waterloo: WLU Press, 1980), chapters 4-8. Also see Gordon, p. 152, and *Hansard*, 1899, pp. 2335-58.
4 Gordon, p. 130.
5 PAC, Hutton *papers*, p. 973, Hutton to Chamberlain, July 28, 1899; ibid., p. 1415, Hutton to Wolseley, Aug. 1, 1899; and Morton, *Ministers and Generals*, pp. 151-52.
6 PAC, pamphlet, no. 2565, "Correspondence touching on the conduct of Lieutenant-Colonel Hughes, MP in connection with his volunteering for active service in South Africa," pp. 7-9, Hughes to Lieutenant-Colonel Montizambert, Sept. 2, 1899. Also see ibid., p. 3, Hughes to F. W. Borden, July 24, 1899; *Hansard*, 1899, pp. 7328-29, and Montreal *Star*, July 14, 1899, p. 5.
7 *Hansard*, 1899, pp. 8992-98; Montreal *Star*, Aug. 5, p. 12; also see Carman Miller, *The Public Life of Sir Frederick Borden*, MA thesis (Dalhousie, 1964), pp. 64-68; Frank Underhill, "Lord Minto on his Governor-Generalship," in the *Canadian Historical Review*, XL, no. 2 (1959), p. 121; editorial comments in *Canadian Magazine*, XIV (1899-1900), pp. 80, 193, 220; PAC, pamphlet, no. 2565, Hughes to F. W. Borden, July 24, 1899.
8 *Militia Report*, 1898, p. 41.
9 PAC, pamphlet, no. 2565, Hughes to Borden, July 24, 1899.
10 PAC, Hutton *papers*, pp. 1101-18; Hughes to Hutton, Nov. 29, 1898; PAC, pamphlet, no. 2565, Hughes to Hutton, Aug. 28, 1899; and Preston, *Canada and Imperial Defense*, p. 249.
11 PAC, pamphlet, no. 2565, Hughes to Montizambert, Aug. 2, 1899; Drummond to Hutton, Aug. 22, 1899; Memorandum, Drummond to GOC, Aug. 22, 1899; and CSO to DOC 3 and 4, Aug. 24, 1899. Carman Miller, unpublished manuscripts on Minto's governor-generalship, pp. 44-48, hereafter cited Miller manuscript; PAC RG 9, II, A 1, f 16203, Hutton to Borden, July 31, 1899; and PAC, Minto *papers*, MG 27, II, B, vol. 15, E. T. Hutton to Minto, Aug. 11, 1899.
12 PAC, pamphlet, no. 2565, Hughes to Hutton, Aug. 28, 1899.
13 Ibid.
14 Ibid., Hughes to Lieutenant-Colonel Montizambert, Sept. 2, 1899; and L. S. Amery *papers*, in the possession of the Hon. Julian Amery, London, England. Canadian Militia Bill file, 1904, Hughes to Amery, May 18, 1904.
15 Penlington, *Canadian Historical Review*, XXIV (1944), pp. 156-71. On the state of the militia, see Hutton's *Militia Report*, 1898, pp. 25-40; also *Globe*, June 9, 1900, p. 18; Hughes to F. W. Borden, Mar. 31, 1900.
16 *Globe*, Sept. 20, 1899, p. 12; Capon, *The Incredible Sam Hughes*, p. 36. Hughes claimed he had the support of J. Israel Tarte, Laurier's Quebec lieutenant and Minister of Public Works, in assisting to mobilize the French-Canadians. Nothing could have been further from the truth. The Montreal *Star*, Sept. 20, 1899, p. 7, contained the following advertisement: "Wanted—Fighters for the Transvaal. Apply to Colonel Sam Hughes MP"; also see Amery *papers*, Canadian Militia Bill file, 1904, Hughes to Amery, Aug. 8, 1904; and Joseph Schull, *Laurier, the First Canadian* (Toronto: Macmillan, 1965), pp. 212-13 and 376-97.
17 PAC, pamphlet, no. 2565, Foster to Hughes, Sept. 25, 1899; and ibid., Foster to Montizambert, Oct. 9, 1899.
18 PAC, Hutton *papers*, Hughes to Hutton, Oct. 10, 1899, and Hutton to Buller, June 18, 1899; PAC, Laurier *papers*, C769, Hughes to Laurier, Oct. 4, 1899, pp. 37831-34; and PAC, pamphlet, no. 2565, Hughes to Montizambert, Sept. 2, 1899, Hughes to Foster, Oct. 11, 1899, and Hughes to Hutton, Oct. 26, 1899.

REFERENCE NOTES TO CHAPTER 5 / 81

19 *Canadian Military Gazette,* Oct. 3, 1899, p. 11; also see ibid., Nov. 7, 1899, pp. 5, 6, 12, Jan. 16, 1900, pp. 6, 9, Mar. 1900, p. 9; and Thomas Pakenham, *The Boer War* (New York: Random House, 1979), pp. 57-103.
20 *Globe,* Oct. 14, 1899, p. 1. Secretly Hutton had notified some of the Permanent Force officers to expect a command in an overseas force a month before the official announcement that it would be raised. For instance, Major Oscar Pelletier received secret warning from the GOC on Sept. 5, 1899 "so that you will not be taken by surprise. Our arrangements here are all thought out and ready." See Hutton to Pelletier, Sept. 5, 1899, confidential, in Colonel Oscar C. Pelletier, *Mémoires Souvenir de Famille, et Récits* (Quebec, 1940), p. 307.
21 PAC, Minto *papers,* vol. 18, p. 2, Hutton to Minto, Jan. 31, 1900. The controversy is well recorded in Miller's *Education of a Viceroy,* pp. 69-75, 80-95 and in C. P. Stacey, *Canada and the Age of Conflict, A History of Canadian External Policies,* vol. 1; 1867-1921 (Toronto: Macmillan, 1977), pp. 57-71; Norman Penlington, "General Hutton and the Problem of Military Imperialism in Canada, 1898-1900," in Carl Berger, ed., *Imperial Relations in the Age of Laurier* (Toronto: University of Toronto Press, 1969), pp. 49-55; PAC, Hutton *papers,* Foster to Hutton, Oct. 13, 1899; and British Museum, Hutton *papers,* "The Memoirs of Lieutenant-General Sir Edward Hutton," pp. 155-59, in the files of Dr. Carman Miller, McGill University. Hereafter cited Hutton, *Memoirs;* and Penlington, *Canadian Historical Review,* XXIV (1944), p. 186. Also see Lindsay *Watchman-Warder,* Oct. 12, 1899, p. 8, Nov. 2, 1899, p. 8, and Nov. 9, 1899, p. 2.
22 Miller, *The Education of a Viceroy,* pp. 80-96.
23 PAC, Minto *papers,* p. 84, Minto to Hutton, Oct. 16, 1899; PAC, pamphlet, no. 2565, Hughes to Foster, Oct. 17, 1899; and ibid., Foster to the GOC, Oct. 17, 1899; and PANS, F. W. Borden *papers,* Official Letters Book (OLB), no. 11, p. 287, Borden to Hutton, Oct. 21, 1899.
24 PAC, Minto *papers,* vol. 15, p. 83, Minto to Hutton, Oct. 18, 1899 (Minto wanted Hughes made a captain); ibid., p. 83. Minto to Hutton, Oct. 20, 1899; and ibid., p. 86, Hutton to Minto, Oct. 21, 1899; also PANS, F. W. Borden *papers,* OLB, no. 11, Borden to Hughes, Oct. 25, 1899; and PAC, Sir Charles Tupper *papers,* MG 26, F, vol. 19, p. 10226, Tupper to Hutton, Oct. 28, 1899; ibid., p. 10270, Tupper to Chamberlain, Oct. 30, 1899.
25 Hutton *Memoirs,* p. 158; also see PANS, F. W. Borden *papers,* OLB, no. 11, p. 291, Borden to Minto, Oct. 23, 1899; and PAC, Minto *papers,* vol. 8, Borden to Minto, Oct. 23, 1899, p. 7.
26 PAC, pamphlet, no. 2565, Hughes to Hutton, Oct. 26, 1899.
27 Ibid., Hughes to Hutton, Oct. 27, 1899; PAC, Laurier *papers,* C-769, p. 38380, Hughes to Laurier, Oct. 27, 1899; and PAC, Richard Scott *papers,* MG 27, D. 14, vol. 4, pp. 1647-54, Hughes to Laurier, Oct. 23, 1899.
28 PAC, W. D. Otter *papers,* MG 30, G 14, GOC Canada to Commander-in-Chief South Africa, Oct. 30, 1899; and Miller, *The Education of a Viceroy,* pp. 72-73.
29 PAC, Laurier *papers,* vol. 30, pp. 38900-04, Hughes to Laurier, Nov. 14, 1899; ibid., vol. 126, pp. 37831-34, Hughes to Laurier, Oct. 4, 1899; also see ibid., vol. 129, pp. 38523-28, Mrs. Hughes to Laurier, Nov. 1, 1899. Great Britain, Colonial Office, 42(874) (188), Hughes to Chamberlain, Dec. 12, 1899; and ibid., 42(880) (7116), Hughes to Chamberlain, Feb. 10, 1900, in the files of Dr. Carman Miller, McGill University, p. 34.
30 *Orange Sentinel,* Nov. 9, 1899, p. 4, and Feb. 15, 1900, p. 4; PAC, Denison *papers,* MG 29, E 29, pp. 4114-15, Septimus to George Denison, Sept. 4, 1900; ibid., pp. 4051-54, Davis-Allen to G. Denison, June 2, 1900; and *Watchmen-Warder,* Oct. 26, p. 1, and Nov. 2, p. 1.
31 Hughes to Methuen, Dec. 6, 1899, in S. H. S. Hughes, *CHAR* (1949-1950), pp. 34-35, and PRO, CO 42(874)(188) Hughes to Chamberlain, Dec. 12, 1899; and ibid., 42(880), 7116, Feb. 10, 1900, in Miller's files.
32 Oxford University, Bodleian Library, Lord Milner *papers* (MS Milner dep.), diary entries for Dec. 20, 1899, Jan. 1, 1900, Feb. 3, 1900, and Feb. 17, 1900. Hereafter cited Milner *papers;* and L. Drummond to Minto, Jan. 12, 1900, in Miller's files.

33 PAC, Governor-General's numbered files, RG 7, G 21, no. 265, Minto to Roberts, Jan. 17, 1900; and ibid., Minto to Chamberlain, July 23, 1903.
34 PAC, Minto *papers*, vol. 18, pt. 2, Borden to Laurier, Feb. 3, 1900; *Watchman-Warder*, Nov. 9, 1899, pp. 2, 8, Jan. 18, 1900, p. 1, and Feb. 18, 1900, p. 2. Among the papers mentioned that supported Hughes were the Toronto *World* and the Ottawa *Journal*. The Toronto *Evening Telegram*, Feb. 3, 1900, p. 4, and Feb. 12, 1900, p. 4, also gave support. The *Orange Sentinel* also gave Hughes a good press. See ibid., Nov. 9, 1899, p. 4; and *Hansard*, 1900, p. 599.
35 PAC, Minto *papers*, vol. 15, p. 90, Hutton to Minto, Jan. 16, 1900; Beckles Willson, *The Life of Lord Strathcona*, pp. 519-22; *Sessional Papers*, 1900, no. 77, Hutton to Borden, Feb. 2, 1900; and *Watchman-Warder*, Mar. 22, 1900, p. 7, Sam Hughes to John Hughes, Feb. 14, 1900.
36 PANS, F. W. Borden *papers*, OLB, no. 13, p. 356, Borden to Strathcona, Mar. 3, 1900. *Canadian Military Gazette* (Jan. 16, 1900, p. 4) did not want Hughes to be recommended for any position in a second force because of his previous conduct.
37 PANS, F. W. Borden *papers*, OLB, vol. 12, p. 922, Borden to Hutton, Feb. 10, 1900; and Morton, *Ministers and Generals*, pp. 155-60.
38 Gordon, p. 168; PANS, F. W. Borden *papers*, OLB, vol. 13, Borden to General Laurie, Mar. 5, 1900; and Miller, *The Education of a Viceroy*, pp. 97-118, covers Minto's role in the crisis.

CHAPTER 6

The Proving Ground: South Africa, 1900

In mid-February 1900, while the dismissal of Hutton was still echoing in Canada, Hughes finally secured his first job in South Africa as a supply and transport officer on the vital lines of communication supporting Lord Roberts' advance northwards from Cape Colony. Likely it was the Field Marshal who gave Hughes the chance, if not out of deference to Minto's and Borden's wishes back in Canada, then out of simple fatigue from hearing the pushy Canadian Colonel's constant plea for employment. On top of this, Hughes' new fortune was very much a product of several larger events then occurring in the course of the war.

If his new duties were rather sedate for Hughes' adventuresome spirit, he did not have them long enough for boredom to set in. The shortage of officers in the British service and the escalation of the war soon made him a more marketable entity, especially after he had shown competence at his first job. In late February, as Roberts' columns pushed hard on the Boer seats of government, their sympathetic Cape Colony cousins in the area of the Orange River to the west of Roberts' lines of march took up arms against the British. The rising in the northwest of the colony posed two major dangers for the British. Every step that Roberts' badly overstretched columns advanced made them more vulnerable to an attack on their vital supply links stretching hundreds of miles back to Cape Town. There was a clear danger of the northwest insurrection spreading into a general Cape rebellion to the rear of the main British forces. The insatiable appetite of Roberts' strategy for men and material had left very little with which to defend

---

Reference notes for Chapter 6 are found on pp. 94-96.

the colony. These events of February 1900 provided Sam Hughes with the opening he had been waiting for.

For the next four months Hughes was involved in two theatres of operation, neither of which can be considered part of the major offensive on the Boer republics, but which were necessary in protecting Roberts' flank and rear and in helping to ensure peace in Cape Colony. From March until mid-May Hughes served with Brigadier-General Herbert Settle in North-West Cape Colony; from May until the end of June he campaigned with Lieutenant-General Sir Charles Warren, in Griqualand West, north of the Orange River, and in Bechuanaland. These operations involved small commands which covered long, tiring distances on foot and horseback. Skirmishes were common and larger actions few. The objective in both cases was the same: to put down the rebellion by occupying the major towns, arresting rebels, confiscating arms and other munitions, and restoring loyal civilian powers as soon as possible. Both campaigns were successful.[1]

With Roberts' columns fully occupied in February in bringing the Boer General Cronje to bay in the dry Modder river bottom near Paardeberg, the added threat of a rebellion in North-West Cape Colony on his west flank and rear was indeed annoying. So was the constant exhortation of Milner from Cape Town to do something about the rebellion before it spread.[2] Consequently, on February 23 Roberts ordered Brigadier-General Herbert Settle, a Royal Engineer and commander of the Orange River Station on the Cape Town to Buluwayo railway, to deal with the rebels south of the Orange River. Settle had to gather up whatever troops he could find before he set out for the western districts. For this operation Settle promoted Hughes, already under his command, from assistant inspector-general of transport to head of the new column's intelligence and scouting section.[3]

As the campaign progressed, Hughes quickly developed a flair for scouting which often put him in the vanguard of Settle's forces, and he was nearly always the first to make contact with the enemy. Hughes' main duties were to find the Boer commandos or any enemy sympathizers and to seize munitions or necessary forage. His role was part of Settle's plans for occupying the major settlements of the disaffected areas which stretched nearly 300 miles along the Orange River to the German West African border. The principal towns were Prieska, Kenhart, and Upington.[4] Hughes' command within the force was not very big, for Settle's column was a small mixed force of infantry, mounted troops, and some guns, made up of many irregular troops and recent volunteers. Most of the time, such forces paid little attention to the rigorous military etiquette and routines which characterized British regular formations. Transport, water, and forage were concerns equal to combating the enemy.

Much of what is known about Hughes's conduct during this campaign comes from Lionel Curtis and Lionel Hichens, both of whom were later prominent either in Milner's "Kindergarten" and in the Round Table movement or in imperial administration elsewhere in the Empire. Along with their Oxford classmate and artist of some talent, Max Balfour, they had joined the cycle section of the City Imperial Volunteers (CIV) as privates in 1899. By March 1900 they were under Hughes' command in Settle's column.[5]

There can be little doubt that Hughes had a common touch which made him a very popular officer among his troops, and he mixed easily with them. Some thought he was "a man among men." Others liked him because he shared all of their privations in the desert-like veld of North-West Cape Colony where dirt, heat, and cold, and sometimes hunger and thirst, were constant companions. Not only was he sympathetic to the plight of his own soldiers; Hughes was often noted for the concern he expressed in the treatment of the enemy. Once when his men looted food from a Boer household, Curtis recorded that Hughes paid the full value of the stolen goods out of his own pocket and apologized profusely. On another occasion, Max Balfour was impressed that after Hughes had to arrest an old Boer rebel named van Schroeder, the Colonel went out of his way to comfort the man's distraught wife and to provide for her well-being.[6]

Most men serving under Hughes admired him greatly, not only because he shared their hardship and did not treat them with the same arrogant aloofness that typified many British officers, but also because, as Lord Milner observed later, Hughes was able to cut through all the red tape that was the curse of the war effort. Sam Hughes was critical not only of the bureaucracy but also of British generalship itself. Both while unemployed and while serving in the field, Hughes frequently wrote letters home to friends condemning the military practices of the British, including their archaic manoeuvres and their inability to ride and shoot. Many of these letters were published in the Canadian press. While campaigning Hughes did not hesitate to impress his views on his soldiers or anyone else who would listen. One such person was the London *Times* correspondent, Leo Amery, whom Hughes had met the previous December in Cape Town. Amery was also a friend of Curtis and Hichens. Amery visited them, and Hughes, in the field where he made an arrangement with the two younger men to send him their impressions of the fighting, which no doubt included many of Hughes' ideas. While Hughes' career in South Africa was not yet affected by his criticism of British leaders, his contacts with Amery while on active service was the beginning of a friendship which lasted many years.[7]

As Settle's plans successfully unfolded, Hughes' reputation in the force grew. He and his scouts covered vast stretches of territory in advance of the main column and often under terrible conditions. He reconnoitred Prieska prior to its occupation; he accompanied Settle to Kenhart; and he was responsible for the occupation and pacification of Upington, the town furthest west and the last one which the demoralized Boers tried to defend before Settle's campaign ended. This last episode demonstrates the qualities some men admired in Hughes: dash, initiative, leadership, audacity, and coolness under fire.[8]

On March 27, 1900, after torrential rain and bad transport had bogged him down forty miles west of Prieska, Settle ordered Hughes, his staff, and a small detachment of irregular cavalry to advance on Upington where reports had located an enemy force of about 300 rebels. When his mounted men proved too slow for Hughes, the impatient colonial galloped on ahead with his interpreter and five others, covering in two days the ninety miles to Upington and exchanging a few shots with the rebels along the way. Approaching the town, Hughes decided not to await reinforcements but to bluff whatever Boer force was there into surrendering by making them believe that his nine-man troop, which now included two captured rebels, was very much larger than it was. As soon as the settlement was in sight, Hughes commanded his troop to gallop "for all they were worth in order to make as much dust as possible, while he put a double team into the cart to make it look like a gun coming into action." These tactics completely surprised the small enemy rearguard; after firing a shot or two, it galloped out one side of the town while Hughes' "column," in extended order, charged into the other. Some thought Hughes' action was reckless; nevertheless he took Upington, then spent an anxious night expecting the much larger Boer force in the area to riposte. Fortunately it did not, but that night held its own special excitement.[9]

After having single-handedly captured eight enemy horsemen who rode too close to the town in the early evening, Hughes armed about twenty Kaffirs, the local blacks, to help defend the town. This unconventional act would have had the blacks killed instantly if caught by the enemy. Nevertheless, Hughes turned this somewhat enlarged force over to Max Balfour of the CIV cyclists, and then disappeared on foot into the night with his two servants "bent on taking the enemy in his own den." Nothing came of either the expected Boer attack or of Hughes' attempt to capture the enemy; and for the next two days, while awaiting the arrival of Settle's main forces, Hughes scoured the farms in the surrounding area looking for weapons and commandeering any forage or transport for British use elsewhere. One of Hughes' most effective means of pacifying the countryside was to wait until the pious but unco-operative Boers were at prayers in their farm houses, then kick in the door, arrest the head of the family, and loudly announce that the man would be promptly shot if weapons were not surrendered immediately. This tactic usually worked. But Hughes would subsequently be overcome by compassion and would then spend substantial time calming down the terrified families.[10]

By the time Settle's forces arrived in Upington, Hughes' three-day bluff had so demoralized the Boer bands in the countryside that many of them simply gave up in the following days. On top of this, the "Kurnel"—as Curtis called Hughes, mimicking his North American accent—had gathered substantial amounts of precious forage and teams to supply Roberts' main advance. Hughes also had arrested the most prominent enemy rebel in the area. There remained little for Settle to do but occupy Upington, then to join up with other British forces already at Kenhart to the south. Hughes' capture of Upington and the pacification of the surrounding area marked the end of the effective rebellion south of the Orange River. The campaign had also demonstrated to many who had served with Hughes that, in Lionel Curtis' words, he was "one of the ablest persons I have come across out here"; although Curtis also admitted that Hughes was inclined at times to act impulsively and unconventionally.[11]

The restoration of British authority in the Prieska and Upington districts set the stage for Hughes' second and last exposure to active combat service in South Africa. After spending about a month in the tedious job of restoring civil administration south of the Orange River, Hughes was ordered to report for duty in Griqualand West, north of the river, under the command of Sir Charles Warren. Warren and Hughes shared one thing in common in South Africa: some important people considered them both pariahs and sought some place to send them where they would cause little harm or antagonism. In Sir Charles Warren's case, he was an aging Royal Engineer like Settle. His greatest moment was lost when, as London's chief of metropolitan police in the 1880s, he had failed to catch Jack the Ripper, in spite of being able to issue most of his orders in rhyming couplets. Afterward he returned to the Engineers where he dabbled pedantically in military cartography and archaeology in South Africa before returning to England to retire.

When war broke out, Warren's obvious first-hand knowledge of South African terrain made him an ideal soldier for the campaign. As fate and the decrepit state of the British forces would have it, he was one of the regular and much overvalued soldiers whom Englishmen felt could save the national honour after the debacle of "Black Week" in December 1899. Having been appointed second in command of the Natal Field Force under Field Marshal Sir Redvers Buller, another irresolute Victorian soldier, Warren faded into ignominy with his chief as a result of their incompetence at the battle of Spion Kop in January of 1900. After that slaughter, when Lord Roberts came out to redeem British arms, the Field Marshal wanted to get rid of Warren. However, with

Milner's constant messages about a possible rebellion in Cape Colony and the shortage of available officers, Roberts decided that Warren, in command of a small force, could yet be both out of the way and of value. In May 1900 he offered Warren a command to pacify Griqualand. The concession also helped silence the bothersome High Commissioner and provided employment for other contumacious soldiers who were otherwise unemployable. Thus Warren and Hughes came together.[12]

Since the conditions north of the Orange River were the same as those that had necessitated action south of it, Warren's campaign plans were very similar to Settle's, as was his force and the terrain over which he had to march. He planned to move against the main rebel force under Commandant-General Piet de Villiers, a Transvaaler who had been inciting the Cape districts to rebellion. Warren wanted to secure the towns of Douglas, Campbell, and Griquatown in Griqualand, and Kuruman in Bechuanaland. Only then could the surrounding countryside be pacified; and in order to do this, it was important for him to capture the Transvaalers since they were the backbone of the insurgency.[13]

The details of Hughes' transfer to Warren's force are not known. Perhaps because the General took his instructions directly from the High Commissioner, Milner had something to do with it. He certainly liked Hughes' forthright manner and shared many of his criticisms of antiquated British military bureaucracy. In mid-May, Hughes was made Assistant Adjutant-General (AAG) and Intelligence Officer in Warren's command. At its largest, the force included less than 2,000 men, and it was pitted against about the same number of Boers. Shortly after his appointment Hughes began his six-week adventure by moving out from Belmont towards Douglas. Again he was to demonstrate to many of his comrades, including his commander, the same "dash and bravery [which] had ... won for him the leadership of the advance party on practically every occasion." On May 29 after fighting several skirmishes and avoiding a Boer ambush en route, Hughes' troops were among the first to enter the town of Douglas.[14]

Although the British managed to seize great quantities of war supplies left by the outmanoeuvred Boers, they failed to capture any rebels, who fell back on Campbell where they were substantially reinforced by de Villiers. After being delayed some days by transport problems, the slow-moving Warren advanced on the town. However, his resolution did not last long. Fearing a tough fight for the settlement, Warren decided on May 29 to stop short of his objective and await supplies at a farm called Faber's Put. But the aggressive de Villiers had far different plans. Believing that the British militia and irregulars, such as Warren's Scouts whom Hughes commanded, would have no staying power if surprised, the Boer commander had no intention of waiting for Warren. Shortly before dawn, while Hughes, Warren, and the troops were just stirring at Faber's Put, about 600 Boers attacked the encampment.

Warren's choice for a bivouac was a poor one, situated as it was at the bottom of a topographical bowl whose rim was a low range of hills. Two farm houses about 800 yards apart looked up the ridges to the north, and Hughes, with his scouts, some men from the Imperial Yeomanry and Paget's Horse, occupied the building on the northwest side. Even though piquets had been placed on the hills around the camp, the undetected enemy had quickly ringed the heights above the British. De Villiers and fifty-six of the best shots had actually penetrated the camp and moved to within 100 yards of its centre. When a surprised sentry finally raised the alarm, the fighting was ferocious and hand-to-hand for about an hour.

Only half dressed when the attack began, Hughes, seeing that some of the enemy were attempting to seize the stone kraal which contained most of the horses of the mounted troops, gathered a few men and stormed it, opening an intense fire at point-blank range. His quick riposte drove the Boers out of the enclosure and eventually back up the slopes. Once at the top, the enemy opened a deadly Mauser fire down the south side. Picking the best shots from the Imperial Yeomanry and Warren's Scouts, Hughes punched in the enemy unit's flank exposed on the bowl's rim, which drove them off the ridges and into the bush toward the south. Elsewhere in the camp, Hughes' actions had been repeated by other officers; and even though most of the horses had been temporarily lost, thus preventing any pursuit, the steadiness of the volunteer troops under fire and their vigorous counter-attacks defeated the Boers.

Warren later reported to Roberts that this repulse was fortunate, for any attack on Campbell or Griquatown would have been considerably more costly than twenty-three dead and thirty-two wounded. He also felt that the bloody expulsion had so demoralized the enemy that they offered very little resistance for the remainder of the campaign.[15] Certainly Warren was right, but had it not been for the solid service performed by Hughes and others of his force, the situation may have been a disaster. Even though Warren claimed that they "were not taken by surprise," they had been.

Hughes knew that the site Warren had picked for a camp only invited attack and that the piquets were hardly adequate. And because of it men had died. When he heard that Warren's reports to Milner and Roberts were tantamount to a whitewash of these mistakes—as he said in later years, reports which were "deceptive and ... absolutely untrue"—Hughes took action. In a highly critical memorandum, he charged that the Boer attack "was a perfect surprise. Few [of our men] were even dressed ready to fight." There is no clear evidence to whom Hughes directed the memorandum, but likely it was leaked to Amery. The criticism soon appeared in Cape newspapers. Warren did not find out for a few weeks after the engagement that one of his severest critics was his own Chief of Intelligence. In the meantime, he continued to praise Hughes for his action at Faber's Put and elsewhere.[16]

Faber's Put was the hottest fight Sam Hughes experienced, and he made a great deal of it in his letters home. In later years, he charged several times that his performance there was never properly recognized. Among other things, he also claimed that on two occasions, one at Douglas and again at Faber's Put, Sir Charles Warren had promised him a Victoria Cross. In the heat of the moment, Warren may have said these things for he could not have failed to realize that it was men such as Hughes who had really saved his hide at the farm bivouac. But if he did promise Hughes any decorations, once he found out about the Canadian Colonel's damning report, it is unlikely that he would have carried it through. After all, in the wake of his Spion Kop disaster, Warren could not afford another blight on his record if he were to salvage anything of his military career. No treacherous Canadian militiamen would stand in his way. In Warren's official dispatches, which were dated after he knew of Hughes' criticism, no such proposal was made; nor is there any evidence of one in his edited diaries. Warren did make one unsuccessful recommendation for the Victoria Cross after Faber's Put, but it was for Lieutenant Claude Lowther of the Imperial Yeomanry, a man who became a favourite of Hughes during the Great War. Although mentioned in dispatches and commended for his vigorous action throughout his service, the official record of Hughes' performance until Faber's Put would remain one of solid and, at times, exceptional service which warranted no further recognition.[17]

During the remaining month of the campaign, Hughes continued to perform well, although he also continued, as Balfour noted earlier, to draw "the Longbow" about his exploits and sometimes to take impulsive actions, which caused some further aggravation with Warren. Hughes led raids on Tweefontein and Knoffelfontein ahead of the main force. These vigorous demonstrations so alarmed the already confused rebels that they fled Campbell without a fight, leaving behind huge quantities of kit and supplies. On June 7 Hughes led the advance scouts on Griquatown and occupied it even though ordered by Warren not to do so if the Boers looked as if they would resist. Once Warren's forces concentrated in Griquatown, he again sent Hughes and eighteen men off towards Kuruman where the General had heard that the last major enemy commando was anxious to surrender. Warren made it clear that Hughes was only to investigate these reports and to screen the enemy, not to enter into parley with de Villiers or his leaders concerning final surrender which, when it came, must be unconditional. Hughes ignored his commander's orders. When he found the Boer laager at Groote Konig in front of Kuruman on June 18, Hughes felt he could capture all of the several hundred rebels, even though he was two days ahead of Warren.[18]

The large number of Boers in the de Villiers force did not deter the zealous Hughes. Leaving his eighteen men behind at a safe distance, he confidently rode into the camp alone and demanded the amazed force's surrender. While these discussions were going on, a message arrived for the chief Boer negotiator reporting that Roberts had suffered a major check on the Rhenoster River further east. With this new information, the Boers decided to continue fighting. Colonel Hughes was now in a tight spot, but his nerve hardly ever failed him. He at once retorted, as he later gloated in a private letter to Warren, "Oh, haven't you heard of that before. . . . Certainly your fellows bagged a few of our yeomanry at Rhenoster but didn't you hear that a superior British force rounded up the whole outfit 24 hours later and they are all prisoners on route for Cape Town." The instant retort worked. Most of the men decided to give up. During the ensuing confusion, however, about fifty Transvaalers, including de Villiers, slipped out of the camp and headed back to the Transvaal; and Hughes did not have enough men to hold them. In spite of the escape of the most important of the Boer leaders and the hard-core of the commando, Hughes took 220 prisoners including a vast train of horses, rifles, ammunition, and other supplies. He managed also to maintain the bluff and keep his prisoners in check until he could regain contact with his main column a few days later.[19]

On June 19 Warren, who had not heard from Hughes for several days, received a message that his errant chief scout was parleying surrender terms with the rebels in spite of Warren's order to the contrary. Perhaps Hughes was trying to soften his violation of orders when he wired Warren that the terms he had imposed were "really unconditional." The irate Warren declared Hughes' terms "totally contrary in every respect to anything I should think of issuing to rebels anxious to surrender." What Warren had hoped would be a complete bag of rebels turned out to be missing de Villiers and fifty of his best fighters. Hughes' settlement also contained terms that allowed a few of the other leaders to be parolled to their homes instead of being transported to the Cape as prisoners of war. Back at the Cape, Milner was angry. The major rebel had escaped, and the High Commissioner wanted an explanation from Warren. Warren filed a detailed report that blamed Hughes and showed clearly that his precipitate actions had cost the expedition its real prize.[20]

In fairness to Hughes, the large bag of prisoners he took before Kuruman and his occupation of that town on June 24, 1900, marked the last major event of the rebellion north of the Orange River. Hughes was pleased with his own effort, and in a private letter, unfortunately published in Canada by some of his enthusiastic friends, he again embellished the deed by claiming that he had captured de Villiers with 400 others and that the surrender was the grand finale of the war. Even Warren was able to commend Hughes for his energy and "smartness." But the events of the entire campaign were hardly helpful to either man's career. Warren had not captured de Villiers and Hughes was the reason. Warren had courted disaster at Faber's Put and Hughes had censored him. Although the evidence remains sketchy, Roberts still considered Warren incompetent. But he allowed Warren to finish his job. By August the area was back to normal and Warren was sent home without much fuss. Hughes, however, was not so fortunate; he had been ordered out of South Africa a month earlier.[21]

The reasons for Sam Hughes' dismissal were the culmination of his fight with Hutton back in Canada and his controversial performance with Warren in South Africa. On top of this, his frequent letters home, which were published in various newspapers, were vain and boastful (many of them read like wild west novels).[22] In March 1900 Hughes lost further ground when the Liberals published in the *Sessional Papers* all of the insulting letters he had written to Hutton the previous year. While such public exposure by the Liberals succeeded in spoiling the Tories' parliamentary attacks on the government over the GOC's dismissal, from South Africa Hughes claimed that Hutton had withheld from the Militia Minister his equally insulting letters to Hughes. When he got no satisfaction from Borden, Hughes went public through the editorial pages of the *Globe*, giving his version of the correspondence. These sensational grievances included all his old military and constitutional charges against the former GOC, who by this time was commanding some Canadians in South Africa. The open letter added more insults and fired more hostile broadsides at the British for their military incompetence in the war.[23]

Until the Hughes letter appeared in the *Globe*, Lord Minto had remained silent on the Hughes-Hutton controversy. But these new charges were too serious a reflection on British arms and the war effort to be allowed to continue. Secretly, via the War Office, Minto cabled Roberts telling him to "take steps to check this as the effect of publication here is most detrimental to the position of any imperial officer in authority." Roberts wired Warren demanding that Hughes either give a satisfactory explanation or be deprived of his command and sent back to Canada "by [the] first ship." The Field Marshal's cable came at the right time for Warren, who by then knew of Hughes' excoriating memorandum on Faber's Put, and who was furious at Hughes for disobeying orders which had cost him the capture of de Villiers. Warren replied that since Hughes had also written some letters "of a very improper character" which appeared in Cape Town papers, he had already ordered Hughes out of his force and down to the Cape. After hearing a rather lame explanation from Hughes, who maintained that his friends had published his correspondence without his authorization, Roberts sent Hughes back to Canada. En route Hughes stopped in London where Curtis, Hichens, and others gave him a testimonial dinner. But when he went to the War Office to see why he was dismissed, he received no co-operation. No doubt this treatment only augmented his distrust of Britons and the regular soldiers.[24]

When Hughes returned to Canada late that summer, he never once publicly admitted that he had been dismissed from the war. Privately he badgered Borden about the circumstances of his service, and the tolerant Militia Minister stayed aloof from debate on Hughes' record or the public disclosure of it. Such was not the case with Minto, whose treatment of the MP—however understandable—was shoddy. Picqued by Hughes' criticism of the efficiency of British arms, the Earl tried to discredit him by leaking the damning details of the MP's firing and reminding the War Office that Hughes was a charlatan.[25] But it did not work.

The public did not pay much attention to the Minto-inspired rumours. Back in Lindsay, the townspeople treated Hughes as a returning hero. So did the Tories of his riding, who nominated him without opposition for the election expected later in the fall. Elsewhere some Liberals poked fun at his boastful letters, especially those describing what "me and my man Turpin" did to the Boers. But it was all vague, normal in political circles, and entertaining. Besides, much of what Hughes said about Hutton and British generalship was true, and he never let anyone forget it.[26]

Hughes' adventures in South Africa reaffirmed his belief in the need for colonial contributions in Empire wars. When the hostilities ended in 1902, it was clear that the colonial volunteer soldiers had done their job well, and frequently better than the British. Hughes took this as evidence of the inherent superiority of part-time soldiers over regulars and of the leadership potential of Canadians. The war also demonstrated that many Englishmen did not receive this message well. There was no doubt that Hughes considered his own case a microcosm of the national one: Canadians had to be recognized and treated as equals in a reborn Empire if the structure was to be saved.

Both during and after the war, Hughes remained the apostle of less military convention, bureaucracy, and ceremony, and of more individuality, field skills, and common sense. Early British disasters verified the validity of many of his observations. But in other ways Hughes missed the mark. The vast spaces of Africa's veld, the need for mobility, and the nature of the enemy made the Boer war ideally suited for the talents of colonial irregulars. But this did not mean that all wars would be like the conflict in South Africa, nor did it mean that irregulars would be as good or as useful in all wars. The best of these soldiers—the Boers themselves—had lost in the end; they had suffered badly because they could not, as could regular soldiers, resolve the need for combining routine, discipline, subordination, and cooperation with individual freedom. Like the Boers, Hughes naively assumed that roles of the citizen and the soldier were the same thing.

But Hughes did not come to any conclusions. He simply thought that the reaction of the British professional soldiers and others to his constant interchange of roles was either a dark conspiracy or mere obstructionism, which made it clear that he had to continue the practice. During the war, because he had been both the victim and the practitioner of personal and political influence peddling, Hughes concluded that such partisan involvement was the only way any war could be directed. In British constitutional practice, the soldier is subordinate to the politician. Hughes had charged Hutton with constitutional usurpation without himself realizing that by giving parity to the two roles of citizen and soldier, he was dangerously close to doing the same thing himself.

The South African experience had also exposed Hughes' startling capabilities as a field fighter and leader. Certainly he was a match for any Boer commander in similar circumstances; and the British had often praised enemy leaders of lesser ability than Hughes. But his military talents had limits. His skills were of a tactical type; they worked best in special cases demanding unorthodox methods, personal leadership, individual initiative, small commands, and limited goals. Milner, Amery, Curtis, and Hichens had seen and admired them, but no doubt knew their limitations.[27] Hughes probably did not. Above all Hughes did not have a personality that allowed him to walk easily along the narrow path of the citizen or the soldier, especially in the role of the government opposition critic.

Reference Notes to Chapter 6

1 *Official History of the War in South Africa, 1899-1902* (London: Hurst and Blackette Ltd., 1906-1910), vol. III, pp. 1-27, provides an overall view of the rebellion in North-West Cape Colony. Hereafter cited as *Official History*.
2 Milner *diaries*, Feb. 20, 1900; and Public Record Office, WO 105/20, Roberts *papers*, Milner to Roberts, Feb. 19, 1900; and ibid., Feb. 20, 1900.

REFERENCE NOTES TO CHAPTER 6 / 95

3 PAC, RG 7, G 21, vol. 142, file 265, Hughes to Connaught, Dec. 20, 1912, "Memorandum—Re Friction Between Colonel Hughes and General Hutton, Culminating in 1900."
4 *Official History*, vol. III, pp. 10-17.
5 Lionel Curtis, *With Milner in South Africa* (Oxford: Blackwell, 1951), pp. v-ix. This volume includes Curtis' war diary from January to June 1900, as well as other contemporary correspondence from South Africa.
6 Ibid., p. 17, Curtis to his mother, Mar. 13, 1900; and ibid., p. 38, unaddressed letter from Max Balfour, Apr. 14, 1900.
7 Milner *papers*, Milner to Hughes, Feb. 11, 1901; and Curtis, p. 27, Curtis to Mary, Apr. 20, 1900. For example, see *Watchman-Warder*, Feb. 15, 1900, p. 10; ibid., Mar. 29, 1900, p. 1; and ibid., Apr. 12, 1900, p. 1. Also see J. F. C. Fuller's *The Last of the Gentlemen's Wars* (London: Faber and Faber, 1937), and Curtis, pp. 10-11, 26-27, Curtis to his mother, Mar. 1, 1900, and Curtis to Mary, Apr. 20, 1900.
8 Curtis, pp. 17-40.
9 *Official History*, vol. III, pp. 15-16; and Curtis, p. 36, Hichens to Walton, Apr. 16, 1900.
10 Curtis, p. 36; and ibid., pp. 36-38.
11 Ibid., p. 27, Curtis to Mary, Apr. 20, 1900.
12 Buller and Warren's role in the Natal Campaign is told in Byron Farrell, *The Great Anglo-Boer War* (New York: Harper and Row, 1976), chapters 19-22; Rayne Kruger, *Goodbye Dolly Gray* (London: Pan Books, 1977), chapter 10; and Julian Symons, *Buller's Campaign* (London: Cresset, 1953), pp. 177-293; Milner *papers*, 175, Roberts to Milner, May 2, 1900; PRO, WO 105/34, Roberts to High Commissioner, May 1900; ibid., Roberts to Milner, Apr. 16, 1900; and ibid., 20, Milner to Roberts.
13 *Official History*, vol. III, p. 17.
14 Watkin W. Williams, *The Life of General Sir Charles Warren* (Oxford: Blackwell, 1941), p. 391. Williams' *Life* is based on his grandfather's (Warren's) diaries and correspondence from the war, of which he reproduces large passages. Also see South Africa, National Library (Cape Town), The *Cape Times*, May 23, 1900, p. 4, Warren to Milner, May 13, 1900. "Colonel Hughes is proving himself an excellent intelligence officer and leader of irregular mounted troops" was the General's assessment of Hughes.
15 The detailed account of Warren's campaign can be seen in L. S. Amery, ed., *The London Times History of the War in South Africa* (London: Sampson, Low Marston and Company, 1905), vol. 4, pp. 214-35, and in the *Official History*, vol. III, pp. 17-26. Also see PRO, WO 32/7994, Warren's "Despatch on the Attack at Faber's Put," Warren to Roberts, June 29, 1900, p. 5. Hereafter cited Warren, "Faber's Put."
16 Hughes' memorandum on the battle of Faber's Put, n.d., in Williams, p. 387; PAC, Laurier *papers*, Hughes to Laurier, Mar. 20, 1908, p. 137987; PRO, WO 105/31, no. 874, Roberts To WO, June 28, 1900; and Amery, *Times History*, vol. 4, pp. 214-35.
17 *Watchman-Warder*, Aug. 19, 1900, p. 6. Letter from Hughes, June 2, 1900; PAC, RG 7, G 21, vol. 142, file 265, Hughes to Connaught, Dec. 20, 1912, "Memorandum"; and Williams, p. 387.
18 PRO, WO 105/10 "Final Report on Sir Charles Warren's Military Operations As Military Governor, Cape Colony, North of the Orange River," Warren to Roberts, Aug. 2, 1900; this contains accounts of Hughes' activities (hereafter cited Warren, *Final Report*). Private letter, Hughes to Major Lennox, Feb. 27, 1901, in the files of Mrs. David Hill, Pembroke, Ontario. Hughes claimed he "challenged" the Boers to surrender.
19 Personal letter, Hughes to Warren, n.d., in Williams, p. 392; ibid., pp. 391-92; and National Army Museum, *papers* of Field Marshal Lord Roberts, 7101-23-110, vol. 3. Roberts to SS for War, June 26, 1900. Hereafter cited NAM, Roberts *papers*.
20 PRO, WO, 105, 10, Warren *Final Report*, Annex A, *Surrender of de Villiers*, Warren to Milner, June 29, 1900; ibid.
21 *Watchman-Warder*, Aug. 2, 1900, p. 6. PRO, WO/105, Hughes to Jack Hughes, June 20, 1900; ibid., Warren to Hughes, June 20, 1900; NAM, Roberts *papers*, 7101-23-110, vol. 3, Roberts to SS for War, June 26, 1900; and Williams, pp. 391-92, Hughes to Warren, n.d.

22 PAC, Arthur Meighen *papers*, MG 26, 1, series 5, vol. 173, C3565, p. 108179, Meighen to R. L. Williams, Apr. 5, 1933; *Globe*, Apr. 20, 1900, p. 2, Hughes to Williamson, Mar. 14, 1900; ibid., June 9, 1900, p. 1, Hughes to Sylvester, Feb. 26, 1900; ibid., Aug. 2, 1900, p. 1, unaddressed letter of June 2, 1900. Also see Curtis, pp. 30-36, unaddressed letter from Mr. Balfour, Apr. 14, 1900, and Hichens to Mr. Walton, Apr. 16, 1900.
23 SP, 1900, no. 77; *Hansard*, 1900, pp. 594-606; *Canadian Military Gazette*, Mar. 6, 1900, p. 9, and ibid., p. 3, Apr. 3, 1900; Toronto *Evening Telegram*, Mar. 26, 1900, p. 8; and *Globe*, Mar. 23, 1900, p. 4; ibid., June 8, 1900, p. 5, Hughes to editor; and ibid., June 9, 1900, p. 18, Hughes to F. W. Borden, Mar. 31, 1900.
24 PAC, RG 7, G 21, no. 265, WO to Roberts, June 19, 1900, confidential; NAM, Roberts *papers*, 7101-23-111-3, no. 607, Roberts to Warren, June 20, 1900; PRO, WO/31, no. 874, Roberts to SS for War, June 28, 1900; NAM, Roberts *papers*, 1101-23-111-3, no. 759, Cowan to Warren, June 25, 1900; ibid., no. 780, A, Mil. Sec. Pretoria to Chowder, June 27, 1900. Also see the *Cape Times*, June 13, 1900, p. 5. The letter was signed "Special Correspondent," however, it was vintage Hughes; *Watchman-Warder*, Aug. 2, 1900, p. 6; Hughes to Jack Hughes, June 20, 1900; and ibid., Oct. 25, 1900, p. 7.
25 *Hansard*, 1900, pp. 10450-51; PANS, F. W. Borden *papers*, OLB, no. 18, pp. 970-72, F. W. Borden to Sam Hughes, June 6, 1901; PAC, Minto *papers*, vol. 21, pp. 159-66, Kitson to Minto, Sept. 15, 1900, and Sept. 30, 1900; and Miller, *The Education of a Viceroy*, pp. 74-75.
26 S. H. S. Hughes, *CHAR* (1949-1950), p. 35; and PAC, Minto *papers*, vol. 21, p. 163, Kitson to Minto, Sept. 15, 1900; *Watchman-Warder*, Oct. 4, 1900, p. 5; ibid., Oct. 18, 1900, p. 1, and Nov. 7, 1900, p. 1. Also see Capon, *His Faults Lie Gently*, p. 38; *Canadian Military Gazette*, Apr. 3, 1900, p. 7; and *Hansard*, Feb. 25, 1900, p. 378.
27 *CAR*, 1901, p. 303. Also see *Hansard*, Feb. 25, 1901, pp. 417-19; and Milner *papers*, 178, Milner to Hughes, Feb. 11, 1901.

CHAPTER 7

A Loyal Veteran, 1900-1911

Sam Hughes returned to Lindsay in the summer of 1900. Official dismissal from the South African war might have spelled ruin for others; not so for Sam Hughes. The forty-seven-year-old veteran resumed his struggles to earn a living and the backing of local supporters for yet another general election. His self-advertised war exploits, local political "know-how," and new worldliness were irresistible. On polling day in November, he won a comfortable majority even though his party trailed the Laurier juggernaut by fifty-three seats in the Commons.[1]

Personal victory as a member of a losing team only made Sam Hughes more vocal. In public, as the war ground through its savage guerrilla stages in 1901, he kept up a constant stream of criticism of the British high command. "Cut the red tape," he often warned; learn how to ride, shoot, and survive on the veld were the tactical messages he preached. He paid scant attention to larger British errors in administration and supply, nor did he question Britain's motives in the war.[2] Though there is no doubt that he could tackle such larger issues, he lacked the ability to sustain an appreciation of the necessary details to give such schemes substance and momentum.

Even after Hughes had been re-elected, he was anxious to return to South Africa. In making an offer directly to Milner, he told the High Commissioner that he could show the British "wooden-heads" how quickly a brigade of good Canadian irregulars under his command could end the war. Milner endorsed Hughes' assessments of British militia management, for both men admired one another's resolve, directness, and inventiveness. Milner, however, also knew that no British general would accept the maverick Canadian, so he neatly put Hughes off. So too did Fred Borden in early 1902 when Hughes

---

Reference notes for Chapter 7 are found on pp. 111-13.

offered his services once more, again in unacceptably critical terms. He argued that Canadians should be given more recognition and should only fight under "competent British Generals." But it mattered little; the war ended two months later.[3]

Part of Hughes' judgment about the British reflected their judgment of him while in South Africa. He was always convinced that Hutton had placed malicious and false information in War Office files and these were the real basis of his being sent home. More galling was the War Office's refusal to admit this and its denial that it held any reports at all. The War Office also refused to award him a war gratuity or to recognize in any official way what Hughes figured was the worth of his war service. Once home he kept up a barrage of memos to the War Office asking for recognition, which by 1903 included at least one Victoria Cross. Nearly all of these windy missives were signed "Lt. Col. Sam Hughes, MP commanding 45th Victoria Regiment" and were sent directly to London. It was a repetition of the same mistake he had made with Hutton. This time it was Minto who wanted to court-martial the Lieutenant-Colonel for ignoring the chain of command. When advised that Hughes was bound to plead that his rights as a citizen would be violated, Minto backed-off but threatened to leak to the press all the messy details of Hughes' South African dismissal.[4]

Evidently the War Office did keep at least one secret dossier on Sam Hughes. Sometime in 1903 the content of the "Colonel Sam Hughes" dossier was important enough "to be taken home by F[ield] M[arshal] Lord Robert's office." (What was in it is now lost.) The British reaction to the Colonel's harangues was a course of polite denial, then stoney silence. Privately some of them decided that Hughes was, in Sir John Anderson's words, "a little bit mad." Nevertheless they seemed to appreciate more than Minto did that Hughes was important enough not to be completely alienated, especially if they needed future political support in the Canadian Parliament. At first Hughes fumed at their inaction. His treatment, he snorted to the War Secretary, has "sown the seeds of more Lexingtons, Saratogas and Yorktowns. Heaven forbid that Canada should ever find it necessary to 'trim' her kinsmen of the British Isles." In time, however, his attention was side-tracked by more immediate and important questions of reform in the Canadian militia.[5]

Neither war's end nor continuing grievances dampened Sam Hughes' enthusiasm for military reform at home. He was in a good political spot to do something about it. Before the war Charles Tupper had made him the party's militia critic; now back in Parliament, his talent for wading through complicated military matters was as impressive as ever. Two issues particularly typify Hughes' domestic defence concerns. He pushed hard to upgrade the quality of the British GOC sent to Canada. As he told the House, these men should not "be sent here to be got rid of in England... or make use of the position [as GOC] as a stepping stone." Pay them a decent wage was the answer. Interestingly, and likely because he recognized the patronage potential of the position, Hughes did not lobby hard for a Canadian soldier in the office of GOC, although he did not oppose one either.[6]

The second issue, running consistently through his many reform demands, was his preference for the volunteer militiaman over the regular soldier, whether Canadian or British. The militiamen, he often asserted, "given equal opportunity with the regular, have trimmed the regular to the finish on every occasion." Regulars, even at their arrogant best, were in a "well-grounded, properly-grounded" plot to "place themselves superior to the active militia." To kill this conspiracy, Hughes demanded that the Liberal government spend much larger amounts on the militia, especially on the rural corps, that marksmanship be taught, and that more armouries be built throughout the countryside. It was the only way the non-permanent force would be made efficient, he insisted. The Boer war had proved to Hughes that long conflict and standing armies had given way to mobile, well-trained, and outfitted citizen-soldiers who could shoot straight and withstand field hardship. While full of specific and frequently correct recommendations about Canada's fighting men, about field units, leadership, tactics, and basic equipment, his arguments never dealt with the larger issues such as senior staff training, logistics, military doctrine, or strategy.[7]

Hughes' constant scrutiny of militia matters was not lost on Fred Borden. The Militia Minister had his own reform streak and, unlike Hughes, the political power to give it form and substance. By mid-1902 Borden was anxious to take advantage of a new mood both in England and in Canada to improve things. By 1903 unpleasant memories of Hutton's blatant political meddling had further increased Canadian awareness of military matters and declining British enthusiasm to defend Canada had caused Borden to begin a major overhaul of his militia structure. By mid-1904 the effort had culminated in a new militia bill, which proposed a far larger, more professional, and more efficient organization firmly under the civilian minister's control.[8] Since the active militia traditionally had a strong Conservative Party bias, Borden needed supporters from both sides of the House. It was this circumstance that made Sam Hughes so important to Borden.

Lord Dundonald thought Hughes important as well. A charming and unorthodox Boer war hero and innovator, in 1902 Dundonald was the newly appointed British GOC to Canada. His views differed from Borden's in as much as he wanted to retain War Office influence in Dominion military affairs, especially through his office. Furthermore, he had his own version of Canada's main enemy, namely, the Americans. He also wanted to build a huge citizen-soldier militia structure as the main line of Canadian defence.[9] None of these ideas impressed Borden, but they did impress Sam Hughes. In spite of his nationalist streak, Hughes' imperial fervour and fear of politicizing the Ottawa headquarters made him want to preserve the office of British GOC. During 1903 and half of 1904, both Borden and Lord Dundonald curried Hughes' favour.

As Borden prepared his militia legislation in 1903, Hughes was conveniently kept from taking mandatory retirement as the commanding officer of the 45th Battalion. In September he was made a brevet-colonel; in November Borden created the unpaid headquarters post of railway intelligence officer for Hughes and appointed him to the board of visitors at the Royal Military College in Kingston. On the British side, the Colonial Office's opinion was that "Hughes has considerable influence in Canada," and with Minto's reluctant support, Hughes was verbally informed that any adverse War Office records detailing his dismissal in South Africa were "withdrawn or have vanished."[10] All of this attention was intended to prime Hughes to support Borden's new legislation. In early 1904 Borden introduced the new bill, then suddenly excised the section that kept the British GOC and replaced it by a general staff system and a militia council with himself firmly at the head. Hughes reacted loudly, but only seriously objected to Borden's abolishing of the post of British GOC and his increases of the size of the Permanent Force. Most of the other reforms Hughes favoured.[11] And his opposition had more to do with his new alliance with Dundonald than anything else.

Dundonald had quarrelled with Borden over policy throughout the previous year; he had far more enthusiasm for retaining some British influence in the Dominion than did his superiors at home, and in this he had the Governor-General's sympathy. All during 1903 Dundonald tested Borden by leaking a confidential portion of his annual report, by making aggressive public utterances about the Alaska Panhandle dispute then in full storm, and in generally favouring Conservative politicians, including Hughes. The two men, perhaps because similar personalities made them blind to their mutual flaws,[12] admired each other's qualities and seemed to sit on the same side of the imperial fence. Yet there was little doubt that the GOC was out to attract Hughes to his side. It was an easy seduction. For Hughes, then in the political wilderness for eight long years, there could be personal and political gains, along with some military reform.

In late 1903 Dundonald helped Hughes with his war record grievances and, as the delighted General confided to Field Marshal Lord Roberts, "he at once began to help me in Parliament."[13] Hughes did reciprocate: he immediately attacked the government for suppressing the GOC's militia ideas. Then with the General's active encouragement, Hughes also concocted a plan for the "Defense of Eastern Canada." Significantly, it not only epitomized Dundonald's pet militia scheme based on a large citizen army, but also identified the General's favourite enemy, the United States. Neither of these aspects was supported by the Canadian government, then in delicate negotiations with the Americans over Alaskan territory. But a pre-emptive strike on the United States by Canadian citizen-soldiers was something Hughes had favoured for years.[14] His 1904 stratagem—if one could label it that— called for 25,000 stalwart Canadians to land at Sacketts Harbor and then to march on Portland, Maine, there to link up with the Royal Navy; meanwhile, Canadian torpedo and gun boats were to ensure Great Lakes control by shooting up the American shore ports.[15] As usual with large schemes details got in Hughes' way, so he ignored them.

Again with Dundonald's urging, Hughes sent the entire ill-considered concoction to Amery at the *Times*, hoping for the usual "leak" in Britain to embarrass the Canadian government into accepting Dundonald's militia ideas. However, Amery passed it to the new British Chief of the Imperial General Staff, Lieutenant-General Neville Lyttleton, who flatly and properly panned it as impractical.[16] Shifting strategic priorities, however, had already doomed Hughes' and Dundonald's hopes. Even if the plan had made sense, English authorities no longer wanted to, and no longer could, defend Canada. If Canada's acceptance of its defence responsibilities meant less direct British control, British support of F. W. Borden's new militia bill, rather than of Dundonald's or Hughes' alternative version, was the only realistic course for imperial administrators in the spring of 1904.

The Canadian government challenged neither the GOC nor Hughes directly over his defence scheme. Yet an indirect confrontation came that spring. The Fisheries Minister, Sydney Fisher, temporarily acting for the absent Fred Borden in the Militia Department, struck the name of a political opponent from Dundonald's slate of officers for a new unit, the 13th Scottish Dragoons, then being organized in Fisher's riding. This was hardly an unusual occurrence by contemporary militia standards. But when Fisher lied about his interference, Dundonald saw the affair as a golden opportunity to condemn Liberal defence policy generally.

As for Hughes, he had already been co-opted by the Dundonald camp for personal and political reasons. There might be some Tory party gain in the scandal if the rumours about a new federal election were true. In June Hughes eagerly sought, and the GOC more than willingly gave, all the documentary evidence necessary to assail the government over the Fisher affair. Blatant political interference eroding honest militia reform was Hughes' charge. In Parliament fellow Tories, including the new leader, Robert Laird Borden, were delighted as Hughes' well-documented case made the seemingly invincible government squirm. But not for long. To Laurier, Hughes' revelations were bad enough, but Dundonald's complicity was "unpardonable." He told Minto so, and then promptly fired the General for the far more serious sin of undermining Canadian political authority. And British officials quietly demurred.[17]

In spite of Hughes' past complaints about Herbert's and Hutton's "unconstitutional" acts, the logic of Laurier's action did not alter the opposition critic's enthusiasm for defending the cashiered Dundonald in and out of the House. As usual Hughes' stubborn defence progressed from a reasoned, but substantially incorrect, claim that the General had a right to expose Liberal meddling to personal attacks on Borden and especially Fisher. Wrapped comfortably in parliamentary immunity, Hughes labelled Fisher an "effeminate . . . sissy" who "doesn't know the butt of a gun from its muzzle," and who wanted to take Canada out of the Empire. Rather than becoming embroiled themselves in the mud-slinging, Laurier and Fred Borden chose the rapier-witted backbencher, Benjamin Russell, the MP for Hants, to demolish Hughes' shaky constitutional defence of Hutton and to ridicule his sacred cow—his Boer war record. In the end Laurier broke his House silence only to add the *coup de grace*; the Canadian government would not be dominated by one of its military servants.[18]

Outside the House, Hughes sputtered on for a few final hot weeks during the late summer, first to the public and then in desperate letters to various British notables, including Prime Minister A. J. Balfour. But there was no redress for Dundonald, for many Canadians knew that Laurier was correct, or more likely they simply did not care; and in Britain, where the "wrong" party was now in power, the British would, and could, do nothing. The War Secretary, Arnold-Forster, summed up the Dundonald affair for Minto in Canada and his colleagues in the Colonial Office: he pointed out that General Dundonald had lost when he put his defence "into the hands of a self-important windbag like Colonel Hughes of the opposition. It amounts to aiding and abetting a government servant in insubordination." Hughes was so angry that he informed Amery that the "British Canadians" were about ready to rebel against Britain for their meddling in "Canadian affairs." But it did not matter; even Amery did not reply.[19]

In the end the Dundonald episode did not seriously injure Hughes. To the public it was really a tempest of parliamentary opposition whose imperial shudders remained unseen. The affair may have even embellished Sam Hughes' public image; after all he had defended the imperial connection and had supported military reform; he had caused the Grits some political discomfort and stalwartly defended an Englishman who continued to have many Conservative friends in Canada. In the fall of 1904, the Dominion was plunged into another federal election campaign where partisan politics often dulled memory as much as they sharpened it.

Unlike the previous electoral contest, the one held in November was no easy walk for Sam Hughes. Two things were against him. First was Laurier's cunning decision to make a politically convenient redistribution of some federal ridings, including Hughes'. The new boundary would lump the two Conservative ridings of Victoria North and South into the much larger new one of Victoria-Haliburton. For Hughes this meant getting the nomination over the similarly deposed fellow Tory of the old southern area, Dr. Adam Vrooman, while avoiding a political split over the issue. The redistribution gerrymandered Hughes' great strength in the northern areas forcing him to run in Lindsay and the south where he was neither as well liked nor as well known. After bitter and fruitless complaints to Laurier, Hughes got down to organizing his succession well ahead of possible Tory competitors or the Liberals themselves. By January 1904 he had the nomination, even though there was a substantial party move to have Vrooman endorsed instead. Eight months later at election call in September, Hughes again had to ward off a small dissident Tory group who tried to draft Vrooman as an independent Tory. When the doctor refused Hughes was relieved, and he got on with what he did best: stumping through the huge new riding.[20]

Hughes' unrelenting campaign style kept the Grits in disarray. Only after Laurier's personal intervention could they field even a lack-lustre candidate. Still Hughes took no chances. His enumerators were out, his lists were carefully prepared, and he adopted a platform that not only took in the main tenets of the national Tory program but also included local issues. The tactics were sound and Hughes won his fourth consecutive victory, this time for Victoria-Haliburton, by over 300 votes.[21]

While Hughes was ecstatic about his own success in the face of adversity, he took little pleasure in the party's national fortunes. Laurier had soundly trounced the Conservatives once more. Their spirits could not have been lower. Given the contemporary circumstances of economic prosperity, it seemed that Laurier was to go on governing the Dominion forever. But this was not all attributable to Liberal popularity. Since the death of Macdonald in 1891, the Conservatives had been plagued by leadership problems, factionalism, and a lack of national representation. Being in the political wilderness without patronage to offer friends of the party since 1896 also took its toll. Two-thirds of the Tory candidates were new in every contest. The party power base was regionally lop-sided. In the 1904 vote, for instance, two-thirds of the new Tory MPs were, like Sam Hughes, from Ontario. The party had no structure, no agreed-upon policy, and had never had a national leadership convention. By 1904, while it was not obvious to many in the party, the quality of the MPs was mediocre; they were an independent lot with little parliamentary experience; their horizons seldom went beyond the constituency level; and they were hard to rule. These features gave successful veterans like Sam Hughes great potential influence on the leader, on other MPs, and on policy. And there can be little doubt that Hughes realized that even in the federal defeat there were opportunities for him.[22]

Sam Hughes had many things besides a safe seat to offer the national party. For years he had been a willing party worker, and he knew the ins and outs of parliamentary practice. There was also the question of support for the new national leader. Robert Borden had succeeded the aging Tupper soon after the last national defeat. At the time Hughes had enthusiastically approved, likely because the quiet Nova Scotian lawyer was not yet tainted by the frequent internal party feuds. More importantly for Hughes, Borden was Tupper's first choice and Hughes had been a long-time Tupper loyalist. Hughes' easy transfer of support suggests that he knew the national party would have to resolve its past ten years of leadership crises if it ever wanted to govern. As for the new chief, he too needed the experience and support of political survivors like Hughes. Over the next decade, these pulls made Sam Hughes a Borden loyalist. Encouraged by his leader, he became a useful senior member of the party, although not at all times would the relationship be free from doubt.

One of Borden's first encouragements for Sam Hughes was his appointment to the powerful Liberal-Conservative Association of Ontario, the senior party group effecting organization and policy. When the ninth Parliament opened in 1901, Borden asked Hughes to sit on several of the House's select standing committees, including four of the biggest: railways; public accounts; banking and commerce; and agriculture. Hughes also continued as the opposition militia spokesman.[23] For his part Hughes consistently supported Borden's controversial stand on railways which called for more governmental control, and he carried the attack for the party over the Dundonald affair in 1904. When the election was called that fall, Hughes stayed with Borden for two precious weeks on the Ontario hustings, introducing him to potential Tory voters and generally smoothing the unknown new leader's way in his most important province.[24] It was a risk Hughes was willing to take even though his own election was not assured. But the Lindsay MP's most unforgettable kindness followed Borden's personal humiliation at the polls.

When Hughes heard the news that the national leader had lost in his own riding, he immediately offered his own seat. It was "a kindness I will always value and appreciate," the despondent Borden wrote back a few days later in turning down his much-needed veteran; and a few months after that, when the resounding national defeat put Borden's leadership in jeopardy, Hughes again stood firm, publicly and emphatically reminding Toronto newspaper reporters that there was only one man who could lead the Conservative Party "and that was R. L. Borden."[25] No doubt such steadfast help buoyed Borden's and others' flagging spirits. By April 1905 the rebuilding process was beginning. Borden created a provisional central committee to give the party a new structure and Hughes and the rest of the caucus supported the idea. Yet significantly Hughes was not among the twenty-five MPs chosen from across the country for the new body, even though only two of Ontario's seven representatives had been in power as long. Whether Hughes realized it then, it was the beginning of his leader's attempt to offset the debilitating effects of the often parochial, mediocre talents of many of his MPs. Nor did the new leader want to be victimized by these men as had Abbott, Bowell, and to some degree Tupper. Equally important were his subtle attempts to infuse the national structure with gifted newcomers of higher principles and larger horizons than those traditionally connected to the partisanship and passion of local politics. Borden wanted men who could stand independently of the old party if necessary, and were in tune with the profound changes then affecting Canadian society. Men like H. B. Ames and G. H. Perley from Quebec and A. E. Kemp from Ontario were wealthy, had broad social and business connections, and often demonstrated reformist tendencies. In time these "new men" came ahead of the senior veterans; they formed a close-knit and small inner advisory body for Borden on major matters. They would also cause some resentment for regulars like Hughes who had spent years in the party's service without many rewards.[26] Nevertheless in April 1905 such a course was not likely obvious to the hopeful and willing MP for Victoria-Haliburton.

For the next several years, Sam Hughes worked hard on party and parliamentary business. Borden appreciated that Hughes' long time in the House rendered him more useful and dependable than many of his newer and far less experienced MPs.[27] He had an active, fertile, and inquiring mind, and he gave the appearance of following debate closely. While he was neither an eloquent nor incisive orator, Hughes was never afraid to speak his mind. And he could defend a position ably and well. Outside of strict political affiliations, he had many acquaintances in militia, business, and fraternal circles. When these were coupled with a reasonably urbane knowledge, Hughes could be good for the party. Moreover, he was often witty, full of puckish charm, and never dull like some of his confrères—a trait that, according to Borden's biographer, ensured the Conservative leader's continued sympathy for Sam Hughes.[28] Finally, Hughes followed Borden's stand on most issues before the House, without either giving up his independence or over-exerting it.

One of Sam Hughes' most important roles was as a political critic. In the give and take of daily Commons tactics, Borden exploited Hughes' talent for hard, behind-the-scenes investigative work. In the House and in various committees, Borden knew that Hughes could be both thorough and brutally blunt with his questioning; and he brought to bear an unrivalled detailed knowledge of many government departments. These qualities were especially useful after January 1906 when the Conservative caucus decided to concentrate on discrediting the Laurier administration in a campaign labelled "Purity in Politics"; they wanted the electorate to know that Tories, even in defeat, were active and if given the chance could govern better than dishonest and inefficient Liberals. Hughes revelled in this sort of attack, and with his quiet leader's blessing, he was often in the middle of it. Over the next several years, scandals in the Departments of the Interior, of Marine and Fisheries, of Railways, of Customs, and of Militia were exposed. Coming from the traditional scrapping school of Ontario constituent politics, Hughes believed that all political opponents by definition were nothing more than a "boodle gang." His leader's purity campaign was particularly enjoyable as he tried to root out the truth about such things as the Liberals' questionable immigration procedures or the activities of the North Atlantic Trading Company, an organization with which the Department of the Interior had a secret and questionable association.[29]

During this time Sam Hughes was no less vigilant in his scrutiny of the government's proposed legislation. The first contentious piece before the tenth Parliament was the Autonomy Bill calling for the formation of the new provinces of Alberta and Saskatchewan. In it were the bitterly contested separate school proposals. In the end Laurier's huge majority ensured passage. Before it did, however, the issue not only caused a Liberal cabinet crisis but also threw the Tories into a dilemma. Once again French-Canadian Conservatives lobbying for central government protection of provincial separate schools were pitted against their English-speaking colleagues, mostly from Ontario, who wanted the new provincial administrations to control their own education. Faced with this solid block, Borden allowed everyone to vote on conscience to avoid a split in the party; he then sided with the Ontario wing. Hughes took his stand with his fellow Ontarians. For years he had resented increasing federal incursions into provincial matters; and he stood on the constitutional interpretation which suggested that all matters of education belonged to the provinces. Yet with his strong Orange leanings, he also knew that most of the western minorities were Roman Catholic and some were French-Canadian. If not protected, they would likely be absorbed into the larger English community. Such a stand was entirely consistent with Hughes' single cultural image of Canadian development outside Quebec. It may have been this narrower view which Borden found repugnant enough to try to change with his "new men" and which also made the leader decide not to give Hughes a position on the new central party organization. Still, to the disgust of his French-Canadians, Borden had backed his Ontario caucus, and he had also used Hughes prominently in the House debate and out in several Ontario ridings broadcasting the party case against the issue.[30]

Much of the remaining legislation in the next three years caused little controversy. Again Hughes' efforts were solid and dependable and within the party line. The legislation was diverse and ranged from such issues as pay increases for MPs and a permanent stipend for the leader of the opposition to federal government encouragement of more trade schools across the country. In the Lord's Day bill in 1906, Hughes could see no use for the vague legislation unless it had some practical and moral use for workers. The next year over the tariff issue, he took the same nationalist stand which he had in the 1890s: protection of Canadian trade. On one hand he opposed any trade preference for the United States, and on the other he consistently advocated avoiding the formation of an imperial economic *zollverein* until the English gave the Dominion equal representation in their councils. When the Industrial Disputes bill came up shortly thereafter, he was more concerned that the militia, especially the Permanent Force, should not be used to break strikes, lest both soldiers' integrity and citizens' rights be violated.[31]

Many of Hughes' parliamentary concerns coincided with Borden's and also clearly underscored Hughes' broader national vision. Among other things Hughes foresaw the emergence of a mature agricultural and industrial nation with modern transport systems. He felt the government should do all it could to encourage such development, if not by persuasion, then by regulation. Private enterprise and individual endeavour, however, still remained for Sam Hughes the vital key to national development. This was the way he continued to look at railway legislation. After he came home from South Africa, Hughes had privately accepted off-session summer employment to augment his meagre Commons income from his friend, William Mackenzie of the Canadian Northern Railway (CNR). Hughes' function was to help choose the route for the new CNR transcontinental. In 1902, and again in 1905, he travelled in Saskatchewan and Alberta for this purpose. On the second trip Amery accompanied him, and the journalist's diaries reveal an interesting comment on Hughes' delight in the prospect of national growth:

Hughes had been engaged since the South African War in selecting for Messrs. Mackenzie and Mann an alternative line across the Prairie Provinces to compete with the Canadian Pacific. He had selected a line well to the North, beyond the border of possible wheat cultivation, so his critics said. But he was convinced with the developing of quicker ripening wheats, the northern country with its higher average rainfall would prove to be more paying in the long run.... At nights we camped under the buggy protected by our canvas fly. One evening Sam told me with great solemnity that we would reach the "city" of Vermilion ... by nightfall. Next morning he called me out from under the buggy and with a magnificient sweep of his arm said "Amery my boy, isn't this the finest city in the whole prairie." I looked across the featureless plain ... inhabited [only] by a few gophers ... and burst into laughter. Sam had his revenge, however, and two months later sent me a photograph of the main street of Vermilion, a double row of matchwood houses, including bank and hotel, put up within a day or two by the arrival of the railhead.[32]

In part Hughes was paid in land, conveniently located along the rail route of his choice. Over the years he sold it to men like Amery and Lionel Curtis. But all existing evidence indicates his "deals" provided him with little more than a moderate return for some years.[33] In spite of these land schemes and his employment by the CNR, he was never a paid lobbyist for Mackenzie and Mann, as some charged. His real concern over railways was to ensure that all Canadian routes and businesses would get lower freight rates and more settlers, all of which would keep the west out of American hands. Such was evident in Hughes' refusal in 1909 to vote for Liberal legislation granting the financially troubled Grand Trunk Pacific a $10 million loan without ensuring some regulation in return, and in this he differed from other party members who voted with the government against state interference in private enterprise.[34]

There were other manifestations of Hughes' particular Canadian vision in his parliamentary performance. In 1906 he succeeded with two Commons motions accepting the principle that any retired British soldier or Empire Boer war veteran be given preference in western land grants. Like-minded imperialists in Canada and England, such as Strathcona, G. T. Denison, and Leo Amery, were enthused about the idea and gave it much play. But in the long haul, British immigrants, with whom such men had hoped to redress the imperial cultural and defence imbalance of Clifford Sifton's schemes, were not as convinced as were the European peasants in "sheepskin coats" that Canada had the "last best west."[35] Ideas that Hughes promoted in the Commons— whether these or the construction of the Trent Canal or the assimilation of reservation Indians into the rest of society—were vehicles

Hughes used to embellish his reputation and to satisfy constituent, party, and personal views on national development.[36]

The same was true of Hughes' major Commons passion—the militia. Regardless of what his contemporaries thought about his pushy personality, few could not be impressed by his command of military details. He read widely, including various military historians such as G. F. R. Henderson, Fortescue, and Napier. He was also interested in the current ideas expressed in the journals of the several military societies, including the Royal United Service Institute or the *Canadian Militia Gazette*.[37] While he often revealed only what matched his particular passions, he brough informed opinion to public debate. Daily question periods were often full of his probing enquiries about everything from Canadian adoption of the latest military spitzer-type bullet, so successfully used in Germany and the United States, to encouraging development of a Canadian militia headquarters mapping and survey directorate so vital to national and imperial defence development.[38] Like the quieter and less nervous progressive educational philosophy of his brother James, Sam Hughes thought that a citizen's social and military responsibilities began with education: military training belonged in the schools, in a cadet corps that created "better men in every respect," as he told the Commons in 1906.[39]

Hughes' push for military reform had two venues: the Non-Permanent Active Militia (NPAM) and the area of imperial defence. In 1905, when the British Halifax garrison finally withdrew, Hughes resisted Sir Fred Borden's increases in the Permanent Force, arguing instead that money should be spent on training the country's youth, and part-time soldiers. The Permanent Corps should be trimmed to "the lowest possible point."[40] Such statements caused regular headquarters soldiers, like Generals William Otter and P. N. Lake, to react, as Sam Steele wrote to his patron Lord Strathcona, as "red rags to [a] bull."[41] Of course they could do nothing to silence or divert the politician, and they did not even try. In a country that paid scant attention to anything military, they may have consoled themselves with the knowledge that Sam Hughes was at least promoting the force, even if by an outdated military idea. Moreover, he was in a far better position than they were to exert direct influence on critical areas such as military spending. As with all political colonels before Sam Hughes, most dedicated soldiers realized they needed someone in political circles who cared about the service.[42]

One thing both Sam Hughes and the regulars could agree on was the need for more Anglo-Canadian military co-operation. For Hughes, closer links promised to encourage military growth; potentially they could forge the channels for more Canadian representation on imperial councils, even if it involved further contributions to the Empire's defence. More importantly, such mutual support implied endorsement of the country's citizen force. In the Commons Hughes wholeheartedly favoured the colonial conferences in 1907 and 1909 which laid the basis of such co-operation. The following year, the first practical manifestation of this new path—the visit to Canada of the Imperial Inspector-General, Sir John French—gave Hughes even more pleasure. Amery had advised French to listen to what Hughes had to say on the subject of a proper Canadian defence policy. No doubt when French inspected the annual camp at Kingston, Ontario, where Hughes commanded three militia brigades, the Lindsay Colonel reiterated what he had been telling Parliament for years. In 1911 when the Imperial Inspector's recommendations were made public, Hughes supported most of them, largely because they clearly endorsed the volunteer militia and suggested many manpower, material, and training reforms.[43]

One of French's recommendations concerned musketry, another subject dear to Hughes' heart. Throughout his adult life Sam Hughes had been a practical and competitive rifle shot, a sport he considered a necessary step in the training of citizen-soldiers. He had climbed steadily through the various government-endorsed provincial and federal shooting organizations, where he fraternized with such important people as millionaire Toronto stock-broker and Tory MP E. B. Osler, and Liberal J. M. Gibson, the Lieutenant-Governor of Ontario. By 1907 Hughes was president of the Dominion Rifle Association. On the practical political side, such participation was good for his career: it brought him into contact with important men and shooters across the country. With some of them being militiamen, some of them soldiers, and all of them voters, they knew that, with the enthusiastic support Hughes gave the sport in and out of the House, their interests were safe.[44]

In all, the decade after his return from South Africa had been good for Hughes. While still in the political wilderness outside government, in Conservative Party politics he had enjoyed obvious success as a hardworking senior member loyal to Robert Borden who in turn liked Hughes, even though he had not taken him into the inner circle of new men. In the militia Hughes had attained a similar level; he was the best-known militia politician in the country and he had a small but influential group of acquaintances in imperial circles; he stood fourth on the list of colonels and was one of the top ten senior officers in the land.[45] Even though he shared their background and most of their ideas, Hughes had a wider and more progressive political philosophy than many of his unsophisticated Ontario party colleagues. He was concerned about all of Canada and he constantly pushed for a development policy that matched his Anglo-Saxon view. But to depict Sam

Hughes' record in terms of general success is to tell only part of the story; in these same years there were moments of disharmony that affected his later career.

Reference Notes to Chapter 7

1 Beck, *Pendulum of Power*, pp. 87-96; and *Watchman-Warder*, Oct. 18, 1900, p. 1, and Nov. 7, 1900, p. 1.
2 *Hansard*, 1902, pp. 1134-38; ibid., 1903, pp. 2403-10; *CAR*, 1901, p. 307; Amery *papers*, "Letters on *Times* History," Hughes to Amery, Dec. 10, 1900; and L. S. Amery, *My Political Life*, vol. 1, *England Before the Storm, 1896-1914* (London: Hutchinson, 1953), chapters 5 to 8.
3 Milner *papers*, C687, Hughes to Milner, Nov. 30, 1900; ibid., 178, Milner to Hughes, Feb. 11, 1901; ibid., 178, Milner to Hughes, Feb. 11, 1901; and PANS, F. W. Borden, *papers*, OLB, no. 21, Borden to Hughes, Mar. 14, 1902.
4 PRO, CO, 42(879), 21227, Hughes to Chamberlain, July 16, 1901; ibid., 42(895), 16252, John Anderson, Hughes minute, May 7, 1903, in Miller files; PANS, F. W. Borden, *papers*, OLB, no. 18, Borden to Hughes, June 6, 1901; and ibid., OLB, vol. 33, p. 66, Borden to Hughes, Mar. 24, 1902; Amery *papers*, 1901-1903, Hughes to Amery, Jan. 30, 1904; PAC, RG7, G21, no. 265, Hughes to Minto, Jan. 14, 1902, and Jan. 16, 1902; ibid., F. S. Maude to Hughes, Feb. 12, 1902, and Mar. 10, 1902; and ibid., Hughes to Maude, Mar. 10, 1902, and Mar. 18, 1902; and PAC, Minto *papers*, vol. 26, p. 62, O'Grady Haly to Minto, Jan. 21, 1902.
5 Douglas Library, Queen's University (QU), Lord Dundonald *papers*, A, 131, microfilm, Dundonald to Roberts, Apr. 27, 1903; ibid., Hughes to Secretary of State for War, Mar. 30, 1903; and CO, 42(895) 16252, John Anderson, Hughes minute, May 7, 1903, in Miller files.
6 *CAR*, 1901, p. 302.
7 *Hansard*, 1902, pp. 861-65, 1134-38, 1141-42; ibid., 1903, p. 13054; and Stacey, *Canada in the Age of Conflict*, vol. 1, p. 69.
8 Preston, *Canada and Imperial Defence*, pp. 317, 321; Morton, *Ministers and Generals*, pp. 182-87; and Miller, *The Education of a Viceroy*, pp. 131-55.
9 QU, Lord Dundonald *papers*, A, 131, Borden to Dundonald, Jan. 31, 1903, and Feb. 21, 1903; and Lord Dundonald, *My Army Life* (London: Arnold, 1931), p. 191.
10 PAC, Minto *papers*, vol. 12, p. 161, Ommaney to Minto, June 17, 1903, private; ibid., vol. 8, p. 151, Borden to Minto, Sept. 29, 1903, private; and ibid., WO to CO, Dec. 23, 1903; *Militia List*, 1904, p. 3; *CAR*, 1904, p. 481; and PAC, RG7, G21, no. 265, Hughes to Maude, Sept. 28, 1903.
11 *Hansard*, 1903, p. 3779; ibid., 1904, pp. 208-12, 274, 289, 5680-81, 6370-74, 6518, 6530, 8190, 8202; *CAR*, 1904, p. 470-72; *Canadian Military Gazette*, Mar. 22, 1904; and *Lindsay Post*, Apr. 1, 1904, p. 5.
12 QU, Dundonald *papers*, A, 131. Dundonald to Lord Roberts, April 27, 1903.
13 Ibid., A, 131, Dundonald to Roberts, Apr. 27, 1903; Hughes to Secretary for War, Mar. 30, 1903.
14 *CAR*, 1904, pp. 410, 438; *Warder* editorials, July 16, 1886, p. 4, July 29, 1887, p. 4, Mar. 29, 1888, p. 4, Apr. 13, pp. 4, 9 and Nov. 16, 1888, p. 4.
15 Amery *papers*, Canadian Militia Bill file, Hughes to Amery, private and confidential, "Memo re Defence of Eastern Ontario and Quebec Border," May 18, 1904.
16 Ibid., Part II of Dundonald's report of 1902, n.d., and R. A. Preston, *The Defence of the Undefended Border* (Montreal: McGill-Queen's University Press, 1977), p. 159.
17 Dundonald, p. 263, Hughes to Dundonald, June 9, 1904; and PRO, CO, 537, 491, Minto to CO, June 10, 1904; ibid., Minto to Lyttleton, June 13, 1904, ibid., Laurier to Minto, June 11, 1904, and QU, Dundonald, *papers*, A, 131, Dundonald to Hughes, June 10, 1904; ibid., Dundonald to Borden, June 10, 1904; PANS, Borden, *papers*, OLB, Borden to Dundonald, June 15, 1904; and PAC, Minto *papers*, vol. 7, p. 146, Laurier to Minto, June 20, 1904.

18 *Hansard*, 1904, pp. 5495-5518, 5531-21, 5545 and 5575-76; and Amery, *papers*, CMB File, Hughes to Amery, July 21, 1904.
19 PRO, CO, 537(491), Arnold-Forster to Cox, June 24, 1904; ibid., 492, Ommaney's minute, June 20, 1904; Amery *papers*, Canadian Militia Bill file, Dundonald to Amery, July 5, 1904; ibid., Hughes to Amery, July 30, 1904; and ibid., Hughes to Chamberlain, July 5, 1904.
20 PAC, Laurier *papers*, vol. 281, Hughes to Laurier, Sept. 12, 1903, pp. 76971-72; Amery *papers*, private letters, 1901-1903, Hughes to Amery, Jan. 30, 1904; *Watchman-Warder*, Oct. 6, 1904, p. 8; and ibid., Sept. 29, 1904, p. 8.
21 *Watchman-Warder*, Oct. 13, 1904, p. 1, Oct. 20, 1904, p. 7, and Nov. 10, 1904, p. 1.
22 John English, *The Decline of Politics, The Conservatives and the Party System* (Toronto: University of Toronto Press, 1977), chapters 1, 2.
23 *CAR*, 1901, p. 436; PAO, James Pliny Whitney *papers*, Mu 3115, R. L. Borden to Whitney, May 20, 1901; and Commons *Journals*, 1901, pp. 31-32.
24 *Watchman-Warder*, Nov. 6, 1900, p. 4; and *CAR*, 1904, pp. 149-150.
25 PAC, Borden *papers*, MG26, memoir notes, vol. XI, p. 5951, Borden to Hughes, Dec. 9, 1904; and *CAR*, 1905, p. 33.
26 Brown, *Borden*, vol. 1, pp. 106-11; and English, chapter 2.
27 Borden, *Memoirs*, vol. 1, p. 75.
28 Brown, *Borden*, vol. 2, p. 17.
29 Ibid., pp. 120-22; Beck, pp. 107-12; *Hansard*, 1906, p. 6918; and Commons *Journals*, 1906, appendix 2.
30 *Hansard*, 1905, pp. 1861-62, 3769-3803, 8831-34; *CAR*, 1905, p. 101; Brown, *Borden*, vol. 1, pp. 97-102; and Commons *Journals*, 1905, pp. 298-99, 476.
31 *Hansard*, 1900, pp. 3500, 5626-35; ibid., 1902, pp. 2946, 3856; ibid., 1904, pp. 210, 277-78; ibid., 1905, pp. 5006-17, 9009, 9190; ibid., 1906-1907, pp. 503, 5619-24, 5642; Amery *papers*, Canadian Militia Bill file, Hughes to Amery, Nov. 27, 1904; Milner *papers*, box 35, Hughes to Milner, Nov. 4, 1908; Commons *Journals*, 1905, pp. 562-66; ibid., 1906-1907, pp. 325-326; and Brown, *Borden*, vol. 1, p. 120.
32 Amery, *My Political Life*, pp. 282-83.
33 Amery *papers*, personal, 1901-1903, Hughes to Amery, Jan. 11, 1902; ibid., Amery to Hughes, May 11, 1910; ibid., private letters 1910, Amery to Hughes, May 17, 1910; Amery, *My Political Life*, vol. I, p. 345; Beaverbrook *papers*, Hughes to Aitken, Oct. 14, 1916, in Hyatt Files, UWO; and J. A. Eagle, "Sir Robert Borden and the Railway Problem in Canadian Politics, 1911-1920," dissertation (University of Toronto, 1972), pp. 6-22; and Regehr, *The Canadian Northern Railway, 1895-1918*—this material covers the background.
34 *Hansard*, 1900, pp. 3500, 4805, 5635, 5626; ibid., 1905, pp. 5006-17, 9543-46; ibid., 1906-1907, pp. 503, 742-43; and ibid., 1909-1910, pp. 130-33, 2718, 3494. Also *CAR*, 1904, pp. 89-90; *Watchman-Warder*, Oct. 20, 1904, p. 7; and Commons *Journals*, May 4, 1909, p. 357.
35 Commons *Journals*, 1906-1907, p. 62; *CAR*, 1902, p. 339; and Berger, *The Sense of Power*, especially chapter 5.
36 *Hansard*, 1906, pp. 5422-28; ibid., 1901, pp. 4402, 5626; ibid., 1903, pp. 8117-18; ibid., 1906-1907, p. 565; and ibid., 1909, pp. 3183-86.
37 *Warder*, July 31, 1885, p. 2; ibid., Aug. 28, 1885, p. 4; Amery *papers*, "Letters on *Times* History," Hughes to Amery, Dec. 10, 1900; *Hansard*, 1909, p. 6418; ibid., 1914, pp. 3418-19; Capon, *His Faults Lie Gently*, pp. 21, 47-48; Winter, pp. 110-17; and S. H. S. Hughes, *CHA*, 1949-1950, pp. 30-40.
38 *Hansard*, 1907-1908, pp. 12154; ibid., pp. 3776-12956; and ibid., 1906-1907, pp. 5724-35.
39 Ibid., 1906-1907, p. 2849; Sam Hughes, "Defense of the Empire," in *Empire Club Speeches*, 1904-1905 (Toronto: Briggs, 1906), pp. 174-84; Berger, *The Sense of Power*, pp. 254-58; and Desmond Morton, "The Cadet Movement in the Moment of Canadian Militarism, 1909-1914," in *Journal of Canadian Studies* 13, no. 2 (Summer 1978), pp. 56-68.
40 *Hansard*, 1905, pp. 9189-95.
41 PAC, Strathcona *papers*, MG 29, D 14, vol. 15, S. B. Steele to Strathcona, June 13, 1909.

42 Morton, *Ministers and Generals*, pp. 199-200.
43 *Hansard*, 1907, pp. 5279-80; ibid., 1910, pp. 132-33; and Amery *papers*, private letters, 1910, Amery to Hughes, May 11, 1910; *CAR*, 1910, pp. 590-94.
44 Morgan, 1912, pp. 97, 443, 875; *CAR*, 1907, p. 487; ibid., 1908, p. 95; ibid., 1909, p. 284; and ibid., 1911, p. 354. Also see PAC, Dominion of Canada Rifle Association, MG 28, I, 243. *Minutes*, 1885-1914.
45 *Militia Lists*, 1908, p. 68.

CHAPTER 8

A Loyal Maverick

Sam Hughes always considered himself to be fiercely independent. His ambition for party promotion and eventual cabinet rank constrained his dissident tendencies, but never totally eliminated them. And they did cause moments of discord in and out of the party.

Instinctively and politically Hughes could never separate race and religion from politics. His mistrust of French-Canadians had been determined in the 1880s by what he saw as their desertion of the traditional Ontario and Quebec Tory coalition. Nor did they share his secular or imperial views. While Hughes was convinced, as he wrote Milner in 1908, that eventually their "dual language" will place them "at the gateway between Europe and America" where they "will shine" in the "new Empire," nevertheless he had little tolerance for French-Canadian culture outside of Quebec. Most French-Canadians in Quebec, he felt, were still "priest-ridden" and parochial, and few had any realistic national or international understanding.[1] One cause of their weakness—at least for Tory Party purposes—was their poor leadership. Hughes once described the new Quebec Conservative leader, F. D. Monk, as "our nominal French Canadian . . . he is a lovely man, clever and wealthy but he has no fight."[2]

Hughes' bigotry, however much he tried to temper it, often embarrassed both him and the party. In 1905 during the bitterly debated Autonomy Bill, Hughes temporarily lost his control. While making an entirely different point, he thoughtlessly claimed that Ontarians were more tolerant of Roman Catholics than the Quebecois were of their Protestants.[3] Two years later, after a heated Commons exchange over loose immigration laws, Hughes charged that Laurier's laws favoured

---

Reference notes for Chapter 8 are found on pp. 131-34.

non-Anglo-Saxons—Catholics, in other words—over good "British stock," and seemingly as an afterthought, he called a few recently arrived immigrant French priests a "curse to Canada." Shocked at what Hughes had said, many of his party colleagues, including Robert Borden, censored him publicly. The incident was further blown out of shape when the *Orange Sentinel* reported that Hughes' actual remark was that these new priests were "only good for breeding purposes."[4]

The unfortunate episode did not end here. Hughes repeated his "curse to Canada" charge at the national Orange Lodge convention in Vancouver that June. The MP was followed by the chaplain, who warned Borden that if he continued to castigate Hughes, he deserved "to be put out of the leadership quicker than he can get out." The threat was evidence that Hughes had rebuilt his damaged standing in the association after his near expulsion in 1896. The chaplain's warning also let Borden know that the Ontario MP had clout, especially in a province that was reported to have several hundred thousand Orange Tory voters.[5]

Hughes' intemperance made Borden's much-needed party revitalization difficult. In 1908 the new Tory leader failed to get a formal alliance with Henry Bourassa who objected "to certain elements within the party." Though there were many other strident and intolerant Ontario Orange Conservative MPs, such as Tom Sproule, the member for East Grey, certainly Bourassa was including Hughes in the lot. Because of Hughes, Borden was having difficulty convincing French-Canadians that the Conservatives could bring about a return to the halcyon days of Macdonald and Cartier; and some from Quebec, with far more enthusiasm than evidence, branded Hughes the "champion of race hatred."[6]

Sam Hughes could also rub many important Ontario Conservatives the wrong way. One of them was James Pliny Whitney whose provincial party finally managed to wrestle the government from the Liberals in 1905 after decades in opposition. The trouble between Hughes, a federal Conservative out of power, and Whitney, a provincial Tory leading the government, was patronage. Some federal MPs wanted their more fortunate provincial colleagues to share the rewards, as they had before 1896 when the situation was reversed. During 1905 and 1906, Hughes bombarded the new Premier with requests for spoils, including appointments for two of his brothers, James as Ontario Public Schools Inspector and William as warden of the penitentiary in Kingston. Every provincial Liberal office-holder, Hughes advised Whitney, should be made "to walk the plank."[7] But Whitney did not entirely share Hughes' view that patronage was the vital link between healthy party organization and continued success at the polls. To Whitney—a new breed of Tory politician—simple party loyalty was not enough; merit had to be considered for any appointment by his government. The obviously irritated Premier responded to one particularly offensive appeal by Hughes that no one could or should be "dismissed without a proper reason."[8]

In September 1905 the two men had a public and embarrassing showdown at a political meeting in Toronto's King Edward Hotel. Hughes collared the Premier and in the loudest terms called him down for his continued support of the Grit "boodle gang" and for being soft on provincial "Micks." The livid Whitney responded in kind and "in a voice that could be heard all over." After accusing Hughes of religious bigotry and blatant partisanship, he and his provincial retinue stormed out of the hotel. That night Hughes wrote a long letter claiming that the Premier had no right to embarrass a veteran party member, especially one who had spent "many a day and many a dollar" getting Whitney elected. Whitney invited the "childish" Hughes to "have it out," but the Lindsay MP did not reply.[9]

Hughes continued to needle Whitney over patronage and to accuse him of prostituting himself to Toronto's Roman Catholics and to Franco-Ontarians by being far too lenient about French-language instruction. Far more than Sam Hughes, James Whitney wanted to accommodate cultural dualism in the province and to play down the disruptive extremism typical of Ontario's intolerant past. Within this distinction, Sam Hughes was far more representative of an older form of politics than Whitney.[10]

Such intolerance had also helped keep Tories out of federal office since 1896, a fact Robert Borden recognized better than Hughes. It is one reason why Borden had brought his "new men" into the party after 1905, and why he tried, unsuccessfully, to forge a working relationship with provincial party teams, especially Ontario. But the activities of men like Hughes kept the provincial Premier distant. Whitney resented any potential threat to the hard-won harmony in his own party; he was suspicious of Borden's attempts at party reforms, especially the much overdue democratic national convention.[11] Because Borden was so dependent on Ontario MPs like Hughes, he was forced to intercede for them and confront Whitney on the issue of his patronage stinginess, even though the national party leader personally thought the MPs' complaints were groundless. Nevertheless patronage was a hard reality for Borden. In the end no accord between the provincial and federal party emerged before 1911 because of men like Hughes. As for Whitney, he tried to have Borden control Hughes and three other MPs, Gus Porter, Bill Northrup, and William Bennett. But he knew that these men were too senior for Borden to censure easily; and Whitney felt sorry for Borden. As he prophetically told his friend, Andrew Broder, the federal MP for the Premier's riding, when Borden takes office "he will have to deal with the gang!"[12]

Perhaps Borden already was. In 1907 Sam Hughes did not get the important new federal post of Ontario liaison officer for the party: instead it went to "a thoroughly loyal and tactful man"—another "new man," J. S. Carstairs. Being passed over hurt Hughes. In later years, if the declining number of his critical letters in the Whitney correspondence is any indication, Hughes may have heeded his leader's warnings about accommodating the independent Ontario Premier for the sake of the federal party.[13]

Sam Hughes' imperial ideas also caused some problems both inside and outside Canada. After the Boer war and also because of it, Hughes' imperial concern intensified. At first it was mostly directed towards co-operative imperial defence and often crowded with hundreds of reform suggestions for both countries. By 1905, however, Hughes was clearly dissatisfied with the slow pace of British progress in this area, as well as by the troubles over his Boer war record and the British approval of Dundonald's dismissal. All of these provoked him to "come out flat-footed for Imperial Union" which demanded more guarantees for Canada. Each year thereafter he sponsored a Commons motion calling for an "equal partnership union" of all members of the Empire.[14] At the core of Hughes' proposal, which was vaguely similar to the modern Commonwealth, was his intensifying nationalism. Canada was to be at least a full partner, if not first among the equals. As inbred and moribund as it had become, Britain must share its power. To Sam Hughes, imperialists had to get it into their "noodles [that] the time is right, the people are stirred." Canadians, he told Amery in 1904, "will be sovereign either as full partners in an imperial machine—or we will be states of the American republic."[15]

Imperial-centralists like Joseph Chamberlain often thought Hughes was one of them, but they were puzzled and frustrated when he refused to accept their ideas. In 1904 Hughes let Chamberlain know that there would be no imperial trade *zollverein* without the partnership.[16] And in 1908, when Milner toured Canada to promote a similar scheme, Hughes still resisted, albeit weakly, when Milner made an unscheduled stop in Lindsay in a vain attempt to flatter Hughes into publicly supporting the idea.[17]

Yet British imperialists continued to think they recognized in Sam Hughes one of their own kind or at least an easy dupe for their imperial purposes. When Grey of Howick replaced Minto as Governor-General in 1905, he too was anxious to get the Tory MP on his side. Even though Hughes is "a vain and impossible fellow, . . . he has his uses," Howick reported to Selborne back in England. He then let it be rumoured that the MP was to be made an aide-de-camp. Had the honour been offered, Hughes would have accepted. But the offer was not made because Hughes remained basically a maverick in imperial circles, convinced that his real purpose was "to educate Britishers. They need it."[18]

And Hughes did try to educate both Britons and Canadians. But the core of his vision remained a full partnership union. Unlike many other imperialists, most of whom were then pushing the economic aspect of imperial consolidation, Hughes was still preaching "colonial assistance in Imperials Wars." As a result of this divergence, Hughes' association with imperial groups, such as Lionel Curtis' Round Table movement, was at best tenuous. In Canada Hughes' constant broadcasting of his imperial ideas made him a sought-after speaker. Typical was an address, supposedly on imperial defence, which he gave to the Empire Club in Toronto in February 1905. But the audience got Hughes' views on Canadian nationalism, on the superiority of Canadian citizen-soldiers over British professionals, and such observations as "taxation" in the form of Canadian military participation in imperials wars "carried with it the right of representation."[19]

From time to time British politicians tried to get Hughes to side with them on divisive imperial issues, such as Irish Home Rule. As a means of pressuring their own government, Andrew Bonar Law and Sir Max Aitken wanted Hughes to speak against conceding to Irish demands. Hughes co-operated willingly, but not in the fashion they wanted. He used the occasions to proselytize his own version of imperial reorganization with Canada clearly in the forefront. "The colonies are already powerful," he wrote Aitken in 1910. Weak, lazy, and ignorant leaders of the old Empire must hand direction over to the colonies by "granting them a free voice and responsibility in a scheme modelled on the Canadian Confederation." Then all problems would be solved and presumably the Irish would not need home rule.[20]

The form of Hughes' imperial scheme was always starkly clear, mostly because his ideas were simple and superficial. In 1904 he described for Amery "a greater British Imperial Parliament meeting in London made up of representatives from each [Dominion] ... elected, say on the basis of population.... It should control foreign policy, army, navy and militia and etc.... The King should be head. The body of Parliament should have power to levy pro rata a duty or tax.... The thing is dead easy, only it requires gradual working out." In 1908 he offered the same scheme to Milner with no more depth and with the aggravating advice that "Britishers" better hurry up and give equality to the colonies before the whole thing collapsed. In 1910 the scheme again showed up in a bitter memo to Aitken, which clearly pointed to Hughes' growing frustration with insensitive Englishmen. The only new item was the suggested devolution of the United Kingdom into four separate states, England, Ireland, Scotland, and Wales, with a mobile parliament meeting in turn in each capital.[21]

Nowhere is there any indication that Sam Hughes thought about the plan's implications. His volatile mind simply trusted that satisfactory details would be worked out. What form would the councils have? How would differing regional interests and wealth be reconciled? How would the international community react? How would taxes be levied? Would the British consider it seriously when more power for the colonies meant less for them? Hughes left too many gaps in his proposal to win converts.

Few men in England could support Hughes' specific schemes largely because there was no single way to accommodate the diverse interests of a huge heterogeneous empire. This fact meant that imperial consolidation was always doomed. As for Canadians, Hughes' brand of imperialism had it supporters, especially in Ontario. Robert Borden understood this, and thus in Parliament the leader often had polite things to say about Sam Hughes' annual motion.[22] But Borden never did anything concrete, for such plans implied the automatic alienation of French-Canada, especially over imperial defence and taxation issues. But Hughes never recognized these subtleties and he continued to be frustrated by his leader's inaction. "Borden really needs to go to England," Hughes wrote Amery in 1908, "it would do him so much good in so many ways."[23]

Compared to the case of the Ross rifle, the Empire question was relatively mild in its effect on Sam Hughes' relationship with his party and leader. As a militia officer, shooting enthusiast, and political critic, Sam Hughes was involved at every level of development of the Canadian-designed and -manufactured weapon. For a variety of practical, military, and economic reasons, Fred Borden adopted Sir Charles Ross' rifle near the end of the Boer war. The expansive Scottish nobleman-inventor was given every encouragement by the Liberal government to establish this new industry in Canada, including tax rebates, cash advances, and a factory site conveniently located on the Plains of Abraham in Laurier's riding. When the British balked at Canada's possible adoption of a rifle other than the Lee Enfield, Fred Borden packed his selection committees with both Liberal and Conservative militia men and rifle enthusiasts who would support his proposal. Hughes was one of the originals in 1901. From then on, when Ross could not meet production schedules and the rifle demonstrated design and manufacturing problems or ran into British opposition, Sam Hughes sprang to its defence for obvious reasons: it was Canadian; it shot better than an Enfield; its straight-pull action fired faster; and it was a modern weapon much needed by equipment-starved militiamen too long dependent on reluctant British suppliers.[24] Ignorance of the complicated military-industrial process of Canada's first sally into major weapons acquisition almost guaranteed that the Ross rifle would be simultaneously elevated into a national passion and submerged in a partisan political debate.[25]

By 1906 the rifle policy had reached that stage. As part of the new "purity in politics" campaign, Robert Borden's party began to question every aspect of the rifle's development. This part of the party's program failed miserably because their own militia critic bolted ranks. To the amazement of Hughes' colleagues, the split started in March 1907, when the Tories thought they had the Grits on the run in a public accounts committee investigating government over-expenditure trying to correct the weapon's manufacturing defects.[26] In defending the arm, Hughes badgered witnesses unmercifully, and thereafter, whenever the rifle question came up in the House, he turned on his own colleagues who could not help but be impressed by the technical details, which he mustered to bury the rifle's detractors. But he could also be critical of the rifle policy and of the strategic location of the factory and of production decisions. Such a course allowed him to retain some party credibility on the issue. But he never once faltered in his belief that the rifle policy was the only sound course for the country.[27]

The critical episode occurred in the spring of 1908 shortly before the federal election. The Conservative attack had been mounting for some time. Two months before it broke, Sir Fred Borden created the Standing Small Arms Committee (SSAC) to investigate, among other things, the fitness of the Ross rifle as the national arm of Canada. In a stroke of political genius, he made Sam Hughes its chairman.[28] That May the Conservatives moved for a vote of censure against the government's handling of the rifle policy. With complete conviction and a flood of emotional and factual responses, Hughes defended the Liberals. He ended up personally slurring the motion's sponsor, a Quebec MP, as a patronage-hungry, jealous, debased politician with a bad military record in the Boer war. In turn Hughes was accused of selling out and of being a paid hack for Sir Charles Ross and Fred Borden.[29] While Hughes' financial connection with Ross has never been established, there was no doubt that F. W. Borden and Laurier favoured him at the time. The chairmanship of the SSAC was one indication; sponsorship as President of the Dominion Rifle Association was another; and the personal intervention of Laurier with the War Office, which netted Hughes retroactive mention in Boer war dispatches, was still another.[30] By the time the House divided, the public brawl among Tory benches, which so greatly amused the Liberal side, left little momentum to the Conservative censure motion: it was defeated overwhelmingly.[31] As a parting gesture before the House adjourned for the summer, Fred Borden quietly made Hughes the railway intelligence officer in the headquarters contingent then organizing the military and imperial spectacle for Quebec's tercentenary celebration.[32] Shortly afterward, Sam Hughes plunged into another federal election—his sixth contest.

By the time the election was called in the fall of 1908, Hughes already had his constituency machine well-oiled and he was eager to get at the Grits on the hustings. His great constituency strength had the local opposition in disarray. It was less than a month before polling day (October 26) before the Liberals could even field a candidate—a Fenelon Falls doctor. The only issue the Grits could realistically aim at was Hughes' extraordinary personality. So they charged him with religious extremism and poked fun at his "continuous vainglorious boast" of how he had won the South African war.[33] It was an uninspired tactic, for there was nothing Hughes and the local constituents liked better than a personal feud in an election campaign, and there were certainly few better at it than Hughes himself.

Hughes issued debating challenges by registered letter, which went unanswered, then published them all in the *Watchman-Warder*. He constantly referred to his main opponents as "cowardly" and "measly creatures" sent out to defame him, the protector of national and local interests. "Please," he wrote in an open newspaper letter, "for once be a man and meet one face to face at all or any of the meetings when you will be treated like a gentleman—though you little deserve it." Once he got into full stride, Hughes set out to show how he was indeed what he claimed, the protector of national and local prosperity. In his twelve-point platform he followed Robert Borden's Halifax manifesto closely, thereby connecting himself firmly with the federal party. He emphasized specific aspects of it, such as "not so much public ownership . . . as rigid public control of corporations." Local interests were also well represented. He called for lumber and agricultural protection; he also blamed Laurier for letting in foreigners so that, as he warned one receptive audience, "in this very country tonight there are 350 or 400 Italians who are taking bread and butter from our boys." Half of his platform was little more than a repetition of the "purity in politics" charges of the last three years. Not surprisingly he failed to mention the Ross rifle. The loyalty theme was there as well as the national one in his traditional call for a full partnership union of the British Empire. In the end Hughes' program was careful to conclude that Whitney, Robert Borden, and Sam Hughes were all one team.[34]

On October 26, 1980, Sam Hughes was re-elected by a margin that tripled his previous victory. For the first time, he took the town of Lindsay and many southern regions of his huge riding. No doubt his prestige was helped by Milner's visit just before the poll. But without a doubt Hughes was a grass-roots politician of no mean proportion; he loved the fray and campaign activity. "In three and a half days," he later wrote a friend, "I travelled 185 miles by buggy, and spoke at 14 meetings, and in 4 days I covered 201 miles in a buggy and 60 by rail and spoke in 15 meetings. The country was lovely, the variegated leaves, the mountains and the lakes—all made the work congenial to my nature."[35]

But once again the federal party failed to win. The distribution during the campaign of the infamous Orange-Order-inspired Hocken pamphlet, which charged that there was a huge Laurier-backed Roman Catholic conspiracy in Ontario, did not help; nor did the Liberal revelations about the scandal involving senior Tory MP George E. Foster released a few weeks before the federal vote. Grits alleged, but did not prove, that "Foster, the Forester" was speculating on blocks of Canadian Northern Railway land with Independent Order of the Forester's funds. Obviously ignoring his own speculation on CNR land, Hughes thought Foster guilty of the charges and a "weakness to us." Ironically he told a friend, "Foster's tongue is too long. He never knows when to stop."[36] The public brawl the Tories had engaged in over the Ross rifle six months before the election may have also contributed somewhat to the Conservative defeat. But on the whole the federal party had advanced. Laurier's majority had been reduced to seven outside Quebec, and Borden quietly put out the word that he was satisfied with the gains.[37]

When Parliament opened in January 1909, Sam Hughes was more determined than ever to fight the Liberals "to a finish." He plunged into routine House and party work, serving on six of the big Commons committees. Again on less controversial but important legislation, Hughes followed his leader's course. Militia issues, however, found him as vigilant and vocal as ever, whether in such larger matters as establishing university militia units across the country or in such minutiae as installing proper plumbing facilities at the Royal Military College.[38] But in the next two and a half years, there were three major questions for Sam Hughes: the Ross rifle, the naval debate, and reciprocity with the United States.

As head of the Standing Small Arms Committee, Hughes became even more devoted to the controversial Ross rifle. By mid-1909 his zealous direction had brought about improvements in the rifle's design which led to a major model change called the Mark III, the final production version of the Ross. His encouraged experimentation with the earlier models continued to improve them as well. That same year when Canadian rifle teams started to win frequently at Bisley, the most prestigious rifle matches in the English-speaking world, Hughes was ecstatic. Not only was the Ross a good national arm but it was, as he often bragged in the Commons, "the best rifle in the world." By having presentation grade samples sent free to imperial statesmen and production models to Canadian MPs to show their constituents, Hughes managed to whip up support and to get more rifles into the hands of militiamen and shooting enthusiasts. Just as importantly, the favourable impression the rifle had on the onlookers at Bisley suggested that Canada might be able to break into the lucrative British small-arms manufacturing monopoly in the Empire. Australians and New Zealanders were very interested in the technological initiatives and self-sufficiency the Canadians were showing with their weapons policy, and there was talk they might even adopt the Ross. Hughes always knew that Canadians could lead the Empire in certain things; perhaps the production of a superior rifle was one of them.[39]

Unfortunately it seemed that when Canadian marksmen won English matches with the straight-pull Ross, the British National Rifle Association, a semi-official military organization, would disqualify the victor on some small technical point, such as light trigger pressures or overweight barrels. When this happened in 1910, Hughes accused the War Office and British small-arms manufacturers of a conspiracy against the Canadian rifle; he even demanded—unsuccessfully—that Fred Borden boycott the matches. Hughes' public campaign spawned national pride and won over the support of many prominent Canadians for the weapon. It kept the imperial authorities sensitive to Canada's budding small-arms industry, and fewer and fewer Ross rifles were disqualified while Canadians continued to win. It also helped force the pace of British improvements in their own small arms development.[40] And Hughes appeared to be making great strides in producing an efficient weapon.

But there were negative effects in all of these developments, many of them caused by Hughes' control of the SSAC. As the real or imagined British conspiracy developed in Hughes' mind, he ordered mechanical changes in the rifle to ensure that the British were defeated on the shooting fields. His technical subordinates pointed out the conceptual flaws in his orders, and when they got nowhere with the stubborn chairman, they resigned or did as they were told. Machine tolerances were tightened; fit was made better; and the weapons won.[41] But close bearing surfaces, complicated and fragile target-type sights, and tight chambers capable of firing only exact dimension ammunition changed the rifle from an efficient combat weapon to an efficient target one. It never occurred to Sam Hughes that fine accuracy was not the sole requirement of a rifle in war. His optimism, his wealth of technical knowledge, and his often vicious defences of the rifle in the Commons and in public stifled any genuinely constructive debate; he made far too many partisans on the issue to help the rifle weather the long peacetime developmental process of all new military equipment.

The great naval debate which shattered Canadian tranquillity in the spring of 1909 made the Ross rifle controversy pale in comparison. Perhaps for Hughes the two issues were manifestations of the same thing: inadequate Canadian preparation for national and imperial defence. For some time many Britons had been alarmed that the Royal Navy was being swamped by German naval construction. The hysteria reached its peak in the British general election the year before it broke in Canada. Sam Hughes did not like the sanctimonious George Foster, but when the Conservative MP for Toronto North resolved in the House in February 1909 to have the Canadian government do something quickly to aid the British Admiralty, Hughes could easily support him. Australia and New Zealand had previously announced direct cash contributions to Britian for ship construction. But both Canadian political leaders dreaded the implications for their respective parties of the entire emotion-filled matter. Forced by Foster to react, Laurier rejected any direct cash contribution; instead he called for the establishment of a Canadian navy under parliamentary control. Robert Borden preferred this course, but it was not the one Sam Hughes wanted. Nor did men like Sir James Whitney, Sir Rodimond Roblin, Premier of Manitoba, Sir Byron Walker, president of the Bank of Commerce, and a host of others, many of them Conservatives. The German challenge, they felt, could only be met by an immediate cash contribution allowing the Admiralty to buy the most modern ships of the dreadnought class.[42]

Several times during the Commons session Hughes made his position clear in the House. It was the immediacy of the peril and the damage that a separate navy could do to the imperial connection that alarmed him. On one occasion, to underscore his dire warnings of German war intentions, he read out long passages from *Cannae*, the book written by the former German Chief of the General Staff, Count Alfred von Schlieffen. Laurier's "tin-pot navy," he thundered across the floor of the House, could not protect Canada now from such a monumental menace. Hughes also carried his message across the province. In April 1909 a large Guelph crowd sympathetically approved when he charged that the threat was so great that the government ought to send enough money to build five dreadnoughts.[43]

As the controversy grew larger, at first Hughes was disappointed, as he so often was, at Robert Borden's initial unenthusiastic response to imperial questions. Instead of pressuring Borden as some other party members were doing, Hughes waited for him to come around. While standing firm in several bitter caucus meetings, he was astute enough not to embarrass the chief by forcing a vote. Outside caucus, as with the jingoistic Orange *Sentinel*'s editors' demands for Borden's resignation, apparently because they thought him a weak Conservative leader, Hughes openly and vigorously defended him as a "future Prime Minister."[44] He was delighted in the spring of 1910 when Borden, after a year of agonizing, rose in the House to condemn the disastrous effect of Laurier's bill on Empire relations; he then called for an immediate cash gift for two dreadnoughts.

Led by F. D. Monk, disappointed French-Canadian Conservatives tried to change their own leader's amendment; but the rest of the party stood against them. After days of stormy debate, which included at least one Tory-inspired singing of God Save the King, the overwhelming Liberal majority passed the bill's second reading amid shouts and cat-calls from the Tory benches; six months later, it slid anti-climactically into law after Sam Hughes attempted the desperate tactic of a six-month hoist.[45] So Canada got its "tin-pot navy"; and in this difficult process Hughes himself managed to remain loyal both to his leader and to his own ideas.

The end of the naval debate did not mean that Sam Hughes was satisfied or that the Tory party escaped unscathed. Hughes wanted Borden to be more sympathetic both to his imperial ideas and to the veteran members, especially those who could attract the support of powerful individuals in Ontario. Obviously the leader's conversion to the naval contributionists' stand had won him the support of the Conservative provincial premiers; and in building this wider base, Sam Hughes suggested another stratagem for Borden. For years Hughes had cultivated a remarkably wide circle of Toronto acquaintances of all political persuasions. In March 1910, he advised Robert Borden that if he adopted a strong imperial policy and a progressive national program, several prominent Toronto Liberal businessmen, like Byron Walker, Thomas White of National Trust, and W. K. George, president of the Canadian Manufacturers' Association, could be lured from Laurier's camp. There was also a rumour that Hughes and John Willison, editor of the influential *News*, might be able to bring over no less a person than Clifford Sifton.[46] For the moment nothing came of these manoeuvres but Borden knew that Hughes' advice was sound and he did not forget it.

There were others in the party besides Sam Hughes who found their leader's waffling and ambivalence hard to take. Perennial antagonisms between the so-called Orange extremists like Sam Hughes continued to gnaw away at French-Canadian Conservatives' sense of comfort with the national organization. Moreover, the tempestuous Monk was now not attending caucus meetings and there were obvious signs of deep discontent among some Ontario veterans. Long-time MPs like J. D. ('Doc') Reid and Bill Northrup wanted to dump Borden.

The revolt came in April 1910. Astutely Borden resigned. His quick riposte stunned calmer members like Hughes who vividly remembered the disastrous squabbles of the Bowell-Tupper era. After six days of acrimonious manoeuvring, in a raucous members' meeting Hughes and a majority of the caucus led by Charles Doherty stood for Borden. The public display quelled the rebels but the caucus warned Borden he would have to change to prevent a recurrence. Yet ten months later when the leader announced the party reorganization that autumn, neither Sam Hughes nor any of the senior members were included in Borden's inner-party circle. Instead George Perley and

H. B. Ames from Quebec became chief party whip and organizer, respectively. As for the veteran Sam Hughes, he was kept busy in the intricate tactical world of daily party routine.[47]

Whatever party dissatisfaction Hughes had, it quickly evaporated in late January 1911 when the Liberal Finance Minister, W. S. Fielding, suddenly announced reciprocal trade proposals with the United States. For Hughes free trade with the Americans was an ancient and dangerous enemy. He knew that Laurier was trotting it out to cover up recent political losses over the naval issue to Henri Bourassa's Quebec nationalists. Hughes also knew that the Grit tactic might work, for there were more than a few Canadians in favour of such an economic agreement. Some of these converts were no doubt in Hughes' own constituency. With an agricultural and lumbering base, the residents of Victoria-Haliburton might find both a buying and a selling advantage in larger and cheaper American markets. Hughes felt he had to attack immediately, even if only to overcome the despair the issue caused among his fellow MPs. Sam Hughes' view was direct and simple: reciprocity was a monumental threat to Canada's survival.[48]

Almost within hours of the bill's first reading, Hughes publicly denounced the Toronto *Globe*'s editor for his open support of the trade idea. By the time the debate resumed in February, the fiery MP was hot on the trail of all "continentalists" in the Commons. He followed Borden then George Foster in a blasting condemnation of the bill; and it was he who read to a hushed Commons the infamous words of Champ Clark, the Democratic leader of the U.S. House of Representatives, who had earlier commented that the trade agreement would be a sure and simple sign that the United States was "preparing to annex Canada." By April Hughes' ire and fighting spirit were at a high pitch; he righteously labelled the trade legislation as a national blasphemy forced upon a democratic people by an arrogant, autocratic, and treasonous Liberal "gang" masquerading as a government.[49] The proposal had to be beaten; the bill, he insisted, must be withdrawn—the future of Canada was at stake. He was right about one thing: as spring came, increasing numbers of Canadians were seeing the issue more in Hughes' terms as a serious challenge to national survival than as an easy road to economic prosperity, and the Tory party was on to a good thing.

The intense political heat of the reciprocity proposal, however, also exposed other considerations for Sam Hughes. One was the aggravating effect which his leader's reaction to the bill could have among the parliamentary party faithful. Since the party fracas the previous spring, Borden had remained aloof and often temperamental. Strains of the trade debate resurrected earlier discontents. They also appeared to be reinforcing Borden's preferences for political novices over the old guard. More than ever Hughes and other regulars regarded these newcomers as political bumpkins the party could ill-afford just when reciprocity had given them a potential winning issue, and when they needed all of the old experience and backroom savvy they could muster. In January, without caucus consultation, Borden had opened talks with provincial Tories on how best to fight the trade issue. By the end of February, he had taken Hughes' year-old advice and secured a working alliance with important anti-reciprocity Liberals from Toronto, including Clifford Sifton, businessman Lloyd Harris, and lawyer Zebulon Lash. In return for their help, Borden promised to appoint Liberals to his cabinet if elected. This last proposal sickened veterans like Doc Reid and William Price; and by March 1911 Borden had another revolt on his hands. Again, to head it off, he threatened to resign.[50]

Hughes came close to open sympathy with the rebels. In a sour seven-page letter to a political friend, he vented his frustrations. Reid, Price, and Northrup, he pointed out, "have more brains and organizational power in five minutes" than Perley or Ames "have in a lifetime." Other newcomers he dismissed as "d[amned] noodles" and "feather-headed fellows" whom he vowed would never set foot in his riding. As for Borden, he was "a lovely fellow, very capable, but not a very good judge of men or tactics and is gentle-hearted as a girl."[51]

But Sam Hughes did not join the rebels. When Borden threatened to resign, Hughes quickly endorsed a round-robin pledging his personal loyalty. His political instincts told him the time was ripe for himself and the party. It was no occasion for a suicidal showdown over leadership. Had he been on the wrong side of the challenge, his political career would have been finished. With sixty-four others signing the loyalty petition, the revolt was quickly suppressed. In Parliament the reciprocity debate had brought a new unity to the opposition benches where the Conservatives were successfully blocking the bill's passage by refusing to vote supply.

At this point Sam Hughes openly displayed his political dissatisfaction. The mild and sulky protest took the form of a partial withdrawal from party functions, and as in the past, the acceptance of a few Liberal favours. The first came at the height of the opposition attack on the trade proposals and shortly after the revolt. Perhaps Fred Borden sensed Hughes' frustration or perhaps he just wanted to remove a very vocal anti-reciprocity advocate. Whatever the case he appointed Hughes to the delegation attending the imperial defence meetings in London that June. Hughes accepted quickly, then publicly exaggerated his role from a mere observer to an official military advisor. Some of his own party colleagues were upset at his easy dalliance with the Grits and said so loudly in the Commons. Once more the Liberals enjoyed seeing the opposition members snapping at their own tails.[52] While hardly as important, it was reminiscent of the tactic used to diffuse the Ross rifle debate in 1908. Towards the end of May, Hughes went off to London. Evidently he gave Robert Borden little or no warning and he left in the company of a Liberal minister while the reciprocity issue was still being hotly debated. The upshot was that Hughes was not included in Borden's small circle of personal friends who since 1906 not only had helped him reform the party but were mobilizing it for the expected general election. The leader knew Hughes was more progressive than most MPs, yet Sam had enough of the old ways to make him unacceptable in Borden's inner sanctum.[53]

By the end of July 1911, sick of Conservative obstructionism over reciprocity, the Liberals called a snap federal election. When the announcement came Sam Hughes had only been home from England for a few days. But for the past five months, he had been saying that the vital reciprocity question could only be answered by polling the people in a national contest; and now that it was here, he was delighted. His party spirits also took on a correspondingly co-operative air. When he started to gather support for his constituency nomination, he played up his loyalty at all levels, promptly forgetting whatever maverick tendencies he had recently shown. He had lots of support. The *Watchman-Warder*'s editor ecstatically reported that "Colonel Sam will get the nomination as the loyalty to the leader is fact and his quality proven." Hughes did get the nomination in a unanimous vote.[54]

As with most other constituencies in the country, there was only one issue in Victoria-Haliburton—reciprocity. During the actual campaign, Hughes met a fairly determined Liberal challenge head-on with the same loyalty tactic. As usual he was charming, witty, and tireless; in one three-day stretch he spoke in forty-five different places; his organization was superb and his message simple. While the implications for the imperial connection were always there, Hughes' basic arguments were directed at the preservation of Canada. The issue was, he made clear to audience after audience, "a battle of ballots against the invasion of Yankees" and it was the nation, the dream of the Fathers of Confederation, that he and Mr. Robert Borden were determined to preserve. When the ballots were counted in the riding on September 21, Hughes had won two-thirds of votes cast.[55] The sweeter victory for Hughes was the Conservative defeat of the Liberals, 134 seats to 87.

It was this ability to win that the national party counted on, and it was Hughes' prompt delivery of votes all solidly connected to Robert Borden's leadership which—as Doc Reid, one of the Ontario strategists, noted to Borden—made the victorious MP hard to ignore.[56] The truth seems to be that Hughes could ill-afford to disconnect from Robert Borden, and for the sake of the party, nor could Borden from Hughes.

The Conservative sweep was really a product of the unlikely alliance of Tories with anti-reciprocity Liberals, big business, and French-Canadian nationalists. Many provincial Conservative administrations, especially Whitney's in Ontario, had lent their political machines to Borden. Besides the normal regional cabinet-making considerations, Borden had to meet all these special interests in choosing his new ministers. As the days went by, F. D. Monk from Quebec, Frank Cochrane and Thomas White from Ontario, Manitoba's Robert Rogers, and British Columbia's Martin Burrell all got portfolios. The new, inner-circle men like George Perley, A. E. Kemp, and Thomas Crothers, the caucus chairman since 1910, were also designated for cabinet.[57] But so far not Sam Hughes.

Hughes wanted the militia portfolio. He felt he deserved it and he was determined to get it. So unabashedly he called in all his credits. He wrote letter after letter, he placed dozens of telephone calls, and made nearly as many personal visits. Four days after the election he laid his case before Borden in a letter that typified Hughes' entire public career. For that reason it is worth laying out in full:

This morning I was phoned from Toronto by one of the most prominent gentlemen there, to inform me that steps were being taken to prejudice me with you by raising the cry that I am not looked upon kindly by a certain ecclesiastical organization.

I do not know what such could have to do with the matter. Everyone has ever had fair play from me; and so long as others do not kick at the appointment of those of that creed, they should be quite content.

The movement I am informed, is boomed not by those of that faith, but by Protestants who would eliminate me from the Government.

It is needless to review here my principles—or my service to the party. For some years, a few so called Tories have made it uncomfortable for me over the Ross Rifle; but when you consider the great success attending that rifle and the fact that today Britain is perfecting a new rifle, and that the vital principles of the Ross as perfected by my committee are [its] essentials, you will realize the futility of the attack. The aim then, was, as I can prove, to "kill Sam Hughes politically," and advance another to be minister under the new Tory leader when you would be driven to retire. Well, neither before their attacks on the Ross rifle, nor when they twice tried to get rid of our Leader, did I flinch—*you found me as true as steel.*

In your coming Cabinet operations difficulties may from time to time arise. It strikes me that it might be that again, my tact, firmness and judgement might come in to help matters along.

My military record is open—and will bear comparison with any. Sir Fred Borden himself has always done me the credit of saying that the vast majority of the democratic and effective changes are due to my suggestions.

It is every honest man's desire to be recognized. Has or has not my line for years been vindicated in this fight. Had our western men begun a year or two years ago, every province would have given us a majority. But anon things will come better out there.

I'll explain personally the work in Ontario.

In my walks through life easy management of men has ever been one of my chief characteristics—and I get the name of bringing success and good luck to a cause.

Hoping you will pardon this.[58]

Shortly after writing this, Hughes telehoned Sir James Whitney for an endorsement. The Premier was just leaving for his own cabinet consultation with Borden in Ottawa. "Say nice things" about me, Hughes pleaded, adding that the Premier should not forget to mention his military expertise. Later he confided to Whitney that he had only requested thirty people to sponsor him, and that he would be "doubly cautious not to make mistakes" if given a cabinet post.[59]

Whitney did not like Hughes and had not for years. Since their break five years previously, in public the Premier had been nothing more than polite to the Lindsay MP. In private he still considered Hughes as a man "so filled with abuse and falsehood you would hardly believe it possible that any man of common sense could think as he does." It is doubtful, therefore, that Whitney recommended Sam Hughes to Borden at all; indeed the Premier thought that he had convinced Borden to appoint Andrew Broder, the federal MP in Whitney's riding, to the militia portfolio. The oblivious Hughes, however, continued to think that the independent-minded Premier had said "good words" to Borden about him.[60]

From Whitney's camp, Hughes went to many others, including Sir William Mackenzie, Clifford Sifton, and the former Liberal Militia Minister, Sir Fred Borden. Borden had been defeated in his own riding in September. Hughes wrote his old Liberal friend a touching letter expressing his "deepest regret at your going down," and then asked Sir Fred to intercede with his Conservative cousin on his behalf.[61]

With no call from Ottawa, Hughes' spirits began to plummet. The signs were ominous. In the traditional newspaper game of guessing about portfolios, Sam Hughes was not frequently mentioned. Even the Orange *Sentinel* did not promote Hughes as ministerial material. One by one Borden made his choices. September gave way to October and Hughes still had no word.[62]

But there were important people who did think that his talent and service should be rewarded with the militia ministry. Sifton was one, so was Sir John Gibson, the Lieutenant-Governor of Ontario. And Sir Fred Borden showed no hesitation at all in telling his cousin that Hughes should get the job. "Whatever success I have had" as Militia Minister, he wrote back to Hughes, "is to a considerable degree due to the patriotic course you ... adopted as military critic in the House. I cannot for the life of me see how your qualifications ... can be overlooked."[63] These endorsements and others were finally enough to convince Robert Borden to consider Hughes seriously. After much agonizing he called the MP to Ottawa. Borden wanted to question Hughes personally about his "erratic temperament and immense vanity." And Sam Hughes—so close to his lifetime political ambition—provided all of the necessary contrition.[64]

In the interview between the two men, Hughes had more support for his case than just the testimonials of others and Robert Borden knew it. Since the early 1880s there had been years of Hughes' tireless party service, more in political famine than in feast. He had been the first to offer the humiliated Borden his seat in the leader's personal defeat of 1904. He had done his duty ably and well in the countless routines and details of the House and on committees. When the party was diluted by new and uninspiring members and suffering from leadership problems, Hughes had provided experience. Many times he had stood up and been counted for Borden and for party solidarity. For nineteen years and through seven electoral contests he had offered the party a strong local constituency. His militia, imperial, and Orange connections gave him a much wider circle of influence than just his political one. Now that Borden had won, he would have to make concessions to them if he was to govern.

But for Borden, while Sam Hughes may have been from the old stalwarts, he was never completely one of them. Borden liked Sam Hughes because he was a proud Canadian with a wider outlook and imagination than most of his parochial-minded fellow MPs; he was forthright, never dull, and, according to Borden himself, a man of "great ability and wide experience," despite his occasional "lack of tact and foolish actions and words."[65] And Sam Hughes seemed to be the MP with the most knowledge about military matters available at the time. The militia portfolio was not a major one; and except for its patronage importance, few Canadians took the militia seriously. The clinching feature of the emotion-filled interview between Borden and Sam Hughes was a promise—a teary promise to the future Prime Minister—that Sam Hughes would be on his best behaviour if granted a cabinet post. Borden accepted his promise. In October 1911 the fifty-eight-year-old Sam Hughes became Canada's fifteenth Minister of Militia and Defence. It was the only cabinet appointment Governor-General Lord Grey criticized.[66]

Reference Notes to Chapter 8

1 Milner *papers*, Box 35, Hughes to Milner, Nov. 15, 1908; and *Hansard*, 1905, p. 1861. Also see PAC, Willison *papers*, Hughes to Willison, p. 15861; and ibid., Hughes to Willison, 1905, pp. 15869-72.
2 Amery *papers*, Hughes to Amery, Aug. 8, 1904.

132 / REFERENCE NOTES TO CHAPTER 8

3 *Hansard*, 1905, pp. 3776-96, 3833-35; and J. W. Dafoe, *Laurier, A Study in Canadian Politics* (Toronto: McClelland and Stewart, 1968), pp. 77-78.
4 Orange *Sentinel*, April 18, 1907, p. 10; ibid., April 25, 1907, pp. 1, 3; *Hansard*, 1907-1908, p. 9330; *CAR*, 1907, pp. 438, 473-74.
5 Orange *Sentinel*, June 20, 1907, p. 1; ibid., June 27, 1904, p. 7; and *CAR*, 1904, pp. 149-50.
6 Orange *Sentinel*, Aug. 29, 1907, p. 1; ibid., Dec. 23, 1909, p. 4; ibid., Dec. 30, 1909, p. 1; *CAR*, 1904, pp. 210-11; Lindsay *Post*, July 22, 1904; *Hansard*, 1907-1908, p. 4420; ibid., 1909-1910, pp. 707, 3219; and *CAR*, 1910, p. 221; PAC, Grey of Howick *papers*, vol. II, pp. 2986-90, Grey to Bryce, Oct. 12, 1911; and Brown, *Borden*, vol. 1, pp. 129, 167.
7 Catherine P. Warner, *Sir James P. Whitney and Sir Robert L. Borden: Relations Between a Conservative Provincial Premier and his Federal Party Leader, 1905-1914*, thesis (University of Toronto, 1967, pp. 33-50; PAO, Whitney *papers*, Mu 3113, Hughes to Whitney, Oct. 19, 1897; ibid., Mar. 2, 1898; ibid., Mu 3115, R. L. Borden to Whitney, May 20, 1901.
8 PAO, Whitney *papers*, Mu 3117, Hughes to Whitney, Mar. 17, 1905; and ibid., Whitney to Hughes, Mar. 20, 1905.
9 Ibid., Mu 3117, Hughes to Whitney, Sept. 14, 1905; and ibid., Whitney to Hughes, Sept. 15, 1905.
10 Ibid., Mu 3121, Hughes to Whitney, Dec. 5, 1906.
11 See Warner, pp. 33-50.
12 Ibid., pp. 48-50; and Brown, *Borden*, vol. 1, pp. 126-28; and Whitney *papers*, Mu 3119, Whitney to Broder, Dec. 6, 1906.
13 PAO, Whitney *papers*, Mu 3119, Borden to Whitney, April 19, 1906; ibid., Whitney to Borden, April 20, 1906; ibid., 3123, Borden to Whitney, May 4, 1907; and ibid., Hughes to Whitney, Mar. 9, 1910.
14 Amery *papers*, Hughes to Amery, Nov. 27, 1904; *Hansard*, 1905, pp. 2335-36; also see ibid., 1903, p. 771; ibid., 1907, pp. 2840-46; and ibid., 1909, p. 6417.
15 Amery *papers*, Canadian Militia Bill, 1904, Hughes to Amery, Aug. 8, 1904.
16 Ibid., private letters, 1908, Hughes to Amery, Nov. 14, 1908.
17 Milner, *diaries*, Sept. 19 to Nov. 6, 1908; and Milner *papers*, Box 35, Hughes to Milner, Nov. 15, 1908.
18 PAC, RG7, G21, no. 265, Hughes to Hanbury-Williams, Jan. 13, 1905, Mar. 20, 1905; and *CAR*, 1905, p. 462; Amery *papers*, Hanbury-Williams to Amery, June 30, 1906; and PAC, Grey of Howick *papers*, vol. 29, p. 007491, Grey to Selborne, May 9, 1907.
19 Sam Hughes, *Empire Club Speeches, 1904-1905*, pp. 176-84.
20 *Hansard*, 1903, pp. 769-71; and House of Lords Record Office (HLRO), Bonar Law *papers*, 81/1/8, S. W. Alexander (Aitken's secretary) to Bonar Law, June 6, 1917; the latter contains Hughes' complete 1910 memo on Irish Home Rule.
21 Amery *papers*, Hughes to Amery, July 30, 1904; and Milner *papers*, Box 35, Hughes to Milner, Nov. 4, 1908; and HLRO, Bonar Law *papers*, S. W. Alexander to Bonar Law, June 6, 1917.
22 *Hansard*, 1905, pp. 2335-36; ibid., 1907, pp. 2840-46; and ibid., 1909, p. 6417.
23 Amery *papers*, 1908, Hughes to Amery, Nov. 14, 1908.
24 Roger Phillips, F. J. Dupuis, and J. A. Chadwick, *The Ross Rifle Story* (Antingonish: Casket, 1984), vol. I.
25 Ibid., Miller, pp. 148-51; *Hansard*, 1901, pp. 378, 1282; Gordon, p. 160; PANS, Borden *papers*, OLB, M.D. no. 18, Borden to O'Grady Haly, June 14, 1901; and ibid., Borden to Hughes, June 17, 1901.
26 Commons *Journals*, 1906-1907, Appendix I, "Report of the Public Accounts Committee respecting payment of $345,091.84 to the Ross Rifle Company," pp. 574-82.
27 *Hansard*, 1906-1907, p. 3794; ibid., p. 3734. For a typical speech on the Ross, see ibid., pp. 3732-801.
28 Ibid., pp. 13505-506; PAC, Grey of Howick *papers*, vol. 5, p. 00138, Grey to Laurier, May 16, 1910; Militia Council *Report*, 1908, p. 112; and *CAR*, 1908, p. 90.
29 Commons *Journals*, 1907-1908, p. 469; *Hansard*, 1907-1908, pp. 9030-31, 9054-57, 9091-92, 9330-33, 9628-52; see Dundonald, p. 205; W. T. R. Preston, *My Generation*

REFERENCE NOTES TO CHAPTER 8 / 133

of Politics and Politicians (Toronto: Rose, 1927), p. 324; and Hector Charlesworth, *More Candid Chronicles* (Toronto: Macmillan, 1928), p. 207. In 1916, R. L. Borden remained highly suspicious that Hughes had received payments from Ross (PAC, R. L. Borden, *private diaries*, Oct. 13, 1916). There is no concrete evidence that Hughes was Ross' paid Commons "hack" to lobby the rifle, yet the above all made the charge.

30 PAC, Laurier *papers*, vol. 510, Hughes to Laurier, Mar. 20, 1908, p. 137987; ibid., vol. 514, Laurier to Haldane, June 12, 1908, p. 138981; ibid., Hughes to Laurier, June 29, 1908, p. 138984-89, and Hughes to Laurier, July 31, 1908, p. 138990.
31 Commons *Journals*, 1907-1908, p. 469.
32 PAC, Otter *papers*, Hughes to Otter, July 22, 1908; and Morton, *The Canadian General*, pp. 282-90.
33 *Post*, Dec. 27, 1907, n.p.; ibid., Sept. 11, 1908, n.p.; ibid., Sept. 25, 1908, p. 1; ibid., Oct. 9, 1908, p. 4; and ibid., Oct. 23, 1904, p. 4.
34 *Watchman-Warder*, Oct. 1, 1908, p. 4; Hughes to R. J. Maclaughlin, Sept. 30, 1908; ibid., Oct. 8, 1904, p. 4, Hughes to the editor; and ibid., Oct. 8, 1908, p. 7.
35 Amery *papers*, private letters, 1908, Sam Hughes to Amery, Nov. 13, 1908.
36 *Watchman-Warder*, Sept. 24, 1908, p. 9; Beck, *Pendulum of Power*, pp. 110-17; PAO, Whitney *papers*, Mu 3126, Borden to Whitney, Nov. 9, 1908; and Amery *papers*, private letters, 1908, Hughes to Amery, Nov. 13, 1908.
37 *Hansard*, 1907-1908, pp. 9030-31, 9054-57, 9330-33.
38 Amery *papers*, private letters, Hughes to Amery, Nov. 13, 1908; *Hansard*, 1909, pp. 357, 406, 7939-40, 681-83, 1179, 2379, 1066; ibid., 1910-1911, pp. 657, 707, 1085, 3219 are samples. Also see Commons *Journals*, 1909-1910, pp. 31-87.
39 Bodleian Library, Oxford, Lewis, First Viscount Harcourt *papers*, Box 463, Hughes to Harcourt, April 25, 1914, p. 326; and *Hansard*, 1909-1910, pp. 338-39.
40 *Hansard*, 1909-1910, pp. 4513-19; ibid., 1910-1911, July 24, 1911, n.p., p. 7553; ibid., p. 9997; and ibid., 1911-1912, pp. 3730-51.
41 SSAC, vol. 2, file 1-562, Greville-Harston to Hughes, 26 June 1908.
42 Brown, *Borden*, vol. 1, pp. 142-69.
43 *Hansard*, 1909, pp. 3769-82, 6418; ibid., 1909-1910, pp. 3763-64, 4888; Commons *Journals*, 1909-1910, pp. 299-301; *CAR*, 1909, p. 94; and *Hansard*, 1909-1910, pp. 3794-98.
44 Orange *Sentinel*, Dec. 23, 1909, Hughes to the editor, n.p.
45 Ibid., 1909-1910, pp. 7528-91; Commons *Journals*, 1909-1910, pp. 299-301, 305, 474-75; Brown, *Borden*, vol. 1, pp. 151-63; and *Hansard*, 1909-1910, pp. 3794-98.
46 PAC, Borden *papers*, vol. 134, pp. 70813, Hughes to Borden, March 23, 1901; ibid., pp. 70892-35, Hughes to William MacArthur, March 23, 1911; and English, pp. 55-56.
47 Brown, *Borden*, vol. 1, pp. 163-69; and *CAR*, 1910, pp. 246, 293.
48 Borden, *Memoirs*, vol. I, p. 303.
49 *CAR*, 1911, p. 230; and *Hansard*, 1910-1911, pp. 3608, 7126-85.
50 Borden, *Memoirs*, vol. 1, pp. 146-47; Brown, *Borden*, vol. 1, pp. 178-80; and R. D. Cuff, "The Toronto Eighteen and the Election of 1911," in *Ontario History* 57, no. 4 (Dec. 1965), pp. 169-80.
51 PAC, Borden *papers*, vol. 134, pp. 7829-35, Hughes to MacArthur, Mar. 23, 1911.
52 Sessional *papers*, 1911, no. 208 d, "Report of a Committee of the Imperial Conference convened to discuss Defence (Military) at the War Office," pp. 465-76 (this contains details of the conference); and *CAR*, 1911, p. 354.
53 PAC, Laurier *papers*, C904, Murphy to Laurier, May 15, 1911, Laurier to Murphy, May 22, 1911, pp. 186208-10; ibid., Hughes to Laurier, May 26, 1911, pp. 186566-69, and Hughes to Laurier, June 2, 1911, p. 186757; *Hansard*, 1910-1911, p. 9072; PANS, Borden *papers*, OLB, vol. 53, p. 34, Borden to Lessard, 1911; Brown, *Borden*, vol. 1, pp. 180-87; and Morgan, *1912*, p. 557.
54 *Watchman-Warder*, Aug. 3, 1911, p. 8, Aug. 10, p. 1, Aug. 24, p. 1.
55 *Post*, Aug. 18, 1911, p. 6; and ibid., Aug. 25, 1911, p. 3. Also see the Lindsay *Post* and the *Watchman-Warder* for August and September 1911 for a description of the campaign; *Watchman-Warder*, Oct. 5, 1911, p. 2; and Robert Cuff, "The Conservative

Party Machine and the Election of 1911," in *Ontario History* 57 (Sept. 3, 1965), pp. 149-60.
56 Warner, p. 87. Reid advised Borden in April that Hughes' seat was a sure thing for the party.
57 English, pp. 61-69 and H. N. McQuarrie, "The Formation of Borden's First Cabinet," in *The Canadian Journal of Economics and Political Science*, III (I, 1957), pp. 90-104.
58 PAC, Borden *papers*, vol. 118, Hughes to Borden, Sept. 25, 1911, p. 65082; cited in Brown, *Borden*, vol. 1, pp. 202, 203.
59 PAO, Whitney *papers*, Mu 3132, Hughes to Whitney, Oct. 8, 1911, and office minute to Whitney, Sept. 26, 1911.
60 Ibid., Mu 3132, Hughes to Whitney, Oct. 8, 1911, Whitney to Hilliard, Oct. 11, 1911, and Whitney to Broder, Oct. 18, 1911.
61 PANS, F. W. Borden *papers*, loose letters, no. 178, p. 15312, Hughes to F. W. Borden, Sept. 29, 1911.
62 Ibid., *CAR*, 1911, pp. 289-91; Orange *Sentinel*, Oct. 12, 1911, p. 1; and Borden, *Memoirs*, vol. 1, p. 33.
63 S. H. S. Hughes, *CHAR* (1949-1950), p. 37; and Brown, *Borden*, vol. 1, p. 179; PANS, F. W. Borden *papers*, loose letters series, no. 179, p. 15374, Borden to Wallace Nesbitt, Oct. 11, 1911; ibid., 178, p. 15372, Gibson to F. W. Borden, Oct. 6, 1911; and ibid., 179, p. 15364, F. W. Borden to Hughes, Oct. 3, 1911.
64 Borden, *Memoirs*, vol. 1, p. 330; and Brown, *Borden*, vol. 1, p. 204.
65 Borden, *Memoirs*, vol. 1, p. 75; and ibid., vol. 1, p. 300, and vol. 2, p. 463.
66 Ibid., vol. 1, p. 330; and PAC, Grey of Howick *papers*, vol. II, pp. 2986-90, Grey to Bryce, Oct. 12, 1911.

CHAPTER 9

The Peacetime Minister, 1911-1914

Hughes wasted no time in impressing his military philosophy on all departmental members. A week after he got Borden's nod, at his first Militia Council meeting he made it abundantly clear to the Chief of the General Staff, Major-General Colin Mackenzie, and the rest of his headquarters staff who were also the military members of the council, that he would expand the role of the volunteer citizen-soldier and confine the Permanent Force soldiers to instructional duties. It was an ominous portent; but it was also one which all these regular officers knew was shared by militia advocates other than Sam Hughes both in Canada and in Great Britain.[1]

Within the month, the Minister started along his declared policy direction. He had told his Militia Council at the first meeting that he intended sometime in the next thirty days to bring together in Ottawa prominent citizens and militia soldiers from across the Dominion to consult on militia matters. Then he took off on a whirlwind tour of his charges in the west, accompanied by a host of reporters and the Chief of the General Staff. During the trip the new Minister formulated the details of his Militia Conference, conveniently slated to start on November 16, the day the new Parliament opened. He also sent a constant flow of ideas and orders back to the capital, setting down the questions for the meeting's agenda and substantially increasing the numbers of invited guests.[2] Once back in Ottawa, he ordered planning for the Militia Conference to proceed at full steam. The delegates, the Minister advised, should submit their suggestions beforehand and bring their court dress so that the entire group could officially witness

---

Reference notes for Chapter 9 are found on pp. 151-53.

the tenth Governor-General, Queen Victoria's youngest son Arthur, Duke of Connaught, open Parliament.

When the group met for the conference, there appeared to be a new mood of co-operation and consultation between the department and its citizen-soldiers. Hughes told his assembled guests that because he was new in the office he wanted to meet them all and to hear their suggestions about military matters, although in fact he had already laid down much of what was to be discussed.

The Minister's long list of topics is the best policy statement of his peacetime ministry. The citizenry and the militia, he thought, should be brought much closer together. In preparation for this fusion, he asked for opinions on such things as establishing a University Officer Training Corps and the building of more drill halls in the smaller militia centres, especially those serving the rural battalions. He emphasized rifle shooting for civilians and better ways to incorporate cadets into the militia structure; he wanted to enhance the military influence at the lower levels of education and to arm the cadets. He asked questions about the establishment of provisional schools of instruction in local centres to make it easier for the non-permanent militiamen to qualify for promotion, and about ways to encourage the closer co-operation between municipalities and their local militia units in sharing defence costs.

Hughes was an engaging host. The wit and charm that had served him so well on the hustings was not lost on the delegates. He could call nearly every representative by his first name as he circulated through the various seminar groups. The delegates welcomed Hughes' proposals; he was talking to the converted. Most of them were non-permanent soldiers and some prominent citizens, men like the Lieutenant-Governor of Ontario, J. M. Gibson, Hughes' brothers, James and John Hughes, and Liberal Senator L. G. Power. The regular soldiers at the conference were few and said little, or were asked to say little. Consequently, the endorsement of the Minister's proposals was nearly unanimous, as was the spontaneous "three hearty cheers for the minister" that ended the meeting.[3]

It appeared that Sam Hughes was off to a good start. Before closing the meeting, he had recommended that similar conferences be held and had proposed, and got unanimous support for, the creation of one military group for the Dominion to speak for the various organizations, such as the Canadian Defence League, and the artillery, cavalry, and infantry associations, all of which had representatives at the meeting. According to the Minister, the new body would be the ultimate step in promoting military virtues in civilian society and in keeping advisory contact with the militia minister.

Although no umbrella defence association developed out of the resolution of the conference until long after Sam Hughes had passed from the scene (the Conference of Defence Associations was created in 1932), his 1911 meeting can be viewed as the genesis of the later group. The Minister did fulfill his promises to have another military gathering in Ottawa. Held during the last week of February in 1913, it was designed to exploit the martial enthusiasm of Paardeberg Week, the anniversary of the Canadian victory over the Boers thirteen years earlier. The Minister had invited no less a personage than the Duke of Connaught to add to the glitter and prestige. Ministerial invitations had also gone to a much wider circle of citizen groups, such as from the Women's Christian Temperance Union. Again the citizens and part-time soldiers traded ideas on the best ways to promote their particular interests within Hughes' amorphous militia philosophy. The few regular soldiers said little because in face of the overwhelming ministerial show they had little to contribute. Nor were many questions asked of the regulars, especially about permanent forces. Most delegates went away satisfied with the frank discussion. The wide national coverage pleased military-preparedness advocates and Conservative politicians, who knew the value of advertising, and in particular the value of Hughes' efforts. While these gatherings had a spectacular social side, they did promote honest exchanges of military ideas, ideas that Canadians had been ignoring for years.[4]

Bringing his converts to Ottawa was only the beginning of what Hughes had in mind for the militia. During the same two and a half years, he took his message directly to the people. With one eye on publicity and one on his message, he accepted most invitations to speak in public, and his willingness to talk made him a favourite if controversial guest from coast to coast. In getting to various destinations, the Minister's whirlwind railroad trips were events in themselves. Aboard his private railcar, and often in the uniform of a full colonel of the Canadian militia, Hughes cut an impressive figure. For the bigger tours, he took a bevy of newspapermen along, reporters like the young Arthur R. Ford of the Tory Winnipeg *Telegram*, whose reports nearly always projected the image of Hughes as a dynamic, no-nonsense man full of good humour, originality, and hard work. The Minister's attractive image also had its negative side: Sam Hughes' popularity meant that his ministry was seldom scrutinized by his colleagues; it also heightened the independent and head-strong tendencies that Borden had worried about when he made him minister. To a party newly arrived in power and based on a fragile and quickly decaying alliance, however, such outward appearances of strength were important.[5]

The message Hughes had for Canadians was always the same: the value of military education in building a strong moral character, and the necessity of developing an efficient, part-time volunteer militia to promote national growth and to defend Canada and the Empire. While addressing audiences from Victoria to Halifax, he emphasized the classless, voluntary, and democratic nature of a part-time force as opposed to the "militarism" of professional armies. In doing so he warned the Permanent Force that its only role was as teachers for the militia. In 1912, for instance, he wrote in *Canadian Defense* that there were three major foci of national morality: the schools, the churches, and the militia. He often expressed surprise that Canadians could spend more money to prosecute crime than to support the militia which would prevent most social evils. Sometimes carried away with his own rhetoric, he even told the Board of Trade of the Eastern Townships in 1913 that war always produced periods of national brilliance in any country.[6]

In his crusade to promote the militia, Hughes did not neglect Parliament or the cabinet. Early in 1912 he circulated a series of memoranda to his cabinet colleagues based primarily on his ideas enunciated at the first Militia Conference a few months before. Since these notes were enclosed along with his substantially enlarged militia budget estimates, Hughes was also clearly trying to justify his spending proposals to the cabinet. To support his case, he could point to the endorsement of his ideas—and implicitly their attending costs—by the delegates of the Militia Conference.[7] The Militia Minister seems to have encountered no serious opposition within the cabinet over his first estimates. Their hopes for militia patronage and his popularity allowed him to go vigorously on his own way. Indeed, in February 1912, he had versions of his cabinet memoranda distributed to every member of Parliament. One outlined the value of cadet corps training for national defence; another exposed the role of intemperance as a major cause of crime and demonstrated how martial discipline could curb it. Military training, Hughes claimed with absolute conviction, was the panacea for the ills of society. One classic example of Hughes' rhetoric reveals particularly well the Minister's sweeping and unsubstantiated generalizations:

The Canadian militia upbuilds manhood, defends homes and loved ones, supplies teachers and instructors all over Canada for the cadet corps, Boy Scouts, physical training, training of school teachers, schools of military instruction and at times police; upbuilds youth—mentally, morally, physically; instills the spirit of obedience, discipline, patriotism, veneration and love for principle; preserves the spirit for liberty and independence and keeps the old flag flying to the breezes and trains boys to be an asset to the nation.[8]

An interesting corollary to the Minister's appreciation of civil-military integration was his creation of advisory committees for the headquarters staff. These bodies were composed of important civilians supposedly with special educational or administrative expertise who were "likely to promote general efficiency in the militia." The experts were rewarded with an honorary rank which previously had been given only to those who had had military service; Hughes simply sidestepped the existing conventions by changing the militia regulations.[9] He formed committees on railways, small arms, remounts, cadet corps and youth training; and their membership included his brother, James Hughes, chief inspector of Toronto's public schools, Sir Charles Ross of rifle fame, and Adam Beck, promoter of hydro-electric power for Ontario's Conservative government. If the Minister's idea was to contribute to the efficiency of the militia, the benefits for his party also loomed large. Most of the positions were given to fellow Tories of their sympathizers or to important men Hughes wanted to flatter. In 1913, he commissioned twenty-six honorary full colonels or lieutenant-colonels, a great many more than his predecessor F. W. Borden. And Hughes' choices were much more obviously partisan.[10] These peacetime commissions, however, were harmless bits of political favouritism not unexpected from militia ministers, before or after Sam Hughes.

In 1912, when Hughes laid his first annual militia report before the House, he made the object of his activity clear: "the one object to be sought is preparedness for war."[11] He envisaged an entire society prepared in a basic military way, not an unprepared society defended by an elite group of professionals. In pursuit of this, one of the most important things he did before the war was to make much more money and men available to the militia. Spending in the department increased from $7 million during Borden's last full year as minister to over $12 million under Hughes in 1913. Although, during this time, some departments did not increase their spending substantially, Hughes' ministry was one of eight that made large increases. In his 1914 estimates, he asked for even more, but with a general decline in government spending, he received a little less than in 1913.[12] At the same time, Hughes greatly enlarged the non-permanent force, until in the summer of 1914 there were 59,000 men undergoing training. He also increased the number of days of militia training,[13] with less time to be spent on parade drill and more on practical field skills. The pay rate for enlisted men was put on a graduated scale to encourage the recruits to fulfill their required three-year enlistment, and efficiency pay of fifteen cents a day was added as a further inducement to mitigate the chronic turnover in the non-permanent ranks.[14] All of these were much needed reforms for creating a more battle-worthy militia. Although few appreciated that fact when the Great War broke out, the Minister's improvements had made the Canadian militia better prepared to fight than it had been in any other previous conflict.

There were many other items of ministerial reform before the outbreak of war. The irregular soldiers got most of the benefits, while the permanent corps actually dwindled in numbers. By March 1913 the decline was so serious that the Adjutant-General, Major-General François Lessard, complained in the Militia Council that the entire force had been adversely affected. Hughes did not agree; he rebutted that the numbers were down only about 250 men. However, Lessard's figures showed clearly that the regulars had fallen off by twice that number, from 3,520 to 2,996 in all ranks.[15] While one reason for the decline may have been the Minister's dislike of the predominantly British-born makeup of the regulars, most likely Hughes simply did not see the need for a large force of regulars; their existence other than as instructors was incompatible with his militia vision. How Hughes reconciled the reductions with the need for more instructors to attain the desired level of battle-worthiness for his expanded militia remains a mystery.

The Minister's preference for his militiamen was never clearer than in his budgets. Between 1911 and 1914, he nearly doubled the amount of money spent on the militia's annual drills, clothing, equipment and stores, while money spent on the permanent corps decreased slightly. Since Hughes believed that the militia would never be efficient if it did not have local training and storage facilities, he initiated a construction program for local armouries and drill halls across the Dominion. By 1914 over fifty had been built, with Hughes correctly reassuring anyone who would listen that these buildings could enhance company-level training and fulfillment of the three-year enlistment term for the non-permanent force. Again the Minister saw the value of this program as more than military. It would stimulate preparedness, encourage local youth training, and, in the words of his Military Secretary, "serve as a public hall, a place of meeting for many local activities not necessarily restricted to members of the militia." By 1914 Hughes had nearly doubled the amount of money which Sir Frederick Borden had spent on construction, buildings, works, and engineering services. In fact, this category showed the largest actual increase of any in Hughes' total expenditure for 1913-1914, including such vital military stores as ordnance, arms, and equipment.[16]

Cadet corps were another of Hughes' major concerns. In 1912 he reorganized and expanded their numbers in each military district and division; he also established a directorate of cadet services under his militia friend, Lieutenant-Colonel R. J. Gwynne, on the headquarters staff at Ottawa. Hughes then began to train both male and female instructors. By the end of 1912, 544 had been certified. That year he also established cadet corps camps run by the Militia Department, and got 7,000 boys under canvas. The number of cadets increased from about 20,000 to 45,000 between 1911 and 1914, and Hughes' budget for the cadets went from a modest $93,000 in 1912 to a whopping $400,000 in the next twelve months, the largest proportional increase of any category in the militia expenditure of 1913 and 1914. Hughes did not stop there. For some time he had been thinking about attaching cadet and reserve battalions directly to the units of the Active Militia, and at the second Militia Conference in late February 1913, he publicly announced the program. The next step was to arm the cadets. Hughes ordered several thousand twenty-two calibre miniature Ross rifles for the cadet corps. Besides being a substantial contract for Sir Charles Ross, the weapons were intended to teach the cadets marksmanship, the promotion of which had undergone a substantial revival in the Empire since the Boer war.[17]

The Minister's plans for expansion covered other areas. After the Inspector-General had complained in his annual report in 1911-1912 of a serious lack of training ground areas, Hughes instituted a scheme to acquire land for that purpose. Not only did he want to fulfill an immediate need; he also wanted to provide a long-term foundation for building his militia structure. This meant land for military use if crises arose. In 1913 he and the Premier of New Brunswick signed an agreement transferring 100,000 acres to the militia department, land that later became the military training grounds surrounding Gagetown. The next year the land that became the Valcartier Camp during the Great War was acquired under a similar deal.[18] In the future, in both peace and war, these two areas proved their worth, thanks to Hughes' foresight.

In 1910 the British Inspector-General had recommended that the number of Canadian units be increased; and Hughes took the suggestion seriously. The pressing need was in the west and there he created both infantry and mounted rifle corps. Across Canada he added not only combat but also new service units such as the Non-Permanent Ordnance Corps. C. F. Winter credits Hughes directly for the expansion of the Non-Permanent Canadian Army Service Corps and the mechanical transport services.[19] From all of this one thing is also obvious: Hughes wanted to improve everyone but the regular soldier. He ignored Sir John French's other most important recommendation: that the Permanent Force be enlarged to fill adequately its "field efficiency, and at the same time properly supervise the training and instruction of the Active Militia."[20] Sam Hughes did not include the regulars in his schemes of reform. He had, however, no such aversions concerning arsenals and rifle ranges.

For many years Hughes had considered the facilities of the Dominion Arsenal near Quebec City to be inadequate. Shortly after coming to office, he had confided to Edward Kemp, Minister without Portfolio from Toronto and a close advisor of the Prime Minister, his desire to build other government munitions plants inland at more defensible locations than the one on the Plains of Abraham. It would be a start to a series of regional arsenals more befitting his decentralized militia scheme. The first was to be built in Lindsay, Ontario. It would be, as he claimed in straining a point, central in the province and on good rail lines. The location was also in his home town and smack in the middle of his constituency. However justified, the construction could not be taken seriously by the public beyond its specific patronage function; and for this reason, Hughes likely could convince neither his headquarters staff nor his cabinet colleagues to accept an expensive second factory when the old Quebec arsenal could answer Canada's needs. Nevertheless, Hughes pushed the scheme hard but vainly in 1912. As a first step, he had a critical look at the original arsenal in the spring of 1913.

Hughes had predicted, again to Kemp, that he would double the militia consumption of rifle and gun ammunition under his enlarged militia plans. He had also heard complaints from both militiamen and civilian shooters about the quality of the Quebec arsenal ammunition. Since imperial authorities were then updating the basic pattern of rifle cartridges, the time was right for an arsenal review. To do it as fast as possible and get the new round into production, the Minister secured War Office ammunition experts to inspect the arsenal. They found production unsettled, organization bad, and great quantities of rifle ammunition defective and too dangerous to use. In spite of substantial pressure from his own cabinet colleagues, Hughes promptly put the plant on a more orderly basis by dismissing its superintendent and creating the first military inspection services there. In the meantime, the condemnation of millions of .303 cartridges temporarily cost the militia nearly all its reserve holdings. But the Minister was confident these could be built up quickly.[21]

Strangely enough for a man convinced that the Dominion Arsenal was vulnerable to sea attack and should be moved inland, less than a year before these reforms Hughes had tried to convince his cabinet colleagues that substantial ammunition contracts should be let out to Sir Charles Ross, whose factory was also at Quebec City and not far from the Dominion plant. Ross had recently expanded into the rifle cartridge business. In the short run, Hughes got neither his Lindsay plant nor any contracts for Sir Charles, but the Dominion Arsenal did reap substantial benefit from his reforms, and the ministry continued to allocate funds in support of rifle-range construction from coast to coast. The immense Connaught Rifle Range north of Ottawa, finished in 1914, was one of the best examples of the Minister's moves to encourage militia and civilian marksmanship.[22]

How did Tory MPs react to Hughes' peacetime program after two and a half years? His fellow cabinet ministers did not seem to strenuously object to much of it. Aside from the occasional embarrassing public outburst by Hughes, most of his colleagues thought little about his department except when it could satisfy their patronage requirements. Certainly this appeared to be the case with Edward Kemp. One of his duties for the Prime Minister was to make sure that the relations between Ottawa and the Ontario federal Tory party association, especially in Toronto, were kept healthy and well greased. Hughes did all he could to co-operate with Kemp by ensuring that militia patronage went to the appropriate party faithful, who immediately after the election in 1911 were not at all reluctant to remind their federal MPs of that duty.[23] Less than two months after gaining his portfolio, Hughes assured Kemp that John Willison of the Toronto *News* would receive his share of government advertising. As Hughes said, "I believe the only one [contract] my department has yet sent out was sent first to his newspaper." Hughes also was careful to consult Kemp before placing firms on the Ontario patronage list. In turn, Kemp seemed satisfied with Hughes' co-operation and even told him to deal directly in patronage matters with A. R. Birmingham, the chief organizer of the Liberal-Conservative Association of Toronto and by 1914 the official organizer of the whole province. All that Kemp asked was to be sent a copy of the final correspondence when the two men had made a patronage deal. Obviously the arrangements worked well.[24]

Apparently Hughes also had a very good relationship with fellow Tory and Orangeman Edmund Bristol, MP for Toronto Centre, who was even more prominent than Kemp in dispensing favours in Ontario. He was a major organizer in Toronto, especially among wealthy Tory businessmen; often Bristol acted as the liaison between the Whitney party machine and the federal party. Frequently he approached Hughes for party favours and Hughes did not hesitate to reciprocate. It seems that Hughes helped keep the connection with the powerful Ontario Tory wing running smoothly, and generally most of them supported him because he did so[25]; and because he did so, the other members of the cabinet were more willing than they might otherwise have been to let him spend money on the militia.

There is little doubt that Sam Hughes used the vigour of his administration to consolidate his party position and to remind other Tory MPs that his program was a powerful aid to the party and to their political fortunes. And legitimate praise often came his way. After receiving congratulations from R. B. Bennett on the success of his militia efforts out west, Hughes bragged to Kemp that "an analysis of the vote of 21 of September last [1911], all over Canada shows that wherever there was a prosperous corps of the militia the vote was strongly increased for the Conservative cause." Everyone knew the party was not strong in Alberta and Saskatchewan, and Hughes went on to remind Kemp that "there were at least 200 places throughout the northwest ... where the people are anxious to establish militia corps."[26] One of the clearest testimonials of 1914 came from the Liberal-Conservative Association of Carleton County in Ontario expressing thanks for "the magnificent new rifle range" Hughes had built there, and grandiloquently adding that the range was a monument creditable to the Dominion, and "to the Imperialism of our present Minister of Militia and Defense, Colonel the Honourable Sam Hughes, and that our sense of gratitude is especially due to him (and through him to the government).[27] Criticism, when it came, came from elsewhere.

Like all cabinet members, the Militia Minister had his critics in the press and in the House. Hughes had more than most, however, and he thrived on it. Usually his detractors felt his policy was too expensive, too militaristic, and blatantly partisan.[28] Both the Liberal spleen of *Globe* editors and the French-Canadian nationalist passions of *Le Devoir* often made him a target. In denouncing the new cadet corps program in 1912, Henri Bourassa charged that Hughes "has invited 25,000 schoolboys to go and make exercises in the fields and train to become debauchees and play the fool at the expense of the state. He has drawn a map of the country as a vast field for manoeuvre where he proposes to enroll the nation and teach them democratically the art of shooting human game at a convenient distance."[29]

Opposition bench criticism of Hughes was always present. In 1914 E. W. Nesbitt, the Liberal member for North Oxford, was so upset that he claimed Hughes was ruining the country with his military madness. The Minister, he warned, "is absolutely obsessed with militarism: it is his one thought and aim from the time he gets up in the morning until he goes to bed at night."[30] Hughes invariably denied that he was militaristic, defiantly rebutting that war was inevitable and had to be prepared for. Convinced that military training created healthy social values in individuals, he insisted that "militarism was the antithesis of what he sought."[31]

The Minister often repeated that he would like to model the Canadian force after the Swiss militia which he greatly admired. In particular he liked the idea of imposing a head tax on all those who avoided military training, an idea that contradicted his views on democracy and voluntarism. The inconsistency did not bother Hughes, if he even recognized it. He was also in favour of having the municipalities contribute financially to the local militia; as far as he was concerned, he would never apologize for one dollar that he spent on the militia. In January 1913 he proclaimed to a Montreal audience that he should really be called "Minister of Peace rather than Minister of War," for one object of his department was to prevent war by training youth and the militia to be upstanding citizens. "I don't find in the history of nations," he added, "that war is averted by being unprepared." He was not alone in holding this view. Some influential military groups supported preparedness, or their version of it. Both the Canadian Infantry Association and the Ontario Artillery Association had already passed motions advocating conscription. Men like Senator James Mason, president of the Home Bank of Canada, were conducting similar campaigns. While Hughes shared their views on preparedness, he remained a staunch advocate of the voluntary principle of military training.[32]

Hughes' announcement that he was ending drinking privileges in the militia camps embroiled him in yet another controversy. Long a temperance advocate, since coming to office he had become increasingly aware of the rising mood of prohibition, especially in Ontario where Whitney was trying to take a moderate stand on the issue with his "local option" tactic. In late 1911 prohibitionists—Ontario Methodists in particular—were pressuring Hughes to declare the militia dry. Seven months later, when some newspapers carried reports that drunkenness was rife among soldiers at the annual camp at Niagara held in June 1912, Hughes vehemently denied it in a letter to the *Globe*. But his goal, he promised, was to achieve a militia with every man a trained soldier and a total abstainer.[33] Any such prohibition alarmed Hughes' headquarters staff who knew that with present canteen rules they could at least control consumption and thereby discipline. They told him so, but Hughes was not anxious to listen. Canteens were now to be dry. No doubt Hughes, himself a Methodist, could see the political advantage for the federal party in coming out strongly against alcohol. The Militia Minister's stand was popular with temperance advocates: the Women's Christian Temperance Union of London, Ontario, passed a resolution thanking Hughes for his solid administration of the militia and for preserving the honour and purity of manhood by imposing a ban on wet canteens.[34]

On the other hand, Hughes lost some support among militiamen. At the Militia Conference in 1913, he arbitrarily ended the debate on the issue by curtly telling the delegates, who thought they were there to establish a new dialogue with the militia department, that "so long as I am minister . . . there never will be allowed . . . any wet messes. You will kindly not waste time discussing this question further. It is settled."[35] In reaction to the Minister's dictate, Lieutenant-Colonel Sir Henry Pellatt showed far more wisdom than Hughes. Sir Henry told the Toronto *World* that "temperance advocates are doing a thousand times more harm in stopping canteens than any good they hope to accomplish. The control of the conduct and drinking of the men is now entirely out of the hands of the proper authorities."

The regular soldiers had more reason to be upset with the Minister. He resented the tradition of the wet messes in the Permanent Force, and once publicly labelled all members of the regular force "bar room loafers," an utterance which received more than the usual comments in the press about the Minister's intemperate tongue. In fairness to Hughes, the label was appropriate for the gathering in Halifax in 1913. According to Arthur Ford, several regular-force officers of the garrison over-fortified themselves in preparation for one of the Minister's dry military dinners, and ended up insulting one of Hughes' teetotalling friends. Hughes, not surprisingly, became the satirized figure of a favourite militia ditty—"Do ye ken Sam Hughes / he's the foe of booze"—which was sung in the militia camps where far more harmful unsupervised drinking undoubtedly took place. In the end Lieutenant-Colonel Pellatt was correct, but Hughes' stubborn decision did little to hurt him politically among the temperance people.[36]

In the late summer of 1912, Hughes managed to involve himself in another fracas by taking a group of militia officers and their wives overseas, at the government's expense, to attend British and European manoeuvres. Such educational trips for a few Canadian professional soldiers had long been departmental policy. Hughes explained to the Commons that now he would send militiamen, "the real fighters," at a much reduced cost. Publicly he promised to choose only those officers he considered to be the most efficient. Besides the obvious educational value, the Minister declared, the honour of being picked to go overseas would encourage the remainder of the militiamen to achieve higher standards of efficiency. It was also true that at least four of the six officers were Tories, and only one, Colonel G. S. Maunsell, was from the Permanent Force.[37]

Not everyone agreed that Hughes selected the most efficient soldiers for the overseas visits, least of all the headquarters staff officers. Unable to move Hughes, they apparently primed the Governor-General who had more than his share of an inclination to interfere in military affairs. Spouting dire warnings of political disaster directly to Borden over what he called Hughes' lavish waste of public funds, the Field Marshal insisted such visits must stop. Connaught's political perceptions were somewhat overblown. Knowing that most Canadians were indifferent to such activities, Borden did nothing except defend Hughes. The headquarters staff winced but could do little. Nevertheless, the former Inspector-General of the Canadian militia, Sir Percy Lake, confided to his old friend, W. D. Otter, then holding that office, that he was "amused at the tail the minister took with him at the English manoeuvres"; and secretly the Chief of the General Staff, Major-General Colin Mackenzie, with more spleen than appreciation of his own correct assessment, bitterly objected both to the Duke of Connaught and to Sir John French in England that Hughes was violating his own dictum about the role of the permanent corps as instructors. If no regulars had the educational experience of attending the overseas manoeuvres, their role as teachers would be seriously eroded.[38] But the Minister remained adament: more Canadian militia soldiers were going to be involved at the higher levels of both training and staff.

While in Britain on the first visit in 1912, Hughes made up his mind to continue and to expand the program. He arranged with Colonel J. E. B. Seely, the new Secretary of State for War, to have a senior British territorial soldier, the equivalent of Hughes' non-permanent militiamen, come to Canada in 1913 to command a cavalry brigade at the annual camp at Petawawa. Lord Brooke was the eldest son of the Earl of Warwick, a friend of Hughes, and more importantly the private secretary to Sir John French, the Chief of the Imperial General Staff and a man Hughes wanted to impress. After the 1913 exchange, the Minister gloated to Seely that never before had the Canadian cavalry learned so much as it had under Brooke, a claim which seemed hard to substantiate. Hughes gave the British War Secretary other reasons for perpetuating the exchanges: they reduced the very severe strain put on Canadian loyalty by the outrageous conduct of British regular officers in Canada. Presumably he meant men like Hutton, Herbert, and especially Colin Mackenzie, who had recently resigned after a terrible row with the Minister. Hughes wanted such exchanges of "decent fellows" made permanent, and he proposed to Seely that the British reciprocate by sending entire battalions of British territorials to Canada. It would improve both forces, he argued, as well as have a beneficial imperial effect. Whatever Seely or his soldiers thought of Hughes' experiments, it was not recorded in the War Minister's reply to Sam Hughes.[39] The War Minister did not endorse the transfer of British territorials to Canada, nor did he discourage having the Canadians come to Britain. Surely Sir John French would have seen little real military value for his troops in such expensive large-scale exchanges, although allowing Brooke to go at least let the Chief of the Imperial General Staff have a first-hand account of what was going on in Canada. For the British it cost little, moreover, they could do little, and at least the trips were a means of maintaining the twin processes of military anglicization and imperial integration. So in 1913 Hughes returned to England with a politically mixed bag of militia officers and optimistically promised an entire brigade of citizen-soldiers for the next year if possible.[40] That year was 1914 and more than a brigade of Canadians would go overseas, but not for the reasons Sam Hughes had imagined.

For some time Hughes had been sure that war with Germany was inevitable and in the not-too-distant future. Many Canadian leaders, including the Prime Minister, shared his growing anxiety about the German threat. Indeed, their appreciation of a Teutonic peril was probably heightened by Hughes' constant exhortations for increased budgets and military preparation. Since advocates of preparation need a reason to be prepared, Hughes' utterances then took on a new relevance. So it must have been with his party's proposal in 1912 for a direct cash contribution to the British navy for the construction of three dreadnought battleships. Even though he hardly spoke on the naval issue in the House, his views were never in doubt and were essentially the same as in the debate of 1909-1910.[41] However, Hughes' public speeches on the subject of the navy and war often caused some irritation, especially at a very sensitive time in Canada's and Britain's relations with Germany.

The Militia Minister's most controversial outburst came in 1912 during a Vancouver address in which he hinted at a pre-emptive military strike by the Empire forces against Germany. Reaction was swift. When many newspapers criticized his comments, the Governor-General requested that the Prime Minister stop Hughes from making such alarmist statements.[42] For their part, the Liberals distributed the Vancouver speech widely in preparation for three by-elections scheduled for Ontario and Quebec in 1913. The damning message for the predominantly French- and German-Canadian constituents of these three ridings was that the Tories either were the willing tools of the English-Canadian imperialists or were anti-German. Though the Conservatives' fortunes seemed rosy when they won six of seven federal by-elections in 1913, in one of the Ontario ridings, South Bruce, the Tory candidate was unexpectedly defeated. The cause, according to several Ontario Tory sources, was Hughes' west-coast comments. A few top party members, like Kemp and Birmingham, quietly complained among themselves that Hughes seemed erratic and unreliable for the promotion of good party relations in the province. But the public knew little of this; and in the end Borden let Hughes' other political merits decide: he supported the Militia Minister.[43]

Borden's cabinet was a fragile coalition, and the rejection by the veteran party MPs of certain parts of it, especially the French-Canadians, set in soon after the 1911 victory.[44] The situation might have escaped public scrutiny had the Liberal opposition not been so quick to exploit it. As an important member of the old Tory party, Hughes had a decisive role to play. It was not that he particularly or publicly singled out any of his confrères for direct criticism. But clearly his often and vigorously expressed views on imperialism and the navy, for example, were in stark contrast to those expressed by Monk and other French-Canadian Tory MPs in their own province. Laurier spotted these anomalies quickly. He pointed to the "two warring factions of the Conservative Party ... to Mr. Monk and to Colonel Hughes, to nationalists and the Imperialists."[45] Though the Prime Minister no doubt privately cautioned his Militia Minister to tread softly in public on various controversies potentially harmful to the government, Borden seemed unable and unwilling to heal the widening schism between his French and English ministers. The reasons are complex. One was that he had little understanding of the French-Canadian mind, hence quickly lost patience with men like Monk; another was Borden's precarious political situation. Above all the Prime Minister wanted his naval aid legislation to pass, and he dared not alienate the powerful Ontario section of the federal caucus which included Hughes. Party discipline became harder to maintain, and the already unequal factions within the cabinet became more lopsided.

A similar situation arose over the Ontario schools issue. In June 1912 Whitney's government announced its new provincial language policy, called Regulation 17, restricting French-language instruction in Ontario schools. Bitter debate followed. Many French-Canadian MPs were alarmed and bewildered at what to them was a threat posed to their culture by English-speaking members of their own party. Once again Borden dared not challenge the much-needed Whitney administration over the legislation. In October 1912 the sick and frustrated Minister of Public Works, F. D. Monk, resigned his cabinet post over the combined naval and education issues; and Borden appeared almost glad to accept it.[46] Without any strong repudiation of the Ontario government's stand, men with views like Sam Hughes' appeared to have been given silent approval. In contrast to his French-Canadian colleagues, the Militia Minister had strongly supported for many years both a public school system and English as the sole language of instruction in it; and for just as many years, Hughes had had a growing reputation as an enthusiastic Ontario Orangeman and a champion, as Henri Bourassa had decided a decade earlier, of "race hatred."

There can be little doubt that Sam Hughes did not entirely deserve all of the charges brought against him by men like Bourassa. Sometimes, however, Hughes made cabinet life needlessly stormy and undermined Tory fortunes in Quebec with his strong secular and Anglo-Canadian views. According to Mason Wade, one good example of the disruptive effect in the cabinet was the row caused by the Militia Minister's refusal in June 1914 to allow the largely French-Canadian 65th Militia Battalion to march in the annual Corpus Christi celebration in Montreal. His refusal was a substantial flip-flop of his public position on such parades announced at the Militia Conference in 1911. Moreover, he nearly always allowed Anglo regiments to participate in Orange parades. The harried Borden finally arranged a compromise allowing the 65th to parade without arms. Later in the month, Hughes again aggravated cabinet relations when he denied the Régiment de Lévis the right to parade in honour of the newly consecrated Cardinal Bégin on his return to Quebec City from Rome.[47]

These were not the only episodes in which Hughes contributed to widening the cracks in the 1911 coalition. He also opposed civil service reform, and at the centre of this were the problems of government organization, patronage, and the new men Borden had brought into the party. Hughes' resistance stemmed from his concept of the role of the party and the government in society. Having served his apprenticeship in the rough-and-tumble world of Sir John Macdonald's constituent politics, many of Hughes' ideas were formed at a time when government organization was unsophisticated and needed to exercise few service functions in society. When they were needed, however, they were conveniently distributed in the form of rewards by individual MPs through the party structure directly to the constituency. Hope of dispensing such rewards also inspired men to gamble on running for otherwise unattractive public offices, the seeking of which imposed its own discipline on the pretender in party service. As Militia Minister, Sam Hughes had for years known of the close bond between party organization, political success, and patronage; and for years it had all worked well.

But Robert Borden did not share his Minister's faith in the old system's efficiency; he and his new men wanted reform. Once in office he immediately tackled the Public Service Commission by first appointing A. B. Morine, a Newfoundland Tory, then at George Perley's suggestion, a top English civil servant, Sir George Murray, to investigate both the service and the government's departments. The Prime Minister wanted more efficiency and co-operation. While this was going on, Borden authorized Kemp to probe the inner workings of each department. As suspected, all three investigations revealed wide variations in spending practices, little co-operation, and general chaos. Murray, in particular, said the only solution was to take appointments out of the hands of politicians and to closely control their departmental spending. Ministers, he strongly recommended, should direct but not try to execute policy as they often now did. Their load should be eased by taking on senior administrators as departmental undersecretaries. Murray also made it clear that if reform was to come, patronage would have to go.[48] But Hughes would have none of this.

The Militia Minister was not prepared to throw out the time-honoured system and refused to co-operate with Kemp. Like Robert Rogers and two other old-party cabinet men, Hughes never replied to the questionnaire Kemp used as the basis of his departmental investigation. Hughes would not support, as Murray had recommended, his departmental estimates and spending being controlled by the Department of Finance under Tom White, another new man and a former Grit to boot.[49]

In all fairness to Sam Hughes, there is no evidence of malfeasance on his part; he did not set out purposely to scupper the reforms or wreck the tender coalition of 1911. Nor was he alone in his attitude towards the political system. A recent study of Borden's tenure as head of the party from 1901 to 1920 maintains that the bulk of the veteran Tory MPs believed in the older system. After 1911 Borden himself quickly discovered that they were not willing to make radical departures from it. Borden, as John English points out, "withdrew almost entirely from party activities and permitted various ministers to build up their own personal fiefdoms whose existence he tried not to notice."[50]

In all Sam Hughes went his own way as a peacetime minister. He seemed popular, dynamic, progressive, and decisive. Yet his self-assumed high profile in the cabinet, his strong public opinions on controversial issues, his lack of understanding of French-Canada—a trait he shared with many colleagues including his indecisive leader— and a particular set of political circumstances born in the election campaign of 1911, all slowly enlarged Hughes' disruptive and independent tendencies. Although it was to be an assessment that received scant attention from most Canadians, ironically the clearest judgment on Sam Hughes as Militia Minister came from three Englishmen, all outside the government and the party: the Governor-General, the Chief of the General Staff, and the Imperial Inspector-General.

Reference Notes to Chapter 9

1 Berger, *The Sense of Power*, p. 234.
2 PAC, RG24, vol. 150, E. F. Jarvis to V. A. S. Williams, Oct. 24, 1911.
3 D. Hist. 500.009, *The Militia Conference, 1911*, transcripts of the general sessions, Nov. 16, 18, 1911, pp. 195-96.
4 PAC, RG9, II, A2, vol. 30, Minutes of the *Militia Council*, Oct. 10, 1911, hereafter cited Militia Council *Minutes. CAR*, 1911, pp. 347-50; ibid., 1913, pp. 213, 216; *Sessional Papers*, 1913, no. 1, Auditor-General's *Report*, 1911-1912, Militia and Defence expenditure, pp. 1-57; "Militia Conference," in *Canadian Defence* IV (Jan. 1913), p. 458, and "Recent Militia Conference" in *Canadian Defence* IV (Mar. 1913), pp. 489-90.
5 English, p. 61; and *CAR*, 1913, p. 25.
6 *CAR*, 1912, pp. 117-19, 176, 177, 293-97; ibid., 1913, pp. 216-17, 284; and Ford, pp. 84-90.
7 PAC, A. E. Kemp *papers*, MG27, II, D9, vol. 1, F5, Hughes to Kemp, Mar. 16, 1912; and ibid., vol. 14, F510, Hughes to Kemp, April 16, 1912, "Memo re cadet corps training."
8 *CAR*, 1912, p. 285.
9 *King's Regulations and Orders for the Canadian Militia*, 1910 (Ottawa: King's Printer, 1910), paragraphs 186-98 (paragraph 198 amended by G. O. 112, 1912, HQ. 970-1-3).
10 *Militia List*, 1913, pp. 6-8, pp. 721-22; and ibid., 1910, p. 589; and *Hansard*, 1911-1912, pp. 5447-50.
11 *Militia Report*, 1911-1912, p. 4.
12 Auditor-General's *report*, 1910-1911, Militia Expenditure, p. b-4, 1912-1913, p. b-6, and 1913-1914, p. b-6. Government expenditure increased from $122,801,064.64 in 1910-1911 to $186,053,919.07 in 1913-1914. *Hansard*, 1914, pp. 3428-29.
13 *Militia Report*, 1914-1915, p. 25. In 1912 Hughes' first year in office, 48,213, the largest number ever to train, went into camps; in 1913, there were 57,527. See *Militia Report*, 1912-1913, pp. 35, 85, 1913-1914, p. 7.

14 Ibid., 1912-1913, pp. 8, 9, 36; and Militia Council, *Minutes*, Nov. 28, 1911. Also see *Hansard*, 1911-1912, p. 5452 and 5447-47a for Hughes' first militia estimates.
15 Militia Council, *Minutes*, Mar. 19, 1913; also see *Militia Report*, 1912-1913, p. 37; and the Auditor-Generals' *reports*, 1910-1914, Militia Expenditure.
16 *Militia Reports*, 1913-1914, pp. 35-36; Winter, pp. 36-37; *Hansard*, 1914, pp. 3401-16; and Auditor-Generals' *reports*, 1910-1914, Militia Expenditure.
17 *Militia Report*, 1913-1914, pp. 28-30, 33-34; *CAR*, 1913, p. 716; Duguid, appendix III; and Auditor-Generals' *reports*, 1912-1914, Militia Expenditure.
18 *Militia Report*, 1911-1912, pp. 109-10; ibid., 1913-1914, pp. 82-83; and ibid., 1912-1913, pp. 85-86; *CAR*, 1913, p. 215.
19 For a detailed description of the expansions, see *Militia Report*, 1912-1913, pp. 1, 14, 19, 22, 97; ibid., 1913-1914, pp. 23-25; *Militia List*, 1913, p. 8; and Winter, p. 45.
20 *Sessional Papers*, 1911, no. 35b. "Reports upon the best method of Giving Effect to the Recommendations of General Sir John French, GCB, GCVO, Regarding the Canadian Militia," by Major-General Sir P. N. Lake, Inspector-General (Ottawa: King's Printer, 1910), p. 9.
21 PANS, F. W. Borden *papers*, LLB, no. 186, F1, p. 17608, Hughes to F. W. Borden, Aug. 7, 1913; Canada, Royal Commission on the Sale of Small Arms Ammunition, *Report* (Ottawa: King's Printer, 1917); and J. Mackay Hitsman, *Inspection Services in Canada* (Ottawa: Queen's Printer, 1959), p. 21.
22 PAC, Kemp *papers*, vol. 1, F5, Hughes to Kemp, June 14, 1912, "Ross Rifle Ammunition Memorandum"—Hughes wanted Ross paid a higher price for the same ammunition which could be produced at the government plant because "this is only fair." Also see *Hansard*, 1911-1912, pp. 5447-48a.
23 PAC, Kemp *papers*, vol. 1, F3, R. D. Greer to Kemp, Oct. 6, 1911; ibid., Kemp to Hughes, Dec. 1, 1911.
24 Ibid., vol. 10, F338, Hughes to Kemp, Dec. 4, 1911; ibid., vol. 1, F2, Birmingham to Kemp, Feb. 20, 1914; ibid., vol. 1, F5, Kemp to Hughes, Dec. 7, 1911; ibid., Fiset to Kemp, Nov. 27, 1911; and ibid., Fiset to Kemp, Mar. 24, 1914.
25 For examples, see PAO, Edmund Bristol *papers*, MU 284-86. Also see ibid., MU 286, Bristol to Birmingham, Jan. 14, 1915.
26 PAC, Kemp *papers*, vol. 14, F510, Hughes to Kemp, May 4, 1912.
27 Ibid., vol. 1, F5, Geo. Flewellyn to Hughes, Jan. 31, 1914, in Hughes to Kemp, Feb. 5, 1914.
28 *Hansard*, 1911-1912, pp. 5447-47a; and *CAR*, 1913, p. 25.
29 *CAR*, 1911, p. 302.
30 *Hansard*, 1914, pp. 3431, 3449-52, 4576-82, 4599-4627; for examples, see *CAR*, 1914, p. 211; ibid., 1912, pp. 286-87; and ibid., 1913, pp. 284-85.
31 *CAR*, 1912, pp. 286-87; ibid., p. 216. See Berger, *The Sense of Power*, pp. 257-58; and Alfred Vagts, *A History of Militarism, Civilian and Military* (New York: Free Press, 1967), pp. 1-37.
32 *Hansard*, 1914, pp. 3418-19; *CAR*, 1912, pp. 286-87; and ibid., 1913, p. 716.
33 *Hansard*, 1911-1912, p. 5462; *CAR*, 1913, p. 216; *Canadian Military Gazette*, June 25, 1912, pp. 6-7; and Margaret Prang, *N. W. Rowell, Ontario Nationalist* (Toronto: University of Toronto Press, 1975), chapters 7, 8.
34 *CAR*, 1913, pp. 217-21.
35 Ibid., p. 216.
36 Ibid., 1912, p. 287; ibid., 1913, p. 218; Morton, *The Canadian General*, pp. 309-10; and Ford, pp. 86-87.
37 *Hansard*, 1914, pp. 316-19, 3416-19; *CAR*, 1913, pp. 218, 718; and *Militia Report*, 1912-1913, appendix G, "Notes on British and French Manoeuvres, 1912," p. 114.
38 PAC, Otter *papers*, Lake to Otter, Oct. 16, 1912; PAC, RG7, no. 265, "A Brief Resumé of Militia Affairs in Canada During 1912," by C. G. S. Colin Mackenzie, Feb. 27, 1913, confidential; ibid., Connaught to Harcourt, Dec. 19, 1913; and ibid., Connaught to Borden, Dec. 3, 1913.
39 Nuffield College, Oxford University, Mottistone *papers*, 21, p. 17021, Hughes to Seely, July 16, 1913; and ibid., Seely to Hughes, July 29, 1913.
40 PAC, RG9, III, "CEF," 203320, HS-20-H-3, Hughes interview, London *Express*

(Eng.), Sept. 1, 1913. Also see Auditor-Generals' *report*, 1913, Militia Expenditure, p. 1-65. It cost $25,572.17 to send the 1913 group.
41 *Hansard*, 1913-1914, pp. 3349-401; and Capt. C. F. Cummins, "Imperial Conferences and Imperial Defence," in *Canadian Defence Quarterly* IV (Oct. 1926); *CAR*, 1911, p. 301; and ibid., 1912, pp. 47-48; and *Journals*, 1912-1913, pp. 311, 509, 604.
42 *CAR*, 1912, p. 61; ibid., 1913, pp. 285-88; and PAC, RG7, no. 265, Connaught to Borden, Dec. 3, 1913.
43 PAC, Kemp *papers*, vol. 10, Birmingham to Kemp, Nov. 30, 1913; Brown, *Borden*, vol. 1, pp. 254, 257; and PAC, RG7, no. 265, Borden to Connaught, Dec. 8, 1913.
44 English, pp. 80-85.
45 *CAR*, 1912, p. 47; and ibid., 1913, pp. 284-85.
46 Brown, *Borden*, vol. 1, pp. 246-47.
47 Mason Wade, *The French Canadians, 1760-1967* (Toronto: Macmillan, 1968), vol. 2, pp. 640-41.
48 PAC, Kemp *papers*, vol. 37, f4, "Committee of Council re purchasing in Government Departments"; ibid., Kemp to Borden, Jan. 11, 1912; and *Sessional Papers*, 1913, no. 57a, *Report on the Organization of the Public Service of Canada* (by George Murray).
49 Brown, *Borden*, vol. 1, p. 215; English, p. 75; J. E. Hodgetts, *et. al.*, *The Biography of an Institution: The Civil Service Commission of Canada, 1908-1967* (Montreal: McGill-Queen's University Press, 1972), chapters 1, 2. PAC, RG7, no. 265, Mackenzie to Hughes, July 15, 1912; and PAC, W. G. Gwatkin *papers*, MG30, G13, F2, copy of an unaddressed letter by Gwatkin, July 1, 1914; and Murray *report*, paragraphs 6-27.
50 English, pp. 74-76.

CHAPTER 10

The Critics

On the night of October 12, 1911, the *Empress of Ireland*, bearing the new Governor-General, the Duke of Connaught, docked at Quebec City. Grey, the departing head of state, secretly came aboard to give the Royal Prince his private impressions of Mr. Borden's six-day-old government. No doubt these frank comments included substantial reservations about Sam Hughes as Militia Minister. Whatever else transpired between the two aristocrats, Connaught was not long in portraying Sam Hughes as "an impossible fellow ... eaten up with conceits and ... very ignorant in military matters."[1] For his part, Hughes claimed that on the day he landed in Canada Connaught had snubbed the Minister and other members of the Militia Council.[2] Clearly their relationship had not got off to a good start, and did not take long to deteriorate further.

Nor was this all Hughes' fault. Connaught was overbearing and arrogant. In the five years he held his office, he ran it like one of his previous military commands, meddling in governmental and military affairs. He also preferred to listen to unhappy British soldiers in Canadian service and he quickly became a too willing tool of their plots against Sam Hughes. Forty years a British professional soldier, the Field Marshal could hardly have avoided knowledge of Hughes' bad reputation among some military men in England over his South African war record or his subsequent charges against the War Office. After being silent on the subject for several years, Hughes began in 1912 to pester the Field Marshal personally with his complaints about his war service. Finally in late December, he wrote a wearisome letter which contained all the old charges and some new demands, not the least which was a request for two Victoria Crosses. Besides the outlandish assertions, what fired the Duke's slow burn was Hughes' dispatch of the

---

Reference notes for Chapter 10 are found on pp. 174-76.

original of the controversial document directly to the War Office without consulting him—the official channel—first. The Duke was sent only a copy.[3]

Neither the War Office nor the Governor-General was willing to accept the Minister's claim. Connaught immediately crushed the appeal with a thinly disguised threat to the Prime Minister that he would reveal all the sordid details of Hughes' earlier dismissal, including the Militia Minister's often compromising efforts seeking redress in the past. Evidently such royal wrath was enough for Borden. No evidence exists that Hughes ever opened the case again. However, it is hard to imagine with his mercurial temperament that he did not resent Connaught's refusal to investigate what for him was a just cause.

The two men continued to quarrel about the smallest things. Clearly the audacious Hughes went out of his way to needle the Royal Prince. One night in Ottawa's Russell Theatre at a white-tie performance attended by the vice-regal couple, Hughes barged into the royal box dressed in a loud blue business suit and flaming red tie, talking all the while. To the delight of his admirers, the Duke refused to acknowledge the improperly dressed Hughes. The next day the Ottawa newspapers were alive with heated editorial letters both in defence of the Minister, whom some said was not tied down by narrow-minded convention, and of the Governor-General, whom others claimed was only protecting the social graces against the philistine Sam Hughes.[4]

Quarrels between Hughes and his humourless and strong-willed chief of staff, Colin Mackenzie, were as immediate as those between Hughes and Connaught, and their clashes often involved that familiar and thorny Canadian question: who rules in the militia and the ministry, the Minister or the General? The confrontation started with Hughes encouraging soldiers to contact him directly at any time on any question. While having dubious democratic and administrative benefits, this approach had a serious effect on militia discipline. By July 1912 Mackenzie was beside himself. Two incidents had been particularly frustrating. In Montreal Hughes' injudicious public comments about a case before the courts produced an innocent verdict for a militiaman charged with desertion; in Saskatoon the Minister publicly censored a commanding officer because he had dismissed a bugler who had broken ranks during a public parade to tear up an American flag being waved in his face—Hughes thought the man showed national spirit. In a militia that had an annual turn-over in excess of 50 per cent, discipline and fulfillment of terms were vital. Divisional commanders, Mackenzie acridly pointed out to the Minister, would no longer accept responsibility because their authority was often undermined by subordinates and the Minister. His plea was ignored.[5]

Even earlier that year, without consulting either his chief of staff or the Militia Council, Hughes had introduced legislation allowing

Active Militia officers to hold permanent ranks higher than that of colonel in peacetime. Clearly he wanted and needed to get more Canadian militia soldiers into these higher ranks as part of his planned changes in the headquarters staff. His legislation allowed for six major-generals, and in time he promoted four Canadians, W. D. Otter, D. A. Macdonald, C. W. Drury, and W. H. Cotton, all on the headquarters staff, as well as Mackenzie to the new rank. This had the advantage of opening their old posts to men of the Minister's choice. But Hughes left one position unfilled, a position he wanted for himself. Immediately after the bill passed, he drafted a general order recommending that the "President of the Militia Council"[6] be among those eligible for the new rank. Sam Hughes wanted to be a major-general as well as defence minister, a combination easily compatible with his distorted view of the dual responsibility of the citizen-soldier.

But for Mackenzie, Hughes' changes were a nightmare: Canadian militiamen now could be senior to the Chief of the General Staff; British influence might be lessened; and militia efficiency could be damaged by unqualified officers and patronage seekers. Mackenzie was right about one thing: the Militia Act never intended the civilian minister to be both soldier and politician or to exercise the role of each simultaneously.[7] Mackenzie decided to try to block his Minister's move. First he solicited Connaught's approval and advice. Once he got both, he lined up the French-Canadian regular François Lessard, the Adjutant-General, to carry the ball directly against Hughes on constitutional grounds. With Mackenzie conspicuously away from Ottawa when the stormy Militia Council meeting took place with Hughes that April, the almost eager Lessard, on written instructions from his Chief of the General Staff, argued that no civilian minister should have the highest substantive rank in the country. "It may be exercised . . . by the heads of states in Russia and Germany but by no individual I know of in the British Empire," Mackenzie had advised Lessard to say. Say it he did; and this time Hughes' attempt at self-promotion was foiled.[8]

Two months later, however, and again without discussion, the Minister successfully passed through the council another but less specific general order which made any member of the Militia Council with certain qualifications eligible for the rank of major-general. Hughes now had the legal channel to promote himself. The device of using a general order to get his own way was a cunning but dubious one. Usually issued only by the chief of the general staff, the Minister often drafted such orders and then *de facto* promulgated them without any prior consultation with his council. Consequently the chief of staff and his officers were frequently forced to approve simply because the orders were for practical purposes already in effect. In the case of promotion to major-general, Mackenzie protested the Minister's action as soon as it happened, but to no avail. By this time the Minister had enough supporters within the Militia Council to ignore Mackenzie if he chose, which he often did. But Hughes did not get the new rank until the opening days of war in 1914. Then he had the appointment made retroactive to May 1912, the date at which he obtained the legal machinery to do it. The reasons for the delay were probably political. It seems that he could not convince the Prime Minister: self-promotion was too blatant, too controversial, and it threatened to upset the proper flow of authority from civilians to soldiers. Whatever the cause, in June 1913 Hughes explained to the Governor-General that even though F. W. Borden and others had "over and over again . . . approached him to become a major-general . . . , for reasons of his own he has so far refused it."9

The question of promotion was not the end of the conflict between the two men. In June 1912, when Hughes again heard that the chief of staff had been corresponding privately with Government House officials about departmental affairs, the Minister went into a rage, demanding that Mackenzie not do it again. But some of Hughes' fury was also reserved for Connaught. At a recent Montreal review, the arrogant Duke had offended the Minister's fragile pride when he would not seat the Minister next to him. Hughes warned the Duke that "under our laws every parade whether in uniform or otherwise is official and the Minister of Militia and Defence for Canada is . . . entitled to due recognition when in military uniform or state uniform or mufti." It may be true that Sam Hughes sometimes masked his strong pride with charges of violated national honour. But at the same time he was correct. The Duke's spokesman had denied that there had been, or would ever be, any collusion between the Governor-General and the chief of staff.10 This was simply not true; and in light of continuing rumours that it was so, the response had little calming effect on Hughes. Certainly the reports heightened his suspicion that both the General and the Duke were treating Canadians and their process of government with a great deal of disdain.

Later that month Sam Hughes had his first opportunity to inspect the militia units turned out for the annual camps that year. Much to the chagrin of the chief of staff, who did not want the Minister on such trips, Hughes did so enthusiastically and in uniform, and was highly critical of what he saw. When he returned to Ottawa, he immediately wrote to Mackenzie criticizing the state in which he found officer training in the militia. Militia officers, reluctant to incur the separation or expense of attending the permanent schools of instruction, he pointed out, would be better trained if more local provisional schools were established. Whether or not the chief of staff, whose bailiwick included training, agreed with its contents, Hughes' request was polite and clear and addressed a very real problem. What he received from Mackenzie six days later was a rude rebuff to his suggestions and an impertinent criticism of his entire administration.[11]

In his reply Mackenzie claimed that, under Hughes' "inadequate" system, efficiency was impossible and that the Minister's assumption of executive duties destroyed morale and incentive. Supported by the Inspector-General, W. H. Cotton, he then identified some valid reasons why provisional schools would not work. Because Hughes kept the Permanent Force below establishment, there were simply not enough instructors for the present regular schools, let alone for new provisional ones. Until there were Mackenzie went on, the permanent schools alone would have to suffice to avoid dangers of Permanent-Force dilution and poorly qualified militia officers. But Hughes pressed on with his scheme. In 1913 he ordered forty-five of the temporary schools set up across the country, nearly five times the number used by his predecessor.

Not everyone agreed with all of Mackenzie's gloomy assessment. While there was certainly no comparison with the quality of staff instruction at the permanent schools, these provisional units provided education where none existed before. During the Great War, this fact proved to be a valuable source of staff officers below the brigade-major level. Because of the watered-down course content, Mackenzie did not like them. In the end after a far longer wait than a ministerial order warranted, he grudgingly staffed them as best he could.[12] Given Hughes' policy of concentrating on the part-time soldier, there was really no other way of teaching local militiamen unless the regular force were greatly enlarged. Moreover, in his report for 1912, W. D. Otter agreed with Hughes that the permanent schools were not doing their job. But the reason he knew, was one the Minister would not admit: the professional force did not have sufficient numbers or training. Mackenzie knew it too.

He was also well aware that Hughes wanted to reduce the permanent corps to training cadres only. Increasing the numbers of provisional schools, then forcing the regulars to take up the posts would quickly accomplish the Minister's aim. On the other hand, the chief of staff wanted the regular force to maintain some semblance of field efficiency, a proposition which Sir John French in his 1910 inspection had considered vital for the health of the entire militia. What was clear from Mackenzie's criticism was that the Minister had a goal but no realistic way of achieving it. If the regulars were to be nothing but teachers, some efficient way would have to be created to allow them to disengage conveniently from all other duties. Who would then fill the garrisons or provide a field force or the staff of the divisions and districts or even a mobilization cadre? No evidence exists that Hughes thought about the outcome of such a radical change. By criticizing Hughes' scheme of provisional schools, Mackenzie had put his finger squarely on one of the basic imperfections in his Minister's administration: in order to have an efficient force of citizen-soldiers, it was necessary to have a competent professional body of sufficient size to instruct them. Hughes was not prepared to do this[13]; and for the remainder of 1912, the two men continued to spar over nearly everything, with Mackenzie always doing just enough to prevent Hughes from firing him on any specific issue.

Perhaps Mackenzie became more incensed when some of the capable Canadian professional soldiers were effectively removed from the headquarters staff that December. General Lessard, the officer who had backed Mackenzie against the Minister's first self-promotion attempt, lost his post as Adjutant-General to Colonel Victor Williams. Both men were regular officers in the Royal Canadian Dragoons. But Williams had strong Tory and militia connections; and Lessard went to a lesser command as head of Second Division based at Toronto. About the same time, the venerable Inspector-General, W. D. Otter, was also retired. According to his biographer, he "perhaps correctly ... saw his premature retirement ... as a political act by Hughes."[14] At least before he left his post, Otter had the satisfaction of writing down in his 1912 report his complaints about the Minister's administration, most of which echoed Mackenzie's. Hughes wanted to get more militiamen into the staff system, but his actions, as in Williams' case, were not always consistent and smacked of partisanship. Finally in February, Mackenzie had had enough; he decided to force the issue. He sent a secret memorandum on Hughes' disruptive administration directly to the Chief of the Imperial General Staff, Sir John French; without a doubt Connaught approved of this conspiracy.[15]

Mackenzie's searing report thoroughly damned both Hughes and the state of the Canadian force. Violations of the Militia Act, congestion in the Minister's office, disciplinary problems, and a confused chain of command were just a few of Hughes' sins. There was hardly any headquarters interdepartmental co-operation, Mackenzie pointed out, because "no action [is taken] unless the customary 'OK, S.H.' is appended" to directives. He also accused Hughes of promoting favoured and unqualified militia officers to responsible and even unneeded positions created for the occasion in the permanent corps. Besides being a reference to Victor Williams,[16] there was also other evidence that it was true. Tories like the seventy-six-year-old Lieutenant-Colonel Henry Smith got a brand new post of judge-advocate-general (JAG); militia gunner and Ottawa *Citizen* editor Edward Morrison replaced the British gunnery expert on the headquarters staff; Colonel Oscar Pelletier, son of a Liberal senator, was retired and quickly replaced by

J. P. Landry, son of a Conservative one; and shooting friends and Ross rifle enthusiasts, Lieutenant-Colonels Charles Greville-Harston and C. F. Winter, respectively, got the new small arms and ammunition inspector's directorate and the vital secretariat of the Militia Council. Hughes knew he could count on their support, especially on the Militia Council, as was the case with Henry Smith who worked out the legal details of Hughes' self-promotion attempt. Hughes often denied that he promoted only favourites and, as Morrison's appointment indicates, Mackenzie first read of these new posts in the newspapers.[17]

Sam Hughes' reasons for all of this were not complicated or unexpected in view of the usual partisan results of any change in political complexion, or the new Minister's long-held military ideas. In addition to wanting more militiamen at the higher levels, Hughes believed that Mackenzie had been discriminating purposely against Canadians, "making it practically impossible for any" to get senior posts. Like the Governor-General, the chief of staff was afraid that Hughes' new men were destroying professionalism and, more importantly, British influence over the Canadian militia.[18] In fairness to Hughes, his appointees on the whole were no less competent than some of the men they replaced.

Mackenzie also told French two other important things. First, that Hughes neglected his experts, the Militia Council. This was true. Called twenty-three times in 1912, Hughes met with his advisors only twice after July. Mackenzie's opposition to ministerial policy was the main reason; that Hughes could or would not delegate power was the other. The council was too slow, he said, and he had never believed in it. Mackenzie's second charge suggested that Hughes was out to destroy the Permanent Force by slow strangulation. Outright destruction was not the Minister's intent—a role change was. If his method continued, however, the effect might be the same. Without paying much attention to Sir John French's 1910 warning that field practice was absolutely vital to regulars and hence the militia, and without even consulting his council, Hughes cancelled the 1912 Permanent-Force camps; he then let the numbers, including particular regular service units like the engineer and service corps, slide by the hundreds without making any attempt to keep the Permanent Force at establishment strength. There was not enough money, he said later to the council. But the real point was that he had already spent his greatly expanded budgets on the militia. In justifying his course, he again pointed to a conspiracy by Mackenzie to make the Permanent Force "a standing army divorced from the militia." This was not true. Mackenzie never denied the training function of his regulars. Nor could anyone reading the Militia Act believe that, as the Minister claimed, their sole function should be only as an "Instructional Force ... throughout the year."[19]

When General Mackenzie finished his confidential report to Sir John French in February 1913, he held out very little hope for the Canadian militia. His last paragraph makes clear his bitterness and frustration:

> With a one year term of service; with a political system which interferes with every detail; destroys discipline and up-roots military authority; with infantry that can neither march nor shoot; with a cavalry (the West excepted) that cannot ride and are poorly horsed; with an artillery that knows nothing of other arms, though some individual batteries shoot fairly well; with an untrained staff, with officers untrained and senior officers unpractised in command; with incomplete administrative services and not sufficient even of these; with wasteful expenditure; with a far too small peace establishment and no organized reserve to complete it to war strength; with no reserve of arms, ammunition, clothing or stores, with no storage accommodation for same, with no settled policy as to provide anything; with a Militia Act which in the event of the British Empire being at war, leaves open to the Government of the day to give assistance or not, and with uncertainty even then as to whether that assistance is to consist of 100 or 10,000 men, with executive command as well as administrative control centred in and exercised by a Minister of Militia who has not the necessary knowledge for it; with a professional force discouraged by an openly expressed contempt; with all this one still hears that the militia is getting on. What must it have been like before?[20]

This catalogue of miseries sent to French also revealed that the dour Scot was unyielding in his opposition to Hughes' policy direction and that he was willing to test the boundaries of Canadian civilian supremacy to block it. The two Englishmen seem to have devised a crisis strategy which they hoped would force Hughes from office.

Mackenzie's memorandum produced no recorded reply from Sir John French, but in a little more than a month after sending it, the chief of staff took another drastic step. On April 7 he suddenly submitted his resignation and, with almost indecent haste, Hughes accepted it. Two events in March and early April seem to have left Mackenzie with no other choice, events that overshadowed all of the Minister's previous transgressions. The first was the critical manpower shortage in the Permanent Force. Natural attrition, no doubt substantially augmented by the Minister's blatant contempt for the regulars, saw the force reduced from 3,520 to 2,996 by March 1913. There were several headquarters staff appeals to reverse the trend, but the Minister remained insensitive. Finally, at a rebellious Militia Council meeting on March 19, Mackenzie and his supporters submitted a signed and elaborate protest, which they wanted recorded officially in the departmental records. Hughes stormed out of the meeting. But he dared not risk any such documentary evidence. Consequently the compromise worked out by the far calmer Deputy Minister, Eugene Fiset, saw the protest filed only within the non-descriptive minutes of the council meeting, while fourteen new officers were added to the regular corps. Mackenzie's small victory stung Hughes to the quick.[21]

The second incident involved a matter of petty patronage. In early April Hughes told Mackenzie to hire for the summer the relative of one of his other employees in the chief of staff's Military Services Branch. Mackenzie resented the interference which had already accounted for a quarter of his vital section's staff; what he needed was qualified cartographers, not unemployed students. He refused. Hughes promptly transferred the section out of Mackenzie's jurisdiction. The next day the chief of staff resigned. As French told the war secretary in Britain, the entire episode pointed out how Hughes was destroying Canadian "military efficiency."[22] Yet this event seemed hardly one to force the Chief of the General Staff out of office, unless he had been planning it for some time.

The Minister's reaction to the General's resignation shows just how deeply the Boer war experiences were burnt into his soul. He treated the Mackenzie episode as if it was the Hutton situation all over again; and it is questionable whether he really appreciated the possible political dangers. Unlike the Hutton or even the Dundonald incidents a decade earlier, the resignation would focus attention on the Minister's acts rather than the General's if there was a public exposure of the facts. The manner in which Hughes accepted Mackenzie's notice also added to the potentially critical political situation. Hughes' speedy reply amounted to a rude dismissal and was initiated without any regard to collective cabinet responsibility or the customary order-in-council. Hughes simply wanted the irksome General out of his way, and he insisted that Mackenzie leave Canada within a week instead of within the customary six months as Mackenzie had requested.[23]

Mackenzie was shocked by Hughes' response and perhaps by the fact that the cabinet was not getting a chance to see the evidence he thought they should. He quickly turned to Connaught for help. Since the General had told the Duke in one of their previous confidential communications that his resignation was inevitable, it came as no surprise. However, the Field Marshal, then in England while the Duchess sought treatment for a chronic illness, could be of no immediate aid. Mackenzie then had to appeal for help against Hughes' discourteous dismissal directly to Sir Charles Fitzpatrick, the Chief Justice of Canada, and in Connaught's absence, the chief administrator of the Dominion. Fitzpatrick immediately summoned the Prime Minister and told him of the circumstances behind the break between the two men. Borden was even more surprised, claiming no knowledge of the quarrel or its causes. But he expressed great dismay that Hughes could write such a letter to Mackenzie. With the naval aid debate in full swing, the Prime Minister needed no Anglo-Canadian quarrel at the moment.[24]

As a consequence of Fitzpatrick's revelations, Borden had to move quickly and quietly on the Mackenzie affair. He eagerly co-operated with the Chief Justice. In spite of being a Liberal, but fortunately for Borden also an imperialist, Fitzpatrick counselled the Prime Minister and the General to keep the affair from the political arena.[25] Fitzpatrick then insisted that Hughes' offensive letter be withdrawn. Later he confided to Connaught that the only real solution to the problem of Anglo-Canadian and civil-military relations in the Militia Department was to have Borden "get rid of his minister." If it came to a show-down with Borden over Hughes' letter, Fitzpatrick promised the Duke that he would stand behind Mackenzie and "take the imperial view."[26] Apparently Connaught agreed with his deputy for reasons similar to one of Borden's: to save the Tory administration political embarrassment so that the naval aid bill might yet be approved by the Canadian Parliament, an unlikely outcome should there be any change in government or if the naval aid legislation was side-tracked while the Liberals probed the militia issue.

Anxious to get to the bottom of this affair, Borden conducted his own investigation and concluded that "General Mackenzie had made offensive minutes on documents, etc., etc., and that there is much friction between imperial and Canadian officers generally." Evidence showed that this was true. There were two specific refusals by Mackenzie to carry out ministerial orders and plenty of others of plain stonewalling tactics, not including the letters sent behind Hughes' back. Mackenzie had also needled Hughes by describing his version of his South African war record, published in the *Militia List* of 1912, as "totally misleading." All these incidents were sufficient to demonstrate to the Prime Minister that Mackenzie not only had aggravated Sam Hughes but had challenged the Minister's authority. Even Connaught was willing to admit, however reluctantly, that "Mackenzie had shown a certain dourness of character in dealing with Colonel Hughes' suggestions."[27]

Fitzpatrick and Mackenzie held their own strong views on why the Prime Minister had sided with Sam Hughes. Fitzpatrick confided to Connaught that Borden could not get rid of Hughes because of his importance to the Prime Minister's political fortunes, especially in Ontario, the key to his power base. With far less accuracy, Mackenzie was convinced that Borden was forced by the economic pressures of the Canadian Northern Railway to keep Hughes in the government. Both men were equally certain that Borden was not strong-willed enough to assert his own dominance over the cabinet, or even knew much of what went on in the militia portfolio. The Chief Justice also thought there was enough scandal in Hughes' administration to "damn any government." Perhaps Borden did not investigate Fitzpatrick's allegation for fear of exposing the whole affair. Last but not least, because Hughes guarded the control of the Canadian force jealously and was very popular among militiamen, Borden may have taken some satisfaction in knowing that his Militia Minister would not let the department fall under the influence of the British soldiers like Mackenzie or Connaught. In the end the Prime Minister thought that the safest solution to the crisis was to have Mackenzie quietly leave his post and to retain Hughes. With great difficulty he persuaded the Militia Minister to withdraw his original letter and to provide an acceptable substitute.[28]

Before Mackenzie left the country, he kept in close contact with Borden. At the Prime Minister's request, in late April the General submitted two statements explaining his resignation. The first was for official records at Government House and was a benign comment that Mackenzie had differed with the Minister. The other was a confidential detailed list for Borden's eyes alone, enumerating all of the flaws in Hughes' record in the Militia Department. In it he told Borden that the only way in which he could find out the real state of chaos and corruption in Hughes' department was to go personally into the files "especially those of the minister's office." Borden balked at this suggestion, partly because he did not want to know and partly because such an investigation would be an act of non-confidence in his Minister. Borden also probably felt that, since he needed Sam Hughes, such a move would be pointless. Since the Prime Minister was not likely to institute an enquiry into Hughes' administration, Mackenzie then advised Borden that Hughes was bent on ending as soon as possible any concrete connection between the Canadian militia and the British War Office. He also cautioned that Borden must get Hughes to agree to an acceptable replacement for him, presumably one who still provided the military link between Canada and Great Britain. Borden replied that he would "settle this with Colonel Hughes" and suggested to Mackenzie that, before returning home, he should quietly make his grievances known to the Inspector-General of the Overseas Forces who was scheduled to visit Canada soon.[29]

Nearly everyone in England was at first sympathetic to Mackenzie, but their support was not enough to make them do anything more than sullenly accept Borden's solution and hope for the best. Along with several other confidential documents of the Militia Department originally (and no doubt secretly) provided to the Duke by Mackenzie, Connaught passed on to Sir John French two long memoranda supporting all of Mackenzie's charges. In turn, French advised his chief at the War Office that he fully agreed with the Duke and that he had known for some time that matters were not working smoothly, "due I think entirely to the distorted view which the Minister of Militia takes of the role he has to fulfill and of his own personal military capabilities."[30]

All of this was indeed true. Another point, however, was also evident, but did not appear so to some of Mackenzie's immediate supporters. As the Minister, Hughes had the right to determine policy. Whether right or wrong, it was Mackenzie's duty to execute the Minister's policy as smoothly as possible. If Sam Hughes wanted to spend all the budget on the non-permanent militia, after notice of dissent, Mackenzie should have carried out the order. Instead he resisted and secretly appealed to offices outside his own jurisdiction. If Hughes' course was ruinous for the militia, then the responsibility to rectify it was the Prime Minister's, not Mackenzie's. As if he recognized Mackenzie's faults, the Secretary of State for War took no overt action in support of Mackenzie's claims. Seely must have realized that in the last analysis the problem was a domestic one and would have to be solved in Canada. In any event he needed much more information than he had, and there was a less direct and hence less offensive method of pointing out to Canadians the problems inherent in Sam Hughes' ministry: exposure by the Inspector-General of Overseas Forces.

The inspection of the Canadian defence establishment in June 1913 was not spawned solely by British reaction to Sam Hughes. Such tours had been normal, if irregular, throughout the Empire since British and Dominion politicians had agreed in 1909 to upgrade and integrate Empire defence through the establishment of an imperial general staff system. Nevertheless at the time of Mackenzie's affair, the military stakes in Canada were important to the British in view of a possible European commitment and complex imperial obligations.

Since the initiation of the imperial defence movement, the War Office felt that substantial progress had been made, especially in increasing the links between Canada's militia and the British Army. Hughes' predecessor, F. W. Borden, had been reasonably easy to get along with in terms of the expectations of the British regular army officers serving in Canada. Men like Sir Percy Lake, a former Chief of the General Staff (1904-1908), and later Colin Mackenzie took it for granted that within certain limitations they could continue to direct the Canadian militia along the lines expected in both the War Office and the Colonial Office. But things had changed after the 1911 federal election.[31] For years nearly everyone in senior British colonial and military service had heard of the cantankerous Colonel Sam Hughes. After he won the portfolio, his clashes with Mackenzie and Connaught and his definite views on the militia produced some concern in British circles. By the summer of 1912 many in the War Office were anxious to have a better look at the Canadian militia through the eyes of the Inspector-General of Overseas Forces.

To get the Inspector into Canada was not as easy as simply putting him on board a ship. First the British needed an invitation from the

Prime Minister, which they got while Borden was in London during the naval crisis talks in the summer of 1912. They also needed Sam Hughes' co-operation. This they secured in the fall when Hughes also went to England with his first lot of militia officers. The persuasion of Hughes was made easier with a little War Office cocktail diplomacy, which included a special banquet in Hughes' honour given by the Inspector-General himself, Sir Ian Hamilton, who cynically confided beforehand to his political chief that it was "an expensive method of ingratiating my billet to them but it must be done."[32] No doubt Connaught's and Mackenzie's increased stream of secret indictments of Hughes, especially the damning February one followed closely by the resignation, made the War Office decide to send Hamilton in June 1913. If Mackenzie had hoped to expose Hamilton to all of Hughes' supposed bungling while guiding the Inspector around the various establishments, such was not to be the case. Hughes had never intended to send Mackenzie on the inspection tour whenever it happened; he had personally arranged the itinerary and had planned to accompany Hamilton himself. In June, however, as Borden had recommended, Mackenzie found a brief opportunity to talk to Hamilton as the two crossed paths.[33] But after that Hughes took over and hardly left the Inspector's side for the next six weeks.

Hughes led Hamilton over 14,000 miles by railway; they inspected 112 units of the Canadian militia, most of which were undergoing training at the annual summer camps. The pace was furious and even the energetic Hamilton found Sam Hughes a hard man to keep up with. The Minister injected into the tour a little cocktail diplomacy of his own. He had invited several parliamentary reporters to travel with them aboard his private rail car. Among them were A. R. Ford of the Winnipeg *Telegram*, John Bassett of the Montreal *Gazette*, and W. E. Grange of the *Globe*, who between them ensured that the ministerial party got top coverage. It was just as clear that Hughes revelled in showing off the Canadian militia to Hamilton and the famous British soldier to impressionable Canadians.[34]

The pace of the trip was tempered from time to time with both controversial and amusing episodes. Hamilton was so impressed with the lavish treatment he received from Hughes that he was afraid there would be a parliamentary enquiry about the cost. It was during the group's stay in Halifax that a furious Hughes levelled his famous "bar room loafer" comments at some rowdy Permanent-Force officers. The following day his comments were much distorted by the local Liberal press. Aboard the train returning to Ottawa Hughes was disconsolate and restless but not, it seems, from the press reaction to his Halifax comments. It was July 12, and he was about to miss his first Orange parade in twenty-five years. Late that evening as the train reached a small New Brunswick junction, Hughes spotted a group of Orangemen returning from a celebration in Saint John. As Ford witnessed, their colour and presence electrified the Minister:

> Our train was still going about twenty-five miles an hour as he jumped off and ran to the station platform. He started shaking hands with all and sundry of the be-ribboned Orangemen saying "I'm Sam Hughes, I'm Sam Hughes." They thought at first he was crazy. But when they became convinced he was the redoubtable Sam, the band played him the "Protestant Boys" and he mounted an express truck and made a 12th of July speech. He was happy the rest of the evening.[35]

At first Hamilton must have been bewildered by such ministerial antics. After a while he started to record a few of them in his daily confidential reports to the War Office. As Hughes and Hamilton watched a sham battle between infantry and dismounted cavalry at Camp Sewell in the west, the foot soldiers caught some of the troopers before they could reach their horses. The Minister sprang to the aid of the mounted rifles but was promptly made prisoner by the opposing side. In his War Office report, Hamilton wrote:

> a militia officer drew his sword and hit the man who held his [Hughes'] reins..., one of the minister's staff also drew his sword and executed a charge in fine style. The comrades of the infantry coming up were greatly excited; in fact everyone was greatly excited and things looked as if anything was possible. However, at last common sense asserted itself and we managed to extricate our Defense Minister in a great state of fury. He said to me that if that man had hung on to his reins one second longer, he would have dashed his brains out, but what he was going to dash them out with I really do not know.

Hamilton not only mused at Hughes' quixotic interjections in training at the camps but—having a sense of humour—he probably laughed outright at evidence of Sam's immense ego being deflated. Not long after the Camp Sewell incident, Hamilton recognized a railway policeman's South African war decoration during a brief stop at a small western station. When the congenial General began a conversation about mutual acquaintances both he and the constable had known in that war, Hughes, not to be "out-recognized" or outdone by Hamilton promptly butted in. "Now," he said to the policeman, "my boy, do you know me?" The man looked at him and drawled out that he did. Then the Minister "beamed all over, for nothing pleases him more than the idea that everyone in Canada recognizes him. 'Well," he said to the man again—'who am I?' 'General Hutton,' replied the constable. 'Hell!', exclaimed the minister and jumped about two feet off the ground."[36]

However entertaining these glimpses may be, there were far more important perceptions in the Inspector's private dispatches, and the vital ones were Hamilton's assessment of Hughes and Mackenzie, and thereby of Hughes' administration. Hamilton was immediately attracted to Sam Hughes. That was predictable. Both men shared a romantic streak and a love of unorthodox and decisive individual action often bordering on impulsiveness; they both believed in united Empire defence and in the social virtues of martial training and military preparedness. During their long hours of discussion, the imperial Inspector-General came to see Hughes as "a very able man whose ideas on the whole are very sound." He thought that the Minister was "doing his level best and is deserving of the sympathy and assistance of all keen soldiers," even though sometimes Hughes was "a prickly sort of personage to handle" and his methods were often "questionable or mistaken." Hamilton was so taken by Hughes that he sent letters praising the Minister to Sir John French and to George V, partly because he felt that Hughes was being underestimated by English authorities. Hamilton believed that such driving individuals, when accorded some understanding, could give the Empire a needed shot of adrenalin. He also realized that Hughes could be persuaded by flattery. "I hear," Hamilton wrote to Seely, "that the Defense Minister has ambitions to be made a major-general. If true, it would be well worth doing. Immense issues may hang on whether we conciliate or antagonize this very powerful personality."[37] No doubt the War Office kept this suggestion in mind.

The War Office read no such praise from Hamilton about Colin Mackenzie. Although Hamilton admitted that the former chief of staff was a fine soldier with a solid character, he "is too uncompromising and too cut and dried in his notions to have any sympathy whatever with a man like Sam Hughes." The problem with Mackenzie, he went on to Seely back home, was that his narrow sense of "fitness and decorum" had been offended by that "representative of a very democratic community," Sam Hughes. "If we are going to hold the Empire together," Hamilton cautioned, Great Britain must teach the officers it sends out to the Dominions to accommodate themselves to types for whom a British officer's upbringing and associations were poor preparation. To a large extent Hamilton was right. Few of the previous British general officers understood the peculiarities of their Canadian commands. As far as Hamilton was concerned, as soon as Mackenzie felt that "he could not stand Hughes, namely within a month or two of Hughes' coming to power, he should have made some good excuse and cleared out." After this harsh indictment, the Inspector went on to suggest to Seely that Mackenzie had stayed in Canada only to accumulate the three years he needed to acquire the permanent rank of major-general once he returned to Britain.[38]

When the exhausting inspection was finally over towards the end of July, Hamilton and Borden secluded themselves at the Algonquin Hotel in St. Andrews, New Brunswick, where they compiled the inspection results. Borden was there more to learn what condition Sam

Hughes' militia was really in than to dictate its terms to the Inspector-General. The "Report on the Military Institutions of Canada," as it was dubbed, was written in less than two weeks and in the hands of the Canadians before the British saw it, a fact that earned Hamilton a substantial rebuke from the British Army Council.

This last point is important for what it reveals not only about the report's limitations but also about Hamilton's attitude: he considered himself purely a servant of the Dominion government through its defence minister. His investigation would "leave untouched" anything the government wished. The Empire's prime ministers, he was sure, would not tolerate his reports being "emasculated first" by the Army Council. This far-sighted stance took the British another thirty years, another war, and Mackenzie King to appreciate.[39]

Hamilton's forty-four page assessment of the Canadian militia contained eighteen major recommendations, and while in places mildly critical of Hughes' program, generally it applauded the Minister's efforts. Hamilton approved of the rapid increases in the number of units, of instructional staff, and of the establishment of provisional schools in local areas. A recommendation that would have horrified Colin Mackenzie was Hamilton's bold suggestion to abolish the central cavalry and infantry schools. As far as the Permanent Force was concerned, Hamilton seemed to waffle but in effect gave Hughes the green light. He said it should be either further dispersed among the part-time units or concentrated into a standing army based on the British regular army model. The Militia Minister's armoury-building and Cadet Corps programs easily won the Inspector's support, as did Hughes' attempts to encourage some training for the rural corps during the year instead of only during the summer camps. Hamilton also looked favourably on and recommended more increases in pay to encourage enlistment and efficiency. He lauded the advances made in organization and training since Sir John French's visit in 1910, and in particular had warm praise for the hard work of the headquarters staff in achieving these improvements. In short, Hamilton's report was anything but an indictment of Sam Hughes' militia.[40] No doubt Borden found it all very reassuring.

But there were two important omissions in the imperial Inspector's report. The central point of Mackenzie's criticism had been the Minister's interference in the jurisdiction and functioning of the headquarters staff; Hamilton nicely side-stepped this issue by commenting in his report that "no proposals have been put forward regarding the organization and distribution of duties at Militia Headquarters at Ottawa. The ommission is intentional. I am anxious to complete my tour of the self-governing Dominions of the Empire before I attempt to discuss a subject so important and contentious as headquarters organization."[41] Without a close scrutiny of the workings of the general staff system and the Minister's relation to it, what was valid in Mackenzie's criticism could never be uncovered.[42] The other point is that Hamilton should have explored the consequences of his recommendations for the Permanent Force. Had he done so, at least in his dispersal suggestion, the necessity of having more and better-equipped and -trained regulars for achieving Hughes' ideal militia force might have been obvious.

Yet Hamilton condemned Mackenzie primarily for not understanding clearly that it was his duty to implement the Minister's orders. His private comments to his chief in England laid much criticism squarely at British feet. Above all he advised that whatever military system operated in Canada, the imperial authorities must develop more tolerance to it; they must send out British officers who were flexible enough "to retain all of [their] importance but as a guiding rather than as a directing force"; and they must recognize that the Militia Minister is master in his own house. On this point Hamilton and, no doubt, Borden, saw clearly what Mackenzie had not: if British authorities continued to turn a blind eye to such nationalist Dominion realities as Sam Hughes, the Empire was doomed.[43]

After reading the Inspector's report, Sir John Anderson, the permanent undersecretary at the Colonial Office, wondered who was to be believed. Hamilton's assessment had sustained neither Connaught's nor Mackenzie's views. While many in the Colonial Office continued to feel that Hughes was "notoriously a very difficult person to deal with" and that the Canadian militia was short of men and equipment,[44] they played down what they could not change. On the surface at least, a similar reaction took place in the War Office. Officially Seely said nothing about the Hamilton report and then apparently decided not to pursue any issue lest it lead to a further alienation of Canadian sympathy for imperial defence integration and planning. Seely knew that Sam Hughes' promotion of the Canadian militia did much to spread the imperial message. And Seely himself was not only a long-time British militiaman but a major proponent of such forces as Haldane's Territorials created a few years earlier in England. In short, he had sympathy with Hughes' direction. In the end the War Office only grumbled a little then acquiesced, as Sam Hughes took the initiative in appointing Colonel Willoughby Gwatkin as the new Canadian chief of staff, without the customary preconsultation with the British authorities.[45]

Colonel Willoughby Gwatkin was a British Army regular who had served on the Canadian general staff as mobilization officer since 1910. The choice of another Briton was likely Hughes' one major concession insisted on by Borden and quietly approved by Seely. But it was also very clear why the Militia Minister accepted Gwatkin. The new chief of staff, Hughes warned the Duke, "had been specially trained to observe rights and functions under responsible government."[46] Even before Mackenzie resigned, Hughes made this point very clear in the Commons. "I am boss while I am here.... So long as I am Minister of Militia, no officer, British or Canadian is going to arrogate to himself the function of Minister of the Crown.... That is why... I am going to supervise the department and every branch of it."[47]

In Canada neither the Mackenzie affair nor the Hamilton report caused much public controversy. Indeed the Conservatives so effectively hid the Mackenzie affair that no one really knew for sure what had happened. Tory newspapers played it down, and the Militia Minister refused to be drawn into public debate. Hard pressed by the naval aid bill, the government remained silent for about a month after the resignation until some rumours spawned opposition questions in May. At first Hughes refused to answer unless the questions were put on the order paper. When they were and six days had elapsed before they came up for consideration, he was absent from the House. Borden answered on the Militia Minister's behalf and in effect misled the Commons by saying that Mackenzie had given no reason for his resignation.[48] After that questions withered away. The Conservatives escaped a more thorough opposition probe on the militia issue in the Commons because, after Hughes' Liberal predecessor had lost his seat in the 1911 election, there was no one in the House who had the intimate knowledge of militia affairs necessary for a sensible critical appraisal of that portfolio. Criticism of the Mackenzie affair also crumbled because it was eclipsed by Hughes' well-orchestrated Hamilton inspection tour during June and July. The tour gathered many more good words than bad, even in some Liberal papers. When Hamilton's report became public, there was nothing substantial in it to condemn Hughes' administration. In the end most Canadians were satisfied by the report and quickly forgot Mackenzie.[49]

Sam Hughes, however, had not forgotten Mackenzie. Even while the inspection was in full progress, he found time to fire a final broadside at his defenceless former chief of staff. In an eleven-page memorandum, Hughes tried to convince the Colonial Secretary, Lewis Harcourt, of the case against Mackenzie. The document was as remarkable for its pettiness as Mackenzie's February memo to French had been for its failure to appreciate Canadian political realities. Hughes accused the dour Scot of being diseased by that "irreconcilable conflict spirit universally existing between the Permanent Force and the Ordinary Militia, the *world over*"; he was, Hughes said, an arrogant, friendless British officer who had no clear understanding that his responsibilities must be subordinate to the cabinet. Moreover, he was a small-minded man who systematically opposed sound recommendations from his minister. Mackenzie was guilty of a whole host of professional sins, including the creation of a Canadian mobilization scheme which was, as Hughes unfairly charged, "absolutely devoid of merit." Hughes went on to deny that he harboured any ill feeling for the former chief of staff because of Mackenzie's refusal "to make Colonel Hughes a Brigadier General," while completely neglecting to mention to Harcourt that he had tried to promote himself at least twice.[50]

The Minister's tirade went directly to the Colonial Secretary bypassing the official channel—Connaught. A copy also went to Seely in the War Office. The Colonial Secretary commented dryly that "it was not a document that should be seen by the Colonial Office or placed in any official file." Obviously the British were not going to risk reopening the affair by rising to Hughes' bait. In fact, when the Minister went to England with his group of militia officers late that summer, he was treated grandly by officials of both offices and they acted as if nothing had happened.[51]

The Governor-General was not so willing to pamper Hughes. All during the fall of 1913, he continued to pressure both Borden and the Colonial Office to do something about the Militia Minister, preferably remove him from office. To Borden, he sent lists of Hughes's transgressions and personally stated that he would be remiss in his duty as Governor-General if he did not say something about the threat the erratic Hughes' regime posed to Borden's government. By this time well-alienated, the Prime Minister had had enough of the Duke's interference in Canadian politics. Politely but firmly, he settled the issue by informing Connaught that "while there has been strong criticism upon matters, alluded to ... there has also been, in important quarters, warm commendation of the minister's administration."[52]

When the Prime Minister would do nothing about Hughes, Connaught sent his own impressions of Colonel Hughes' administration and all of the documents of the Mackenzie affair to the Colonial Office with the excuse that he wanted to ensure that his fellow officer's career was in no way harmed. Other than to assure the Duke that Mackenzie was unscathed, Harcourt made no attempt to support the Governor-General. By January 1914, after Hughes' appointment of Gwatkin was confirmed by the War Office, the Duke reluctantly accepted the decision as a sign that British authorities wanted the case closed.[53] And apparently it was.

In the six months of peace which remained for Canada, Hughes' ministry was relatively quiet. In the two and a half years of his administration, however, that had hardly been the case. It was clear that he could not delegate power easily and that often he was above consulting his military experts or realizing that he had obligations within the confines of collective ministerial responsibility. Sometimes he practised blatant favouritism. While his appointments were generally no worse than his predecessors had made, there were some that excluded the talented and included the unqualified. At times the Minister assumed military prerogatives not normally given to a politician. Certainly there was growth and improvement in the militia, but the two were not synonymous nor were they necessarily due to the Minister's ideas. Hughes, however, believed that one naturally went with the other, and improvement was his political justification for expansion. Not all previous militia ministers had accepted either expansion or reform; yet it is true that many others had pushed both for as long as Hughes, especially the regular soldiers. The fact does not detract from the importance of Hughes' contribution, and after 1911 he had the political power to implement his views. Hughes accepted others' suggestions if they fitted in with his concept of the militia force; and by the time he came to office, civilian authority was strong enough that they could not have been implemented without his approval.

In struggling to create his ideal of a volunteer militia, the Minister lost sight of the tool that could do most to realize his dream—the Permanent Force. A larger militia and a reduced regular force negated gains achieved by more equipment and facilities and caused an unevenness in the units. Most of these problems had been identified by the Canadian Inspector-Generals, Otter and Cotton, in their annual reports on the militia. As Ian Hamilton pointed out, there was nothing wrong in focusing on either part-time or regular soldiers. But the Minister's mistake was not letting one grow in proportion to the other.

Not only was Hughes' attitude to the regular force harmful to his militia, but the Minister's image of the moral value of military training contained some naive and simplistic assumptions. If military training produced better citizens or reduced crime and corruption (and there was no hard evidence that it did), then it followed that military training was desirable for all citizens. This, however, conflicted with other Hughes ideas—voluntarism and individualism. The Minister's particular view of democracy was itself antithetical to discipline, sound administration, and subordination—qualities vital to military efficiency. This is especially true of his appreciation of the general staff system, which he progressively ignored and subverted. To his credit he wanted to make his headquarters staff more representative of Canadian military talent and less dominated by the British, and he did that. Consequently, like F. W. Borden, Hughes ranks as a positive force in the nationalization of the higher levels of the military structure. But with this he mixed his conspiratorial attitudes about regular and militia soldiers, which threatened the efficiency of his military dream and undermined the system that would have given the part-time force the best chance at efficiency.

Some of Hughes' contemporaries claimed that the Minister's tumultuous administration threatened to kill Canada's relationship with Great Britain. Perhaps it is more accurate to say that, while the Minister's activities certainly tested that connection, Hughes in his own way was only proceeding along lines that had been growing more autonomous since the Boer war. There was never any doubt that Sam Hughes would participate in Empire defence, as was the fear of Connaught, Mackenzie, and others, but Hughes insisted that it would be on terms advantageous to Canada, not to England. Like most other Canadians who wanted a role in "Greater" Britain, however, Sam Hughes suffered from imperial fervour which clashed with his growing nationalism. In spite of how much Sam Hughes pressed for recognition of Canadian personnel, he actually helped increase the anglicization of the militia forces and hence Canadian fortunes by his ready co-operation with the British Army in other areas, like training.

In some ways Hughes' strong personal traits complicated his peacetime career, especially his insatiable vanity and need for public recognition; in other ways they protected him from close critical examination, as the press campaign he orchestrated around Hamilton's tour in part masked the Mackenzie affair. Although Robert Borden can in no way be held responsible for Hughes' personal foibles, the Prime Minister did give Hughes a virtually free hand. Hughes took it, and in doing so not only revealed his flaws but also his greatest assets: enthusiasm, conviction, and boundless energy. Surrounded by people who, in W. D. Otter's words, did not take "the militia seriously,"[54] Hughes believed in the potential efficiency of the force, and worked as hard as possible to attain that goal, never once shirking a difficult task. However, two questions remain. Was Sam Hughes' concept of the militia force realistic? Was he doing his job efficiently and within the bounds of responsible government? Only a bloody war would provide the answers.

Reference Notes to Chapter 10

1 PAC, Grey *papers*, vol. 30, D8, F18, p. 7685, Connaught to Howick, Feb. 19, 1913; and R. H. Hubbard, *Rideau Hall* (Montreal: McGill-Queen's University Press, 1977), pp. 125-26.
2 Militia Council, *Minutes*, Oct. 19, 1911.
3 PAC, RG7, G21, vol. 142, no. 265, Hughes to Connaught, Dec. 20, 1912; ibid., Hughes to Connaught, Feb. 3, 1913; and ibid., Connaught to R. L. Borden, Feb. 17, 1913.
4 Ibid., Rogers to Lowther, Mar. 10, 1913; and ibid., newspaper clippings: "Colonel Sam Hughes and his Red Tie" and "Concerning Conventions."
5 Ibid., Hughes to the Governor-General, "Memorandum Re General Mackenzie," June 1913; ibid., Mackenzie to Hughes, July 12, 1912; *King's Regulations*, 1910, paragraphs 360, 362; and *CAR*, 1913, p. 218.

REFERENCE NOTES TO CHAPTER 10 / 175

6 *Hansard*, 1911-1912, p. 6061; *Militia Act*, 1904, paragraph 43; Canada, *Statutes*, 1912, p. 279, 2 Geo. V. Chap. 34; Militia Council, *Minutes*, Mar. 12, 1912; and PAC, RG7, G21, no. 265, Hughes to Governor-General, June 1913, p. 11.
7 *Militia Act*, 1904, paragraph 5.
8 PAC, RG7, G21, vol. 142, no. 265, Mackenzie to Lowther, Mar. 10, 1913; and ibid., "Note on the Rank of Major-General to the President of the Militia Council," CGS to AG, April 19, 1912.
9 PAC, RG7, G21, no. 265, "Memorandum Re General Mackenzie," June 1913, p. 11; and PRO, CO537, 498, "Resignation of Major-General C. Mackenzie," enclosure B, Mackenzie to Borden, April 25, 1913.
10 PAC, RG7, G21, no. 265, Hughes to Lowther, June 3, 1912; and ibid., Lowther to Hughes, June 6, 1912.
11 Ibid., Hughes to CGS, July 9, 1912.
12 Ibid., Mackenzie to Hughes, July 15, 1912; *Militia Report*, 1912-1913, pp. 93-98; and see *Militia Report*, 1913-1914, for W. H. Cotton's comments. Kenneth Charles Eyre, *Staff and Command in the Canadian Corps: The Canadian Militia, 1896-1914 as a Source of Senior Officers*, thesis (Duke University, 1967), pp. 36, 80, 95-96.
13 Ibid.
14 Morton, *The Canadian General*, p. 312; see also pp. 308-14.
15 *Militia Report*, 1912-1913, pp. 93-113; and PAC, RG7, G21, vol. 142, no. 265. "A Brief Resumé ... 1912," C. Mackenzie, Feb. 27, 1913; and ibid., Connaught to Harcourt, Colonial Office, Dec. 19, 1913.
16 Ibid., "A Brief Resumé ... 1912," C. Mackenzie, confidential, Feb. 27, 1913, p. 2.
17 Militia Council, *Minutes*, Oct. 19, 1911, July 16, 1912, Nov. 15, 1912, and Jan. 28, 1913; *Militia List*, 1912, p. 10; and *King's Regulations*, 1910, paragraph 22, rev. G.O. 132, 1912; PAC, RG7, G21, no. 265. "A Brief Resumé ... 1912," C. Mackenzie, confidential, Feb. 27, 1913, p. 3; Morton, *The Canadian General*, pp. 310-13; and *Militia Report*, 1912-1913, p. 69. Morton, in *War and Society*, p. 94, claims Pelletier was retired by Hughes as revenge on professional soldiers. Pelletier (p. 370) says only that he was growing very deaf and asked to be placed on the retirement list because his malady was interfering with his duty. Winter, pp. 25-29, 65-66.
18 PAC, RG7, G21, no. 265, "Memorandum Re General Mackenzie," p. 8; ibid., "A Brief Resumé ... 1912," C. Mackenzie, Feb. 27, 1912.
19 *Sessional papers*, 1911, no. 35b, p. 9; PAC, RG7, G21, no. 265, "A Brief Resumé ... 1912," pp. 4-5; ibid., "Memorandum Re General Mackenzie," June 1913, pp. 9-10; *Militia Report*, 1912-1913, pp. 15, 35; and *Hansard*, 1914, pp. 3428-29. Concentration of the PAMC, by Hughes' own estimate, would have cost only $70,000; Militia Council, *Minutes*, June 2, July 16, 1912, and Feb. 4, June 28, and Dec. 4, 1913; *King's Regulations*, 1910, pp. 250-51; Winter, pp. 25, 28. PAC has no record of the minutes of the Militia Council for the first two years of the war. It is more likely that Hughes never called the Council together, as Winter implies.
20 PAC, RG7, G21, no. 265, "A Brief Resumé ... 1912," C. Mackenzie, Feb. 27, 1913.
21 Militia Council, *Minutes*, Mar. 19, 1913.
22 Seely *papers*, Box 20, French to Secretary of State for War, May 2, 1913; and ibid., enclosure E.
23 PAC, RG7, G21, no. 265, Mackenzie to Hughes, April 7, 1913; ibid., Hughes to Mackenzie, April 16, 1913; ibid., Mackenzie to the Governor-General, April 9, 1913.
24 Brown, *Borden*, vol. 1, pp. 242-43.
25 PAC, RG7, G21, no. 265, Fitzpatrick to Connaught, April 18, 1913; and ibid., Sladen to Connaught, April 18, 1913. Sladen was one of the Duke's secretaries.
26 Ibid., Fitzpatrick to Connaught, April 21, 1913; and ibid., Fitzpatrick to Connaught, April 18, 1913.
27 Ibid., Sladen to Connaught, April 21, 1913; ibid., "Memorandum Re General Mackenzie," June 1913, and "Summary of two Memoranda by Major-General Mackenzie and one by Colonel Hughes," Connaught to the Colonial Office, Dec. 3, 1913, secret; ibid., Mackenzie to Lowther, Feb. 10, 1913; and ibid., Connaught to Colonial Office, Dec. 3, 1913, secret.
28 Ibid., Fitzpatrick to Connaught, April 18, 1913; and ibid., Hughes to Mackenzie, April 21, 1913, and Borden to Fitzpatrick, April 28, 1913.

29 Seely *papers*, Mackenzie to Sir John French, April 21, 1913; and PAC, RG7, G21, Box 142, no. 265, Mackenzie to Borden, April 25, 1913.
30 PAC, RG7, G21, no. 265, French to Secretary of State for War, May 2, 1913, and enclosures A and B.
31 John Gooch, *The Plans of War, The General Staff and British Military Strategy, 1900-1916* (New York: Wiley, 1974), especially chapter 5, "The Imperial Design."
32 Seely *papers*, Box 18, Hamilton to Seely, Aug. 30, 1912; and Hamilton, *The Happy Warrior*, p. 256.
33 Seely *papers*, Box 20, Mackenzie to French, April 21, 1913; ibid., Box 18, Hamilton to Seely, June 7, 1913; and PAC, RG7, G21, Box 142, no. 265, Mackenzie to Borden, April 25, 1913.
34 Seely *papers*, Box 18, pp. 31-59; and Ford, pp. 84-90.
35 Ford, p. 87.
36 Seely *papers*, Box 18, Hamilton to Seely, July 5, 1913.
37 Ibid., Box 18, Hamilton to Seely, June 7, 1913; and ibid., Hamilton to Seely, June 11, 1913; and ibid., Hamilton to Seely, June 7 and 21, 1913.
38 Ibid., Hamilton to Seely, July 18, 1913.
39 Hamilton, *The Happy Warrior*, pp. 257-58.
40 "Report on the Military Institutions of Canada," by General Sir Ian Hamilton, Inspector-General of the Overseas Forces (Ottawa: King's Printer, 1913). He also recommended a National Reserve; re-implementation of muster rolls, and a paper organization for the Reserve Militia. Sir Ian placed special emphasis on maintaining the imperial connection and in having Canada make more concrete its imperial defence responsibilities. He also identified large shortages in equipment of all sorts as well as men.
41 Hamilton, *Report*, 1913, p. 5.
42 Hamilton, *The Happy Warrior*, p. 258.
43 Seely *papers*, Box 18, Hamilton to Seely, June 21, 1913; and ibid., Hamilton to Seely, July 18, 1913.
44 PRO, CO537, 498, HMO 07860, Canada 44607; and Gooch, *Plans for War*, p. 155.
45 PAC, RG7, G21, no. 265, CO Letter no. 42496/1913, Dec. 12, 1913; and J. E. B. Seely, *Adventure* (London: Heinemann, 1930), pp. 46-47, 125-27, 227.
46 Ibid., Hughes to Connaught, Jan. 30, 1914.
47 *Hansard*, 1912-1913, p. 4942.
48 *CAR*, 1913, pp. 216-17; and *Hansard*, 1912-1913, pp. 10418-19, 10824.
49 Seely *papers*, Box 18, Hamilton to Seely, June 21, 1913; and Hamilton, *Report*, 1913, p. 34.
50 Oxford, Bodleian Library, Lewis Harcourt *papers*, Box 463, "Memorandum Re General Mackenzie," by Sam Hughes, June 1913.
51 PAC, RG7, G21, vol. 142, Harcourt to Connaught, Jan. 7, 1914, private and personal; and *CAR*, 1913, p. 218.
52 PAC, RG7, G21, vol. 142, Connaught to Borden, Dec. 3, 1913, private and personal; and ibid., Borden to Connaught, Dec. 8, 1913, private and confidential.
53 Ibid., Connaught to Harcourt, Dec. 19, 1913, secret; and Harcourt *papers*, Box 476, Seely to Harcourt, Jan. 23, 1913, pp. 124-25, secret; and ibid., Harcourt to Connaught, Jan. 27, 1914.
54 *Militia Report*, 1912-1913, p. 113.

CHAPTER 11

War and Mobilization: One Man's Show, 1914

However much the British declaration of war on August 4, 1914, may have come as a shock to most Canadians, few questioned their country's constitutional or moral obligations. Still fewer had given much thought to the possibilities of anything but a short war. Given the minuscule size of its regular force—about 3,000 in all ranks—it was assumed that Canada's military role would be to reinforce and complement Britain's.[1] While Sam Hughes' prewar efforts were sufficient to meet the traditional demands of Canadian defence and perhaps even to send abroad a small volunteer expeditionary force, much as had been done in the Boer war, no one could foresee then the great forces that were about to be unleashed. Four years later, amid the casualties and carnage, these had radically and painfully changed Canada and the Empire.[2]

Yet in early June 1914 when Parliament adjourned for the summer recess, the country seemed serene, despite the strains of the previous year's naval aid debate and the first signs of a serious recession setting in. Balkan politics were remote and so was the assassination near the end of the month of the Austrian Archduke in Sarajevo. The Governor-General, the Duke of Connaught, had headed west towards Banff; the Prime Minister relaxed bass-fishing in Muskoka; and like so many other MPs, Sam Hughes had gone home. July was hot; the weather was good; so were the crops. But by the middle of the month the slow diplomatic movements of the moribund Austrian Empire let loose a series of events that picked up a war momentum. Hughes knew that if the situation deteriorated into conflict between the powers of the

---

Reference notes for Chapter 11 are found on pp. 194-97.

Grand Alliance and the Entente, it would be war between England and Germany—and war for Canada.[3]

On July 28 the British flashed a message to the Empire to adopt the precautionary stage of war planning which had been agreed upon two years before by the Committee for Imperial Defence. Hughes rushed to Ottawa to meet with his militia staff. He told newsmen that, if needed, Canada had plans to send an overseas contingent. There was no doubt in his mind that if war came Canada's role would be a fighting one. By mid-day on August 1, and five days before the British asked for them, the Militia Minister advised his Prime Minister that troops were immediately available. The less excitable Borden waited for others of his cabinet to return to Ottawa before he made any decision.

Germany's war declarations against Russia and France came on the first and third of August. Sitting in his office at militia headquarters, Hughes grew so impatient with Britain's hesitancy to join the fray that he bawled to his embarrassed military secretary, C. F. Winter, to take down the Union Jack atop the building proclaiming, "By God I don't want to be a Britisher..." if they would not back France. When war finally was declared on the evening of the fourth, it came as a relief for Hughes. The Prime Minister and the rest of the cabinet also seemed caught up with the Militia Minister's enthusiasm. The next day Hughes made the announcement that Canada would send Great Britain one division—and public opinion all over the Dominion applauded the decision. Even Quebec, where such obvious foreign military involvements had never been received enthusiastically, seemed to support the declaration. Almost caught in France by the German invasion, Henri Bourassa, the tireless French-Canadian nationalist, added his endorsement when he got home. In Parliament during the special war session called in mid-August, the eloquent Laurier also promised, perhaps over-generously, that the Liberal opposition would loyally refrain from political partisanship until the war's end; and Borden had reciprocated with his own testament of patriotic government neutrality in its course. In 1914 it seemed as if Canada was united as never before.[4]

To Hughes the announcement of the division meant mobilization, such considerations as arms, equipment, establishments, reserves, transportation schedules, and recruiting organizations. The year before the war, when he had reviewed mobilization plans, Sir Ian Hamilton had gone to great pains to warn Canadians about the dislocation any haphazard methods would cause.[5] Considerable strain would be put on most government departments. What was needed was calm, efficient planning and teamwork, the very essence of sound administration.

In 1911, under General Mackenzie's orders, Colonel W. G. Gwatkin, then mobilization officer, began confidential plans for raising a small military force for service outside Canada. This scheme was secret and separate from the already evolving domestic mobilization project. In the Gwatkin overseas plan, a division of infantry and a mounted brigade totalling 24,000 were either to concentrate at Petawawa or to go directly to the point of embarkation depending on the season. The scheme was decentralized and highly dependent on the local divisional and district commanders for most things including recruiting, remounts, and equipment. The Militia Council was to determine the senior officers while the commanders of the military divisions would advise on lesser appointments. By the onset of the 1914 crisis, the Gwatkin plan, although still incomplete in some of its details, was in the hands of the local commanders.[6] When Hughes arrived in Ottawa on July 28, he had two choices: accept Gwatkin's arrangements or make his own. By the time the Prime Minister arrived two days later, Hughes had made up his mind to scrap the existing plan and to run what was tantamount to a one-man show.

This decision would have a major impact on Canada's participation throughout the entire war. On July 31 Hughes ordered all the divisional commanders across Canada to discard Gwatkin's 1911 plan. Then he set in motion his own program. First, the Minister sent 226 night telegrams directly to the local unit commanders in the Active Militia directing them to remit to Ottawa, for final approval, rolls containing the names of volunteers willing to go overseas. On August 10 the Minister apparently restored the military chain of command by ordering the divisional commanders to mobilize certain formations and units. Three days later he again modified these instructions. Conflicting messages continued to emanate from general headquarters and the office of the minister. Hughes interfered in the smallest details. He ordered troops to be sent directly to Valcartier, Quebec, where as yet there was neither a camp nor a rail line. Arms were not handed out at the local level. The Minister took away the local commanding officer's task of acquiring remounts and similar equipment and placed it instead in the hands of many of his own special agents. By calling for rolls to be prepared and sent to Ottawa, Hughes complicated mobilization. For instance, as the commanding officer of the 31st British Columbia Horse, C. L. Flick, protested, his squadron leaders got the mobilization order two days before he did.[7]

Several things probably saved Hughes from making a complete blunder of mobilization. Most important was a flood of enthusiastic volunteers anxious to aid Britain. During the next six weeks after the mobilization order, young men across Canada swamped local recruiting offices. "Recruits are simply pouring in from all quarters," one B.C. lieutenant-colonel pointed out. Another from Ontario happily reported that, with lots of men offering, he knew "that we would have no difficulty in getting all we required." As these volunteers paraded through the streets of many towns throughout the Dominion, the excitement was overwhelming. "Young ladies carried the men's rifles," J. A. Currie, commander of the 48th Highlanders witnessed, "others decorated them with flowers; others clung to their arms and the sidewalks were a mass of excited cheering humanity." Militia headquarters itself was deluged with personal letters from those who could not get accepted into the units but who did not want to miss the "great adventure." Such demonstrations supported the public impression that Sam Hughes' way got results.[8]

The Minister also had a very hard-working headquarters staff who helped smooth out the ambiguities caused by his interference. He also knew how to manage the press. At the beginning of the crisis, he initiated daily press conferences in his office for the hordes of reporters anxious for any story. Often called "seances" by the newsmen, these informal gatherings were very popular—and they were easy news. Often in the late evening with his shirt sleeves rolled up and amid the clutter and clatter of a very busy office, Hughes described what had been done that day and what would happen the next. To uninformed readers, such reports suggested that all war activity was in Hughes' hands. Many of his colleagues disapproved of his limelighting techniques; and they did not like reading in the press what he later asked them to approve in council. Borden simply thought that "Hughes [is] doing well but gives too many interviews."[9]

There are complicated reasons why Hughes improvised the first contingent. Not many of them excuse his ways, but they make them at least somewhat understandable. Hughes could not delegate power, and as Desmond Morton suggests, the Minister's motives remain impenetrable. This is not the case when his militia concepts and his proving ground, the Boer war, are considered. In addition to his personality, these are the controlling features of the Minister's controversial activities for the next two years. At a time when one could buy Stand Fast whisky, and John Player's cigarette sailor had "Hero" inscribed on his hat band, Hughes had a romantic vision of war in which local battalions responded spontaneously to a call to arms, as they had always done. Past experiences, supported by the militia myth, provided evidence that impromptu methods were all that responsible citizen-soldiers needed; and the South African war was the only precedent for sending Canadians out of the country in any numbers. The bulk of those, the Minister knew, were easily recruited through the battalions.[10]

But there were other reasons for Hughes' impromptu methods. Traditionally Canadian militia forces had been highly political. The Northwest Campaign and the Boer war had proven that reality, nearly

Hughes, the "black lad" (number one), was aggressive and tough at lacrosse and politics.
Toronto Public Library, Early Canada Picture Collection

Hughes loved to shoot, and thought that most citizens should as well to ensure that Canada was well defended.
Public Archives Canada/PA-16121

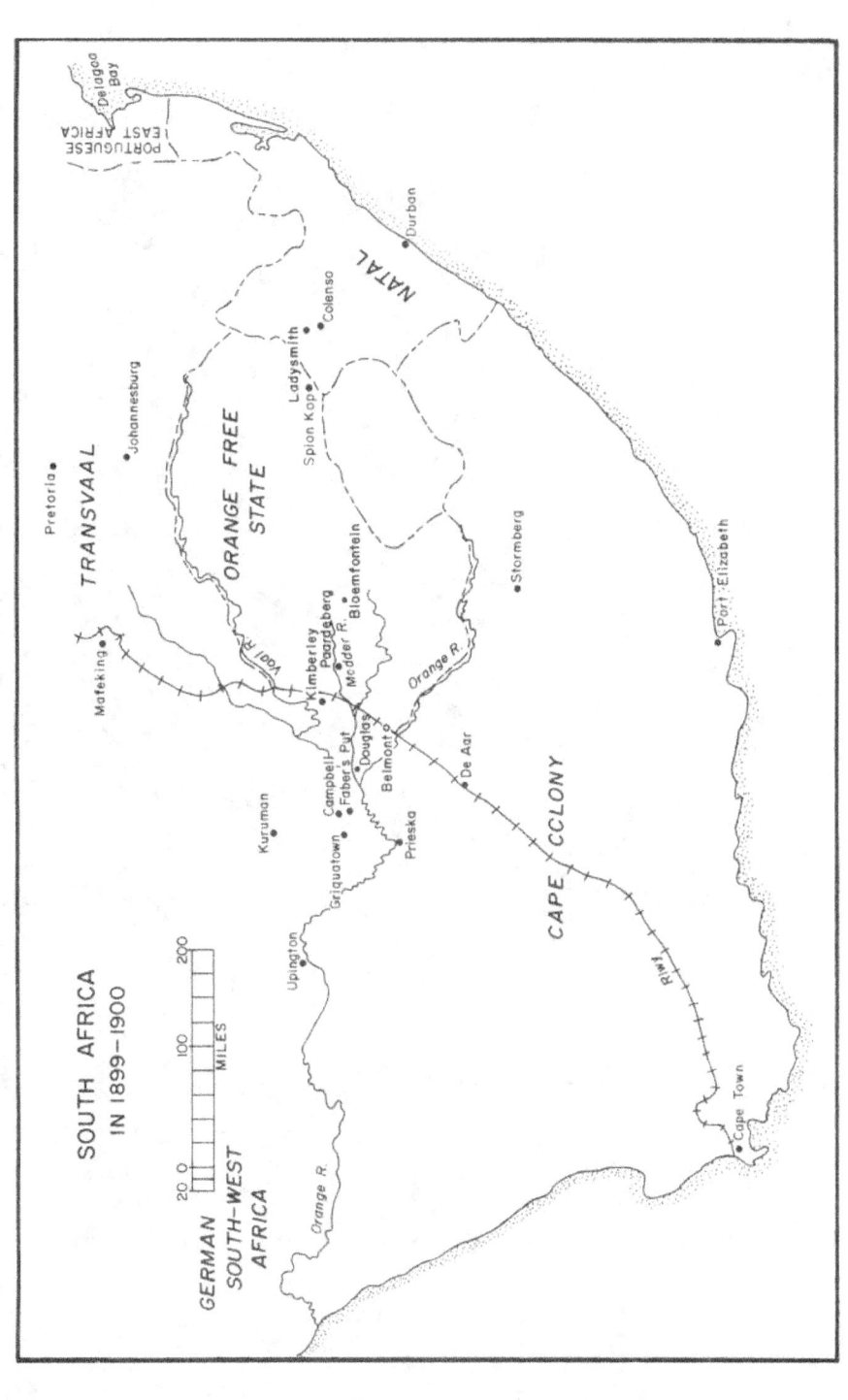

Although Hughes was fired from his post in South Africa, he received a hero's welcome from the citizens of Lindsay when he returned in 1900.
From the collection of A. R. Capon

Senior Conservative M.P. and official militia critic, 1904.
Public Archives Canada/PA-12223

Colonel Sam on the hustings, c. 1911.
From the collection of A. R. Capon

Mr. Borden's first cabinet, October 1911.
Public Archives Canada/C-23913

Hughes and Connaught review troops in front of the Parliament Buildings, 1914. R. L. Borden looks on (centre).
Public Archives Canada/PA-25088

The Ross rifle being fired through a MacAdam shield-shovel before a satisfied Hughes at Valcartier, 1914. From the collection of A. R. Capon

Hughes and some of his family early in the war aboard the private car that served as his "command post." From the collection of A. R. Capon

"Hughes' boys" of the CEF on their way to the "Great Adventure," October 1914.
Public Archives Canada/PA-22731

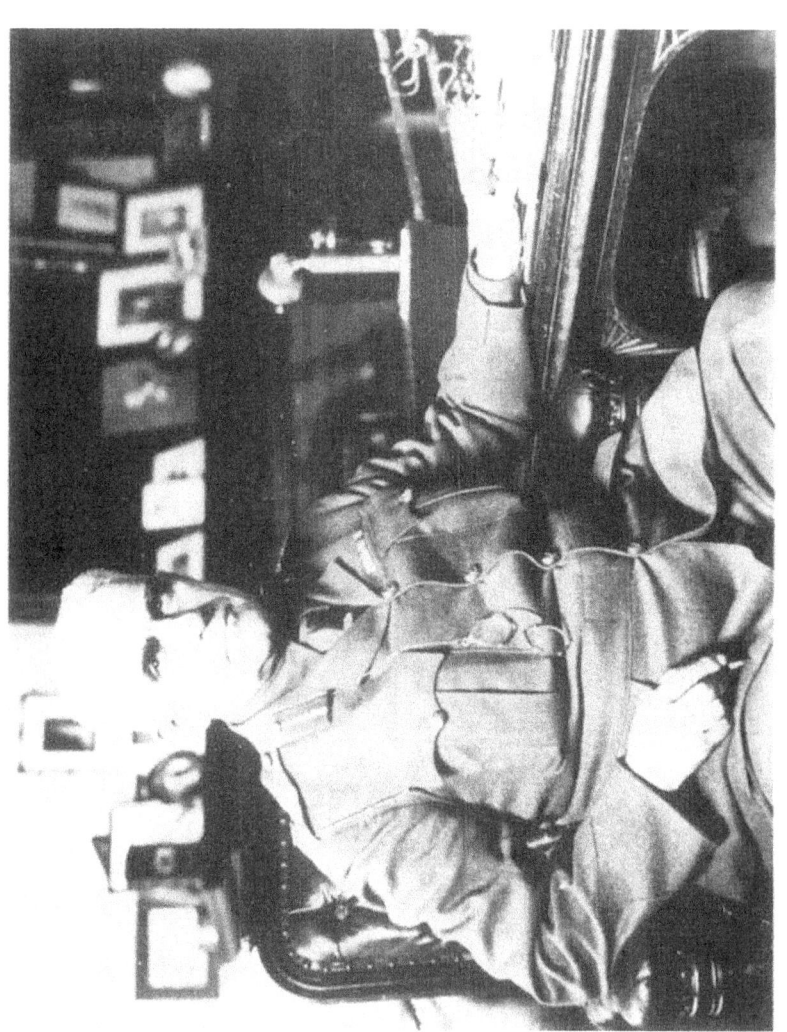

Hughes at his ministerial desk, in uniform, 1914.
From the collection of A. R. Capon

The three Hughes generals in France. On Sam's left, Garnet and William.
Public Archives Canada/PA-4881

The minister teaches bayonet drill in France in 1916.
Public Archives Canada/PA-596

TROUBLE WITH THE DECEASED

The newspapers had a field day when Hughes was sacked, and the Tories were frightened about what he might reveal.
From the collection of A. R. Capon

*Hughes' funeral parade, Lindsay, Ontario, August 1921.
From the collection of A. R. Capon*

disastrously so for Hughes in the latter case. And in 1914 when the political shoe was on the other foot, the Minister was determined to follow the traditional pattern. Furthermore, the year before he had told Connaught that Mackenzie had kept the overseas plan from him and that it was devoid of all merit. Mackenzie had denied the Minister's charge. But whatever the case, Hughes' personal control of the plan and of the slate of officers' appointments guaranteed that no Hutton-style manipulation of government would take place in the new war.[11]

There were also some serious shortcomings in the Gwatkin plan. The divisional staff used for the overseas unit was the same one that governed the domestic militia forces. To send the former out of the country would seriously erode the ability of the home forces to mobilize quickly. Sir Ian Hamilton had commented on this flaw in 1913; Loring Christie, the Prime Minister's personal advisor on legal affairs, gave the same advice. Several years later, in looking back on those hurried events, Christie also reminded his chief that the legal implications of a force mobilized to fight outside Canada were in serious doubt, sufficiently so that the Governor-General had to raise the question with the Colonial Secretary on August 2, 1914. In the special war session of Parliament called on August 18, Hughes told the members that there was no authority to send the militia out of the country. Consequently only volunteers, as distinct from the Dominion's forces, were acceptable. Perhaps Hughes jettisoned the 1911 scheme because he wanted to avoid such time-consuming pitfalls. In 1916 he explained to the Commons that Gwatkin's plan was just too slow for the first contingent, but since there was no hurry with the subsequent divisions, he used normal channels. He had also caught, he said, the sense of patriotic response of English-speaking Canadians in their willingness to enlist in 1914, and at the same time admitted his compulsion for crusading when he told the Commons that his mobilization "was really a call to arms, like the fiery cross passing through the highlands of Scotland, or the mountains of Ireland in former days."[12]

That the practical mobilization questions weighed heavier than Hughes' personal or political ones seems improbable. Yet they were there. In some ways Hughes resembled his British counterpart, Lord Kitchener, who at the same time was also ignoring his professional soldiers and an existing mobilization plan. But the best explanation for his action remains the fact that Sam Hughes was an egotistical and grand improvisor, led on by an archaic war concept and encouraged by a particular view of a citizen's martial responsibilities, by existing military moods, and by his own experience.[13]

Possibly Hughes' greatest achievement in the mobilization process was the creation of Valcartier Camp. Since 1912 the Militia Department had planned to build a training camp for the Quebec militia and had selected the wide valley where the Jacques Cartier River joins the St. Lawrence above Quebec City. But as of the summer 1914, nothing had been done at all in the area. When mobilization was announced, Hughes decided that with the apparent rush to get Canadian troops to England the contingent would best be situated close to an embarkation point—a fact not present in Gwatkin's scheme, which would have had the troops assemble at Petawawa in Ontario. On August 7 Hughes ordered his friend and the Quebec Tory party organizer to build a camp and have it completed by the time the entire force assembled there. It was a tall order. But armed with a new honorary lieutenant-colonelcy, Price plunged into the work. Hughes also helped him along by ordering the construction contractors with their heavy equipment, who were then putting the finishing touches to the Connaught Rifle Ranges a few miles above Ottawa, to move down to Valcartier. Price's valuable business connections also eased the situation, and no doubt a substantial number of Quebec's Conservative subcontractors got welcome business. But whoever got them, 400 workmen built the camp in thirty days, including installing sewers, water mains, rail links to Quebec City, and three miles of rifle ranges. It was a dusty and busy place, with the first troops arriving by the third week in August. In all it accommodated nearly 33,000 troops; and Canadians and most of the cabinet, especially the Prime Minister, were amazed at the speed with which Hughes got it done. Borden was "well pleased." Even Hughes' old enemies, such as the dour Trade Minister, George Foster, thought it was "a fine site," and the Governor-General was grudgingly forced to admit that it was a splendid performance all round.[14]

However, problems lay behind the Valcartier accomplishment; some were beyond the Minister's control, others were not. The troops were meant to do little training in the camp; the British wanted them sent to England in a hurry. With expected shortages of equipment and much of their brief stay taken up by giving the 33,000 soldiers some organization, including officers, medicals, and attestations, there was confusion, made all the more evident by the constant construction and the influx of new troops.[15]

Yet Sam Hughes could not leave the process alone. Dressed in his colonel's uniform, he was frequently at Valcartier living in his specially constructed brick bungalow. Around him were numbers of assistants and newspaper reporters. Indeed he tried to carry on simultaneously the duties of his Ottawa office and those of the camp; and there were always swarms of citizens delegations and contractors buzzing around the Minister looking for benefits for their regions or businesses. The many surviving photographs suggest that Hughes liked the publicity and commotion. Sometimes his peculiar personality and arbitrary methods were both depressing and abrasive. Canon F. G. Scott felt that "the dominating spirit was General Hughes who rode about with his aides in great splendor like Napoleon. To me it seemed that his personality and despotic rule hung like a dark shadow over the camp." Hughes also interfered with the smallest details of camp life, from the inspection of horses to giving lessons in the art of bayonet fighting. The average onlooker could not be certain whether Sam Hughes was acting as a soldier, a politician, or a simple camp guide. During September he held four well-publicized troop reviews to which he invited the public and his cabinet colleagues. There were even special excursion trains from Quebec City. On the last one, the weekend of September 20, some 10,000 visitors showed up along with Connaught, Princess Patricia, Borden, and other ministers to watch Hughes—instead of the camp commandant—lead the march-past before the Duke.[16]

The spectacle certainly did not amuse Connaught. Yet since the outbreak of the war, the Field Marshal had taken his nominal role as head of the militia far too literally. He also felt that he could offer Canadians his military expertise. At first others had thought so too: in early August Borden had asked Connaught to attend the cabinet meetings as the government mobilized for war. But by the end of the month, the Prime Minister had lost his enthusiasm. As he confided to his diary, "the Duke [is] very fussy about being consulted on every detail."[17] As for Hughes, he no doubt thought he recognized another Boer war, Minto-style meddling in a purely Canadian affair, and he told the Duke, in no uncertain terms, what his constitutional role allowed him to do in Ottawa or in Valcartier Camp. The horrified Borden had to warn Hughes not to repeat his abuse; and he did not—for a while. But he went out of his way to ignore the sensitive Connaught. By mid-September the Duke thought Hughes was "mentally off his base" and when the troops departed for England, his wounded vanity and bloated sense of place made him complain secretly to the Colonial Office that his advice was "seldom taken." It was the start of two years of wartime quarrels between the two men.[18]

Connaught and Scott were not alone in their complaints about Hughes' "overbearing manner." Even before Valcartier Camp was begun, the nearly continuous round of cabinet meetings spawned by the war were often stormy. Several members including George Foster tangled with Hughes over his determination to run the force himself. There had been sharp altercations with Thomas White in the Finance Department over Hughes' letting of war contracts without first seeking cabinet approval. No doubt some of the objections emanated from his colleagues' jealousy over the Militia Minister's new patronage potential, but cabinet members also felt that they too had something to offer the war effort. While Borden's diary entries during these days are full of admiring comments about Hughes' "wonderful" drive and "splendid work," they are also full of notes of exasperation about his heavy-handed manner and loose tongue. At Valcartier there were enough complaints that Borden felt compelled to intervene several times to smooth raised hackles among maritime officers the Minister had offended. But it was also true that Borden spent some time quieting two others of his political brood, Sam Sharpe, MP for Ontario North, and David Watson, managing director of the Quebec *Chronicle*, who were at each other's throats over conflicting military ambitions; and as the Prime Minister was willing to admit, Hughes had often been provoked into his unfortunate outbursts by equally antagonistic officers.[19]

Hughes was no diplomat in dealing with men. He had to cope with organizational problems which had no precedent nor easy solutions. The root of these lay in the parochial and political nature of the old militia out of which most of the Valcartier soldiers had come. At the camp the volunteers had to be formed into battalions. Many of the militia officers who brought up their troops lost their expected commands; others, good Tories, expected Hughes to favour them. Given his personal control, he easily could and often did give favours, none of which lessened the scramble. One of the less partisan observers, the Liberal A. W. Currie, then a newly appointed brigadier in the Canadian Expeditionary Force (CEF), noted how Hughes bore the brunt of all the manoeuvring during those hectic days: "The minister's life must have been a misery for days on end ... every squirt of a politician in the country and especially those in camp were trying to arrange things to their own selfish ends. Everyone was at everyone else's throat." In addition, since the Canadian militia could not legally be involved at Valcartier and since Hughes tried to build a division with national representation, as in the Boer war, none of the new overseas battalions had any direct connection with the traditional militia units of Canada. To those who expected to go overseas wearing the insignia of their militia regiments, the remustering process was a bitter disappointment.[20]

Often the selection of officers was arbitrary. Hughes felt he knew the military quality of these men and he did not hesitate to use his power. It seemed he was handing out on-the-spot promotions, many of them to favourites and Tories. J. A. Currie who commanded the 48th Highlanders and who also sat on the same side of the Commons as Hughes, was appointed commanding officer of the 15th Overseas Battalion. But John Currie had also brought over 800 men of his militia regiment to Valcartier and was probably the best man for the job. Hughes also made his son Garnet a staff officer in the third brigade, the command of which went to another Tory, Richard Turner, a Victoria Cross winner in South Africa. But the Minister did not exclude Liberals. A. W. Currie, destined to become Canada's greatest soldier, was one. But besides being the friend of the Minister's son, he was also a talented militiaman. Currie was assigned command of the second brigade. C. G. "Chubby" Power, son of a Liberal Senator, pointed out later that Hughes had simply yelled at an assistant to "find Chubby Power and give him a commission"; and Lieutenant-Colonels F. W. Hill of the 1st Battalion and W. J. Buell of the 4th Battalion were also Grits.[21]

Yet there were other ministerial appointments which adversely affected sound administration. One of them came when Colonel Victor Williams, the Adjutant-General of the militia, and a Tory-leaning friend who had sided with Hughes during the Mackenzie feud the year before, was made camp commandant and then led the contingent to England at the end of September. This action robbed the Canadian militia of the services of one of its senior administrative officers at a very critical time. The Adjutant-General's post was not filled for five months. During this period, Hughes did not employ his professional soldiers effectively. Only his personal choice from their ranks were allowed to join the overseas contingent. Later Hughes claimed that he had kept the regulars in Canada for constitutional and training reasons. But in August, when Connaught wanted the Royal Canadian Regiment (RCR) sent to Bermuda, thereby freeing a British unit for action in Europe—a fact that makes the Duke little better than his Minister—Hughes eagerly complied. Since the RCR was the only regular infantry regiment in Canada, the Minister's action denied the Valcartier troops much needed professional expertise.[22] As a result, the first contingent sent overseas suffered from a lack of trained officers at the senior staff level. There was little choice but to fill this need with British soldiers, a proposition to which the Minister was also strongly opposed. But in fairness to Hughes, it is doubtful if the few Canadian regulars could have provided many senior staff-trained officers to the first contingent.

When criticized for any of his impulsive acts, Sam Hughes only became more aggressive. The work load was tremendous. He got little sleep and was involved in virtually everything that went on with the contingent. Nor was the news from Europe good. The British wanted the troops soon; and the Canadian public, as Lieutenant-Colonel J. A. Currie remembered, easily deluded themselves into thinking that once a man was in uniform he was fully trained. They too wanted the contingent sent overseas right away. But of the 33,000 volunteers, the War Office wanted only a heavy division, in all about 25,000. As minister Hughes was badgered by those pleading special cases to go. The often conflicting political and military considerations substantially increased the strain. So did Hughes' still solidifying vision of a massive response by a national contingent. He wanted everyone to go. But that decision was not his to make. Fortunately for the Militia Minister,

Robert Borden also had a similar and yet just as vague view of Canada's effort. In time, military participation would be used as a way into British councils. But whatever the case, on September 22, after Borden had seen the large Valcartier force parade the previous weekend, and where he had no doubt listened to Hughes' and others' pleas to go overseas, he announced that the entire force would be sent to England. It was the best solution to a political and military dilemma; it answered the urgency of the times. When Borden told his Minister, Hughes "broke down and sobbed."[23] Thereafter Hughes' disposition improved noticeably; now he could get on with moving the troops to England.

Late in September when the CEF marched down their tent lines towards Quebec City, they were moving into an embarkation scheme that also bore the stamp of the Minister's improvisations. As with the mobilization, there had been a prior plan, one that had been updated by the Director of Supplies and Transport to handle 31,200 troops, their baggage and kit. Hughes discarded it. Instead he again put the departure arrangements in the hands of William Price. Considering the immensity of the task, Price did a remarkable job. Thousands of waiting troops and hundreds of horses, along with piles of equipment and throngs of curious and patriotic onlookers, crowded Quebec City's streets and docks. The Militia Department took any ship that was offered or could be commandeered. When the men went aboard, some vessels were overloaded; some were loaded with equipment separate from units using it; and some had to take on water for ballast. Sorting it all out in England caused more confusion. Yet Price and his assistant, A. J. Gorrie, another prominent Montrealer with good business and party connections, accomplished their task in record time even though Gorrie himself thought chaos had "reigned supreme." But Hughes did not argue; he told the Prime Minister's wife that he had made "perfect arrangements" for the departure.[24]

Nevertheless the ships got away, and one by one dropped down the river to anchor in the Gaspé Basin to await the others until they could sail as one big convoy. During this time, Hughes never lost contact. As the flotilla waited and grew, he travelled by his ministerial steam launch to each vessel offering words of praise and encouragement. He had thousands of copies of a departing address, called "Where Duty Leads," handed out to the soldiers. The content was maudlin and hardly original, and was structured after Napoleon's famous address to the Army of Italy. Even the Prime Minister privately lamented in his diary that the Minister's theatrics "did not enhance his prestige and was a laughing matter."

In spite of the confusion and Hughes' pretentiousness, a great many people gave him full credit for the speedy organization of the CEF and its safe arrival in England when it landed a week and a half later. His popularity lasted well into 1915 in both countries. The partisan press could rant all it wanted about his eccentricities—and it did plenty of that—but most Canadians outside the grip of partisanship genuinely thought that Sam Hughes was the embodiment of the expeditionary force. Unfortunately this success reinforced Hughes' tendency to think himself infallible and indispensable to the war effort.[25]

Even before he received the public acclaim for the quick formation of the contingent, Hughes, perhaps trying to recoup his lost Boer war chances, had hinted at leading the force into battle himself. In August he had his friend Robert Rogers approach Borden asking if this was possible. Borden had no strong personal objections; he sent the request off to the War Office through the High Commission. Like Lord Kitchener, Hughes could see nothing wrong with holding both jobs. In later years, when he challenged anyone in the Commons to "point to an instance where I overstepped my rights as Minister of Militia or as Officer Commanding the forces," he unconsciously admitted that he could not tell the difference between his civil and military roles. Yet the initial attempt at command was thwarted, not by Borden, but by Lord Kitchener who cabled the Prime Minister that "it would be a mistake to change the minister [of] militia at this juncture."[26]

The rejection did not dampen Hughes' enthusiasm once the force set sail for England. In early October he persuaded Borden to let him go over. Borden agreed for several reasons. First, both men wanted to keep watch over the force once it left Canadian shores; to Sam Hughes this meant personal control. Second, the Minister had convinced Borden that he had vital information about Canadian officers to give to the newly chosen British commander of the contingent, General E. A. H. Alderson. Most importantly, Borden hoped that, while Hughes was out of the country, the aggravations he had aroused within the party and elsewhere in the country would subside. Closely associated was the strong push by some in the caucus to go to the polls that fall. An election would be constitutionally mandatory in a year. With the war enthusiasm and Hughes' bright public image and equally important absence, the time might be right.[27]

At the beginning of October, just after the CEF convoy sailed out of the Gulf of St. Lawrence, Hughes rushed to New York to board a liner bound for England. Before going Borden had warned him that he had no official military role and that he was not to aggravate the English authorities. Hughes, however, remained as vocal as ever. When he arrived in New York, he grandly announced to the newspapers that Canada could "send enough men to add the finishing touches to Germany without assistance from either England or France."[28]

Hughes actually arrived in England before the contingent did; but he did not stay out of military affairs at all. Still in the uniform of a full colonel, he had a large military staff accompanying him. These were hardly the trappings of a tired man on a holiday (the official reason for his trip) or one who wanted to avoid military involvement. While laying the beginnings of what was to be a very personal and elaborate overseas administration, Hughes constantly promoted the Canadian war effort in aid of Britain. He was given what amounted to a hero's reception from the English people.

But in private some British politicians were less than happy about the visit, in particular Harcourt at the Colonial Office and Kitchener in the War Office. Still, as the Colonial Secretary confided to the Governor-General, "I am keeping on the best possible terms with him and hope that he will return to Canada shortly in a fairly good temper." Aided by deliberate public priming, Hughes' tour around England proved less painful than some of his enemies feared. His enthusiasm was infectious, and coming as it did after the long retreat from Mons, his optimism was welcome. At several flattering public functions, he promised eager audiences large numbers of stalwart young Canadian volunteers, varying anywhere from the 70,000 he cited at a Bexhill, Sussex, military review to 300,000 before the Royal Automobile Club. Even the venerable London *Times*, got carried away by tales of a million if necessary. Whatever the offer, Hughes nearly always left the impression that the success of the CEF was his own personal triumph.[29]

But it hardly seemed fitting that such praise should fall on a mere colonel. Having been thwarted in trying to get himself promoted by Mackenzie in 1913, the Minister tried again soon after the war was declared. In August he sent his Deputy Minister, Eugene Fiset, and the Adjutant-General, Victor Williams, to ask for the Prime Minister's consent. Hughes wanted the highest rank he could get, lieutenant-general, but Borden was reluctant and Connaught outright opposed. However, by autumn Hughes' success with the CEF strengthened his case, and in late October 1914, after receiving an urgent telegram from his Minister in England stating that being a colonel was just not suitable, Borden finally gave in and promoted both him and Gwatkin to major-general. The Militia Minister's appointment was made retroactive to 1912 when he had originally tried to get the promotion, which gave him seniority over his chief of staff. Still Hughes was not satisfied. He wanted a high rank in the British Army as well; so with the support of Max Aitken and other British politicians, including Lloyd George, he tried for that too while still in England but failed.[30]

Once Hughes got his Canadian promotion, he renewed his agitation to get an overseas command. With the mounting complaints about the Militia Minister and the dilemma over an election, Borden briefly dallied with getting rid of Hughes that October. At most he could insist on a ministerial resignation as the price of command, and at least,

Hughes might be shunted off to an obscure military theatre away from Canadian troops as he had been in the Boer war. The Prime Minister secretly advised Perley in London to clear the way for "political reasons." But he lost his resolve when Kitchener refused. The British remembered their last experience with the feisty colonial in the field. Kitchener told Borden that Hughes should go home and "attend to work" there. None of it mattered much. By this time Hughes' acute political instinct had caused him to back-track. He was not going to sacrifice his government career with an election possible; so he safely retreated into ambiguity on the command issue and Borden gave up for nearly two years any attempt to remove him.[31]

Hughes got home from England early in November 1914. The flattering English accolades and the prestige of his new rank did little to temper his aggressive acts or vanity. Nor did they curb his enthusiasm for mobilizing Canadians for war and for recruiting as many as he could under arms. For the next several months, he went back and forth across the country in his private rail car giving speeches and interviews to anyone who would listen about the need to get involved. He resumed his highly personal and controversial style, all of which provided grist for his detractors' mills. In late November, for example, he told a London, Ontario, audience that he favoured shooting dishonest contractors and "rawhiding" any civilian who doubted the Canadian military capacity. Not only had he arranged the miracle of the first contingent, he told one audience, but he also personally had saved it from destruction by German submarines while sailing overseas. The British, he went on, were not at first willing to give the Canadian troop convoy adequate naval protection and finally did so only after his vigorous protests. Again in November, newspaper reports claimed that three Turks were arrested in London, Ontario, with instructions to assassinate the dynamic Canadian Militia Minister. His reaction was to say that he was glad they were not armed with Canadian Ross rifles or they would have got him for sure.[32]

Hughes' relations with his professional soldiers continued to be poor and distrustful. Often he publicly criticized them, as he did General Lessard in November when the General ran a practice mobilization for Toronto militia units. With all of the wild German sabotage and spy rumours then circulating in the city as elsewhere in the country, none of which Hughes did much to dispel, the test was indeed alarmist. Hughes was correct in his condemnation of it, but not in publicizing it, nor in labelling Lessard's act before a Toronto patriotic society as "ridiculous nonsense" and as "the worst military tactics possible." Though Borden was forced to defend Lessard in public, the Minister's outburst did little to instill public confidence in the regular soldiers. Moreover, the incident had pointed the finger at a senior officer of French-Canadian background commanding in English-Canada.[33]

Sam Hughes continued to ignore his headquarters staff. In July 1914 Gwatkin had complained to an unknown correspondent that, in spite of two dire Colonial Office warnings, the Minister could see no need for interdepartmental defence planning; and the war crisis only heightened Hughes' neglect. It was not until late September that the Minister informed the CGS who the senior officers of the first contingent were, and then he did so only after the latter had complained about not knowing. By the early new year 1915, Gwatkin was even more worried about Hughes allowing vital departmental administration to "drift" and treating his military staff as so many "informal" associates. More and more the Chief of the General Staff had to seek information through unofficial and indirect channels to find out what his Minister was doing. Seven months into the conflict and during a period of acute shortage in rifle ammunition, the desperate Gwatkin wrote to the Governor-General's secretary, "Stanton, will you please ask the Duke to ask the Premier what is being done toward obtaining one-hundred million rounds of small arms ammunition, the purchase of which was authorized by order-in-council."[34]

During this time, as afterwards, Hughes' absences from Ottawa could only have added to the "drifting." Between August 1914 and November 1916, Sam Hughes was out of the country one-third of the time. Perhaps one of the longest periods that he remained in Ottawa was the two weeks he spent in the hospital early in 1915. On at least two occasions, the Prime Minister had to go to the hospital to find what was going on in the department because the staff did not know. The Minister's military secretary remembered that during Hughes' "many absences from Headquarters visiting camps, inspections etc. the departmental files awaiting his decisions would accumulate to alarming piles." None of this made for orderly or efficient administration.[35]

Sam Hughes sometimes appeared oblivious to the bewilderment he created. In December 1914, on the suggestion of Connaught while Hughes was in England, the headquarters staff established military inspection services under regular soldiers François Lessard and Sam Steele to ensure that the first contingent and another one just offered had a constant flow of reinforcements and supplies. The services also covered training, recruiting, equipment, and discipline. When Hughes found out about the Duke's role he was upset. Instead of getting rid of the offending system, which he could have easily ordered as minister, he simply appointed another one headed by his brother, John Hughes, and a Liberal militia colonel, Sydney Mewburn. For over two months, the two agencies existed side by side each trying to do the same job. By January their clash brought orderly inspection services to a standstill with Lessard bitterly complaining to the Militia Council that unless things were cleaned up he would refuse to do his job. Someone also must have complained directly to the Prime Minister, for he had to ask Fiset about Hughes' scheme. Fiset had little knowledge of what Hughes had done and he in turn had to query the chief of staff, who replied that the Minister had never bothered to consult anyone on the matter. But Gwatkin made his position clear: "I am not in favour of the board [Hughes' creation] nor is the AG nor I believe are you." When Hughes showed no inclination to retire his body or fire the other one, Borden was forced to override Hughes to re-establish Steele and Lessard to their rightful position. The Prime Minister then reminded the Minister that he had no legal authority to act without cabinet approval, that his personal agents had no qualifications, and that "the question ... arises who is responsible to the Government of Canada."[36] More to the point, Borden clearly preferred the Duke's agency, likely because it was not under the Minister's thumb.

Such incidents had little effect on Sam Hughes. Nor did they help to harmonize his relations with militia headquarters, the cabinet, or Rideau Hall. The problem, as E. M. Macdonald, the Liberal militia critic, correctly noted, was that Hughes' appointments appeared so obviously partisan when many other politicians and private citizens had called for an end of political abuse for the duration of the war.[37]

No matter how well Sam Hughes tried to run an efficient department during the war, he was a contributor to and was encumbered by the dilapidated machinery of state which retarded efficient administration in many departments. As the Canadian war effort grew to unexpected proportions, the predictions of Sir George Murray and others finally came home to haunt many in Borden's government; and not the least of these was Sam Hughes. In 1912 Murray had said that the traditional practice of departmental improvisations caused great inefficiency. Often ministers, he noted, gave more time to administering small details than to general policy and planning. Department heads, he went on, should delegate their power and only act in the political capacity of dictating policy. He also had recommended the appointment of political undersecretaries to relieve their chiefs of some of the routine departmental burdens. But Hughes for one had refused to share his portfolio with any such individual. Murray had also reminded Canadians of the principle of "the collective responsibility of the cabinet for the actions of individual ministers." Neither then nor during the war could Hughes ever see the need for such reforms; and he often gloated that his methods were "unorthodox" and "unique," as if there was some inherent efficiency and good in their practice when, indeed, they were really anachronisms.[38]

By the late autumn 1914, Hughes' highly controversial public activities threatened the fragile tranquillity of the senior party organization. The nearly exhausted Borden was flooded by complaints. Even earlier when J. D. Hazen, the Minister of Fisheries and the Naval Service who had run Hughes' department while he was overseas, told Borden flatly that Hughes' administration was "most unbusiness-like and irregular," the Prime Minister decided to keep a watching brief on Hughes thereafter. One first act was to announce the formation of a second contingent while Hughes was still in England and unable to interfere. Yet complaints continued to come in.[39]

On November 19 E. B. Osler, the influential and veteran Tory MP for Toronto West, came to see Borden to object to Hughes' public outbursts. So did J. S. Willison, editor of the Toronto *News*. The next day Sir Richard McBride penned his thoughts on the Militia Minister. "There is no question," he wrote confidentially, "of a very pronounced feeling in many quarters against one of your colleagues [Hughes]. He is a great personal friend of mine and I value the relationship—still under all obtaining conditions, it is best to speak frankly." On November 23 Borden recorded in his diary that there were "many violent letters from Toronto as to his conduct."[40] The following day Kemp and Lougheed came to his office to object to Hughes' "eccentricities."They were followed by the Governor-General on November 26. By the end of the year Borden also witnessed Hughes in a first-class row with the Auditor-General and Thomas White in Finance over Hughes' erratic Militia Department spending without cabinet approval. He also heard the first reports that one of the Militia Minister's long-time friends and newly commissioned honorary colonel, J. Wesley Allison, from Morrisburg, Ontario, was making huge profits on British war contracts with Hughes' written endorsement. In spite of these denunciations, Borden continued to support Sam Hughes, both in the Militia Council and in public. During that December, in a series of speeches across the country promoting the war effort and his own government performance, Borden praised Hughes' tremendous war energy in building Valcartier and mobilizing the first contingent, although when the Prime Minister spoke before Toronto's Empire Club, he mentioned neither Hughes nor his office by name. Indeed Borden demonstrated a strange ambivalence about the Militia Minister for the next two years. In early 1915, he thought Hughes "quite unbalanced" in things which touch upon his "insane egotism"; other times he felt that the Militia Minister was "on all other matters, able and sometimes brilliant." Later he noted that "Hughes seems lately much less excitable and impulsive and much saner than usual."[41]

Why if Sam Hughes seemed such a political impediment so soon in the war did the Prime Minister not do something about the stumbling block? There are many reasons. At that early point, in a war which few expected to be as large as it became or last as long as it did, the general public considered Hughes to be the very personification of the national war effort. Though there were violent outbursts in the Liberal press, most Canadians were used to such partisan abuse. While they were well aware of the failings of Hughes, pressmen like A. R. Ford, parliamentary reporter of the Toronto *News*, P. D. Ross of the Ottawa *Journal*, Colonel J. B. Maclean of *Maclean's Magazine*, the urbane Toronto author, Augustus Bridle, and the prolific J. Castell Hopkins of the *Canadian Annual Review* applauded Hughes' early efforts. There were others. Clifford Sifton, who would remain a Hughes admirer because of the Minister's commitment to the Allied cause and his refusal to be bullied by anyone, advised Borden that the Minister had accomplished more than any other man in mobilizing the first contingent. Another was Robert Rogers. During the excitement of Valcartier many others of the cabinet had also expressed their faith in Hughes.[42] Yet it was much more than their support which made Borden stick with his Militia Minister. There was hard political reality. To fire Hughes meant that Borden's war administration would be exposed as inefficient and irresponsible from the start. There would also likely be a political crisis created by Hughes' not inconsiderable if somewhat silent supporters. As his reluctance to leave the Militia Ministry for active military command indicated, Hughes would not give up his post voluntarily, nor would he probably accept a cabinet shuffle which tried to reject him quietly. When Borden did reshape his ministry in mid-October 1914 in preparation for a general election that was not called, he never even considered that Hughes should be replaced. Instead Borden planned to get rid of two of his French-Canadian members whom he believed did not have much political value left for his government. The plain truth seems to be that the naturally hesitant Borden both liked Sam Hughes and was intimidated by his real or imagined power. The Prime Minister could not bring himself to bold action when all the evidence was not in.[43]

And at least until the Canadians were shocked into objective criticism by the slaughter of their own soldiers at Ypres in the spring of 1915, there was the screen of Hughes' powerful public image. Even after that, it took a long time for evidence to accumulate which could erode Hughes' reputation. To many defenders, Hughes was the specific manifestation of the same electricity which the war had sparked in many other Canadians in 1914; he was absolutely confident that the nation could do anything in pursuit of victory. When Hughes went to England in 1915, he was rewarded for his effort with a knighthood. Sir Reginald Brade, Lord Kitchener's secretary, expressed to his chief the grudging admiration many Englishmen felt for Hughes, no matter how exasperating he often was. "Sam's energy," he told Kitchener, "has added a corps of good troops to our fighting forces ... no one else could have done this in Canada." Borden thought this was true and he knew Sir Sam had "earned it."[44]

To the less discerning of 1914, Hughes' prewar predictions all seemed to fall into place. Furthermore Robert Borden was not a military man. He deferred to Hughes and even protected him from others, such as White and Foster, on grounds that Hughes knew what he was doing. It was a powerful argument. Sam Hughes talked and lived the war; he portrayed himself as the creator of the effort; his enthusiasm to extract such an effort from the country almost exactly coincided with a large public desire to give it and the Prime Minister's belief it should be so. Most Canadians knew there were bound to be mistakes and irregularities, but within limits they were willing to tolerate them. Hughes had not yet reached those bounds. The criticism of Hughes, at least until early 1915, was more about what he said than what he did. What he had done, of course, was to give to the easily converted the miracle of Valcartier and the first contingent. Nobody, least of all an overly indulgent Prime Minister, could fire a man of Hughes' accomplishments when as yet his errors were mostly words and rumours.[45]

Reference Notes to Chapter 11

1 R. Mathew Bray, "'Fighting as an Ally': The English Canadian Patriotic Response to the Great War," in *Canadian Historical Review* LXI, no. 2 (1980), pp. 141-47; and J. L. Granatstein and J. M. Hitsman, *Broken Promises, A History of Conscription in Canada* (Toronto: Oxford, 1977), pp. 22-23.

2 Beck, p. 139. For an overall view of the war, see Brown and Cook, chapters 12 to 15; and John Swettenham, *To Seize the Victory, The Canadian Corps in World War One* (Toronto: Ryerson Press, 1965).

3 Cook and Brown, pp. 210-11.

4 Lord Hankey, *The Supreme Command* (London: George, Allen and Unwin, 1961), vol. 1, p. 133; Winter, pp. 133, 135-36; and Borden *private diaries*, August 4, 5, 6, 1914. Also see *Hansard*, special session, 1914, pp. 8-10 and Schull, *Laurier*, p. 557.

5 Stanley, p. 317; and PAC, pamphlet, no. 4039, pp. 11-12.

6 Stanely, pp. 307-309.

7 PAC, Loring Christie *papers*, MG 30, E 15, vol. 2, f 3, p. 120; and ibid., p. 1168, "Memorandum on Mobilization," n.d.; ibid., pp. 1132-33, "Memorandum on Daily Events," n.d.; Duguid, p. 5, and appendices 10, 17, and 44; and G. W. L. Nicholson, *The Official History of the Canadian Army in the First World War, The Canadian Expeditionary Force, 1914-1919* (Ottawa: Queen's Printer, 1964), pp. 10-20. Also see historical section, General Staff, Canadian War Records, vol. I, *A Narrative of the Formation and Operations of the First Canadian Division to the End of the Second Battle of Ypres, May 4, 1915* (Ottawa: King's Printer, 1920), p. 3; hereafter cited *Canadian War Records*.

8 C. L. Flick, *Just What Happened* (London: privately published, 1917), p. 14; J. A. Currie, *The Red Watch: With the First Canadian Division in Flanders* (Toronto: McClelland, Goodchild and Stewart, 1916), pp. 32, 39; *CAR*, 1914, pp. 136-41; and PAC, *Department of National Defence* (DND), RG 24, vol. 373, 54-21-1 to 24-21-4. These are a few of the sources testifying to the enthusiasm of Canadians to aid Britain.

9 Winter, pp. 76-77; and Borden *private diaries*, August 6, 1914.

10 Morton, *A Peculiar Kind of Politics*, p. 19.

11 Private letter, Desmond Morton to the author, Mar. 25, 1969; and PAC, Laurier *papers*, A, vol. 710, p. 196734, Bostock to Laurier, Aug. 17, 1917; PAC, W. A. Gries-

bach *papers*, MG 30, G 44, f 1, Hughes to Griesbach, May 13, 1915; PAC, RG 24, no. 265, vol. I, Hughes to Connaught, June 1913. Mackenzie himself did not believe in the viability of the plan; and PAC, Christie *papers*, vol. 2, f 3, p. 1167, "Memorandum on Mobilization," n.d.
12 Duguid, appendix II; and Colonel J. S. Brown, "Military Policy in Canada, 1905-1924 and suggestions for the Future," in *Canadian Defence Quarterly* (July 1924), pp. 24-25. See PAC, Christie *papers*, vol. 2, f 3, p. 1164, "Memorandum on Mobilization," n.d., and pp. 1260-68, "Memorandum on Employing Forces Outside of Canada," June 6, 1917; PAC pamphlet, no. 4039, pp. 9, 31; Governor-General to Colonial Secretary, Aug. 2, 1914, cited in Duguid, appendix 17. In *Hansard*, special session, Aug. 18, 1914, p. 95, Hughes said he had no authority to send anyone except volunteers out of the country; also see ibid., 1916, p. 287.
13 Philip Magnus, *Kitchener: Portrait of an Imperialist* (London: Penguin, 1968), pp. 374-75, and private letter, Captain John Swettenham to the author, Mar. 15, 1969.
14 PAC, RG 24, vol. 413, 54-21-1-29, "Report on the Construction of Valcartier Camp"; Nicholson, p. 20; *Hansard*, 1915, pp. 522-26; Duguid, appendix II; PAC, Borden *private diaries*, Sept. 6, 1914; *CAR*, 1914, pp. 200-201; PAC, Sir George Foster *diaries*, MG 27, 11, D 7, Sept. 19, 1914; and Ford, pp. 88-89.
15 PAC, Gwatkin *papers*, F 1, Gwatkin to Elliot, Oct. 2, 1914; RG 24, vol. 142, 54-21-10, Gwatkin to Rowley, Nov. 3, 1914; Winter, p. 11; Duguid, appendix 98, CO to Governor-General, Sept. 1, 1914; ibid., appendix 64, CO to Governor-General, Aug. 14, 1914,; and ibid., appendix 65.
16 Canon F. G. Scott, *The Great War As I Saw It* (Toronto: Goodchild, 1922), p. 17; *CAR*, 1914, pp. 200-201; and Borden *Memoirs*, vol. 1, pp. 462-63.
17 PAC, Borden *private diaries*, Aug. 25, 1914.
18 Ibid., Sept. 16 and Aug. 17, 1914; and Harcourt *papers*, 476, no. 29, Connaught to Harcourt, private and confidential, Oct. 5, 1914, pp. 175-79.
19 PAC, Borden *private diaries*, Aug. 4, 5, 6, and 25, and Sept. 14, 17, 19, 21, and 24, 1914; and Foster *diaries*, Sept. 19, 1914.
20 Duguid, appendix 85. Each numbered CEF battalion had members of militia units in it; some, like the 15th, had mostly one militia regiment (48th Highlanders); while others, such as the 2nd was composed of personnel from nineteen different militia units drawn from MD 2 and 3.
21 Currie, *The Red Watch*, chapters 1-5; Morgan, 1912, pp. 168, 534; Johnson, p. 147; A. M. J. Hyatt, *The Military Career of Sir Arthur Currie*, dissertation (Duke University, 1964); Norman Ward ed., *A Party Politician, The Memoirs of Chubby Power* (Toronto: Macmillan, 1966), p. 44; and Duguid, pp. 91-92.
22 Nicholson, pp. 21, 537; Canada, Department of the Secretary of State for Canada, *Copies of Proclamations, Orders-in-Council and Documents Relating to the European War* (Ottawa: King's Printer, 1915 and 1917), PC. 2164, Aug. 17, 1914; hereafter cited State Department *Documents. Hansard*, 1902, pp. 1138-39; ibid., special session, 1914, p. 95; *New York Times*, Feb. 17, 1916, p. 3; PAC, DND, RG 24, "Army," vol. 486, "Memorandum of Compostion of CEF," GO 106, May 5, 1915, 54-21-4-44; PAC, Gwatkin *papers*, Gwatkin to Rutherford OC:RCR, Halifax, Aug. 1914. Later, Hughes was reluctant to have the RCR transferred to France in spite of Gwatkin's urging (ibid., F 2, Gwatkin to Christie, Mar. 17, 1915); and Critchley, p. 49.
23 Borden *Memoirs*, vol. 1, p. 462; Currie, pp. 43-44; and Brown, *Borden*, vol. 2, p. 15.
24 For a description of the confusion, see Duguid, pp. 94-99 and appendices 130, 131; Flick, pp. 46-47; PAC, Sir David Watson *diaries*, 1914-1919, MG 30, G 13, Sept. 29, to Oct. 6, 1914; Currie, *The Red Watch*, pp. 45, 64; PAC, Sir George Perley *papers*, MG 27, II D 12, vol. 3, p. 47, Perley to Borden, Jan. 24, 1915; PAC, Borden *private diaries*, Sept. 26, 1914; and Morgan, *1912*, p. 460.
25 Borden *Memoirs*, vol. 1, p. 465; and Duguid, appendix, 149; *CAR*, 1914, pp. 200-202, 1914, pp. 186-87; PAC, Kemp *papers*, vol. 39, f 9, "clippings 1914"; and Swettenham, pp. 39-40.
26 *Hansard*, 1917, p. 267; PAC, Borden *private diaries*, Aug. 8 and 25, 1915; and Canada, Department of External Affairs, *Documents on Canada's External Relations, 1909-1918* (Ottawa: Queen's Printer, 1967), vol. 1, no. 64, Perley to Borden, Aug. 18, 1914, p. 44.
27 PAC, Borden *papers*, OC 318(2), pp. 35860-62, Hughes to Borden, Nov. 1, 1916. George Perley, the Acting High Commissioner, was convinced that the force should

be entirely under the War Office and part of the British Army "in every sense of the word." See PAC, Perley *papers*, vol. 2, p. 26, Perley to Borden, Sept. 18, 1914, and p. 29, Borden to Perley, Oct. 20, 1914; PAC, Borden *private diaries*, Aug. 11, 17, and 25, 1914; Harcourt *papers*, 476, no. 29, pp. 175-79, Connaught to Harcourt, Oct. 5, 1914; and Brown, *Borden*, vol. 2, pp. 18-20.
28 Harcourt *papers*, 465, p. 37, Perley to Harcourt, Oct. 9, 1914; and *CAR*, 1914, p. 217.
29 Ibid., 476, pp. 193-96, Harcourt to Connaught, Oct. 28, 1914, confidential. For an example of the favourable impression created by Hughes see PAC, RG 9, III, *CEF* box 203320, HS-20-H-3, inspection tour, Bexhill, Sussex, Oct. 1914; and *CAR*, 1914, p. 214; Stephen Gwynn, ed., *The Anvil of War: Letters Between F. S. Oliver and his Brother, 1914-1918* (London: Macmillan, 1936), p. 46. Oliver was a founder of the Round Table group; his brother Frank sat in the Canadian Parliament. London *Times*, Oct. 16, 1914, p. 9.
30 PAC, Borden *private diaries*, Aug. 11, Sept. 12, 22, 1914 and Oct. 12, 1914; PAC, III, *CEF*, Box 203320, HS-20-H-3; Lord Beaverbrook, *Men in Power, 1917-1918* (London: Hutchison, 1956), pp. 273-74; Nicholson, p. 209; and *Militia List*, July 1917, pp. 57, 107.
31 PAC, Perley *papers*, vol. 2, p. 29, Borden to Perley, Oct. 20, 1914, cable, and Perley to Borden, Oct. 23, 1914, cable. Also see Harcourt *papers*, 476, 34, pp. 193-96, Harcourt to Connaught, Oct. 28, 1914, private.
32 PAC, RG 9, *CEF*, Box 203320, HS-20-H-3, extract from *Canada*, Nov. 28, 1914; and the clippings file, in PAC, Kemp *papers*, 39, f 9, especially the *News*, Nov. 25, 1914.
33 *CAR*, 1914, p. 219.
34 PAC, Borden *papers*, OC 277, p. 31527, Gwatkin to Fiset, Jan. 21, 1915; and PAC, Gwatkin *papers*, F 2, unaddressed copy of a letter by Gwatkin, July 1, 1914; ibid., Gwatkin to Hughes, Sept. 21, 1914; and ibid., Gwatkin to Stanton, Apr. 5, 1915; and PRO, C0694/27, circular letter to Dominions from C.J.D., Nov. 10, 1913, and Apr. 3, 1914.
35 The best description of Hughes' travels is in *CAR*, 1914-1916. He spent nearly seven months overseas during the period; PAC, Borden *private diaries*, Jan. 2 and 8, 1915; and Winter, p. 16.
36 PAC, Borden *papers*, OC 277, p. 31521; ibid., I. G. East to secretary of Militia Council, Jan. 20, 1915, pp. 31508-509; ibid., Borden to Fiset, Jan. 21, 1915, p. 31526; ibid., Gwatkin to Fiset, Jan. 21, 1915, p. 31527; ibid., Borden to Hughes, Jan. 20, 1915, pp. 31511-12, and ibid., Christie memorandum to Borden, n.d.
37 For instance, see ibid., OC 318, clipping, Montreal *Mail*, Aug. 11, 1916, which states that while on tour, Hughes called for Major Boyer out of his entourage. Boyer replied that he was only a captain. Hughes responded quickly, "You're a Major now" (PAC, RG 9, III, A1, *Carson File*, 8-1-70, Major John Basett [ADC to Hughes] to Carson, Aug. 9, 1916). Boyer was a journalist, a Liberal, and a militiaman in the 17th Hussars. See Morgan, *1912*, p. 132. Hughes ordered three promotions in this letter alone. There are many other examples such as Power, *Memoirs*, p. 44; and Flick, p. 33. After Hughes' abortive attempt to make his brother, John Hughes, I. G. East, the Minister made him commandant of Valcartier Camp, June 8, 1915 (*CAR*, 1915, p. 190). Also see *Saturday Night*, Feb. 13, 1915, p. 4; ibid., Sept. 4, 1915, p. 1; PAC, Foster *diaries*, Dec. 15, 1915; Macdonald, pp. 273-74; *CAR*, 1915, p. 192; and G. M. Lefresne, *Pegasus: The Canadian Department of Overseas Transport and the Movement of Imperial Supplies from Canada to Europe, 1914-1920*, graduate paper (Queen's, 1971).
38 *Sessional paper*, 1913, no. 57a, "Report on the Organization of the Public Service of Canada," by Sir Geo. Murray, paragraphs 6-27; and Capon, p. 70.
39 PAC, Borden *private diaries*, Oct. 16, 17, and 21, 1914; and Borden *papers*, 31, pp. 15664-66, Hughes to Borden, Oct. 25, 1914.
40 Public Archives of British Columbia, Sir Richard McBride *papers*, Add Mss, 347, Box 1, f 8, McBride to Borden, Nov. 20, 1914; and PAC, Borden *private diaries*, Nov. 19, 23, 24, 26, and 27, 1914.
41 PAC, Borden *private diaries*, Oct. 21, 1914, Jan. 2, Feb. 12, Mar. 19, and June 5, 1915; Brown, *Borden*, vol. 2, p. 16; and Sir Robert Borden, "Canada and the Great War," in *Empire Club Speeches, 1914-1915* (Toronto: Dent, 1915), pp. 6-15.
42 PAC, Borden *private diaries*, Mar. 18, 1915; Floyd Chalmers, *A Gentleman of the Press* (Garden City, N.Y.: Doubleday, 1969), pp. 202-208; Ford, pp. 88-89; Ross, pp.

200-210; Domino, *The Masques of Ottawa* (Toronto: Macmillan, 1921), pp. 141-52; *CAR*, 1914, pp. 200-202; ibid., 1915, pp. 186-87; J. W. Dafoe, *Clifford Sifton in Relation to his Times* (Toronto: Macmillan, 1931), p. 387; D. J. Hall, *Clifford Sifton*, vol. 2, *The Lonely Eminence 1901-1929* (Vancouver: UBC Press, 1985), pp. 276-77; and PAC, Borden *private diaries*, Aug. 8, 1914.
43 Brown, *Borden*, vol. 2, pp. 16-17.
44 PAC, Borden *private diaries*, Feb. 26, 1915 and Aug. 15, 1915; and PRO, Kitchener *papers*, 30/57/56, WG 21, Brade to Kitchener, Aug. 16, 1915.
45 Sir Andrew Macphail, *The Official History of the Canadian Forces in the Great War, 1914-1918: The Medical Services* (Ottawa: King's Printer, 1925), p. 190.

CHAPTER 12

Recruiting, 1914-1916

Military records show that by the end of the Great War 619,636 Canadian men and women had served with the army. It took four years to raise such a number, and well over half enlisted while Sam Hughes was War Minister. By late 1916 when he was fired from the cabinet, the army overseas had four divisions and another ready for organization. But Canadians at home had lost much of their enthusiasm for volunteering to feed the field force. However, two years earlier the opposite had been true when the majority of Canadians seemed determined to do their duty. After the first contingent left Valcartier, the Prime Minister authorized a second one in mid-October. The next month militia headquarters decided to maintain 30,000 men under arms in Canada. By July 1915 the overall total was 150,000 and three months later 250,000. On New Year's Day 1916, the Prime Minister announced that the national establishment of the Canadian Expeditionary Force (CEF) would be a half million men. It all looked so easy. But by mid-1916, the volunteer system began to falter all over the country. As the war effort stepped up, the demands of the other equally vital forces of industry and agriculture competed for the men. Enlistments slowed down. In English-Canada pessimistic conscription rumours turned into open demands; and as enlistments dried up before the mounting casualties in Europe, French-Canadians recoiled at the prospect of being drafted for a foreign war, which by 1916 they no longer considered much of their concern.

To avoid a national schism—perhaps even an open rebellion—the government desperately tried other solutions. By the fall of 1916 national registration to co-ordinate the wealth of the nation had come and gone. In early 1917, amid the crescendo of English-Canadian voices

---

Reference notes for Chapter 12 are found on pp. 222-24.

demanding conscription, the harried Borden administration attempted to free volunteers for the front by establishing the Canadian Defence Force for domestic duty, but it too failed. That spring, after the British authorities predicted the need for more and more troops, the Prime Minister finally resigned himself to military conscription. In May 1917 he announced his intention and padded the blow by promising to bring in conscription through a union government. In the next six months, the declaration split the country along French and English lines, irrespective of party; and by the general election in December 1917, Canada had both coalition government and conscripts.[1] The story of these events involves Sam Hughes, and to a large degree he, like his Prime Minister, must bear both praise and blame.

Sam Hughes' one-man mobilization effort in 1914 set the tone for recruiting in the next two years. Hughes gave to the recruitment effort nerve-end leadership—spirit, enthusiasm, vigour, hope, and confidence—but little order and less administration. He conceived of Canada's war contributions mainly in terms of fighting troops in a national army. But he never appeared to understand fully the modern needs of such a force. He could not see, first, that national war must have at least a semblance of consensus of the nation's people—both French and English—and second, that limits on the size of the force and the method of keeping it at established strength were problems which eventually would have to be faced. Force size was a political problem that belonged to the government as a whole but one for which Sam Hughes as Militia Minister must give sound and realistic advice to the cabinet. Maintenance of strength, however, was an administrative question that for the most part belonged to Sam Hughes. Instead of understanding these dimensions, he seemed governed solely by a desire to show Canada's martial prowess on the battlefield in a huge patriotic and volunteer army without regard for the effects of unrestrained recruiting on industry, agriculture, or the combat efficiency of the force.[2] But in 1914 and 1915 the faults of Sam Hughes' recruiting system were not immediately obvious because the demands of war were not known; and in all fairness to Hughes, few of his fellow ministers in the beginning had any more of an accurate conception of how best to respond to the crisis. For months all of them worked in the dark using dilapidated tools of state. Some found both light and better utensils; Hughes never did.

When the first contingent had sailed in October 1914, Hughes had been thankful that Borden had allowed all the volunteers to go, a sure sign that both men agreed in the limited and archaic view that the best way to pursue the war effort was with soldiers in large numbers. When Hughes returned from England early the next month he immediately plunged into the organization of the second contingent, recently announced by the Prime Minister. In terms of manpower, he swung back to the old decentralized recruiting arrangements that had been with the militia since Confederation. In the scheme, authority rested with the officers commanding the divisions, who in turn gave quotas to each of the militia units of their areas. The quotas were supplied by headquarters, but beyond that there was little help from Ottawa in personnel, funds, or organization. In the first three years of the war, Ottawa spent only $27,000 on recruitment, most of it in 1917. But then little help was expected.[3]

The months from August 1914 to July 1915 are best described as ones of enlisting rather than recruiting. Nearly 60,000 had joined in 1914 alone. By February 1915 Hughes announced that a third contingent would be sent and optimistically told the Commons that "I could raise three more contingents in three weeks if necessary." As yet there was no perceived shortage of manpower in industry or agriculture. But it was the off-season for agriculture, and others presumed that the recession-induced unemployed were being conveniently syphoned off into CEF units. By June 1915 the overseas force had 100,247 officers and men. During the special session of Parliament the year before, Hughes had made it clear that as far as he was concerned this war would be one of volunteers, not conscripts. The Prime Minister had agreed when he told a Halifax audience in December that "there has not been, there will not be compulsion or conscription." The only technique Hughes applied during this period was to keep close watch on who got the commands of each new battalion.[4] Sometimes the divisional commanders asked that units be allowed to organize in their districts; other times—and increasingly so—Hughes made arrangements himself with specific individuals, then informed the divisional organization to expect a new unit in the area. True to his romantic view of war, the Minister was convinced that in a crisis a citizen's patriotic sense of duty would be sufficient to supply all the volunteers necessary. All he had to do was constantly remind them of it. As soon as he recovered sufficiently from the illness that had put him in the hospital in late December, Hughes took to his private rail car late in January to encourage volunteering. He had to get back to Ottawa by the opening of the new session on February 5, but before that he covered 7,000 miles in two weeks and delivered over twenty-five recruiting speeches across the country.[5]

Hughes gave out the stuff that many wanted to hear: the Empire was threatened; Canada had to do its duty. Canadians could do it and would do it; it was the moment of national greatness; Canada was a principal in the war, not a colony. Hughes' battle message, mixing national pride and imperial obligation, was contagious. No wonder Castell Hopkins considered him during those early days to be the single most visible and enthusiastic recruiting agent in the country.[6] The Minister's confidence, pride, and cajoling also added to the impression that manpower resources were infinite and no other government facilities except Sam Hughes' sermons were necessary in raising the country to war.

    The illusion was substantially aided by patriotic citizens themselves. The fervour seemed so great that the problem was not in stirring it up but in controlling it. The various gifts of money and food sent to the Belgian Relief Fund and to the British government in the early days were ample evidence of that spirit; so were the campaigns in many communities to contribute to the well-being of the soldiers. Local councils quickly arranged for gifts of money, clothing, and the small amenities like cigarettes and socks. Many churches and women's organizations across the country did their bit as well. The Ontario government donated a half million dollars to the Imperial War Fund in Great Britain. The same special session of Parliament that brought the ominous War Measures Act into being in August 1914 also created the Canadian Patriotic Fund, of which Hughes was one of the honorary vice-presidents. This group was dedicated to raising and distributing money to soldiers' families and it expanded and carried out this function throughout the war. In fact, the general shortage of equipment produced such a spontaneous public response of private donations, like "the machine gun movement," that militia officials and Borden were so embarrassed by the summer of 1915, they refused to accept such gifts. Hughes, however, had no such pangs. His role, he knew, was to encourage the people on to new heights of patriotic effort. In fact, Robert Borden's biographer claims that this sort of decentralized war responsibility was a calculated "policy decision at the beginning of the war." Hughes' activities in recruiting, therefore, were not out of tune with the rest of the government's general view of its role in promoting active citizen participation in the war effort.[7]

    However, by the spring of 1915 there were signs that these time-honoured concepts were not adequate. There were 36,000 Canadians already overseas, with an entire division in the trenches after February 1915. The war had lasted longer than the predicted six months; Christmas had come and gone and there were yet no victories. Then in mid-March, the British reported 13,000 casualties, including 100 Canadians, at Neuve Chapelle, and bungled the opportunity for the elusive "breakthrough" on the western front to regain the magic mobility every general sought. Even though few Canadian were victims, the 25,000 lost on both sides was a terrible omen for Canadians. The CEF did not have long to wait: a few weeks later the Canadians held a bulging section of the line near Ypres in Belgium. Late in the day of April 22, the Germans smashed into the French colonial troops to the left of the Canadians with artillery and the dreaded chlorine gas. In a ferocious defensive battle lasting nearly a week, Canada's tenacious amateurs restored the line at the terrible price of nearly 6,000 men. They won the admiration of all. Their effort was quickly followed by smaller but similarly expensive defences at Festubert in May and Givenchy in June. The Germans torpedoed the supposedly unarmed British liner *Lusitania* off the coast of Ireland on May 8. It took 1,200 lives, 100 of them from Ontario. This was indeed war; Canadians were stunned.[8]

Back home the successes of the CEF in these battles stirred the Canadian soul; but they also were a rude awakening to the true sacrifices. The Canadian Ross rifle, it was reported, had not worked well. Some said gunners had not had enough artillery shells to give adequate support to the Canadian infantry. But the most shocking revelations were the casualty lists. An increasing number of Canadian homes mourned the loss of loved ones; and it was not likely to stop. At the end of May, the British government announced, largely as a result of the jolt to its own complacency caused by the German spring offensive, that "His Majesty's Government would accept with deep gratitude" any number of troops the Canadians could send.[9] Hughes took it as a personal signal.

But would Hughes' non-system of recruiting provide the reinforcements? Even before Ypres there were signs that the rural militia units were having trouble filling their enlistment quotas. *Globe* columnist Peter McArthur demanded that it was time the Militia Minister co-ordinate his actions with the Agriculture Department in some definite recruiting policy. Part of the flash of enthusiasm which had given nearly 60,000 volunteers in 1914 was that most of the ranks—over 70 per cent in the first contingent—were not Canadians, but British-born immigrants. Initially native Canadians had little enthusiasm to fight for king and Empire in Europe. This fact made no impression on Hughes, at least not one that he nor anyone else admitted publicly. Yet suspicions indicated something extra was needed. Other citizens began stepping into the breach with or without Sam Hughes. The same month as Neuve Chapelle, the Speakers Patriotic League, the joint brainchild of H. A. Ames, a Quebec Conservative MP, and N. F. Davidson, an Ontario Tory Organizer, was created in Toronto. It was the first of many private civilian associations designed to promote all facets of the patriotic response to the war, including a more systematic recruiting organization. From this point, private recruiting leagues appeared all over English-Canada. Their proliferation in Ontario was so rapid that by November 1915 they combined into a central organization—the Ontario Recruiting Association with branches throughout the province working hand in hand with local militia authorities.[10]

Hughes was all for the local organizations and a personal approach to the war effort, as he had been since he had sent out his famous 226 night telegrams mobilizing the first contingent shortly after the war started. After that he had used the existing local militia structure to funnel into the CEF whole battalions closely associated with particular areas. But he did not do it without opposition. Since September 1914, the Chief of the General Staff had warned Hughes that he could not keep adding such units to the overseas force. What should be done, Gwatkin had then protested, was to establish modern centrally located depots providing basic training for the unbrigaded troops before they were syphoned off as reinforcements for the veteran line units. Before the war Sir Ian Hamilton had also warned Hughes about this lack of depots. Their reasons were solid. More efficient training and use of manpower and a smaller casualty rate were three important ones. As well, authorities would have some accurate idea of available resources on hand, a fact not always present in the anachronistic and decentralized method which Hughes had followed since the outbreak of hostilities. The American Civil War, of which Hughes claimed to be a student, had pointed out the perils of constantly raising new battalions, then sending these fresh but green troops into battle. But the Minister did not believe it was so; the Boer war had needed no such elaborate and soulless depots to produce good fighting men, so he ignored his staff.[11]

After the spring battles of 1915, the shocking casualties and increased demands reaffirmed Hughes' resolve to secure more men. The second contingent had lingered long in Canada awaiting transport and billets in England. Hughes was anxious to get it overseas. By the middle of June it sailed, but the recruiting news at home, while gratifying, was not as spectacular as it had been. It seemed that just as the manpower demands were rising remarkably, the will to supply them was faltering. The possibilities of a substantial short-fall were obvious after it became clear at the end of June that Hughes wanted to form a Canadian corps of two divisions. The thought horrified Connaught; he secretly confided to Kitchener that the move was a ruinous one contrived by Hughes for no other reason than to satisfy his ego for a Canadian national force "possibly with a view of obtaining the command... himself." The Duke also suffered from his own form of exaggeration: he was afraid of an invasion by German-Americans from the still neutral United States, and even more of a revolt in the west by recent immigrants from enemy countries. Troops should therefore be kept in Canada. More accurately, Connaught worried about the disastrous effect on vital agricultural and industrial production caused by Hughes' wholesale recruiting. Connaught protested to Lord Kitchener that it was "extremely doubtful" if the Dominion could "keep an Army Corps in the field up to its proper establishment."[12]

It was not probable that Hughes had duped Borden into supporting the formation of a Canadian corps, as the Governor-General also imagined. The Prime Minister was himself determined to send more troops. Nevertheless, the Governor-General had put his finger on the exact point that caused the regular soldiers so much anxiety. An army corps meant at least 50,000 troops in France. A corps was also the natural precursor of an army. Gwatkin and Deputy Minister Fiset had been greatly alarmed at the wastage of the CEF in the spring of 1915. At that time, Canada had to contend only with one division. The possibility of twice as many casualties came with the formation of a corps. An army, if it came out of that, would be impossible to maintain. Gwatkin wanted no more than a corps, and certainly not an army. In June when he told Borden that Hughes' grandiose plans were a "mistake," it had made no impression. A few days later, in responding to an enthusiastic militia colonel, who like many of the patriots wanted many more men sent, Gwatkin bluntly stated that it was wrong "to go on adding to the number of regiments, batteries, and battalions at the front." Better, he thought, to train reinforcements and produce war material rather than to be drawn into an intolerable and exhausting war effort because of a commitment to an unrealistic combat force.[13] The true import of his and the Duke's message was that Sam Hughes' vision of a massive field effort was courting ruin, and that there were different ways to make war other than by sending warriors. Also implicit was that Hughes should advise Borden that a realistic establishment had to be determined and then adopt an efficient method of maintaining it that was in tune with national capabilities.

It was not to happen. On July 8, 1915, Robert Borden increased the CEF force to 150,000.[14] The new figure meant more recruits. While the monthly enlistments had gone up in June, they were not sufficient to allow for even normal wastage in the new national goal.

In response Hughes remained largely on the old personal course. But a few weeks earlier, he had made some small concessions in applying direct government aid for recruiting when he decided that central rather than regimental recruiting offices would be set up and that recruiting would be continuous. In August, as a further inducement for volunteers, he approved from afar a national recruiting poster campaign; 100,000 of them were distributed from coast to coast. After that no other national advertising went on out of the militia headquarters for over a year, and even then the Minister rejected the Canadian Press Association's offer to co-operate in a national newspaper campaign to stimulate recruiting.[15]

In the summer of 1915, Hughes spent two months in England. Like the Prime Minister who was also there, Hughes went to the front where he saw the magnitude, the horror, and the deadlock of the war situation. When he got back to Canada in early September, what he had seen and heard only cemented his determination to step up the national effort. Canada now had a corps, but victory was not close; the British had not handled the first year at all well. What was needed was more and more troops. At the end of September, enlistment figures dipped threateningly. Hughes told reporters about his new local battalion and billeting plans. Modelled in part on Lord Derby's battalions in England, Hughes promised to house and train troops in any centre that could raise twenty-five or more district recruits. Surely, he reasoned, it would help the citizens realize the importance of the war as well as comfort men anxious about doing initial duty in a strange place. But the other aspect of the scheme had its roots in the traditional local unit structure of the non-permanent militia. Indeed, that was its very essence and the sum of Sam Hughes' forty-one years of experience in the Canadian volunteers. Hughes believed in the time-honoured technique of raising citizen-soldiers by appointing prominent politicians and businessmen as lieutenant-colonels to enlist battalions in their own local areas.[16] Sometimes these men were the Minister's personal and political friends who had no particular military knowledge. Over the next year, because recruiting "was continuous" and the men were penny-packeted across the country, the training was a hit and miss affair. The first man to enlist trained most, the last man hardly at all. Often those early volunteers, in effect, immediately became recruiters themselves in the desperate rush to get other men. The local billeting made the plan costly. In some cases supervision was nearly impossible and consequently discipline was often poor. Evidently the plan also deviated from the central recruiting centres set down earlier in the summer. Implicit in Hughes' scheme was the suggestion that recruits raised from the same locality would go overseas and fight together. As it turned out, the units were broken up in England to maintain the strength of the corps in France. A. M. J. Hyatt and Desmond Morton have called Hughes' scheme variously a "confidence trick" or a hoax. Since the labels both imply deliberate intent to defraud, such charges are not fair to Hughes any more than they are to Borden who supported the method. Yet continuous recruiting until the moment of departure made retraining in England almost a certainty. Nevertheless, these problems were not Hughes' concern; and even though they should have been, his mind could not handle those sorts of details, if he saw the flaws at all. He wanted men, and at October's end, Borden followed Hughes' lead, again raising the national commitment to 250,000.[17]

Why Borden did this is not clear. His biographer suggests the cause was rising casualties, more and more demands, poor leadership in London and Ottawa, and the lack of decisive victory. The papers of Captain Harold Daly, Hughes' assistant, explain more:

Once toward the end of 1915, he [Hughes] decided to raise another 100,000 men. He went over to see Sir Robert Borden, got authority for it, and told me to send over and get an atlas showing the different [political] constituencies. He then dictated about a hundred telegrams to different people, one in each constituency and out of that I think we got 60,000-70,000 men. He knew everybody all over the country who was popular and who could raise men.[18]

If Daly's memory is correct, the comment epitomizes the personal improvised nature of Hughes' recruiting ideas. But more than that, Daly's observations point out the scope of political party organization; with its emphasis on patronage as the means, the party system had traditionally performed many of the social duties that, in later days, Canadians expected the state to undertake. When war was declared this party machinery geared up to help solve the country's recruitment problem.

Hughes was one of the chief supporters and users of this traditional party system. In 1914 it was at the root of his 226 night telegrams; it was present in his retention of control over military offices and later recruiting. As represented by Sam Hughes, the government provided the impulses to the party structure to secure volunteers. What was in the interest of the party was good for the country. On that October day in 1915, when he told Daly to get out the constituent map, he was really calling for a stepped-up effort by the old party system as one of the normal pieces of machinery running that portion of the war effort. The episode also illuminates the relationship and similarity of ideas between Hughes and Borden. For a short time at least, it appeared that Hughes' recruiting rationale was paying off. With the new establishment set that October, enlistments jumped by 5,000 in November, and again in December.[19]

While men like Daly may have thought the Minister's recruiting accomplishments "wonderful," the other powerful reasons for the success remained the loyal and hard work of the volunteer citizens, recruiting leagues, and sufficient men who were willing to join. Yet Hughes remained, with his continuous touring, speeches, and inspections, the most visible single national recruiting figure in the entire improvised scheme. The apparent success of the combination, which he believed was mostly due to his own efforts, stirred the Minister to make bigger promises and more boastful claims. Already on record the previous February as claiming that he could raise three more contingents in three weeks, a little later he told a Montreal audience that he could "send a fifth [division] a sixth, a tenth or a twentieth." In Toronto in October, he declared to an enthusiastic recruiting rally: "We are coming General Kitchener, 500,000 strong." By the end of the year, Borden had translated that optimism into a half-million-man establishment for the CEF.[20]

On December 30, when Hughes and two other cabinet colleagues, White and Reid, met with Borden, the Prime Minister proposed that the overseas forces' establishment should be raised to 500,000. The move, Borden was convinced, would be welcomed by English-Canadians who were beginning to think that the Conservative administration, except for Hughes' activities no doubt, was not fighting the war vigorously enough. He also believed that the larger the physical contribution the greater would be Canada's influence over British war policy. With the way events were going at the front, the Prime Minister went on to reason, surely such a force would be needed. If all three visitors were surprised by the proposal, Hughes at least expected and wanted the new commitment; and he supported it fully. By January 12, the establishment of the CEF was put at 500,000 men. The question was: Could it be done?[21]

By now there were even Canadians who felt that it was too dangerous and too difficult a task; and as for others, maybe because they were Englishmen or professional soldiers or both, no one had bothered to consult General Gwatkin, the Governor-General or the people at the War Office; all of them were opposed. Borden also ignored R. B. Bennett, his parliamentary secretary, who had complained earlier that December that the new figure was impossible. Evidently few other ministers were consulted before Borden's decision was made. The new goal had been an impulse supported by Hughes, by White and Reid, and indirectly endorsed by Sir George Foster in the trade department, who naively thought that if 40 per cent of the population of about eight million was of military age then a 500,000-man CEF was not unrealistic. Ironically, Foster also thought that Hughes' recruiting methods were unrealistic and chaotic.[22]

But there was no doubt in the Militia Minister's mind that they could get the half million. Neither a challenge to the Prime Minister's judgment nor a doubt of its subsequent effect on other vital sectors of the war effort came from Hughes. Privately he told Borden, "we can easily live up to your offer, if right systems are pursued." Immediately he plunged into the new challenge by commissioning more local battalions and more local prominent citizens, friends, and businessmen. In 1915 alone, beyond the elements of the second contingent, Hughes had already approved of 141 CEF units; in 1916 the same method added 79 more; and as the local sources were no longer as fruitful, Hughes encouraged special interests, which encouraged the proliferation of Highland battalions, "Pals" and "Bantams" formations, and Irish regiments. Early in 1916 Hughes also promised that he would bring the best of the overseas officers home from the front to raise new units, a proposal which must have alarmed CEF commanders already suffering from serious shortages of reinforcements and experienced officers. As before, the Minister rejected using only the regular military structure; what he sought, he said, was "strong men who have successful business or professional training ... the best soldiers are such men as engineers, barristers, contractors, large businessmen with military training.... They far surpass the professional soldier."[23]

Ministerial optimism knew no bounds. In January 1916 Hughes easily convinced Borden to approve the establishment of a fourth Canadian division; the announcement sparked Max Aitken, the Minister's chief overseas agent, to wire flatteringly: "Your exertions may save the Empire." Certainly the accolade spurred the Militia Minister on; in February he told a New York *Times* reporter that he could raise one and three-quarter million men without compulsion in a matter of a few months. In Ottawa he laid out an elaborate plan to raise nearly twenty more divisions. It was unrealistic. Toronto was to give five, Ontario four; Manitoba and Saskatchewan, Quebec, British Columbia, and the Maritimes each gave two.[24]

By then the magnitude of Hughes' plans started to frighten his cabinet colleagues. Frequently council meetings, already stormy, became even more bitter. Thomas White was now alarmed. Hughes, he complained, "wants to press recruiting regardless of other considerations." It was true. Even the Prime Minister was finally having doubts about his own national pledge in the hands of Sam Hughes. He asked the Militia Minister not to recruit so that it dislocated other national priorities or denuded some localities of their manpower. Hughes paid little heed, but continued to cajole the country into sending more of its sons. From January to March 1916 over 90,000 Canadians joined up.[25]

But in the spring of 1916 there were pressing public arguments against unrestrained enlistments. Ironically much of the discontent came from those groups which had often been the Minister's most fervent recruiting aids—the civilian recruiting leagues. Dissatisfied for some time, they all agreed that the government could no longer count on volunteering to provide the resources. Now that Canadian industry, agriculture, timber, and mining resources were beginning to feel the strains of full wartime employment, the government had to impose a centralized and integrated recruiting policy to avoid harming the effort of the home-front. Moreover, the burden had to be distributed so that all parts of the Dominion were sharing it equally; and many identified Quebec as delinquent in doing its share. To some, what was needed was a national registration of the manpower, to others, an inventory of all wealth of the nation including human, and to even others, complusion if necessary. But they all agreed that the Borden government could no longer avoid direct involvement in recruiting and national mobilization.

Two of the most prominent critics were Lord Shaughnessy, president of the CPR, and Senator James Mason, the seventy-three-year-old former commanding officer of the 10th Royal Grenadiers. Both men had been great supporters of the war effort. But by March they were sceptical about meeting the new national pledge of half a million men. When Shaughnessy spoke out in Montreal about the goal's harmful effect on national production, Hughes scornfully dismissed the warning as "piffle," and publicly told Shaughnessy to mind his own business. Privately Borden agreed, choosing to believe that Shaughnessy's statement was nothing more than a political conspiracy against his administration. But then James Mason laid bare for his senate colleagues the hard realities of Borden's goals and the weaknesses of Hughes' improvised recruiting. "This large number [500,000]," he told a hushed chamber, "means that we shall have to provide each month . . . at least 25,000 new men—or 300,000 a year. There can be no question that the additional 250,000 to bring our quota up to 500,000 and the 300,000 if required annually to keep it at that figure will not be obtained under the present system of enlistment."[26] To Hughes it was still "piffle."

But it was not so to others. Many of the provincial governments had organized their war effort far better than Hughes had his own department. The Canadian Manufacturers' Association followed up Shaughnessy's predictions in a memorandum critical of Hughes' unlimited and unorganized recruiting. Various patriotic and recruiting leagues called for conscription or at least creation of a national register of wealth. So did Sir John Eaton, and executives of the Nova Scotia Steel Company, Consumers Gas, and the Dominion Steel Corporation. In April the New Brunswick Legislature passed a resolution asking Borden to employ "scientific means" in recruiting to protect industry and agriculture; and many national newspaper editorials carried similar messages. The old Tory, Castell Hopkins, sadly reported to readers of his *Canadian Annual Review* that during these months "the arbitrary policy and personality of Sam Hughes sometimes worked against recruiting as his enthusiasm and efforts worked for it." There was more alarming evidence long before the year was through. By April the monthly recruiting figures started to plummet from over 34,000 in March to a low of about 6,000 by September 1916, where they remained for some time. However, the previous spring while the protest was rising and the enlistments falling, Borden had done little publicly to change Hughes' improvised methods. In April the Prime Minister refused to hear a delegation of recruiting league members who had come to him hoping that he would do something in terms of registration and compulsion. When he refused to act, as Sir George Foster confessed to the delegates the next day, it was because the cabinet was afraid of riots in Quebec. In the same month, the frustrated recruiters formed the Canadian National Service League and openly lobbied for the draft.[27]

While Hughes remained in effective control of his department through 1915 and 1916, he continued to ignore the criticisms that his method of recruiting did not work. But many of his newly minted colonels who were raising local battalions were increasingly aware that there were serious problems. Frequently Hughes had authorized several units in the same area, and the battalion commanders ended up in cut-throat competition for men. Many used any method they could to secure the quotas; and it varied from bribing to shaming the individual into enlisting. None of it encouraged the hesitant volunteer. Two examples seem typical of those who had problems. Late in 1915 the Militia Minister let his old friend, William Price, raise a unit, the 204th in Quebec's Eastern Townships. After spending three months and a great deal of his time and money, and still never forming much of a battalion, Price lost his enthusiasm. His complaints to Hughes' aide in February 1916 sum up many unit commanders' frustrations and the Minister's inability to give recruiting some structure:

> I can now see that there will be difficulty in raising many men in this province. The organization is rotten and there is a complete misunderstanding of how to get French-Canadians to recruit. Each battalion should be given a certain district and should be forced to recruit from there and not allowed outside. This would force the battalions to recruit their localities thoroughly; at present, they do as they like and steal from each other. The way things go I am going to have a hard time to raise my men.... You might tell Sir Sam after what I have, it is impossible with the present organization to raise twenty thousand men from the district. To do so requires a complete new system and some slave driver at the head with the power of sacking.[28]

This unit never completed its establishment. Further west, where recruiters did not have to contend with reluctant French-Canadians, Lieutenant-Colonel W. A. Griesbach, commanding officer of the 49th (Edmonton Regiment), had much more success. But he still complained of the lack of organization and the disastrous effects of inter-battalion competition.[29] One of the problems was that Hughes would not establish a centrally controlled system. The "slave driver," as Price said, also needed to be one who was willing to delegate authority and to pay close attention to routine detail.

But it was not only the home-front that suffered under Hughes' recruiting improvisations. Once in England the supposedly trained Hughes battalions were mercifully broken up and retrained by the British, then transferred to France as drafts. Consequently, now unemployed, bitter, and increasingly vocal officers were an embarrassment to the Canadian government. Hughes ignored, then denied their existence as a problem, but the complaints continued to embarrass all. So too did the slowly emerging realization that Hughes' labyrinth of an overseas organization was starving the front of desperately needed reinforcements. One side-effect was to encourage Hughes to try to add more divisions to the Canadian corps as a simple solution. Yet the corps commander, General Alderson, knew that this was not the answer; steady and adequate reinforcement of his existing divisions was. By mid-February 1916, he actually returned to England to try to solve the reinforcement bottleneck. But with little help from Hughes' appointees there, and desperate in the expectation of huge casualties in the spring and summer fighting, the frustrated Alderson circumvented Hughes by placing his grievances directly before his old army friend, the Duke of Connaught. The facts, he told the Governor-General, spoke for themselves: of the 1,476 officers and 25,087 men in the Canadian camp at Shorncliffe, only 75 and 2,385, respectively, were trained to go to France. The problem, according to Alderson, was due not only to Hughes' multi-headed overseas administration, but also to the poor state of the recruits coming from Canada.[30]

By then Hughes was not insensitive to the reinforcement problem, but he would not let anyone else try to resolve it. In March, when Parliament was halfway through its 1916 session—and at a time when rumours of Militia Department scandals were growing steadily— Hughes decided to rush over to England to straighten out personally the problems in reinforcement and administration. In the meantime, Gwatkin, who had likely been alerted by Connaught, informed Hughes' temporary replacement, A. E. Kemp, of the dangerous reinforcement situation due to the Minister's snafu in training. If Kemp had hoped to improve things during Hughes' absence, a severe political storm focusing directly on Hughes prevented it. Before he could solve anything in England, the attacks on his administration became so acute that Borden had to order him back to Canada in April. It left the situation in England and at the front unresolved. On his return Hughes commissioned General Lessard to make a confidential inspection of training depots in England. After touring the camps for several weeks in April and May, Lessard confirmed Alderson's and Gwatkin's charges. But Hughes never made public Lessard's damning report. To do so would have been to admit the failure of the Minister's local recruiting and training program. If the Prime Minister knew about it, there was also certain benefits for the government in keeping silent on Lessard's findings. Opposition attacks during the parliamentary session, which had ended in mid-May, were very heavy. Most of them were focused on the Militia Minister and, thereby, the entire Conservative administration. Two royal commissions also were still pending; and both were concerned with Sam Hughes' office. With the recent high casualties coming from the Battle of St. Eloi in March and April, Lessard's news would not be welcomed by the public. But whatever the motives for suppressing the report, the problems of the surplus officers and the quality and training of the troops continued for more months—the months of Mount Sorrel and the Somme.[31]

If Sam Hughes' recruiting policy caused problems in English-Canada where the majority viewed the war as a national crusade, then it proved calamitous in French-Canada where there was no such passion. As the war progressed, the difference in attitudes between French- and English-Canada became more and more obvious; and with the imposition of conscription in 1918, it led to near open rebellion that spring. During the previous three years, with a population of about two million, French-Canada had given far fewer soldiers to the overseas battalions than had English-Canada. Soon there were charges that Quebec was not doing its duty. In response, the province became increasingly more sullen: it was a foreign war; Canada was not threatened; there were more pressing problems at home, especially when English-Ontario was trying to take away the French-language school rights of her French-speaking citizens. There was also little attraction for most Quebecois in giving their lives for either Great Britain or France. Of the 14,000 or so French-Canadians who actually joined during Hughes' tenure, many did so not because of patriotism, but for economic and other practical reasons. Yet in the end, the Quebecois in particular—for French-Canadians in other parts of the Dominion had enlisted in about the same proportion as their English-speaking confrères—were more seriously divided from the rest of the nation than they had ever been since Confederation. Whose fault was it? As Desmond Morton has pointed out, since Confederation the militia had become increasingly anglicized in men, manners, and equipment. Consequently fewer French-Canadians joined its ranks.[32]

Sam Hughes was an important part of the process that led to that alienation. It did not matter much in peacetime, but it did in war. The Minister had always been remarkably insensitive to French-Canadians. For a long time Hughes foolishly believed that his remote Huguenot ancestry and his friendship with nationalists like Armand Lavergne made him acceptable to Quebec. He was peculiarly unaware that his previous campaigns against separate schools, French priests, Canadian Papal Zouaves, French-Canadian military representation in Catholic ceremonies, and his Orange Lodge activities had overpowered the limited attractions of ancestry or friendship. Nor was he aware that his image as an imperialist, however nationalistic, was not attractive to many French-Canadians, who were not at all concerned about defending the Empire outside of Canada.[33]

None of it augered well for a war in 1914. It was not that Sam Hughes did not want to recruit French-Canadians. He did. But he did not realize that by scrapping the Gwatkin mobilization scheme, which gave a balanced national representation to French-Canada in the form of their own units, he scuppered separate French-Canadian battalions in the first contingent. Still he wanted Quebec's numbers. One of the first things he did was visit Cardinal Bégin of Quebec in September 1914 in an attempt to secure priests for the initial force, but the Cardinal gave him little hope of obtaining any number for overseas service.[34] With this warning, the Minister should have seen that Quebec was going to need special care if recruiting for a foreign war was to succeed in the province.

Yet the outbreak of the war did produce some initial sympathy in Quebec for participation; and Hughes wanted a national effort. That had been part of the rationale behind his nationalistic "fiery-cross" call to arms in August. But as the response to it poured into Valcartier he allowed for no separate identity by giving privileges as well as responsibilities to members of the various French-Canadian regiments who turned out. Instead units like the Carabiniers Mont-Royal, the Chausseurs Canadiens, the Voltigeurs de Quebec, and the Carabiniers de Sherbrooke were absorbed into the 12th and 14th Battalions, both of which were English-speaking. Only the 14th went to France where it was reinforced by French-Canadians from the 12th Battalion. When Liberal MP and former cabinet minister Rodolphe Lemieux requested the creation of a separate French-Canadian unit with its own officers in the first contingent, Hughes refused. Even the attestation documents were worded in such a fashion that no French-Canadian volunteer could record his racial origin. There were over 1,200 French-Canadians at Valcartier in 1914, sufficient to assemble one complete battalion including officers.[35]

At the beginning of the war, the Militia Minister had two ready-made native sons of Quebec and generals at his disposal to rally the Canadiens: François Lessard and Oscar Pelletier. Both were regular soldiers of substantial experience. But while Hughes was in office, no meaningful role was ever given them, in spite of pleas by prominent English-Canadian Tories, like Toronto MP and patronage co-ordinator Edmund Bristol, who wanted Lessard to command the second contingent. All Hughes gave him was public abuse over his Toronto mobilization trials and a bitter ministerial squabble over inspection services. As late as 1916, Hughes again refused to make him an overseas brigadier, or even use him in the disastrous Quebec recruiting drives of that year. Only after Hughes was fired did Lessard get a Quebec battalion to recruit. But by then it was too late; he secured only ninety-two men, and he had no battle experience, so was unsuitable for overseas command. As for Pelletier—the son of a Liberal senator and the man whom Hutton had chosen as commander of one of his Boer war infantry columns—in 1914 the Minister could only give the

Major-General command of a half dozen troops guarding a wireless station on Anticosti Island—and that was all.[36]

If Sam Hughes made little use of individual French-Canadians, he had not much greater concern for their units. Once the first division got into the fighting, it was this bloody experience that trained many of the future officers of the subsequent divisions. Because the first contingent had few middle and senior level French-Canadian officers beyond the company level, there never would be enough of them to lead other units of their own culture, even if Hughes had wanted to send them. He seemed to think of Quebec with its two-million population only as a place to get numbers, not French-Canadians. But the Canadiens themselves had been concerned in September 1914. Then Rodolphe Lemieux and Dr. Arthur Mignault, a wealthy Quebec pharmaceutical manufacturer, led a delegation of fifty-eight influential Liberal and Conservative Quebecois to Ottawa to make sure that at least the second contingent had an identifiable battalion. They warned Borden that if care was not taken to give Quebec representation on the national fighting force, there was a strong risk of losing its active support. Apparently with hardly more sympathy than Hughes, Borden only consented after the Militia Minister had sailed for England. The result was the formation of the 22nd Battalion commanded by F. M. Gaudet, which went to France with the second contingent the next spring. By then even it was having trouble: 10 per cent of the number were English-speaking, and French-Canadian troops had to be transferred from two other battalions recruiting in Quebec before it could sail. In the first two contingents, then, French-Canadians were represented only by one battalion and it was to remain the only official one in the Canadian Corps during the entire war.[37]

There was hardly any doubt about the potential enthusiasm for enlistment in French-Canada just before and after the 22nd was announced. However, Hughes appeared unappreciative of it. In February 1915 he could only give vague answers about establishing a French-Canadian brigade when questioned in the Commons, and he even seemed unsure of the number of French-Canadians who by then had enlisted. Just before the second division sailed for France in mid-1915, a French-Canadian lawyer and militia soldier, Colonel J. P. Landry, who had been given command of one of its brigades as a small conciliation to Quebec, was removed. To replace him came a Tory journalist friend of the Minister, Brigadier David Watson, fresh from the First Division. It was inevitable that Landry should lose out. His fate was one of the earliest consequences of Hughes' not including French-Canadians of middle and high command in the first contingent the previous year. Landry had no battle experience, and no one willingly was going to jeopardize lives and efficiency with an untested brigadier. Watson had nearly a year under his belt. Back in Canada, however, no one in Quebec would question Landry's competence. To them there was another obvious reason for his removal. The deposed brigadier's father, Conservative Senator Philippe Landry, had been a major spokesman in the defence of the Franco-Ontario's fight against their Tory government's infamous Regulation 17 denying them French-language rights; to many French-Canadians Hughes, the vengeful Orangeman, had simply retaliated.[38]

After mid-1915 when Hughes was trying to recruit the Third and Fourth Divisions, to encourage Quebec enlistments he brought home some of the few French-Canadians who had served with the corps overseas. But there were never enough veterans even to begin the job. Mostly he had to use the same method employed in the rest of Canada—prominent citizens and promises of local battalions.[39] From October until the summer of 1916, twelve such groups canvassed in various areas of the province. Most of them had little success. By then an unmoved or lukewarm clergy, stories of the horrors waiting on Flanders' battlefields, and the general shortcomings of the Militia Minister's recruiting system, all made the Canadiens stubbornly resist any foreign military service. The new munitions industries with their steady and lucrative employment represented a far safer calling. The sneers and accusations of English-Canada and the relentless antiwar campaign of Henri Bourassa and his nationaliste allies were strong inducements for many Quebecois to stay away from the colours. Nevertheless Hughes pressed for the numbers.

Wealthy French-Canadians were not so willing to become some of Sam Hughes' recruiting colonels as were many in English Canada. As a result, many whom Hughes chose were less than worthy and their units were often doomed. One such example was the 41st Battalion. After a scandalous record both in Canada and England, which included desertion, two murders, and many court-martials, the unit was finally broken up to feed the 22nd in France.[40] Others were little more successful. In the fall of 1915, Hughes asked Armand Lavergne to raise a unit in Montreal. The year before he might have done it, but now his response was an embarrassing public letter in the columns of Bourassa's *Le Devoir* in which he refused to accept what he said was nothing more than an interesting adventure in a foreign country. Unexpectedly, the offer was then accepted by Olivar Asselin—an ardent nationaliste. Whatever his real motives for doing it, Asselin had a little more success than many others. His energy, popularity, and discipline got recruits and better officers, but not full ranks. Only too quickly Asselin discovered that Hughes had authorized a Conservative lawyer, Tancrède Paquelo, to raise the 206th Battalion in the same area. Paquelo was a former commanding officer of the 85th militia regiment and was representative of the declining quality of French-Canadian officers brought about by increasing anglicization in the militia. While Asselin brought men into his unit by hard work and discipline, Paquelo seduced his by appealing to baser values and promises of being "le dernier regiment à parter, le premier à profiter de la victoire." Asselin was so frustrated at the cut-throat competition between the two rivals, he demanded that Hughes get rid of Paquelo's battalion. Asselin's unit was transferred to Bermuda, not France; and Paquelo's was disbanded, with the bulk of them being transferred to the distraught Asselin. When the furious Paquelo heard what was to happen, he paraded his men and told those few who had not already disappeared to desert. For this he was court-martialled, and during the trial it was found that he and some of his officers had also defrauded the unit of funds. Paquelo went to jail.[41]

On other occasions, when Hughes could not get suitable French-Canadian colonels, he chose English-Canadian ones to recruit in Quebec. William Price was one. In spite of the general popularity the Price family had had in Quebec for years, there was little attraction to serve an imperialist "English" colonel in a foreign war; and Price, already encumbered by Hughes' bad system, added his own insensitivities, and so failed. According to Price: "I tell them what no politician dare tell them, that they are away behind all the other provinces and that though they have a double duty, one to the Empire and one to France, yet they are laggards and that they should as a matter of fact furnish more than any other province."[42]

In the summer of 1916, the half dozen battalions still trying to reach their quotas were really only fragments of military units. With a lack of discipline and equipment and ranks thinned by desertion and drafts to other battalions, few were sent to England. Of those who got there, they were broken up to reinforce the 22nd in France. In all, by 1916 the possibility of having a French-Canadian brigade, native sons in senior command, or any serious encouragement for national war participation had all but disappeared under Sam Hughes. Instead the spectacle of most of those French-Canadian battalions stumbling incompetently and often dishonestly through a vain quest for full establishments caused the Quebecois to withdraw further into demoralized and sullen inaction in the province; outside of it, the show reaffirmed the belief that French-Canadians were incompetent and unpatriotic.

If Hughes was a major cause of the situation, others must also share the guilt with him. During his first two years, Borden in particular had little more appreciation of cultural politics than did Sam Hughes. Since the Prime Minister had scant support in the province even after the 1911 election, he should have realized that Quebec would be a special case in a national crisis. Just before the war, he and Monk had parted. The Prime Minister's failure to respond to the Quebec delegation that wanted a French unit in the first force, his failure to find any post for Lessard, his securing the resignation of two of his three French-Canadian cabinet ministers in the fall of 1914—all these actions held little evidence of an understanding of French-Canada. His position on the imperialist side in the naval debate in 1910, and in 1913 the question of cash contributions to the Admiralty only confirmed the nationalistes' charges after 1914 that French-Canada was being tossed into a foreign war. So did Borden's quick acceptance of sending more and more troops thereafter. Even after the reshuffle in 1914, his cabinet had no French-Canadians with any credibility to defend war participation. Nearly all of them had campaigned for votes in the 1911 election by attacking Laurier's naval bill as conscriptionist. After 1914, how could these same men persuade their confrères that they must participate in a British war? Similarly, Borden and his cabinet seemed to be incapable of or unwilling to support the Franco-Ontarians against the English-speaking "Boches" in the Ontario schools question.[43]

Like Hughes, Borden tried to enthuse Quebec. Early in 1916 he told Hughes that he should be sure that French-Canadians who had distinguished themselves at the front were rewarded with decorations that the French government had put at his disposal. The Prime Minister also suggested that, if Hughes would authorize a Quebec unit for service in the French army, recruiting would be greatly encouraged. But General Gwatkin knew better and so advised against it; he recognized that French-Canadians had no particular loyalty to France and that pay difference between the two forces would discourage any chance of success. No one seemed to listen to Gwatkin. Overseas Max Aitken, the government "Eye-Witness" in France, offered Hughes and Borden "a French mission... sent to Canada by the Jesuits or other religious orders for religious purposes but really to assist recruiting in Quebec." In all, these schemes represented the bankruptcy of Hughes' and Borden's attitude to French-Canadians. To them France was never an attraction; Canada was. But in order to gain French-Canada's support of an external policy, national leaders first would have to give the minority a definite, identifiable, and responsible role and to ensure its well-being at home. Neither Hughes nor his Prime Minister seemed aware of this. What came from them came too little and too late.[44]

But one of the most objectionable things about Borden for French-Canadians was that he would not or could not control Sam Hughes. Most of the time Hughes continued to proclaim his belief that French-Canada would measure up to his expectations, or, as Mason Wade puts it, Hughes kept his honest opinion about French-Canada to himself. That may be true, but from time to time he made some stupid public moves, often in themselves small but collectively lethal, concerning recruiting in Quebec. When again unsuccessful in obtaining support from Cardinal Bégin in mid-1916, the Minister uttered his infamous statement in Lindsay that Quebec had not done its duty. Earlier he had countered questions from an opposition MP, asking why western French-Canadians were not organized into a battalion, by saying that their numbers were too small, that they would be better off in English-speaking battalions, and that the local French-Canadian officer of the proposed unit was incompetent. When the same member confronted Hughes with the 1911 census figures indicating that there were over 40,000 French-Canadians in the west, Hughes replied that he would order two French-Canadian "half-breed" battalions to be raised. Perhaps the most celebrated and distorted case of Hughes' neglect of sympathetic organization in French-Canada occurred in August 1916 when the Minister was again out of the country. Military authorities wanted a new enlistment drive in the Montreal area to be jointly headed by two clergymen as representatives of both cultures and faiths. By that time, however, no French-Canadian priest would accept the post. But the campaign proceeded anyway, headed by a Methodist clergyman, Reverend C. A. Williams. Williams was hardworking and far more tolerant of French-Canada than many have given him credit for. But predictably his efforts ended in failure. The Williams affair was not as it was portrayed by extreme nationalists—an example of Hughes' anti-Catholicism. Nor was Williams a bigoted Orangeman sent by the Minister to ride herd on French-Canada. The entire episode represented what was tragic about the Minister's methods. He could not understand that French-Canada required a different approach than the rest of the population. Quebec, because it provided the basis of Laurier's power, was suspect to an old party politician like Hughes. In the past two years he had given Quebec nothing except discrimination to be enthusiastic about. Soon the province was not interested and soon Hughes and his local military officers had run out of prominent French-Canadians for such duties; authorities had to use whomever they could get. So they got men like Williams. Common sense, however, should have dictated that it not be a Methodist clergyman. But by then it was a vicious circle.[45]

The Militia Minister showed more creative imagination in recruiting foreigners for military duty than he did French-Canadians. For example, there was the Minister's "American Legion" scheme. Soon after the war began, Hughes offered and had accepted for overseas service a battalion of American citizens living in Canada; the offer was a substantial mental somersault for Hughes' usual anti-Americanism. A few weeks later, he extended the project to three "corps of splendid fighters," numbering "sixty thousand," which now included Russians and Serbs.[46]

The British authorities could not co-ordinate their reaction. The Colonial Office authorities were hesitant because they said that such a force would violate the U.S. Foreign Enlistment Act of 1818, and that they did want to keep relations as cordial as possible with the neutral republic. By the same token they did not want to tread on Canadian sensitivities, especially those in the hands of the prickly Sam Hughes. Consequently, the British referred the question back to the Governor-General, whom they said was free to act as he saw fit. Connaught, who had never seen the first communications between Hughes and Kitchener, and did not like being left out, was puzzled. So he enquired at militia headquarters. The Deputy Minister said he knew nothing about the scheme either; nor did the Militia Council, but if such a proposal had been made by Hughes, they recommended it be quickly dropped. Meanwhile, Kitchener, supported by the king, Churchill, Sir Richard McBride, and Acting High Commissioner Perley gave Hughes permission to send at least one American unit, providing no recruiting went on outside of Canada.[47]

Hughes did not move on the issue until domestic volunteering started to slow down in the fall of 1915. Then he allowed the limited acceptance of American citizens resident in Canada to mushroom ultimately into plans for a full-fledged American brigade of five overseas battalions. The Minister had created a special cap badge with an American flag surrounded by clusters of maple leaves. As the first of these units, designated the 97th Overseas Battalion, quickly filled up its ranks during the winter of 1915-1916, Hughes got the idea that he could recruit unlimited numbers. As a result he authorized four more by the late spring (the 211th, 212th, 213th, and the 237th) and labelled them the "American Legion." Their cap badge was a variation of the 97th and all of them wore American Legion shoulder flashes. As was the case elsewhere, none of these units had much success. The Minister created each new battalion long before the others finished recruiting, and so they competed, often viciously, with each other for volunteers and none of them ever reached establishment—most of them reached less than half of it. During June 1916, 20 per cent of the legion deserted. Hughes also used the typical special agent to organize the entire scheme. C. W. Bullock, who had suggested the brigade idea to the Minister, was an American citizen and a Unitarian minister whose military career, as General Gwatkin scornfully commented, "is remarkable. Appointed chaplain with the honorary rank of captain in October last [1915], he is now a lieutenant-colonel commanding an overseas battalion." Whether Hughes ordered it or not is not known, but recruiting took place on American soil. Certainly the Minister aided it by making a personal arrangement with customs officials to turn a blind eye to these recruits when they were brought across the border.[48]

These frequent abuses of American neutrality aggravated and embarrassed the Washington and London authorities equally. Every time Connaught confronted Hughes about the foreign recruiting, the Minister denied it and then blatantly let it continue. American authorities increasingly objected to the continued use of the U.S. flag displayed at various Canadian recruiting offices; and so there were several stiff diplomatic notes exchanged with British diplomats over Hughes' scheme. In Ottawa, Gwatkin, Fiset, and the Governor-General had no more success in stopping the plan. For their part, the British would not let the legion come to England until all outward connections with the United States were cut.[49]

By the mid-spring 1916, tired of the long wait, endless changes in officers, and constant haggling, the legionnaires were frustrated. Desertions and resignations mounted while enlistments nearly stopped. Like some of the other battalions Hughes had authorized, the legion had its share of scandal. The Toronto chief of police described the 97th as the "worst behaved battalion in the city." Drunkenness, fraud, embezzlement (including the decamping of the 97th's first commanding officer with all the unit funds), and incompetence plagued the force. In May Fiset said he would be pleased to send the legion overseas before "they all desert," but not until they got rid of American insignia. Connaught's constant complaints and Hughes' lack of response finally brought the Prime Minister into the picture.[50]

Like many others, Borden was totally surprised at what had so far taken place. Hughes had not told him much in the previous two years and precious time was now wasted while he tried to sort through the Minister's mess. In the process, it involved Borden in a first-class row with the Governor-General, whom the Prime Minister felt was exerting far too much pressure in a domestic Canadian matter. By late July, when Hughes was out of the country, Borden ended the affair by consolidating the legion's five battalions into one, the 97th, and sending it overseas, shorn of all its insignia. The process only added to its further demoralization. With financial and leadership problems still festering in its ranks, in the end it was broken up to feed the corps' battalions in France.[51]

The Prime Minister's decision on the American Legion was part of a larger judgment on Hughes' entire domestic administration. In August 1916 he took recruiting out of Sir Sam's hands. First Borden tried a director-general of recruiting to give order to the chaos and to secure the vital enlistments; then in the autumn he tried the National Service Board which was responsible to the cabinet and dedicated to the same causes. Both had little success. By the spring of 1917, large numbers of casualties and the conviction that it was essential to have a Canadian voice in imperial councils made a reluctant Prime Minister believe that only conscription could do it. By year's end compulsory service had arrived at the hands of the newly elected union government. The war would be pursued to bitter victory. But over a year before, Borden had got rid of Hughes, a major cause of his bad luck; and before Hughes had gone in 1916, he too had come out hotly for conscription—typically without consulting anyone and apparently oblivious to its party or national cost.[52]

By the end of 1916 there were over 250 overseas battalions. Hughes had authorized most of them while he was minister. But earlier that summer, the Canadian Corps was complete at forty-eight battalions. Except for some reinforcements, it remained at that level in spite of Hughes' attempts to add two more divisions before he left office. The remaining battalions either suffered collapse before they left Canada or were doomed to be broken up in England. Over the previous two years, Sam Hughes had taken the declaration of war as a personal challenge to lead a national crusade to raise as many men as possible. In doing so, he had little regard for dislocation, or for the advice of his professional staff, or for responsibility to his government. He showed no more awareness of the cultural politics of French-Canada. While trying to heighten patriotism and enlistment by throwing responsibility to the citizens, he left them confused and adrift when the war demands transcended the ability of individuals, of the party structure, and of local groups to handle them on a national scale. Yet he constantly interfered even in this process because he could neither delegate the necessary authority nor apply himself to the daily routine of co-ordinating a national effort. Moreover, the local battalions ended up being destroyed by the same spontaneity that created them and that helped sour and alienate the two cultures, both from the government and one from the country. Certainly Hughes' Prime Minister must bear some of the blame. In part Borden put up with Hughes' recruiting ways because in those early years the Militia Minister gave the most vitality to a pale and hesitant war administration. But neither man checked each other with sound advice or firm control. That Sam Hughes demonstrated initiative, confidence, and an unrelenting energy, which helped rally many Canadians to the early war effort, cannot be doubted. But there was also overwhelming evidence that he lacked the skills of sound administration which the larger war—the one of 1916 and after—demanded. Ironically he was a major force in creating the particular size of the Canadian war effort but he could not cope with its demands. He was a spirited improviser, intolerant of criticism, jealous of power, and imbued with the philosophy of the citizen-soldier in a conflict which no longer belonged to individual citizens. He did not see that Canada had created, with the masses of his recruits, professional demands and a professional modern army. As long as the spirit and manpower were in abundance, and the sophisticated needs few, Sam Hughes' local talents remained unchallenged. When these lagged, Hughes' regime collapsed.

Reference Notes to Chapter 12

1 Desmond Morton, *Canada and War: A Military and Political History* (Toronto: Butterworth's, 1981), chapter 3.
2 *Hansard*, 1917, pp. 261, and 269-70 for Hughes' own description of his recruiting methods.
3 Brown, *Borden*, vol. 2, pp. 27-28; and Wilson, p. xxxi.
4 *CAR*, 1915, p. 188; Granatstein and Hitsman, p. 34; *Hansard*, special session, 1914, pp. 17, 95; Duguid, appendix 55; and PAC, Borden *papers*, address, Dec. 18, 1914, p. 34672.
5 *CAR*, 1915, pp. 187-88.
6 Murray Donelly, *Dafoe of the Free Press* (Toronto: Macmillan, 1968), p. 76.
7 Wilson, pp. xxi, xxix-xlii; G. N. Tucker, *The Naval Service of Canada* (Ottawa: King's Printer, 1952), chapter 13; PAO, Bristol *papers*, 283, Armour file, note on CEF; *CAR*, 1915, pp. 213-14; and Brown, *Borden*, vol. 2, pp. 68-69.
8 Swettenham, pp. 71-95; Wilson, p. xxx.
9 External Affairs, *Documents*, pp. 73-74, Perley to Borden, May 29, 1915.
10 *Globe*, Jan. 22, 1915, p. 6; Wilson, pp. xxxv-1, 6-8, B4; Duguid, appendix 86; Senate *Debates*, 1916, p. 406; Granatstein and Hitsman, pp. 23-24; and Bray, pp. 147-49.
11 PAC, Gwatkin *papers*, F4, Gwatkin to Hughes, Sept. 21, 1914; PAC, pamphlet, no. 4039, p. 8; and Winter, pp. 88-89.
12 PRO, Kitchener *papers*, 30/57/56, FNG 43A and B, Connaught to Kitchener, July 1, 1915.
13 PAC, Gwatkin *papers*, f2, Gwatkin to Mason, July 3, 1915; and PAC, Borden *papers*, p. 109601, Gwatkin to Christie, May 24, 1915.
14 Brown, *Borden*, vol. 2, p. 28.
15 Wilson, pp. xxxii, 8, B5; Militia Order no. 340, July 12, 1915; PAC, John Bassett *papers*, MG 30, E 302, Basset to Winter, Aug. 19, 1915; *CAR*, 1915, p. 190; and P. D. Ross, pp. 206-11.
16 PAC, Borden *papers*, OC313, "Memorandum on Recruiting in England Prior to the Derby Recruiting Scheme" claims Hughes' method was similar to that in Britain; an improvised, local volunteer response with little government planning. Also see Nicholson, p. 109; and PAC, RG 24, vol. 6999, 593-1-40.
17 *Hansard*, 1916, pp. 3288-89; PAC, RG 24, vol. 413, "Report on the work of the Department of Militia and Defence to Feb. 1, 1915," Memorandum no. 1, Gwatkin to the Prime Minister, Feb. 1, 1915; ibid., Memorandum no. 3, Gwatkin to the Prime Minister, Dec. 1, 1916; PAC, Borden *papers*, OC313, McCurdy to Borden, Oct. 7, 1916; *Hansard*, 1917, p. 263; *Canadian War Records*, p. 3; and Morton, *Peculiar Kind of Politics*, p. 44.
18 PAC, Harold Mayne Daly *papers*, MG 27, III, f9, D, "Memoire notes."
19 Nicholson, pp. 213-14, 546; and English, pp. 95-105.
20 *CAR*, 1915, pp. 187-93, 222-27; and *Hansard*, 1915, p. 438.
21 State Department *Documents*, no. 556; PC 36, Jan. 12, 1916; and Brown, *Borden*, vol. 2, pp. 32-34.
22 PAC, Perley *papers*, vol. 5, Bennett to Borden, Dec. 7, 1915; Borden *Memoirs*, vol. 1, p. 529, Stanton to Blount, Dec. 31, 1915; PAC, Foster *diaries*, Aug. 10, 1915; PAC, RG 24, vol. 413, Memorandum no. 3; and Brown, *Borden*, vol. 2, pp. 33-35.
23 *Hansard*, 1917, pp. 269-71; PAC, Borden *private diaries*, Jan. 18, 1916; Morton, *Canada and War*, p. 60; Wilson, pp. xxxvi, xlv; *Winnipeg Free Press*, May 29, 1916; and *CAR*, 1916, p. 256.
24 *New York Times*, Feb. 27, 1916, p. 3; *CAR*, 1916, p. 303; and HRLO, Lord Beaver-

brook *papers*, General Hughes, no. 2; IP, Hughes to Aitken, Jan. 15, 1916; and ibid., Aitken to Hughes, Jan. 19, 1916.
25 PAC, Borden *private diaries*, Jan. 18, 1916, and Feb. 5, 1916; Queen's University, Joseph Flavelle *papers*, B2, Flavelle to W. E. Rundle, June 14, 1916, pp. 1500-502; and *Hansard*, 1917, pp. 269-70.
26 Senate *Debates*, 1916, pp. 127-32; PAC, Perley *papers*, vol. 5, Borden to Perley, Mar. 14, 1916; *CAR*, 1916, p. 319; *Hansard*, 1917, pp. 269-71; and Calgary *Daily Herald*, Mar. 11, 1916, p. 6.
27 For instance, in Ontario see Wilson, pp. li-ii. Also see *Hansard*, 1916, pp. 145, 440, 498-500, 3550; Nicholson, p. 219; *CAR*, 1916, pp. 310-24; Ottawa *Citizen*, Apr. 14, 1916, p. 1; *Globe*, June 28, 1916, p. 6; Calgary *Daily Herald*, Mar. 29, 1916, p. 6.
28 PAC, Bassett *papers*, vol. 5, Price to Bassett, Feb. 25, 1916. On the recruiting methods in Ontario, see Wilson, pp. xlii-liii.
29 PAC, Griesbach *papers*, vol. 1, Griesbach to Hughes, May 13, 1915.
30 PAC, F. L. Lessard *papers*, MG 30, G 47, Report of IG (Imperial) on Canadian Troops, no. 47/560/MT2, June 16, 1915, appendix A, in Lessard to Hughes, May 1916; ibid., Hughes to Lessard, Apr. 16, 1916; Nicholson, pp. 202, 225; Duguid, appendix 8; PAC, Kemp *papers*, vol. 110, Alderson to Governor-General, Feb. 17, 1916; PAC, Borden *papers*, OC 318, McCurdy to Hughes, July 21, 1916; and ibid., Hughes to Borden, Aug. 2, 1916. When Hughes was fired, Perley resolved the problem of surplus officers by sending them home or letting them go to France with a lesser rank. Nicholson, pp. 223-24.
31 PAC, Kemp *papers*, Gwatkin to Kemp, 1916; PAC, Lessard *papers*, Hughes to Lessard, Apr. 16, 1916 and Lessard to Hughes, May 1916; PAC, Borden *papers*, OC 318, Borden to Hughes, Aug.19 1916; and ibid., OC 322, Gwatkin to Christie, June 27, 1916.
32 For an overview, see Granatstein and Hitsman, pp. 22-34; Desmond Morton, "French Canada and the War, 1868-1917: The Military Background to the Conscription Crisis of 1917," in J. L. Granatstein and R. D. Cuff, eds., *War and Society in North America* (Toronto: Nelson, 1971), pp. 84-103.
33 Mason Wade, *The French Canadians, 1760-1967* (Toronto: Macmillan, 1968), vol. 2, pp. 640-41. See ibid., pp. 640-726 for the trials of French-Canadians during the war. Also Elizabeth A. Armstrong, *The Crisis of Quebec, 1914-1918* (Toronto: McClelland and Stewart, 1974), pp. 35-160.
34 Winter, p. 140.
35 Duguid, appendix 85, "Composition of Provisional Infantry Brigades and Battalions, Valcartier Camp, Sept. 3, 1914," and appendix 88, "Questions to be put before attestation"; Morton, in *War and Society*, p. 96; *Hansard*, 1916, p. 3283; PAC, Gwatkin *papers*, F2, Gwatkin to Sladen, Aug. 27, 1915; and Duguid, appendix 86.
36 PAO, Bristol *papers*, 285, political 1914, Bristol to Borden, Oct. 17, 1914; and ibid., Bristol to Hazen, Oct. 17, 1914; *Hansard*, 1916, p. 3281; Morton, in *War and Society*, p. 102; and Wade, vol. 2, pp. 668, 708, 709; and Oscar Pelletier, *Memoires, Souveniers de Famille et Récits* (Quebec: 1940), pp. 382-90.
37 Duguid, appendices 74, 711, 843; and Armstrong, pp. 70, 83-84.
38 *Militia List*, Sept. 1914, p. 204; Morgan, *1912*, pp. 436 and 447; Morton, in *War and Society*, p. 97.
39 Desmond Morton, "The Limits of Loyalty: French Canadian Officers and the First World War," in Edgar Denton, ed., *Limits of Loyalty* (Waterloo: WLU Press, 1980), pp. 92-93.
40 PAC, Gwatkin *papers*, F2, Gwatkin to Sladen, Aug. 27, 1915; and Desmond Morton, "The Short, Unhappy Life of the 41st Battalion CEF," in *Queen's Quarterly* XLLLI, no. 1 (1974), pp. 70-80.
41 *CAR*, 1916, p. 194; *Hansard*, 1916, p. 3283; Oliver Asselin, *Pourquoi Je m'enrole*, Montreal: n.p., 1916, especially p. 32; and Morton, in *Limits of Loyalty*, pp. 92-94.
42 PAC, Bassett *papers*, vol. 5, Price to Bassett, Feb. 24, 1916.
43 Granatstein and Hitsman, p. 30.
44 HLRO, Beaverbrook *papers*, E, 7-8, Aitken to Borden, May 17, 1916; PAC, Borden *papers*, OC68, Borden to Hughes, Jan. 25, 1916; PAC, Gwatkin *papers*, F1, Gwatkin to Kemp, spring 1916; and *CAR*, 1916, p. 258.

45 Wade, vol. 2, p. 727; Macdonald, p. 335; *Current Opinion*, Sept. 1917, p. 158; London *Free Press*, June 12, 1916, p. 4; Calgary *Daily Herald*, July 18, 1916, p. 6; *Hansard*, 1916, pp. 1373-74; Mason Wade, *The French Canadian Outlook* (Toronto: McClelland and Stewart, 1964). p. 52; Nicholson, p. 221; and Morton, in *War and Society*, pp. 98-99.

46 PAC, Borden *papers*, Law to Governor-General, Aug. 30, 1914, Kitchener to Hughes, Sept. 7, 1914; and Duguid, appendix 87, Hughes to Kitchener, Aug. 29, 1914.

47 Ibid., OC322, vol. 70, Fiset to Sec. External Affairs, Oct. 24, 1914; ibid., McBride to R. L. Borden, Nov. 25, 1914. Also see NDHQ, Directorate of History, Edwin Pye *papers*, F1, f5, W. S. Churchill memo, Sept. 5, 1914; and Harcourt *papers*, Box 465, p. 49, Perley to Borden, Dec. 2, 1914.

48 PAC, RG 24, vol. 1542, 684-1-174-1, Minute of Militia Council, Jan. 13, 1916; ibid., vol. 14071, vol. 461, Gwatkin to Sladen, July 31, 1916; PAC, Borden *papers*, OC322, vol. 70, Gwatkin to Christie (HQC 1562), June 18, 1916; ibid., Connaught to Borden, June 25, 1916, and DMD memo, July 4, 1916; D. Hist, Pye *papers*, F1, f5, J. G. Mitchell, Department of Interior to Sam Hughes, Nov. 3, 1915; and PAC, RG 24, vol. 1383, 593-6-1-93.

49 HLRO, Beaverbrook *papers*, E/18, 97th Battalion, F? to Spring-Rice, July 17, 1916, and RG 7, 14071, vol. 452, Spring-Rice to Connaught, May 2, 1916, U.S. Department of Justice to U.S. Secretary of State, Jan. 17, 1916; ibid., vol. 455, Spring-Rice to Governor-General, July 1, 1916; and Detroit *Free Press*, Dec. 19, 1915, Dec. 24, 1915, and Jan. 6, 1916, editorial.

50 PAC, D. Hist, Pye *papers*, "Notes by Pye," CGS to AG, Mar. 3, 1916; and PAC, Borden *papers*, OC322, vol. 70, Fiset to Christie, Mar 27, 1916.

51 R. G. Haycock, "The American Legion in the Canadian Expeditionary Force, 1914-1917: A Study in Failure," in *Military Affairs*, XLIII, no. 3 (Oct. 1979), pp. 115-19.

52 Morton, in *Limits of Loyalty*, p. 91; PAC, Borden *papers*, OC318, Hughes to Borden, Oct. 23, 1916; and *CAR*, 1916, pp. 265-66. For a review of Borden's course after 1916, see Brown, *Borden*, vol. 2, chapters 8, 9, 10. As early as August 1914, Sir Charles Ross had protested the loss of his skilled machinists in Hughes "fiery cross" mobilization. See PAC, Sir Charles Ross *papers*, MG30, A95, vol. 5, Ross to Hughes, Aug. 6, 1914.

CHAPTER 13

"Done in Our Own Country": War Supplies, 1914-1916

In some ways supplying the war machine with material was similar to supplying it with men: industry had to be recruited, resources gathered and distributed, finances taken care of, facilities laid down, and the actual production undertaken. All of it needed the appropriate organization, co-operation, and planning. But in 1914 there was little industrial planning. Those in Canada's small manufacturing base thought that the expected short war would only allow them to replace the German producers on the domestic market. The peacetime Canadian munitions industry was embryonic. Sir Charles Ross' factory and the Dominion Arsenal in Quebec were the only munitions plants in the Dominion.

A deepening economic recession promised a bleak winter for many unemployed Canadians in 1915. The increase in government spending for clothing, feeding, housing, and arming the expeditionary force meant some relief for Canadian business. But all of it could be quickly satisfied by private concerns in Canada. So there was not much thought about radical industrial reorganization or of government involvement for war purposes. Well into 1915 Canadians could still afford to export skilled labour to England and Russia. If the war was short, expensive retooling would be a disaster. But by mid-1915, with the Western Front's monstrous casualties and insatiable demand for more men and munitions, and still no victory in sight, the forced mobilization of industry came as a shock. As with military manpower, industry did not achieve efficiency equal to the expanding demands until it was regulated and co-ordinated fairly by a centralized authority; and Sam Hughes was a major factor in the transitional process.[1]

Reference notes for Chapter 13 are found on pp. 253-57.

The official historian of the CEF has suggested that generally government buying methods were sound during the war "except in [the] early stages when haste and ignorance were in evidence." Lack of war experience, he infers, and the decrepit system of government organization within departments and the civil service in general contributed a large share to the initial abuses.[2] It is also true that the prevailing party system, dependent on patronage distribution to provide services for the war effort, did not help the situation; nor did the sense of urgency. Added to these factors was Sam Hughes holding a portfolio which was the single most important one in early wartime government. In peacetime and during previous wars, with what little there was beyond rifles, ammunition, and uniforms, munitions orders had been placed through the Militia Department's structure with the Minister exercising close patronage surveillance.

It was much the same in Great Britain. Munitions were handled by the War Office alone, and produced by various Royal Ordnance Factories and a small list of preferred manufacturers such as Vickers and Armstrong. When war was declared, the monumental task of arming the British Expeditionary Force (BEF) and the new armies fell on the War Minister, Lord Kitchener, and his Master General of the Ordnance Sir Stanley von Donop. As in Canada, there was no separate organization—either a cabinet committee or a government portfolio—which handled war material. During 1914 and early 1915 the munitions shortages became staggering. Kitchener and von Donop struggled vainly to outfit the new armies, refusing to delegate their power either to the cabinet or to civilians. Only the political threat to Asquith's government over the severe shortage of shells forced the British in May 1915 to organize a separate munitions ministry and a reformed supply organization.[3]

In Canada the war brought about a frantic search for equipment and escalated the business opportunities for the Militia Ministry. As had the political opposition in England, Laurier had promised in 1914 that his party would "offer no criticism" of the government's administration until the danger had passed. But the endless lines of contractors and job seekers outside Hughes' doors sparked party hacks, like Edmund Bristol, to expect all sorts of favours from the Militia Minister. Hughes' potential power as a bestower of patronage created resentment among some of his less well-endowed colleagues. Consequently Borden set up an ad hoc cabinet subcommittee of veteran political hands including Doc Reid, George Foster, and Robert Rogers—the "Minister of Elections"—as well as Hughes to help dispense militia patronage more equitably to the party faithful.[4]

By the end of August, White in the Finance Department complained to the Prime Minister that Hughes had ignored his earlier promise to consult the cabinet before issuing contracts. Hughes had also promised the subcommittee and the Auditor-General that he would seek orders-in-council and use public tenders in business transactions. He was not alone; Borden himself had made such public commitments. But not being as forthright as he sounded, Borden quietly allowed that orders-in-council could be sought after the transaction, and public tender used only "as far as was practicable." As for Hughes' reaction to contract sharing, he complained to Borden that his colleagues were abusing the subcommittee's patronage potential and that the entire awkward system only slowed down the acquisition of urgently needed military kit.[5]

However, during the first eight months of the war, the differences in the complaints and counter-complaints from within the party seemed to be directed not at ending patronage per se but at altering its degree and control. John Bassett wrote one of the best descriptions of how the various departments, including Militia and Defence, dispensed war patronage in those early days: "You might tell your friend," he wrote to an eager Tory businessman, "that his firm was on the list which was presented to the subcommittee of the cabinet.... Contracts are sent to a great extent to those firms who have political pull.... The only way to get anything is by coming to Ottawa, securing an interview with the minister and if he thinks it worthwhile, keeping in touch with the contracts branch all the while." What is also evident from Bassett's advice was that Hughes had no better alternative to the subcommittee but to keep it all under his personal control.[6]

By late November 1914, A. E. Kemp was even more hostile to Hughes' patronage stinginess. Besides letting the other members of the subcommittee know that Hughes was not doing his party duty fairly, he indignantly claimed that Hughes had even given some Grits contracts. Borden was far more tolerant of Hughes' choices than most of the cabinet, and Hughes had his military expertise and the urgency of the hour arguments, which were both convincing. This squabbling, the disgusted Chief of the General Staff secretly told Connaught's military secretary, was because of the entire cabinet's thinking that "a nice adjustment of patronage is more important than the production of goods."[7]

This favouritism might have passed without serious consequences had there been only one overseas contingent and a quick victory. But two things in 1914 intensified the situation: first, the speedy escalation of the Canadian troop contribution; and second, the enquiries in late August of the hard-pressed Lord Kitchener directly to Hughes asking whether or not Canadian industry could produce desperately needed eighteen and twenty-five pounder shell components. Hughes saw this request as an opportunity, not only to show the British that the country could produce war goods, but also to benefit the depressed private domestic sector. He was convinced that Canadian entrepreneurs might as well share in the lucrative international war supplies market in view of the host of British agents who were then profitably scouring it for goods.

The Prime Minister agreed. Canadians, he complained to Perley in late 1914, were making sacrifices "heretofore undreamed of to support the Empire in this war." Why, he went on, were men "going without bread in Canada while those across the line [in the U.S.] are receiving good wages for work that could be done as efficiently and as cheaply in this country"? Perley, Borden instructed, was to make that point clear to the British for "public opinion here is being so seriously aroused as to most gravely affect our future action." Like his nationalist Militia Minister's, Borden's view—if less obviously partisan—was consistent throughout the war and he appreciated Hughes' early efforts in this direction for the rest of his days.[8] When Kitchener's urgent cables arrived asking about shells, Borden quickly gave Hughes, who was acting anyway, vague instructions to fill all British and Allies war orders "with as little delay as possible," using "such persons as may be appointed for the task." At that point Hughes had two distinct roles in war supplies, one for the Canadian government, and one for the British government. Both were potentially powerful patronage positions. Neither function was shared initially by the cabinet; and Hughes never made the differences in these roles clear to the public, nor to many of his cabinet colleagues. Furthermore, the new tasks only reinforced his tendency to act alone.[9]

In pursuit of his twin duties, Hughes frequently did not consult his own military staff on how best to procure equipment. Instead, as was the general practice in government, he placed his trust in the hands of men of business, often friends, whom he felt had the expertise. Before the war he had laid down that principle in his militia conferences and had attached prominent citizens with specialized knowledge directly to the headquarters staff in preparation for such a crisis. Now that it had arrived, he simply triggered the mechanism. Most of the time Hughes gave each individual an honorary commission so, as he later said, "I could get a hold of him in case he did not play the game square." Unfortunately, the Minister was not consistent in giving force to this threat; sometimes he was also not a very good judge of character. Criticisms of the activities of some of these personal representatives— always in larger numbers than in other departments—were among the first complaints about Hughes' wartime administration. A few of these men took advantage of the trusting Hughes. The most notorious was honorary Colonel John Wesley Allison—a Morrisburg, Ontario, entrepreneur and Conservative who had wide connections among

American steel manufacturers. At one time he had also been in business with James Pliny Whitney, the Premier of Ontario.[10]

In October 1914, soon after Hughes had chosen Allison to make purchases in the United States and England for the Allied governments, rumours reached Ottawa of his profiteering on contracts. When warned by the Prime Minister about these activities, Hughes denied that he had appointed anyone as a special agent. However, it seems that more than one of the Minister's acquaintances were using their association with Sam Hughes for profit. As their activities increased, the British ambassador in Washington complained to the Governor-General that such agents as "Allison, Murphy, Morgan, MacAlpine, Sifton, Wright and Maclean were charging exorbitant prices, supplying bad products and spoiling the market." Given Hughes' denial about any connection with these men, Borden and Connaught, through ignorance or political fears, denied the existence of such a group. In private, however, Borden kept tabs on Allison through investigations involving the Dominion Police Commissioner. He then warned the British authorities through Perley that Allison was not an agent for the Canadian government and that neither the War Office nor any Allied munitions buyers should have anything to do with him in that capacity. The effect on Washington and London of the Allison crews' high pressure sales pitch was most harmful to the Canadian government's image. "Whether rightly or wrongly," Perley hurriedly advised Borden, "these men are by many considered to be backed by Hughes [and by implication that means the Canadian government]. . . . You would be sorry if you hear the way big men here speak of Hughes." Two days later he again broached the subject: "If Hughes is their friend and sponsor you should either control or get rid of him." Convinced that Allison was doing vital war work, Hughes continued to ignore the Prime Minister's warnings and to endorse Allision, even using his private rail car to carry the entrepreneur to the United States; and Allison usually got the urgently needed goods.[11]

All through the first winter of the war, rumours about Hughes' chaotic administration and partisan business practices continued to circulate. In December an irate Auditor-General temporarily cut off Hughes' departmental credit because of the confusion in contrasts, a complaint already registered by cabinet colleagues such as Hazen, Foster, and Lougheed; and by January the orderly Thomas White and Hughes were making cabinet meetings rowdy with their quarrels. When Parliament opened on February 4, the Liberals had picked up the scent and were far more aggressive than expected. By spring the Canadian contingent in France was in action and complaints about its equipment started to give public substance to the rumours. This pressure forced the harried Borden to accept some public investigations of

Hughes' equipment, and all the while the Public Accounts Committee, spurred on by the opposition, rooted around in the Militia Minister's other supply practices.[12]

The first of the 1915 controversies centred around the soldiers' boots. Even before the first contingent left for France in early February, reports said that their footwear fell apart while the troops were still stationed on Salisbury Plain in England. Encouraged by the many lurid newspaper accounts, the opposition wanted to know why Hughes had ordered such bad footgear. Pressure was so great by the end of the second week of the Commons session that Borden conceded and appointed a commission. The parliamentary enquiry found that Hughes was not responsible for the condition of the boots; they had been manufactured according to a pattern accepted by his predecessor, F. W. Borden, and that only very few of them were produced with inferior materials. Most footwear was up to the Canadian standard, but the standard itself proved too light for the severe weather experienced on Salisbury Plain and in the conditions in France.[13]

Testimony before the boot committee, however, did make certain other things evident. There were too few boots for the troops to change frequently during wet weather, and too few cobblers, or too little waterproofing to prevent irreparable damage. Most of those omissions led back to Hughes. The Minister admitted to the enquiry that he had acted in a summary fashion in acquiring shoes for the forces, but said: "I have to do things in a summary way. I have done so all my life and I will go on doing so until the end." He also took appropriate steps to improve the boots, lashing out in a typical verbal broadside that he would publicly shoot any manufacturers caught short-changing on equipment for "our boys." Personally Borden thought the Militia Minister had handled himself well at the hearings. In the meantime Canadians overseas were issued the British service pattern boot, a fact that Hughes resented.[14]

While the 1915 parliamentary session lasted, the Public Accounts Committee and the Auditor-General continued to probe militia spending. Borden had cautioned Hughes to prepare himself well when he answered in the House. Hughes did not. Instead he preferred to argue with White, Foster, and the others in council or not to attend at all. There was a "very strong feeling against Hughes," Borden wrote in his diary on February 12, "everyone accuses him of discourtesy, pomposity, vanity to an absurd degree, [and] favouritism, arrogance and lack of business methods. On March 25, the Prime Minister was again referring to the "sharp quarrel[s] in Council between Foster and Hughes. Casgrain much excited about the Public Accounts Committee and wanted a royal commission, Foster also." Two weeks later Hughes was still treating "scandals affecting his Department very casually and does not seem to realize situation."[15]

Not that the stories coming out of the Public Accounts Committee needed any cabinet squabbles to reinforce them. In April the worst of these revelations involved two Tory MPs who were buying drugs and horses in Nova Scotia for Hughes' department. William Garland who sat for Carleton in Ontario and Dewitt Foster, the member for Kings in the Annapolis Valley, were caught red-handed and Borden had no choice except to read them out of the party in the Commons on April 15. The two MPs had no direct connection with Hughes, but they were selling to his ministry, which was so poorly and partisanly run that it could not detect such abuse. The case also exposed some of the larger details of Hughes' horse-buying methods. In the 1914 mobilization, he had ignored the existing military provisions for obtaining the animals and had substituted his own remount committee headed by two of his honorary colonels. One of them was Allison. They superintended the purchase of over 8,000 horses for the CEF, of which Dewitt Foster's were likely some.[16]

Shortly after the Garland and Foster firings, the Prime Minister concluded that he had to do something to head off the situation before it broke into a major political scandal. Publicly imposing his own organization on war buying in general and on Sam Hughes' department in particular could also help. But political pressure for change was not the only motive. Borden and some others were having their first vague suspicions that the normal peacetime patronage method was inappropriate for such a large war effort. The Prime Minister's answer was to get rid of the ad hoc cabinet subcommittee on buying established the previous August. He substituted a War Purchasing Commission, headed by his trusted friend and Minister without Portfolio, A. E. Kemp, and two associates, neither of whom was Sam Hughes. The new body was the product of an investigation Kemp had made for Borden at the end of April of the Militia Ministry's facilities to handle munitions procurement. He had found Hughes' department undermanned and overworked, with no internal organization and no apparent attempt by the Minister to give it one. There was no inventory; war supplies were piled up across the country; and there were no inspection services. However, the War Purchasing Commission—the result of Kemp's recommendations—was to have jurisdiction over all purchases under the War Appropriations Act and all future purchases by or for the British or allied governments, except for munitions for the British. While there were some exemptions for emergencies, public tender and lowest-price contracts were to be the norm. The new commission quickly took on the characteristics of a modern government department; its members had authority and responsibility, and they set up procedures for doing business on a routine basis. There can be no doubt that the news of the organization's creation in early May pleased the public and helped stifle the opposition. But Hughes did not like it, although he knew that something had been wrong with the old method.[17]

In January he had been so anxious to get urgently required material to the troops that he had begged Borden to set up a better organization than the cabinet subcommittee, whose other members slowed down the decision-making process because they were not in the Militia Department. Their patronage concerns also bothered Hughes, and he was sincerely worried about such unfortunate episodes as the Garland and Foster affair. However, it was equally clear that he did not want to end the old patronage system; nor did he want to give up his personal control. Consequently, in January, his suggestion to Borden for reform of the contract-letting aspect (and one repeated four months later) was simply another version of the traditional patronage organization: he wanted a new committee of prominent "businessmen" in his Militia Department. When the Prime Minister took the idea to the council, the members were "aggrieved by the suggestion," likely because Hughes would control the new committee. Nothing happened until Borden's War Purchasing Commission came about in May, and then Hughes fought it all the way. The Militia Minister saw its independence as a slap at his "dignity." These comments, Borden caustically noted, "angered me excessively and I spoke very sharply; his eyes filled up." However, by June 1915 the new committee was functioning. It did not end patronage in war spending—far from it. If Kemp's files are any indication, many of the old practices continued. But the new body ended Hughes' monopoly, reduced the most blatant incidences of patronage, and in general dispersed, regulated, and controlled war spending, and made munitions procurement much more efficient. For the public and opposition, especially after the sacrifices of Ypres and Festubert that spring, the committee demonstrated that some in Borden's administration were moving towards a less partisan direction in a bloody war than Sam Hughes was willing to do.[18]

No doubt Hughes was sincere in his complaints about the slowness of the new purchasing committee and the persistent and blatant patronage considerations of colleagues. Men like Edmund Bristol, Senator Lougheed, and Bob Rogers continued to exert pressure. Even Kemp, as head of the War Purchasing Committee (WPC), was able to promise the Ontario party organizer, Robert Birmingham, that while his patronage requests would be "somewhat" more difficult "to carry out to the full, be assured I will do the best I can." Six months later the Prime Minister, who was still exasperated over Foster's constant and self-righteous council bickering with Hughes over political spoils, admitted that "Foster has no more political sense than a turnip ... his speech about patronage was eloquent mouthing; in everyday practice no one is keener about petty patronage than he is." But Foster and

Kemp did realize that during war—this war at least—the usual vague and wide patronage boundaries were going to have much more definite and narrow limits.[19]

As for Hughes, he would continue to act alone, resenting his loss of patronage and resisting the need for more government organization. The Liberal press continued to focus on Hughes' extravagance in war purchasing. But the criticism was substantially mitigated in 1915 because the Commons session was over in mid-April, and Parliament would not meet again for another nine months. And in early June 1915, the Prime Minister had appointed Sir Charles Peers Davidson, recently retired from the Quebec Superior Court, to investigate munitions purchasing for the Canadian government. The report would take over a year to complete. All the moves of that spring had helped satisfy the public and dampen the opposition for a while. But Borden gloomily wrote in his diary on June 5 that he was still receiving reports "as to Hughes' favouritism and unbridled temper; [he] cannot help making a fool of himself."[20]

During the next eighteen months, even though there is no evidence of ministerial malfeasance, Sam Hughes continued to tangle with one and all over war supplies, most of which went the same route as the boots. Oliver equipment and motor and wagon transport were just as controversially handled. The Canadian-designed Oliver harness, the body strapping from which a soldier suspended his personal equipment, was condemned shortly after the Boer war and Hughes himself had been replacing it with the new web imperial pattern since 1911. Yet in early 1915, to the disgust of his colleagues, he spent without their approval $700,000 in rebuilding the obsolete Oliver harness, declaring that it would be issued to all Canadians. Besides informing no one about the expenditure, the problems of the reworked kit were not solved, nor did the harness fit the imperial pattern or even carry the same amounts of things like rifle ammunition—a nightmare for any quarter-master worried about his troops in battle. Hughes wanted Canadian manufacturers to benefit and to show off their design capabilities; but when the Canadian soldiers complained and the British discarded it, Hughes' nationalism bristled, and Canadians were sent overseas wearing the useless harness until 1917.[21]

In the case of motor vehicles and wagons, which the War Office had requested accompany the first contingent, Hughes ordered T. A. Russell, a Tory supporter since 1911 and the wealthy manager of the Canada Cycle and Motor Company, to buy up whatever available ones he could find. Specifications, the Minister told the anxious Russell, did not matter. Such was the case with the notorious Bain wagon, which Hughes got from a Grit firm in Ontario, and with his impulsive purchase of a single aircraft and the commissioning of its civilian owner and pilot. None of these items conformed to any imperial standard; often there were no spare parts, and they could not be repaired. They were rejected first by the Canadian soldiers and then by the War Office. The Minister did not admit that it was often "his boys" who were passing these judgments; for him the rejections remained a well-developed British conspiracy to rob Canadians of business opportunities and their excellent equipment.[22]

Sometimes Hughes brought disaster on perfectly sound munitions ideas which he could not or would not follow up. One was the MacAdam shield-shovel. In 1913, while on European manoeuvres, Sir Sam's young secretary suggested to the Minister that the Swiss troops she saw laboriously digging trenches should combine their shovels in a convenient shield-shovel tool. The following year fifty tons of shield-shovels appeared at Valcartier with Hughes proudly proclaiming them a Canadian-designed miracle device for the first contingent. But they had no handle and could not be suspended from the Oliver harness; they were heavy, expensive, and above all, not bullet proof. Overseas, Canadian and British soldiers, including Alderson, Currie, and Sir John French, condemned and replaced them. According to *Saturday Night*'s editor, the shovel was useful only for "opening tins . . . cleaning a pipe [or will even] . . . come in handy when rush operations for appendicitis are necessary." Such gadgets proliferated in the Great War, but their success usually had men of orderly and innovative minds behind them, men who could pay close attention to larger details, something Hughes could not do well.[23]

The same problem arose with rifle ammunition in the spring of 1916, when the news broke that Allison had sold to Vickers five million rounds of desperately needed .303 rifle cartridges at a price of $15 per thousand less than Canada was paying in the United States, and that he had kept a $5 per case commission. No one could placate the anxious public or opposition, and Borden added the affair to the list of Mr. Justice Davidson's investigations. In time, the commissioner revealed that Hughes had been justified. The ammunition had been condemned in 1913 as part of Hughes' arsenal reforms that year; it was also the obsolete Mark VI ball for which no Canadian or British weapons were any longer sighted, and Allison's profit was normal. Hughes had not told anyone what he was doing or why; nor had he used the War Purchasing Commission to dispose of the cartridges. He had simply ordered one of his personal agents to give substance to a sound idea, then he forgot about it. Davidson did not report until well into 1917; all the while the public imagination festered. In spite of Davidson's exoneration of Hughes, the damage had already been done when the cartridge charges were laid in the spring of 1916 just as Hughes was under suspension and the Commons was in an uproar over two other, far larger scandals concerning shells and the Ross rifle.[24]

When Lord Kitchener cabled Sam Hughes on August 24, 1914, urgently requesting him to obtain artillery shell components from the United States, Hughes was already convinced that Canadian industrialists could make anything. Shortly after receiving Kitchener's request, the Minister had asked two American representatives of the U.S. Steel Corporation to help in the organization of Canadian steel production for shells. When the arrogant Americans told Hughes that Canadians could never produce such steel, Hughes angrily yelled, "By God, the work shall be done in our own country; we are not so dependent as you think," and he ordered the pair out of the militia headquarters. In early September 1914, while he was bustling around Valcartier Camp, Hughes gathered together a small group of steel manufacturers headed by his friend, Colonel Alex Bertram of John Bertram and Son, Steel Works, in Dundas, Ontario. Hughes gave all the members honorary ranks and simply told them to organize Canadian industry for shell production. He legitimized the committee on a scrap of paper written in pencil and signed, "For Action, S.H." One member, Thomas Cantley of Nova Scotia Steel, remembered that "Sam . . . asked Alex [Bertram] and myself if we could undertake the job. He said our expenses would be paid but not a damn cent by the way of remuneration." Another member also recalled that the committee was not formally organized because its members were convinced that the war would be over in six months. Also feeling the urgency of the times, the Prime Minister had sanctified Hughes' creation vaguely with the words "All orders for arms, equipment and munitions of war should be filled by the Department of Militia and Defence with as little delay as possible . . . contracts, etc., should be prepared that the purchase may be made in a systematic fashion and according to business methods." Hughes sought no advice, although many people did not feel Canada had the facilities to produce such items in quantity.[25]

The work of Hughes' Shell Committee established the foundations of the Canadian munitions industry. By May 1915, from nearly a dead start, the body had produced and shipped to the front 675,000 eighteen pounder artillery shell bodies, and had laid the basis for continuing work by granting orders for $170 million to over 250 firms across Canada. The committee had set up specifications for its contractors and a central organization for receiving and shipping. It was ironing out the manufacturing processes and, indeed, made some innovations in shell manufacturing by using unheard of steel processes. All the while David Carnegie, the committee's Woolwich Arsenal-trained ordnance adviser and brother of one of the members, was actively soliticing more and more war orders in Great Britain and the British, more willingly than wisely, gave them.[26]

In February 1915 the War Office wired Hughes asking about the "advisability and feasibility of the manufacture of armaments" of all sorts in Canada. This was what the Minister wanted to hear; he immediately struck a sub-group of the Shell Committee to find out. Headed by Honorary Colonel and Tory Frederick Nicholls of Canadian General Electric, the body noted the initial reluctance of Canadian industry to respond to the war crisis as well as the very limited basis of its capacity. The Shell Committee had gone a long way in rectifying this hesitancy, the report said, but still more had to be done. More war contracts from Great Britain was the only way. Because of the small and dispersed nature of Canadian factories, any new orders, the sub-group concluded, should be spread across the country to give all regions a better share and to promote industrial response.[27]

The net result was a British order in May for five million rounds of fixed gun ammunition. The Shell Committee was also encouraged in their expanded enterprise by Borden and other cabinet ministers equally anxious to have Canadian industry share in the lucrative munitions market. Such national participation, they reasoned, would be more commensurate with the sacrifices made in terms of troops and would certainly help mitigate resentment caused by the War Office's placement of the largest war orders in the U.S. Moreover, unemployment would be reduced and, as both Hughes and the Prime Minister quickly saw, contract dispersion would satisfy the economic demands of the regions, particularly the west which had already provided a remarkable number of volunteers for the overseas divisions. Hughes' positive activities as the major political promoter of economic recovery in 1914 and 1915 contributed to the Prime Minister's high tolerance level for the Militia Minister's other faux pas.[28]

But to paint such a glowing description of the positive features of the Shell Committee in the spring of 1915 is to ignore both its faults and influential events elsewhere. As R. J. Q. Adams details, the sensational British shell scandal in the spring of 1915 forced Prime Minister Asquith into a coalition government with a new ministry of munitions under the fiery little Welshman David Lloyd George. To solve the crisis, the new Minister was determined to shake both the domestic and the Empire munitions supply system by radically departing from respected laissez-faire practices and involving the government directly in private enterprise.[29] Once that fundamental decision was made in England, Sam Hughes' Shell Committee, with its reliance on private business and personal agents, was destined to change as well.

The Canadian committee's problems paled in comparison to those faced by the British. Yet they were similar, and they grew as the demand for munitions increased. The organization of the Shell Committee was at best primitive. Its two executive officers were Bertram and Carnegie, with the chairman's son Harry acting as a sort of chief of staff. For the first nine months, the willing and hard-working Bertram conducted the committee's business out of his own company's offices in Montreal. After May 1915, at Hughes' insistence, the obvious need to regularize their accommodation brought the committee into new quarters in the Stephen Building in Ottawa. But the move did not streamline the headquarters. On any day one could see the harried Bertram immersed in paperwork, while outside his office dozens of contract-hungry manufacturers sat on shell boxes waiting to see him. While $170 million in orders had been received, the committee had shipped only $5.5 million worth of shells. Only 2 per cent of them were delivered on time; and there were tremendous backlogs of various shell parts awaiting other components. In some cases, records were chaotic and Bertram did not seem to know exactly what he had accomplished or who or what was under his control.[30]

After the unpleasant revelations of the Public Accounts Committee earlier that spring, further gossip during the summer suggested that the Shell Committee had the same diseases as Hughes' department. Some manufacturers complained that the committee's executive let contracts to their own firms and did not use tenders in awarding orders. Rumours had it that Hughes' special agents were taking huge profits, while some contracts were even being let out to American companies, thereby defeating the original purpose of the Shell Committee to promote Canadian business. Certainly the former charge was true, but it was not so damning as it seemed. Since at least four members of the committee were among the most prominent of the manufacturers, it would be hard to avoid giving contracts to their own concerns. As for the lack of tenders, the British seldom used them in the early war effort in order to encourage industrial response. In Canada the experience was much the same, but it was compounded by the lack of experience of most of the country's small firms—by far and away most of them—in having any idea of how to submit an accurate estimate. By the summer of 1915, many had learned to evaluate cost, and as the initial bottlenecks were overcome, actual production expenses had declined substantially. As for rumours of graft, they would have to wait for more concrete proof. But it was evident that most Canadians did not understand that the Shell Committee was not responsible to the Canadian government; nor did they know that it was not buying munitions for Canadian soldiers. What they also did not realize was that the Shell Committee was the agent first of the British War Office and then of Lloyd George's new munitions ministry, and that Hughes was its sole liaison with British authorities. When it contracted, the British government notified Hughes, who as agent in turn placed the order with the members of his own committee which then subcontracted to manufacturers across the country.[31]

By spring 1915 Sam Hughes knew that his creation was not working well and that criticism had to be allayed somehow. But Hughes could not think of much else besides moving the body closer to him in Ottawa. Or at least other events did not give him time. By June Canadian businessmen finally realized the potential of Hughes' optimism for domestic production; they pressured Borden for still more orders. But Borden was equally frustrated by the Shell Committee's slowness, disorganization, and failure to give him concrete information. In England so was Lloyd George. Anxious to get the most out of Canadian resources, he refused to place any more orders with Canadian firms until Hughes' committee was reformed. With these points among others in mind, in late June 1915 Borden went to England as a contract procurer, and Lloyd George sent D. A. Thomas, a rich Welsh coalmine owner, to Canada to see what could be done.[32]

As soon as Thomas arrived in Canada, he got to work with Sir George Foster, who was sick of Hughes' bragging, erratic, and haphazard ways, and who was determined to bring some order to the war effort. Since Hughes had rushed over to England behind Borden in early July, neither the Welshman's nor Sir George's activities were impeded by the Militia Minister's presence. Fuelled by Foster's biases, the hard-nosed Thomas ruthlessly uncovered all of Hughes' Shell Committee weaknesses, and he spared few words in telling the shocked members his opinion. The investigations also included listening to manufacturers' complaints and rumours of corruption. As he wrote later, he found that "considerable uneasiness existed in the minds of the [Canadian] cabinet ... as to the manner in which the Shell Committee were discharging their functions and to the probable effect of their activities upon the Government itself." On top of this, Thomas thought that the British taxpayer had been charged exorbitant prices in Canada because of a lack of a method of tendering and the nationwide dispersion of contracts to small producers. The only answers for efficiency, he believed, were competitive tenders and large national factories; and he told Bertram that no more orders would be placed in the country until such reforms took place. He also wanted a new, independent, and British chairman for the committee. His attitude was insensitive to the committee's past hard work and to the Canadian political, economic, and manufacturing reality of munitions procurement during the first year of the war: there were no large industries; decentralization had been supported by the government for political and economic reasons; and few Canadian firms had any hope of ever making accurate estimates on contracts before production because of inexperience. However, Thomas' view was an accurate assessment of what would be needed in the future. Times had indeed changed.[33]

Thomas' bluntness and arrogance won him few friends on the Shell Committee. Cantley called him "a Welshman with all the crookedness pertaining to that race." Bertram was no less bitter. He would not budge on the tenders issue, and he strongly resented Thomas' attempts to control Canadian contracts "when jurisdiction was clearly in the purview of the Shell Committee." By October, four months after the British had decided to reform the committee, nothing had been done; nor had any more orders been placed. Three weeks before, Hughes and Borden had arrived back in Canada. Thomas had gone to New York to meet them and the three took the train back to Ottawa while Thomas made his case for reorganization. But he did not get the co-operation he expected. He was shocked at the "hostility" on the part of both ministers: "Sir Robert mentioned in the course of his conversations with me that Canada had been drawn into this war without any previous consultation on the part of the Imperial Government, and the Minister of Militia did not attempt to disguise his feelings toward the War Office and the Secretary of State for War." But Hughes and Borden had more in common than their nationalism. After confidential briefings in England, both were well aware of the need for shell reform; by the time they got to Ottawa, both also knew of the rumours haunting their own committee, especially ones involving Hughes' friend Allison, who although not a member was one of its contractors. At first Hughes was unwilling to give up his control of the Shell Committee or to hand it over to the British. He also resented Thomas' lack of praise for the previous work of the committee and for his constant harassment of Bertram's methods. "The Shell Committee," as Hughes flatly put it to Thomas, "was his baby and it had been a model to the whole world." But the stakes all around—political, economic, and military—were higher than Hughes' passion and grudgingly he admitted it. The compromise came from Lloyd George when he sent out a replacement for Thomas to break the stalemate in late October 1915.[34]

Lionel Hichens, the chairman of Cammell-Laird, the great British steel-shipbuilding company, was the same Hichens who had served under Sir Sam in the Boer war and one of those who thought him "a man among men." In his seven weeks in Canada, Hichens found more to commend the Shell Committee's record than the intemperate Welshman ever admitted. Certainly it was no worse, Hichens reported to Lloyd George, than similar early agencies created in Britain. Nevertheless, inherent executive weaknesses now made it inefficient. Hughes already knew this, but it took the diplomatic Hichens to effect the change in Sir Sam's mind; he pointed out that the advantages of reorganization would be to regularize its existence, explain its function, and rectify its command faults. Similarly, it had to be brought into phase with the new conditions both in the war and in British munitions administration. The key to Hichen's success with Sir Sam was his emphasis upon evolution and continuity between the Shell Committee and whatever new body was agreed upon, rather than destruction and reconstitution. It was also clear that the new group could have no direct political, military, or munitions connections. Borden was firm in this and Hichens could point to the British reorganization as a precedent to calm Hughes' doubt. There were two choices, he suggested: a munitions portfolio of the Canadian government modelled on the British one, or a board in Canada responsible to the ministry in England. Either way, Hughes was to have nothing more to do with it. Personally he preferred the latter course; so did the rest of the cabinet, probably to ward off further Liberal press accusations of favouritism. Borden himself refused to accept a Briton as head of the new board; no doubt Hughes wanted Bertram to superintend the new concern, but he was no longer politically acceptable. When the Prime Minister offered the willing Senator Lougheed as the new chairman, Sir Sam refused, probably because Lougheed had been very critical of Hughes' militia administration in the past and because the Senator was just as capable of using the patronage mill as was the Militia Minister. Borden declined to push Lougheed in the face of his unhappy Militia Minister.[35]

Again there was a compromise. This time it was over a man Hughes had known for years and clearly did not like. Joseph Wesley Flavelle was the millionaire president of the William Davies Company and a man respected and admired in Canada and England for his business acumen and organizational ability. Back in the spring of 1915, he had already been considered by the British to be part of the whatever reorganization took place in Canada. Flavelle also was the nephew of J. R. Dundas—the Militia Minister's old rival in his early days of Victoria county Tory politics and journalism. They had nearly driven Hughes out of the newspaper business and politics in the 1890s. But in 1915, however reluctantly, he did accept Flavelle as head of the new Imperial Munitions Board (IMB). He could neither do much about it, nor deny that Flavelle was a competent businessman. In his favour, he was not a politician, nor was he in the steel business.[36]

By the end of November the old Shell Committee had resigned. To save face, the unhappy and by now sullen Hughes was made honorary president of the IMB with Bertram as deputy and David Carnegie as ordnance adviser. While all of this was going on, Borden had quietly investigated the corruption rumours about the old group. There was nothing that proved the members guilty of anything save errors of judgment during hurried times. Nor was the Militia Minister involved in any graft. Other complaints by disgruntled businessmen—that the committee had discriminated against them—generally proved to be "sour grapes." Hichens also advised the Prime Minister in December that he was convinced "that the Shell Committee had carried out its work well" under the existing conditions. It was an opinion he continued to hold in later years and to which both he and Borden added their appreciation of Hughes' initiative, energy, and optimism in laying the basis of Canada's early munitions industry. Still, rumours about Allison's huge profits made on a committee fuse contract let out in the U.S. in early June persisted throughout the fall of 1915.[37]

Since the summer Tory strategists had predicted that the party could not win an election. The government's image had been tarnished not only by shells but by many other things, including a bankrupt rail system and the Ontario schools question. What Borden needed in 1916 was to avoid both scandal and an election and to persuade the wily Laurier to grant an extension of Parliament, preferably until the end of the war. So far the opposition leader had remained silent. Yet during the first days of January 1916, the unofficial word was that the Liberals would soft-pedal their criticism and the session would be short. It did not turn out that way.[38]

The IMB's creation did not stop controversy over Hughes' Shell Committee; and it was the Allison fuse contracts that did it. On January 18, six days after the Commons session started, the Liberals attacked Hughes. At first, the vague accusations bothered neither him nor Borden. The Prime Minister's advisers still said that the Grits had nothing to go on, and Hughes responded in the House with what Borden thought at times to be an excellent defence of the Shell Committee. But the gains here were marred by Sir Sam's constant defence of Allison.[39]

In private, if Flavelle's biographer is correct, Hughes was frightened because he knew that neither the fuse contracts nor Allison's activities would bear much scrutiny. More likely, he did not know about the real corruption, and the dictates of personality kept him loyal to a friend whom he thought was a patriotic businessman. All the rest was "piffle." Whatever the case, about this time Flavelle thought he detected a Hughes-inspired whispering campaign against the competence of the new IMB. If true, perhaps it was done because the Militia Minister still resented his loss of patronage and the eclipse of one aspect of his miracle of Valcartier—the Shell Committee. Another interpretation suggests that Hughes simply wanted to move the Liberal attacks from him to Flavelle's organization. While the first explanation seems the more probable, one thing is sure: Hughes never understood that "his ... model to the world" was gone forever, as total war replaced limited battle. Flavelle was not, as Hughes thought of Foster, just a self-righteous moralizer with no military qualifications; rather, he was, as John English so succinctly puts it, representative of the new non-military war leaders then emerging who were "simultaneously the masters of the machine and the embodiment of national purpose, where virtue and knowledge become one." As one of the old order,

Sam Hughes was not alone in his resentment of Flavelle. Businessmen accustomed to Hughes' practices disliked the new chairman's neutrality. Probably they, rather than the Minister, were the source of the several complaints about the IMB in the newspapers and elsewhere which appeared in early 1916. As such they were testament to the fact that many still believed that party interest, profit, and patriotism remained the best servants of the state.[40]

In the next two months, although Laurier finally agreed to prolong Parliament for a year, there was much political capital to be made. Consequently the Liberals pressed hard on Hughes with the still undefined shell charges. In spite of them, Sir Sam persuaded Borden that he was urgently needed in England to sort out his administrative jumble there. Before he left in early March, he also assured Sir Robert that it was safe to leave with the House in session, claiming he had arranged a backroom deal with the Liberals to hold off any specific charges until he returned. In fact, Sir Sam had met with Laurier and his militia critic, E. M. Macdonald, but they denied any deal. As Macdonald remembered the encounter, Hughes had stormed out of the room when reminded that Allison was a "heeler." Moreover, his almost indecently hasty departure from Canada looked to many on both sides of the House as if he was running away to avoid the issue. The Conservative members were not long in expressing their disgust at Hughes' exit and at Borden for allowing it. But whatever the motives, or whoever misled whom, the Liberal member for Richmond, Nova Scotia, G. W. Kyte, dropped the bomb of the "fuse scandal" shortly after Hughes departed, alleging that Allison had made "fabulous profits" on fuses from American companies and that Hughes was also involved. Sir Sam got the news while he was having supper with Bonar Law in London, and as Harcourt witnessed, "General Sam . . . was white as a sheet and looked an utterly broken man, as indeed he is likely to be in the future. . . ."[41]

Borden weakly tried to refute the charges but to no avail. The Conservative Party whips reported that "our members are practically in open revolt against Hughes' continuance as minister." Conservatives everywhere were horrified and frightened. The caucus and cabinet wanted a thorough investigation of the entire shell business. Hughes had caused the trouble and left them to bear the brunt. Important men like Flavelle thought that Borden was weak and "short on imagination" and his entire cabinet "a wobbly lot," But he saved most of his sanctimonious spleen for Hughes: he was a "degenerate without moral sense.... I believe him to be mentally unbalanced with the low cunning so often found in the insane." The scandal, if left unchecked, could bring down the government. Already saddled with a lack-lustre and tainted image, it could not possibly withstand much more of Hughes' activities.[42]

The alarmed Borden finally moved. He ordered Hughes home immediately, then appointed a royal commission. These acts greatly steadied the caucus; but the last one inflamed Sir Sam. Earlier he had sent Borden a private letter defending Allison and the Shell Committee and describing "himself as the only strength of the Conservative Party"; and he was in a high emotional state when he returned to Ottawa on April 16. His interview with Borden the same day was both unpleasant and pathetic. "He wept at one time and laughed at another" and claimed that he would come through any investigation with flying colours. Personally Borden doubted that and mentioned taking over the Militia Department until the air was cleared, suggesting that Hughes tell the Commons that he had asked his chief to relieve him only during the enquiry. Hughes gave in because he had little choice. But in three days he was back in Borden's office; he "was quite excited when he came to see me," Borden recorded, "he says he is regarded as suspended. Why did I not suspend Rogers? He swore at Meighen and Ames, especially the latter." But Borden held firm.[43]

Outside of the prime minister's office, the temporarily dethroned Militia Minister kept up a constant barrage denying Kyte's charges and defending Allison and the Shell Committee in the Commons and in the newspapers. In one emotional tirade, he publicly proclaimed that his friend Allison had more honour in his little finger than the Auditor-General had in his entire body. Such outbursts at a time when most cabinet and caucus members had already written Allison off as a complete scoundrel drove Borden to consider "resigning as Prime Minister in favour of Foster and taking the portfolio of Militia with two Party secretaries." Amid the storm, however, there were some signs that he could avoid such drastic action.[44]

On April 26 the Royal Commission began its sessions and continued to hear evidence well into the late spring. The two commissioners, Sir William Meredith, Chief Justice of Ontario, a Tory provincial leader in the 1890s, and a man "sharply prejudiced against Hughes," and his Liberal co-chairman, Lyman Duff from the federal Supreme Court, gave the Hughes affair a thorough scrutiny. They heard testimony from Allison in mid-May, the same day the 1916 parliamentary session closed, and two weeks later, they listened to Hughes' two days of spirited defence. The fact that Allison admitted to the commissioners that he took profits of $220,000 to be divided among four of his colleagues, including $105,000 for his secretary, and that Sir Sam later still defended one and all before the same body, underscored the Militia Minister's inability to see that party affiliation, profits, and patriotism were not an efficient mixture in wartime administration. As the investigation progressed, however, Hughes gave a reasonable defence of the Shell Committee in the Commons, except for his outbursts on behalf of Allison; and the Conservative lawyer serving on the Royal Commission privately told Borden that "nothing of importance will develop over Hughes or the Shell Committee's activities." Even Flavelle, who continued to despise Hughes, admitted privately that the old committee members were "honest men" and the naive Hughes was likely "duped."[45]

Both Duff and Meredith agreed with Flavelle. In their final report Hughes and the Shell Committee were exonerated of any wrongdoing. Allison and his gang were severely condemned for taking large commissions and for deceiving both the Militia Minister and his committee. The findings gently refrained from commenting on Hughes' gullibility and his continued association with the Morrisburg entrepreneur. Because the Shell Committee was not connected with the Canadian government in any way, the commissioners felt that no action could be taken against Allison. Certainly the idea of a Shell Committee was an inspired one. Its function had rendered valuable service in mustering a reluctant and inexperienced small domestic industry. The report also pointed out that the country had undergone substantial change in its attitude since the innocent and impromptu days of 1914. "Informal" organization and "the absence of a specific definition of ... functions and duties," the commissioners suggested, were no longer tolerable; and the trouble with Allison from the beginning, as John Bassett perceptively noted at the time, "was that he wished to pose as a patriot and not as a real businessman. Allison without wings is a person we can understand"; and Sam Hughes' continued praise of Allison was not just loyalty, it was the defence of a traditional, moribund political system.[46]

Four months earlier, immediately after the Kyte charges had rocked both the party and the public, Borden realized that his Militia Minister could "not remain in government" much longer. But he could hardly fire Sir Sam without indicting his own administration—at least not just yet. Late that spring, however, Borden did insist that the Militia Minister accept a permanent undersecretary. F. B. McCurdy, the talented MP for Queens-Shelborne in Nova Scotia, was the Prime Minister's personal choice and he was to handle the routine business of the Militia Department from then on. But Sir Sam did not want McCurdy; he even tried to have the new post made a "military position"—a proposition the Prime Minister refused. Nevertheless, McCurdy's appointment brought an immediate stabilizing and ordering effect to an office which Hughes had all too often left vacant; and the Militia Council started to meet formally and regularly, and once more began to advise the department—its function, long lapsed under Sam Hughes.[47]

Hughes got himself into hotter water. While privately upset about Allison's betrayal of trust, the Minister continued to praise him until an embarrassed Borden ordered him to shut up. Then came the needless controversy over the construction of Camp Borden in Ontario. Early in the spring construction had begun, under Hughes' orders, with almost indecent haste and in the fashion of Valcartier. By July the rolling pine plains fifty miles northwest of Toronto had over 30,000 troops sweating and cursing the heat, sand, and flies. At a review Hughes called for July 11, the unhappy troops booed him, a few even rioted; and the next day Hughes left in haste. There was no Valcartier triumph here; indeed, the discontent was a clear sign that the war had changed in the minds of most Canadians, but not in Sir Sam's. At hearing the news the Deputy Militia Minister told Borden he was not surprised: "Hughes is very unpopular in the country."

After the camp fiasco, Borden let Hughes go to England where he promised to mend his equally tattered organization there. No doubt glad to have him out of the country for the summer, the Prime Minister continued to feel the increasing cabinet discontent over the unrepentant Militia Minister; and the Liberal press lampooned him fairly and unfairly, while some usually supportive reporters noted how fast "the universal military hero of Canada was becoming plainly insufferable."[48]

The Ross rifle scandal broke almost at the same time as the small arms ammunition and shell issues in the spring of 1916. To the public, the three were all the same thing. But in the Ross case, unlike the Shell Committee goods, the rifle was used by Canadian troops. The fate of the Ross in war had been largely determined by Sam Hughes' control of it in peacetime. By 1914 it was already the most celebrated, hated, and debated military rifle of its time. Its military serviceability eroded by partisan politics, nationalism, and the target shooting mania coming out of the Boer war, the Mark III model was put in the hands of the first overseas contingent. Both from Valcartier and later Salisbury Plain, complaints about the rifle trickled in: it jammed, there were few spare parts, and even fewer competent military armourers. But Hughes did little except to assert that "his boys" were trained to use a rifle as "no man ever handled a rifle before."[49]

Early in 1915 General Alderson, the CEF's first commander, saw the defects and, more importantly, the lapsing confidence in the weapon while the troops were still in England, and he requested its exchange for the Lee-Enfield. However, the British authorities, deferring to the obvious preference of Hughes, sent Alderson's contingent to France armed with the Ross, which was a pound and a half heavier and nearly nine inches longer than the Lee-Enfield. There were valid reasons why Hughes was not bothered by the weight and length of the Ross. The rifle was similar to the standard infantry pattern of most other countries. In the Boer war Hughes had seen that a long, heavy, and accurate weapon was the ideal rifle to accomplish the long distance shooting. Unfortunately, as Winter says, in 1914 no one expected that trench warfare would demand a weapon that was short, light, and easily pointed and that would endure dirt and rapid fire.

The Ross rifle's first combat test came with the second battle of Ypres in April 1915. During the fighting over one-third of the frantic Canadian troops threw the Ross away when it jammed on British ammunition. After this, unit commanders, including Hughes' son Garnet of the Third Brigade, flooded Alderson with complaints which he passed on to the British commander-in-chief, Sir John French. This weapon, the Canadian commander warned his superiors in a grave covering note, "cannot be allowed to stand in the way when the question may be of life or death or of victory and defeat." British rifle tests then showed the Ross indeed did jam but only with certain lots of British ammunition—usually the over-dimension type about which Hughes had been warned years previously. French concluded that since the appropriate low limit Canadian ammunition supplies could not be guaranteed for the expected summer offensives, the first contingent would be rearmed with the Lee-Enfield. The Second Division could keep the Ross if properly fitting ammunition was procured. To help ease the problem of dependence on British cartridges Sir John also suggested enlarging the Ross chamber a bit.[50]

Hughes was outraged at the unilateral and wholly unnecessary action. He stormed to Borden that the Ross had no faults, only "bad" British ammunition. What he said was true, but what he did not say was that the straight-pull bolt actions of the Ross inherently had less chance of removing defective and stuck cases than Enfield turn bolts, and that the Ross chambers were notoriously tight, making the problem even worse. Often too willingly victimized by Hughes' technical barrages, Borden was also aware that the Canadian rifle was good Canadian business in bad times, and he felt that the British had not often consulted Canadians adequately in such matters. Certainly he was not prepared to see the rifle scrapped for a British one without adequate Canadian proof. He quickly pointed this out to British authorities who no doubt had already heard directly from Hughes that he would not tolerate French's cavalier discrimination against Canada's national weapon. The Field Marshal was astute enough to know that once confidence in any military item is lost in a combat situation, it is not easily rewon. But the Field Marshal stuck to his guns—the Lee-Enfields for the First Canadian Division.[51]

Hughes appointed his own committee to discover the fault and he chose the rifle's inventor, honorary Colonel Sir Charles Ross, as one of the examiners. At the end of June, this group came to a different conclusion: besides bad British ammunition, the other culprits were Flanders mud, too few armourers, and too much ignorance among officers to correct the situation. Hughes, Ross added critically, should have ensured a better public educational program in Canada so that soldiers knew how to care for their rifles. For the time being, the best thing to do was to issue British pattern "breech sticks" to keep the mechanism clear. Obviously there was confusion as to what was the real problem or the best solution. The British rearming, nevertheless, was one of the reasons Hughes wanted to get over to England in the summer of 1915.[52]

Both there and while he was still at home, he did little to counter effectively the alarming number of reports by returned soldiers of the disastrous role the Ross had played at Ypres, Festubert, and Givenchy. These ruinous stories fell hard on the Canadian psyche, already stunned by the casualties and indignant over the revelations of Hughes' munitioning inefficiency that spring. In spite of Sir John French's plea to Hughes in June that he would most "heartily welcome an authoritative statement which will carry conviction to the men that their apprehensions are unfounded," Hughes made no such reasoned explanations to anyone in public. For the next year, he gave only emotional broadsides, claiming that the Ross was so popular that Canadian soldiers had to sleep on the weapons to keep their envious British allies from stealing them. Nevertheless, when the problems persisted, Hughes decided to have the receivers of all rifles enlarged a few thousands of an inch to ensure easier extraction of British ammunition.[53]

In the meantime, Hughes' chief cabinet antagonist, Sir George Foster, who was Acting Prime Minister while Borden was in England, and the Chief of the General Staff, Willoughby Gwatkin, seemed to have quietly joined forces to have Hughes' rifle policy overthrown. Their first target was to expose the faults in production and supply of the weapon to the British. The previous October, during the onset of the critical shortage in nearly all military hardware, the War Office had made a contract with Sir Charles Ross for 100,000 rifles at the rate of 200, then 300 per day. Sir Charles' appetite for orders was far larger than his ability to fill them. He had neither the skilled craftsmen nor the plant. Over the winter his obligations to produce for the Canadian government clashed with his British commitments and he was constantly late in his deliveries for both. By spring 1915, he was nearly 13,000 rifles in arrears to the War Office. And knowledge of the rifle's problems in the field was already widespread in British circles. They did not need much pressure to look at it critically.

At this point, the shell shake up in Britain saw Lieutenant-General L. T. Pease, an ordnance expert, sent out to assess the trouble with munitions supply in North America. Quickly he got around to the Ross. The delays, he said, were caused by poor organization of the factory and the constant failure of the rifle to pass British inspection services;

he recommended the Ross contract be cancelled. Nothing was done as Sir Charles Ross played a delaying action in Britain. Later that summer, after D. A. Thomas came out from England, he, Pease, Gwatkin, and Foster co-operated quietly in a further investigation of the state of affairs at the Ross factory. In August Gwatkin privately went another step by notifying Pease that the Canadian government was "sick to death of the Ross Company," perhaps hoping he could have the British put enough pressure on the Canadians to switch to the British arm. Yet nothing came out of their secret attempts to scupper the Canadian side of the venture. Nevertheless, they continued to exert pressure against the weapon with Foster in the cabinet the most vocal opponent. In June he had demanded that Borden abandon the whole affair, while proclaiming that "the blood of half our slain is more precious than an idea." The dour New Brunswicker, of course, would have wanted Borden to dump Hughes along with the rifle.[54]

Sir Charles Ross never managed to deliver more than 1,000 rifles to the English authorities in the first year, although he constantly asked for more money and larger orders from the War Office. At the same time, he also negotiated with the Russians for a similar sized contract. Before Thomas went back to England in the fall of 1915, he advised the British to cancel their agreement with Ross. In the end they did, but it took them another sixteen months because of the labyrinthine vagaries of Sir Charles' negotiations and the unresolved fate of the rifle in Canadian hands. During this time Ross delivered less than 67,000 rifles. Thomas at the same frustrated Foster and Gwatkin by abruptly suggesting to Lloyd George that there should be no interference with the existing arrangement between the Ross Company and the Canadian government; they are "satisfied with this output... General Hughes was opposed to changing the Ross rifle for the British rifle, and Mr. Thomas thought his faith in the rifle was genuine and was largely due to his share in evolving the present design." In short, the British did not now want the weapon because it cost too much but they still needed Canadian men, so they would not interfere too heavily.[55]

Hughes' order, during the summer of 1915, that the Ross chambers be enlarged was sound, but his interference caused confusion and more serious problems. Again the Minister appointed Sir Charles Ross to handle the enlargements and even he could complain of Hughes' interference and specifically that the Minister's reaming instructions were "at variance with the militia department's latest instructions and the War Office figures." During the rest of the year, adverse reports about the weapon's refitting were added to those of its continued malfunctioning—and all got back to Canada.[56]

But in January 1916, Sir Sam misinformed the Commons that all the rifle's faults were corrected and complete confidence in it restored.

There was no truth, he told Borden, to any rumours about continued malfunctions. The British, he went on, were so impressed with his rechambering scheme that they had their Lee-Enfields enlarged to the new Ross breech dimensions. This was not true, but the British were having difficulties with the quality of their ammunition and rifles, and they did rectify the problem by easing the Lee's chamber. Nevertheless, Hughes confidently assured Borden that "with good ammunition, that is proper brass, neither rifle had the slightest trouble."[57]

Hughes' personal agents overseas were responsible for some of the false information leading to Hughes' inaccurate statements on the rifle. Perhaps feeling it was what Sir Sam wanted to hear, J. W. Carson and Max Aitken fed Hughes favourable information about the Ross. Their most notorious deception, whether or not intentional, happened in late October 1915. Earlier that fall, when the Canadian First Division was involved in the Battle of Loos, one of its Canadian officers wrote a searing criticism of the Ross' performance. Currie, the divisional commander, passed it on to the British headquarters. Always vigilant, the busy Sir Max Aitken quickly cabled Hughes of the episode and added that there was a great deal of prejudice in the Canadian Corps concerning the weapon. Hughes' response was to try to quash the document by ordering that its initiator be fired. "I will have no intrigue on the part of ignorance," he told Aitken. "Such men are a menace to any service; the fellow, whomever he may be, knows nothing of rifles. What is his name?" It is not clear if the Minister ever found out, but the rifle was tested against the Enfield at the end of the month. The trials showed the Lee less prone to malfunction than the Ross; Canadian ammunition helped but did not stop the jamming. Carson's assessment of the trials to the Militia Minister, however, implied that the problem seemed solved. Over the next few months Max Aitken also advised his Minister that there was no case for the malfunction charge; and he warned that there was a conspiracy afoot. At best the net result was that Hughes and Borden got conflicting information, and the soldiers at the front got to keep the Ross whether they wanted it or not. As for Borden, although he had an unadorned copy of the test in his possession by January 1916, he still deferred to the judgment of his Militia Minister.[58]

There were other problems with the quality of the rifle which were not so widely known as its jamming. But again rumour took its toll. In late October 1915, an ordnance officer in France reported that bolts on a recent number of 1915 Ross rifles "are coming in dead soft, in fact are running from glass hard to dead soft." The reports were confirmed in England. On his own initiative in the opening months of 1916, Carson ordered the parts retempered; then he informed Hughes that all was well. But it was not. Many military experts thought the ad hoc process used to do the retempering was dangerous. In a later investigation,

Professor W. D. Bancroft of Cornell University, a metallurgist appointed by the Canadian government after Hughes was fired, found that such irregular tempering methods "would be criminally careless in times of peace."[59]

With the expected offensives in 1916, field commanders were alarmed about their troops' reactions if still armed with a rifle in which they had no faith. In February 1916, when it was clear that neither Hughes nor any of his agents were going to pay any attention to the previous October's tests, Alderson decided he would not wait any longer. He bundled up all of the adverse evidence on the Ross and sent it off to Gwatkin in Canada. His covering note contained all of the reasons why the Enfield rifle was the better one. When Hughes found out, he was furious at both his chief of staff and the corps commander. His immediate reaction was to send a rude letter of censure to the corps commander accusing him of ignorance and saying that "few officers knew anything about any rifle, especially the Ross rifle." Later in the Commons, Hughes told the members that Alderson did not "know the butt from the muzzle." After sending the letter, the Minister had 281 copies of it delivered to most of Alderson's officers in the field. This action had the effect of undermining confidence in the corps commander, as well as confirming the troops' suspicions about the rifle. Alderson's stand on the weapon probably contributed to Hughes' consenting to his dismissal after the ferocious battle of St. Eloi Crater two months later—a struggle in which so many Canadian servicemen threw away their Ross rifles that some officers in the Second Division vainly threatened to court-martial offenders.[60]

Canadian battles later that spring only produced pleas to rearm, especially from the Third Division. In early May Max Aitken advised both Hughes and Borden that the situation was critical. But he implied that the trouble was because of the fact that "most British officers attached to Canadian Corps and Divisions have persistently attacked Ross rifle due, no doubt, to greater familiarity with existing rifle [the Lee-Enfield] and dislike of innovation [the Ross]." Such reports only confirmed Hughes' suspicions about a British conspiracy. On May 26 he fired a chauvinistic salvo at the War Office through Aitken: "Do you mean to tell me that Canada, furnishing already one-third of a million men and paying for everything, is to be interfered with in the matter of rifles and equipment of every description. The thing is unbearable." The next day he charged that Alderson had promised favours to Canadian officers if they would report adversely on the rifle: "I further respectfully deny," he thundered on, "authority of the British Government to interfere with our rifle... it will create more serious issue than had arisen since 140 years [1776]—[Alderson], thinking my star was descending, took advantage to play on weak officers; please remember my star is merely on the ascendant."[61]

Hughes was still not going to listen to anyone. And the concurrent Allison and shell scandals made him politically vulnerable. Sensing this, Gwatkin forced the Ross rifle issue by discreetly taking Alderson's letter to the Governor-General's secretary who, on May 17, 1916, the day before the Commons session ended, had Charles A. Bowman, editor of the independent Ottawa *Citizen*, publish all of its damning evidence. The sensational disclosure came as a complete surprise to the Militia Minister, but it came just a little late for the Liberals to exploit it in the Commons. Hughes was so incensed he tried to fire Chief of the General Staff, Gwatkin, by telegraphing Sir Max Aitken to pressure the British government to have him recalled. Fortunately and ironically, Hughes' wire got garbled in the transmission. Sir Max must have thought his time as Eye-Witness was up when he read the cable in London: "Please have G. W. Aitken recalled immediately otherwise I shall insist on his dismissal." Sir Max immediately wired back: "War Office and Foreign Office deny any knowledge of G. W. Aitken. What is his post." By that time the Militia Minister said he was "dealing with the matter" in other ways. How he did was never revealed, for Gwatkin outlasted Hughes in office, and Sir Sam had to face the onslaught of public opinion on the Ross rifle.[62]

While it was too late for Parliament to have a thrust at Hughes, the Liberal printing offices and many of the newspapers were in an uproar over the Bowman rifle revelations. In desperation Borden had defended the Ross rifle and Hughes, stating that all the faults had been corrected. By this time the Prime Minister knew that this was not true; for five days he had been in possession of transcripts of Alderson's tests. To some in the caucus and cabinet, Borden's defence of both Hughes and the rifle was lame. Foster thought that "Sam's pets and Sam are the peril of this government and with the Premier's strange compliance will in the end likely destroy it."[63]

By the end of May 1916, opposition attacks and public indignation over the rifle policy were so intense that Borden could not leave the matter in the Militia Minister's hands, even though he was sympathetic to Hughes' nationalist motives about Canadian equipment. Reluctantly the Prime Minister told the British he would accept their decision on the fate of the rifle. Canadians, they responded, had no confidence in the weapon; it was decidedly inferior to the Lee-Enfield. The War Office instructed the Canadian government not to send any more troops to England armed with the Ross. Back in Canada Borden thought he had convinced Hughes to accept the Army Council's decision. While Hughes may have told Sir Robert that he had, in fact, he was still lobbying through Aitken. On June 10, the day after Borden told Aitken that he and Hughes had agreed to the British decision, the Militia Minister secretly wired Aitken: "I am absolutely firm, make no concessions, as far as I am concerned; will be over soon." A month later Hughes went to England, but his efforts came to nothing. By the end of September, the British had completed the re-equipping of the Second, Third, and Fourth Divisions. Ironically, just before the weapon's complete abandonment, its jamming problem was easily corrected when a Canadian ordnance officer found that by doubling the surface area of the bolt stop, the locking mechanism did not get deformed. But it was too late. The Prime Minister knew he had made the right political decision. A relieved Newton Rowell, Ontario Liberal opposition leader, summed it up to Borden by saying simply that he did "not think any announcement could be made which would give greater satisfaction to the men at the front."[64]

The man who had so much exaggerated confidence in the Ross rifle destroyed other people's faith in it. The point about the rifle which Hughes could never see was the psychological one. By mid-1916 the debate about mechanical merits or faults or nationalistic comparisons no longer mattered. British munitions production had then exceeded demand. The British could supply Canada with rifles; nor did they need Hughes to supply the men. To the soldier in the field who entrusted his life mostly to his rifle, if he did not believe in it, he would not use it. With the lack of solid and unbiased information for the public to make a sensible judgment, the Ross rifle was doomed. With its reputation gone, with manually operated small arms suspect, with huge surpluses and no domestic or foreign markets, the expensive Ross would never be revived.

In the spring of 1917, the government expropriated Sir Charles Ross' factory after legal advisers had cautioned that his sixteen-year-old Liberal-initiated contract would be legally hard to end. Sir Charles promptly sued for $3 million and in 1920 settled out of court for $2 million cash. His factory was torn down as a Depression relief project in the 1930s; and his rifles, after twenty years of storage, were dispersed all over the world as emergency second standards in another German war. More than any other factor, the ignominious end of the rifle was due to Sam Hughes.[65]

In 1914 the declaration of war had been Sam Hughes' private mandate to direct its course personally. With munitions, much like men, there was little he felt Canadians could not do. After the Duff-Meredith findings in 1916, the business community was still very sympathetic to Hughes for his foresight and imagination in creating what turned into a spectacular munitions mobilization—one which was to change the very nature of the country.

Unfortunately in their execution his good ideas—the Shell Committee, the Ross rifle—frequently tripped over his administrative disabilities, or foundered on his nationalism and apparent unwillingness to give Canadians intelligent and accurate appreciations of predictable munitions snafus. But as a junior, and not yet considered even a partner, in the Empire alliance, Canada's war production and supplies were bound to face an uphill climb made steeper by the demands for military uniformity. Sam Hughes did not create these spoiling factors; he inherited them. But if he wanted to have Canadian goods used by Canadian fighting troops, he should have realized that spleen and speed could not replace the efficiency of order and reason. Hughes' personal leadership style could succeed only as long as he remained credible and above partisanship. In supplying the war, Sam Hughes undermined his own position and threatened that of his government. By late 1916, as one contemporary observer noted, Canadians

> looked upon as inevitable that at the beginning there should be delays and such petty graft as that discovered in the case of some shoe contracts. But at this date [1916] the official machinery should be running smooth. Every fifth or sixth home in Canada has sent its representative to the front, and the population will deal sternly with those found at fault.[66]

Reference Notes to Chapter 13

1 Michael Bliss, *A Canadian Millionaire, The Life and Business Times of Sir Joseph Flavelle, Bart. 1858-1939* (Toronto: Macmillan, 1978), chapter 10; John Herd Thompson, *The Harvests of War, The Prairie West 1914-1918* (Toronto: McClelland and Stewart, 1978), chapter 1.
2 Duguid, pp. 112-13, 169; Brown and Cook, pp. 193-95; and J. A. Corry, "Growth of Government Activities in Canada 1914-1918," in CHA *Annual Report*, 1940, p. 63.
3 R. J. Q. Adams, *Arms and the Wizard, Lloyd George and the Ministry of Munitions 1915-1916* (London: Cassell, 1978), chapters 2, 3.
4 English, p. 89; Adams, pp. 28-29; PAO, Bristol *papers*, are full of such requests, especially MU 283 to 286; Borden *Memoirs*, vol. 1, p. 466; and PAC, Borden *private diaries*, Oct. 16, 1914.
5 PAC, Sir Thomas White *papers*, MG 27, 11, D 18, vol. 2, F 10, White to Borden, Aug. 27, 1914.
6 Public Accounts Committee, 1915, *Evidence*, pp. 15-17, especially White to Auditor-General, Sept. 3, 1914; and PAC, John Bassett *papers*, MG 30, E 302, vol. 7, Bassett to Smeaton White, Nov. 25, 1914.
7 PAC, Gwatkin *papers*, F 1, Gwatkin to Connaught's secretary, Sept. 28, 1914; PAC, Borden *papers*, OC318, Hughes to Borden, Jan. 2, 1915; PAC, RG 24, vol. 412, 54-21-1-10, Gwatkin to Rawley, Nov. 3, 1914; PAC, Kemp *papers*, vol. 4, F 58, Kemp to Borden, White, Foster, Reid and Rogers, Nov. 27, 1914; and ibid., Borden to Kemp, Nov. 18, 1914.
8 Harcourt *papers*, vol. 465, pp. 40-43, confidential cable, Borden to Perley, Nov. 27, 1914; and PRO, Munitions Ministry *Records*, MUN 5, 173, F 1142/36, Borden to Lloyd George, Feb. 10, 1916; ibid., f 1142/2, Borden to Colonial Secretary, Aug. 23, 1915 (hereafter cited as MUN 5).
9 PAC, RG 24, vol. 502, 54-21-5-10; Borden to Fiset, Sept. 30, 1914; and PAC, Gwatkin *papers*, F 4, unaddressed letter by Gwatkin, July 1, 1914.
10 PAC, Gwatkin *papers*, F 2, Gwatkin to Stanton, Apr. 5, 1915; and PAC, Borden *papers*, 466 (1), vol. 90, Fiset to Christie, Feb. 15, 1915, and Brown to Fiset, Feb. 15, 1915. Also see Duguid, p. 83; and PAO, Whitney *papers*, MU 3116, J. W. Allison to Whitney,

May 9, 1905; and Morgan, *1912*, p. 19. The company was the Canada Tin Plate and Sheet Metal Company of Morrisburg, Ontario.
11 PAC, Borden *papers*, OC 318, McAdam to French Ambassador, Washington, Oct. 13, 1914; ibid., Borden to Hughes, Oct. 7, 1914, and Hughes to Borden, Oct. 23, 1914; ibid., 446, vol. 90, Perley to Borden, Dec. 16, 1914; ibid., Borden to Perley, Nov. 7, 1914, vol. 90, contains most of the relevant details on Allison's activities in 1914; PAC, Borden *private diaries*, Oct. 21, 1914; and PRO, Foreign Office, 371/2224/61688, Spring-Rice to Foreign Office, Oct. 20, 1914; Duguid, appendix 172, Spring-Rice to Governor-General, Nov. 1, 1914; ibid., appendix 173, Governor General to W.O. and H.M. Ambassador in Washington, Nov. 13, 1914; and ibid., Private Secretary, Minister of Militia to Russian Ambassador, Washington, Nov. 13, 1914 (also see appendices 175 and 176).
12 PAC, Borden *private diaries*, Oct. 16, 1914, Oct. 21, 1914, Feb. 10, 1915, Mar. 25, 1915; PAC, Borden *papers*, OC69, White to Borden, Feb. 5, 1915; and PAC, Foster *diaries*, Sept. 12, 1914. Public Accounts Committee, 1915, *Evidence*, p. 15, Auditor-General to the Deputy Minister of Finance, Dec. 4, 1914.
13 *Canadian Liberal Monthly*, vol. 2, Feb. 1915, p. 71; *CAR*, 1915, pp. 188-89; and Duguid, appendix 204, Perley to Borden, Nov. 24, 1914; these contain details on the boot scandal.
14 *Journals*, 1915, part 3, "Proceedings and Evidence of the Special Committee on Boot Inquiry," pp. 1013-17 (hereafter cited as *Journals*, 1915, "Boot Inquiry"); and ibid., pp. 5-27; *Hansard*, 1915, p. 1678; PAC, Borden *private diaries*, Apr. 12, 1915; and *Saturday Night*, Apr. 17, 1915, p. 1.
15 PAC, Borden *private diaries*, Feb. 12 and 13, 1915, Mar. 19, 20, 24, 25, 1915, and Apr. 8, 1915.
16 Ibid., Apr. 14, 15, 1915, Public Accounts Committee, *Evidence*, 1915; *CAR*, 1915, pp. 177, 188; and Duguid, pp. 84-88.
17 PAC, Kemp *papers*, vol. 4, F 58, Kemp to Borden, Apr. 20, 1915; and Brown, *Borden*, vol. 2, p. 38.
18 PAC, Borden *papers*, OC318, Hughes to Borden, Jan. 2, 1915; and PAC, Borden *private diaries*, Jan. 4, 1915 and Apr. 17, 1915; Hughes to Borden, May 13, 1915 in Duguid, appendix 721. Also see *Hansard*, 1916, pp. 1351, 1361, 3288; PAC, Kemp *papers*, vol. 1, F 2, contains much evidence of continued patronage; and English, pp. 96-97.
19 Ibid., PAC, Borden *private diaries*, Jan. 4, 1916.
20 *CAR*, 1915, p. 192; PAC, Borden *private diaries*, June 5, 1915; Brown, *Borden*, vol. 2, p. 38; *Saturday Night*, Sept. 4, 1915, p. 1; and the *Canadian Liberal Monthly*, issues for August through October 1915.
21 Preston, *Canada and Imperial Defense*, pp. 270-71; Militia Council Report, 1910, p. 75; and PAC, RG 24, vol. 1202, HQ. 130-23-2, QMG to OC:MD's, Nov. 8, 1911, repeated in 1913 and 1914; ibid., HQ. 130-11-5, PC, no. 532, Mar. 8, 1915; ibid., HQ. 130-32-2, QMG:Cdns, Eng. to QMG Ottawa, Jan. 12, 1917; Duguid, appendix 216, Alderson: Order 1164, Feb. 2, 1915; ibid., 219, Hughes to Carson, Feb. 9, 1915; ibid., p. 446; and PAC, Borden *private diaries*, Jan. 28, 1915.
22 S. F. Wise, *Canadian Airmen in the First World War; The Official History of the Royal Canadian Air Force* (Toronto: University of Toronto Press, 1980), vol. 1, pp. 25-30. Also see the Public Accounts Committee, *Evidence*, 1915.
23 Great Britain, Parliament, *Debates of the House of Commons 1915* (London: King's Printer, 1915), p. 1563; F. J. Dupuis, "The McAdam Shield Shovel," in the *Canadian Journal of Arms Collecting* 11, no. 4, pp. 117-19; personal interview, Ena McAdam Macdonald and the author, Ottawa, Dec. 12, 1984. She had grown up in a family of iron workers. The idea, she said, simply made sense. Also see Duguid, appendix 218, Carson to Hughes, Feb. 10, 1915, and appendix 219, Hughes to Carson, Feb. 9, 1915. PAC, RG 24, vol. 1202, HQ. 130-19-2-3, GOC:BEF France to WO, Feb. 12, 1916; and *Saturday Night*, Oct. 3, 1914, p. 1.
24 Canada, Royal Commission on the Sale of Small Arms Ammunition, *Report*, Sir Charles Davidson, Chairman (Ottawa: King's Printer, 1917), pp. 4-5, Auditor-General to Minister of Finance, Apr. 3, 1916; *Sessional Papers*, 1916, no. 276, p. 96, cited in Davidson Commission, 1917, pp. 10, 29. Also see ibid., pp. 5, 33, 56, 70.

REFERENCE NOTES TO CHAPTER 13 / 255

25 Duguid, pp. 112-13; David Carnegie, *The History of Munitions Supply in Canada* (London: Longmans, Green and Company, 1925), pp. 2, 112; Winter, p. 94; *Review of Reviews* (December 1915), pp. 743-44; Bertram *papers*, Shell Committee file, Cantley to Henry Bertram, Dec. 10, 1932; Borden *Memoirs*, vol. 1, pp. 467-68; Winter, p. 94; Jean Graham, "The Story of the Shells," in *Saturday Night*, Sept. 15, 1915, p. 10; and *CAR*, 1915, pp. 228-40.
26 Bertram *papers*, Shell Committee file, Alex to Henry Bertram, June 5, 1915; Great Britain, *Hansard*, 1915, p. 1204; PAC, Christie *papers*, vol. 2, F 3, p. 1216; and PAC, RG 24, vol. 413, HQ. 54-21-1-20, MGO to DM:DMD, Jan. 31, 1915—for a report on Shell Committee activities to date.
27 PRO, MUN 5, 173, 1142/8, "Report of the Committee Appointed by the Minister of Militia and Defence to Consider the Advisability and Feasibility of Manufacture of Armaments in Canada," Feb. 15, 1915.
28 Ibid., 370, 1141/5, D. A. Thomas, *Final Report*, Dec. 9, 1915; Carnegie, p. 87; Bliss, pp. 246, 252; and Thompson, chapter 3, challenges the effectiveness and the amount of this help in the prairie provinces.
29 Adams, chapters 1-5.
30 Bliss, pp. 244-52.
31 Ibid.
32 PRO, MUN 5, 173, 1142, Minute, "Purchase of Army Supplies in Canada," June 1915; ibid., 1142/2, Borden to Law, Aug. 23, 1915; and ibid., 1142/4, R. H. Brand to Montagu, July 18, 1916.
33 Ibid., 370, 1141/5, Thomas, *Final Report*, Dec. 9, 1915.
34 Bertram *papers*, Shell Committee file, Cantley to A. Bertram, Dec. 10, 1932; and ibid., Alex Bertram to Hughes, Dec. 17, 1915; PRO, MUN 5, 173, 1142/30, Memo, Oct. 30, 1915; ibid., Thomas to Bertram, Oct. 9, 1915, and Bertram to Thomas, Oct. 5, 1915; ibid., 370, 1141/5, Thomas, *Final Report*, Dec. 9, 1915; and PAC, Borden *private diaries*, Sept. 1, 4, 7, 8, 1915, and Oct. 27, 1915.
35 PRO, MUN 5, 370 1141/5, Thomas, *Final Report*, Dec. 9, 1915; ibid., 371, X/Mo7389, "The Establishment of the Shell Committee," Hichens to Lloyd George, Nov. 15, 1915.
36 PRO, MUN 5, 173, 1142/29, "War Office Armaments Committee Recommendations," May 28, 1915; and Bliss, pp. 69, 14-18, 30, 36.
37 Carnegie, pp. 96-108; PAC, Borden *papers*, 446(1), Lloyd Harris to Borden, Oct. 2, 1916, "Memorandum of Negotiations of the Russell Motor Car Company with the Shell Committee ie. fuses," Oct. 2, 1916; Bliss, pp. 251-52, especially notes 34, 35; PAC, Borden *private diaries*, Nov. 1, 20, 1915; PAC, Borden *papers*, Hichens to Borden, Dec. 8, 1915, p. 24024; PRO, MUN 5, 371, 1142/10, "Introduction to the History of the Imperial Munitions Board" by R. H. Brand, 1921; and ibid., 173, 1142/36, Borden to Lloyd George, Feb. 10, 1916.
38 Brown, *Borden*, vol. 2, pp. 46-48.
39 PAC, Christie *papers*, vol. 2, pp. 1220-27, "Memorandum on Shell Committee Attacks"; and PAC, Borden *private diaries*, Jan. 26, 1916 and Mar. 2, 1916.
40 Bliss, pp. 267-69; and English, pp. 97-98, 106.
41 PAC, Foster *diaries*, Mar. 9, 1916; Borden *Memoirs*, vol. 2, p. 556; Macdonald, p. 306; PAC, Borden *papers*, Borden to Hughes, Mar. 31, 1916; and ibid., Hughes to Borden, Mar. 31, 1916; Harcourt *papers*, 462, Harcourt to Connaught, Apr. 13, 1916; PAC, Borden *private diaries*, Mar. 9, 10, 1916; and the diary of Mrs. Ena McAdam Macdonald (March 30-31, and April 1, 1916) notes the flurry that the news caused.
42 PAC, Borden *private diaries*, Mar. 29, 1916, Apr. 3 and 7, 1916; Queen's University, Flavelle *papers*, 83, Flavelle to Willison, Apr. 6, 1916, pp. 1684-85; and ibid., Mar. 30, 1916, pp. 1681-83. Flavelle records that many cabinet colleagues would "welcome his disappearance." For other comments on Hughes, see PAC, Foster *diaries*, Mar. 29, 1916.
43 PAC, Borden *papers*, 318, Borden to Perley, Mar. 29, 1916; ibid., Hughes to Borden, Mar. 27, 1916; ibid., Willison to Borden, Apr. 1, 1916; and PAC, Borden *private diaries*, Apr. 16, 17, 19, 1916.
44 PAC, Borden *private diaries*, Apr. 9, 1916; and Queen's University, Flavelle *papers*, B 2, Flavelle to Willison, May 29, 1916, pp. 1490-91.

45 PAC, Borden *private diaries*, Apr. 11, 1916; ibid., Apr. 23, 25, 1916; PAC, Perley *papers*, vol. 5, p. 155, Borden to Perley, May 13, 1916; Queen's University, Flavelle *papers*, B 3, Flavelle to Willison, Apr. 28, 1916, pp. 1693-94; and D. R. Williams, *Duff: A Life in Law* (Vancouver: University of British Columbia Press, 1984), pp. 83-87.
46 Canada, Royal Commission on Shell Contracts, *Report*, R. M. Meredith and Sir Lyman Duff Commissioners (Ottawa: King's Printer, 1916), pp. 3-27 (hereafter cited Shell Report). Also see Brown, *Borden*, vol. 2, pp. 55-56; English, pp. 97-98; and PAC, Bassett *papers*, vol. 1, Bassett to Aitken, May 2, 1916.
47 PAC, Borden *private diaries*, Apr. 3, 1916; ibid., June 23, 1916; and ibid., July 1, 1916.
48 McAdam Macdonald interview, Dec. 12, 1984; Militia Council *Minutes*, 1916, p. 185; PAC, Borden *papers*, OC318, Borden to McCurdy, Aug. 1, 1916; and ibid., Hughes to Borden, Aug. 9, 1916; and PAC, Borden *private diaries*, June 23, 1916; ibid., July 1, 6, 12, 13, 24, and Aug. 23, 29, 1916; *CAR*, 1916, pp. 262-64; and Wilson, pp. xlix-l. Camp Borden documents are in PAC, RG 24, particularly HQ. 67-19-1, and in PAC, Kemp *papers*, vol. 90; *Nation* 52 (April 13, 1916), p. 399; "Canada Stirred by War Graft," in *Literary Digest* 52 (April 22, 1916), pp. 1137-38, for a survey of the Canadian press on Hughes' administration. Also see "Sam Hughes' Way," in *Literary Digest* 52 (May 27, 1916), p. 1556; the *Canadian Liberal Monthly*, issues for July, Aug., and Sept. 1916; and PAC, Foster *diaries*, July 6, Aug. 10 and 29, 1916.
49 *Hansard*, 1915, pp. 1429-30; Duguid, appendix 111, p. 85; *CAR*, 1914, p. 221; Winter, p. 157; PAC, RG 24, SSAC, vol. 7, f 2-5-5-2, Harston to Hughes, Dec. 10, 1910; *Militia Report*, 1910, p. 116; PAC, Sir Charles Ross *papers*, MG 30, A 95, vol. 5, Ross to Hughes, Oct. 23, 1914; PAC, Perley *papers*, vol. 2, p. 27, Borden to Perley, Oct. 3, 1914, private and confidential memo, updated, unsigned, written at Valcartier, likely by Ross; and PAC, Borden *papers*, III (3), pp. 5766-67, Nesbitt to Borden, Jan. 31, 1916.
50 Duguid, appendix 3, pp. 81-87; and Haycock, *Canadian Defense Quarterly* 14, no. 3 (Winter 1984/85), pp. 48-57 (more details about the Ross).
51 PAC, Borden *private diaries*, June 12, 1915; *Sessional Papers*, 1917, no. 44, pp. 9-10, French to the War Office, June 19, 1915; and PAC, Borden *papers*, III (2), 5629, Carson to Steele, July 31, 1915, and p. 5624, Hughes to Craig, July 16, 1915.
52 PAC, Ross *papers*, vol. 5, Ross to Hughes, June 23, 1915; Allan, *Ordeal by Fire*, p. 98; and PAC, Gwatkin *papers*, F 2, Ross to Gwatkin, June 30, 1915.
53 *CAR*, 1915, p. 197; and Galt *Daily Reporter*, June 25, 1915, pp. 1, 9, and July 9, 1915, p. 6; *Hansard*, 1916, p. 1349; Duguid, appendix 3, p. 89; PAC, RG 24, SSAC, vol. 6, Aug. 23, 1915, "Tests made on Ross Rifles and Ammunition," and PAC, Borden *papers*, III (2), p. 5624, Hughes to Craig, July 16, 1915.
54 PRO, MUN 5, 173, X/MO7362, "The Ross Rifle Contract," pp. 2-4; PAC, Gwatkin *papers*, F 2, Gwatkin to Pease, Aug. 5, 1915; ibid., F 1, Gwatkin to Foster, July 25, 1915; and PAC, Foster *diaries*, June 25, 1915.
55 PRO, MUN 5, 173, X/MO7362, appendix E.
56 PAC, Borden *papers*, III (3), pp. 5747-48, Ross to the War Office, Aug. 15, 1915. Also see R. H. Roy, ed., *The Journal of Private Fraser, 1914-1918: Canadian Expeditionary Force* (Victoria: Sono Nis Press, 1985), pp. 12, 26, 32-33, 56, 69, 115.
57 *Hansard*, 1916, pp. 292-93, and PAC, Borden *papers*, III (4), Hughes to Borden, Feb. 18, 1916.
58 HLRO, Beaverbrook *papers*, E/6, "Ross Rifle," nos. 1, 2A, Aitken to Hughes, Oct. 4, 6, 1915, cable; ibid., no. 2, Hughes to Aitken, Oct. 5, 1915; ibid., no. 5, Sims to Aitken, Jan. 21, 1916; ibid., no. 7, Aitken to Alderson, Feb. 11, 1916; ibid., no. 8, Aitken to Gwatkin, Feb. 11, 1916; PAC, Borden *papers*, III (2), Carson to Hughes, May 19, 1916; and PAC, Perley *papers*, vol. 4, p. 107, Perley to Borden, Jan. 14, 1916 (this contains a complete copy of the Alderson test of Oct. 27, signed by Carson and marked secret).
59 PAC, Borden *papers*, III (3), p. 5638, Captain G. Mortimer to DAA:OS, 2 Cdn. Div. HQ., Oct. 2, 1915; ibid., p. 5639, Harkom to Carson, Feb. 3, 1916; ibid., p. 5654, Carson to Hughes, Feb. 9, 1916; ibid., p. 5689, Northover to White, Apr. 16, 1916; ibid., Perley to Dominion Government, June 14, 1916; ibid., pp. 5757-58, "Report on hardening of bolts in England, 1916," and ibid., pp. 5754, 5755, Bancroft to Parker, Dec. 16, 1916.

60 *Hansard*, 1917, p. 485; PAC, Borden *papers*, III, Ross Rifle file, p. 40; ibid., III (4), p. 6057, Perley to Borden, Apr. 20, 1916; Duguid, appendix 3, p. 93; and PAC, Griesbach *papers*, F 4, Carson to Griesbach, Mar. 24, 1916, enclosure.
61 HLRO, Beaverbrook *papers*, E6, Aitken to Hughes, May 12, 1916, no. 12; ibid., Hughes to Aitken, May 26, 1916, no. 28; ibid., Hughes to Aitken, May 27, 1916, no. 30; see ibid., E5 and E6 for Aitken's involvement in the rifle issue in 1915-16.
62 Bowman, pp. 40-42; and Charles Bruce, *News and the Southams* (Toronto: Macmillan, 1968), pp. 94-95; Beaverbrook *papers* (in Dr. A. M. J. Hyatt's files), Hughes to Aitken, May 20, 1916; and ibid., Aitken to Hughes, May 22, 1916.
63 *Winnipeg Free Press*, May 19, 1916, p. 9; *Globe*, May 19, 1916, p. 4; and ibid., May 25, 1916, p. 6; Galt *Daily Reporter*, May 23, 1916, p. 2; and *Le Devoir*, May 22, 1916, p. 1; also see *Hansard*, 1916, pp. 4112-16; PAC, Borden *papers*, III (4), pp. 6072-73, Alderson to Borden, May 13, 1916; ibid., p. 5693, "Confidential report on Alderson's Rifle Investigation," C. H. Harrington, GS:CC, May 2, 1916; and PAC, Foster *diaries*, May 19, 20, 1916.
64 HLRO, Beaverbrook *papers*, E/5, Hughes to Aitken, June 10, 1916, ibid., Borden to Aitken, June 9, 1916, no. 5; ibid., Hughes to Aitken, July 15, 1916, no. 30; PAC, Borden *private diaries*, Oct. 13, 1916; Great Britain, Parliament, House of Commons, Cmd. paper no. 8429, *Correspondence Relating to the Use of the Ross Rifle by Canadian Troops in France* (London: King's Printer, 1916), p. 3, Haig to the War Office, May 28, 1916; *Sessional Papers*, 1917, no. 44, pp. 4-5, Bonar Law to Governor-General, July 11, 1916; PAC, Kemp *papers*, vol. 154, R 9, Rowell to Borden, Sept. 18, 1916.
65 Commons *Journals*, 1917, LIII, p. 115; Stent, in the *American Rifleman*, Apr. 1945, p. 27; and Duguid, appendix 3, pp. 98-99.
66 *Hansard*, 1917, pp. 262-63; ibid., 1919, p. 630; British *Hansard*, 1916, p. 1011; PAC, White *papers*, vol. 2, F 8, p. 901, "Memorandum for the Canadian Government," Jan. 1916—Perley told Borden that we "were all informed that the War Office had undertaken to provide everything needed for the men in the contingent and that the Canadian government had no responsibility in that regard." Ibid., Perley to Borden, Feb. 11, 1916; PAC, RG 24, vol. 1205, HQ. 130-1-2, Kemp to Gwatkin, Mar. 22, 1916—Gwatkin ordered the CGS to accept the policy if possible to use Canadian made equipment for Canadian troops. *CAR*, 1916, p. 286; *Saturday Night*, Jan. 8, 1916, p. 13. In mid-1916, J. H. Sherrard, president of the Canadian Manufacturers' Association, declared that "Canada's debt to the Minister of Militia in connection with the making of munitions will only be fully known when the history ... is written. ... He has made mistakes of judgement which are easy to criticize now but the percentage of error should be regarded in proportion to his vast accomplishment" (*CAR*, 1916, p. 286), and *Nation* 102 (April 13, 1916), p. 400.

CHAPTER 14

Hughes' Hydra Overseas, 1914-1915

The purpose of military administration is to provide the necessities that allow the fighting soldiers to achieve full efficiency. There must be clear jurisdictions, open communications, and willing co-operation between soldiers of the bureaucracy and those of the line. By Armistice 1918 Canada controlled its entire war effort, except for operational deployment of its troops. But achieving this in the previous four years meant creating certain administrative processes and organizations. This progress was all the more difficult because the conflict turned out to be one of unexpected length and unimaginable violence. All nations had trouble achieving efficiency. Some leaders never found it. Sam Hughes was one of them. Yet facing the absence of national experience and machinery and labouring under the encumbrances of established political norms, Hughes tried.[1]

When the Minister arrived in England in October 1914, he spent most of his time promoting the national image of the expeditionary force even though at the time neither he nor the Prime Minister was claiming to have independent strategic or tactical control of the troops outside of Canada. Their main concern initially was to keep the units together as an identifiably Canadian fighting force, a concern not everyone shared. Men like the anglophile George Perley, and Gwatkin and Fiset of the headquarters staff in Ottawa wanted the CEF to be "entirely under the War Office" and "with the same status . . . as British regular troops." Given the lack of both equipment and administrative staff in the CEF, Gwatkin and Fiset were especially convinced that the British government would do all that was necessary in administering

---

Reference notes for Chapter 14 are found on pp. 284-87.

and supplying the contingent—including looking after the casualties. These sentiments immediately clashed with and reinforced Hughes' national image of the force.[2]

In December 1914 Colonial Secretary Lewis Harcourt suggested to Lord Kitchener that the Canadian contingent should be dispersed to "train them in different places with the better portions of your new army. I do not believe that you will dare use them as a single unit together at the front." The next month Kitchener tried to do exactly that, and he was supported by Canada's Acting High Commissioner, George Perley. Kitchener thought that some of the CEF units should be attached temporarily to British formations. But Hughes quickly stopped the disintegration and insisted on training for the entire contingent as a unit. Again three months later, over a different question of service appointments, the Minister bluntly told Kitchener that Canada had "supreme control of her troops."[3]

There was no British conspiracy to rob Canadians of their identity, as Hughes was all too ready to charge. Still the threat of no Canadian control was there. Imperial statesmen did not understand that Canadians wanted to be Canadains as a group. Eventually Hughes' instincts were supported by such necessities and circumstances as accountability for expenditure, Canadian home defence, growing national pride, increased size of the force, number of casualties, effort and safety of troops, local opinion, and the realities of patronage. The net effect of all of these was not only the increasing momentum of Hughes' nationalism during the next two years, but a similar and clear trend in the Prime Minister's thinking and that of the nation as a whole.[4]

The few precedents for action when the war began, and the few existing Canadian overseas agencies, would have presented problems for any militia minister. With no hint of what numbers would be expected in the next four years, Sam Hughes established only rudimentary arrangements for the initial contingent while overseas that October. He made no regular administrative appointments other than those of two Permanent-Force soldiers then serving on the headquarters staff in Ottawa. Major C. D. Spittal of the Canadian Army Service Corps was to look after transport and supply arrangements, and Lieutenant-Colonel W. R. Ward headed CEF records and pay offices. However, Hughes did begin to set up an unofficial and vaguely defined structure of his own agents to guide the operation of the force through its time in England. The *ad hoc* appointments in England created confusion and clashed with the jurisdictional ambitions of George Perley in the High Commission.[5]

The Acting High Commissioner and the Militia Minister had disliked each other for some time. By October 1914 it looked as if Hughes was going to force the same prewar controversy into Perley's placid bailiwick in England. The month before Hughes had succeeded in obtaining direct communication with the War Office and later with the CEF's British commander without going through either Government House or the High Commission. Perley complained to the Prime Minister that not only Hughes but other cabinet ministers were working at cross purposes in their relations with the CEF in Britain. He wanted the power of an overseas ministry with complete authority to co-ordinate the administration there. Yet the Prime Minister refused this not unjustified request. The confusion was only temporary, he said; he would arrange things better when the tension relaxed. Shortly after that exchange, as if he knew that Hughes could not be counted on to lay down any orderly system, Gwatkin quietly pressured Borden through his legal advisor, Loring Christie, to ensure that Perley was the main contact for the CEF's administration overseas. But nothing happened, nor did tensions relax.[6]

By the spring of 1915 Hughes' disruptive ways had so severely jarred the well-organized Perley that he frequently begged Borden for some relief. The Prime Minister did little, beyond securing his acting High Commissioner a knighthood on the 1915 New Year's Honours List, perhaps to help calm Sir George's protests. It did not have any such effect. Instead Perley charged that the Militia Minister's uncoordinated, impromptu methods in Britain made him "squirm." Many in the British government, he pointed out, felt that there were "two governments in Canada, one which is represented here by various people sent out by Hughes and not under the control of the other." Apparently the Prime Minister dismissed Perley's complaints as personal ambition. Hughes was still riding high enough on the popularity of his Valcartier feat that a radical change would be hard to effect politically.[7]

The cause of many of Perley's complaints was Hughes' growing network of personal overseas representatives. One of the first was the portly Montreal mining promoter, strong Conservative, and former commander of the Canadian Grenadier Guards, Lieutenant-Colonel John Wallace Carson, whom Hughes had favoured in September as one of the advance party for the CEF sent to England. A month later, when a second contingent had been announced and Hughes had returned to Canada, he left the underemployed Carson in charge of "financial and other matters" pertaining to his ministry, the CEF, and British authorities. He told few, and Perley was not among them. But soon it would be clear that Hughes had really appointed Carson as his personal agent because it was the traditional way and because war information was hard to get out of the British, who were beginning to reject some of the Minister's officers and his proudly if expensively acquired Canadian equipment. By December 1914 Carson was carrying stories back to Canada of the bad living conditions which the British were forcing Canadians to endure on Salisbury Plain and of the contingent's British commander's criticism of his Canadian officers. Handicapped by the aura of the Valcartier success and British silence, this information alarmed Hughes and Borden. So did Carson's warnings that the contingent was to be broken up. When Perley denied Carson's charges, explaining that extraordinarily bad weather rather than British bungling was the cause of Salisbury Camp's poor conditions, and that there were some unsuitable officers among Hughes' choices, his reassurances quieted Borden but they did not satisfy Hughes who because of Carson never forgot what the "horror" of Salisbury Camp or Alderson had done to "his boys."[8]

Part of the problem in this confusing welter of information, Perley was sure, was Carson's ambiguous terms of reference. But Borden's solution was to have Hughes regularize Carson's position through an order-in-council. The Minister got the order passed but it was far from clear. After February 1915 Carson was to be the Minister's personal representative and to act for the Militia Department in securing "supplies and other equipment" for the CEF "in the United Kingdom and at the seat of war." The Prime Minister, like Hughes, was satisfied that this "competent and faithful man," Carson, would act in Canada's best interest overseas. No doubt he did, but by the summer of 1916 he also had managed to promote his own career into a major-generalcy and was by then calling himself vice-minister of the Militia Department overseas.[9]

The appearance of ministerial agents like Carson was caused by more than British reluctance to share information, old political methods, and the rejection of equipment. Perhaps it was even the legacy of Herbert, Hutton, and Mackenzie; but Connaught had been convinced since 1912 that Hughes was destroying the links of Empire by his erratic and nationalistic demands in the Canadian militia. The war, the Duke wrote secretly to Kitchener in November 1914, would likely increase the "ignorant and conceited" Militia Minister's tendencies. Gwatkin must be kept in Canada if for no other reason than to ensure the flow of vital if confidential Canadian military information direct to the War Office. About this, the chief of staff was far less enthused than Connaught; but he agreed, and in the next two years he often did circumvent, and at times try to undermine his Minister's position. While it was all done in the name of a greater cause, it was still a violation of the principle of superior civilian authority. Its insidious continuence made Hughes more determined to go his own way; and Borden was far more tolerant of Hughes because of it.[10]

In his turn, Gwatkin reacted to Carson. As he quietly warned Loring Christie, this man holds "over our minister, an evil influence.

Should friction be set up between the militia department and the War Office, he will be responsible." As for Connaught, he was absolutely convinced, as he again warned Kitchener shortly after the Ypres battles, that Hughes was a "conceited lunatic"; "Borden is hypnotized by Hughes," and "the latter is carefully fanning the flame here against anything English and especially against the English army whom he abhors on account of its honesty, gentlemanly behaviour and good discipline." "Colonel Carson," Connaught raved on, "is his henchman." It was quite the opposite for Hughes and Borden. With the British showing no inclination to establish a better system with Canada, Canadians forged their own with *ad hoc* appointments like Carson's. By the summer of 1915 Borden was convinced that Carson "has obviously been of great service to the country [and he] handles W[ar] O[ffice] officials particularly well." So Hughes, Borden concluded, must be correct. But what the Prime Minister did not yet sense was the danger inherent in his Minister's belief that Carson was not only a national agent but Hughes' personal one as well.[11]

If Carson was Hughes' special agent looking into British circles, then Sir Max Aitken was the Minister's inside representative looking out. Long connected to the Canadian Conservative Party, in 1914 the wealthy expatriate had rushed back to Canada to help the government. But after he had talked to Hughes and Borden, they made it clear that they wanted him to serve, as Aitken's biographer says, as "the voice of Canada in Great Britain. He would be less official and more adroit" than the anglophile Perley. Aitken owned Britain's mass circulation *Daily Express* and, for several years, was a Union-Conservative MP in the British Parliament; and he moved easily in top political circles there. In December Hughes jumped at Aitken's suggestion to propagandize the Canadian war effort, especially the Valcartier triumph in the United Kingdom. Sir Max was confident he could do it, as he said "with Kipling's assistance." The Minister knew the value of a good press for himself, the country, as well as for the government. In January 1915, through another ambiguous ministerial-inspired order-in-council, Aitken became the official Eye-Witness, doing much the same promotional job which F. E. Smith, another English press baron, was then doing in the United Kingdom for the British armies in France.[12]

Unfortunately Aitken's vague commission clashed with Colonel W. R. Ward's records and pay section. But the diplomatic Sir Max made a private deal with Colonel Ward to take over the records section; and Hughes insisted that all Canadian casualties be announced through Aitken's office under the Minister's signature. This was another step in Hughes' national war, so too was Aitken's growing stable of journalists, such as Major Sir Charles G. D. Roberts and Beckles Willson. Soon an elaborate and highly effective group was telling the national story of

Canada's soldiers overseas, grinding out daily communiqués issued through Hughes' office in Canada.

In time this effort, much of it paid for by Aitken, also included war art and other forms of national record. One of the most popular was a book series, entitled *Canada in Flanders*, which was widely sold in the Dominion. While the first volume heaped substantial praise on Hughes as Canada's fighting Militia Minister, the publications said far more about the country at war. Yet as late as 1916, Canadian news correspondents still felt that the War Office was limiting their access to the front. But the real point is that Hughes and Aitken got a foot in the British information door in France the year before, and would not let it close. For national as well as political reasons, Borden was as grateful for the Minister's and Sir Max's role as he was for Carson's. The "splendid story," he commended Aitken in September 1915, "would have been lost" or told only in "fragmentary form" had it not been for the Canadian Eye-Witness.[13]

The power-loving Aitken was willing to help Hughes for reasons other than simple patriotism or friendship: he was after a higher British, not Canadian, political position. But he would stay with Hughes as long as the Militia Minister was of value. In the process he would assume, again like Carson, functions he did not legally have; and he would sometimes lead the too-willing Minister in dangerously inflated nationalistic directions. In the end, neither as pretentious nor as obvious as Carson in his ambition, Aitken was more important to Hughes' overseas administration.

By the spring of 1915, Aitken believed that neither Asquith nor Kitchener was capable of pursuing the war effectively, as evidenced by acute munitions shortages, many casualties, and bloody stalemate. These were the same forces that brought Hughes and Borden to England and then France that summer. The spectre of the slaughter of more and more Canadians meant that a closer audit of the newly proposed Canadian Corps with its burgeoning posts and promotions was essential. In September, with Borden's support, Hughes made Aitken the "General Representative for Canada at the Front." The post was another attempt to put a second Canadian foot inside the exclusive British general headquarters. It worked because Aitken had excellent political connections, especially with Lloyd George and Andrew Bonar Law.[14]

But a few in England and Canada did not like Aitken's dual roles. Perley was both surprised and piqued by the Eye-Witness himself. The War Office did not know what to make of his vague terms of reference—or so they said. Borden's legal adviser recommended a clarifying order before there was trouble. In Canada Connaught was upset at Aitken's rapidly expanding functions, likely because he knew how lethal Sir Max's backroom political lobbying could be, especially when aimed at his friend and fellow officer, Lord Kitchener. As well, the Duke resented losing to Hughes the flow of war information which normally came out of Rideau Hall. For certain, Connaught thought Aitken would make the Minister even more independent and conceited while Canada's troop integration with the British army would be seriously impeded.[15] But Borden, very upset by the deteriorating war situation, knew that his watchful Militia Minister and his agents were challenging British exclusiveness and incompetence.[16]

Sir Max was not the first watchdog appointed by the Militia Minister. In early 1915, as soon as he thought that the first contingent might be submerged in the British Expeditionary Force (BEF) in France, and receiving very little information from them, Hughes arranged his own Canadian connection at British headquarters. A flamboyant land speculator from Port Arthur, J. J. Carrick, was a Quaker and the Tory MP for Thunder Bay and Rainy River. Euphemistically labelled "intelligence officer," with the CEF, he was Hughes' man making sure that there was some Canadian political influence being exerted directly on the national force. But Carrick had no military experience, and his contumacious nationalism soon rankled the British soldiers. To the Liberals at home, he was simply another Conservative bagman promoted to an influential position.[17]

They were not too far wrong. Late in 1914 Carrick had actively lobbied for any job that would get him to the front with a substantial rank. Just before Christmas Hughes arranged Carrick's appointment with the War Office. Then both men set to work to convince Borden of the need to have contact with the troops in the field. Borden agreed, and by January Hughes had made Carrick an honorary colonel but had not advised many others beforehand. Nor did Hughes clearly define to either Kitchener or Carrick himself exactly what his functions would be. Later that spring, like so many in Hughes' overseas retinue, Carrick carried out his imprecise mandate as he saw fit, while the British grimaced. Connaught fought the appointment, but finally seeing that he would have to accept the advice of his council, he pressured Borden to use an order-in-council, written in his own vice-regal hand. Probably Connaught hoped that this sign of official displeasure would cause Hughes to back down. It did not. Hughes pressed on and Borden backed him because he resented Connaught's interference and because he too wanted some channel manned by Canadians through which the government could address its field soldiers as it could now communicate with its organization in England through Carson.[18]

When the First Division went to France in February 1915, Carrick went with it. In fact, Hughes appointed Carrick "Official Recorder, Canadians," a job which, if taken literally, intruded on Max Aitken's and the Adjutant-General's duties. Neither British nor Canadian field headquarters knew who Carrick was or what to do with him. In Canada the frustrated Gwatkin again circumvented his Minister's authority trying to get Carrick removed, but that failed. Nevertheless, the aggressive honorary colonel found his own duties.[19]

Carrick claimed he was "collecting information for General Hughes and acting as a link between home, headquarters here, and the War Office." And he got plenty of opportunities after Ypres and Festubert in April and May. According to Carrick, the British would not provide adequate data about the Canadian involvement in those battles. Since there was no proper link between the Militia Minister and British headquarters, Carrick wanted Hughes to promote him to brigadier-general to give him more clout. The Colonel also made the same appeal to Sir Robert Borden: "It has certainly been a strange situation hitherto that the Government of a country making such sacrifices as is Canada, should be not only without control or jurisdiction over its forces in the field but even lacking a source of prompt official information as to their welfare and achievements." What Carrick said was true. British field headquarters was already notorious for not talking to politicians, whether Canadian or British. For different reasons, both countries had no proper links between their political centres and their field forces. While Hughes' personal, vague, and improvised appointments helped forge channels, they failed to address the problem of central organization. Carrick played on Hughes' nationalism; his political posturing and ambition tainted his credibility, and his abrasive personality irritated many, including Sir George Perley.[20]

For some time the ambitious Perley, who wanted to be "more than just a clerk," had been pestering Borden to give the High Commission the power to co-ordinate the entire overseas effort. Carrick's pushy presence and unclear duties bothered him, and he was sure that the Militia Minister was at fault. "Everyone expects that this war," Perley went on to warn Borden, "will bring great changes in Empire relations, and it is especially necessary here that we are both sane and capable in the management of our own affairs which is certainly not consistent with [Hughes'] double barrelled authority."[21]

By June 1915 any possibility of co-operation between Carrick and Perley had ended. Like Hughes, Carrick thought Perley acquiesced too readily to British authority. In a blunt comment, especially for a Quaker, Carrick growled to his friend and cabinet patron Robert Rogers that Sir George was "certainly a D.F. and a H.A. You know what D.F. stands for and 'H' is for horses and you will likely be able to guess what the 'A' is for." All of this bickering forced Borden to devote much of his precious two months in England smoothing out relationships ruffled by the heavy-handedness of Hughes and his appointees. Finally Sir Robert solved the Carrick-Perley problem, not by giving Sir George what he wanted, but by getting rid of Carrick. The compromise did nothing to solve the organizational problems, but it did get rid of one abrasive personality. Borden again sided with his Militia Minister by reaffirming Hughes' personal agent technique, but this time through the much more adroit and less obviously partisan Sir Max Aitken.[22]

Carrick's short-lived overseas posting was typical of Sam Hughes' application of the old political system to wartime. Urged on by many similarly inclined cabinet colleagues, the Minister made hosts of other such appointments. As in the case of Captain H. M. Daly or Major John Bassett, some were in positions as personal aides to the Minister or as special service officers, as with Colonel Sir Charles Ross. In January 1915, after Hughes had given J. W. Carson his job, he immediately tried to make his Boer war friend, English part-time soldier and Conservative MP, Lieutenant-Colonel Claude Lowther, Carson's special assistant. Twice the War Office, which knew how prickly Lowther could be, blocked the move. At the end of March the Militia Minister recommended Lowther to command the Second Canadian Division. This too failed. Finally the exasperated Hughes gave the British MP the temporary rank of lieutenant-colonel in Canadian service, which he held until 1919 without serving in any Canadian post. It was much the same with W. Grant Morden, another wealthy expatriate living in London. For over two years he held a rank without real employment. A retired British regular living in Canada, Major R. F. Manly Sims, found a more useful function under Hughes' influence. A junior business associate of Carrick's, he was quickly attached to the Thunder Bay MP's office at headquarters in France. Later Sims also served Aitken in that post and succeeded him in 1917.[23]

Hughes also made appointments directly to the military structure overseas. As often a matter of personal selection as a response to cabinet or party pressures, the Militia Minister's choices reflected his preference for militia men or certain regulars who were politically safe and sufficiently malleable. Two such regulars were Colonel Victor Williams and Colonel J. C. MacDougall, both of whom had strong party and militia links; they also had been on the Minister's side during General Mackenzie's dismissal in 1913. When war was declared, Hughes yanked Williams out of his headquarter's adjutant-general's job, and leaving that vital post unfilled, gave him various and not very useful camp commandant's functions at Valcartier and in England. When Williams finally got a combat command as a brigadier in the Third Division, which Hughes opposed, he was wounded and captured at Mount Sorrel in June 1916. MacDougall faired better. Left behind by the departure for France of the First Division in February 1915,

Hughes gave him an important-sounding post as officer commanding all Canadians in England at the big camp at Shorncliffe. Training was also part of his nebulous responsibilities. But Hughes put nothing in writing; so when the new "temporary" Brigadier-General tried to assert himself, he ran into a jealous and politically lethal John W. Carson who quickly put him in his place.[24]

It all became very complicated when the Second Division under Major-General Sam Steele arrived in England in the spring of 1915. In picking Steele, Hughes had relented to Robert Rogers and to western Tory feeling to give the venerable old soldier this command. Since Steele was already famous and had many of the Canadian militia qualities which the Minister cherished, it was an easy choice. No doubt it helped recruiting. But by the summer when the British baulked at letting him lead the division in combat, Hughes' compromise was to let Steele have a British command in England overlapping MacDougall's training division at Shorncliffe. The Minister let it be known that Major-General Steele had control of all Canadians in England. He out-ranked MacDougall, and it was not long before the two men were at loggerheads, the War Office thoroughly confused, and Carson, the chief beneficiary, claiming to be the only man with authority to sort it all out. Adding to the confusion were the independent commands of the Canadian Cavalry Brigade under the British politician and part-time soldier, J. E. B. Seely, and another, the Canadian Training Depot, under W. R. W. James, a British regular.[25]

In November 1915, for no apparent reason other than to spread the political largesse, Hughes created another big camp, called Bramshott. This one went to Lord Brooke, the eldest son of the Earl of Warwick. Hughes had taken away one of the Second Division's brigades from the Canadian regular, Septimus Denison, and given it to Brooke earlier that summer. Alderson was not impressed by the aristocrat's fighting abilities in the field, but Hughes liked him, perhaps because he was a territorial soldier or because he owned large acreages in the Canadian west or because he had been Sir John French's secretary. Soon there was a debate about whose command Bramshott fell under; and nobody really seemed to know for sure. Vital reinforcements from England started to suffer from such bureaucratic arguments, and the bickering reinforced Carson's conviction that he alone could save the situation by heading a senior co-ordinating central command in England. In the meantime the Minister's relationship with his line soldiers was under stress.[26]

Sam Hughes had cooled towards Edwin Alderson, the CEF's British commander who had indiscreetly let it be known towards the end of 1914 that he was not impressed with the quality of some of the Minister's officer choices. In February 1915 Hughes received a brief through Carson which claimed that Alderson still felt that some Canadian officers of the First Division were "not qualified or clever enough to perform their duties" and that Canadian soldiers in turn looked upon Alderson as "not big enough to command the Division." The report probably came from a disgruntled officer among the Canadians who had not been chosen to go to France. None of the various reports was true, as Perley quickly assured the concerned Prime Minister. However, until mid-April when the division moved into the British line on the Ypres Salient, a strategic bulge in the allied front in Flanders, relations between Hughes and Alderson were fairly even. They did not remain so for long.[27]

During the German gas attack on the Ypres position later that month, the fighting had been vicious. But the Canadians had held onto the area, saving most of the position and preventing the collapse of two entire divisions of neighbouring British units. For this the Canadians won the admiration and praise of the British high command. But their gallant defence cost half their strength—nearly 6,000 casualties in a few days. However much pride came out of the feat, the casualties stunned Canadians back home. Two weeks after the Ypres defence, Sir John French again ordered the Canadians into action around Festubert to the southeast of Ypres. The offensive was designed to take pressure off both their French allies and the Salient. It failed. Five times the Canadians "broke their teeth" on German barbed wire amid a torrent of enemy bullets and shell fire. There was not enough high explosive gun ammunition to carry the positions, but the enemy had more than enough of everything to defend it. Nearly 3,000 more casualties were added to Canadian lists. British generals were still optimistic that the same direct assaults over a wide front would work; it was just a matter of more guns and ammunition. However, some Canadians were not convinced.[28]

The most violent reaction came from Sam Hughes. Taking his cue from the militia myth and his Boer war experience with these "woodenheads," the Minister delivered a searing condemnation of British generalship; it was an opinion he held for the remainder of the war and one which he often made public. In late May in a letter to Borden, parts of which Hughes had eagerly read to newsmen gathered in his office, the Minister singled out Edwin Alderson as chief perpetrator of the slaughter. He sent copies to Kitchener, with the comment, "I make no profession of being a 'competent soldier', but if such performances as this St. Julien battle display competency, then heaven prevent my being in the competent class." St. Julien, he said, was a "soldiers battle—a kind of Inkerman." Hughes also as much as accused Alderson of cowardice by charging that the commander had remained "in his office, miles to the rear." The diatribe analysed in detail where the General had gone wrong and offered solutions. When they read the letter, Perley was embarrassed, Kitchener amazed, the King angry, Sir John French resentful, and the Duke of Connaught wanted the "conceited lunatic" court-martialled.[29] Even though Sam Hughes' passions often threatened his reason, his instincts were sound—there had to be a better way than this slaughter.[30]

When copies finally reached Alderson in late June, he began to build a solid defence for what happened at Ypres, blaming bad terrain, the division's recent arrival in unprepared positions, and the psychological effect of gas. He was not miles behind the lines, nor was a battle run by brigadiers, as Hughes suggested, a soldiers' battle. With two cavalry brigades and forty-seven battalions under his command, Alderson was where he should have been—in his command post. Alderson's reasoned and eloquent defence once again exposed Hughes' limited and tactical view of war.

Yet in light of what transpired in the war's next three years, Hughes had made some interesting and justified observations about British methods. He too wanted more and more shells, but he also wanted more machine guns and more trench bombs; he advocated defence in depth, with hidden machine gun positions "for miles in the rear." Well before the April fighting, when he had recommended such a disposition to the War Office, Hughes exclaimed to Borden that "Earl Kitchener, himself, informed me that such were deemed impracticable." "This nibbling at a drive is costly," he turned to chastise Kitchener. "The one attacking is always the loser in such affairs." He also pointed out to the Prime Minister that "within a week [at Fesubert] we have again lost upwards of two thousand men in silly attempts to gain a few yards here or a few yards there, with no preconceived plan or effective drive to smash the enemy." What was needed was far less "imbecile" frontal bayonet attacks and more penetration by a thrust "cooly planned, at a narrow front, but with force enough behind it, power enough to carry it fifty miles into the enemies' rear, and hold every foot of the way, or it should not be attempted at all." Hughes left much unexplained as usual, but his advocacy of penetration in depth on a narrow front with massive support and then cutting "behind the Germans and round[ing] them up"[31] are reminiscent to later observers of Liddell Hart's Expanding Torrent, a theory developed out of the same war by a similarly horrified participant. While Hughes may have had his principles correct in early 1915, there is no supporting evidence to show how he would have given the forces breaking the enemy line the necessary momentum to accomplish and sustain his version of the torrent. For one thing the technological innovations of the mechanized troop carriers or armoured combat vehicles were not yet appreciated.

That remained the later contribution of J. F. C. Fuller and Liddell Hart, to name a few.

But for the moment Hughes wanted Alderson sacked and replaced by his friend, Richard Turner, then commanding the division's Third Brigade. After his condemnation of Alderson, Hughes congratulated the men of the CEF for their gallant stand at Ypres, in spite of their commander. Then on the suggestion of Carson and to the consternation of military authorities, the Militia Minister ordered Carson to "provide a step in rank [for] lieutenant-colonels at the front." Carson tried his best to carry out the instructions but when constant appeals to Hughes failed to clarify the vague order and when the resistance and confusion of the field commanders became apparent, Carson dropped the idea.[32] By that time the Minister too had forgotten about it.

Hughes took few pains to conceal his contempt for the present CEF commander or for British generalship. Ironically, if there were any serious mistakes at Ypres made by soldiers within the division, they were made by Canadians Richard Turner and his brigade major, Garnet Hughes, the Minister's son.[33] What the effect of Hughes' charges on Borden was can only be derived from events later that summer, although it is fair to say that while the Prime Minister was not then willing to blame Alderson, he did share his Militia Minister's revulsion over the casualties. So did many others in Canada and Great Britain; and to be master of one's own hand in a high stakes game was one reason why the worried Prime Minister sailed to England the same day Alderson penned his rebuttal to Sam Hughes.

By the time Borden left Canada, units of the Second Division had already landed in England. Who was to command them in the field was a major question going back several months while the Second Division was still in Canada. That February, after the War Office had given Jack Seeley command of the Canadian Cavalry Brigade without consulting Ottawa, Canadians had not been pleased. Above all Hughes was not going to let that happen to the Second Division. For the next five months he agitated to get a Canadian in the spot against substantial British resistance. First he told Borden that he would take command of the entire force, but when Sir Robert insisted on Hughes' resignation as minister, the idea was promptly dropped. At this point, bowing to Robert Roger's cabinet pressure and western sentiment, he put up the sixty-six-year old Sam Steele of Lord Strathcona's Horse and North-West Mounted Police fame, even though he thought Steele too old and inexperienced with large formations. On Sir John French's advice, Kitchener refused Steele. The Minister sent the War Secretary a hot reminder that for every British officer in Canadian units—there were "fifty Canadians better qualified." Yet Kitchener remained firm: Steele could bring the Second Division only as far as England, but he would never take it to France.[34]

That blunt riposte sent Hughes into a rage. In late March he shot off another message that surprised even the imperturbable Kitchener:

I am not in the habit of deceiving and Steele will know the exact situation.... I know many of our major-generals, some good and capable but many absolutely reverse, far inferior in office or capability in the field to Steele or a dozen other of my officers. Have calmly and loyally remained aloof from interference with Salisbury horror and disintegration of 1st Canadians but please do not ask too much to be borne. Claim no authority to manage Force in Field, but under Army Act Canada has absolute authority in respect to appointments. Further offensiveness and contemptuousness of some army officers in 1st Division became almost intolerable. I look to see that courtesy and even-handed justice and fair play are accorded to all my deserving officers.

The wire upset the King, and Louis Harcourt thought an issue should be made with Sir Robert Borden about the "intolerable" impertinance and "the behaviour of his so-called subordinate." But the calm Kitchener just passed the correspondence along to Perley with the observation that "this seems extra-ordinary even from Hughes." To Sir George, it was just another example of Hughes' needless aggravations about which his Prime Minister was apparently prepared to do little. What Perley missed was that Borden wanted a Canadian in command as well.[35]

All that spring Hughes kept up his pressure on the command issue from Ottawa. In June Carson aggravated the situation, already tender over the Minister's infamous Ypres charges, by advising Hughes that Steele was to be purposely side-tracked with a position on Kitchener's staff, "the inference being ... that he [Kitchener] wished a British officer to take over [the Second Division] command."[36] No evidence of a plot exists but evidence of a British offer to Steele does.

During the final stages of selection for the field command of the Second Division, Kitchener offered to accept Hughes' choice of any British officer on the unemployed list. But the Minister would only accept a Canadian and shifted his support from Steele to Richard Turner, then serving in Flanders. He now had Borden's active support. In late June the Prime Minister ordered Perley to impress on Kitchener "the wisdom of giving the appointment to a Canadian brigadier." When Kitchener responded that Currie was "the most suitable," it was again a dilemma for Borden who too often hesitated when faced with the pressure of his Militia Minister on one hand and the contrary advice on the other. Sir Robert cabled Kitchener to do nothing until he arrived in England in early July.[37]

Once Borden was in England, he was surprised to find that Hughes had followed him over; and with him he had the makings of a good compromise over the command question. Why not form the two divisions into an army corps? Borden seized on its potential to work out the solution to the various commands, not all of which everyone liked but which everyone would accept. Hughes convinced Steele to accept Kitchener's convenient offer of south eastern army command including all Canadians, with the rank of major general and with the qualification that all incompetent staff and those "antagonistic to Canadians" be gotten rid of. Turner, Hughes' candidate, got command of the Second Division; A. W. Currie was to head the First Division. And the two divisions were to be formed into the Canadian Corps that autumn headed by Major-General Alderson.[38]

Substantial credit for urging the creation of the Canadian Corps belongs to Sir Sam Hughes. The idea was the outcome of Hughes' view of a unified and unlimited troop participation. When allied with his nationalist streak, his desire to lead all troops himself, and his tendency to concentrate control as close to himself as possible, there could hardly be any other result. In later years he confided to his son that early in the war he had had a dream of a Canadian Army of two corps, each of three divisions. But the first specific mention of the corps came in early April 1915, when Carson, probably again exploiting his Minister's tendencies in this direction, wired Hughes suggesting the formation of a corps "with your good self in command."[39]

Once struck with the idea, Hughes cabled J. J. Carrick, who was at general headquarters in France, to tell Sir John French that it was "the earnest desire of all in Canada ... to increase the existing division in this country [France] into an army corps first of two, later of three divisions." Both French and Kitchener consented enthusiastically in recognition of the splendid service the First Division had given at Ypres that April. Nothing was firmed up, however, until Hughes and Borden arrived in England in July. If a Canadian Corps was created Hughes did not want Alderson to head it, and Carson fuelled the Minister's conspiracy theory by advising him that Kitchener and French had already decided that Alderson was to have the post. "It almost seems," he protested to Hughes in June, "as if they are going to run this show according to their ideas or inclinations without considering our likes or dislikes on the premises." Carson also maintained that Alderson had been ignoring the Minister's representative, and that since the commander was in Canadian pay, he was therefore a servant of Canada bound to its direction. Indeed the overseas representative was correct about one thing: British soldiers had decided on Alderson because he was capable and, above all, experienced. But war is never a purely military event. It is as much one of national and political considerations. Recognition of this was what Hughes in his erratic way was pushing for and one which British soldiers did not see easily. Consequently the political compromise between Hughes and Alderson came at the hands of Borden.[40]

Once in England the Prime Minister had a long talk with Kitchener and Alderson over the charges Hughes had made after the Ypres battle; and he found the General's explanations quite plausible. Again contrary to Hughes' opinion, Borden also found Alderson capable, straightforward, and popular with the troops, and thus chose him to lead the new corps, ordering Hughes to reconcile with the new commander. So the Canadian Corps was formed that September—granted, with a British GOC, but with two Canadians leading its divisions. Sam Hughes received a knighthood on Borden's recommendation, because he "has earned it."[41]

This honour made Alderson's continuance more palatable to Hughes. It pleased his insatiable vanity to be dubbed Sir Sam by the King that August. Of course Hughes did deserve it. He had worked hard at making the British war Canada's war, and the British knew it was true, if somewhat galling to accept. It took Borden, Max Aitken, and Bonar Law (the new Colonial Secretary) over a month to convince the King and Connaught to concede the honour. The Duke would not give his approval because of Hughes' scandalous association with J. W. Allison. In truth, Connaught did not like the pushy Militia Minister's nationalist bent and erratic behaviour. But Borden pressured the Duke to reconsider. Law also assured him that he had checked "very carefully ... Allison's files in the Colonial Office and "in my opinion no evidence exists whatever that he [Hughes] had any interest in the transactions of Allison." In the end Hughes got his reward because Borden admired Sir Sam's total commitment to the war, which aimed at protecting and augmenting Canada's position in proportion to its responsibilities.[42]

A new corps and a knighthood did not mean that Hughes was satisfied with the way the British were conducting the war. Both he and Borden had been appalled by their visits to the European battlefields and the hospitals of France. To Hughes, British generals seemed incapable of devising a strategy which could do anything except fill up those hospitals and cemeteries with Canadian "boys." During that summer the evidence he saw and heard in England pointed to the same conclusion. Borden concurred. Both men had asked straightforward questions of the British; they got vague or conflicting answers. Churchill, for instance, confided how incompetent and apathetic the officers were at Gallipoli. Everyone knew there was a critical shortage of munitions, but no one could agree when it would be resolved, except that it would be a long while. There was still the problem of a lack of information supplied to Canadians. As well as damning past British war administration, Lloyd George gave only a bleak forecast about the future. Hughes had been saying such things for some time; to Borden it was a revelation.[43]

By August the Militia Minister had seen and heard enough. Perhaps with Borden's approval—at least in principle—he wrote another of his notorious memos, this time to the Colonial Office, but it was widely distributed elsewhere. Instead of singling out Alderson, he aimed at the entire British administration, repeating much of what he had said to Kitchener in May: the acute shortage of munitions of the proper type, ridiculous frontal assaults with the bayonet, faulty defence and attack methods, the incompetency of the officers, and poor domestic munitions production all got roundly slammed. "To meet all of these," he said, "calls for much not now possessed by either Sir John French or General Joffre." The attitude in England was all wrong: "Complacency is observed in every hand" while men are dying by the thousands. "To some, the Empire seems on the verge of disaster," he warned; "energetic action is absolutely essential." Hughes' memo was typically full of self-aggrandizement and national praise, but the core charges were hard to ignore. The reformers of Asquith's coalition, like Lloyd George and Bonar Law, encouraged Hughes because they knew and admitted that much in the Minister's memo was true; and Borden was convinced that Hughes knew what he was talking about. More slaughter and no victory at Loos the next month only corroborated the charges. Not much changed on the battlefield.[44]

What did change was the size and formation of the Canadian fighting force at the front. Predictably and immediately, Sir Sam tangled with the new corps' commander and those in British military circles over the vastly increased number of appointments. There were two important considerations in judging these particular appointments. The first was the inexperience of Canadian soldiers. Since the beginning of the war, not enough trained and experienced officers had been available for the contingents, and one-third of the staff officers in the corps were on loan from the British Army. The shortage was less apparent at the command than at the staff level, and by the fall of 1915 it existed mostly in the senior positions of brigade-major to general staff officer, first grade. The second consideration was Sir Max Aitken, after August 1915 the Minister's new "General Representative for Canada at the Front." Sir Max had no military training whatsoever, but he possessed Hughes' distrust of British soldiers, although for different reasons, and he also resented their exclusiveness which at any time made it hard for a civilian like him to get inside their circles. He was no less convinced in the fall of 1915 than he had been that spring that these soldiers had bungled the war effort. As well they were, he felt, remarkably insensitive to Canadian's national aspirations concerning their own force, and had difficulty in seeing much beyond narrow military considerations. Aitken had powerful political aspirations of his own, and one way of influencing things was to make sure Canadian politicians were not swamped by British soldiers. To ensure this, he quickly set up his own private organization both at the War Office in England and at general headquarters in France.[45]

The day Sir Sam was knighted, he authorized Aitken to organize a "Canadian Headquarters in France" as "my representative" there replacing the quarrelsome Carrick who had been sent home at Borden's insistence. This new post also gave Sir Max a room at the War Office in London which brought him closer to the seat of British military decision-making. All the while, according to his later assistant, Beckles Willson, Aitken's Lombard Street offices continued to grow as an unofficial Canadian headquarters. It quickly became, in effect "the real center and immediate source of authority of the Canadian Corps in Europe"; and Sir Max exercised that authority with the "same audacity and arrogance which made Sam Hughes supreme and omnipotent in military affairs in Canada" and caused "resentment among military people" who had to deal with him.[46]

During the fall of 1915, Hughes' major concern was to make sure that Canadians got posted into the corps. He devised an elaborate code system with Aitken so that they could transmit secret messages. In time, Aitken was also leaking War Office information as well as information from other British departments directly to Sir Sam through the Lombard Street centre. Again Willson described it as like a corps headquarters where the personnel, in uniforms, worked "at high pressure examining files, typing out documents, coding and decoding messages which were constantly being brought in by dispatch bearers" and all of which "was not only unauthorized, but neither the Canadian Government nor the War Office knew anything" about its activities in any detail. Such clandestine functions were no more condemnatory than Connaught's "leaks" to Kitchener or Alderson's to Gwatkin, and they seemed necessary because there were no defined channels or any organization to exchange vital information between the two governments.[47]

The Canadian Corps officially came into existence on September 13, 1915. Seven days later Sir Sam ordered Aitken to ensure that he, not the British, had control of promotions. Aitken quickly informed Hughes that he had taken the initiative to expand the principle to include for the Minister all "rewards for forces not under Alderson's Command." He also cautioned, "please do not indicate my proposals to anyone and nothing will be known if you reject my whole plan." Over the next several months Hughes and Aitken made sure acceptable men were put into the corps; and in their minds the choices were synonymous with the national good. But other things emerge from the extensive correspondence between the two men. Sometimes Max Aitken was the prime mover and Sam Hughes the follower. At times and despite his love of aggressive action, Hughes was beginning to be indecisive. He could not make up his mind when the British asked if one division of Canadians could be spared from the western front to go to Egypt. "Would it be better," he queried Sir Max in December 1915,

> to have four divisions on western front making two army corps or three divisions on western front and twelve battalions in Egypt or two divisions plus corps troops on western front and twelve battalions in Egypt with balance of four divisions in England? Would troops in Egypt be under Canadian command, and what duties are anticipated for them? Would it not be better to hold them together?

Aitken wired back, "definitely refuse to send troops to Egypt. When spring comes you may find it convenient to increase troops in France to three divisions or possibly four."[48] That is exactly what happened.

Not to Hughes' surprise, Aitken soon ran afoul of British headquarters and General Alderson. A week after Hughes told him to secure Canadian posts, Aitken was protesting that his attempts were being stifled by Sir John French's staff, in particular by Sir Neville Macready, the Adjutant-General. The initial case occurred when Canadian Major J. F. Homer Dixon, who was the deputy Assistant Adjutant-General of the Second Division, was replaced without consultation by British Major R. J. Stewart. Aitken rushed to headquarters only to be kept waiting and then was told by an aide that "there is no room for discussion." When the General Representative replied that in the view of the Canadian government "where vacancies occurred on the staffs of our Canadian units the positions should be filled by Canadians," the aide accused Sir Max of "attempting to introduce political considerations into a purely military affair." He went on to inform Aitken that "there must be at least one experienced English officer on the administrative staff of every division in the BEF." When Hughes heard this, he was furious; he kept pushing for Canadians and ultimately succeeded in protecting many positions, though the senior staff posts had their share of British regulars out of necessity. What contributed to the problem was that Aitken and Hughes did not fully appreciate staff requirements and the British concern over them; in turn the British showed little sensitivity to the political-cultural aspects of what was really coalition warfare.[49]

While such episodes played on Hughes' mind as evidence of a conspiracy, nothing bothered him more than the opposition he faced over his son's promotion to brigadier. The evidence is not quite clear who initiated the request for the young Hughes' promotion, but it seems to have been the Minister. On September 28, Aitken cabled Sir Sam that Turner, Currie, and Alderson had all agreed to give

Lieutenant-Colonel Garnet Hughes the first brigade. Then in his other role as Eye-Witness, he let the information out to the Canadian newspapers. Hughes wired back the same day: "universal verdict of troops as reported by friends is that Garnet did much to save situation at St. Julien and Festubert. Was repeatedly urged in England and France to ask for his promotion brigadier-general instead of Watson and others.... Please thank Alderson." Within hours Alderson privately denied to Aitken he had recommended any such course. In the next two weeks he put his objections in writing. "I am told," he wrote to Sir Max in mid-October, "that it has been published in the Canadian papers that I especially asked for Hughes to be made a brigadier!"

> I do not think this is right or fair; all I have ever written on the subject was in a private letter to Lowther and in that I said that I did not think Hughes has the necessary experience to command a brigade, although he has brains and if insisted upon by Canada, as he probably would be, he might do as well as some others. To say that I asked specifically for him is putting me in a very wrong position with several gallant commanding officers who have done real solid good work.

In short, there were several men in the new corps who did not want Garnet Hughes. Aitken warned the corps commander that he was "disappointed" and noted that Alderson had lost a great opportunity to strengthen his own position with the Militia Minister by not agreeing to the scheme. After Alderson refused Aitken's offer to get rid of Lord Brooke, who then commanded the fourth brigade, if the GOC would yet accept the young Hughes in the vacated spot, Aitken threatened that Alderson must keep in mind that, since Canada was paying for all of the corps, he was obliged to carry out their wishes. Then Aitken threatened to quit "unless I am in complete sympathy with you and your wishes concerning officers serving under you!" It was a threat that would make Alderson's position nearly untenable.[50]

The two men sparred for nearly a month over Garnet Hughes. In mid-November there was even an offer from the War Office "to command a column in EastAfrica." In view of what Paul von Lettow-Vorbeck was doing to British and South African forces there, it was fortunate that Garnet did not accept. Apparently someone was trying to side-track him from the Canadian Corps. Aitken flatly told Sir Sam, "Garnet... will decline." Perhaps as the genesis of Brooke's new command at Bramshott, by the end of the month the General Representative had worked out a deal with Alderson that gave Garnet the first brigade in Currie's division.[51] Sir Max had kept Hughes under the impression that little was wrong with Alderson and the younger Hughes' relations; and he had not said anything to Sir Sam about Arthur Currie's opinion of Garnet's military talent. When Garnet ended up in Currie's division, Currie did not want him. All too well the new divisional commander remembered his exposed left flank at Ypres six months before. But finally, now under pressure from his own corps commander as well as Sir Max, Currie reluctantly conceded.

Why did Alderson change his mind? He obviously resented the Minister's interference with his right to choose or reject officers for the good of his troops. For one thing he realized that in the end he would have to accept this political appointment and that he might as well bargain for the best circumstances in a bad situation. Though the corps commander yielded, he would not give Garnet a brigade in Turner's division, which both Sam Hughes and Max Aitken wanted. Perhaps the harried GOC also remembered the Turner-Hughes combination at Ypres or even sensed its political potential; he may have felt that any such further alliance would be trouble in the battles to come. He insisted then that if Garnet was promoted, he should go with Currie whom he may have felt could prevent any such reoccurrence as St. Julien. Whatever the case, Aitken bent on this point; so did the unhappy Currie.[52]

As if he knew of Currie's dislike of Garnet, Sir Sam vigorously protested the decision; he wanted Garnet to be a brigadier under his friend Turner. Hughes even tried to order Alderson to put Garnet in Turner's division, but in the end he sullenly accepted Aitken's advice not to reopen the issue. As for Aitken, he got the young Hughes promoted; he coerced and cajoled the corps commander; he hid things from his minister, as he later said to Borden, to preserve harmony; he moved people in and out of corps positions for political reasons; and he made decisions with which Sir Sam did not agree but finally accepted because of distance and a generally correct direction. Aitken was right in one thing: to keep the lid on the overseas harmony jar was better than allowing Sam Hughes to ram in his ministerial fingers. Still Hughes knew by October that Alderson had held up his son's advancement.[53]

While the positioning of his son occupied a lot of Hughes' attention that fall, so did the matter of other Canadian appointments to the corps. One might even argue that Hughes saw the former problem as a particular manifestation of the latter, and he was bent on promoting the national character of the corps. As soon as the corps was formed, he insisted that the Princess Patricia's Canadian Light Infantry be included in it. At first the British showed no willingness to accept the request until he, through Aitken, kept pushing the point. In late December his emphatic protests succeeded in preventing British Army medical authorities from breaking up the Canadian Dental Corps. Three months later Aitken was assuring Sir Sam that after a "stout fight" he had finally managed to get British approval for an official Canadian photographer on the battlefields.[54]

Over these several months, Hughes carried his criticism of British attempts to overshadow Canadians in the corps well past what it really was. In part, the fault for this has to be shared by Carson and Aitken. At the end of November, both men urgently wired Ottawa exposing a concerted British plot with Alderson's aid to unseat more Canadians. In particular, Aitken cited four cases that month where Canadians had fallen victim to staff-college-trained British officers. The language of the wires was that of a conspiracy; the person who received them wanted to believe it. The Minister's response to Aitken was instant and insistent:

You will protest most emphatically against staff and other positions in the Canadian force being filled by British officers. We have soldiers fit for the highest positions—it is discreditable to have British officers run the Army Corps and Divisional positions. It would be insulting to have them brought into the brigades. The new men who fought so well at St. Julien and Festubert require no staff college theorists to direct them; on the contrary it is the general opinion that scores of our officers can teach the British for many moons to come. You must stand firm. If the feeling of returned soldiers were known, another Boston tea party might be looked for. Surely they can find positions for their pets among the British but I will not submit to our forces being burdened with them. They were no strength whatever in any of the big fights.

Six days later he fired off a similar but private message to Sir John French. Just as he had in the Boer war, he reminded Sir John that colonial troops invariably proved better than British professional soldiers. The arrogance of the British in trying to rob Canadians of their corps posts smacked of trying to keep them in permanently inferior positions. It was a risky business, Hughes warned; after all, forcing colonials to be "hewers of wood and drawers of water" had caused the American Revolution. He would not stand for it in the Canadian Corps. He also took a substantial swipe at Alderson, implying he was responsible for the so-called plot. Hughes almost convinced Borden there was a plot. The Prime Minister was particularly susceptible because by then Hughes controlled nearly all the direct channels of information about the war; and the British were not yet willing to provide alternatives, and did not until 1917.[55]

When Borden found out about Hughes' wire, although aghast at "some of the expressions contained in your telegram . . . ," he thought, as he told Sir Sam, "the principle for which you contend . . . is quite correct and I am prepared to support it." But he also cautioned the Militia Minister: "you are speaking not for yourself alone but as a member of the government." Then Borden instructed the Acting High Commissioner to tell the British government that "we will not permit anything of the kind"; yet it took Bonar Law a month to reply that everything possible would be done to meet the wishes of the Canadian government. Significantly Bonar Law still did not see the need to create any better apparatus from the British side to give substance to his soothing words.⁵⁶

From a military point of view, the truth of the issue about posts in the corps came from General Alderson who pointed out the necessity of including British officers in it. The problems, he said, stemmed from a lack of trained Canadians, especially brigade majors. He was wholeheartedly supported by his two Canadian divisional commanders, Turner and Currie. Turner recommended that the appointment of regular British officers as brigade majors continue until such time as "selected Canadian officers could be trained"; as for Currie, he made it clear that "it is not a question of whether a man is Canadian or otherwise. It is a case of the best man for the job."⁵⁷

By early January 1916 Aitken was again counselling both Hughes and Borden that the appointments situation had been rectified—"I am happy to say as a result of my action." The Adjutant-General's policy, he went on, before "I approached him, was to insist on appointing British officers to important positions on the administrative staff." However, with the formation of the Third Division (then organizing in England), he claimed, the practice has stopped. It was true, Aitken admitted, that Turner and Currie supported such British officers as brigade majors but "this attitude is due ... to the manner in which the question was put to them" by Alderson: it was not made clear that the Canadian government wanted to nationalize the corps. On the other side of the coin, R. B. Bennett, then Borden's parliamentary secretary, was convinced that to some degree Aitken had duped both Hughes and Borden into taking too strong a position on the issue of Canadian appointments. "Aitken was," Bennett felt, "at war with what he calls the Trade Union of the soldiers. I fear that we are being used to aid him in that quarrel."⁵⁸

Some good results came out of Hughes' exertions to maintain Canadian identity. According to the official historian of the CEF, efficiency and national morale would not have reached the height they did had Hughes, among others, not taken strong, although sometimes poorly executed, stands; and surely Hughes' constant demands could do little but make the British sensitive to Canadian problems. When Aitken pointed his accusing finger in December 1915, British headquarters itself was in a state of flux. Sir John French had just been sacked largely because of his military failure; he had also been removed to prove that "the men on top cared." His replacement as head of the British armies in France was Douglas Haig. This shake-up may have helped the British realize that in their Canadian cousins they needed content and happy allies. Whatever the case, after December 1915 the controversy over Canadian posts never reached the same level again. By that time Hughes' problems within his own overseas administration far overshadowed those that he imagined were caused by the British.⁵⁹

Orderly Canadian administration in England had nearly stopped by the end of 1915. All that autumn the pretentious Carson had tried to aggrandize his way out of the jurisdictional jealousies and the plethora of vague positions seen in Steele's, MacDougall's and Brookes' commands by making all of them subordinate to him as vice-minister of militia overseas. It did not work. Everyone continued to bicker and the British did not know where real authority lay. Complaints were legion. In November Colonel W. R. Ward recommended to Carson the creation of a complete headquarters system similar to Ottawa's as the only way out of the present plight. The idea became Carson's; but for the time being he was not willing to share it with Hughes.[60]

The reason seems to have been the Minister himself. Increasingly aggravated by reports of the snarls in England, he first blamed MacDougall's, then Carson's personal ambitions. He ordered Carson to file a complete report on all organization in Britain. Carson did so; and the shock waves rolled down the chain and back up in about a week. By then the Minister's agent seemed willing to share Colonel Ward's wisdom. "We have to," Carson urgently wired Hughes on December 15, "carry on this organization on this side of the Atlantic Ocean until we have almost a duplicate of your complete organization in Ottawa." Of course Carson saw himself as head of it.[61]

On Christmas Eve Aitken urgently underscored Carson's message by wiring Hughes that it was "positively urgent you come here. In my opinion, things are bad." Typically he added a cynical assessment of general British affairs and one flattering to his chief:

We have had a remarkable escape from the Dardenelles. Haig has disappointed everybody by his personal appointments. Robertson is in control of the War Office. If you come here now I think your recommendations will have great weight and I believe you can benefit the entire situation on the Western Front and in the east. Your telegram expressing disappointment and anxiety had profound effect on cabinet ministers. Everyone ready to make sacrifices.

Several times before, as in October when Aitken offered to arrange Sir Sam's promotion to lieutenant-general in the British Army, and later in January when he told Hughes that he could secure command of the Fourth Division for Garnet if David Watson was brought back to England as Commander-in-Chief of all Canadians there, the wheedling aspect of his relationship with Hughes had been demonstrated. There is no doubt his assessment of this man was correct. Perhaps more attention should be paid to R. B. Bennett's judgment that Aitken was only using Hughes in his political "war" against the "trade union of the soldiers."[62]

In the face of all these disturbing reports from his overseas empire, Sir Sam remained remarkably indecisive. He would not make up his mind who was to have command of the Fourth Division once it was formed; and he did not reply to Carson's or Aitken's December wires to do something about the set up in England. He gave no clear response at all to Carson except to chastise him for inefficiency and to say that in the future he was not to allow any promotions "whatever... without... my final consent." Finally after a two months delay, Hughes got an order-in-council passed which made it impossible for anyone in France or England to be promoted without his permission.[63] The order was a revelation of more than just his ability to convince Borden that it was necessary. The situation had reached such a state in England that desperate reform was needed. While Sir Sam was far away, he could not do it personally and he would not give authority for anyone else to do it. Moreover, the Canadian overseas war effort had reached such proportions that one man could not handle it all, yet that one man was not willing to let others try. The demands which finally brought the administrative crisis to a head came from the fighting soldiers.

In early 1916 the deteriorating administrative situation overseas reached a crisis. The Canadian field forces were in dire need of reinforcements. They were unable to get sufficient troops from the large numbers held in the organization in England even though Gwatkin and Alderson had pleaded for a reform of the recruiting, training, and distribution system in Canada and England. With the expectation of the great offensives in the winter and spring of 1916, Alderson was desperate to fill out the expanded corps. When little response came through normal channels, he finally appealed in February directly to the Governor-General. "All this trouble" he told the Duke, "is due to the fact that weak and inexperienced men are commanding training divisions both at Shorncliffe and Bramshott." The men were two of Hughes' favourites, Brooke and MacDougall, and Aitken was the man who had arranged to put Brooke in charge of some of those training battalions as part of Garnet Hughes' promotion manoeuvres.[64]

Alderson also had serious complaints about Aitken which, perhaps too trustingly, he had put on paper to the Canadian representative in early March. He found that he was forced to serve "two masters," Canada (Aitken and Hughes) and GHQ. Because Aitken was frequently away from his post at GHQ on political and personal business, Alderson found that these absences made his job very "complicated." He made it clear to Sir Max that if this was the inefficient way Hughes and he were going to run their administration overseas then Alderson would act in the best interests of the corps irrespective of what the Canadian representative or the Minister thought. On top of that, he warned Aitken, since he knew senior officers far better than anyone else, then his decisions were what is best for the units and they should be free from "outside" influences. Undoubtedly Sir Max transmitted the corps commander's tough message to Sir Sam. Clearly there was going to be a final confrontation between the General and Hughes. To some of Aitken's assistants who were watching the situation deteriorate that winter, Alderson was going to lose.[65]

At the same time, other channels touched by the Minister were equally clogged by neglect. The chief of staff in Canada and the Acting High Commissioner in England suffered from the reluctance of Hughes or his appointees to co-operate with them. In December, when Carson and Aitken were vainly trying to get Hughes over to England, Perley was having no more luck convincing Borden that the situation had to be reformed. At least three times in the previous nine months he had asked Borden to make his position into an overseas cabinet portfolio to co-ordinate Hughes' chaotic hydra—but to no avail. Borden had kept Hughes' system and simply tampered with it from time to time to smooth it out. Yet there is some indication that Borden may have thought Hughes correct when the Militia Minister accused Sir George of having a submissive colonial mind. Early in the war Perley had advocated that the Canadian contingent be entirely under the War Office "in all things"; the previous January he had cautioned Borden to accept a decision which the British had already made to put the command of the Canadian Cavalry Brigade in the hands of an Englishman, J. E. B. Seely. "I do not know how you will look at it," he advised Sir Robert then, but appointments "of this kind should rest entirely in the hands of Lord Kitchener as our men are simply part of a great whole, and the Secretary of State for War must have full control." Sir Robert was so incensed at Seely's appointment that he swore to Sir George that "I shall see to it that the next mounted corps that goes from Canada is placed in the command of one of our men as brigadier." In the summer of 1915 Borden thought Perley's complaints about the lack of organization and the need to give him control of it were tiresome to the point of "exasperation," although he promised Sir George he would consider the problem. He may also have thought it was a touch of personal ambition that made Perley so persistent. By December 1915, when Perley pleaded again for reorganization, Sir Robert replied that he could not establish an overseas ministry. Laurier, he said weakly, would never support it because it would bring Canada closer to the United Kingdom. Evidently the administrative crisis was not yet acute enough for Borden. But the political one at home was; so he would not rock the overseas boat.[66]

Bewilderment had already spread to the Colonial Office and the War Office because of Carson's claims. In January the Colonial Secretary enquired whether Connaught could shed any light on Carson's proper status. No one knew—except General Carson who was absolutely convinced, as he told Hughes the month before, that "I am your special representative and agent with wide powers and as such I must act for you in all business matters and military matters." In February Perley was again complaining to Borden that neither Aitken nor Carson co-operated easily with him. Things continued to deteriorate. The same month Major Beckles Willson recorded in his diary the truth of Sir George's grievances. He also noted another important thing. Sir Max, he wrote, had confided "to me that he thought the moment propitious to get... confirmation of the fact that he was the Minister's Chief, and indeed, exclusive representative and that the establishment in Lombard Street was the chief administrative headquarters of Canada in Europe... we were to absorb the chief functions of the Records branch previously established to supersede General Carson's Military headquarters, and to restrict the activities of the Canadian High Commissioner in London to the merest civilian formalities...." Elsewhere a disgruntled Canadian officer serving in England wrote to his MP: "the senior officers, General Carson, General MacDougall, General Steele and Lord Brooke, are all working at cross-purposes, that there is no head of Canadians in England."[67]

Reference Notes to Chapter 14

1 The fascinating story of Canada's overseas military administration is very ably told by Desmond Morton, in *A Peculiar Kind of Politics*, especially chapters 1 to 4. While recognizing that Hughes' nationalism helped assert Canadian autonomy, he felt that Hughes' extraordinary personality made progress in this direction "more costly and humiliating than the most supercilious Englishman could have wished" (p. viii). The assessment is not inaccurate, but perhaps it is unfair in as much as it undervalues what is commendable in Hughes' motives and actions; its retrospective basis adjudicates the wartime experience as if it happened in a vacuum and downplays the absence of national machinery and experience.
2 PAC, Christie *papers*, F 1, Gwatkin to Christie, Oct. 1, 1914; *Sessional Papers*, 1914, no. 40a, Colonial Secretary to Governor-General, n.d.; *Hansard*, Special Session, 1914, p. 36; PAC, Borden *papers*, OC 318 (1), Hughes to Borden, Oct. 23, 1916; and PAC, Gwatkin *papers*, F 1, Gwatkin to Christie, Mar. 3, 1915, confidential.
3 PRO, Kitchener *papers*, 30/57/56, Harcourt to Kitchener, Dec. 16, 1914; Nicholson, p. 35; and *Hansard*, 1917, p. 259.
4 Great Britain, *Hansard*, 1916, pp. 1522-26; PAC, Perley *papers*, vol. 2, Perley to Borden, Oct. 23, 1914; ibid., vol. 5, Borden to Perley, Jan. 4, 1916; Preston, *Canada and Imperial Defense*, pp. 465-66, 475-78, 503-14; Duguid, appendicies 118, 119, 121; and Vince, *CJEPS* 20 (August 1954), p. 369.
5 PAC, RG 24, "Army," vol. 502, HQ. 54-21-5-8, Fiset to Perley, Sept. 1914; PAC, RG 9, III, CEF, 203-319-12-J-9, "Memorandum on the History of the Formation and Growth of the Canadian Records Office, London"; also PAC, Gwatkin *papers*, F 1, Gwatkin to Christie, Oct. 1, 1914; Winter, p. 100; and Nicholson, pp. 17, 18, 29.
6 Cook and Brown, p. 183; *Hansard*, 1917, p. 4199; Duguid, appendix 49, Colonial Secretary to Governor-General, Aug. 10, 1914; PAC, Perley *papers*, vol. 1, Perley to Borden, August 15, 1914; ibid., Borden to Perley, Sept. 5, 1914; and PAC, Gwatkin *papers*, F 1, Gwatkin to Christie, Oct. 1, 1914.
7 PAC, Perley *papers*, Perley to Borden, May 9, 1915; and PAC, Borden *private diaries*, July 18, 1916.
8 *Militia List*, 1913, pp. 95, 194; PAC, RG 24, vol. 24, HQ. 54-21-5-7, PC 107, Jan. 15, 1915; ibid., vol. 502, HQ. 54-21-5-8, Fiset to Perley, Sept. 1914; and Nicholson, pp. 203-204.

REFERENCE NOTES TO CHAPTER 14 / 285

9. PAC, RG 9, III, A 1, Carson file, Carson to WO, n.d., and Carson to Hughes, June 10, 1915; MacPhail, p. 24; PAC, Perley *papers*, vol. 3, Borden to Perley, Jan. 12, 1915; ibid., Perley to Borden, Jan. 25, 1915; and Nicholson, pp. 35-38.
10. PRO, Kitchener *papers*, 30/57/56, Connaught to Kitchener, Nov. 7, 1914; and PAC, Gwatkin *papers*, F 1, Gwatkin to Christie, Mar. 3, 1915.
11. PRO, Kitchener *papers*, 30/57/56, Connaught to Kitchener, May 31, 1915; and PAC, Borden *private diaries*, July 9, 1915.
12. Taylor, p. 87; HLRO, Beaverbrook *papers*, E. General Hughes, no. 1, Aitken to Hughes, Dec. 28, 1914; ibid., no. 4, Curry to Hughes, Dec. 31, 1914; and ibid., no. 6, Hughes to Aitken, Dec. 30, 1914. Canada had used the editor of the Canadian Militia Gazette as an "Eyewitness" in the Boer war.
13. Duguid, appendix 229, Taylor, pp. 81-90; Nicholson, p. 356; PRO, CO 532/90, F. A. Mackenzie to Lord Durnham, "Memo on Granting Greater Canadian Press Access to Information from the Front," Dec. 8, 1916; and HLRO Beaverbrook *papers* c/50, Borden to Aitken, Sept. 14, 1915.
14. Taylor, see chapters 4 and 6, and Duguid, appendix 229.
15. PAC, Christie *papers*, Perley to Borden, Feb. 1, 1915; ibid., Christie to Borden, Feb. 18, 1915; and Taylor, p. 98.
16. Morton, *A Peculiar Kind of Politics*, p. 46.
17. Morgan, 1912, p. 203; and PAO, Bristol *papers*, 204, personal, Bristol to Wolvin, July 7, 1915.
18. PAC, Borden, *private diaries*, Dec. 31, 1914 and Jan. 2, 1915; PAC, RG 9, III; CEF, 203319, 12-J-9, Hughes to Kitchener, Dec. 22, 1914; ibid., PC, no. 16, Jan. 7, 1915; and PRO, Kitchener *papers*, 30/57/56, WG 41, Hughes to Kitchener, Jan. 16, 1915, and Connaught to Kitchener, May 31, 1915.
19. Duguid, appendix 229; and PAC, Gwatkin *papers*, F 2, Gwatkin to Stanton, Jan. 5, 1915.
20. PAC, RG 9, III, CEF, 203319, 12-J-9, Carrick to Rogers, May 25, 1915; ibid., Carrick to Hughes, n.d.; ibid., Carrick to Hughes, May 28, 1915; ibid., Carrick to Borden, June 7, 1915; Correlli Barnett, *Britain and Her Army 1509-1970: A Military, Political and Social Survey* (New York: Morrow, 1970), pp. 387, 399-400; Magnus, chapters 15 to 17, especially pp. 438-440; and Hankey, vol. 1, p. 208.
21. PAC, Perley *papers*, vol. 3, p. 79, Perley to Borden, May 9, 1915.
22. PAC, RG 9, III, CEF, 203319, Carrick to Rogers, June 6, 1915; PAC, Borden *private diaries*, June 26, July 10, 12, 21, 1915; and Duguid, appendix 229.
23. Duguid, appendix 229.
24. HLRO, Beaverbrook *papers*, E. General Hughes, 1, Hughes to Aitken, Nov. 25, 1915, no. 47; Nicholson, pp. 148-49, 539; Morgan, *1912*, pp. 687-88, 1170; and Duguid, appendix 188.
25. Nicholson, pp. 201-205.
26. Swettenham, pp. 127-128.
27. PAC, Perley *papers*, vol. 3, Borden to Perley, Feb. 17, 1915 and Mar. 9, 1915; and PAC, Borden *private diaries*, Feb. 24, 1915, and Mar. 1, 1915. About this time, Alderson had written to Connaught ranking the Canadian Brigadiers according to merit: Currie, Turner, and Mercer; while in the artillery, he said, Mitchell was best and Morrison worst.
28. Nicholson, pp. 55-104, covers the details.
29. PRO, Kitchener *papers*, 30/57/56, Hughes to Kitchener, May 28, 1915; ibid., Hughes to R. L. Borden, May 28, 1915. See the Alderson file in ibid., WG 22 to WG 41, which contains reactions to various people who saw the memo.
30. Ibid., Alderson to Lempton, WG 28, June 28, 1915.
31. Ibid., Hughes to Kitchener, May 28, 1915.
32. PAC, RG 9, III, AJ, Carson file, 8-1-35, Hughes to Carson, July 2, 1915; ibid., Hughes to Carson, Apr. 25, 1915; and ibid., Carson to Hughes, Nov. 1, 1915.
33. Hyatt, *Currie*, pp. 86-91; and Swettenham, *To Seize Victory*, pp. 80-90.
34. PRO, Kitchener *papers*, 30/57/56, WG 28, Alderson to Lampton, June 28, 1915; PAC, Borden *private diaries*, Feb. 24, 1915; ibid., Feb. 26, 1915; the Winnipeg *Free Press*, May 6, 1915; Nicholson, p. 112; Duguid, appendix 243; PAC, Perley *papers*, vol. 3, Hughes to Kitchener, Mar. 29, 1915; ibid., Hughes to Kitchener, Mar. 20, 1915; ibid., Hughes to Kitchener, Mar. 22, 1915; and ibid., Kitchener to Hughes, Apr. 1, 1915.

35 PAC, Perley *papers*, vol. 3, Hughes to Kitchener, April 8, 1915, and Kitchener's marginalia; and PRO, Kitchener *papers*, 30/57/56, Wigram to Fitzgerald, Apr. 7, 1915; ibid., WG 8, Apr. 10, 1915; and ibid., WG 10, Harcourt to Kitchener, Apr. 28, 1915.
36 PAC, RG 9, III, A1, Carson file, 8-1-5, Carson to Hughes, June 1, 1915; and Nicholson, pp. 114-15, and 203.
37 PAC, Perley *papers*, vol. 4, Perley to Kitchener, June 22, 1915; ibid., Kitchener to Perley, June 24, 1915; ibid., Borden to Perley, June 28, 1915; and ibid., Perley to Kitchener, June 29, 1915.
38 PAC, Borden, *private diaries*, Aug. 15, 1915; PRO, Kitchener *papers*, 30/57/56, Steele to Hughes, July 24, 1915; and ibid., Hughes to Steele, July 25, 1915.
39 Nicholson, p. 114; Canadian Forces Historical Section (CFHS) f 990.009 (D2), Hughes to Garnet Hughes, Mar. 7, 1917; and PAC, RG 9, III, A1, Carson file, 8-5-8, Carson to Hughes, Apr. 1, 1915.
40 PAC, Perley *papers*, vol. 3, French to Kitchener, Apr. 27, 1915, in Nicholson, p. 114; PAC, RG 9, III, A1, Carson file, 8-1-5, Carson to Hughes, June 2, 1915; and ibid., 8-1-22, Carson to Aitken, n.d.
41 PAC, Borden *papers*, OC 69, Borden to Connaught, July 18, 1915; and PAC, Borden *private diaries*, July 11, 12, 13, 1915.
42 HLRO, The Davidson *papers*, CO, 1914-1916, Hughes file, Law to Connaught, July 20, 1915, p. 26; and ibid., Law to Connaught, Aug. 18, 1915. See the entire Hughes file for negotiations surrounding the honour; HLRO, Andrew Bonar Law *papers*, 53/6/34, Law to Henry Wilson, July 22, 1915; and ibid., Wilson to Bonar Law, July 24, 1915.
43 Brown, *Borden*, vol. 2, pp. 30-31.
44 Harcourt *papers*, 463, no. 100a, Hughes to Colonial Office, Aug. 15, 1915, "Memorandum on the War Situation at the Western Front"; Morton, *Canada and War*, p. 67; and Brown, *Borden*, vol. 2, pp. 30-31.
45 Eyre, pp. 113-27; Nicholson, pp. 114-15, 127; Beaverbrook, *Politicians and the War, 1914-1916* (London: Thornton Butterworth, 1928), chapters 7-14; and Taylor, chapters 5 and 6.
46 HLRO, Beaverbrook *papers*, E, General Hughes, 1, Hughes to Ward, Aug. 24, 1915, no. 8; and Beckles Willson, *From Quebec to Piccadilly* (London: Jonathan Cape, 1929), p. 201.
47 HLRO, Beaverbrook *papers*, E/12, General Hughes, 1, Hughes to Aitken, Oct. 11, 1915; ibid., General Hughes, 2, Aitken to Hughes, Feb. 28, 1916, no. 47; PRO, Kitchener *papers*, 30/57/56, WG 33 to 41 (samples of Connaught's frequent letters). Also see Willson, p. 201.
48 HLRO, Beaverbrook *papers*, E. General Hughes, 1, Hughes to Aitken, Sept. 20, 1915, no. 11; ibid., Aitken to Hughes, Aug. 20, 1915; ibid., Aitken to Hughes, Oct. 6, 1915, no. 12; ibid., Aitken to Hughes, Oct. 19, 1915, no. 21: ibid., Hughes to Aitken, Oct. 21, 1915, no. 27; ibid., Hughes to Aitken, Dec. 11, 1915, no. 71; and ibid., Aitken to Hughes, Dec. 13, 1915, no. 73.
49 Ibid., Aitken to Hughes, Sept. 26, 1916, no. 126.
50 Ibid., Aitken to Hughes, Sept. 25, 1915, no. 12A; ibid., Hughes to Aitken, Sept. 28, 1915, no. 12C; ibid., Aitken to Hughes, Sept. 28, 1915, no. 12D; ibid., E/18, F/3/6, Alderson to Aitken, Oct. 18, 1918; and ibid., E/19, Aitken to Alderson, Sept. 28, 1915.
51 Ibid., General Hughes, 1, Aitken to Hughes, Nov. 18, 1915, no. 43; and ibid., Aitken to Hughes, Nov. 29, 1915.
52 Ibid., Aitken to Hughes, Oct. 30, 1915, no. 31; ibid., Hughes to Aitken, Nov. 2, 1915, no. 32; ibid., Aitken to Hughes, Nov. 2, 1915, no. 33; and H. M. Urquhart, *Arthur Currie, The Biography of a Great Canadian* (Toronto: J. M. Dent, 1950), pp. 117-118.
53 HLRO, Beaverbrook *papers*, E, General Hughes, 1, Hughes to Aitken, Nov. 12, 1915, no. 42; ibid., Aitken to Hughes, Dec. 28, 1915, no. 81; ibid., Hughes to Aitken, Dec. 4, 1915, "purely personal and unofficial" and ibid., E/1, 7-8, Carson to Aitken, Oct. 12, 1915.
54 Ibid., General Hughes, 1, Hughes to Aitken, Sept. 17, 1915, no. 9; ibid., Hughes to Aitken, Dec. 17, 1915, no. 74; ibid., General Hughes, 2, Aitken to Hughes, Jan. 4,

REFERENCE NOTES TO CHAPTER 14 / 287

1916; ibid., Aitken to Hughes, Mar. 3, 1916, no. 30, no. 9; and Beaverbrook, *Men in Power*, pp. 270-71.
55 PAC, Borden *papers*, OC 318, Hughes to Aitken, Nov. 30, 1915; and HLRO, Beaverbrook *papers*, E/18, F/3/6, Hughes to French, Dec. 6, 1915, personal.
56 PAC, Perley *papers*, vol. 4, Borden to Hughes, Nov. 30, 1915; ibid., Borden to Perley, Dec. 2, 1915; and ibid., Law to Perley, Dec. 31, 1915.
57 Ibid., Alderson to Perley, Dec. 13, 1915.
58 HLRO, Beaverbrook *papers*, E/7-8, Aitken to Hughes, Jan. 11, 1916; ibid., Aitken to Borden, Jan. 20, 1916; and PAC, Perley *papers*, vol. 5, Bennett to Borden, Dec. 7, 1915.
59 Nicholson, p. 128; and Bullitt Lowry, "French and 1914: His Defence of his Memoirs Examined," in *Military Affairs* 45 (April 1981), pp. 79-83.
60 PAC, RG 9, III, A1, Carson file, 8-5-43, Carson to Steele, Aug. 27, 1915; ibid., Carson to Hughes, Oct. 4, 1915; ibid., Carson to Hughes, Nov. 15, 1915; ibid., 8-1-55, Carson to Hughes, Nov. 19, 1915; ibid., Ward to Carson, Nov. 27, 1915; PAC, RG 24, HQ. 54-21-5-7, Carson to MacDonald, Aug. 17, 1915; Duguid, appendix 188; Nicholson, pp. 200-204; and Swettenham, *To Seize Victory*, pp. 124-30.
61 PAC, Borden *papers*, OC 183 (2), pp. 14865-66, Gwatkin to Connaught, Jan. 22, 1916; PAC, RG 9, III, A1, Carson file, 8-1-55, Carson to Hughes, Dec. 2, 1915; and ibid., Carson to Hughes, Dec. 15, 1915.
62 HLRO, Beaverbrook *papers*, General Hughes, 1, Aitken to Hughes, Dec. 24, 1915, no. 76; ibid., Aitken to Hughes, Oct. 16, 1915, no. 15; and ibid., General Hughes, 2, Aitken to Hughes, Jan. 20, 1916, no. 2.
63 PAC, RG 9, III, A1, Carson file, Hughes to Carson, Dec. 17, 1915; and ibid., 8-1-70, PC 273, Feb. 23, 1916. See PAC, J. J. Creelman *diaries*, MG 30, G 34, Feb. 20, 1916, for one Canadian field soldier's reaction to Sir Sam's stranglehold on promotions. Also see PAC, Christie *papers*, pp. 1229-34, memo by Hughes on "Canadian control over appointments and promotions."
64 PAC, Kemp *papers*, vol. 110, Gwatkin to Kemp, Mar. 11, 1916; and ibid., Alderson to Governor-General, Feb. 17, 1916.
65 HLRO, Beaverbrook *papers*, E/19, Alderson to Aitken, Mar. 3, 1916; and Willson, pp. 213-15.
66 PAC, Perley *papers*, vol. 3, p. 56, Borden to Perley, Feb. 6, 1915; and ibid., Perley to Borden, Jan. 26, 1915. Hughes' reaction is not recorded but Seely was a territorial soldier which made him better than most in Hughes' mind. Also see ibid., vol. 4, p. 124, Perley to Borden, Dec. 6, 1915; and ibid., Borden to Perley, Dec. 29, 1915; PAC, Borden *private diaries*, July 31 and Aug. 14, 1915, and July 18, 1916.
67 PAC, RG 24, vol. 502, HQ. 54-21-5-7, Colonial Secretary to Governor-General, Jan. 11, 1916; PAC, RG 9, III, A1, Carson file, Carson to Hughes, Dec. 2, 1915; PAC, Perley *papers*, vol. 5, p. 129, Perley to Borden, Feb. 17, 1916; Willson, p. 211; PAC, Kemp *papers*, vol. 110, Hazen to Kemp, Mar. 16, 1916; and Kemp to Borden, Mar. 21, 1916; and PAC, Borden *private diaries*, Mar. 15, 1916.

CHAPTER 15

A Nightmare Removed: Reform and Resignation, 1916

In December 1915 when Sam Hughes ordered that major appointments overseas could not be made without his approval, he was at the highest point of his ministerial power. In overseas matters he thought he was on the threshold of another major accomplishment—a repetition of his feat of Valcartier—where, with a superior hand, he would step in and swiftly bring order out of chaos. For the first two months of 1916 Sir Sam seemed unable to do anything about conditions in England except promise to go over himself in the near future. Liberal probes into his Shell Committee's activities, however vague, kept him busy in the Commons during January and February, and he had thrown himself with equal passion into recruiting drives across the country; but he arranged for nothing different overseas until he could do it personally.

Robert Borden was making some private and careful moves of his own within Sir Sam's department. His decision may have stemmed from the promise to Perley the previous summer that he would look into creating a separate overseas department. With strong evidence of Hughes' domestic confusion over the shells question and his deteriorating relations with Kitchener's soldiers that fall, the Prime Minister had been keeping a watch on Sir Sam's overseas arrangements as well as those at home. But the reports were often contradictory. He received information directly from Aitken. Usually it was much more optimistic than Sir George Perley's which urgently warned of faltering communications among all parties.[1]

Finally in January 1916, Borden did two things that signalled his determination to reform Hughes' machinery. He asked a legal opinion

---

Reference notes for Chapter 15 are found on pp. 310-12.

of E. L. Newcombe, Deputy Justice Minister, about Canada's jurisdiction over its troops outside of the country. At the end of the month, Newcombe responded that the CEF legally came under control of Canadian law "as if these operations were being carried out within Canada." A year before Newcombe had held a far different position; he had told Borden then that Hughes' method of administration should "be allowed to govern so long as there was no complaint from the other side of any lack of authority there." Complaints were now rife. Newcombe's 1916 memorandum meant that Borden had the means to reorder the overseas administration officially from the Canadian side. This produced the Prime Minister's second step that month: he asked Gwatkin and Fiset to prepare a reform proposal for the English set-up, which they did, promptly and willingly. Their scheme, generally referred to as Gwatkin's, would create a local council to superintend the overseas administration; importantly, it would diminish Sir Sam's control in it. Although Borden had both these opinions in his hands by the end of January, he did not take action. With no guarantee that Laurier would agree to extend Parliament's life, the political situation was still fragile. Perhaps the Prime Minister had also ordered Hughes to clean up the situation overseas himself, or Hughes had convinced Borden to let him try first. That he still had faith in his errant Minister seems probable.[2]

In early March during the middle of the Commons session, Hughes suddenly left Canada amid cries from his own party members that he was "running away" leaving them to face the Shell Scandal. Yet he had his own credible excuses. Several days before he sailed, he complained to Borden of "being ill [with] insomnia and some affection of the heart." Such appeals always seem to have touched Borden's soft spot, but he also knew the rigours of the job first hand. Hughes' constant activity, long hours, and sixty-three years were finally beginning to tell on him. Close to nervous exhaustion twice in the past two years, he had spent several weeks that winter in hospital suffering from a fall and a lung infection. After several appeals, Borden finally approved Hughes' trip.[3]

Sir Sam arrived in London on March 20 where he established himself and his military suite at the Ritz Hotel. Borden was doubtful that Hughes could make the necessary reforms smoothly. Before his Minister left, the Prime Minister had warned him not to aggravate anyone; and Sir Robert's hopes were bolstered by Aitken who had advised him that all was well in Hughes' relations with the English authorities. However, Borden was not taking any chances; he cabled Perley to keep a close watch on the unpredictable Minister: "Send me a secret message," he hurriedly wired, in case Hughes' "impetuous temperament should lead him into difficulties." Borden's suspicions were well founded. People on the other side found the Militia Minister with fire in his eyes and in a fighting mood. He had come over "to settle a few matters that needed his personal attention"; he knew, he told members of Aitken's organization, "what Canada wanted and he was going to get it."[4]

There were three things in particular that Sam Hughes believed Canada wanted: a new Canadian administrative structure overseas under his auspices and run by Sir Max Aitken; long-term details worked out on the command and structure of the corps, and especially of the new Fourth Division recently announced; and finally the extrication of Canadians from the dreadful Ypres Salient. On this last point, Hughes was most concerned, for he did nothing concrete about reorganizing his United Kingdom network until he spoke to Kitchener about the Salient which he did the day he arrived at the Ritz. Bluntly, Hughes told the War Secretary that the Salient was indefensible. To keep the Canadians there would call for "great and unnecessary" sacrifice. It should be abandoned with the surrendered ground intensively mined before the withdrawal. Hughes only wanted "his boys" in a position that made some sense. According to his later press statements, he also told Kitchener that the position "was being held more out of sentimental reasons than military considerations." On hearing Hughes' plea, Sir Sam claimed, Kitchener's eyes "filled up with tears; he was deeply affected by what I said.... He told me to give him my proposition in writing and he would communicate it to General Sir Douglas Haig," the British Commander-in-Chief.[5]

If Kitchener did send the letter, Hughes could not follow it up because he was called home to face the Shell Committee charges. If Haig received it, it had little effect on him for the Canadians stayed in or around the Salient. Bloody events kept them there for the next three months. In early April and again in June the corps was heavily involved, first at St. Eloi, then at Mount Sorrel, and casualties were heavy.

Meanwhile, no one knew for sure what Hughes was going to do about reorganizing the administrative set-up in England. Again he appeared indecisive. On March 24 he cabled Borden that he was "bringing Dave Watson [Brigadier-General then commanding the fifth brigade in Turner's division] back to England to make him Inspector-General and knock the whole thing into shape." Watson came back but Sir Sam did not make him inspector-general. In fact, he still waited, most likely while negotiating with Watson who had some definite opinions about the causes of the snafu in England, namely Steele and MacDougall.[6]

The appearance of Watson in England had another dimension which Hughes did not confide to the Prime Minister—the formation of a Canadian army made up of two corps. If the scant information on this subject is correct, Watson was to be given the Fourth Division, which in turn was to become one of the divisions of the Second Corps. Again Sir

Max seems to have acted as the prime mover, perhaps after hearing his Minister talk of his hopes for a national army. There had been long discussion on the subject earlier that winter among Aitken, Hughes, Turner, and Watson; and it was all done through the two men's secret channel using the Minister's home-grown codes, which Aitken thought Sir Sam was "as clever at compiling . . . as Mr. Bonar Law is at playing bridge." When Hughes arrived, they started to push the army idea.[7]

If an army were to be formed, it would be necessary to protect the surplus battalions by some action such as putting the Canadian battle troops in a less costly position. Certainly Sir Sam hated to see the continued death on the Ypres Salient, but that "unnecessary" bulge was also a threat to his army idea. And there were other advantages for Hughes besides national ones in creating a new corps. It would be a place to put Turner, whom he felt should have got the First Corps; Aitken had also suggested the shuffles could get Garnet a division; and it would have the political advantage of preventing the break-up of his local battalions, thereby calming the many surplus, dissatisfied, and unemployed officers in England who had been unceremoniously shorn of their commands; and, of course, it gave Hughes power to deal with the British in the name of Canada.[8]

None of this happened while Hughes was minister. Ironically, this was partly because his administrative system was so inefficient and because the losses at the front were so high. Yet the effect of the Minister's intention was to aggravate further the critical reinforcement problem for the existing corps because Hughes and his agents tried to hold back the battalions necessary to form new divisions.

It was the chaos in England that brought Alderson to London while Hughes was there. The General's immediate concern was to pry loose some of the desperately needed reinforcements from MacDougall's training morass, although he may have also got wind of the Minister's Canadian Army plan. What transpired between Hughes and Alderson is revealing for what it demonstrates about the support and co-operation between Hughes' network and the fighting soldiers. By the time Hughes and Alderson were in London, the Minister already knew of the commander's condemnations of the Ross rifle, the Minister's administrative machinery, and his frequent political interference in staffing the corps. The strains were so great that Alderson refused to call on Hughes unless "he was sent for"; to which Hughes responded, "Send for him? I'll be d--d first"! Again Aitken, who had helped cause the schism in the first place, tried to close it a bit. Towards the end of March, he arranged a dinner for Sir Sam at the Marlborough Club, of which Alderson had been a long-time member, hoping to get the two together, but he apparently had little success. The day before the dinner, accompanied by Beckles Willson, Aitken met Alderson there. The corps commander appealed to Sir Max "to support the best interest of Canada and the Canadian troops against Sir Sam's high-handed conduct" which, he said, was having "a most disastrous effect on esprit de corps." Aitken's reply was short and absolute—at least for the time being: "I am sorry General but please understand, I am first, last and all the time with the Minister." When they parted company, Willson recorded that "Aitken said to me, I fear Alderson must lose his command."[9]

Hughes' reaction was to remain inflexible and unco-operative. "I won't have any conflict of authority," he commented on hearing of Alderson's appeal. "If General Alderson don't like my ways he has the remedy in his own hands." Clearly Hughes and Aitken now saw Alderson not only as an impediment to their nationalization process but also as a challenge to civilian supremacy—perhaps a miniature of the concurrent British politicians' fight with their generals, or at least reminiscent of Hughes' struggles with Hutton in an earlier war. Over the next several days, Willson again recorded conversations between Sir Max and Sir Sam which bandied around the names of several "imperial officers" as possible successors to the corp's top post; these included Sir Julian Byng, a man to whom Hughes evidently was not as attracted as Aitken. The Minister's only comment about Byng was, "He's a Lord's son ain't he?" Willson's conclusion was that it "made me certain Alderson's supersession had been resolved upon."[10]

Apparently again indecisive, Hughes did not take a definite step towards reform in England until March 31, and he did so only the day after Borden had ordered him home to face the Kyte charges. Seeming to fulfill Sir Max's expectations, Hughes ordered Aitken to set up a local council responsible to the Militia Minister personally, which included such favourites as Carson, Watson, Brooke, and MacDougall, as well as Aitken. Except for Hughes' ministerial control and its informality, the scheme looked very much like the one Gwatkin had recommended to Borden two months before, and one which the CGS back home had continued to promote ever since.

Indeed it may have been this pressure supported by Perley's and Connaught's continued exhortations about the mess in England that made Borden very interested in hearing what Gwatkin had to say on the overseas issue; Hughes had never kept the Prime Minister well briefed on what went on in militia matters. Two days after Hughes had left Ottawa, the CGS was called before the cabinet to give an assessment of why the front remained starved of reinforcements when nearly 250,000 Canadians were in uniform. He pointed the finger squarely at Hughes' hydra and especially at incompetent men like Carson, MacDougall, and Steele. Borden's sudden interest made it seem that if Hughes did not solve his overseas problem as promised the Prime Minister would do it for him. But after hearing Gwatkin's ideas, Sir Robert did little for over two weeks. Only after the Kyte shell charges rocked the Commons on March 28 was he once more jolted into activity. He asked Fiset to get together all of Gwatkin's notes of January. When he tried the Deputy Minister could not find them anywhere. A search of Hughes' files produced nothing; nor did Captain Daly, Hughes' aide, know where they had gone. The inference was, as Daly put it, that there was some "hanky pank" by the Minister or his staff to hide the files, which if implemented would have instituted an overseas structure separate from Hughes' jurisdiction. It was flatly and hotly denied by most of Hughes' men on the staff. But the missing files were never uncovered; so Gwatkin went on to produce some more.[11]

In England, that Hughes would ask Max Aitken to form the new local council was seen as a foregone conclusion. Carson was not as high in ministerial estimation as he had been. With MacDougall and Steele still fighting with each other, Hughes looked more and more to Aitken for any calmness overseas. The incredible web of Sir Max's private Lombard Street headquarters with its attachments to various British departments had already become the major source of Hughes' information. Furthermore Aitken had the money and political connections to exploit this area more than any of the other Hughes appointees; and unquestionably he was on the same nationalist wavelength as Sir Sam. Consequently Hughes' dependence on and trust in Aitken grew. If Taylor's and Beckles Willson's assessment is correct, the ambitious Sir Max wanted to be the Minister's chief agent and had clearly set out to get it long before Sam Hughes returned to England in March.[12]

Unfortunately the local council idea solved nothing; nor did it last long—less than five weeks, in fact. Ironically the main reason for its demise was Max Aitken. The body only held two meetings—both in April. Aitken never went to either; the reasons seem to be that the council did not give Sir Max all that he wanted. While Hughes may have asked Aitken to set it up and had included him as a member, the organization gave power to no one as its chairman, let alone to Sir Max. The group was also "informal," to use the Minister's word—hardly a description to impress people who wanted an official and concrete order laid down. In the same vague message, Hughes had tossed in another confusing addition to his ramshackle organization: "Brigadier Watson to be given," Hughes ordered, "the rank of major-general and made chief military commander of the Canadian Forces in England." It was the third commander of Canadians in a year; the other two were still there and claimed to have some sort of endorsement from Hughes to prove it. A week earlier Hughes had told Borden he was going to make Watson inspector-general; now maybe either Sir Sam or Sir Max had someone else in mind.[13]

According to Aitken, he could see no chance of success for this council. During April while the fighting raged around the St. Eloi craters in Flanders, Hughes' new councillors were bickering among themselves. As a condition of his acceptance of the "Chief Military" command, Watson wanted both Steele and MacDougall removed. But neither would accept that with any grace. Back home Borden had temporarily removed Hughes from his portfolio so that things had stalled from Hughes' end, even if he was inclined to remove Steele or MacDougall. It seems that the Prime Minister was not willing to move either. As a result Watson, who by then had also been appointed by Hughes to command the new Fourth Division being formed at Bramshott, saw the handwriting on the wall and backed out of the council. As for Sir Max, on May 10 he wired Hughes that, given the obvious weakness in the body, he had "decided on my own account to place every obstacle in the way of that committee and this I have done." In the end Hughes' attempt at reorganization that spring had been the victim of his own ad hoc methods and of Aitken's own precipitous decisions.[14]

While the informal council was sputtering to an indefinite end, again the Prime Minister took a few more steps towards imposing his own form of reorganization. As attacks on Hughes mounted in the Commons, he drafted an order-in-council for Gwatkin's revised scheme. The draft, submitted to the Governor-in-Council on April 8, 1916, claimed that "the present system of command and administration fails to secure the best results; there is no central authority properly constituted, and a want of co-ordination is apparent." The plan put Perley firmly and officially at the head of the overseas organization and Fiset, Lessard, Ward, and Carson, among others, were to be members. But most important, the Overseas Military Council, as the new agency was called, would be severed completely from Sir Sam's control; and among its membership only Carson could be called a Hughes' man since Aitken was not there either.[15]

The Prime Minister, however, did not implement his program. He lost a splendid opportunity once he knew that Aitken had scuppered Hughes' informal group. This recurrent hesitation was in part understandable. A series of crises largely involving Hughes' record again intervened to make a move inopportune. Apparently Sir Robert was waiting until the Royal Commission on Shells and the Ross rifle investigations were completed before taking any step which would pass judgment on Hughes and thereby on the Conservative government. The Prime Minister was convinced that Hughes could not long remain in the government and that reform must come to the Canadians overseas. He seemed to be waiting and administering Hughes' department until Sir George Perley could return from England with further advice on what was needed there. Still there is also evidence that Borden could not act decisively against Sir Sam. Foster's diaries provide the proof: in late April Sir Robert agreed to let Hughes go back to England once again.[16]

Though Hughes had given Borden his resignation pending the outcome of the investigations, the Militia Minister was far from silent or calm. Just before he left Ottawa for London in March, Hughes had once more quarrelled with the Governor-General. This time it was a genuine crisis: Connaught threatened to resign if Hughes did not publicly apologize.

The cause of these remarks had long been in the making. Since the war began, the Duke had encouraged Alderson, Gwatkin, and others secretly to pass on departmental information to Government House without ministerial approval. Just as frequently, Connaught had leaked such information to British friends and had often expressed opinions based on it which did not accurately reflect those of his Minister. Alderson's February communication with the Duke, which painted such a black picture of the Hughes' overseas hydra, represented to Sir Sam hard evidence of the conspiracy of professional soldiers against their civilian masters, as well as the arrogance which he imagined some Englishmen had for Canadians.

That is what Sir Sam thought about Connaught and that is what he told the members of his headquarters staff in March at one of their infrequent and informal meetings. By the time Connaught heard these remarks—probably transmitted by Gwatkin or Fiset—Hughes was in England. Borden had difficulty quieting the apoplectic Duke and he spent a great deal of his valuable time trying to sort out who had said what to whom. When the Prime Minister questioned Hughes, his response was, as Borden recorded in his diary, not very satisfactory. After taking the time to call in all of the headquarters staff who heard the controversial statements, Borden decided that Hughes had said more about the Duke than "he realized."[17]

But Borden did not side with Connaught either. The same searches also pointed out that what Sir Sam had said was true and that the Duke often spoke disparagingly of Hughes to the Minister's own staff. Furthermore the Prime Minister was convinced that Connaught was really "guilty himself" and was "by no means a brilliant intellect." In April when Hughes got home, they laboured over the issue some more. The Minister made an indirect apology and the Duke did not resign, although he continued to press for Hughes' resignation—a fact which only confirmed Borden's opinion of Connaught's unconstitutional acts. The complaint had clearly backfired on the Governor-General. Borden had Christie prepare a memorandum to remind the Duke of his "titular position," and he told Perley that the next Governor-General was going to be a Canadian. Ironically it was Connaught's fight with Hughes with its constitutional revelations that may have sparked Borden to have the Duke recalled later that summer, long before he acted decisively on Hughes. But that spring it was Hughes' essentially correct judgment on Connaught which helped keep the Militia Minister in the cabinet a while longer.[18]

In June Hughes again aggravated Connaught and more than a few Canadians. The new wrangle got emotionally wound up in the drowning of Lord Kitchener in the North Sea on June 6, the same day soldiers of the Canadian Third Division were blown out of their positions at Mount Sorrel near the Ypres Salient. When the news of the heavy casualties of Mount Sorrel came hard on the heels of Kitchener's death, Hughes told a newspaper reporter that the British were holding on to the Ypres bulge for no more than sentimental reasons while Canadians were being slaughtered for a strategically useless bit of ground.[19]

Hughes revealed that he had asked the War Secretary in March to straighten the line to save Canadian lives and that this had not been done even though two more costly battles had taken place, which implied that recent Canadian deaths were the fault of Kitchener and the British high command. It certainly questioned the rationale behind most Canadian battle involvements in the past year. Again Connaught bristled, sputtering to the Prime Minister that if Sir Sam had been a British officer he would have been arrested and court-martialled for such subversive statements. Again Borden took no action against Hughes, except to record the inappropriateness of the comment so close to Kitchener's death. At the time Connaught and Hughes were also sparring over Sir Sam's American Legion scheme in which Borden thought the Duke was being far too meddlesome. And Borden did not like Connaught's pressure on the Ypres issue. The Prime Minister agreed with Hughes; the Ypres area was "a dangerous and useless salient in which we have recently lost five thousand and upwards." He also wired that message to Perley knowing that the English authorities would soon hear of his opinion. It is doubtful if he was convinced by Perley's reply that the Salient was important strategically.[20] The question on which both Hughes and Borden concurred was that Canadians were dying for a spot not of their own choosing, and without even being asked or advised why it had to be defended at such a cost.

Not only did Hughes condemn the importance and motives of the British defence of Ypres, he also offered a solution. It was the same as his March plan: mine and withdraw—leave the bad ground to the "boche," then blow him up "quietly from time to time." On the surface Hughes' tactical Ypres plan made sense, but he ignored many of the facts, most of them strategic. For example, the Ypres Salient followed the only high ground in the area. By 1916 mining was virtually impossible and highly dangerous. The Canadian officers as well as others at the front agreed with the British that the ground must be held. A withdrawal could be almost as costly as an attack. If it turned into a rout in the process, the ports of Calais, Dunkirk, and Boulogne would be seriously threatened, if not lost. Allied resupply and reinforcement would be very difficult at best. Moreover the Ypres Salient was on the last bit of territory the Belgians held; for the sake of their continued participation and in light of the possibility of a negotiated peace, the area had to be defended.[21] Still Hughes was not alone in his criticism; there were a great many people who had Sir Sam's instinctive revulsion about the slaughter and who had not yet come to know the full impact of total war. As for Borden, he spent more valuable time trying to quieten the Duke and to soften Hughes' press comments.

As the debate on Hughes' departmental administration reached a crisis in Canada in the spring of 1916, his relationship with Alderson reached its climax. It came suddenly but not unexpectedly. The participation of the Second Division in the battle of St. Eloi Craters, from March 27 to April 16, 1916, provided the immediate background for the crisis, although a variety of previous events point out that Hughes and Aitken had long wanted to get rid of the independent General. During the battle there was a costly fiasco that raised doubts about command ability within one of the Canadian divisions. When it was over Alderson, acting on the advice of his superior, British General Sir Herbert Plumer, tried to fire General Turner, commander of the Second Division, and one of his brigadiers, H. D. B. Ketchen. Their incompetence, it was alleged, caused the failure of an operation that accomplished little and cost much. Turner refused to accept any of the charges made about their performance and countered with accusations of higher British bungling which had handed him an impossible situation. Significantly, he appealed, not to Carson, but to Aitken in England.[22]

When Aitken received Turner's complaints that he and his brigadier were being sacrificed by Alderson and Plumer to cover up the mess which British command—not Canadian soldiers—had made of the issue, Sir Max headed immediately to see some of his friends on the Army Council, where he explained Turner's case and apparently made it quite clear that the Canadian government would be upset if any of their men were removed. As to the truth of who botched up at St. Eloi, there is ample evidence that everybody did, Turner's men and the British included. But the way Alderson would have it, the Canadian General was to bear all the responsibility, and what Alderson wanted in reality was simply to get rid of Turner. Their relations had been publicly bad for some time. However, in choosing the St. Eloi incident where so many others were also clearly at fault was tactically a bad move, and the corps commander played directly into Hughes' and Aitken's hands. The previous March Alderson had notified Aitken that he alone would decide for the good the corps who would be its commanders. In late April after the St. Eloi crisis broke, he again pushed the issue in front of Sir Max: "My report on General Turner distinctly states... that I did not consider that the one incident [St. Eloi] alone justified General Turner's removal but that incidents arising from and brought up by operations, showed General Turner to be unfitted for the responsible position of a Divisional Commander." As far as Alderson was concerned, what had been suggested about Turner's competence at Ypres the year before should now be decided upon. All the evidence was in.[23]

One interesting aspect of the episode is that Aitken told the Army Council of Canada's desires before he told Canada—namely Hughes. But once Hughes found out, he made it clear that he had "great confidence in Turner" and that his removal was an "unnecessary step." In all fairness to Sir Sam, none of the correspondence reveals that he specifically asked for Alderson's removal. That initiative came from his overseas agent. The same day that Hughes in Ottawa was reading Aitken's first messages about the crisis, Sir Douglas Haig in France had already received the Aitken-initiated Army Council's warnings about firing Turner. As Haig recorded in his diary that night, he had received notice that "some feeling against the English exists amongst Canadians." Under this pressure the Field Marshal simply decided to retain both Turner and Ketchen because there was no Canadian officer with enough experience to replace Turner. More importantly Haig was beginning to realize the importance of Canadian nationalism and goodwill. He believed that "the main point is whether the danger of a serious feud between the Canadians and the British is greater than the retention of a couple of incompetent commanders." At least Haig's action showed he was not party to any British conspiracy to hold back Canadians.[24]

The crisis was far from over. Hughes' insistence on Turner's retention and General Plumer's demands that someone in the Canadian Corps had to be blamed meant that Alderson himself now became the likely candidate. Again ignoring the military chain of command, Turner wired Sir Max to come over to France to intervene personally on his behalf. In the meantime Haig was faced with the probable resignation of Plumer, his Second Army commander, if something was not done to appease him. Aitken and Haig got together at British GHQ on April 26, and Aitken told Haig that it was Sir Robert Borden's personal request that Turner be retained. But none of the correspondence indicates that at that date Borden had suggested any such thing, or that even he or Hughes knew what was then going on. The first mention of Turner's name in Borden's letters appears after the decisions were already made. The only one in Canada who to that point had promoted Turner's case was Hughes. In short, it was Aitken's pressure on Haig that determined the outcome. During the rest of the meeting, major reshuffles were decided. The entry in Haig's diary indicates how he saw the problems of Canadian military administration and what happened in light of what Aitken led him to believe would take place:

> I had an interview with Sir Max A. representing the Canadian Government. He took a very reasonable attitude. The Prime Minister of Canada makes a personal request that General Turner should not be removed but . . . I told him then that I had decided to retain Turner. We then discussed the organization of the Canadian Forces in Europe and the difficulty which the Commander of the Canadians in the field suffered through having so many administrative and political questions to deal with in addition to his duties in the field. It was agreed that an Inspector General [or Commander in Chief] of Canadian Forces in Europe be appointed with HQ in England to deal with the organization and administration of the Canadian Army in Europe. This appointment seems all the more necessary as a 4th Division will shortly be added to the Canadian Corps and 32 battalions are soon to arrive from Canada as draft finding units. General Alderson is to be asked by the Canadian Government to become Inspector General of their forces in Europe and General Byng would be most acceptable to the Canadians as successor to Alderson in the field. After lunch I saw Plumer commanding Second Army. He agreed to the necessity of an Inspector General of Canadian Forces.[25]

Besides pointing out what a strangling impediment Hughes' administrative network was to the fighting corps and the ministerial prejudice against Alderson, the diary entries made other things clear. First, Haig and Plumer thought that Alderson was being promoted to an important military position; second, they believed he was to straighten out the various problems plaguing the orderly functioning of the Canadian forces; and third, they obviously thought he was going to lead the new military organization in England. He may have been removed but he definitely was not fired.

In the cables to Canada—one to Hughes and a secret simultaneous one to Borden—Aitken told them only that Alderson was to be "Inspector-General of Troops in England." There was no mention that the purpose was to reform Hughes' entire system of overseas administration. In the end Alderson was awarded the hollow title of inspector-general of troops in England; Aitken remained the personal representative of Hughes at the front. In light of the passing of Hughes' "informal council," Sir Max also effectively superintended much of what went on in England and France. The Canadian Corps got Sir Julian Byng. The Canadian cabinet approved of Sir Max's plan; and Alderson returned to England where his new position, as Aitken later claimed to Hughes, clashed with the other three officers supposedly commanding Canadians there.[26]

As for command of the corps, Hughes did not want Byng. He wanted a Canadian, probably Turner. But Sir Max's strong initiative, especially his notice to Borden that he "could not complete the arrangements on any other basis," generated a momentum made stronger by distance and time, a momentum the Minister could not resist. Aitken's decisions gave Hughes a ready-made solution to the problem of a troublesome Englishman who was continually testing his—and therefore Canadian—control over the corps and who was always questioning the Minister's judgment on men, organization, and material. It was a splendid chance to get rid of a man he did not like and whom he thought St. Eloi had once again proven incompetent. On May 28, 1916, British General Julian Byng replaced Alderson who was given the nominal duty of inspector-general of Canadian troops in the United Kingdom, a job he quit four months later because there was so little for him to do. Hughes never bothered to inform his Militia Council of the new Inspector-General's appointment. Finally the council had to appeal to the Prime Minister to ascertain "whether Lieutenant-General Alderson's appointment had been officially recognized by the Canadian Government and his duties defined."[27]

Three days before Haig and Aitken had their fateful interview at St. Omer, France, Hughes contacted François Lessard, who was then in England. The General had been unknowingly kept there by Borden in preparation for becoming a member of the Prime Minister's unborn and secret local council. When it did not materialize, some employment had to be found for him; Hughes' message had the advantage of doing that. "Please," the Minister said, "make confidential inspection and report to me before returning on command under General MacDougall and also under Lord Brooke." Lessard had no indication that Borden was not going to initiate his own reforms. The French-Canadian was yet hopeful, indeed eager, to see the end of Sir Sam's system and of the Minister himself. In early April he had dined at the Junior Naval and Military Club with Willson whom he told, "I am out for this man's [Hughes'] blood. He is disgracing Canada and jeopardizing relations with the Imperial Government and the Army." "Lessard's friends," Willson recorded, "would like to see him in Sir Sam's place." Nevertheless, like the soldier he was, Lessard carried out Hughes' orders, the findings of which no doubt privately pleased him. Hughes' training system both in England and at home was inefficient. This accounted for the reinforcement bottleneck at the front and meant that Canadians virtually had to be retrained. Hughes did not make the General's findings public and it is not clear if he told Borden of the full details. That Sir Sam had commissioned Lessard in the first place, however, was an indication that Borden would not impose his will on Sir Sam just yet. Indeed when he had given Hughes permission to return overseas, it was the signal that Sir Sam had started to plan again.[28]

But he had to do something, especially after Lessard's report. By then the informal council of March was moribund, and British officials continued to be confused by Carson's and all the others' activities. Again the War Office pleaded to have some order imposed to overcome the increasing delay and confusion. Carson also perplexed the Canadian militia headquarters staff by keeping back information about his appointments. The same frustration existed at British headquarters in France whose soldiers resented Carson's liaison directly with the corps concerning important decisions which they found out about only later. For his part, Byng was far from malleable; he reacted strongly to Hughes' and his agents' constant interference in promotions.[29]

One of them, in Turner's division, was the Minister's younger brother, William, who had commanded the 21st Battalion (Eastern Ontario) of Rennie's fourth brigade at the St. Eloi battle. At the time Turner had written a report on Colonel Hughes' failure to defend adequately part of the cratered salient. In part this may explain Aitken's eagerness to settle the affair quickly in Turner's favour. If Turner had been fired, Sir Sam's brother's role would have been exposed. It is not known if the Minister was privy to these facts. But if he felt that Alderson was covering up larger British incompetence by sacrificing Turner, then his brother would be just another national martyr. Whatever the case, by May and June the recently redeemed Turner had completely reversed his opinion of Bill Hughes; he worked through Carson's and Aitken's networks to make Colonel Hughes a brigadier in the new Fourth Division. Hughes got the command. Yet Byng continued to make the point that since he was "responsible for the Corps and for the safety of the men in it," he informed Sir Max's assistant, "he proposed to make his own recommendations to the Commander-in-Chief."[30]

Because Sam Hughes had done little to reorganize the situation in England, the corps was even more critically starved of reinforcements. In June Manly Sims confided to Aitken that there was a distinct possibility that, because of the manpower shortage, the Third Division would have "to be pulled out all together." The corps, he went on, needed about 7,000 replacements to bring it up to strength. But at Shorncliffe, training and administration were so encumbered by overlapping and small commands that there were "only 100 men available" with "3,100 having completed only the musketry" part of the training syllabus. The situation at the front was so critical, Manly Sims warned, that "we are sending these men over anyhow." However, Sam Hughes could do little personally until the Royal Commission investigating the Shell Committee exonerated him in July. Once that verdict was in, the over-tolerant Borden decided to give Hughes another chance. Thinking he could do it and convinced that some of his cabinet colleagues were conspiring to oust him, Hughes hurried off to England to begin the reorganization in earnest. But the Prime Minister specifically warned Sir Sam not to take any final action until the cabinet approved.[31]

After Hughes left Canada, Borden again reconsidered Sir Sam's value in the government. The Prime Minister's timidity apparently sprang not only from his tendency to avoid controversial action but also from his fear that Hughes could harm the administration if forced from the government. Above all the Prime Minister wanted no public break in the Conservative Party. With Sir Sam at a safe distance, Borden cautiously tested his colleagues' opinion about a cabinet reconstruction. He may still have hoped to resolve the overseas problem without getting rid of Sir Sam Hughes.

Sir George Perley conveniently arrived in Ottawa soon after Hughes left, and he pleaded with the Prime Minister to let him take over the English operations. At first Borden felt that Sir George was "consumed with desire to be appointed High Commissioner." But he soon thought differently. By mid-August Hughes did not appear to be changing his ways as his denials to the Prime Minister about surplus officers indicated; and many cabinet ministers were near revolt. White was "crying out against Hughes" in cabinet meetings; Foster thought the Militia Minister was "crazy constitutionally and in part unbalanced and absolutely untruthful"; Borden himself wrote that Sir Sam's "recent interviews have begun to disgust his best friends." John Willison, who always seemed to have his fingers on the pulse beat of Ontario, advised the Prime Minister to divest himself of the unpopular Hughes. Even the Deputy Militia Minister admitted to Sir Robert after Hughes got soundly booed by the troops at Camp Borden—supposedly "his boys"—that the Minister was "very unpopular in the country."[32]

On August 18 Perley and Borden discussed the Militia Minister and the reconstruction of the cabinet over breakfast. The Acting High Commissioner made it quite clear to his chief that Sam Hughes was "a very dangerous passenger." Yet at the same time, Sir Robert was still encouraging Hughes to submit to the cabinet a plan for an effective organization in England. Apparently Borden was keeping open as many avenues as possible. But whatever his reasoning, the Prime Minister's diaries indicate that sometime during the next few days he offered Perley an overseas portfolio probably as head of the resurrected Overseas Military Council; privately he also felt that "Hughes [is] doing nothing in England but [making] a fool of himself."[33] If Borden wanted to set up an organization in England free of Hughes' control, Perley, as the only man independent of Hughes and yet knowledgeable, was the only choice.

Two events may have pushed events along faster than Sir Robert preferred. First, Perley refused "to take a portfolio with Hughes";

second, Hughes was far from inactive overseas. As usual Sir Sam kept a high and busy public profile. He spent plenty of time reviewing huge parades; he visited all of the camps in England, France, and Belgium; and he even taught a little bayonet fighting at one of the training establishments. Back home Borden was getting impatient. All of this visiting was good press for Hughes but it had little to do with the task at hand. Hearing nothing, twice in August the Prime Minister cabled Sir Sam to ask him about his progress; the Minister's replies always skirted the issue. But in fact, Hughes was secretly reorganizing.[34] Contrary to Borden's specific instructions, Sir Sam had set up the Acting Sub-Militia Council with Carson as president. Other members were mostly drawn from Hughes' old gang which now included his son-in-law, Major Byron Greene, who was to be in charge of all promotions. He was also secretary of the new body; and the committee was responsible solely to the Militia Minister for all final decisions.

Although the group had been functioning for several days, Borden first learned of the council through the newspapers, where it was said the Minister was settling "all difficulties in England with the jud[gment] of Solomon." Borden had to cable Hughes asking if the reports were true and Hughes flatly denied them. Because of these inconsistencies, Borden seemed disposed to accept Perley's advice of September 6 that "the only salvation is to take it [administration in England] completely out of Hughes' hands." The next day Borden consulted several cabinet colleagues who agreed that he should establish his own overseas militia committee under a separate cabinet minister, and on September 8 he ordered Hughes home.[35] At the same time he tried to get information from Sir Sam about the Sub-Militia Council.

It took Hughes three days to reply by cable but not before he had asked Aitken to determine Borden's reaction to the council. When Sir Max described the new set-up, he told Borden, "it appears to me that the scheme of organization ... is very good. If you object to any names on Council suggest you communicate your views to Sir Sam ... as minister is disposed to accept suggestions." Hughes then denied to Sir Robert that he had set up any council: "Know nothing whatever about our own composition of proposed council," he wired, "and cannot understand your peculiar message.... Absolutely understood nothing settled until approved by order-in-council." The Militia Minister had actually admitted to Borden that he set up an overseas council on September 8, but instead of using the wire service, Hughes had written a letter to Borden giving the details of the council. It took Borden ten days to get it; and by that time, Hughes probably hoped, the Sub-Militia Council idea would be too entrenched to change.[36]

For the next month and a half, Borden and Hughes continued to circle each other. Hughes was certain that he could force Borden to accept his organization, while the Prime Minister was equally determined to establish Sir George Perley in an independent overseas ministry. Since both plans were similar, their individual details were not in question. Further, both schemes accomplished what both men agreed on: a separate agency materializing out of action taken by Canadians which was recognized by British authorities. Either scheme would have satisfied the desire to have more recognition from Great Britain.[37] However, there the similarities ended; and only Canadian political moves counted.

What did matter was that one group was dominated by an erratic minister 3,000 miles away who had little regard for the wishes of his government and who had little appreciation of efficient overseas administration. As long as Sir Sam held office, co-operation with Sir George Perley in the new portfolio was unlikely.

Perley's body would be a ministry directly responsible to the Canadian cabinet. Sir Sam's was responsible to him alone. Perley's was officially sanctioned by the due process of the Canadian government; Hughes' was not. The Minister created it in spite of his instructions. In Sir George's structure, executive and administrative action would normally be taken by the overseas council within the guidelines of cabinet policy and collective responsibility. In Hughes' structure, regardless of what cabinet wanted, nothing could happen until he said so. But by association the government would be marked by any of the Minister's mistakes. A case in point was Hughes' order to his own council in October 1916 that "all reports must be carefully prepared, and must be endorsed from here [Hughes in Ottawa] before final adoption." Again when Hughes' body tried to alleviate the urgent reinforcement problems of the corps, by using the battalions Hughes had set aside in England for his dream of a two corps Canadian army, the Minister overruled it from afar and ordered two new divisions made ready. Efficiency was of course the most pressing problem for the men at the front and Hughes' Sub-Militia Council gave no indication that it would come as long as he had hold of the reins—reins which, as he heard rumours of Sir Robert's separate plans, he grasped more desperately. However, the long-term question for the Canadian administration was who governed in Ottawa, Sam Hughes or Robert Borden and his cabinet.[38]

Although the Prime Minister had been considering a reconstruction of the cabinet for some time, he took further action on September 12. After making sure that his cabinet was behind him, Sir Robert approached E. L. Newcombe in the Department of Justice for advice. By September 26, Newcombe had confirmed the legality of Borden's proposal to establish a militia ministry in England, separate from the one in Canada. Even though Hughes returned to Ottawa on October 7, Borden hesitated for ten days before informing Sir Sam of his intention. When the two did meet, the Prime Minister recorded in his diary that Hughes took the news "better than I anticipated," but "I think he will resign."[39]

Sir Sam took two days to digest the fact that Perley was to get the new portfolio. At first he denounced Sir George and many other cabinet colleagues, then he tearfully informed Borden that the new scheme would humiliate him—a tactic he sometimes used to break down the Prime Minister's resistance. Perley, Hughes charged, had no ability, was a toady for the British, and an enemy of Canadian national interests. At the same time Sir Sam claimed "that everything he had done himself was perfect." The humiliation would be so great, lamented Hughes, that he would have to leave the government if Perley won the portfolio, a claim which he repeated in a telegram to Aitken.[40] Obviously Sir Sam had no appreciation of his own unpopularity.

During the entire unpleasant affair, there was one constant theme in Hughes' letters to Borden: he was patriotically protecting Canadian interests and securing national control, in spite of many British obstacles. No doubt Hughes believed it. Earlier that summer he had stated in print that "the present relationship between Great Britain and the Dominions is untenable. A Dominion which sends to a European war an army immeasurably greater than the allied armies sent to the Crimea can not again have issues of peace and war determined for her by a government in which she is not represented...." He went on to call for his old scheme of a full partnership union.[41] During his October moves he tried to exploit this aspect, knowing full well that Borden was susceptible to such a claim. Indeed Sir Sam was right; he had done much to protect and identify the country's national interests. But in doing so he had confused his personal power with the national good. The question now was efficiency and government control, not personal patriotism. Most ministers in the cabinet had had enough of that.

As it became clear that Borden was not going to listen, whatever the appeals, Hughes took several desperate counter-moves. He deluded himself into believing that if he left Borden's administration, it would collapse. As he was manoeuvring in Ottawa's circles, he secretly tried to get support in England for a new coalition government headed by himself and "recognizing certain Liberals." Borden, he proposed to Sir Max, would be shunted off to the Supreme Court or some other quiet spot; and he wanted Aitken to head the new ministry overseas.[42]

Aitken was cunning enough not to reply too soon. By mid-1916 his entire relationship with Sam Hughes had changed, though he was still doing Hughes flattering favours. In September he had run interference with Borden over the Sub-Militia Council in England; as well he had advised Hughes on its details and helped him set it up. In early October he fulfilled his year-old promise to get Hughes a lieutenantgeneralcy in the British Army. He did so through Bonar Law by announcing the promotion in Canadian papers before the King even knew about it. This precipitous action caused a minor British cabinet crisis. After several stern regal warnings never to usurp the royal prerogative again, the King grudgingly promoted Sir Sam to the honorary rank. He did so only because he did not want to cause "simply disastrous" friction in Anglo-Canadian relations and because he was put in such a compromising position he could hardly refuse. He said that he would have refused under normal circumstances: Hughes did not deserve the rank.[43]

But Sir Max was not a member of the Sub-Militia Council. Although he continued in his capacity as the representative at the front until early 1917, by the previous autumn he clearly had cut himself loose from Hughes. The reasons were obvious; he knew Hughes' star was waning. British politics, especially with the promotion of the Lloyd George-Bonar Law team, had taken on a new perspective. It helped bring Lloyd George to the British Prime Minister's office later that December and Sir Max to a cabinet portfolio in his government the next year. To stay with Hughes would have been ruination. Whether he liked it or not, Aitken was tainted as a Hughes' man; he was better off elsewhere. As well there was a much more powerful game in London than in Ottawa and Aitken liked high stakes. When Sir Max got Hughes' late October offer to head the overseas militia ministry, he waited, consulted with several people including Clifford Sifton, then turned Sir Sam down a week later. "I cannot accept," he wrote on October 28, "I am not qualified to fill the post. I strongly recommend you accept Prime Minister's proposal and on no account resign."[44] It ended that alternative for Sam Hughes.

Suddenly Hughes threw his support publicly behind compulsory military service as a method of solving the acute manpower shortage.[45] He may have hoped that his stand on the issue would regain him some cabinet and popular support of like-minded conscriptionists and consequently sanction for his overseas scheme. He was again mistaken. Even Aitken had warned him the time was not yet right for such a move.

While Hughes continued to believe he could replace Borden, he still tried to persuade the Prime Minister not to appoint Perley to the overseas militia ministry. At the end of the month, he told Sir Robert he would accept the scheme if Aitken headed it. He even went so far as to draft an order-in-council setting up such a proposal. But without cabinet support it went nowhere.[46]

During the next few days, Hughes displayed typical erratic behaviour in an attempt to get his own way. Through a mixture of crying fits, complaints of conspiracy, unfounded charges of public humiliation, and more to the point, pleas against losing power, he continued to pressure Borden. On one occasion, after storming out of a cabinet meeting, he refused to return and telephoned his personal abuse to the Prime Minister, who was still trying to preside over the gathering. Indicative of Hughes' blind determination was his sustained effort by letters and interviews with his colleagues to have Borden's scheme overturned even though the majority of the cabinet was in favour of it. Hughes either ordered or persuaded his Deputy Minister, Fiset, to plead with Borden to accept an Aitken-led overseas ministry, although two days before Hughes had learned that Sir Max had refused the position.[47]

On October 31 Borden had had enough of Hughes' manoeuvres; he announced that Sir George Perley would head the new overseas ministry. The next day Hughes wrote the Prime Minister, claiming, among other things, that Borden had lied to him about creating an overseas militia council and that for over a year he had been conspiring with Perley to remove him from his control overseas. Hughes deplored Borden's penchant for orderly methods and claimed that if in 1914 he had waited for orders-in-council the first contingent would still be in Valcartier.[48]

If Borden was looking for a way to rid himself of Hughes, Sir Sam's insulting letter of November 1 provided him with the opportunity. After formulating two replies, one asking for an apology and one asking for a resignation, Borden again polled his cabinet on Hughes. Most believed that he should resign and, because of his unpopularity in the country, most thought he would not be a threat to the government thereafter. Many, including Borden himself, hoped that the whole administration would receive a much needed public lift if Hughes were fired. Finally on November 9 Sir Robert demanded Hughes' resignation. In his letter, Borden stated the reasons for the dismissal:

My time and energies, although urgently needed for much more important duties, have been very frequently employed in removing difficulties ... unnecessarily created. You seem actuated by a desire ... to administer your department as if it were a distinct and separate government ... which has frequently led to a well-founded protest from your colleagues as well as a detriment to the public interest. The latest of these [instances] is the establishment of a militia Sub-Council in Great Britain. All members of the Government have full and direct responsibility in respect to the very important matters which the proposed Council would advise upon and direct. You proceeded to disregard [my instructions].... Such an attitude is wholly inconsistent with and subversive of the principle of joint responsibility upon which constitutional government is based.[49]

The Militia Department was in a great state of commotion when Hughes arrived Saturday morning, November 11, and received Borden's letter. The Minister quickly concocted an even more impertinent response, repeating most of his previous contentions, but also tendering his resignation. When Borden received it the following Monday, he read it to his cabinet, most of whom thought it foolish. If co-operation with Perley's new ministry could not be accomplished, then, as the Prime Minister said, "conditions at this end must change." Even the patient Gwatkin had reached the limit with his Minister and had threatened to resign if Hughes did not go. Hughes had lately bragged that Borden dare not dismiss him; but in firing Sir Sam, the Prime Minister took the only course possible.[50]

Indeed Borden should have done it much sooner. By early 1916 Sir Sam Hughes' overseas administration had reached an impasse, while his domestic ministry was faltering under various scandals and manpower pressures. Greater efficiency had to be achieved if the war was to be fought successfully. Over the past two years, more and more of the responsibilities with which Sir Sam started the war had had to be taken over by others. But he had kept the overseas organization under his personal control. He would not delegate power and he did neglect collective cabinet responsibility. Sir Sam's inordinate suspicion of British professional soldiers and some real evidence of England's insensitivity to Canada's growing maturity also added to the degeneration of the Minister's organization. Overseas Hughes was too far away to be an effective personal leader yet he had set up a system there that only a personal leader in close contact with the situation could run. Sir Sam neither understood nor sympathized with the fact that the Canadian Corps had become a professional army with professional needs.

Borden did not dismiss Hughes during these two years for many of the same reasons he had kept him on during the early months of the war despite all the complaints about the Minister. Not the least of the reasons was the political debt for Hughes' past loyalty, his nationalist temper in the face of arrogant British unco-operativeness, and his complete commitment to rallying the nation to war. Hughes had also made some perceptive judgments about bad British generalship; he was never afraid to tackle any of these problems head on in expressing Canadian concerns, which were often shared by Borden himself. Hughes was a fighter. He was colourful and he was good for business. Surrounded by the heady aura of Valcartier sentiment, he was also good for the image of an often dull party. When controversy arose in his ministry, it was not always politically wise to try to remove Hughes at every revelation, lest judgment be passed on the entire Conservative administration. Furthermore, Borden appeared to defer to Hughes' judgment because, in Sir Andrew MacPhail's words, "Sir Robert Borden was protesting continually and correctly that he was not a military man ... [and] ... he placed full reliance upon the Minister of Militia who in virtue of that position had imputed to himself all military knowledge and was allowed to assume the double role of Minister and commanding officer."

MacPhail's judgment was correct, but Borden was over-cautious and did not clamp down on Sir Sam. The Prime Minister also had an inordinate fear of Hughes' potential political power being used against his administration.

The disarray of the overseas organization was mostly the fault of Sam Hughes, but Sir Robert must bear some of the responsibility for not allowing it to have an orderly growth from the start. In August 1914 he had ignored Perley's request to set things off on a regular basis. Again that October he had advised the Colonial Secretary, who agreed with him whole-heartedly, that he was "not confident that any more definite programme can be prepared." The English then and thereafter agreed with allowing amorphous growth until they too had to do something about Hughes' mess. For well over a year Borden continued to follow Newcombe's 1915 advice not to do anything overseas until someone complained; so he let Hughes' informal agent system fill the widening gap until the system proved so inefficient that he was forced to take it out of Hughes' hands. And since Hughes would never give up, only abrupt and long overdue political action would suffice.[51]

In the days following the dismissal, Borden was still afraid that Hughes would cause trouble outside government, and he tried to placate Sir Sam by ordering "Kemp to have our press drop Hughes or use soft pedal in dealing with him." The new Governor-General, the Duke of Devonshire, also expressed the concern of the government to British authorities. He told Law that Hughes "will endeavour to cause trouble to the Government at the next session is possible and even probable."[52] Even after the resignation, Borden went a long way to smooth over the situation. In February 1917 he helped Hughes' son gain promotion to the command of the Fifth Canadian Division in England in spite of the recommendations by Perley that Canada could not reinforce five divisions. As late as the summer of 1917, the Prime Minister wanted to give the First Canadian Division to the junior Hughes, presumably as an additional sop to his father.

But at the time of the firing, it had looked as if Hughes would fight. On November 11 he had asked Borden for permission to publish the correspondence which had passed between them. Since Hughes would have done it anyway, Borden took the first step in publishing the material himself. The Prime Minister's action had shown Canadians that he had nothing to hide; and the move had also taken the wind out of the opposition's sails.[53]

By mid-November Sir Sam Hughes had vacated his offices in the Militia Building.[54] Public reaction to his dismissal was all that Borden hoped for. There were few regrets. Devonshire assured the Colonial

Office that the government had enhanced its prestige by the move. The Duke also believed that Hughes' past record and his waning popularity meant his end as a political force. Many newspapers praised Sir Sam's initial energy in rallying the nation to war in the early days of the struggle, but nearly all realized that what was needed in 1917 was a smoother, more efficient ministry. Privately some men indicated the full extent of their relief. John Creelman, then serving with the Canadian Field Artillery, articulated the severest thoughts of many soldiers when he wrote:

There is a new contentment among us all. We walk with sprightlier step. We have clearer eyes and are generally of a cleaner-cut get-up now that the inevitable has really happened. The mad mullah of Canada has been deposed [Sir Sam has lost his job]. The Canadian Baron Munchausen will be to less effect. The Louis de Rougement of Lindsay will in vain seek supporters. The greatest soldier since Napoleon has gone to his gassy Elba and the greatest block to the successful termination of the war has been removed. Joy, oh Joy! I do not like to kick a man when he is down but I am willing to break nine toes in kicking Sam in the stomach or in the face or anywhere else.

Sir George Foster simply claimed it was a "nightmare removed."[55]

Reference Notes to Chapter 15

1 For examples, see PAC, Perley *papers*, vol. 5, Perley to Borden, Feb. 17, 1916; and HLRO, Beaverbrook *papers*, C/50, Aitken to Borden, Dec. 3, 1915.
2 Vince, in *CJEPS* 20 (1954), pp. 365, 362; PAC, Borden *papers*, OC183(2), pp. 14863-68, Gwatkin to DM:DMD, Jan. 1916; and PAC, Kemp *papers*, vol. 115, F10a, Christie to Kemp, Apr. 10, 1916.
3 PAC, Borden *private diaries*, Mar. 3, 9, 1916; and PAC, Perley *papers*, vol. 5, Borden to Perley, Mar. 15, 1916, private and confidential.
4 PAC, Perley *papers*, vol. 5, Borden to Perley, Mar. 14, 1916, private and confidential; and Willson, pp. 211-12.
5 Ibid., p. 162, Hughes to Kitchener, Mar. 24, 1916; and Willson, p. 227.
6 Nicholson, p. 206; and PAC, Sir David Watson *diaries*, MG 30, G 17, Apr. 4, 24, 25, 1916.
7 HLRO, Beaverbrook *papers*, E/18, F/3/6, Watson to Aitken, Mar. 26, 1916; ibid., E. General Hughes, 2, Aitken to Hughes, Mar. 3, 1916, no. 55; ibid., Aitken to Hughes, Feb. 14, 1916, no. 31; and ibid., Hughes to Aitken, Feb. 22, 1916, no. 36.
8 Ibid., WO, CRF, E/3, General Macdonough to Aitken, June 22, 1916.
9 Willson, p. 214.
10 Ibid.
11 HLRO, Beaverbrook *papers*, General Hughes, 2, Hughes to Aitken, Mar. 31, 1916, no. 64; and PAC, RG 24, HQ. 54-21-5-7, Daly to DM:DMD, Apr. 1, 1916.
12 HLRO, Beaverbrook *papers*, General Hughes, 2, Hughes to Aitken, Feb. 1, 1916, no. 23; Willson, pp. 207, 211; and Taylor, p. 89.
13 HLRO, Beaverbrook *papers*, General Hughes, 2, Hughes to Aitken, Mar. 31, 1916, no. 64.
14 PAC, Watson *diaries*, Apr. 24, 25, 1916; and HLRO, Beaverbrook *papers*, E/12, Aitken to Hughes, May 10, 1916.
15 PAC, Kemp *papers*, vol. 115, f10a, Christie to Kemp, Apr. 10, 1916; and Vince, in *CJEPS* 20 (1954), pp. 357-70.

16 PAC, Foster *diaries*, Apr. 29, 1916; CFHS, HS 990-009 (D2), Hughes to Borden, July 24, 1916; PAC, Borden *private diaries*, Apr. 3, 1916; and Nicholson, p. 207.
17 PAC, Borden *private diaries*, Mar. 22, 1916.
18 PAC, RG 7, 265, vol. 1, "Hughes Memorandum on the Connaught Quarrel," Apr. 20, 1916; ibid., "Transcript of Connaught-Borden Audience, Government House," Mar. 24, 1916; ibid., Borden to Connaught, Apr. 21, 1916; and ibid., Connaught to Borden, Apr. 18, 1916; PAC, Borden *papers*, OC322, undated, unsigned, "Memorandum on the Powers and Duties of the Governor-General of a Self-Governing Dominion"; PAC, Perley *papers*, vol. 5, p. 143, Borden to Perley, Mar. 14, 1916; PAC, Borden *private diaries*, Mar. 14, 24, 1916, and July 2, 1916; and PAC, Laurier *papers*, vol. 706, p. 19423, Woods to Laurier, Feb. 27, 1917.
19 *CAR*, 1916, p. 261; and Queen's University, Flavelle *papers*, B2, Flavelle to Rundle, June 19, 1916.
20 PAC, Borden *private diaries*, June 6, 8, 12, 1916.
21 PAC, Perley *papers*, vol. 5, p. 162, Hughes to Kitchener, Mar. 24, 1916; Nicholson, p. 92; and Willson, pp. 219-34.
22 See Nicholson, pp. 137-47, for a complete description of the battle.
23 The National Library of Scotland (NLS), *Papers* of Field Marshal Sir Douglas Haig, ACC3155, no. 104, vol. 8, diary entries, Apr. 3, 8, 1916; and ibid., Plumer to Haig, Apr. 12, 1916; and HLRO, Beaverbrook *papers*, E/12, Aitken to Hughes, Apr. 21, 1916; ibid., E/18, F/3/6, Alderson to Aitken, Apr. 25, 1916; Nicholson, pp. 80, 145; and Willson, p. 216.
24 HLRO, Beaverbrook *papers*, Aitken to Hughes, Apr. 20, 1916; ibid., Aitken to Hughes, Apr. 21, 1916; ibid., Hughes to Aitken, Apr. 21, 1916; and NLS, Haig *diaries*, Apr. 21, 1916.
25 NLS, Haig *diaries*, Apr. 21, 1916.
26 PAC, Borden *private diaries*, Apr. 26, 1916; and HLRO, Beaverbrook *papers*, E/12, Aitken to Hughes, May 20, 1916. On Byng's appointment, see Jeffery Williams, *Byng of Vimy: General and Governor-General* (London: Cooper, 1983), pp. 115-31.
27 HLRO, Beaverbrook *papers*, E 7/8, Aitken to Borden, Apr. 26, 1916; Willson, p. 216; PAC, RG 9, III, A, Carson file, 8-1-70, Hughes to Borden, Sept. 15, 1916; ibid., 8-1-122, Cubitt to C-in-C Home Forces UK, May 30, 1916; ibid., Alderson to Carson, Sept. 21, 1916; and Militia Council, *Minutes*, July 18, 1916.
28 PAC, Lessard *papers*, Hughes to Lessard, Apr. 23, 1916, cited in "Confidential Report on Troop Training for General Hughes," May 1916; Willson, p. 215; and PAC, Foster *diaries*, Apr. 29, 1916.
29 PAC, RG 9, III, A 1, Carson file, 8-1-70, War Office to Carson, May 3, 1916; ibid., CO to MMD, May 12, 1916; Militia Council, *Minutes*, May 8, 1916; and HLRO, Beaverbrook *papers*, E/16, Manly Sims to Aitken, June 30, 1916.
30 HLRO, Beaverbrook *papers*, E/16, Manly Sims to Aitken, June 18, 1916; and ibid., Manly Sims to Aitken, June 8, 1916.
31 Ibid., Manly Sims to Aitken, June 6, 1916; and PAC, Borden *papers*, OC318(1), Borden to Hughes, July 31, 1916.
32 PAC, Borden *papers*, OC318(1), Hughes to Borden, Aug. 2, 1916; ibid., Borden to Hughes, Aug. 19, 1916; PAC, Borden *private diaries*, July 18, 1916, June 22, 1916, July 1, 1916, and Aug. 23, 31, 1916; and PAC, Foster *diaries*, June 10, 1916, July 6, 1916, and Aug. 29, 1916.
33 PAC, Borden *private diaries*, Aug. 18, 19, 28, 1916.
34 Winter, pp. 165-67; and Swettenham, pp. 135-36.
35 PAC, Borden *papers*, OC318(1), clipping from the Ottawa *Journal*, Sept. 7, 1916. For details of the council see Morton, *A Peculiar Kind of Politics*, pp. 76-83; Vince, in *CHR* (Mar. 1950), pp. 1-24; PAC, RG 9, III, A 1, Carson file, Hughes to Carson, Sept. 18, 1916; and ibid., Carson to Reid, Oct. 2, 1916.
36 HLRO, Beaverbrook *papers*, E7-8, Hughes to Borden, Sept. 8, 1916, letter.
37 Vince, in *CJEPS* 20 (Aug. 1954), p. 369.
38 PAC, RG 9, III, A 1, Carson file, 8-1-106, Hughes to Greene, Sept. 20, 1916; HLRO, Beaverbrook *papers*, E7/8, Hughes to Aitken, Oct. 13, 1916; ibid., Carson to Aitken, Nov. 7, 1916; and Nicholson, pp. 208-10.

39 PAC, Borden *private diaries*, Sept. 8, 9, 12, 13, 27, 1916, and Oct. 17, 1916; PAC, Perley *papers*, vol. 6, p. 1906, Perley to Borden, Oct. 11, 1916; PAC, Kemp *papers*, vol. 157, Rowell to Borden, Sept. 18, 1916; and PAC, Borden *papers*, OC318(1), Borden to Hughes, Oct. 18, 1916.
40 PAC, Borden *papers*, OC318(1), Hughes to Borden, Oct. 23, 1916; ibid., Hughes to Borden, Oct. 26, 1916; PAC, RG 24, vol. 430, HQ. 54-21-1-64, Hughes to Governor-General, Oct. 23, 1916; and PAC, Borden *private diaries*, Oct. 19, 1916.
41 Sir Sam Hughes, "Canada's Future in the Empire," in E. A. Victor, ed., *Canada's Future* (Toronto: Macmillan, 1916), pp. 10-11.
42 HLRO, Beaverbrook *papers*, E/12, Hughes to Aitken, Oct. 21, 1916.
43 HLRO, Davidson *papers*, CO 1914-1916, Hughes file, Law to Brade, Oct. 4, 1916; ibid., Law to George, Oct. 4, 1916; and HLRO, David Lloyd George *papers*, F/29/1/6, Stamfordham to Asquith, Oct. 6, 1916.
44 HLRO, Lloyd George *papers*, cataloguer's notes; Taylor, chapters 6 and 7; HLRO, Beaverbrook *papers*, E/12, Hughes to Aitken, Oct. 21, 1916; ibid., E/18, F/3/12, Sifton to Aitken, Oct. 18, 1916; and ibid., E/12, Aitken to Hughes, Oct. 28, 1916.
45 PAC, Borden *papers*, OC218(2), Hughes to Borden, Oct. 23, 1916; and *CAR*, 1916, pp. 265-66.
46 Ibid., Hughes to Borden, Oct. 26, 1916; and PAC, RG 24, F1, HQ. 54-21-1-64, Hughes to Governor-General's Office, Oct. 23, 1916.
47 PAC, Borden *private diaries*, Oct. 27, 30, 1916.
48 PAC, Borden *papers*, OC318(2), Hughes to Borden, Oct. 23, 26, 30, 1916, and Nov. 1, 1916.
49 PAC, Foster *diaries*, Nov. 9, 1916; PAC, Perley *papers*, vol. 7, Borden to Perley, Nov. 15, 1916; PAC, A. E. Blount *papers*, MG 27, II, E 6, "Borden memoirs, annotated pages, 1916," p. 569; Brown, *Borden*, vol. 2, p. 58; and PAC, Borden *papers*, OC69, pp. 35884-85, Borden to Hughes, Nov. 9, 1916.
50 PAC, Borden *private diaries*, Nov. 11, 13, 1916; PAC, Borden *papers*, OC69, Hughes to Borden, Nov. 11, 1916; PAC, Foster *diaries*, Nov. 16, 1916; PAC, Perley *papers*, vol. 7, Borden to Perley, Nov. 3, 6, 1916. Also see Militia Council, *Minutes*, Nov. 10, 1916, which points out that control of policy was an important consideration in getting rid of Hughes; PAC, Gwatkin *papers*, Gwatkin to War Office, Dec. 20, 1916; and ibid., War Office to Gwatkin, Dec. 30, 1916. They refused to accept his resignation; *CAR*, 1916, pp. 265-66; and Borden *Memoirs*, vol. 2, p. 571.
51 MacPhail, p. 190; and CFHS, 990.009 (D2), Hughes to G. B. Hughes, Mar. 7, 1917. He called Perley and Borden weak and White "a mental epileptic" (ibid., Hughes to Borden, July 24, 1916); and Harcourt *papers*, vol. 462, Borden to Perley, Oct. 22, 1914, and Harcourt's marginalia.
52 PAC, Borden *private diaries*, Nov. 16, 1916.
53 PAC, RG 7, 265, vol. 1, Devonshire to Bonar Law, n.d., confidential; PAC, Perley *papers*, Borden to Perley, June 13, 1917; PAC, Borden *papers*, vol. 268, Borden to Macdonnell, Dec. 2, 1933; PAC, Borden *private diaries*, Nov. 14, 1916; and PAC, pamphlet, no. 4633, "Correspondience of General Sir Sam Hughes and the Right Hon. Sir Robert Borden at the time Sir Sam resigned," Liberal Information Office, 1917.
54 PAC, Borden *private diaries*, Nov. 16, 1916. On this day the Prime Minister recorded an interesting comment: "McCurdy . . . reports that Sectrys [secretaries] of ministers are still busy destroying."
55 PAC, RG 7, no. 265, vol. 1, Devonshire to Bonar Law, n.d., confidential; Winnipeg *Free Press*, Nov. 14, 1916, pp. 1, 7, 11; and ibid., Nov. 15, 1916, p. 11. Also see Calgary *Daily Herald*, Nov. 14, 1916, p. 6; *Le Soleil*, London *Times*, Nov. 15, 1916, p. 10; The *Globe*, Nov. 11, 1916, p. 10; *CAR*, 1916, pp. 254, 318, 447-49; PAC, Creelman *diaries*, Nov. 19, 1916; and PAC, Foster *diaries*, Nov. 14, 1916.

CHAPTER 16

Eclipse

Although Sir Sam Hughes was dismissed from the cabinet in 1916, he did not leave politics. He continued to sit in the House of Commons as a backbencher until his death in August 1921. When the Commons reconvened in January 1917, many people were anxious about what the disgruntled ex-Minister might have to say about his expulsion. When it came, it was nowhere near as strident as some had feared. Hughes' general, albeit reluctant, statement of support for Borden in the new session of Parliament disappointed the opposition critics. Still the ex-Minister's implied criticism of the Conservative administration was often bitter and he did not hesitate to defend his past actions.[1]

And the controversies lingered for years. But the first post-resignation one came in early 1917 when Canadians were shocked by sensational newspaper allegations about the poor treatment of wounded Canadians by the British and the Canadian Army Medical Corps (CAMC). The public did not know that Hughes had been displeased with the CAMC overseas since 1915 when its Director-General, Colonel Carleton Jones, after an urgent request from the War Office, had transferred some of the Canadian hospital units to British service in the operations at Gallipoli. At the same time the Minister had been dissatisfied that many of the Canadian casualties were being separated from Canadian jurisdiction and treated in small British Volunteer Aid Detachments (VAD) dispersed throughout the British Isles. Again it was his old nationalist hobby-horse: Hughes wanted greater Canadian control.[2]

After complaining to Borden in the spring of 1916 that the CAMC had to be reorganized, Hughes ordered a politically ambitious fellow Tory and well-known Toronto surgeon, H. A. Bruce, to make an

---

Reference notes for Chapter 16 are found on pp. 323-24.

investigation. Except for a brief earlier tour at the front where he had tangled with Carleton Jones over some missing x-ray plates, Bruce had little military experience. He wanted to make a point with the medical director and to return overseas, this time in a high position. As for Hughes, once more he was under considerable cabinet pressure to find Bruce a post in the summer of 1916. In July the doctor's willingness coincided with the Minister's desire to change things in the medical corps. In preparation for his investigation in England, Bruce became one of Sam's "colonels."[3]

By September 20, after a month's whirl-wind tour of Canadian medical services there, Colonel Bruce submitted to Hughes' Sub-Militia Council a full report on what he considered to be the corp's failings; and he scored some valid points. Among other things, he recommended sweeping reforms which centralized Canadian casualties under Dominion jurisdiction. To ensure his personal control, Hughes then replaced Carleton Jones, a long-time regular soldier, with Bruce. But when Bruce tried to carry out his changes in the fall of 1916, he had little success, partly because of his grating and aggressive personality. While his report was far better than most contemporaries wanted to admit, he caused a great deal of resentment among those in the CAMC who agreed neither with his harsh accusations nor with the Minister's heavy-handed firing of Jones. In fact the eminent surgeon Sir William Osler resigned his CAMC commission in protest and returned to Canada. It caused quite a stir; but by this time Hughes was gone from cabinet, and Sir George Perley had to face the problem. The determined yet diplomatic Sir George resolved it in less than four months. He had Sir William Baptie of the British medical services conduct an enquiry into the Bruce allegations, then he removed Bruce and temporarily reinstated Carleton Jones to rebuild the CAMC's shaken confidence. He found other employment for the smouldering Bruce and discreetly implemented many of the recommendations contained in Bruce's report. During 1917 Perley rectified much of Hughes' overseas administrative chaos in a similar fashion. He brought back from France capable corps officers whose reputations were built on merit and who were untainted by Hughes' favouritism. Between them they had the administration working smoothly by the end of the year.[4]

During this time Hughes made a number of controversial statements about the overseas medical corps. Two days before he was dismissed, he told a meeting of the Empire Club in Toronto about a general British conspiracy to take over the medical services, and about inferior medical treatment for wounded Canadian soldiers. After he and Bruce had been ousted from power, Sir Sam continued to stir up public opinion in defence of his special agent's charges. Some of his former cabinet colleagues suspected that Hughes purposefully leaked

Bruce's confidential report to the Canadian press. However, in February 1917 the Prime Minister forestalled any opposition attack on the issue by tabling all the documents together with Perley's solution. Nevertheless Hughes tried to discredit Perley's actions by spreading slurs about Sir William Baptie's competence. Some of what he said about Baptie was true and even Bruce could point out that most of his recommendations had been adopted. Such revelations caused both Perley and Borden some tender moments. Yet in the end their prompt action satisfied most Canadians that the nation's wounded sons were receiving the best possible medical services, even if some were outside national control.[5]

But the medical service was not the last subject on which the former Militia Minister tried to reassert his lost influence. In June 1917 Arthur Currie succeeded General Byng as commander of the Canadian Corps. Currie was the first Canadian to reach such an exalted operational command. In supporting the appointment, Perley and Borden suggested that Currie give Garnet Hughes, then commanding the Fifth Division in England, a division at the front, hoping perhaps that it would keep Sir Sam quiet. Currie again refused to have the young Hughes under his command, rightly claiming that there were more experienced and capable commanders available. There was strong opposition, but in spite of it Currie remained firm. Hughes wanted Garnet to have a senior field command. Sir Sam also had supported the claim of his old friend, Sir Richard Turner, to Currie's new post. Hughes' dream of a Canadian army of two corps, each with three divisions, was opposed by Currie because of the limitations of manpower and experienced officers, among other things. Since Currie was the impediment to Sir Sam's hopes in all three cases, a further controversy between the two seemed inevitable.[6]

Concurrent with the events surrounding Currie's command overseas was the domestic issue of conscription. In May 1917, after much hesitation, Sir Robert Borden decided that compulsory military service must come if victory was to be achieved. But Laurier was opposed and refused to join a coalition government dedicated to conscription without a national plebiscite on the issue. Nevertheless, aided by the Military Service Act and the Wartime Voters Act, the Prime Minister formed a coalition with some dissident conscriptionist Liberals. Then he called an election on conscription for December 1917. Publicly Sir Sam Hughes had favoured compulsory military service for some months. In fact he was so dissatisfied with Borden's hesitations on the issue before May that he attempted to start a third party that month. Presumably as its head he would impose some sort of compulsory service. After Sir Clifford Sifton and others refused their support, Sir Sam abandoned the project.[7]

In spite of getting nowhere with his new party, Hughes did continue to support compulsory service. Although he preferred the enforcement of the compulsion clauses in the Militia Act, Sir Sam backed conscription throughout 1917. Where he differed sharply with Borden was on the idea of a union government. Convinced that the Conservative administration could win an election on its past performance if coupled with a pledge to introduce conscription, Hughes predicted to Borden that a coalition would destroy the Conservative Party. His position was not unexpected. As an old-line Tory, he had resisted other changes that risked political success and his view of what party norms should be. When the federal election was called for December, Hughes ran in his own riding as a Conservative conscriptionist. But as the local campaign progressed, the unionists in Victoria-Haliburton promoted a different conscriptionist candidate. The possibility could have been disastrous for Hughes' re-election because it would have split the vote and forced the conscriptionist electors to choose between the Tory Hughes and a union conscriptionist who had the federal government's endorsement. However, three weeks before the election Sir Sam prevented the emergence of a union candidate by abruptly becoming one himself. Borden had little choice but to endorse Hughes' move and his victory was assured. After conducting a campaign which included accusations about poor French-Canadian military efforts and charges of the influence of "German gold" in Laurier's campaign, Hughes won his last election contest with the largest majority ever.[8]

Perhaps the most irresponsible and petty episode of Sir Sam's career was his charge of cowardice and murder against Lieutenant-General Sir Arthur Currie in 1919. Although the roots of the accusations can be traced to Currie's performance in the second battle of Ypres in 1915, which also involved Garnet Hughes and Richard Turner, Hughes launched his strongest attack in 1919. First in March and then in September, Sir Sam told a stunned Commons that Currie purposely had allowed thousands of Canadian soldiers to be killed in needless attacks on unimportant objectives. Ultimately Hughes charged that Currie had doomed many Canadians by ordering an attack on Mons on November 10 and 11, 1918, even though he knew the Armistice would take effect within hours. In these rambling speeches Hughes also devoted much time to defending his administration and talking about the British discrimination against Canadian men and equipment. During all such Hughes' diatribes, Currie kept a public silence, refusing to become involved in a "mud-slinging contest with the such as he." The viciousness and falseness of Sir Sam's charges are obvious. But his claims, partially supported by the absence of a clear government defence of Currie, continued to plague the corps commander long after Hughes' death. Ultimately they led to a show trial in

Cobourg in 1928 where Currie's smeared reputation was finally and absolutely cleared.[9]

What caused the former Militia Minister to make such outrageous claims? During the war when men like Currie opposed Hughes, the Minister created fantasies about conspiracies against him or about their incompetency impeding the war effort. Perhaps by 1919 these machinations were compounded by failing health, by bitterness over his son's and Sir Richard Turner's appointments, by his loss of power and his dismissal, and by Currie's success as commander of the Canadian Corps. Above all Currie may have represented the triumph of military professionalism which Sir Sam could not understand.

Little time remained to Sir Sam Hughes after his accusations against Currie. His health declined rapidly during 1920, although Winter thought it was obvious soon after he had lost the militia portfolio. The doctors pronounced Hughes anaemic. When visitors came to see him after 1919 they found him often "pale, listless and emaciated." Several times he had to have blood transfusions, but they did little good and the blood poisoning continued to take its toll. His appearances in the Commons were progressively less frequent. Finally in the late autumn 1920, he was bed-ridden but remained in his Ottawa residence until Parliament dissolved the next summer, when he returned to Lindsay. He died on August 24, 1921.[10]

The military funeral was the final episode in one of the most dynamic and controversial careers in Canada. Historically, the most important years of Sam Hughes' life were those in the war ministry, but the formative ones—those that laid the basis of his successes and failures—were the years in local politics and militia circles.

Sam Hughes' greatest success was in politics. Above all else he was a very potent constituency politician, with a string of seven consecutive local election victories. He sat for thirty unbroken years in the House of Commons. There were few more exhilarating experiences for him than the rough and tumble world of riding battles—and few were better at it. His wit, charm, forthright manner, and hard work were combined with a clear talent for the more direct forms of organization and for personal leadership. Hughes was also keenly competitive and had a knack for exploiting the public mood to get votes. These instincts pushed him more and more into influential party circles. At the same time he was able to use his increasing clout to support his militia activities.

Sam Hughes was a very ambitious man, so he also learned that to advance publicly he had to check some of his pet ideas. Consequently he became a reluctant moderate over the Jesuits Estates question and the Manitoba schools issue. In turn he earned the party reputation as a good team player concerned about national unity. After 1901 sustained loyalty to Robert Borden's fragile leadership more than anything else attached Sam Hughes to a cabinet post and kept him there until 1916. Elsewhere in the party, especially during the long lean years in opposition, Hughes consolidated his position because he was an experienced veteran who knew how to use Parliament and the prevailing patronage system. Even though Borden did not agree with the traditional patronage devices in politics, most of his parliamentary colleagues, including Sam Hughes, did; and powerful men, like Price, Lougheed, Rogers, Reid, and even Kemp supported him because of it. When the new Prime Minister selected his first cabinet in 1911, Hughes was an obvious choice because he represented a talented, loyal, and conventional old-line Tory from Ontario, the province from which Borden had to choose many of his ministers. Yet Hughes had an urbanity, a national outlook, and a progressive streak that many of his colleagues lacked. On one hand, Hughes' loyalty, experience, and wider view gave the new government strength; on the other, his deep-rooted political methods contributed to the rejection of reformist and French-Canadian elements within the coalition, which had given the party a victory in 1911.

In order to rally Canadians to the fight during the Great War, Hughes invoked the traditional rules which he knew so well and which had been valid at other times. But by 1916 in the face of huge sacrifices, Canadians would no longer tolerate the wasteful excesses of the Minister's volunteerism and partisanship. Other ministers in Borden's cabinet moved with the changing conditions; Hughes did not. And so he was ruined by the war itself.

But during all of his thirty years of parliamentary activity Hughes was more than just a successful politician; he was a militia politician. The key to understanding this phenomenon lies in Hughes' idealization of the militia itself. Hughes probably would never have foresaken a political career for a military one. But as a politician, he was well aware of the advantage of militia service. However, he was genuinely committed to the belief that the defence of Canada could best be served by the volunteer efforts of individuals whose main preoccupation was the ordinary business of living, but who also accepted as a social obligation volunteer, part-time military training. In addition, for Hughes military training also built character and thereby prevented moral decline in society; and to him only citizen-soldiers had sufficient investment in the country through their civil vocation to guarantee that they would act in the nation's best interest.

On his way to power and while he held it, Sam Hughes' constant publicizing of his military ideas made him a leading spokesman of a school of thought which preached the merits of the citizen-soldier. He became the self-appointed leader of a group of militia enthusiasts who were convinced that the militiaman could probably teach the regular soldier, whether Canadians or British, a thing or two. He fed on the myth that part-time soldiers were the real backbone of Canadian defence during the War of 1812; and to it he could personally add the Fenian Raids, the North-West Campaign, and above all the Boer war. The militia, he felt, should be liberated from meaningless routine, red tape, and out-dated disciplines associated with regulars. This concept flattered his and others' growing sense of national pride, and helped confirm the rightness and righteousness of their ideas.

Fortunately, a contrary philosophy of the militia emanated from others such as William Dillon Otter. His early battle experiences as a militiaman had clearly pointed out the necessity of achieving a hard core of professionalism through routine, discipline, and subordination. Otter also felt that when a man became a soldier he "parts for a time with the privilege of citizenship, having no will of his own, no liberty of action, [and] no unrestrained freedom of speech... for obedience and self-control are indispensable to his duties...." No doubt Sir Arthur Currie also held Otter's views.[11]

Through the early decades of this century, the two concepts continued to be debated until well after both Hughes and Otter passed from the scene. Following the South African War and the First World War, Hughes' viewpoint seemed commendable to a great many who were anxious to dismantle the army and lower defence expenditure. But in the last analysis, the same wars also overtook the validity of Hughes' ideas. Ultimately they proved that the inherent virtues of a militiaman became valuable only after he had acquired the tough substance and training of the professional soldier. These were the qualities which Sam Hughes despised because he failed to understand them.

By 1911 Hughes had brought most of his ideas into the Militia Ministry. Certainly he helped reduce the apathy of many Canadians to the armed service. He did expand the militia in numbers, and by 1914 there is no doubt that Canada was better able to fight than it had ever been. In addition, he continued the nationalization process that had been going on for some years, by bringing more of the part-time soldiers into the higher levels.

However, Sam Hughes' near blind faith in a citizen militia was dangerous for the country's regular soldiers. Yet it is doubtful that he could have ever destroyed the Permanent Force. Countervailing military trends were too strong for that. But he did impede the force's growth and efficiency. In this process, he had equally strong supporters and critics. Yet few contemporaries, not even Sir Ian Hamilton, were able to grasp a complete view of the basic contradiction of his militia policy; perhaps it was so because only retrospective sight through four years of bloody war could clearly discern that an erosion of the professional force would equally rob Sam Hughes' militia dream of its life-giving fibre and substance. Whatever the case, with his continued ministerial discrimination, and his confusion of professionalism with red tape, the regulars steadily lost ground as teachers and leaders.

Throughout most of his career, Sam Hughes was never in a position to affect the nation profoundly. But the First World War amplified his power, and his position became central to the successful pursuance of the conflict. During the war's early days Hughes received credit for more success than he deserved. Afterwards he found it nearly impossible to accept that his methods could be wrong. Moreover, in visualizing a huge volunteer army of citizen-soldiers, Sir Sam did not allow for considerations such as planning, the bicultural political relations of the Dominion or of collective cabinet responsibility—or, most importantly, of fighting by other means than combat. So long as spirit and manpower were in abundance and the sophisticated needs few, the Minister's military concepts and administrative improvisations sufficed. In the end, however, his regime collapsed before the demands of total war.

Hughes' conception of the citizen-soldier is central to an understanding of his career. It may even add a new dimension to the man's historical image, an image which to date has come mostly from those who have concentrated on his remarkable personality. A less subjective response to the man emerges when one looks at his view of the citizen-soldier as he attempted to relate this to his own political life. In combining in politics the responsible citizen role with that of the soldier, Hughes joined two ideas which, although very attractive on the surface, are antithetical in a democracy. The former emphasizes individual responsibility, promotes freedom of action and speech; the latter demands discipline and subordination to a clearly structured system of authority. As a politician, Hughes often seemed a kind of North American democrat; as a militia officer, he often took on the role of an autocratic soldier. But this paradoxical union did not seem inconsistent to Sam Hughes. On one hand, it allowed him to function as a democratic citizen and take independent action; on the other, it let him be a militia officer and function authoritatively as a soldier with the full weight of the military structure behind him. Indeed, the combination afforded him a substantial field of operation. Undoubtedly, the mixture seemed quite plausible to Hughes because he was never a man to explore the full ramifications of his ideas, and because it had strong historical roots within the North American militia tradition.

Once Hughes got cabinet power, this symbiotic combination gained a new potency. In his peacetime ministry, he managed to sustain the appearance of success largely because the militia portfolio was not of vital national concern and few outside the militia took it seriously. Consequently, the paradoxical and sometimes confusing actions of the Militia Minister generally were ignored by others, while Hughes himself rationalized them in the light of his understanding of the civil, military, and moral responsibilities of the soldier-politician as derived from the citizen-soldier.

During the war, however, it became increasingly apparent that, as Sir Sam tried to play the role of the soldier-politician in the context of a national and international crisis, the combination did not work. His decisions and actions were often quite inconsistent on critical matters. They aggravated civil-military relations to an almost unprecedented degree, and caused confusion and embarrassment that impeded departmental administration and military development. Some of Hughes' major achievements, such as the establishment of the Canadian war industries, were certainly diminished. Moreover, the effects of his personality traits—vanity, love of power, inflexibility, and a propensity for improvisation, among others—added to the chaotic effects of Hughes' inherently faulty concept. Nevertheless, Hughes continued to believe in it to the point where it became a source of blind inspiration. It shaped his actions and gave strength to his resolve and commitment.

But what about Sam Hughes' strengths? Of his admirers, a great many considered that he bordered on genius. They were wrong, but he did have obvious merits. His drive and energy, his political success, his constant defence of education as a form of social improvement, and his faith in the country were some of them. So too were his military reform instincts, however extreme their implementation. In the last two decades of the nineteenth century, he was a constant battler to improve the force. In the Boer war, he spotted—and fatefully criticized—archaic British practices so that his voice contributed to the growing crescendo demanding change; once in office he made his policy clear then carried it out. During the Great War, still profoundly influenced by his earlier South African experiences, he was in the vanguard of criticism of English practices and the struggle for national recognition. Indeed, in both the conflicts, what had appeared to many to be typically erratic Hughes' generalizations, proved true, if overstated, and ultimately his growing dissatisfaction became a caricature of the country's view of things.

But these talents, whether expressed in military or political ways, were special and limited. They are best described in military terms as being of the tactical type; he was tough and could inspire, yet he could never raise himself beyond the level of a battalion commander on independent service. In politics it was much the same. For years, these gifts brought him success in the battalions and the brigades, in the ridings and the associations, and even as an MP and as a minister. But the Great War demanded more than his limited capabilities could give. By early 1916, he realized they were not working and he frantically scrambled doing the things which he had always done to rectify the problems. But by then it took more than his tactical and special skills, so he had to go. Since he would not give up because he had never given up, only a long and painful political excision could do it.

Inseparable from Hughes' military and political ideas were his views of Canada and the Empire. Although he sounded like an imperialist and accepted the title proudly, Sir Sam's stand was essentially nationalistic as his controversy with Hutton would indicate. However, part of the trouble with his imperial notion, like all of his visions, was that it was not entirely clear. Whether he realized it or not, this presented a real dilemma throughout his career. He wanted closer military, political, and economic co-operation with Great Britain so that Canada might influence imperial policy and share imperial glory. Yet he objected to traditional British leadership. As in the wars in 1899 and 1914, Hughes' over-willingness to aid Britain ultimately posed the question of Canadian control which in itself should have tempered his response. As a result, he was always a source of amazement and chagrin to nationalists and traditional imperialists alike who mistook him to be a kindred spirit.

In spite of some of the vagaries in Hughes' thinking, he had a strong sense of nationality based on both the appreciation of Canada's history and national character and a belief in its future. A conviction that Canada could and would escape from colonialism and play an important role in the Empire were major precepts in his dream of the nation as an equal partner with Great Britain. Ultimately Sir Sam's design was left behind by men like Sir Robert Borden. However, there can be little doubt that his promotion of it contributed to a growing sense of Canadian maturity which may have helped other men to seek a more autonomous path.

Finally, Sam Hughes has been persistently traduced as a chronically wrong-headed character. A number of observers have gone so far as to question his sanity. Yet the evidence denies that claim.

Obviously Hughes was never a disinterested player in the demanding game of military politics. He was prone to eccentricity, conceit, and exaggeration born of a single-minded devotion to a limited stock of powerful guiding principles. This myopia was married to an aggressive and abrasive manner that often irritated more than it converted. Such a personality operating from a limited base did not make for easy relationships or commonly shared viewpoints. For Hughes' opponents, the normative was missing in his actions and assessments: hence their sense of estrangement and anger and their tendency to over-react when faced with this formidable phenomenon.

And Hughes was formidable. During a crisis, this side of his character was all the more striking because it showed up in long periods of calm, routine behaviour which sometimes was inspired and occasionally bordered on the brilliant.

Certainly at the height of the Great War, there were increasingly more frequent times when his extreme actions appeared to those who had already felt his sting to be the product of a demented mind. However, these incidents were more likely the contortions of a man in over his head who did not know what to do. And there were others in Borden's cabinet who did not meet the mark. Besides, the conflict was terrifying for all. In a later war, to name just one, an Australian prime minister would be so frightened that he would take to his bed for days on end while a hard-nosed, abrasive, and volcanic external affairs minister ran the country. In Sam Hughes' case, he struck out at those around him because, as a desperate fighter losing power, he would not admit that his peculiar brand of leadership was no longer effective. This fact and an appalling war had concentrated his idiosyncrasies.

After 1918 Hughes was physically ill, in part because of exhaustion, age, and even disappointment at his rejection. But his diagnosed and lethal "pernicious anaemia" may have ravaged his mind as well as his body and thereby spawned his public meanness to Currie in the last years of his life. However, to account for Sam Hughes before this time as being anything but sane simply cannot be substantiated. To do so would be to proffer a simplistic and convenient explanation for an always complicated and individualistic personality.

Reference Notes to Chapter 16

1 *Hansard*, 1917, pp. 225-27, 254-55; and ibid., 1919, p. 624. His first major speech to the House was on Jan. 30, 1917 (*Hansard*, 1919, pp. 254-68); it contained no startling charges.
2 Nicholson, pp. 497-98; and MacPhail, p. 189. This is clear in Hughes' report to Borden charging serious inefficiency in the CAMC. See PAC, Perley *papers*, vol. 6, Hughes to Borden, Sept. 2, 1916. Hughes also told Borden that he had to reorganize the CAMC because, among other things, "our officers... will persist in pursuing what they call the "regular army system" instead of business methods." An interesting memo by MacPhail exists in PAC, Meighen *papers*, vol. 114, pp. 66969-74 in which Sir Andrew in 1926 defends himself against serious charges by Conservatives that his condemnations in the official history of the medical services of Hughes' war administration were the result of his prejudices against Sir Sam.
3 Morgan, *1912*, p. 161; and PAC, Kemp *papers*, vol. 104, Bruce to Hughes, May 25, 1916, June 21, 1916, and July 3, 1916. See ibid., Lougheed to Hughes, July 15, 1915, and Hughes to Bruce, July 31, 1916.
4 *Militia List*, Sept. 1914, p. 6; PAC, Kemp *papers*, vol. 104, Carson to Jones, Oct. 13, 1916; ibid., Reid to Bruce, Aug. 27, 1916; and MacPhail, pp. 168-213. Also see Morton, *Canada and War*, p. 68, and especially his *A Peculiar Kind of Politics*, pp. 86-87, 103-105 on Bruce.

5 *CAR*, 1916, pp. 265-66 (speech to the Empire Club, Nov. 14, 1916); also see ibid., pp. 455-58; *Hansard*, 1917, pp. 201-202, 264, 537-48, 601-602, 3845; and PAC, Kemp *papers*, vol. 104, Perley to Borden, Nov. 7, 1916, confidential. *CAR*, 1917, pp. 516-17. In 1919, H. A. Bruce published his personal version of the controversy. See H. A. Bruce, *Politics and the Canadian Army Medical Corps* (Toronto: William Briggs, 1919). MacPhail's official history six years later labelled Bruce's publication as private grievances of "no public concern," MacPhail, p. 202. PAC, Kemp *papers*, vols. 103-104, among others, hold the documents of the entire CAMC controversy.
6 PAC, Perley *papers*, Borden to Perley, June 13, 1917; and A. M. J. Hyatt, "Sir Arthur Currie and Conscription: A Soldier's View," in *Canadian Historical Review* 50, no. 3 (Sept. 1969), pp. 285-96. Also see Urquhart, pp. 118-20, 163-65; CFHS, HS. 990-009 (D2), Hughes to G. B. Hughes, Mar. 7, 1917; Eyre, pp. 141-42; and Swettenham, pp. 147, 170-73, 239-40, which discuss the details surrounding Currie's appointment.
7 PAC, Borden *papers*, OC(318), Hughes to Borden, Oct. 23, 1916; and *Hansard*, 1917, p. 270. PAC, Laurier *papers*, pp. 193521-22, Aylesworth to Laurier, May 10, 1917. In May 1917, Hughes presented a motion in Parliament that compulsion should be employed. Also see Macdonald, pp. 323-25.
8 *CAR*, 1917, pp. 313-14, 337; *Militia Act*, 1904, paragraphs 11-12; PAC, Borden *papers*, OC(363), Hughes to Borden, July 27, 1917; *Watchman-Warder*, Nov. 1, 1917, p. 1; and the Lindsay *Post*, Nov. 9, 1917, p. 1. For a narrative of Hughes' 1917 campaign in Victoria-Haliburton, see R. G. Haycock, "The 1917 Federal Election in Victoria-Haliburton: A Case Study," in *Ontario History* 67, no. 2 (June 1975), pp. 105-18.
9 After the battle of Ypres in 1915, Hughes had confused A. W. Currie with J. A. Currie, a Conservative MP (Simcoe North) who commanded the 16th Battalion. Hughes attacked J. A. Currie in the Commons. By 1917, he reversed himself and defended J. A. Currie and then attacked A. W. Currie. See Swettenham, pp. 8, 11, 88 (on the charges); and Morgan, *1912*, p. 289 (on J. A. Currie). *Hansard*, 1919, pp. 195-215, 624-42. Also ibid., 1920, pp. 3647-56. See PAC, Sir A. W. Currie *papers*, MG30, G25, vol. 5, Currie to Parkinson, June 15, 1920. Swettenham, pp. 1-20, tells the story of Currie's trial at Cobourg, Ontario, in 1928. Major-General Milton Gregg reported that, when he returned to Canada in 1919, he met Hughes and some of his "cronies" in the lobby of the Chateau Laurier in Ottawa. Hughes hailed Gregg and asked him to tell "these men how Currie murdered men around Mons when he knew the armistice was coming." Gregg stated he was not in the habit of gossiping about his superior officers and walked away. Gregg also testified in Currie's defence at the Cobourg trial. Personal interview with Major-General Milton F. Gregg, Major John Hasek on behalf of the author, Feb. 11, 1976.
10 PAC, Borden *private diaries*, Mar. 9, 1916; Winter, pp. 171-74; Capon, *The Incredible Sam Hughes*, pp. 13-18; and Winter, pp. 171-77.
11 Morton, *The Canadian General*, pp. 80-81; and W. D. Otter, *The Guide: A Manual for the Canadian Militia* (Toronto: Copp Clark, 1914), p. 8.

Bibliography

Primary Sources

Government Sources

Canada

Department of Corporate and Consumers Affairs, Patent Office, patent no. 51024, 26 Sept. 1889.

Department of External Affairs. *Documents on Canada's External Relations 1909-1918.* Vol. 1. Ottawa: Queen's Printer, 1967.

Department of Militia and Defence. *King's Regulations and Orders for the Canadian Militia,* 1910. Ottawa: King's Printer, 1910.

Department of Militia and Defence. *The Militia Lists of the Dominion of Canada, 1875-1920.*

Department of the Secretary of State. *Copies of Proclamations, Orders-in-Council and Documents relating to the European War.* King's Printer, 1915 and 1917.

House of Commons. *Debates,* 1892-1920.

⎯⎯⎯. *Journals,* 1904-1917.

⎯⎯⎯. *Journals.* "Proceedings and Evidence of the Special Committee on Boot Inquiry," in *Journals of the House of Commons,* 1915, pt. III. Ottawa: King's Printer, 1915.

⎯⎯⎯. *Journals.* "Report of the Public Accounts Committee Respecting Payment of $354,091.84 to the Ross Rifle Co.," in *Journals of the House of Commons,* 1906-1907, appendix I. Ottawa: King's Printer, 1907.

Senate. *Debates,* 1916.

Parliamentary Sessional Papers, 1900, no. 77, "Copies of all correspondence, telegrams, and cablegrams that may have been passed between Major-General Hutton and Lieut.-Col. Samuel Hughes, M.P., or between these officers and any member of the Government of Canada, or others, touching the conduct of Lieut.-Col. Hughes, M.P. in connection with his volunteering for active service in South Africa...."

⎯⎯⎯. 1911, no. 35b, "Report Upon the Best Method of Giving Effect to the Recommendations of General Sir John French, G.C.B., G.C.V.O., Regarding the Canadian Militia," by Major-General Sir P. N. Lake, K.C.M.G., C.B.

⎯⎯⎯. 1911, no. 208d, "Report of a Committee of the Imperial Conference Convened to Discuss Defence (Military) at the War Office."

———. 1913, no. 35G, "Notes on British and French Manoeuvres, 1912."
———. 1913, no. 57a, "Report on the Organization of the Public Service of Canada," by Sir George Murray.
———. 1916, no. 231, "Memorandum No. 2 Respecting the Work of the Department of Militia and Defence—European War, 1914-1915, From 1st February, 1915 to 31 January, 1916."
———. 1916, no. 276, "Return for a Copy of all Letters, Telegrams, Offers, Tenders, Reports, Contracts and Documents Relating to the Sale of Small Arms Ammunition Since 4th August, 1914."
———. 1917, no. 44, "Correspondence Relating to the Withdrawal of the Ross Rifle from the Canadian Army Corps."
———. Auditor-General. *Reports.* 1910-1914.
———. *The Annual Reports of the Department of Militia and Defence,* 1898-1916.
Public Accounts Committee, 1915. *Evidence.* Ottawa: King's Printer, 1915.
Royal Commission on the Sale of Small Arms Ammunition. *Report.* Sir Charles Davidson, Commissioner. Ottawa: King's Printer, 1917.
Royal Commission on Shell Contracts. *Report.* Sir William Meredith and Lyman Duff, Commissioners. Ottawa: King's Printer, 1916.
Statutes of Canada. 1905. "An Act Respecting Militia and Defence of Canada," chapter 24. 4 Edward VII.
———. 1912. "An Act to Amend the Militia Act," chapter 32. 2 Geo. V.

Great Britain

Parliament. House of Commons. *Correspondence Relating to the use of the Ross Rifle by the Canadian Forces in France.* Cd. 8429, 1916.
Parliamentary Debates (Commons), 5th series (1915, 1916).

Personal Papers and Records

Canada

Directorate of History, National Defence Headquarters, Ottawa

Historical Section. HS. 990-009, D2, Beaverbrook to G. B. Hughes, 27 Jan. 1937; Sam Hughes to R. L. Borden, 24 July 1916; and Sam Hughes to G. B. Hughes, 7 Mar. 1917.
———. HS. 500.009(D.29). The Militia Conference: 1911. Transcripts: the Minister's copy.
———. Edwin Pye. *Papers.*
———. *Canadian War Records.* Vol. 1: *A Narrative of the Formation and Operations of the First Canadian Division, to the End of the Second Battle of Ypres, May 4, 1915.* Ottawa: Historical Section, General Staff, King's Printer, 1920.

Public Archives of Canada, Ottawa

Aitken, William Maxwell. *Papers.* MG27, II, G1. Also some extracts taken from the Lord Beaverbrook *Papers* by Dr. A. M. J. Hyatt, University of Western Ontario, London, Ontario.
Bassett, John. *Papers.* MG30, E302.
Blount, A. E. *Papers.* MG27, II, E6.
Bonar Law, Andrew. *Papers.* MG27, A1.
Boyd, Mossom. *Papers.* MG28, III, I.

Borden, Sir Robert Laird. *Papers.* MG26.
———. *Private diaries*, 1913-1916.
Bowell, Mackenzie. *Papers.* MG26, E.
Caron, Sir Adolphe-Phillipe. *Papers.* MG27, I, D3.
Charter of Incorporation, Hughes to Ventilator Car Company, 1894. RG68, Liber 132, folios 432, 433, 434.
Christie, Loring. *Papers.* MG30, E15.
Cotton, W. H. *Papers.* MG29, E79.
Currie, Sir A. W. *Papers.* MG30, G25.
Creelman, J. J. *Diaries.* MG30, G34.
Daly, Harold Mayne. *Papers.* MG27, III, F9.
Denison, G. T. *Papers.* MG29, E29.
Department of Militia and Defence. RG9.
Department of National Defence. RG24.
Dominion of Canada Rifle Association. MG28, I, 243.
Foster, Sir George. *Diaries.* MG27, II, D7.
Governors-General. *Numbered Files.* RG7, G21.
Griesbach, Major-General W. A. *Papers.* MG30, E15.
Gwatkin, W. G. *Papers.* MG30, G13.
Herbert, Ivor John Caradoc. *Papers.* MG29, E61.
Home Bank of Canada. *Papers.* MG28, II, 11.
Grey of Howick, Lord. *Papers.* MG27, II, B2.
Hutton, Sir E. T. H. *Papers.* MG21, G3.
Kemp, Sir Edward. *Papers.* MG27, II, D9.
Laurier, Sir Wilfrid. *Papers.* MG26.
Lessard, F. L. *Papers.* MG30, G47.
Macdonald, Sir John A. *Papers.* MG26, A.
McCarthy, Dalton. *Papers.* MG27, 1E7.
Meighen, Arthur. *Papers.* MG26, I.
Minutes of the Militia Council, 1910-1913 and 1916. RG9, II, A2.
Minto, Earl of. *Papers.* MG27, II, B1.
Otter, W. D. *Papers.* MG30, G14.
Perley, Sir George. *Papers.* MG27, II, D12.
Pope, Sir Joseph. *Papers.* MG30, E86.
Porteus, Charles E. L. *Papers.* MG29, A32.
Ross, Sir Charles. *Papers.* MG30, A95.
Scott, Richard. *Papers.* MG27, D14.
Sifton, Sir Clifford. *Papers.* MG27, II, D15.
Smith, Henry H. *Papers.* MG27, I, 19.
Standing Committee on Small Arms. RG24, A.
Strathcona, Lord. *Papers.* MG29, D14.
Thompson, Sir John. *Papers.* MG26, D.
Tupper, Sir Charles. *Papers.* MG26, F.
Turner, R. E. W. *Papers*, MG30, G20.
Watson, Sir David. *Diaries*, 1914-1919. MG30, G17.
White, Sir Thomas. *Papers.* MG30, D18.
Willison, J. S. *Papers.* MG30, D14.

Public Archives of British Columbia
McBride, Sir Richard. *Papers.* Add. MSS, 347.

Public Archives of Ontario, Toronto
Bristol, Edmund. *Papers.*
Whitney, Sir James Pliny. *Papers.*
Wallace Family *Papers.*
Willison, John. *Papers.*
Belcher, A. E. *Papers.*
Jennings, C. A. C. *Papers.*
PAO Scrapbook collections. No. MS417 and 82.
PAO Miscellaneous collection. MU2126.

Public Archives of Nova Scotia, Halifax
Borden, Sir Frederick W. *Papers.*

Queen's University, Douglas Library, Kingston
Dundonald, Lord. *Papers* (microfilm).
Flavelle, Joseph Wesley. *Papers.* C25.

University of British Columbia, Special Collections Library, Vancouver
Tupper, Sir Charles Hibbert. *Papers.*

Wentworth County Historical Society Museum, Dundas, Ontario
Bertram Family. *Papers.*

Diary of Ena MacAdam Macdonald, Mar.-Apr. 1916 in the possession of her niece Mrs. Lois Hope, Ottawa. The spelling of the family name was changed, as McAdam said, after the Irish troubles in 1916.

Great Britain

British Museum, London
Hutton, Sir Edward. *Memoirs.* Extracts in the files of Dr. Carman Miller, McGill University.

Colonial Office, London
Copies of letters relating to Sir Sam Hughes in the files of Dr. Carman Miller, McGill University. 42(874), 42(819), 42(880), 32(895).

The House of Lords Record Office, Westminster
Beaverbrook, Lord. *Papers* (BBK).
Bonar Law, Andrew. *Papers.*
Davidson Family. *Papers.*
Lloyd George, David. *Papers.*

National Army Museum, Chelsea
Roberts, Field-Marshal Lord. *Papers.*

The National Library of Scotland, Edinburgh
Haig, Field-Marshal Sir Douglas. *Papers.* ACC3155.

National Registry of Archives, Chancery Lane
Historical Manuscripts Division, catalogues.

Oxford University
Bodleian Library
Asquith, Lord. *Papers.*
Curtis, Lionel. *Papers.*
Harcourt, First Viscount. *Papers.*
Milner, Lord. *Papers.*

Nuffield College
The Mottistone *Papers.*

Public Records Office, London
Balfour, Lord. *Papers.* PRO 30/60.
Buller, Sir Redvers. *Papers.* WO132.
Colonial Office files.
Foreign Office files.
Kitchener, Lord. *Papers.* PRO 30/57/56.
Milner, Lord. *Papers.* PRO 30/30.
Ministry of Munitions. MUN5.
Roberts of Khandahar. *Papers.* WO105.
War Office files.

Amery Family Archives, London
Amery, L. S. *Papers.*

Republic of South Africa
The National Library, Capetown
The Cape *Times* and the Cape *Argus*, 1899-1900.

Pamphlets and Reports

PAC no. 2565. "Correspondence touching on the Conduct of Lieut.-Col. Hughes, M.P., in connection with his volunteering for active service in South Africa."

PAC no. 3625. "Report on the Best Methods of Effecting Sir John French's Militia Recommendations by Maj.-Gen. Sir P. H. N. Lake, Insp.-Gen." 1910.

PAC no. 4628. "War Scandals of the Borden Government as told in the House of Commons and sworn to before the Public Accounts and Other Committees." 1917.

PAC no. 4629. "An Administration of Extravagance in Patronage." 1917.

PAC no. 4630. "Shell and Fuse Scandals." No. 49, 1917.

PAC no. 4633. "Correspondence of General Sir Sam Hughes and R. L. Borden at Hughes' Resignation." No. 52, 1917.

PAC no. 4034. "Report on the Military Institutions of Canada by General Sir Ian Hamilton G.C.B., D.S.O." 1913.

Memoirs and Contemporary Accounts

Aitken, Sir Maxwell. *Canada in Flanders.* Vols. 1 and 2. London: Hodder and Stoughton, 1916, 1917.
Amery, L. S. *My Political Life.* Vol. 1. London: Hutchinson, 1953.
Asselin, Olivar. *Pourquoi je m'enrôle.* Montreal, 1916.
Beaverbrook, Lord. *Men in Power, 1917-1918.* London: Hutchinson, 1956.
———. *Politicians and the War, 1914-1916.* London: Butterworth, 1928.
Borden, Sir Robert Laird. "Canada and the Great War," in J. Castell Hopkins, ed., *Empire Club Speeches, 1914-1915.* Toronto: J. M. Dent, 1915.
———. *Robert Laird Borden: His Memoirs.* Vols. 1 and 2. Ed. by Henry Borden. Toronto: Macmillan, 1938.
Bowman, Charles A. *Ottawa Editor.* Sidney: Grasy's, 1966.
Bridge, James Howard. *Millionaires and Grub Street.* New York: Brentano's, 1931.
Bridle, Augustus. *Sons of Canada.* Toronto: J. M. Dent, 1916.
Bruce, Dr. H. A. *Politics and the Canadian Army Medical Corps.* Toronto: Macmillan, 1919.
Capon, Alan R. (Picton, Ontario). Personal files on Sam Hughes.
Carnegie, David. *The History of Munitions Supply in Canada, 1914-1918.* London: Macmillan, 1925.
Charlesworth, Hector. *More Candid Chronicles.* Toronto: Macmillan, 1928.
Cosgrove, Lt.-Col. L. Moore, D.S.O. *Afterthoughts of Armageddon: The Gamut of Emotions Produced by the War, Pointing to a Moral That Is Not Too Obvious.* S. B. Gundy, 1919.
Critchley, A. C. *Critch: The Memoirs of Brig.-Gen. A. C. Critchley.* Toronto: Nelson, Foster, and Scott, 1962.
Currie, J. A. *The Red Watch.* Toronto: McClelland and Stewart, 1916.
Domino. *The Masques of Ottawa.* Toronto: Macmillan, 1921.
Dundonald, Earl of. *My Army Life.* London: Edward Arnold, 1926.
Flick, Lt.-Col. C. L. *Just What Happened.* London: Privately printed, 1917.
Ford, Arthur R. *As The World Wags On.* Toronto: Ryerson, 1950.
Fuller, J. F. C. *The Last of the Gentlemen's Wars.* London: Faber and Faber, 1937.
Griesbach, Maj.-Gen. W. A. *I Remember.* Toronto: Ryerson Press, 1946.
Gwynn, Stephen, ed. *The Anvil of War: Letters Between F. S. Oliver and his Brother, 1914-1918.* London: Macmillan, 1936.
Hankey, Lord. *The Supreme Command.* 2 vols. London: George, Allen and Unwin, 1961.
Hopkins, J. Castell, ed. *Canada, an Encyclopedia of the Country.* Vol. 6. Toronto: Linscott, 1900.
Hughes, Sir Sam. "Canada's Future within the Empire," in E. A. Victor, ed., *Canada's Future.* Toronto: Macmillan, 1916.
———. "The Defence of the Empire," in J. Castell Hopkins, ed., *Empire Club Speeches, 1904-1905.* Toronto: Briggs, 1906.
———. "Some Observations on the War," in *Empire Club Speeches, 1915-1917.* Toronto: Ryerson Press, 1917.
MacDonald, E. M. *Recollections: Political and Personal.* Toronto: Ryerson Press, 1939.
Magurn, Arnold J., ed. *The Parliamentary Guide, 1898-1899.* Ottawa: Hope, 1898 (including the volumes from 1900 to 1916).

BIBLIOGRAPHY / 331

Marquis, T. G. *Canada's Sons on Kopje and Veld*. Toronto: n.p., 1901.
Meighen, Arthur. *Unrevised and Unrepented*. Toronto: Clark Irwin, 1949.
Morgan, Henry James, ed. *Men and Women of the Time: A Handbook of Canadian Biography*. Toronto: Briggs, 1898.
―――――. *The Canadian Men and Women of the Time: A Handbook of Living Characters*. Toronto: Briggs, 1912.
Mulvaney, C. P. *The North-West Rebellion*. Toronto: Hovey, 1886.
Murray, W. W. *The History of the Second Canadian Battalion*. Ottawa: CEF, Historical Committee, 1947.
Otter, W. D. *The Guide, A Manual for the Canadian Militia*. Toronto: Copp Clarke, 1914.
Pelletier, Col. Oscar C. *Mémoires, Souvenirs de Famille et Récits*. Quebec, 1940.
Preston, W. T. R. *My Generation of Politics and Politicians*. Toronto: Rose Publishing, 1927.
Ross, P. D. *Retrospects of a Newspaper Person*. Toronto: Oxford, 1931.
Scott, Canon F. G. *The Great War As I Saw It*. Toronto: Goodchild, 1922.
Seely, J. E. B. *Adventure*. London: Heinemann, 1930.
Willson, Beckles. *From Quebec to Picadilly*. London: Jonathan Cape, 1929.
Winter, Gen. Charles F. *Lieutenant-General the Hon. Sir Sam Hughes, K.C.B., M.P., Canada's War Minister 1911-1916*. Toronto: Macmillan, 1931.

Contemporary Newspapers

Berlin (Kitchener, Ont.). *Daily Telegraph*. 1911.
Berlin (Kitchener, Ont.). *News Record*, 1916.
Calgary. *Daily Herald*. 1914, 1916.
Detroit. *Free Press*. 1916.
Fenelon Falls. *Gazette*, 1917.
Galt. *Daily Reporter*, 1914-1916.
Lindsay. *Post*, 1885-1911, 1917.
Lindsay. *Victoria Warder*, 1885-1899.
Lindsay. *Watchman-Warder*, 1899-1911, 1917.
London. *Times*, 1914-1917, 1921.
London (Ont.). *Free Press*, 1916.
Montreal. *Le Devoir*, 1916.
Montreal. *Star*, 1899.
Montreal. *Le Soleil*, 1914-1916.
New York. *Times*, 1914-1916.
Ottawa. *Citizen*, 1914-1916.
Toronto. *Globe*, 1896-1917.
Toronto. *Telegram*, 1900-1916.
Winnipeg. *Free Press*, 1914-1916.

Contemporary Periodical Literature

"At Five O'Clock," in *Canadian Magazine* 35 (1910), pp. 38, 279.
Black, Robson. "General-The Honourable-Sam," in *Maclean's Magazine*, January 1915, pp. 38-40.
"Canada and the Empire, a Symposium," in *Canadian Magazine* 19 (Aug. 1902), pp. 307-13.
"Canada and the Munitions Scandal," in *Outlook* 112 (April 1916), pp. 878-79.

"Canada—Stirred by War Graft," in *Literary Digest* 52 (April 22, 1916), pp. 1137-38.
"Canada's Munitions Scandal," in *Nation* 102 (April 13, 1916), pp. 399-400.
Canadian Defence Magazine, 1910-1915.
Canadian Liberal Monthly, 1914-1917.
Canadian Military Gazette, 1892-1909, 1911-1912.
Cooke, B. B. "Major-General Sam Hughes, Minister of Militia and Defence," in *Canadian Magazine* 45 (September 1915), pp. 388-94.
"Dismissal of Sir Sam Hughes," in *Outlook* 114 (November 29, 1916), pp. 695-96.
"Editorial Comment," in *Canadian Magazine* 46 (Dec. 1915), pp. 144-50.
"First Contingent in South Africa," in *Canadian Magazine* 14 (March 1900), pp. 417-22.
"Glory of the Princess Pats," in *Literary Digest* 51 (August 14, 1915), p. 314.
Graham, Jean. "The Story of the Shells," in *Saturday Night*, Sept. 11, 1915, p. 10.
Hamilton, Capt. C. F. "The Canadian Militia," in *Canadian Magazine* 31 (July 1908), pp. 230-33.
Hopkins, J. Castell, ed. *The Canadian Annual Review of Public Affairs*, 1901-1917.
Laut, Agnes C. "Borden, the New Premier of Canada," in *Review of Reviews* 44 (Nov. 1911), pp. 445-60.
MacCartney, M. H. H. "Political Career," in *Living Age* 271 (Dec. 2, 1911), pp. 559-63.
MacLaren, J. A. "The Cost of Training Canada's Army," in *Saturday Night*, Sept. 19, 1914, pp. 5 and 12.
MacTavish, Newton. "Cynic at Valcartier," in *Canadian Magazine* 44 (Nov. 1914), pp. 3-12.
"Man who Raised Canada's Army," in *Review of Reviews* 61 (Dec. 1915), pp. 742-45.
Matthews, C. A. "Portrait of F. W. Borden," in *Canadian Magazine* 14 (March 1900), pp. 448-52.
"Militia Council," in *Canadian Magazine* 25 (May 1905), pp. 3-6.
"Most Misunderstood of the Dominion Militarists," in *Current Opinion* 60 (May 1916), pp. 322-23.
Mowat, Maj. H. N. "A Citizen Army," in *Selected Papers of the Canadian Military Institute*, 1916-1921, pp. 77-89.
"Nation's Business," in *Financial Post*, Nov. 28, 1914, p. 8.
Orange Sentinel, 1897-1902, 1905, 1907-1911.
Patterson, N. "The Boer War and Canada," in *Canadian Magazine* 19 (July 1902), pp. 204-11.
_____. "Second Canadian Contingent for South Africa," in *Canadian Magazine* 14 (March 1900), pp. 423-33.
"Personnel of the Militia Council," in *Canadian Magazine* 25 (May 1905), pp. 7-10.
Power, L. G. "The Defence of Canada," in *Canadian Magazine* 46 (Dec. 1915), pp. 144-51.
Redford, Elsie. "Grant and the Nation," in *Canadian Magazine* 31 (1908), pp. 43-48.
"Sam Hughes' Way," in *Literary Digest* 52 (May 27, 1916), pp. 155-56.
Saturday Night, 1914-1918.
Strathcona, Lord. "Stepping Stones to Closer Union," in *Canadian Magazine* 19 (August 1902), pp. 291-302.

"Vindication of General Hughes," in *Literary Digest* 53 (Aug. 12, 1916), p. 346.

Personal Interviews and Letters

Capon, Alan R. Interview with the author. Lindsay, Ontario, Feb. 8, 1969.
Gregg, Major-General Milton F. Interview with Major John Hasek, on behalf of the author. Tape-recorded, Feb. 11, 1976.
Frost, Leslie M. Letters to the author, Oct. 11, 1968 and Jan. 3, 1969.
Hughes, S. H. S. Letter to the author, Aug. 24, 1973.
Lyall, Ken. Letter to the author, Nov. 22, 1968.
Macdonald, Mrs. Ena MacAdam. Interview with the author, Dec. 11-12, 1984. Macdonald died Apr. 1, 1985.
Mitchell, Mrs. E. Letter to the author, Jan. 24, 1969.
Morton, Desmond. Letter to the author, March 25, 1969.
Preston, Percy J. Letter to the author, March 5, 1969.
Regehr, T. D. Interview with the author, Ottawa, Ontario, Dec. 13, 1980.
Swettenham, Capt. John. Letter to the author, March 5, 1969.

Secondary Sources

Books

Adams, R. J. Q. *Arms and the Wizard: Loyd George and the Ministry of Munitions, 1915-1916*. London: Cassell, 1978.
Allen, Ralph. *Ordeal by Fire: Canada, 1910-1945*. Toronto: Macmillan, 1962.
Amery, L. S. ed. *The Times History of the War in South Africa, 1899-1902*. London: Sampson, Low, Marston, 1905.
Armstrong, Elizabeth H. *The Crisis of Quebec, 1914-1918*. Toronto: McClelland and Stewart, 1974.
Barnett, Corelli. *Britain and Her Army, 1509-1970, a Military, Political and Social Survey*. New York: Morrow, 1970.
Berger, Carl. *The Sense of Power, Studies in the Ideas of Canadian Imperialism, 1867-1914*. Toronto: University of Toronto Press, 1969.
Blake, Robert, ed. *The Private Letters of Douglas Haig, 1914-1919*. London: Eyre and Spottiswood, 1952.
Bliss, Michael. "A Canadian Businessman and War, the Case of Joseph Flavelle," in J. L. Granatstein and R. D. Cuff, eds., *War and Society in North America*. Toronto: Nelson, 1971.
————. *A Canadian Millionaire: The Life and Business Times of Sir Joseph Flavelle, Bart. 1858-1939*. Toronto: Macmillan, 1978.
Brown, R. C. *Robert Laird Borden, a Biography*. Vol. 1, 1854-1914, and vol. 2, 1914-1937. Toronto: Macmillan, 1975, 1979.
———— and Ramsay Cook. *Canada, 1896-1921, A Nation Transformed*. Toronto: McClelland and Stewart, 1974.
Bruce, Charles. *News and the Southams*. Toronto: Macmillan, 1968.
Capon, Alan R. *His Faults Lie Gently: The Incredible Sam Hughes*. Lindsay: Floyd Hall, 1969.
Chalmers, Floyd. *A Gentleman of the Press*. Garden City, N.Y.: Doubleday, 1969.
Dafoe, J. W. *Clifford Sifton in Relation to His Times*. Toronto: Macmillan, 1931.
————. *Laurier, A Study in Canadian Politics*. Toronto: McClelland and Stewart, 1968.

Denton, Edgar, ed. *Limits of Loyalty*. Waterloo: Wilfrid Laurier University Press, 1979.
Donnelly, Murray. *Dafoe of the Free Press*. Toronto: Macmillan, 1968.
Duguid, Col. A. F. *The Official History of the Canadian Forces in the Great War 1914-1919*. Vol. 1 and appendices. Ottawa: King's Printer, 1938.
Earle, E. M., ed. *The Makers of Modern Strategy: Military Thought from Machiavelli to Hitler*. Princeton: Princeton University Press, 1943.
English, John. *The Decline of Politics: The Conservatives and the Party System, 1901-1920*. Toronto: University of Toronto Press, 1977.
Farrell, Byron. *The Great Anglo-Boer War*. New York: Harper and Row, 1976.
Frost, L. M. *Fighting Men*. Toronto: Clark, Irwin, 1967.
―――. *The Record on Sir Sam Hughes Set Straight*. Fenelon Falls: Gazette, n.d.
Gooch, John. *The Plans of War: The General Staff and British Military Strategy, 1900-1916*. New York: Wiley, 1974.
Goodspeed, D. J. *The Armed Forces of Canada: A Century of Achievement*. Ottawa: Queen's Printer, 1967.
―――. *The Road Past Vimy: The Canadian Corps, 1914-1918*. Toronto: Macmillan, 1969.
Gordon, D. C. *The Dominion Partnership in Imperial Defense, 1870-1914*. Baltimore: Johns Hopkins, 1965.
Graham, Roger. *Arthur Meighen*. Vol. 1. Toronto: Clarke, Irwin, 1960.
Granatstein, J. L. and J. M. Hitsman. *Broken Promises. A History of Conscription in Canada*. Toronto: Oxford University Press, 1977.
Hall, D. J. *Clifford Sifton*. Vol. 2, *The Lonely Eminence, 1901-1924*. Vancouver: University of British Columbia Press, 1985.
Hamilton, Ian B. M. *The Happy Warrior: A Life of General Sir Ian Hamilton*. London: Cassells, 1966.
Harkness, Ross. *J. E. Atkinson of the Star*. Toronto: University of Toronto Press, 1963.
Haycock, Ronald G. *The Image of the Indian*. Waterloo: Wilfrid Laurier University Press, 1971.
Hitsman, J. McKay. *Inspection Services in Canada*. Ottawa: Queen's Printer, 1959.
Hodgetts, J. E., et al. *The Biography of an Institution: The Civil Service Commission of Canada, 1908-1967*. Montreal: McGill-Queen's University Press, 1972.
Hubbard, R. H. *Rideau Hall. An Illustrated History of Government House Ottawa from Victorian Times to the Present Day*. Toronto: McGill-Queen's University Press, 1977.
Johnson, J. K., ed. *The Canadian Directory of Parliament, 1867-1967*. Ottawa: Queen's Printer, 1968.
Kirkconnell, Watson. *Victoria County Centennial History*. Lindsay: *Watchman-Warder*, 1921.
Kruger, Rayne. *Good-Bye Dolly Gray*. London: Cassells, 1961.
Liddell Hart, B. H. *Strategy*. New York: Praeger, 1972.
Lower, A. R. M. *Canadians in the Making*. Toronto: Longmans, Green, 1958.
Lucas, Sir Charles. *The Empire at War*. Oxford: Oxford University Press, 1921.
MacPhail, Sir Andrew. *The Official History of the Canadian Forces in the Great War, 1914-1919: The Medical Services*. Ottawa: King's Printer, 1925.
Magnus, Philip. *Kitchener, Portrait of an Imperialist*. London: Penguin, 1968.
Miller, Carman. *The Canadian Career of the Fourth Earl of Minto: The Education of a Viceroy*. Waterloo: Wilfrid Laurier University Press, 1980.

Morris, James. *Farewell the Trumpets: An Imperial Retreat.* Harmondsworth: Penguin, 1979.
Morton, Desmond. *The Canadian General: Sir William Otter.* Toronto: Hakkert, 1974.
―――― . *Canada and War.* Toronto: Butterworths, 1981.
―――― . "French-Canada and War, 1868-1917," in J. L. Granatstein and R. D. Cuff, *War and Society in North America.* Toronto: Nelson, 1971.
―――― . *Ministers and Generals, Politics and the Canadian Militia, 1868-1904.* Toronto: University of Toronto Press, 1970.
―――― . *A Peculiar Kind of Politics: Canada's Overseas Ministry in the First World War.* Toronto: University of Toronto Press, 1982.
Morton, W. L., ed. *The Shield of Achilles: Aspects of Canada in the Victorian Age.* Toronto: McClelland and Stewart, 1969.
Nicholson, G. W. L. *Official History of the Canadian Army in the First World War: The Canadian Expeditionary Force, 1914-1919.* Ottawa: Queen's Printer, 1962.
Pakenham, Thomas. *The Boer War.* New York: Random House, 1979.
Penlington, Norman L. *Canada and Imperialism, 1896-1899.* Toronto: University of Toronto Press, 1965.
―――― . "General Hutton and the Problem of Military Imperialism in Canada, 1898-1900," in Carl Berger, ed., *Imperial Relations in the Age of Laurier.* Canadian Historical Readings, no. 6. Toronto: University of Toronto Press, 1969.
Phillips, R., F. Dupuis, and John Chadwick. *The Ross Rifle Story.* Sydney, N.S.: Casket, 1984.
Prang, Margaret. *N. W. Rowell, Ontario Nationalist.* Toronto: University of Toronto Press, 1975.
Preston, R. A. *Canada and Imperial Defense: A Study in the Origins of the British Commonwealth Defense Organization, 1867-1919.* Durham: Duke University Press, 1967.
―――― . *Defence of the Undefended Border.* Montreal: McGill-Queen's University Press, 1977.
Regehr, T. D. *The Canadian Northern Railway: The Pioneer Road of the Northern Prairies, 1895-1918.* Toronto: Macmillan, 1976.
Roberts, Charles, G. D. and A. L. Tunnell, eds. *A Standard Dictionary of Canadian Biography.* Vol. 1. Toronto: Transcanada Press, 1934.
Roy, Reginald H., ed. *The Journal of Private Fraser, 1914-1918: The Canadian Expeditionary Force.* Victoria, B.C.: Sono Nis Press, 1985.
Schull, Joseph. *Laurier, the First Canadian.* Toronto: McClelland and Stewart, 1965.
Senior, Hereward. *Orangeism: the Canadian Phase.* Toronto: McGraw, Hill, Ryerson, 1972.
Stacey, Col. C. P., ed. *Introduction to the Study of Military History for Canadian Students.* 3rd ed. rev. Ottawa: Directorate of Training. C.F.H.Q., 1973.
―――― . *Canada and the Age of Conflict, a History of Canadian External Policies.* Vol. 1, 1867-1921. Toronto: Macmillan, 1977.
―――― . *The Military Problems of Canada.* Toronto: Ryerson Press, 1940.
Stafford, Ellen, ed. *Flamboyant Canadians.* Toronto: Baxter, 1964.
Stanley, G. F. G. *Canada's Soldiers 1604-1954: The Military History of an Unmilitary People.* Toronto: Macmillan, 1954.
Swettenham, John. *To Seize Victory: The Canadian Corps in World War One.* Toronto: Ryerson Press, 1965.

Symons, Julian. *Buller's Campaign.* London: Cresset Press, 1963.
Taylor, A. J. P. *Beaverbrook.* New York: Simon and Schuster, 1972.
Thompson, John Herd. *The Harvests of War, The Prairie West, 1914-1918.* Toronto: McClelland and Stewart, 1978.
Urguhart, Hugh M. *Arthur Currie: The Biography of a Great Canadian.* Toronto: Dent, 1950.
Tucker, G. N. *The Naval Service of Canada.* Vol. 1. Ottawa: King's Printer, 1952.
Vagts, Alfred. *A History of Militarism, Civilian and Military.* New York: Free Press, 1967.
Wade, Mason. *The French Canadians, 1760-1967.* 2 vols. Toronto: Macmillan, 1968.
Waite, P. B. *Canada, 1874-1896: Arduous Destiny.* Toronto: McClelland and Stewart, 1971.
Ward, Norman, ed. *A Party Politician: The Memoirs of Chubby Power.* Toronto: Macmillan, 1966.
Wallace, W. S. *The Memoirs of the Right Honourable Sir George Foster.* Toronto: Macmillan, 1933.
Williams, D. R. *Duff: A Life in Law.* Vancouver: University of British Columbia, 1984.
Williams, Jeffery. *Byng of Vimy: General and Governor-General.* London: Leo Cooper, 1983.
Williams, Watkin. *The Life of General Sir Charles Warren.* Oxford: Blackwells, 1941.
Willson, Beckles. *The Life of Lord Strathcona and Mount Royal.* London: Cassell, 1915.
Wilson, Barbara M. *Ontario and the First World War 1914-1918: A Collection of Documents.* Toronto: Champlain Society, 1977.
Wise, S. F. *Canadian Airmen in the First World War: The Official History of the Royal Canadian Air Force.* Vol. 1. Toronto: University of Toronto Press, 1980.
Worthington, Mrs. Larry. *Amid the Guns Below: The Story of the Canadian Corps, 1914-1919.* Toronto: McClelland and Stewart, 1965.

Articles

Allen, A. R. "In this Corner Sir Sam Hughes," in *Maclean's Magazine*, May 20, 1961, pp. 13-17, 60-66.
_____. "Misfortunes of War," in *Maclean's Magazine*, June 3, 1961, pp. 18-19, 39-40.
Beahen, William. "Filling out the Skeleton: Paramilitary Support Groups, 1904-1914," in *Canadian Defence Quarterly* 13, no. 4 (Spring 1984), pp. 34-39.
Bray, R. Mathew. "Fighting as an Ally: The English-Canadian Patriotic Response to the Great War," in *The Canadian Historical Review* 61 (Nov. 2, 1980), pp. 141-47.
Brown, Col. J. S. "Military Policy in Canada, 1905-1924 and Suggestions for the Future," in *Canadian Defence Quarterly*, July 1924, pp. 18-32.
Brown, R. Craig and Desmond Morton. "The Embarrassing Apotheosis of a 'Great Canadian': Sir Arthur Currie's Personal Crisis in 1917," in the *Canadian Historical Review* 60, no. 1 (1979), pp. 41-63.
"Canadian Heritage," in *Maclean's Magazine* 54 (Dec. 1, 1941), pp. 30, 64.
Capon, Alan R. "The Incredible Sam Hughes," in *The Post* (Lindsay, Ont.). Serial began Oct. 25, 1968.

Carliss, P. "What Happened to Business and Finance in the Great War? Here's the Answer," in *Saturday Night* 54 (May 13, 1939), pp. 11, 13.
Clark, Lovell C. "The Conservative Party in the 1890's," in the Canadian Historical Association, *Annual Report*, 1961, pp. 58, 74.
Corry, J. A. "Growth of Government Activities in Canada, 1914-1921," in the Canadian Historical Associaton, *Annual Report*, 1940, pp. 63-73.
―――――. "Some Aspects of Canada's War Effort," in *Queen's Quarterly* 47, no. 3 (1940), pp. 356-68.
Cuff, Robert. "The Conservative Party Machine and the Election of 1911," in *Ontario History* 57, no. 3, pp. 149-54.
―――――. "The Toronto Eighteen and the Election of 1911," in *Ontario History* 57, no. 4, pp. 169-80.
Cummins, Capt. J. F. "Imperial Conferences and Imperial Defence," in *Canadian Defence Quarterly* 4 (Oct. 1926), pp. 13-20.
Dupuis, F. J. "The MacAdam Shield-Shovel," in the *Canadian Journal of Arms Collecting* 11, no. 4, pp. 117-19.
Ellis, F. H. "Canada's First Military Aeroplane," in the *Beaver*, Autumn 1974, pp. 48-53.
Gooch, John. "Great Britain and Defence of Canada, 1896-1914," in *Journal of Imperial and Commonwealth History* 3 (May 1975), pp. 369-85.
Globe and Mail, Oct. 31, 1939. (Clippings in the Great War File of the Kitchener Public Library, Kitchener, Ontario.)
Haycock, R. G. "The 1917 Federal Election in Victoria-Haliburton: A Case Study," in *Ontario History* 67, no. 2 (June 1975), pp. 105-18.
―――――. "The American Legion in the Canadian Expeditionary Force, 1914-1917: A Study in Failure," in *Military Affairs*, 43 (Oct. 1979), pp. 115-19.
―――――. "Early Canadian Weapons Acquisition: 'That Damned Ross Rifle'," in *Canadian Defence Quarterly* 14, no. 3 (Winter 1984/1985), pp. 48-57.
Howard, Capt. H. C. "Canada's Costly Mistakes in the Great War," in *Saturday Night* 52 (Sept. 10, 1938), p. 2.
Hughes, Sam H. S. "Sir Sam Hughes and the Problem of Imperialism," in the Canadian Historical Association, *Annual Report*, 1949-1950, pp. 30-42.
Hyatt, A. M. J. "Sir Arthur Currie and Conscription: A Soldier's View," in *Canadian Historical Review* 50, no. 3 (Sept. 1969), pp. 285-96.
Lee, Betty. "The Second Battle of Ypres," in *Globe and Mail Magazine*, Sept. 15, 1964, pp. 12-13, 19.
Lowry, Bullitt. "French and 1914: His Defence of His Memoirs Examined," in *Military Affairs* 45 (April 1981), pp. 79-83.
MacQuarrie, Heath N. "The Formation of Borden's First Cabinet," in *Canadian Journal of Economics and Political Science* 22, no. 1 (1957), pp. 90-104.
―――――. "Robert Borden and the Election of 1911," in *Canadian Journal of Economics and Political Science* 25 (Aug. 1959), pp. 271-86.
―――――. "Robert Borden—Party Leader," in *Canadian Forum* 37 (April 1957), pp. 14-17.
Morton, Desmond. "The Short Unhappy Life of the 41st Battalion C.E.F.," in *Queen's Quarterly* 81, no. 1 (1974), pp. 70-80.
―――――. "'Junior But Sovereign Allies': The Transformation of the Canadian Expeditionary Force, 1914-1918," in *Journal of Imperial and Commonwealth History* 8 (October 1979), pp. 56-67.

─────── . "The Cadet Movement in the Moment of Canadian Militarism," in *Journal of Canadian Studies* 13, no. 2 (Summer 1978).
Nicholson, G. W. L. "Three Ways to Slip into War; Enthusiasm for Empire in 1914," in *Saturday Night* 79 (August 1964), pp. 12-15.
Pearkes, G. R. "The Evolution of the Control of His Majesty's Canadian Forces," in *Canadian Defence Quarterly*, July 1933, pp. 465-80.
Penlington, N. "General Hutton and the Problem of Military Imperialism in Canada 1898-1900," in *Canadian Historical Review* 24 (June 1943), pp. 156-71.
Phillips, Roger and Jerome Knap. "Sir Charles Ross, Bart, and his ill-fated Rifles," in the *Gun Digest* 21 (Chicago, 1966), pp. 264-75.
Roberts, G. E. I. G. "Those Ammunition Boots," in *Saturday Night* 54 (Oct. 14, 1939), p. 6.
Stacey, C. P. "Canada's Last War and the Next," in *University of Toronto Quarterly* 7 (April 1939), pp. 247-54.
Underhill, F. H., ed. "Lord Minto on his Governor-Generalship," in the *Canadian Historical Review* (no. 2, 1959), pp. 121-32.
─────── . "Some Reflections on the Liberal Tradition in Canada," the Presidential Address in the *Report* of the Annual Meeting of the Canadian Historical Association. Toronto: University of Toronto Press, 1946.
Vince, D. M. A. R. "The Acting Overseas Sub-Militia Council and the Resignation of Sir Sam Hughes," in the *Canadian Historical Review* 31 (March 5, 1950), pp. 1-24.
─────── . "Development in the Legal Status of the Canadian Military Forces, 1914-1919," in *Canadian Journal of Economics and Political Science* 20 (August 1954), pp. 357-70.
Watt, A. M. "Imperial Defence Policy and Imperial Foreign Policy, 1911-1939—a neglected paradox," in the *Journal of Commonwealth Political Studies* 1, no. 4 (1963), pp. 266-81.
Willms, A. M. "Decision-Making: the Case of the Ross Rifle," in the *Canadian Public Administration* 2 (December 1959), pp. 202-13.

Unpublished Material

Allen, J. H. "Make Ready Thine Arrows: Ammunition Policy and Practice in the Canadian Forces, 1867-1974," M.A. thesis, Royal Military College, 1976.
Brazeau, J. B. D. "A Study of the Relationship of the Duke of Connaught with R. L. Borden and S. Hughes during his Tenure as Governor-General," B.A. History thesis, Royal Military College, 1980.
Ellis, Robert J. "Relationships of MacKenzie and Mann with the Laurier Government," M.A. thesis, University of Western Ontario, 1965.
Eagle, J. A. "Sir Robert Borden and the Railway Problem in Canadian Politics, 1911-1920," Ph.D. dissertation, University of Toronto, 1972.
Eyre, Kenneth Charles. "Staff and Command in the Canadian Corps: The Canadian Militia, 1896-1914 as a Source of Senior Officers," M.A. thesis, Duke University, 1967.
Frost, Leslie M. *The Record Set Straight on Sir Sam Hughes* (privately printed, 1964).
Gagan, Paul David. "The Queen's Champion: The Life of George Taylor Denison III: Soldier, Author, Magistrate and Canadian Tory Patriot," Ph.D. dissertation, Duke University, 1968.

Hyatt, A. M. J. "The Military Career of Sir Arthur Currie," Ph.D. dissertation, Duke University, 1964.
Johnson, A. D. "The Imperial Federation League in Canada, 1885-1899," B.A. thesis, Royal Military College, 1972.
Kelly, Peter, producer. "And We Were Young." CBC television, Nov. 11, 1968.
Lane, Barry W. "The Effects of Sir Sam Hughes and His Administration Upon the Canadian War Effort of World War I: His Faults do not Lie Gently," B.A. thesis, Royal Military College, 1974.
Lefresne, G. M. "Pegasus: The Canadian Department of Overseas Transport and the Movement of Imperial Supplies From Canada to Europe, 1914-1920," graduate history paper, Queen's University, 1971.
Miller, Carman. Unpublished, untitled manuscript on Minto's governor-generalship.
———. "The Public Life of Sir Frederick Borden, M.A. thesis, Dalhousie, 1964.
Warner, Catherine L. "Sir James Pliny Whitney and Sir Robert L. Borden: Relations between a Conservative Provincial Premier and His Federal Party Leader, 1905-1914," M.Phil. thesis, University of Toronto, 1967.

Index

Abbott, John, 41, 43, 51, 52, 105
Aberdeen, Lord, 58. *See also* Governor-General of Canada
Academie Parisienne des Inventeurs, 35
Acting Sub-Militia Council, 303; and Borden's reaction to, 303-306. *See also* Sub-Militia Council
Adams, R. J. Q., 236
Advisory committees (headquarters staff), 138. *See also* Headquarters staff (Ottawa)
Agricultural development, 11
Aitken, Max, 118, 188, 208, 217, 250, 263, 273, 281, 288, 290, 292, 293, 294, 300, 301, 303, 305; and Alderson's removal, 298; and Battle of St. Eloi, 297-98; as Canada's voice in Great Britain, 262ff.; and Canadian Army, 290-91; as "Eye-Witness," 262-63; and Hughes' conspiracy theory, 274ff.; and Hughes' Lt.-Generalcy in British Army, 305-306; and Hughes' overseas military ministry, 306; influences Hughes, 275-76; and local military council, 294; and Lombard Street organization, 275, 284; personal ambitions of, 293; and Ross rifle, 249, 251. *See also* "Eye-Witness"; Lombard Street headquarters
Alaska boundary dispute, 100, 101
Alberta, 106, 107, 143. *See also* Autonomy Bill

Alderson, General E. H. A., 23, 187, 211, 245, 246, 260, 267, 268, 273, 274, 275, 276-77, 278, 280, 285n; and Aitken, 282; Borden on, 273; commands Canadian Corps, 272; criticizes Canadian officers, 261; as Inspector-General, 299-300; quarrels with Hughes, 268, 291, 292, 297, 298, 299, 300; and reinforcements, 282, 291-92; removed from office, 296-300; and Ross rifle, 250-51; and Ypres, 268-73. *See also* Canadian Expeditionary Force; Reinforcements
Allan, Ralph, 6
Allison, John Wesley, 192, 228-29, 231, 241, 242, 243, 244, 273; Borden on, 229; and contracts in Great Britain and the U.S., 228-29. *See also* Auditor-General; Royal Commission; Shell Committee; Shell Scandal
"American Legion," 218-20
Amery, Leopold, 78, 85, 94, 102, 108, 117, 119
Ames, H. B., 105, 126, 127, 202, 243
Ammunition, 142
Anderson, Sir John, 98, 170
Anticosti Island, 214
Armistice (1918), 258
Arnold-Forster, H. O., 102
Artillery association, 136
Asquith, H. H., 226, 263
Asselin, Oliver, 215, 216

Auditor-General of Canada, 192, 227, 229, 243
Austrian Empire, 177
Autonomy Bill, 106-107, 114. *See also* Alberta; Saskatchewan
Australia, 123, 124, 323; and colonial government, 68

Bain wagon, 233-34
Balfour, A. J., 102
Balfour, Max, 85, 86
Balkan politics, 177
Bancroft, Prof. W. D., 250
Banff, 177
Baptie, Sir William, 314, 315
Barron, J. A., 28, 37, 38, 39, 40, 41, 43, 44, 45
Bassett, John, 166, 227, 266; and J. W. Allison, 244
Batoche, Battle of, 18, 21
Battalions (CEF), Princess Patricia's Canadian Light Infantry, 278; 12th, 213; 14th, 213; 22nd, 215, 216; 31st (British Columbia Horse), 179; 41st, 215; 48th Highlanders, 180, 184; 97th, 219; 204th, 210; 206th, 215; 211th, 219; 212th, 219; 213th, 219; 237th, 219
Beaverbrook, Lord, 5. *See also* Aitken, Max
Bechuanaland, 84, 88
Beck, Adam, 139
Bégin, Cardinal, 149, 213, 218
Belgian Relief Fund, 201
Belleville (Ontario), 9
Belmont (South Africa), 88
Bennett, R. B., 143, 207, 280, 281
Bennett, William, 116
Berger, Carl, 24
Bermuda, 216
Bertram, Alexander, 235, 236, 238, 240. *See also* Shell Committee
Bexhill (Sussex), 188
Birmingham, Robert, 17, 32, 34, 35, 36, 41-42, 44, 54, 143, 148, 232
Bisley rifle matches, 122
Blake, Edward, 14 n, 23
Bliss, Michael, 6
Bloemfontein (South Africa), 73, 79
Bobcaygeon (Ontario), 17, 36
Boer commandos, 84, 90

Boer republics, 79, 84
Boer war, 99, 117, 119, 177, 180, 183, 184, 187, 203, 213, 233, 239, 268, 279, 319, 321; as Hughes' model, 93-94, 180; and rifle shooting, 245
Boers, 64, 68, 70, 73, 78, 83, 86, 88. *See also* Boer commandos; Boer war; de Villiers; Kruger; Boer republics; Warren; Settle
Bonar Law, Andrew, 118, 242, 263, 273, 274, 279, 291, 306
Boot enquiry, 230, 253, 254 n
Borden, Dr. F. W., 62-63, 68, 69, 71, 74, 75, 76-77, 78, 79, 82 n, 83, 92, 93, 97, 99, 100, 101, 102, 119, 120, 127, 129, 130, 139, 140, 157, 165, 173, 230
Borden, Laura (Mrs. R. L.), 186
Borden, Robert Laird, 1, 5, 6, 102, 110, 115, 116, 119, 120, 121, 128, 130, 135, 137, 146, 149, 150, 151, 157, 166, 168, 169, 171, 174, 178, 182, 188, 191, 199, 201, 204, 206, 208, 211, 240, 260, 261, 265, 271, 278, 283, 289, 293, 297, 312 n, 315, 318, 322; and British-Canadian war relations, 228, 264; and cabinet complaints about Hughes, 183-84, 301-302; and Carrick replacement, 266; decision to fire Hughes, 244; embarrassed by Hughes, 229-30; and Hughes-Connaught quarrel, 154-57, 172, 295-96; and Hughes' conspiracy theory, 279-80; and Hughes' loyalty, 104-106, 124-25, 127, 129, 131; and Hughes-Mackenzie quarrel, 161-64; and Hughes' mobilization efforts, 183-84; and Hughes' patronage, 226-32; and Hughes' party position, 116-17; and Hughes' recruiting schemes, 205-206, 207; and Hughes' resignation, 307-309; loses Commons seat, 105; and munitions controversies, 233; and his "new men," 105, 107, 116, 125-29, 150; 1915 trip to England, 263, 270; orders Hughes home, 290, 292, 294; and overseas militia ministry, 288-89, 294, 306-308; and party

politics, 116-17; and party reform, 104-105; and party revolt, 125-26; and Ross rifle, 251; and Shell Scandal, 242-45; and war effort, 186, 192-94
Bourassa, Henri, 115, 126, 144, 149, 178, 215
Bowell, Mackenzie, 25, 54, 55, 105, 125
Bowell government, 56
Bowman, Charles A., 251
Bowmanville (Ontario), 8, 9, 12
Boyd, Mossom, 36, 37
Brade, Sir Reginald, 193
Bramshott Camp (England), 277, 282, 294
Bridle, Augustus, 193
Brigades (CEF), "American Legion," 218-20; Canadian Cavalry Brigade, 267, 283; and French-Canadians, 216
Bristol, Edmund, 143, 213, 226, 232
British Admiralty, 124, 217
British Army, 165, 196n
British Army Act, 72
British Army Council, 169, 251, 298
British Army manoeuvres, 146-47, 172
British Army units; and City Imperial Volunteers, 85, 86; and Imperial Yeomanry, 89, 90
British Army veterans, 108
British Empire, 2, 23, 24, 25, 26, 93, 178. *See also* Hughes, Sam; Imperialism
British Empire League, 25. *See also* Imperial Federation League; Denison; Hughes, Sam
British Expeditionary Force (BEF), 226, 264, 276
British Headquarters (France), 264, 265, 266, 282, 298
British high command, 97
British immigrants, 108. *See also* Hughes, Sam
British regulars, 21. *See also* Hughes, Sam
British Second Army, 298
British small arms manufacturers, 123

Broder, Andrew, 130
Brooke, Lord, 147, 267, 277, 281, 284, 292, 300
Brown, R. Craig, 6
Bruce, H. A., 313-14, 324n
Bruce Report, 314-15
Buchan, Lt.-Col. Lawrence, 73, 76
Buell, Lt.-Col. W. J., 185
Buller, Sir Redvers, 64, 87
Bullock, C. W., 219
Buntin, Reid and Company, 41
Burk, Harvey William, 10, 14n
Burk, Mary, 10
Burrell, Martin, 129
Bury's Green (Ontario), 44
Business, Canadian; complaints about British, 227-28; reaction to war, 225
Byng, Sir Julian, 292, 300, 301, 315; as Canadian Corps Commander. *See also* Alderson; Aitken

Cabinet, 148-51, 162, 178, 191, 299, 318; complains about Hughes, 183-84, 301-302; French-Canadians resign from (1914), 217; on Hughes' recruiting methods, 208; and patronage, 226-27, 232
Cadet Corps, 4, 13, 136, 138, 140-41, 169; and female instructors, 2, 140; and Hughes, 13; and youth training committee, 139
Calvinism, 15
Campbell (South Africa), 88, 89
Camp Borden, 302; riots at, 245
Camp Niagara, 145
Camp Petawawa, 179, 182
Camp Sewell, 167
Camp Shorncliffe, 211, 267, 282, 301
Camp Valcartier, 5, 141, 179, 181-86, 192, 213, 234-35, 245, 288
Canada Cycle and Motor Company, 233
Canada in Flanders, 262
Canada Mutual Company, 61
Canadian Annual Review, 193, 209
Canadian Army, 290, 291, 315; and Aitken, 290-91; and First Corps, 291; Hughes' plan for, 272; and Second Corps, 290

INDEX / 343

Canadian Army Dental Corps, 278
Canadian Army Medical Corps (CAMC), 313-15, 323 n. *See also* Bruce; Jones
Canadian cavalry, 147, 267, 283
Canadian Contingents (CEF), 258-59, 274-76; First, 198; Second, 199, 203
Canadian Corps (CEF), 203, 204, 205, 214, 215, 250, 263, 273, 275, 277, 298, 299, 315; formation of, 272
Canadian Defence, 138
Canadian Defence Force, 199
Canadian Defence League, 136
Canadian Expeditionary Force (CEF), 177, 178, 179, 182, 184, 188, 195 n, 198, 201, 202, 206, 231, 245, 259, 260, 261, 267, 280; break-up of battalions, 221; and flotilla, 186-87; legal status of, 289; and special battalions, 207; size of, 199, 204, 205, 206, 207. *See also* Battalions (CEF); Brigades (CEF); Canadian Contingents (CEF); Canadian Corps (CEF); Divisions (CEF); Non-Permanent Active Militia; Permanent Active Militia
Canadian Infantry Association, 145
Canadian Manufacturers' Association, 125, 209, 257 n
Canadian military aircraft, 233-34
Canadian Military Gazette, 74, 82 n
Canadian Militia Gazette, 19, 109
Canadian National Service League, 210
Canadian Northern Railway, 38, 61, 107, 108, 122, 163
Canadian Pacific Railway, 19, 36, 108
Canadian Patriotic Fund, 201
Canadian Press Association, 204
Canadian Training Depot, 267
Canadian Training Depot (U.K.), 267
Canadian war industries, 321
Le Canadien, 55
Cantley, Thomas, 235, 238-39
Cape Colony (South Africa), 83, 84, 88
Cape Colony, Northwest (South Africa), 84
Cape Colony rebellion, 83
Cape Town (South Africa), 76, 77, 78, 82, 84, 85, 90, 93
Carnegie, David, 236, 240
Caron, Adolphe, 31
Carrick, J. J., 264-65, 272, 275
Carson, John Wallace, 249, 260-61, 263, 266, 267, 268, 270, 272, 279, 281, 282, 283, 284, 292, 294, 297, 300, 303
Carstairs, J. S., 116
Cartier, Georges-Etienne, 115
Cavalry association, 136
Chamberlain, Joseph, 64, 67, 68, 69, 70, 71, 72, 73, 117. *See also* Colonial Office; Colonial Secretary
Chief of the General Staff (Canadian), 151
Christie, Loring, 181, 261, 295
Chronicle (Quebec City), 184
Churchill, Winston, 219
Citizen (Ottawa), 78, 159, 251
Citizen-soldiers, 1, 318-19, 320
Civil-military relations, 173
Clark, Champ, 126
Coalition government, 199; Hughes on, 316
Coboconk (Ontario), 39, 42-43
Cochrane, Frank, 129
Colonial conferences, 1907, 1909, 110
Colonial Office, 64, 70, 100, 102, 190, 273, 274, 283. *See also* Chamberlain; and Colonial Secretary
Colonial Secretary, 181, 309
Committee of Imperial Defence, 178
Conference of Defence Associations, 137
Connaught, Duchess of, 162
Connaught, Duke of, 136, 137, 162, 172, 177, 181, 182, 190, 191, 192, 204, 207, 211, 219, 220, 229, 261, 262, 263, 264, 269, 273, 275, 282, 292, 297; Borden on, 183, 295; early career and character, 154; fear of German-American invasion, 203; interference in war effort, 183; opinion of Hughes, 4; quarrels with Hughes, 154-57, 295-96; reaction to patronage, 227; relationship with Borden, 172; and secret memoranda to Sir

344 / SAM HUGHES

John French, 164-65. *See also* Governor-General of Canada
Connaught rifle ranges, 182
Conscription, 198, 199, 200, 221, 315, 324 n; Hughes on, 221, 306, 315-16
Conservative Party (federal), 79, 103-104, 110, 114
Conservative Party (Ontario), 115
Constituent politics, 2, 317-18
Cooper, Joseph, 31, 32
Corpus Christi celebrations (Montreal), 149
Cotton, W. H., 156, 158, 173
Creelman, A.R., 25
Creelman, John J., 310
Cronje, General, 84
Crothers, Thomas, 129
Cubitt, Fred, 22, 48
Currie, General Arthur W., 185, 234, 271, 272, 276, 280, 316, 317, 319, 323, 324 n; as CEF brigadier, 184; commands Canadian Corps, 315; Hughes' charges against, 315-16, 317; on Garnet Hughes, 277-78; on Ross rifle, 249
Currie, Lt.-Col. J. A., 180, 184, 185, 324 n
Curtis, Lionel, 4, 78, 85, 87, 93, 94, 95 n, 108, 118
Customs, Minister of, 29

Daly, Harold M., 205-206, 266, 293
Daily Express (Britain), 262
Darlington Township, 10
Davidson, Sir Charles, 233. *See also* Davidson Commission
Davidson, N. F., 202
Davidson Commission, 233, 234
Department of Agriculture, 202
Department of National Defence, 6
Delemere, John H., 59
Denison family, 77. *See also* Denison, George T.; Denison, Septimus
Denison, George T., 20, 24, 25, 26, 77, 108
Denison, Septimus, 77, 267
Le Devoir (Montreal), 144, 215
Devonshire, Duke of, 309, 310. *See also* Governor-General of Canada
Diamond Jubilee, 63, 78
Dickey, Arthur, 50

Divisions (CEF); and controversy over command, 270-71; Fifth, 309; First, 249, 266, 268, 272, 309; Fourth, 208, 215, 281, 290, 294, 301; and Lee-Enfield rifles, 246; and reinforcements, 301; and St. Eloi, 297; Second, 246, 250, 266-67, 270-71, 276; Third, 215, 250, 266, 280, 296
Dobson, John, 33 n
Doherty, Charles, 125
Dominion Arsenal, 225, 234; Hughes' reform of, 142. *See also* Ammunition; Government Arsenals
Dominion Police, 229
Dominion Rifle Association, 4, 110, 120
Dominion Steel Corporation, 209
Dominion Trust Company, 61
Donop, Sir Stanley von. *See* von Donop
Douglas (South Africa), 88
Dreadnoughts, 124
Drill halls, 136, 140
Drill squad, 13
Drury, C. W., 156
Dry canteens, 145-46
Duff, Lyman, 243, 244, 252
Dundas, J. R., 30, 31, 34, 36, 39, 43, 240
Dundonald, Lord, 99, 100, 102, 104, 117, 162; and Hughes, 101-103; and quarrel with Fisher, 101-103. *See also* General-Officer-Commanding
Durham County, 8, 9, 12
Durham East (constituency), 18

Eaton, Sir John, 209
Echo (Minden), 59
Economic recession, 225
Egypt, 276
Electoral Revisions Court, 44
Embarkation plan (CEF), 186
Empire (British), 137, 200
The Empire, 25
Empire Club (Toronto), 118, 192, 314
Empire defence, 174. *See also* Imperial defence
Empress of Ireland, 154
English, John, 2, 6, 151, 241

English-Canadians, 215
Entente, 178
"Equal partnership union," 117-18
Equal Rights Association, 29, 35, 52
European manoeuvres, 146
Evening Star (Toronto), 62
"Eye-Witness," 217, 277, 285 n; and Boer war, 74. *See also* Aitken

Faber's Put, battle of, 88-90, 92, 93
Fairbairn, Charlie, 37, 45
Fashoda, 64
Federal elections, 1887, 23; 1891, 38; 1892, 34; 1896, 59-60; 1900, 97; 1904, 103; 1908, 120-22; 1911, 128, 143; 1913 by-elections, 148; 1917, 315. *See also* Victoria-Haliburton (constituency); Victoria North (constituency); Victoria South (constituency)
Fenelon Falls (Ontario), 17, 38, 44
Fenian raids, 12, 78, 319. *See also* Fenians
Fenians, 26, 27
Festubert, battle of, 202, 232, 247, 268, 269, 277, 279
Fielding, W. S., 74
First World War, 158, 177-258, 313, 319, 320, 321, 322, 323
Fisher, Sydney, 101, 108
Fiset, Eugène, 161, 188, 191, 204, 219, 245, 258, 289, 294, 295, 302, 307
Fitzpatrick, Sir Charles, 162-63
Flanders, 215, 268, 271
Flavelle brothers, 43. *See also* Flavelle, Joseph Wesley
Flavelle, Joseph Wesley, 6, 240, 242, 255 n. *See also* Flavelle Brothers; Imperial Munitions Board
Flick, C. L., 179
Ford, Arthur R., 137, 146, 166, 167, 193
Forestier-Walker, General Sir Frederick, 78
Fortescue, Sir John, 109
Foster, Dewitt, 231
Foster, George, 6, 56, 57, 122, 124, 126, 182, 183, 207, 226, 229, 230, 238, 241, 243, 294, 302, 310; and patronage, 232; on Ross rifle, 247-48

France, 178, 211, 212, 216; and colonial troops at Ypres, 201-202; and French-Canadians, 217; and Quebec units, 217
Franco-Ontarians, 116, 217. *See also* French Canada; French-Canadians; Ontario schools question
Free trade, 23
Freemasons, 16
French, Sir John, 110, 141, 146, 147, 158, 159, 160, 161, 164, 168, 169, 234, 246, 247, 267, 268, 269, 270, 272, 274, 276, 279, 280. *See also* Imperial Inspector-General
French-Canada, 119, 151; and French-Canadian units, 213; and recruiting, 210. *See also* French-Canadians
French-Canadians, 26, 106-107, 114, 124, 125, 129, 148-49, 198, 318; attitude towards France, 217; and British war, 217; and cabinet shuffle (1914), 193; and the Empire, 212, 216; military efforts, 316; and nationalism, 68, 144; participation in war, 216-17; reaction to Hughes, 148-49; and recruiting, 212-18; and western recruits, 218. *See also* Franco-Ontarians; Ontario schools question
French priests, 115, 217
Frost, Leslie, 5
Fuller, J. F. C., 270

Gagetown (New Brunswick), 141
Gallipoli, 313
Garland, William, 230
Gascoigne, Maj.-Gen. Sir William, 63. *See also* General-Officer-Commanding
Gaspé Basin, 186
Gaudet, F. M., 214
Gazette (Montreal), 166
General-Officer-Commanding, 98-99, 100. *See also* Dundonald; Gascoigne; Herbert; Hutton; Middleton
George V, 168, 219, 269, 273
George, W. K., 125
German East Africa, 277

German naval construction, 123, 124
German Southwest Africa, 84
German threat, and Hughes' reaction to, 147-48
German war intentions, 124
Germany, 109, 124, 147-48, 178, 189
Gibson, J. M., 110, 130, 136
Givenchy, Battle of, 202, 247
Globe (Toronto), 92, 126, 144, 145, 166
Gorrie, A. J., 186
Government Arsenals, 141, 142. *See also* Dominion Arsenal
Government House, 157. *See also* Governor-General of Canada; Rideau Hall
Governor-General's Bodyguard, 20
Governor-General of Canada, 38, 39, 58, 146, 151, 160, 188. *See also* Aberdeen; Connaught; Devonshire; Grey; Minto
Graham, Roger, 6
Grand Alliance, 178
Grand Orange Lodge of British America, 28
Grand Trunk Pacific, 108
Grange, W. E., 166
Grant, G. M., 25, 26
Great Britain, 23, 39, 170, 178, 212, 225, 262; Anglo-Canadian military co-operation, 109-10, 147; British investigations of Ross rifle, 247-48; and British reaction to Hughes' overseas organization, 259-60, 301; British reaction to Shell Committee, 238-40; Canadian financial and food aid to, 201; and Canadian volunteers, 179; declaration of war (1914), 177; discriminates against Canadian troops and equipment, 316; early method of munitions contracting, 231-32; Hughes' criticism of British generalship (1915), 268-70; munitioning experience, 226; munitions history, 236; policy in South Africa, 67-69; opposition to "American Legion," 219-20; rearming of Canadian divisions, 230, 245-47; and reinforcements, 182, 199, 202; and Ross rifle contracts, 247-48; support for Hughes' war effort, 196 n; war contracts, 207; war policy, influence over, 207
Great War. *See* First World War
Greene, Major Byron, 303
Gregg, Maj.-Gen. Milton, 324 n
Grevelle-Harston, Charles, 160
Grey, Lord, 117, 131, 154. *See also* Governor-General of Canada
Griesbach, Lt.-Col. W. A., 3-4, 210
Griqualand West (South Africa), 84, 87, 88
Griquatown (South Africa), 88, 89, 90
Groote Konig (South Africa), 91
Groote Schuur (South Africa), 78
Guelph (Ontario), 124
Gulf of St. Lawrence, 187
Gwatkin, Maj.-Gen. Willoughby, 170-71, 172, 190, 195 n, 203, 204, 207, 211, 217, 220, 227, 250, 258, 260, 261, 265, 275, 283, 292, 293, 296, 308; as mobilization officer, 178-79, 181, 213; and proposal to reform overseas administration, 289; and reaction to "American Legion," 219-20; on Ross rifle, 247-48, 251
Gwynne, Lt.-Col. R. G., 140

Haggert, John, 42, 47, 54
Haig, Douglas, 280, 281, 298-99
Haldane, Lord, 170
Haliburton (provisional county), 16
Halifax, 109, 138, 146
Halifax Manifesto, 121
Hall, Chris, 44
Hamilton, Gen. Sir Ian, 4, 173, 178, 181, 203, 319; and assessment of Hughes, 166-70, 176 n; and reaction to Mackenzie, 164-70
Harcourt, Lewis, 171, 172, 188, 242, 259
Harris, Lloyd, 127
Hastings County, 9
Hazen, J. D., 192, 229
Headquarters staff (Ottawa), 135, 138, 146, 169, 173, 190-91, 203, 228, 258, 295
Headquarters (England), 281
Henderson, G. F. R., 109
Herbert, Maj.-Gen. Ivor, 48-49, 50, 147

INDEX / 347

Hichens, Lionel, 85, 93, 94, 239-40
High Commissioner (London), 51, 187, 219, 259, 260, 265, 279, 283, 284
Hill, Lt.-Col. F. W., 185
"Hockin Pamphlet," 122
Homer Dixon, Maj. J. F., 276
Hong Kong, 50
Honorary Commissions, 139, 210, 228
Hopkins, J. Castell, 25, 193, 200, 209
House of Commons (Canada), 97, 109, 110, 114, 171, 214, 234, 248-49, 289, 313, 317. *See also* Currie; Hughes, Sam; Shell Committee; Ross rifle; Medical scandal; Parliament
Hudspeth, Adam, 25, 30, 31, 32, 34
Hughes, Aileen, 13
Hughes, Garnet, 13, 184-85, 246, 270, 277-78, 282, 291, 309, 315, 316, 317
Hughes, James L., 10, 13, 24, 29, 58, 109, 115, 136, 139
Hughes, John (brother), 12, 18, 21, 22, 48, 136, 190, 196 n
Hughes, John (father), 8
Hughes, Roby, 13
Hughes, Sam; and absences from Ottawa, 180; and Anglo-Canadian military co-operation, 109; assessment of, 1-7, 85-87, 93-94, 171-79, 252-53; and Australasian tour, 64; and belief in British conspiracy, 274ff.; and business concerns, 60-61, 107-108; on Canadian nationalism, 2, 117-18, 284 n, 322; and complaints on Boer war record, 90, 93, 98, 100, 117, 120, 154-55; on Canada, 5, 11, 22-24, 26, 30, 107-109, 126, 128, 322; and civil-military relations, 69, 70, 72-73, 79, 94, 173, 187, 320-21; criticism of British war performance, 89, 90, 92-94, 94 n, 97-98, 273; death, 8, 313, 316-17; and "Defence of Eastern Canada," 101; dismissal, 1, 8, 92-94, 309-10, 312 n, 313; duties in 45th, 12-13, 62-63; and early life, 7-14, 16, 20; and French-English relations, 5, 26-31, 114-15; and formation of coalition and third party, 305, 315-16; and Hughes Ventilator Car Company, 60-61; and inventions, 35-36, 38, 40-41, 60-61; illness, 289, 317, 324; imperial ideas, 5, 23-26, 70, 117-19; and knighthood, 273; and lobbying for cabinet post, 3, 129-31; and loss of popularity, 245, 302; and medical scandals, 314-15; on militia and training, 11-12, 17-20, 47-48, 99-100, 109-10, 135-42; and militia exchanges, 147; and mobilization, 179-82, 203; historical opinion on, 5; debts, 40-41, 60-62; and personal ambition, 3, 129-31, 156-57, 160, 188-89; political talent, 4, 15-16, 34, 42-44, 57, 60, 104-109, 131, 317-18, 321-23; and ideas on religion, 4, 31, 34-37, 53-55; and resentment of British equipment replacements, 232-33, 279ff.; romantic view of war, 9, 19, 180, 200; his sanity, 6, 183, 242, 322-23; seeks overseas command, 69, 79, 188-89; and separate schools, 57-58; and the Tory Party, 2-3, 50, 104-109, 116-17, 143-44; trips to England, 63-64, 127-28, 146-47, 187-88, 196 n, 204-205, 211, 242, 258, 271-72, 289ff., 303; Victorian ideas, 1, 4, 9, 10, 20
Hughes, S. H. S., 6
Hughes, William, 115, 301
Hughes Ventilator Car Company, 60-61
Hutton, E. T. H., 64, 67, 68, 81 n, 92, 93, 98, 147, 162, 167, 181, 213, 322; and Canadian militia, 71; and constitutional violations, 74-77, 79; quarrel with Hughes, 69ff.; relations with Minto, 75-76
Hyatt, A. M. J., xi, 205

Imperial defence, 109, 165; and Canada, 76. *See also* Committee of Imperial Defence; Empire defence
Imperial federation, 23-26. *See also* Imperial Federation League
Imperial Federation League, 23-26, 37
Imperial General Staff system, 165

Imperial Inspector-General, 110, 141, 151. *See also* French; Lake
Imperial Inspector-General of Overseas Forces, 164-65, 170. *See also* Hamilton
Imperial Munitions Board, 240-42. *See also* Flavelle, Joseph Wesley
Imperial sentiment, 71-72
Imperial trade, 107, 117
Imperial War Fund (Great Britain), 201
Imperialism, British, 64; Canadian, 23-26; Hughes on, 117
Indian reservations, 108
Industrial development, 11, 225
Industrial Disputes Bill, 107
Infantry association, 136
Inkerman, battle of, 268
Intercolonial Railway, 35, 36, 38
Irish Home Rule, 118, 132n

Jacques Cartier River, 182
James, W. R. W., 367. *See also* Canadian Training Depot (U.K.)
Jameson, Dr. L. S., 78
Jesuit Estates, 27, 29, 35, 40, 51, 52, 55, 317; Hughes on, 28-30. *See also* Jesuit Order
Jesuit Order, 217
Joffre, General, 274
John Bertram and Son, Steel Works, 235
Jones, Colonel Carleton, 313, 314. *See also* Canadian Army Medical Corps
Journal (Ottawa), 4, 56, 82n
Judicial Committee (Queen's Privy Council), 55
Justice, Minister of, 28

Kaffirs, 86
Kemp, A. E., 6, 105, 129, 141, 142, 143, 148, 150, 192, 211, 233, 309, 318; and patronage, 227; and War Purchasing Commission, 231
Kenhart (South Africa), 84, 87
Ketchen, Brig. H. D. B., 297-98
Kimberley (South Africa), 78
King, William Lyon Mackenzie, 169
Kingston District Headquarters, 12, 71

Kingston (Ontario), 69, 110, 115
Kinmount (Ontario), 44
Kipling, Rudyard, 262
Kirkconnell, Watson, 26
Kirkfield (Ontario), 17, 37
Kitchener, Lord, 187, 188, 189, 193, 203, 206, 219, 226, 227, 228, 235, 259, 261, 262, 263, 264, 268, 269, 270, 271, 272, 273, 275; death, 296; and Hughes, 181, 290
Knoffelfontein (South Africa), 90
Kruger, Paul, 71, 74
Kuruman (South Africa), 88, 90-91, 92
Kylie (blacksmith), 27-28
Kyte, G. W., 243, 244; and fuse scandal, 242; and shell charges, 292. *See also* Shell Scandal

Lake, General Sir Percy, 109, 146, 165. *See also* Imperial Inspector-General
Land grants, 108
Landry, Colonel J. P., 160, 214-15
Landry, Senator Philippe, 215
Langevin, Hector, 31
Lash, Zebulon, 127
Laughlin, Caroline, 9
Laurent, P. D., 31
Laurier, Wilfrid, 5, 23, 26, 60, 64, 68, 70, 71, 72, 74, 75, 77, 97, 102, 103, 120, 122, 124, 126, 148, 241; and Hutton, 79; and extension of Parliament, 242; initial opposition to war, 178; and Naval Bill, 123-25; offer to send troops to South Africa, 73-74; position on Uitlanders, 69; promise not to oppose war effort, 226; Quebec political power base, 218; and South Africa, 71-72
Lavergne, Armand, 212, 215
Lee-Enfield rifle, 119, 245, 246, 249
Lemieux, Rodolphe, 213, 214
Lessard, Maj.-Gen. François, 140, 156, 159, 213, 217, 294, 300; and criticized by Hughes, 189-90; as inspector of military services, 190-91; as inspector of training depots in England, 211; opinion of Hughes, 300; report on training scheme in England, 300-301; squabble with

INDEX / 349

Hughes, 213; and Toronto trial mobilization, 213
Lettow-Vorbeck, Paul von, 277
Liberal-Conservative Association of Ontario, 104
Liberal-Conservative Association of Toronto, 143
Liberal-Conservative Union (Ontario), 16, 29, 39, 41, 50, 54, 58, 60
Liberal Post, 26, 28
Liberal press: and Ross rifle, 245
Liddell Hart, Basil, 269-70
Lifford (Ontario), 9
Lindsay (Ontario), 8, 12, 17, 25, 54, 77, 103, 117, 142, 218; and Board of Trade, 16
Lindsay, Haliburton, Mattawa Railway Company, 61
Lindsay, Pontypool and Bobcaygeon Railway Company, 61
Lloyd George, David, 188, 236, 237, 238, 239, 248, 263, 273, 274, 306
Local battalion scheme, 203, 207, 211, 215, 221 n, 241; and local billeting, 204-205; need for retraining in England, 210-11; and surplus officers in England, 223 n. *See also* Recruiting
Lombard Street headquarters, 293. *See also* Aitken, Max
London (Ontario), 145, 189
Loos, battle of, 149, 274
Lord's Day Bill (1906), 107
Lougheed, Senator James, 192, 229, 232, 318
Lowther, Lt.-Col. Claude, 90, 266, 277
Lusitania, 202
Lyttleton, Lt.-Gen. Neville, 101

MacAdam, Ena, 3, 7 n
MacAdam shield-shovel, 234
McArthur, Peter, 202
McBride, Sir Richard, 192, 219
McCarthy, D'Alton, 24-25, 28-30, 32, 52-53, 55, 57, 59
McCarthy, Osler, Hoskin and Co. (law firm), 25
McCurdy, F. B., 244
Macdonald, D. A., 156
Macdonald, E. M., 191, 242

Macdonald, Ena MacAdam. *See* MacAdam
Macdonald, Sir John A., 1, 5, 16, 19, 21-22, 24-25, 28-32, 34-36, 38-39, 103, 115; correspondence with Hughes, 17; death, 51, 54; and militia reform, 19
MacDougall, Colonel J. C., 266-67, 281, 284, 291-94, 300; quarrel with Sam Steele, 293
Mackenzie, Maj.-Gen. Colin, 135, 146-47, 166, 169, 174, 181, 266; British reaction to, 165; and Hughes' war record, 163; and mobilization, 178; and petty patronage, 162; public reaction to his dismissal, 171; quarrel with Hughes, 171-72; resignation, 161-64; secret memorandum on Hughes' administration, 159-61
Mackenzie, Sir William, 37-39, 41-42, 52-54, 60-62, 130; and Donald B. Mann, 107-108; quarrel with Hughes, 39-43
McKinley Tariff, 39
Maclean, Col. J. B., 193
Maclean, W. F., 54
MacPhail, Sir Andrew, 308-309, 323 n
Macready, Gen. Sir Neville, 276
Mail (Toronto), 21
Manitoba schools question, 50-51, 53-60, 317; and Hughes, 5
Manly Sims, Maj. R. F., 266, 301
Mann, Sir Donald B., 38, 61, 108
Manpower, 200, 225
Marine and Fisheries, Minister of, 17
Mason, James, 145, 209
Maunsell, Col. G. S., 146
Meighen, Arthur, 6, 243
Meredith, Sir William, 243-44, 252
Merritt, William Hamilton, 25
Methuen, Lord, 77
Métis, 18-19
Mercier, Honoré, 28, 58
Mewburn, Sydney, 190
Middleton, Lt.-Gen. Sir Fred, 18-21, 48; quarrel with Hughes, 21-22. *See also* General-Officer-Commanding
Midland District, 60
Mignault, Dr. Arthur, 214

Militarism, 144
Militia, budgets (1911-1914), 140; legislation, 100; myth, 1-2, 18, 180, 268; Hughes on, 20, 70, 76; reform, 99-100; training camps, 141, 145. *See also* Hughes, Sam; Macdonald, John A.; Non-Permanent Active Militia
Militia Act, 12, 156, 159
Militia Bill (1904), 99-101
Militia Conferences, 135-38, 141, 145, 149, 228
Militia Council, 135, 140, 154-57, 160-61, 175n, 179, 191-92, 244
Militia and Defence; Department of, 6, 18; Minister of, 1, 8, 131, 319. *See also* Patterson
Militia Headquarters (Ottawa), 135, 169-70, 180. *See also* Headquarters staff
Militia Policy, 142-44
Military Service Act, 315
Military Services Branch, 162
Miller, Carman, 75
Milner, Lord Alfred, 64, 73, 78, 84-85, 88-89, 91, 94, 97, 114, 117-18, 121
Minto, Lord, 64, 68, 70, 75-76, 78-79, 80n, 83, 92-93, 98, 100, 102, 117; quarrel with Hughes, 98; relations with Hutton, 75-76. *See also* Governor-General of Canada
Mobilization, 178-82, 224n. *See also* Gwatkin; Hughes, Sam; Militia; Non-Permanent Active Militia; War Office; War supplies
Modder River, battle of, 84
Monk, F. D., 114, 124-29, 148-49, 216-17
Mons, 316
Montreal, 26, 206, 209, 215
Morden, W. Grant, 266
Morine, A. B., 150
Morrisburg (Ontario), 192, 228
Morrison, Edward, 159-60
Morton, Desmond, 6, 18, 180, 205, 212, 284n
Morton, W. L., 1
Mount Sorrel, battle of, 212, 266, 290
Mulock, William, 74

Munitions; acute shortage of, 226-27, 274; and Hughes, 228; and industries, 215, 252; and small arms scandal, 234-35. *See also* Ammunition; Dominion Arsenal; Government Arsenals; Hughes, Sam; Ross rifle; Shell Committee; Shell Scandal; War Office; War supplies
Murray, Sir George, 150, 191
Muskoka (Ontario), 177

Napier, Sir William Francis Patrick, 109
Napoleon, 183, 186
Natal (South Africa), 67
Natal Field Force, 87
National Policy, 11, 16, 20, 23, 39
National registration, 198
National Service Board, 220
National Trust, 125
Naval Aid Bill, 148
Naval Bill (1910), 123-25, 217
Naval debate (1909-1910), 122-23, 148
Nesbitt, E. W., 144
Neuve Chapelle, battle of, 201-202
New Brunswick, 209
"New men," 105, 107, 150
New South Wales, 69, 71
New York, 187
New Zealand, 123-24
Newcomb, E. L., 289, 304, 309
News (Toronto), 125, 143, 192
Niagara Peninsula, 12
Nicholls, Frederick J., 62, 236
"Noble Thirteen," 28-29
Non-Permanent Active Militia (NPAM), 11, 18, 47-49, 71, 109-10, 137-39; and Canadian Militia Mobilization Scheme, 172; enlistment, 11-12; Hughes on, 318-19; legality of international service, 181; mobilization, 178; political influence on CEF, 184; quotas, 202. *See also* Hughes, Sam; Militia; Mobilization; Recruiting
Non-Permanent Active Militia units; Canadian Grenadier Guards, 260; Carabiniers Mont-Royal, 213; Carabiniers de Sherbrooke, 213; Chaussiers Canadiens, 213; Mid-

land Regiment, 18, 21; Régiment de Lévis, 149; Tenth Royal Grenadiers, 209; Voltigeurs de Quebec, 213; 45th, 12, 16, 21-22, 48, 62-63, 69, 73, 98, 100; 46th, 22, 48, 62; 49th, 12; 65th, 149; 85th, 215
Non-Permanent Canadian Army Service Corps, 141
Non-Permanent Ordnance Corps, 141
North Atlantic Trading Company, 106
North Oxford (constituency), 144
Northrup, William, 116, 125, 127
Northwest Campaign, 19-20, 180, 319
North-West Mounted Police, 270
Nova Scotia Steel Company, 209

O'Brien, William, 32 n
Oddfellows, 16
Old party politics, 2, 116, 266, 318; effect on industrial mobilization, 226, 232-33; effect on recruiting, 206; and Hughes, 2, 16, 150-51; influences on Shell Committee, 241-42
Oliver equipment, 233
Oliver, Frank, 196 n
Ontario, 26-27, 114; government, 201; and Methodists, 145; and patriotic response, 202
Ontario Artillery Association, 145
Ontario Liberal-Conservative Union. See Liberal-Conservative Union (Ontario)
Ontario schools question, 149, 212, 215, 217
Orange Free State, 73
Orange Lodge, 16, 26, 28, 41, 53-54, 56, 58, 59, 77, 115, 122, 149, 166-67, 218; and Hughes, 51-52, 58-59; and Manitoba separate schools issue, 81. See also Grand Orange Lodge of British America
Orange River (South Africa), 83-84, 87, 92
Orange River Station (South Africa), 84
Orange Sentinel, 115, 124, 130
Osler, B. B., 31

Osler, E. B., 110, 192
Osler, Sir William, 314
Ottawa (Ontario), 16, 73
Otter, Gen. William Dillon, 17-18, 20, 109, 146, 156, 158, 173-74, 319; as Inspector-General, 159
Overseas Council, 290-94, 300, 302. *See also* Aitken

Paardeberg, battle of, 84, 137
Pacific Scandal, 10
Paget Horse, 89
Paquelo, Tancrède, 215-16
Parkin, G. R., 26
Parliament (Canadian), 2, 28, 38-39, 41, 47, 60, 98, 106, 177, 200, 229-30, 241, 318; and Shell investigation, 240-42; secret session, 181; and special war session, 178. *See also* House of Commons; Hughes, Sam
Patriotic citizen groups, 201-202
Patronage, 2, 16-17, 30-31, 37, 47-48, 61, 99, 103, 131, 254 n, 259; and Hughes, 115-16, 143, 150-51; and Liberal press, 233; and munitioning, 226-27; and old party politics, 2, 150
Patterson, J. C., 42; as Minister of Militia and Defence, 49-50
Pease, Lt.-Gen. L. T., 247
Pellatt, Lt.-Col. Sir Henry, 145
Pelletier, Oscar, 81 n, 159, 175 n, 213
Perley, Sir George H., 6, 105, 125, 127, 129, 150, 189, 195 n, 219, 257 n, 258-59, 261, 265, 269, 271, 288-89, 294-96, 302-309, 312 n, 314-15; on Allison, 229; clashes with Carrick, 265-66; clashes with Hughes, 259-60; heads new administration, 304-307; lack of co-operation from Aitken and Carson, 284; pleas for overseas reorganization, 283
Permanent Force, 11, 19-20, 48-49, 100, 107, 109, 135, 141, 146, 158, 166, 173, 177, 185, 195 n, 245, 319; Hughes on, 160-62, 171. *See also* Canadian Expeditionary Force
Plains of Abraham, 119, 141
Plumer, Gen. Sir Herbert, 297-98

Pontifical Zouaves, 49, 212
Porter, Gus, 116
Porteus, C. L., 61-62
Portland (Maine), 101
Powell, Col. Walker, 49
Post (Lindsay), 17, 28
Power, C. G., 185
Power, Senator L. G., 136
Preston, Caroline, 9
Price, William, 127, 182, 186, 210, 216, 318
Prieska (South Africa), 84, 86-87
Prohibitionists, 145
Public Accounts Committee, 120, 230-31, 237
Public Service Commission, investigation of, 186
Pullman Railcar Company, 60
Purity in politics campaign, 106, 120-21

Quebec, 26, 114, 120, 126, 210, 214. *See also* French Canada; French-Canadians
Quebec City, 142, 149, 154, 182-83, 186
Queen's Regulations and Orders, 12
Queen's University, 25

Railcar ventilator system, 35-36, 38, 40-41, 60-61
Reciprocity, 39-40, 47, 122, 126-29
Recruiting, 199ff., 288; depot system, 203-204; in English-Canada, 212; effect on industry and agriculture, 200, 208; in French Canada, 210-12; and Hughes' leadership, 199; local battalion scheme, 203-204; Lord Derby's scheme, 205, 205n; national poster scheme, 204; and public alarm, 208-10; public support for, 206; recruiting leagues, 209; retraining in England, 205, 210-11. *See also* Hughes, Sam
Red Ensign, 25
Reform Party, 16, 26
Reid, J. D., 41, 125, 127-28, 207, 226, 318
Reinforcements, 207-208, 210-12, 282, 291, 292, 296, 300, 301, 304

Regulation 17, 149, 215
Remount Committee, 139
Rhenoster River (South Africa), 91
Rhodes, Cecil, 78
Rideau Club, 54
Rideau Hall, 55, 191, 264
Ridgeway, battle of, 12
Riel, Louis, 13, 24
Riel Rebellion, 18, 21
Rifle ammunition, 142, 234
Rifle ranges, 141, 144
Rifle shooting, 4, 13, 110, 136, 141-42
Roberts, Field Marshal Lord, 3, 64, 70, 77-79, 83-84, 87, 89, 91-93, 98, 100
Roberts, Maj. Sir Charles G. D., 262
Roblin, Rodimond, 124
Rogers, Robert, 129, 150, 187, 193, 226, 232, 265, 267, 270, 318
Roman Catholics, 26, 114-16, 122. *See also* French-Canadians; Hughes, Sam; Orange Lodge
Ross, Sir Charles, 119-20, 139, 141-42, 152n, 224n, 248, 266; and factory at Quebec, 225; and expropriation settlement, 252-53
Ross, James, 60, 61
Ross, P. D., 4, 10, 193
Ross rifle, 119-23, 120n, 128-29, 152n, 189, 202, 234, 245ff., 256n; and Borden, 249; British opinion of, 122-23; for cadet corps, 141; troop complaints about, 252, 255; Hughes' faith in, 246-52; investigations of, 294; and the Liberal press, 245; and low quality of British ammunition, 246, 249; modifications, 248-50; public complaints about, 251-52; replaced by Lee-Enfield, 252; Russian contracts, 248; scandal, 251-52. *See also* Aitken; Alderson; Lee-Enfield rifle; Ross, Sir Charles
Round Table Movement, 4, 85, 118, 196n
Rowell, Newton W., 252
Royal Automobile Club, 188
Royal Canadian Dragoons, 159
Royal commissions, 211; on shells, 243-44, 301. *See also* Shell Committee; Duff; Kyte; Davidson

Royal Military College of Canada, 20, 100, 122
Royal Navy, 101, 123
Royal Ordnance factories, 226
Royal United Services Institute, 109
Russell, Benjamin, 102
Russell, T. A., 233
Russia, 178, 225, 248

Sacketts Harbour, 101
St. Eloi Craters, battle of, 212, 250, 290, 293, 297-98, 300-301
St. Julien, battle of, 268, 277-79
St. Lawrence River, 182
St. Omer (France), 300
Salisbury Plain, 230, 261
Sarajevo, 177
Saskatchewan, 106-107, 143. See also Autonomy Bill
Saskatoon, 155
Saturday Night, 234
Schlieffen, Count Alfred von, 124
Schools of Instruction, 20, 157-59
Scott, Canon F. G., 182-83
Scott, Richard, 74-75
Seely, Col. J. E. B., 147, 168, 170, 267, 270, 283, 287 n
Selborne, Lord, 117
Settle, Brig.-Gen. Sir Herbert, 78, 84-87, 88
Sharpe, Sam, 184
Shaughnessy, Lord, 209
Shell Committee, 235ff., 238, 243-45, 252, 288, 290, 294; and Bertram's administration, 236-37; and Borden, R. L., 238; and Canadian business, 235, 238; criticism of, 237; and Hughes, 5, 239-40; political and economic advantages of Canadian production, 236; relations with Canadian government, 237; reorganization, 244
Shell Scandal, 289
Sifton, Clifford, 108, 125, 127, 130, 193, 306, 315
Smith, Sir Donald, 56, 58, 63-64, 79, 108-109
Smith, F. E., 262
Smith, Lt.-Col. Henry, 159-60
Somme, battle of, 212

South Africa, 64, 107, 126. *See also* Boer republics; Orange Free State; Transvaal
South African war, 3, 121, 277. *See also* Boer commandos; Boer republics; Boer war; Boers; Hughes, Sam; Kruger, Paul
South Bruce (constituency), 148
Spanish-American war, 70
Speakers Patriotic League, 202
Spion Kop, battle of, 87, 90
Spittal, Maj. C. D., 259
Spitzer-type bullet, 109
Sproule, Tom, 115
Standing Small Arms Committee, 120, 122-23, 139
Stanton, Edward, 190
Star (Montreal), 71
Steele, Sam, 190-91, 267, 270-71, 281, 284, 292, 293, 294
Stewart, Maj. A. B., 277
Sub-Militia Council, 304, 306; and Bruce report, 314-15. *See also* Acting Sub-Militia Council
Supplies and Transport, Director of, 186
Surplus officers, 210, 212, 223 n, 302
Swiss Militia, 144
Sudan, 64

Tarte, J. Israel, 80 n
Telegram (Winnipeg), 137, 166
Thomas, D. A., 238, 239-40, 248
Thompson, John, 28, 31, 36, 51-55, 61; and his death, 55; and relationship with Hughes, 51-55
Times (London), 101, 188
Times (New York), 208
"Tin Pot Navy," 124
Toronto (Ontario), 12, 24-25, 189, 202, 220
Toronto Collegiate, 13
Toronto Normal School, 9, 10
Toronto Shamrocks, 10
Toronto Street Railway Company, 42, 61
Transcontinental railway, 11
Transvaal (South Africa), 68, 73, 88
Trent Canal, 108
Tupper, Charles, 17, 51, 56, 58, 72, 75, 98, 104-105, 125

Turner, Lt.-Gen. Richard, 184, 270-72, 276-78, 280, 291, 298, 301, 315-17
Tweefontein (South Africa), 90

Uitlanders, 69, 73
Underhill, Frank, 1
Union government, 199
University of Toronto, 10
University Officer Training Corps, 136
United States, 11, 18, 23, 99-101, 109, 229; and "American Legion," 220; American Revolution, 279; Civil War, 203; Foreign Enlistment Act (1818), 219; and neutrality, 203, 219
Uphill (Ontario), 44
Upington (South Africa), 84, 86, 87
Upper Canada College, 26
U.S. Steel Corporation, 235

Valcartier. *See* Camp Valcartier
Van Straubenzie, Lt.-Col. Bowen, 21
Vancouver (British Columbia), 115
Vatican, 28
Vermilion (Alberta), 108
Victoria (British Columbia), 138
Victoria-Haliburton (constituency), 103, 105, 120, 126, 128
Victoria County (Ontario), 9, 13, 23, 25-26, 27, 29
Victoria County Rifle Association, 16
Victoria Cross, 90, 93, 154, 184
Victoria North (constituency), 16, 34, 39, 45, 53, 103; and by-election (1892), 41; and Conservative leadership race (1890), 37-45; and federal election (1896), 59-60; and Hughes' campaigns, 40, 59-60; and nominating convention (1890), 38
Victoria South (constituency), 16, 30, 32, 36
Victoria Warder (Lindsay), 7, 13, 15, 17, 19-20, 26-28, 30-32, 37, 41, 52, 56; and *Watchman*, 31-32; sale of, 60-61. *See also* *Watchman-Warder*
Villiers, Piet de, 88, 89, 90-92, 93
Volunteer Aid Detachments, 313

Volunteers. *See* Non-Permanent Active Militia
von Donop, Sir Stanley, 226
Vrooman, Dr. Adam, 103

Wade, Mason, 149, 217
Walker, Byron, 124, 125
Wallace, N. Clark, 41-44, 47, 51-54, 56, 58, 60; and Hughes, 51-52, 58-60
War casualties, 198, 201-202, 211-12, 220, 225, 259, 263, 268, 290
War contracts, 230-31
War of 1812, 18, 319
War enthusiasm, 192-94, 194 n, 198, 202; and Hughes, 181, 186-87, 189, 192-94
War Measures Act, 201
War Office (Great Britain), 92-93, 98-100, 120, 123, 142, 164-66, 168, 170, 172, 185, 187, 196 n, 207, 226, 234, 236-37, 248, 250, 257 n, 260-65, 269, 275, 277, 283; and Hughes, 98; and Canadian munitions production, 235-36
War Purchasing Commission, 231-33
War supplies, 257 n. *See also* Munitions; Shell Committee
Ward, Lt.-Col. W. R., 259, 294, 262, 281
Warren, Lt.-Gen. Sir Charles, 78, 84, 87-88, 90, 95 n; and Hughes, 87-92
Warren's Scouts, 88-89
Wartime Voters Act, 315
Warwick, Earl of, 147, 267
Washington Treaty (1871), 11, 19
Watchman (Lindsay), 30-31, 32, 34, 39, 43. *See also* *Watchman-Warder*
Watchman-Warder, 121, 128. See also *Victoria Warder*; *Watchman*
Watson, Brigadier David, 184, 214, 277, 281, 290-92, 293
Web equipment, 233. *See also* Oliver equipment
White, Thomas, 125, 129, 150, 183, 192, 207-208, 226, 229-30, 312 n
Whitney, Sir James Pliny, 60, 115, 121, 124, 130, 149, 229; and Hughes, 115-17; and Borden, 116
Williams, Arthur, 18, 21, 32 n

Williams, Reverend C. A., 218
Williams, Colonel Victor, 159, 185, 188, 266
Willison, John S., 57, 125, 143, 192, 302
Willson, Beckles, 262, 275, 284, 291-92, 300
Winnipeg (Manitoba), 52, 56
Winter, Colonel C. F., 3, 5, 141, 160, 178, 245, 317

Wolsely, Sir Garnet, 64, 68
Women's Christian Temperance Union, 137, 145
Wood, Dr., 38, 39, 42-43
World (Toronto), 25, 82 n, 145

Ypres, 193, 201-202, 232, 246-47, 262, 268, 270, 272, 273, 298; and Hughes, 273, 296, 297; and Salient, 290-91

www.ingramcontent.com/pod-product-compliance
Lightning Source LLC
Chambersburg PA
CBHW052009070526
44584CB00016B/1681